Contents

Introduction to
San Francisco
& the Bay Area

One of America's most iconic cities, San Francisco sits poised on the 47-square-mile fingertip of a peninsula at the western edge of America. The city has much to gloat about, from the rugged coastline, fog-capped hills and dense woods that surround it to the steep streets of the city itself, whose distinct neighbourhoods, by turn quaint or hip, are lined by rows of preserved Victorian houses or dotted with chic clubs in converted warehouses. Residents rightly think of their home as the liberal-minded Northern alternative to glitzy Los Angeles – this is a place that will forever be associated with the epoch-defining writers of the Beat Generation and the free-loving hippies that followed in their wake. More recently, it has become a haven for once-disenfranchised groups, most notably its gay residents.

From its earliest days as a stop on the Spanish chain of missions, through its explosive expansion during the Gold Rush, up into the internet boom of the 1990s and beyond, San Francisco's turbulent history is relatively short. The city sprang up almost overnight in the late 1840s from a sleepy fishing village, whose hilly terrain did not daunt the rough-and-ready prospectors, who built on it according to a grid pattern that ignored even the steepest inclines. The late nineteenth-century city defied the elements, luring writers, architects, immigrants and thousands of transient sailors eager to "make it" in the newest, westernmost metropolis. Though earthquakes, fires, droughts, landslides and other natural disasters have put the city's very existence to the test, residents have never taken long to rebuild and re-settle, refusing to give in to nature's tantrums. And San Franciscans themselves are known for the same unbreakable character, infusing their city with an activist, can-do attitude.

ABOVE ALCATRAZ (P.71)

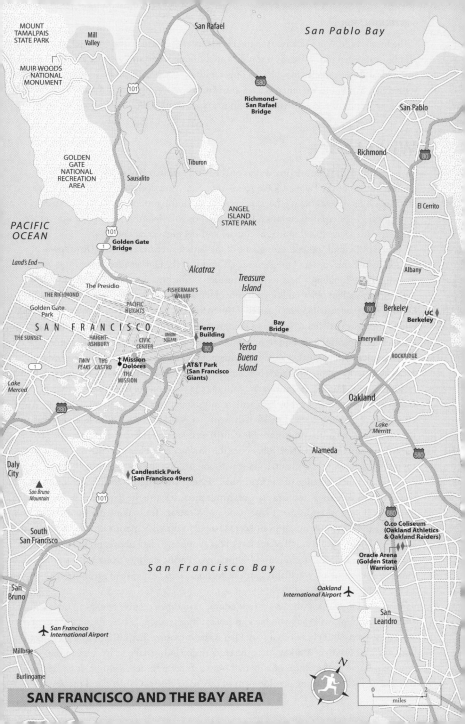

SAN FRANCISCO AND THE BAY AREA

The locals aside, San Francisco's main asset is its easy charm – quaint pastel street scenes and blossoming parks, offset by a sophisticated dining scene and world-class clubs, make it the ideal American city in which to linger without a serious agenda. Indeed, despite all its activity, San Francisco remains a small town, where having a car is a liability. Provided you don't mind hills, every major sight in town is a short walk, bike or bus ride away.

What to see

Surrounded by the shimmering waters of the San Francisco Bay to its east and the crashing waves of the Pacific Ocean to its west, San Francisco sits on a hilly peninsula. The city's hills serve as handy markers between its shifting moods and characters. As a general rule, geographical elevation is synonymous with wealth – the higher up you are, the better the views (barring fog, of course) and the higher the rents.

Created by landfill and bulldozing, one of the flattest stretches of land is **Downtown**, at the top right-hand corner of the Peninsula. Capped at the **Embarcadero** waterfront by the towering Ferry Building – boat terminus turned gourmet market – Market Street is lined with the city's tallest office buildings; it runs alongside the boxy high-rises of the **Financial District**, and past the shopping quarter of **Union Square**, also home to a number of boutique hotels. Just north of Union Square is **Chinatown**, a tight cluster of apartments, restaurants, temples and stores built around historic Portsmouth Square. Nearby, the towering **Transamerica Pyramid** makes a useful landmark to orient yourself by, shadowing historic **Jackson Square's** restored redbrick buildings. Columbus Avenue separates Portsmouth from Jackson Square, heading northwest and forming the backbone of **North Beach**, the old Italian enclave once haunted by Beat writers and still popular among espresso drinkers. To either side of Columbus stand peaks of three of San Francisco's steep hills: **Telegraph Hill** to the east, the perch of the unmistakeable Coit Tower; **Russian Hill** to the west, reached by curvy Lombard Street; and **Nob Hill** – once the province of robber barons – to the southwest, topped by stately Grace Cathedral, along with some of the city's poshest hotels.

Along the northern edge of the Peninsula, **Fisherman's Wharf** is loathed by locals, yet draws hordes of visitors to its tacky waterfront piers. It's also the departure point for ferries to the notorious former island prison of **Alcatraz**. Trails along the water's edge lead west past the clutch of museums in **Fort Mason** and the ritzy **Marina** district, home of the Palace of Fine Arts and some of the city's best shopping. High above, on the hills just to the south, the ornate mansions and Victorians of **Pacific Heights** make for splendid views; from this perch you'll also spot the **Presidio**, a vast expanse of green stretching west to the Golden Gate Bridge.

Back near Downtown, the gritty **Tenderloin**, a rundown section of cheap hotels and sleazy porn shops, will snap you back to reality. It rests uneasily next to the **Civic Center**, where the painstakingly restored City Hall is the imposing focus. Cross Market Street and you'll hit **South of Market**, once the city's major industrial enclave and, in the Nineties, home to the offices of a myriad now-defunct internet start-ups. It has retained its cultural cachet with the development of the Yerba Buena Gardens and the San

Francisco Museum of Modern Art. The area's waterfront, long-neglected South Beach, has been rezoned for housing and businesses, anchored by the Giants' baseball park.

Inland, the **Mission District** was built around Mission Dolores, the oldest building in San Francisco. The neighbourhood's diverse population, which includes a large Hispanic community, holds a concentration of lively cafés, restaurants and bars. Just west is the energetic **Castro** quarter, hub for San Francisco's gay population. North of the Castro, **Haight-Ashbury** was once San Francisco's Victorian resort quarter before the hippies and flower children took over; today it's a rag-tag collection of used-clothing stores and laid-back cafés. Nearby are a few areas of only marginal interest to visitors: tiny **Japantown**, the slightly tatty **Western Addition** and the **Lower Haight**, best known for its nightlife.

The western and southern sides of San Francisco are where many of the city's locals live, in neighbourhoods like the **Richmond**, liberally sprinkled with some of the city's best ethnic restaurants. The Richmond is hugged by the Golden Gate National Recreation Area to the north, along the coast of which you can pick up the four-mile Pacific Coast Trail. Expansive **Golden Gate Park** borders the south of the district and holds a number of fine museums and gardens. South of the park, the **Sunset**'s homogenous single-storey houses stretch on relentlessly; relief can be found on the western coast, home to the city's best **beaches**.

Though San Francisco is undoubtedly the focus of the Bay Area, there's much in the surrounding parts to take in, too. The **East Bay** is centred on the gritty, up-and-coming

THE HILLS OF SAN FRANCISCO

Along with a breezy waterfront setting and persistent fog, the city's fifty-plus high points are its defining natural characteristic, providing heart-thumping exercise, astonishing vistas and behind-the-wheel thrills for locals and visitors alike. A trio of prominent hilltops stands above the crowd (see below); other hills particularly worth a climb include **Bernal Heights**, with largely unimpeded vistas to the north and east, **Nob Hill**, a quiet repose of luxury hotels and distinguished high-rise residences, and **Russian Hill**, full of classic San Francisco residences and vintage apartment towers.

Telegraph Hill To the east, topped by Coit Tower, this is the finest natural vantage point in the area, its 288-foot rocky mound affording excellent views of Downtown's skyscrapers and the central neighbourhoods.

Twin Peaks Towards the centre of the city is the pair of 900-foot promontories known as Twin Peaks, from which a number of major points are visible across the Bay on clear days, most notably Mount Diablo.

Sutro Heights Park High atop a bluff along northwest San Francisco's rocky shoreline, Sutro Heights Park overlooks the Pacific Ocean 200ft below. A set of benches along the park's westernmost edge offers unlimited views of sandy Ocean Beach, which yawns for several miles towards the city's southern border.

port city of **Oakland** and the University of California's flagship campus in hipster **Berkeley**. To the south, the bayside of the **Peninsula** contains **Palo Alto**, dominated by prestigious Stanford University, while the coast offers some surprisingly unspoilt beaches on either side of delightful **Half Moon Bay**. North of San Francisco, across the Golden Gate Bridge, **Marin County** boasts the postcard-perfect towns of **Sausalito** and **Tiburon**, plus prime biking and hiking trails in the **Marin Headlands**. Further north is the lush beauty of California's famed **Wine Country**, whose principal valleys, **Napa** and **Sonoma**, trace gentle crescents through the countless vineyards.

When to go

San Francisco does not belong to the California of endless blue skies and slothful warmth. Flanked on three sides by water, it is regularly invigorated by the fresh winds that sweep across the Peninsula. The **climate** is among the most stable in the world, with a daytime temperature that generally hovers around 15°C (60°F), but can drop much lower at night (see box, p.30). Spring and autumn usually have the sunniest days, while summer often sees heavy **fog** roll in through the Golden Gate. This thick mist does much to add romance to the city but it can also dash any hopes of tanning at the beach. Winter brings most of the city's rainfall, sometimes in torrential storms. Almost everywhere else in the Bay Area is warmer than San Francisco, especially in the summer when the East Bay basks in sunshine, and the Wine Country and other inland valleys are baking hot.

To avoid the crowds, do not come in the summer, although even then the tourist congestion is rarely off-putting. The **best times to visit** are late May and June, when the hills are greenest and covered with wildflowers, or in October and November, when you can be fairly sure of good weather and reduced crowds.

18

things not to miss

It's not possible to see everything in and around San Francisco in one trip – and we don't suggest you try. What follows, in no particular order, is a selective taste of the city's highlights: from major museums and iconic architecture to vibrant festivals and great day-trips. Each highlight has a page reference to take you straight into the Guide, where you can find out more.

1

1 PAINTED LADIES
Page 112

Sooner or later, all visitors to San Francisco come to Alamo Square to view the six colourful Victorians known as the "Painted Ladies".

2 SAN FRANCISCO MUSEUM OF MODERN ART
Page 88

The dazzling modern exterior of SFMoMA is as much of a draw as its renowned collection of abstract Expressionist and California School art.

3 AÑO NUEVO STATE RESERVE
Page 259

No matter what time of year, you'll see clusters of elephant seals lounging on the beach, but to see hundreds of them at once stop by during the December to March mating season.

4 BASEBALL
Pages 89 & 223

From the upper seats at AT&T Park you can enjoy a fine view of the Bay in between innings when the Giants have a home game. With fun, fact-filled tours of the ground and even a play area for children, there's something here for everyone.

12 CABLE CARS
Page 43

Famous for good reason, these glorious old trams provide irresistible photo opportunities, as well as a leisurely way of climbing Downtown's steepest hills.

13 CHINATOWN
Page 50

Chinatown bustles with dim sum restaurants, traditional herbal stores and steamy teahouses.

14 ALCATRAZ
Page 71

Take a boat ride out to "The Rock" and tour the famous maximum-security prison, where Al Capone and Machine Gun Kelly did time.

15 LEGION OF HONOR
Page 115

This celebrated museum holds an impressive collection, notable for its Rodin sculptures.

16 THE FERRY BUILDING
Page 48

This foodie paradise sells gourmet produce and offers superb views over the Bay.

17 GOLDEN GATE PARK
Page 118

It's easy to spend hours unwinding in the green expanses of Golden Gate Park, whose Japanese Tea Garden is one of its main attractions.

18 GAY PRIDE
Page 227

If you're here in late June, be sure to check out the exuberant Gay Pride parade, which takes over the Castro district.

Itineraries

It doesn't take long to realize that Bay Area residents place a premium on two elements of local life: eating well and taking advantage of the region's wealth of outdoor opportunities. You could easily find yourself riding a cable car to catch an Alcatraz ferry in the morning, enjoying a gourmet picnic and bike ride in the afternoon, and capping it all off with an outstanding dinner that evening.

A WEEKEND IN SAN FRANCISCO

DAY ONE
Ferry Building and the Embarcadero Grab an early bite inside the Ferry Building before enjoying a morning stroll along the adjacent waterfront promenade. **See p.48**

Filbert Steps and Coit Tower Climb a garden-studded path up the steep east flank of Telegraph Hill to a gorgeous Art Deco promontory. **See p.61**

North Beach While away a few hours wandering San Francisco's charming Italian-American enclave, where cafés, bakeries and trattorias evoke Old World atmosphere at every turn. **See p.57**

Chinatown A true feast for the senses: barbecue chickens dangling inside market windows, oceans of local shoppers along Stockton St and, amid it all, tranquil temples high above the side streets. **See p.50**

Dinner Head out to a San Francisco Giants baseball game at bayfront AT&T Park, where the diverse food options and extraordinary views compete for your attention with the action on the field. **See p.89**

DAY TWO
Alcatraz Get tickets in advance for the day's first ferry to this wind-lashed island, which for

decades was home to the most infamous stockade in the US. **See p.71**

Palace of Fine Arts Find a bench near the adjacent lagoon and marvel at this newly restored c.1915 beauty. **See p.75**

Crissy Field This flat wetlands area near the Golden Gate is the top spot in town for a short, easy walk that reveals stunning vistas. **See p.80**

Cable car ride Hop aboard one of the city's famed trolleys and trundle around – and over – hill after hill. **See p.43**

Asian Art Museum Browse the vast collection of artefacts on hand, including the world's oldest Buddha image. **See p.94**

Dinner Take a short BART ride to *Papalote* in the Mission District, home of what is arguably San Francisco's finest burrito. **See p.162**

THE GREAT OUTDOORS

Although one of the most populous urban regions in the US, the Bay Area has few rivals when it comes to outdoor activities. With a week at your disposal, you could take in many of the region's highlights.

Hiking Mount Tamalpais Anyone game for an invigorating workout can mount an assault on this 2571ft Marin County peak from one of

ABOVE WINE COUNTRY VINEYARDS (P.271); CABLE CAR **RIGHT** HOUSE OF NANKING, CHINATOWN (P.141)

several trailheads far below. And for those who want to take in the peerless view without breaking a sweat, you can simply drive up to a few hundred feet short of the summit. **See p.264**

Biking around Angel Island Hop aboard a ferry to San Francisco Bay's largest land mass, where a perimeter road traces an easy, five-mile route around the island's lower reaches. Bike rentals are available steps from the boat landing. **See p.265**

Whale watching If you're in the Bay Area between January and May, reserve a spot aboard a tour boat to view California grey whales as they push through the Pacific's churning waters along their yearly migratory route. **See p.267**

Elephant seals Another top winter wildlife-watching activity is at Año Nuevo State Reserve along the Santa Cruz coast, where these enormous pinnipeds engage in violent annual mating battles. **See p.259**

Sailing on San Francisco Bay Assuming your wealthy uncle hasn't invited you out for a day on the water, the visitor-friendly Cal Racing Club, based at the Berkeley Marina, offers affordable instruction and access if you'd like to bob about the Bay's choppy whitecaps. **See p.246**

BAY AREA GASTRONOMY

In a region known for its love of all things culinary over just about anything else, you certainly won't go hungry. Allow five days to explore the Bay Area's epicurean delights.

San Francisco farmers' markets Earmark a couple of hours one morning to visit one of the city's farmers' markets, where vendors sell everything from artichokes to fresh flowers, much of it organically grown. **See p.211**

San Francisco restaurants Whether it's world-class pizza at *Tony's Pizza Napoletana* (see p.149) in North Beach, a five-star meal at *Gary Danko* (see p.151) at Fisherman's Wharf or a super burrito at *Gordo Taqueria* (see p.169) in the Inner Sunset, you're never far from a memorable culinary experience in the city with more restaurants per capita than anywhere else in the US.

Picnic at Sutro Heights Park Go the DIY route by packing your own lunch before trekking out to this quiet hilltop park set in the lovely (if sometimes fogbound) northwest corner of the city. **See p.117**

Chez Panisse Make a pilgrimage to the north Berkeley restaurant that played as significant a role as any in the rise of California cuisine. The menu changes daily, but you can always expect fresh ingredients used in unimaginably creative ways. **See p.248**

Fentons Creamery If you're one to scream for ice cream, don't miss Oakland's top ice-cream parlour, where a long list of handmade flavours includes both time-honoured favourites (chocolate marble, rocky road) and left-field choices (pomegranate, rum raisin). **See p.239**

Wine Country Once you've had your fill of winery-hopping in Napa and Sonoma, choose from a full slate of eating options, from the wonderfully low-brow such as *Puerto Vallarta* (see p.280) in Calistoga, to the sophisticated, such as *Bouchon* in Yountville (see p.281).

ONE OF SAN FRANCISCO'S FAMOUS CABLE CARS

Basics

Getting there

Unless you're coming from nearby on the West Coast, the quickest way to San Francisco is via one of its two major airports, San Francisco International Airport or Oakland International Airport (see p.238). Taking a train comes a slow second, while travelling by bus is the least expensive method, but also the slowest and least comfortable.

Airfares always depend on the **season**, with the highest average prices charged from June to August – ironically, when San Francisco's weather is often at its most unpredictable. Fares drop during the "shoulder" seasons – March to May, September to October – conveniently, just as the weather becomes more dependable. You'll get the best prices during the low season, November to February (excluding Thanksgiving, Christmas and New Year when prices are hiked up and seats are at a premium). The competition between airlines means that much cheaper fares are sometimes available, while a sudden spike in fuel prices can lead to a sudden general increase. The fares quoted in the sections below are representative averages.

Flights from the UK and Ireland

There are daily nonstop flights to San Francisco from **London Heathrow** with British Airways and Virgin Atlantic, and regular services by United, Continental and American Airlines. These flights take about eleven hours, though tailwinds ensure return flights are always an hour or so shorter. Flights out usually leave Britain mid-morning, while flights back from the US tend to arrive in Britain early in the morning. Most other airlines serving San Francisco, like Air France and KLM, fly from London via their respective European or American hubs. These flights take an extra two to five hours each way, depending on connection times.

Return **fares** to San Francisco can cost more than £800 between June and August and at Christmas, though £500–550 is the average range. Prices in winter often fall to around £300. More flexible tickets to San Francisco, requiring less advance booking time or allowing changes or refunds, cost from £150 more whenever and from whomever you buy.

Aer Lingus offers a direct service from **Dublin** to Los Angeles (anywhere from €600–1000, depending on your proposed itinerary), with connecting services to the Bay Area.

Flights from the US and Canada

Many domestic flights into and out of the Bay Area use San Francisco International Airport (SFO); carriers offering the most frequent services here include United (with its West Coast hub at SFO), American and Delta Air Lines. Smaller, more navigable Oakland International Airport (OAK) across the Bay is often a better bet for snagging a bargain fare on airlines such as JetBlue, Southwest and US Airways. There's also a regular shuttle service from Los Angeles: American, United and Alaska Airlines operate the most frequent services.

Fares for nonstop round-trip flights from the Northeast and Mid-Atlantic (New York, Boston, Washington DC) to the Bay Area are around $350–400, although with a little luck and flexibility, you might be able to find something closer to $300. From southeastern cities like Miami and Atlanta, expect fares to hover between $375 and $500. Round-trip fares from Chicago range around $350–450, while shuttle fares from **Los Angeles** are $140–175.

If travelling from **Canada**, Air Canada has direct flights to San Francisco from Vancouver (around Can$350 return) and **Toronto** (Can$550).

A BETTER KIND OF TRAVEL

At Rough Guides we are passionately committed to travel. We feel that travelling is the best way to understand the world we live in and the people we share it with – plus tourism has brought a great deal of benefit to developing economies around the world over the last few decades. But the growth in tourism has also damaged some places irreparably, and climate change is exacerbated by most forms of transport, especially flying. All Rough Guides' trips are carbon-offset, and every year we donate money to a variety of charities devoted to combating the effects of climate change.

Flights from Australia, New Zealand and South Africa

From **Australia and New Zealand**, Los Angeles and San Francisco are the main points of entry to the US, with Los Angeles better served. Seat availability on these international flights is limited, so it's best to book at least a couple of months ahead.

There are daily direct flights to San Francisco with United Airlines from Sydney, and on Air New Zealand from Sydney and Melbourne. Qantas, Japan Airlines and Korean Air typically fly out of several major Australian cities, with the latter two making en-route stops in Asia. Expect flights to start around Aus$1500 in low season, adding as much as Aus$400 if originating from Perth. Tack on an additional Aus$500–700 at peak times.

Starting from Auckland or Christchurch, Air New Zealand flies via Sydney, Los Angeles, or Honolulu. Off-season fares hover around NZ$2200 – add NZ$300 or so for Wellington.

Travel to San Francisco is not particularly cheap from **South Africa**; prices are about the same out of Cape Town or Johannesburg, but up to ZAR500 more from Durban and other smaller cities. Fares start at around ZAR10,000 and rise as high as ZAR15,000 at peak times. Direct flights with US or South African carriers invariably involve a refuelling stop (often in Cape Verde), though a more roundabout route on one of the national airlines from further north in Africa is usually cheaper.

RTW flights

If San Francisco is only one stop on your longer journey, consider buying a **Round-the-World (RTW) ticket**. This can either be an "off-the-shelf" RTW ticket that will have you touching down in about a half-dozen cities or a more expensive tailor-made itinerary. Many of the major international airlines have allied themselves with one of two globe-spanning networks: the "Star Alliance" now has 27 members, including Continental, United, US Airways, Air Canada, Air New Zealand, Lufthansa, Thai, SAS, South African Airways and Swiss; while the dozen "One World" members include British Airways, Qantas, American Airlines, Aer Lingus, Cathay Pacific, Iberia, JAL and LAN. Both networks offer RTW deals with three stopovers in each continental sector you visit, with the option of adding additional sectors relatively cheaply.

Trains

Amtrak (☎1 800 USA RAIL, ⊛amtrak.com) services into San Francisco are more picturesque than punctual, best for those looking for a leisurely alternative to flying. There's only one long-distance train per day from the north or east, and only a couple more from the south; all three routes are among the most scenic on the entire Amtrak system.

The most spectacular is the **California Zephyr**, which runs all the way from Chicago via the Rockies, Salt Lake City and Reno in a scheduled 52 hours. There's also the **Coast Starlight**, where San Francisco is the midpoint on a breathtaking, mostly coastal route between Seattle and Los Angeles. Note that the other LA–SF Amtrak route heads inland by bus to Bakersfield, then by rail north through the comparatively dull San Joaquin Valley.

Note that Amtrak trains don't stop in San Francisco proper but rather across the Bay in Oakland – there's a free shuttle bus that runs over the Bay Bridge and drops passengers at San Francisco's Ferry Building.

Rail passes

One-way cross-country coach-class **fares** start at around $200 one-way if booked in advance online but can cost well over $300 at short notice in high season. If San Francisco is part of a longer journey, Amtrak offers **USA Rail Passes** (15 days/8 segments/$389, 30 days/12 segments/$579 or 45 days/18 segments/$749). There's also a **California Rail Pass**, which allows 7 days travel in a 21-day period for $159. Check Amtrak's website for the various senior, student, child and other discounts.

Buses

Taking a bus is usually the cheapest option for getting into San Francisco and only takes around the same time as the train, although it can

---

ONE-WAY TICKETS

A word of warning: it's not a good idea to buy a one-way ticket to the US. Not only are they rarely good value compared to a return ticket, but US immigration officials usually take them as a sign that you aren't planning to return home; as such, they'll probably refuse you entry. And with increased airport security checks, it's unlikely you'll be allowed to board your flight to begin with.

seem longer. **Greyhound** (☎1 800 231 2222, ⓦgreyhound.com) is the sole cross-country operator servicing San Francisco; 21-day advance purchase prices for one-way tickets should cost around $120 from New York or Boston (3 days), $100 from Chicago (2 days), or $40 from Los Angeles (8–11hr), but considerably more if you book less than a week in advance. **Greyhound Discovery Passes** buy unlimited travel on the entire Greyhound network, but are only really worthwhile for travellers including San Francisco as part of a longer itinerary. Check the website for details.

The other option is to catch one of **Green Tortoise**'s funky buses (☎415 956 7500 or 1 800 867 8647, ⓦgreentortoise.com) – they all arrive at the Transbay Terminal in South of Market. These buses come complete with bunks, foam cushions, coolers and sound systems, and offer a couple of useful routes to get you to the Bay Area. The company's "Hostel Hopper" links San Francisco with Los Angeles ($42) and Las Vegas ($62), and they also run various tours around the state.

Driving

Driving your own car gives the greatest freedom and flexibility, but if you don't have one (or don't trust the one you do have), one option worth considering is a **driveaway**. Companies operate in most major cities and are paid to find drivers to take a customer's car from one place to another, most commonly between New York and California. The company will normally pay for your insurance and your first tank of fuel – after that, you'll be expected to travel the most direct route and average 400 miles a day. Many driveaway companies aren't keen to use foreign travellers, but if you can convince them you're a safe bet, they'll take something like a $250 deposit, which you'll get back after delivering the car in good condition. It makes obvious sense to get in touch in advance, to spare yourself a week's wait for a car to turn up. Search online by "Automobile transporters and driveaway companies", phone around for the latest offers, or simply try one of the ninety branches of Auto Driveaway, based in Chicago (☎312 341 1900, ⓦautodriveaway.com).

If you're looking to **rent a car** to drive to the Bay Area, be sure when booking to get free unlimited mileage, and be aware that rates can skyrocket if you want to pick up the car in one location and leave it at another.

Airlines, agents and operators

AIRLINES

Aer Lingus ⓦaerlingus.com.
Air Canada ⓦaircanada.com.
Air France ⓦairfrance.com.
Air New Zealand ⓦairnewzealand.com.
Alaska Airlines ⓦalaskaair.com.
American Airlines ⓦaa.com.
British Airways ⓦba.com.
Cathay Pacific ⓦcathaypacific.com.
Continental Air Lines ⓦcontinental.com.
Delta Airlines ⓦdelta.com.
Frontier Airlines ⓦfrontierairlines.com.
Hawaiian Airlines ⓦhawaiianair.com.
Iberia ⓦiberia.com.
JAL (Japan Airlines) ⓦjal.com
JetBlue ⓦjetblue.com.
KLM (Royal Dutch Airlines) ⓦklm.com.
Korean Air ⓦkoreanair.com.
Lan Airlines ⓦlan.com.
Lufthansa ⓦlufthansa.com.
Qantas ⓦqantas.com.au.
SAS (Scandinavian Airlines) ⓦflysas.com.
Southwest Airlines ⓦsouthwest.com.
Thai Airways ⓦthaiair.com.
United Airlines ⓦunited.com.
US Airways ⓦusairways.com.
Virgin Atlantic ⓦvirgin-atlantic.com.

AGENTS AND OPERATORS

Abercrombie & Kent ⓦabercrombiekent.com. Well-tailored, rather upmarket tours.
Adventure Center ⓦadventurecenter.com. Hiking and "soft adventure" specialists.
American Holidays ⓦamericanholidays.com. All sorts of package tours to the US, including San Francisco, from Ireland.
Backroads ⓦbackroads.com. Cycling, hiking and multisport tours.
Bridge the World ⓦbridgetheworld.com. Specializing in RTW tickets, with good deals aimed at the backpacker market.
Contiki Travel ⓦcontiki.co.uk. West Coast coach tours aimed at partiers in the 18-35 age group.
Journeys Worldwide ⓦjourneysworldwide.com.au. Can make all travel arrangements to the Bay Area and other US destinations.
Kuoni ⓦkuoni.co.uk. Flight-plus-accommodation-plus-car deals, often geared toward families.
Madison Travel ⓦmadisontravel.co.uk. Specializing in gay and lesbian travel packages, including trips to the Bay Area.
Mountain Travel Sobek ⓦmtsobek.com. Conducts hiking, kayaking and rafting tours.
North South Travel ⓦnorthsouthtravel.co.uk. Nonprofit agency offering friendly and efficient service.
Peregrine Adventures ⓦperegrine.net.au. Specialists in active small-group holidays.

REI Adventures ⓦ rei.com/travel. Climbing, cycling, hiking, paddling and multisport tours.

Sydney International Travel Centre ⓦ sydneytravel.com.au. Individually tailored holidays, flights, bus and rail tours.

Trailfinders ⓦ trailfinders.com. One of the best-informed and most efficient agents for independent travellers.

TrekAmerica ⓦ trekamerica.com. Adventure touring holidays looping through San Francisco – usually small groups in well-equipped 4WD vans.

USIT ⓦ usit.ie. Ireland's premier student travel centre, which can also find good nonstudent deals.

Arrival

The Bay Area airports are well served by public transport, with a plethora of options to get you quickly into San Francisco or the East Bay. Besides BART (Bay Area Rapid Transit), there are plenty of buses, minivans and taxis, all of which will deliver you into the centre of the city in around thirty minutes.

Those arriving by bus in San Francisco pull into the centre of Downtown; if you're coming on Amtrak, you'll need to hop onto the free shuttle bus from Oakland in the East Bay. If arriving by car, San Francisco is well signposted, though it's best to stick to major routes such as I-280 for as long as possible; the one-way network of roads Downtown can be devilish to navigate the first time (see opposite).

By plane

All three major airports in the Bay Area are served by a host of airlines, both international and domestic.

San Francisco International Airport

There are several ways of getting into town from San Francisco International Airport (SFO; ☎650 821 8211 or 1 800 435 9736, ⓦ flysfo.com), each of which is clearly signed from the baggage reclaim areas. The easiest option is **BART**: the effortless thirty-minute nonstop train journey whisks you from the airport to the heart of Downtown for $8.10 (ⓦ bart.gov) and leaves every ten to twenty minutes; add ten to twenty minutes to Oakland ($8.40) or Berkeley ($8.55). There are signs within the airport directing you to the station.

A slightly cheaper, yet less convenient choice is the San Mateo County Transit (SamTrans) buses (☎1 800 660 4287, ⓦ samtrans.org), which leave every half-hour from the upper level of the airport.

The KX express ($5) takes around thirty minutes to reach the Transbay Terminal Downtown, while the slower #292 ($2) stops frequently and takes nearly an hour. On the KX, you're allowed only one carry-on bag; the advantage of the slower #292 is that you can bring as much as you want. Buses leave from level one (Arrivals), Terminal 2 centre island, and Terminal 3 curbside; at the international terminal, they stop on Level One next to Bus Courtyard G.

Due to their door-to-door service, many people opt to take **minibus shuttles** into the city – companies include Supershuttle (ⓦ supershuttle .com) and American Airporter (ⓦ americanairporter .com) – which depart every five minutes from the upper level of the circular road and take passengers to any central destination for around $17 a head; follow the signs for "Door to Door Vans" on the lower Arrivals level. Various **Airporter** services travel directly to the wider Bay Area: Evans Airport Service (Napa; 1hr 30min; $29; ⓦ evanstransportation.com); Marin Airporter (Sausalito and Mill Valley; 50–55min; $20; ⓦ marinairporter.com); and Sonoma County Airport Express (Santa Rosa; 2hr; $34; ⓦ airport expressinc.com).

Taxis from the airport cost around $35 (plus tip) for any Downtown location, more for East Bay and Marin County – definitely worth it if you're in a group or too tired to care. If you're planning to pick up a **rental car**, the usual car–rental agencies operate free shuttle buses to their depots, leaving every fifteen minutes from the upper level. Driving from SFO, head north on gritty US-101 or northwest on prettier I-280 for the twenty- to thirty-minute drive Downtown.

Oakland International Airport

Several domestic airlines (including America West, Southwest and United) fly into Oakland International Airport (OAK; ☎510 563 3300, ⓦ oaklandairport .com) across the Bay. As close to Downtown San Francisco as SFO, OAK is efficiently connected with the city by the **AirBART** shuttle bus ($3; exact change only), which drops you at the somewhat seedy Coliseum BART station. From there San Francisco's Downtown stops are fifteen minutes away ($3.80) – take the train that terminates at Daly City or SFO. For Oakland ($1.75) or Berkeley ($2.35), take the Richmond line. Otherwise, a taxi should cost $50–55 into San Francisco, $40 into Oakland or $45 to Berkeley.

Norman Y. Mineta San Jose International

The third regional airport, Norman Y. Mineta San Jose International (SJC; ☎408 501 7600, ⓦ sjc.org), also serves the Bay Area, but should only be considered if you plan to begin your stay in Silicon Valley or lower Peninsula. Fares in and out of SJC are comparable to the airports north, and public transport to the city is inconvenient and time-consuming. The frequent VTA SJC Airport Flyer bus runs to Downtown for $4.

By train

All Amtrak trains stop in Oakland at the **Bay Area terminal** (📞 1 800 USA RAIL, 🌐 amtrak.com) at Jack London Square. From here, free shuttle buses run across the Bay Bridge to the Transbay Terminal, or you can take BART into town. A more efficient route is to get off Amtrak at Richmond to the north, where you can easily pick up BART nearby. Although it's technically closer to San Francisco, don't get off at Emeryville, the train stop before Oakland, as regular public transport to the city doesn't exist, though you can hail a cab there or take an Amtrak bus across the Bay Bridge. An hour late counts as on time for Amtrak, so don't make plans for tight connections.

By bus

At the time of writing, all of San Francisco's **Greyhound** services use the Transbay Terminal at 425 Mission St at First, South of Market (📞 1 800 231 2222, 🌐 greyhound.com). Plans are afoot to redevelop the terminal, so call to confirm first. To connect to the BART network, walk one block north to the Embarcadero station on Market Street; to reach CalTrain, take Muni bus #10 to the

station on Fourth King Street. **Green Tortoise** buses (see p.21) stop behind the Transbay Terminal at the corner of First and Natoma streets, South of Market.

By car

If you're driving into town from the east, the main route by car is I-80, which runs via Sacramento all the way from Chicago. I-5, passing fifty miles east of San Francisco, serves as the main north–south route, connecting Los Angeles with Seattle; the I-580 spur from I-5 takes you to the Bay Area. **SFO airport** has car-rental facilities (see opposite).

City transport

San Francisco is a rare American city where you don't require a car to see everything. Indeed, it is best viewed on foot. Given the chronic shortage of parking Downtown, horrible traffic and zealous traffic wardens, it makes more sense to avoid driving altogether. The public transport system (though unpredictable at times) covers every neighbourhood inexpensively via a system of trains, cable cars, buses and trolleys. If you have stout legs to tackle those hills, consider cycling – but, frankly, walking the city is still the best bet. Expect pavements to have steps on steeper hills for easier climbing.

THE STREETS OF SAN FRANCISCO

San Francisco's **street system** can seem maddeningly idiosyncratic at first, since, unlike many American cities, Downtown streets have names rather than numbers (the only grid of numbered streets is that radiating into the dock area south of Market). Throughout this guide, we've provided the street address, its cross street and the city neighbourhood to make it as easy as possible to locate any listings.

If you need to find another address, there's a basic formula that will help pinpoint your destination. Streets work on blocks of 100 from their Downtown source, which on north–south streets is Market; on east–west streets it's the Embarcadero (or Market in the case of those streets that don't extend all the way east to the Bay). For example, 950 Powell St is on the tenth block of Powell north of Market; 1450 Post St is on the fifteenth block of Post west of Market; 220 Castro St is on the third block of Castro south of Market. Further out from Downtown, in the Richmond and Sunset districts, the avenues all have their origin at the foot of the Presidio and travel south in increasing blocks of 100.

Handily, block numbers are usually also posted above the street sign, with an arrow indicating if the numbers are increasing or decreasing. When pinpointing an address verbally to a cab driver or when giving directions, San Franciscans always give the cross road rather than the number, and you'd do well to follow their example.

MAIN MUNI & CABLE-CAR ROUTES

USEFUL BUS ROUTES

#5 From the Transbay Terminal, west via Fulton alongside Haight-Ashbury and Golden Gate Park to the ocean.

#22 From the Marina up Pacific Heights and north on Fillmore.

#28 & #29 From the Marina through the Presidio, north through Golden Gate Park, the Richmond and Sunset.

#30 From the CalTrain depot on Third Street, north to Ghirardelli Square, via Chinatown and North Beach, and out to Chestnut Street in the Marina district.

#38 From Geary Street via Civic Center, west to the ocean along Geary Boulevard through Japantown and the Richmond, ending at Cliff House.

#70 (Golden Gate Transit) From Civic Center to the Golden Gate Bridge.

#71 From the Ferry Terminal (Market St) to the end of Haight Street and to Golden Gate Park.

MUNI TRAIN LINES

Muni F–Market Line Restored vintage trolleys from around the world run Downtown from the Transbay Terminal up Market Street and into the heart of the Castro. The extension along the refurbished Embarcadero to Fisherman's Wharf is one of MUNI's most popular routes.

Muni J–Church Line From Downtown to Mission and the edge of the Castro.

Muni K–Ingleside Line From Downtown through the Castro to Balboa Park.

Muni L–Taraval Line From Downtown west through the Sunset to the Zoo and Ocean Beach.

Muni M–Ocean View From Downtown west by the Stonestown Galleria shopping centre and San Francisco State University.

Muni N–Judah Line From the CalTrain station, past Pac Bell stadium, along South Beach to Downtown west through the Inner Sunset to Ocean Beach.

Muni T-Third Line From the Castro station through Downtown along the Embarcadero and Third Street to the Dogpatch area in the southeast corner of the city.

CABLE-CAR ROUTES

Powell-Hyde From Powell Street/Market along Hyde through Russian Hill to Fisherman's Wharf.

Powell-Mason From Powell Street/Market along Mason via Chinatown and North Beach to Fisherman's Wharf.

California Street From the foot of California Street at Robert Frost Plaza in the Financial District through Nob Hill to Polk Street.

If you have questions on any form of public transport in the Bay Area call ☎511 or check ⓦ511 .org – there's a point-to-point bus/train route planner online, as well as live operators to answer any questions on public transport and even traffic conditions. See the colour **map** at the back of this book for transport routes in the centre of town.

Muni

The city's public transport is run by the San Francisco Municipal Railway, or Muni (☎415 673 6864, ⓦsfmta.com). A comprehensive network of buses, trolleys and cable cars runs up and over the city's hills, while the underground trains become **streetcars** when they emerge from the Downtown metro system to split off and serve the outer neighbourhoods.

Currently, there are seven tramlines (see above), which run underground along Market Street and above ground elsewhere. Environmentally conscious buses, powered by overhead electric cables rather than petrol, cover all the areas not served by street-cars. There are three historic **cable-car lines** (see above), which are more for cruising than commuting but still an unmissable treat.

On buses and trains, the flat **fare** (correct change only) is $2; with each ticket you buy, ask for a free transfer which is good for another two rides on a train or bus in any direction within ninety minutes to two hours of purchase. Even if you don't plan to transfer, make sure to pick one up, as you must be able to produce proof of payment at any time when asked by a Muni inspector. Note that cable cars cost $6 one-way ($3 before 7am and after 9pm) and do not accept transfers. The best option if you're planning on using Muni often is to buy a **Muni Passport**, available for one, three, or seven days ($14, $21, $27). It's valid for unlimited travel on the Muni system. A **Fast Pass** costs $62 for a full calendar month and for $72 also allows travel within the city limits on BART. These passes must be loaded onto the new electronic **Clipper card**, which you can also use as a convenient way to load cash for pay-as-you-go cash fares.

Muni trains run throughout the **night** on a limited service, known as the Owl Service, except the street-cars, which stop around 1am when above-ground buses take their place, and the F-Market Street line, which runs 6am–midnight; most buses run all night, but services are greatly reduced after midnight. For the most reliable information on schedules, you can buy a handy, up-to-date Muni map ($3) from the Visitors Information Center at Hallidie Plaza, the cable-car turnaround at Beach and Hyde or at most bookstores; it's also available online.

BART and CalTrain

Along Market Street Downtown, Muni shares station concourses with **BART** (Bay Area Rapid Transit; ☎510 465 BART or 415 989 2278, ⓦbart.gov), which is the fastest way to get to the East Bay – including downtown Oakland and Berkeley – and south of San Francisco, not to mention the bustling Mission District. **Tickets** aren't cheap ($1.75–10.90 depending on how far you ride), but the service is efficient and very dependable, with a fixed schedule. Trains usually arrive every ten minutes, although fewer trains run after 8pm and at weekends. There are four routes that run through San Francisco and across to the East Bay, while a fifth has its entire route in the East Bay. Tickets can be purchased on the station concourse; save your ticket after entering the station, as it is also needed when exiting the station via the turnstiles. Free schedules are available at BART stations: trains operate Monday to Friday 4am–midnight, Saturday 6am–midnight, and Sunday 8am–midnight, meaning the last trains leave their departure stations at midnight.

The **CalTrain** commuter railway (depot on Fourth St at Townsend, South of Market) links San Francisco south to San Jose; call ☎650 508 6200 or 1 800 660 4287 or see ⓦcaltrain.com for schedules and fares ($2.50–12.50).

Ferries

A picturesque if not particularly quick or cheap way of touring the Bay is by boat: three companies

operate regular services from the city centre. The **Blue & Gold Fleet** leaves mainly from Pier 41 at Fisherman's Wharf (☎415 705 8200, ⓦblueand goldfleet.com), along with a few weekday runs from the Ferry Building. It runs boats to Tiburon and Sausalito (both $10 one-way), while **East Bay Ferries** (☎510 747 7963, ⓦeastbayferry.com) operates services to Oakland ($6.50 one-way) and Angel Island ($14.50 one-way). **Golden Gate Ferries** are based at the Ferry Building on the Embarcadero (☎415 455 2000, ⓦgoldengate.org), offering trips to Sausalito and Larkspur (both $8.25 one-way).

For trips to Alcatraz, **Alcatraz Cruises** (☎415 981 7625, ⓦalcatrazcruises.com), run frequently to and from the island during the day from 9am to 3.55pm, departing from Pier 33 just southeast of Fisherman's Wharf. The last day-tour ferry returns at 4.30pm in winter, 6.10pm in summer; the night-tour ferries leave at 6.10pm and 6.45pm and return at 8.45pm and 9.25pm (day tour $26, night tour $33).

Taxis

Taxis ply the streets and while you can flag them down (especially Downtown), finding one can be difficult. The granting of more taxi licenses is a contentious issue in San Francisco, many arguing that the streets are clogged enough. Your best bet is to head for one of the larger Downtown hotels, where taxis are often waiting at a taxi stand, or to call ahead.

If you want to call a cab, try DeSoto (☎415 970 1300), ⓦdesotogo.com), Luxor (☎415 282 4141, ⓦluxorcab.com), or Green Cab (☎415 626 4733, ⓦ626green.com). Green Cab represents the environmentally friendly mindset of San Francisco and has the distinction of being the city's only cab company to use all hybrid vehicles. **Fares** (within the city) begin with a fee of $3.10 to start the meter, plus 45¢ for each additional 1/5th of a mile or 60 seconds' waiting time. There's a $2 surcharge from SFO airport; it's customary to add a fifteen-percent tip to the final amount.

Driving and car rental

The only reason to **rent a car** in San Francisco is if you want to explore the greater Bay Area, the Wine Country or the landscape north or south along the coast. If you're heading out of the city by car, pick up your vehicle at the end of your stay at one of the Downtown desks rather than at the airport on arrival. When driving in town, pay attention to San Francisco's attempts to control

Downtown traffic, all of which effectively make driving diabolical. The posted speed limit is 30mph, speeding through a yellow light is illegal, and pedestrians waiting at crossings have the right of way. In addition, it's almost impossible to make a left turn anywhere Downtown, meaning you'll have to get used to looping the block, making three rights instead of one left.

The American Automobile Association (☎1 800 222 4357, ⓦaaa.com) provides free maps and assistance to its members, as well as to British members of the AA and RAC.

Parking and tolls

Cheap, available **parking** is even rarer than a left-turn signal, but it's worth playing by the rules: police issue multiple tickets for illegally parked vehicles and won't hesitate to tow your car if it's violating any posted laws. Downtown, plenty of garages exist, most advertised rates beginning at $2.50 for fifteen minutes: note that new public garages – under Union Square Downtown, Portsmouth Square in Chinatown, or Ghirardelli Square near Fisherman's Wharf – are cheaper than the private ones. One of the cheapest is on Broadway east of Stockton, next to the *Pacific Motor Inn*, another is on Pacific Ave in Jackson Square. The smartest overnight option if you have a rental car to stash is the Sutter Stockton garage above the Stockton Street tunnel: rates start at $8 at weekends. Metered spots on the street fill up fast and usually have a limit of two hours; be careful to avoid restrictions denoted by the kaleidoscopically confusing **curb colours**. Also, beware of posted no-parking hours, which could be late-night for street-sweeping or high-traffic commuting hours in the middle of the day.

Take care to observe the San Francisco **law of curbing wheels** – turn wheels into the curb if the car points downhill and away from the curb if it points up. Violators are subject to a $50 ticket. If you're towed, the minimum release fee is $194: to reclaim your vehicle, call AutoReturn Customer Service Center (☎415 865 8200) or head to its walk-in office at 450 Seventh St, where you can pay your fine and get your car back. For assistance or questions, contact the Department of Parking and Traffic (☎415 553 1235).

Bridge tolls are collected only when entering San Francisco by car; the Golden Gate Bridge toll costs $6, while the Bay Bridge one is $4–6, depending on the time.

CAR-RENTAL AGENCIES

Advantage ⓦadvantage.com
Alamo ⓦalamo.com
Avis ⓦavis.com
Budget ⓦbudget.com
Dollar ⓦdollar.com
Enterprise ⓦenterprise.com
Hertz ⓦhertz.com
National ⓦnationalcar.com
Payless ⓦpaylesscarrental.com
Rent-a-Wreck ⓦrentawreck.com
Thrifty ⓦthrifty.com

Cycling

Cycling is a great way to experience San Francisco. Throughout the city, marked bike routes – with lanes – direct riders to all major points of interest but note that officials picked the routes for their lack of car traffic, not for the easiest ride. If you get tired, bikes can be carried on most BART trains (during non-rush hours), and newer diesel and trolley Muni buses have bike racks on the front of the bus. You can also **rent a bike** at several outlets (see p.219).

THE 49-MILE DRIVE

If you have your own car, you can orient yourself by way of the breathtaking **49-Mile Drive**, a route that takes in the most important scenic and historic points in the city in around half a day. Marked by blue-and-white seagull signs, it circuits Civic Center, Japantown, Union Square, Chinatown, Nob Hill, North Beach and Telegraph Hill, before skirting Fisherman's Wharf, the Marina and the Palace of Fine Arts, after which it passes the southern approach of the Golden Gate Bridge and winds through the Presidio. From here it sweeps along the ocean, past the zoo, and doubles back through Golden Gate Park, vaulting over Twin Peaks and dipping down to Mission Dolores, then back to the waterfront for a drive past the Bay Bridge, the Ferry Building and the Financial District.

Some of the signs are missing along the route, so having a **map** is essential at times. Maps of the entire route are available for $1 from the Visitors Information Center at Hallidie Plaza, at the Powell Street cable-car turnaround, or you can download a free copy at ⓦonlyinsanfrancisco.com.

The media

San Francisco's media are surprisingly parochial: newspaper and TV coverage of all things Californian, especially the Peninsula, may be in-depth but events elsewhere in the country or the world will often receive little attention. It's worth picking up a newspaper, though, to understand the Byzantine bureaucracies that cripple local government and learn about the people who have a stranglehold on local politics.

Newspapers and magazines

San Francisco's only full-scale daily is the *San Francisco Chronicle* (daily $1, Sun $3; **W**sfgate .com). It's most useful for its Sunday edition's *Datebook* (known locally as the "Pink Section"), which contains reviews and previews for the upcoming week. An often-overlooked alternative is the peppy and well-reported *San Jose Mercury News* (daily 50¢, Sun $2; **W**mercurynews.com), the thick daily that focuses on the Peninsula but also provides terrific international news.

San Francisco is justly proud of its **alternative press**, which picks up the slack from the *Chronicle* and co, and results in two fine free weekly papers: *The San Francisco Bay Guardian* (**W**sfbg.com) and *SF Weekly* (**W**sfweekly.com), available from racks around town. Both offer more in-depth features on local life and better music and club listings than the dailies. The glossy *San Francisco Magazine* is often free in hotels; better is its upstart rival, *7x7*, another monthly with a trendier edge and a more in-depth restaurant review section. However, savvy locals eschew both of these ad-heavy magazines in favour of the more down-to-earth weeklies.

Detailed information on the East Bay can be found in its dailies, the *Oakland Tribune*, the *Berkeley Daily Planet*, or the *Examiner*-style *East Bay Daily News*. There's also an alternative weekly, the *East Bay Express*, as well as UC-Berkeley's two free daily student newspapers.

Television

In San Francisco, you'll have access to all the usual stations: from major networks like ABC (channel 7), CBS (channel 5), NBC (channel 3), and Fox (channel 2) to smaller netlets like the WB and UPN. Expect talk shows in the morning, soaps in the afternoon, and big-name comedies and dramas in primetime.

If that's all too maddeningly commercial-heavy, there's always the rather earnest, ad-free **public broadcasting** station KQED (channel 9), which fills its schedule with news, documentaries and imported period dramas.

There's a wider choice on **cable**, including CNN for news, and well-regarded premium channels like HBO and Showtime are often available on hotel TV systems, showing original series and blockbuster movies.

Radio

Listening to the radio is often one of the smartest ways to gauge the character of the local area. It's best to skip most speciality stations on the **AM** frequency – although there may be the occasional interesting chat programme. An intriguing addition is 1550 KYOU Radio, the world's first podcasting radio station. It offers bite-sized listener-submitted content simultaneously broadcast over the radio and online.

On FM, you'll find the usual mix of rock, Latin and r'n'b – these commercial-laden stations are too numerous to list. College stations such as UC Berkeley's KALX (90.7 FM) and University of San Francisco's KUSF (90.3 FM) are good picks for finding random local bands and eclectic music. The best way to find satisfying local, national and some international news is to tune in to **National Public Radio** (NPR), the listener-funded talk station with a refreshingly sober take on news and chat (try KQED 88.5 FM and KALW 91.7 FM).

Travel essentials

Costs

Accommodation will be your biggest single expense: the cheapest reasonable double hotel rooms go for $100 or so a night, although hostels will of course be cheaper. After you've paid for your room, count on spending a minimum of $40 a day for public transport, three budget meals and a beer but not much else. Eating fancier meals, taking taxis, and heftier bar tabs will mean allowing for more like $70–75 per day. If you want to go regularly to the theatre or major concerts, rent a car, take a tour or seriously shop, double that figure. As usual, students and people under 26 will receive good discounts on museum entrance fees and some other services such as travel costs, if they carry a valid International Student ID Card (ISIC, ⓦ isiccard.com) or International Youth Travel Card through (IYTC) through STA Travel.

Remember that a **sales tax** of 9.5 percent in San Francisco itself and slightly less in the surrounding counties is added to virtually everything you buy except for groceries and prescription drugs; it is seldom included in the quoted price.

Crime and personal safety

San Francisco is largely a safe and easy place for visitors to wander round, whatever the time of day or night. However, some central areas, such as the Tenderloin, especially along Turk and Eddy streets, are unpleasant day or night. Similarly, take care throughout South of Market and along Mission Street (between 14th and 19th streets) and 24th Street (between Potrero and Mission streets); taxis are the best transport option around Lower Fillmore and the Western Addition after dark.

As for **drugs**, possession of under an ounce of marijuana is a non-criminal offence in California: the worst you'll get is a $200 fine. Being caught with more than an ounce, however, means facing a criminal charge for dealing and a possible prison sentence. Other drugs are completely illegal; it's a much more serious offence if you're caught with any.

If you find yourself in need of **legal advice**, contact the Lawyer Referral Service, 465 California St at Montgomery, Financial District (Mon–Fri 8.30am–5.30pm; ☎415 989 1616).

Mugging and theft

Most visitors will have few (if any) problems but you shouldn't be complacent. Take the usual precautions: keep your wits about you in crowds; know where

> # EMERGENCY NUMBERS FOR LOST CARDS AND TRAVELLERS' CHEQUES
> **American Express cards**
> ☎1 800 992 3404
> **American Express cheques**
> ☎1 800 221 7282
> **Citicorp** ☎1 800 645 6556
> **Diners Club** ☎1 800 234 6377
> **MasterCard** ☎1 800 826 2181
> **Thomas Cook/MasterCard**
> ☎1 800 223 9920
> **Visa cards** ☎1 800 847 2911
> **Visa cheques** ☎1 800 227 6811

your wallet or purse is; avoid poorly lit parks, car parks and streets at night; and avoid using ATMs in untouristed areas or at night. And if you have to ask directions, choose carefully who you ask (go into a shop, if possible).

Always store valuables in the **hotel safe** when you go out. In hostels and budget hotels, you may want to keep your valuables on you, unless you know the security measures to be reliable. Should the worst happen, hand over your money and afterwards find a phone and dial ☎911, or hail a cab and ask the driver to take you to the nearest police station. Here, report the theft and get a reference number on the report to claim insurance and travellers' cheque refunds.

Having bags that contain travel documents, especially your passport, snatched is the biggest headache. Make photocopies of everything important before you go and keep them separate from the originals. If your passport does go missing, visit the nearest consulate and have them issue you a temporary passport to travel home.

Keep a record of the numbers of your travellers' cheques separately from the actual cheques; if you lose them, call the issuing company on the toll-free number below. All being well, you should get the missing cheques reissued within a couple of days – and perhaps an emergency advance to tide you over.

Car crime

Crimes committed against tourists driving **rental cars** have garnered headlines around the world in recent years but there are certain precautions you can take to keep yourself safe. Any car you rent should have nothing on it – such as a particular license plate – that makes it easy to identify as a rental car. When driving, under no circumstances should you stop in any unlit or seemingly deserted urban area – and especially not if someone is waving you down and suggesting that there is something wrong with your car. Similarly, if you are "accidentally" rammed by the driver behind, do not stop but drive on to the nearest well-lit, busy area and phone the police on ☎911. Keep your doors locked and windows never more than slightly open. Hide any valuables out of sight, preferably locked in the trunk or in the glove compartment.

Electricity

Electricity runs on 110V AC and most plugs have two flat pins, although some have a third

ESTA

Citizens of the UK, Ireland, Australia, New Zealand and most Western European countries who are eligible to travel under the **Visa Waiver Program** and who are staying for up to ninety days must now apply online for **ESTA** (Electronic System for Travel Authorization) before setting off. The process is quite straightforward – simply go to the ESTA website (ⓦ https://esta .cbp.dhs.gov), fill in the application and pay the $14 fee – the authorization is valid for two years. The process should only take a matter of minutes but it's best to apply at least three days before you travel. Make a note of the authorization number you are sent, in case you are asked for it at immigration.

round one. If coming from outside the USA, make sure you have an adapter that will fit the American sockets.

Entry requirements

Citizens of the thirty-six countries – including the UK, Ireland, Australia, New Zealand and most Western European countries – covered by the **Visa Waiver Program** must now apply online for **ESTA** (see box above) before travelling.

To use this system, all passports must now be machine readable and any issued after October 2006 must include a digital chip containing biometric data. Each traveller must undergo the US-VISIT process at immigration, where fingerprints are taken digitally and a digital headshot is also taken for file. At your port of entry, you are likely to be asked to confirm your departure date and prove you have onward travel arrangements, as well as sufficient funds. You will probably also be asked for a US address, for which the hotel you plan to stay for the first night is fine.

Canadian citizens are still exempt from the US-VISIT process but should present valid documentation. A valid passport is best, although an enhanced secure driver's licence is still an acceptable alternative. This may change though, so check for updates.

Prospective visitors from other parts of the world not mentioned above require a valid passport and a non-immigrant **visitor's visa** for a maximum ninety-day stay. How you obtain a visa depends on which country you're in and your status on application, so contact your nearest US embassy or consulate. Whatever your nationality, visas are not issued to convicted felons and anybody who owns up to being a communist, fascist, war criminal or drug dealer.

On arrival, the date stamped on your passport is the latest you're legally allowed to stay. The Department of Homeland Security (DHS) has toughened its stance on anyone violating their visa status, so

even **overstaying** by a few days can result in a protracted interrogation from officials. Overstaying may also cause you to be turned away next time you try to enter the US.

To get an **extension** before your time is up, apply at the nearest Department of Homeland Security office, whose address will be under the Federal Government Offices listings at the front of the phone book. In San Francisco, the office is at 630 Sansome St at Washington, Jackson Square (☎ 1 800 375 5283; ⓦ dhs.gov). INS officials will assume that you're working in the US illegally, so it's up to you to convince them otherwise by providing evidence of ample finances. If you can, bring along an upstanding American citizen to vouch for you. You'll also have to explain why you didn't plan for the extra time initially.

US EMBASSIES AND CONSULATES ABROAD

Australia

Online ⓦ canberra.usembassy.gov
Melbourne 553 St Kilda Rd, PO Box 6722, Vic 3004
☎ 03 9526 5900
Sydney MLC Centre, 59th floor, 19–29 Martin Place, NSW 2000
☎ 02 9373 9200

Canada

Online ⓦ canada.usembassy.gov
Montréal 1155 Rue de St Alexandre, Québec, H3B 1Z1
☎ 514 398 9695
Toronto 360 University Ave, ON M5G 1S4 ☎ 416 595 1700

Ireland

Online ⓦ dublin.usembassy.gov
Dublin 42 Elgin Rd, Ballsbridge ☎ 01 668 8777

New Zealand

Online ⓦ newzealand.usembassy.gov
Auckland Citibank Building, 3rd floor, 23 Customs St
☎ 09 303 2724
Wellington 29 Fitzherbert Terrace, Thorndon
☎ 04 462 6112

AVERAGE MONTHLY TEMPERATURES

	Jan	Feb	Mar	Apr	May	Jun	Jul	Aug	Sep	Oct	Nov	Dec
Max/Min (°F)	55/45	59/47	61/48	62/49	63/51	66/52	65/53	65/53	69/55	68/54	63/51	57/47
Max/Min (°C)	13/7	15/8	16/9	17/9	17/11	19/11	18/12	18/12	21/13	20/12	17/11	14/8
Rainfall (mm)	119	97	79	38	18	3	0	0	8	25	63	112

South Africa

Online Ⓦ southafrica.usembassy.gov
Cape Town 2 Reddam Ave, Westlake 7945 ☎ 021 421 4280
Johannesburg 1 River St, Killarney 2041 ☎ 011 644 8000

UK

Online Ⓦ http://usembassy.org.uk
London 24 Grosvenor Square, W1A 1AE ☎ 020 7499 9000; visa hotline (£1.50/min) ☎ 09061 500590
Edinburgh 3 Regent Terrace, EH7 5BW ☎ 0131 556 8315

FOREIGN CONSULATES IN SAN FRANCISCO

Australia Suite 1800, 575 Market St, Financial District (Mon–Fri 8.45am–1pm & 2–4.45pm; ☎ 415 644 3620)
Ireland Suite 3350, 100 Pine St, Financial District (Mon–Fri 10am–noon & 2–3.30pm; ☎ 415 392 4214)
New Zealand Suite 400, One Maritime Plaza, Embarcadero (appointment only; ☎ 415 399 1255)
UK 1 Sansome St, Financial District (Mon–Fri 8.30am–5pm; ☎ 415 617 1300)

Health

Foreign travellers should be comforted to learn that if you have a serious accident while in San Francisco, emergency services will get to you sooner and charge you later. For **emergencies**, dial toll-free ☎ 911 on any phone. If you have medical or dental problems that don't require an ambulance, most hospitals have a walk-in emergency room: for your nearest hospital, check with your hotel or dial information at ☎ 411. Some of the main hospitals are listed below.

Should you need to see a **doctor**, lists can be found in the *Yellow Pages* under "Clinics" or "Physicians and Surgeons." Be aware that even consultations are costly, usually around $75–100 each visit, which is payable in advance. Keep receipts for any part of your medical treatment, including prescriptions, so that you can claim against your insurance once you're home.

For minor ailments, stop by a **pharmacy**: we've listed some that are open 24 hours below. Foreign visitors should note that many medicines available over the counter at home – codeine-based painkillers, for one – are prescription-only in the US. Bring additional supplies if you're particularly brand-loyal.

Travellers do not require **inoculations** to enter the US, though you may need certificates of vaccination if you're en route from cholera- or typhoid-infected areas in Asia or Africa – check with your doctor before you leave.

For a free referral to the nearest **dentist**, call the national Dental Society Referral Service (☎ 415 421 1435 or 1 800 511 8663) or check Ⓦ dentalreferral.com.

HOSPITALS

California Pacific Medical Center Castro and Duboce streets, Lower Haight ☎ 415 565 6060. Has 24-hour emergency care and a doctors' referral service.
Castro-Mission Health Center 3850 17th St at Prosper, Mission ☎ 415 487 7500. Offers a drop-in medical service with charges on a sliding scale depending on income, plus free contraception and pregnancy testing.
Haight-Ashbury Free Clinic 558 Clayton St at Haight, Haight-Ashbury ☎ 415 487 5632 (phones answered Mon–Wed 9am–9pm, Thurs 1–9pm, Fri 1–5pm except from 12.30–1pm & 5.30–6pm). Provides a general health-care service with special services for women and detoxification, by appointment only.
San Francisco General Hospital 1001 Potrero Ave at 23rd, Potrero Hill ☎ 415 206 8000 or 206 8111 emergency. Has a 24-hour emergency walk-in service.

PHARMACIES

Walgreens 24-hour pharmacies 498 Castro St at 18th, Castro (☎ 415 861 6276); 3201 Divisadero St at Lombard, Marina (☎ 415 931 6415).

Insurance

Although not compulsory, international travellers should have some form of **travel insurance**. The US has no national healthcare system and prices for even minor medical treatment can be shocking. It's wise to verify if benefits will be paid during treatment or only after your return home, and whether there is a 24-hour medical emergency phone number. If you need to make a claim, keep receipts for medicines and medical treatment. Also,

ROUGH GUIDES TRAVEL INSURANCE

Rough Guides has teamed up with WorldNomads.com to offer great travel insurance deals. Policies are available to residents of over 150 countries, with cover for a wide range of adventure sports, 24hr emergency assistance, high levels of medical and evacuation cover and a stream of travel safety information. Roughguides.com users can take advantage of their policies online 24/7, from anywhere in the world – even if you're already travelling. And since plans often change when you're on the road, you can extend your policy and even claim online. Roughguides.com users who buy travel insurance with WorldNomads.com can also leave a positive footprint and donate to a community development project. For more information go to Ⓦroughguides.com/shop.

if you have anything stolen from you, you must obtain an official statement from the police.

A typical travel insurance policy also provides coverage for the loss of baggage, tickets and a certain amount of cash or travellers' cheques, as well as the cancellation or curtailment of your trip. Most policies exclude so-called dangerous sports unless an extra premium is paid; in the Bay Area, this can apply to rock climbing, windsurfing and even off-road mountain-biking. Therefore, if you're planning to do watersports or similar activities, you'll probably have to pay extra. Before buying travel insurance, American and Canadian citizens should check that they're not already covered. Credit-card companies, home-insurance policies and private medical plans sometimes cover you and your belongings when you're travelling.

Most travel agents, tour operators, banks and insurance brokers will be able to help you, or you could consider the travel insurance offered by Rough Guides (see box above).

Internet

There's free internet access at almost all hostels and most hotels but there's often a wait to get on a machine; likewise, the Public Library offers fifteen minutes' free access, but again often with a long wait. You can pick up an exhaustive list of almost every internet café for free from the information desk or check at Ⓦworld66.com. Most cafés in the city are tech-savvy enough to offer **wireless access** for laptop-toters, usually just for the price of a coffee – check Ⓦzrnetservice.com for locations.

Laundry

There's a laundry on nearly every other residential block in town. Two standouts are Brainwash, 1122 Folsom St at Langton, South of Market (☎415 861 3663), a combo bar-and-laundromat, and The Little Hollywood Launderette, 1906 Market St at Guerrero,

Mission (☎415 252 9357), which is open until midnight, with last wash at 10.45pm. There's no better **dry cleaners** in town than Gary's, 1782 Haight St at Shrader, Haight-Ashbury (☎415 387 2035).

Mail

Ordinary **mail** sent within the US currently costs 44¢ for letters weighing up to an ounce (28g), while standard postcards cost 29¢. It's important to include the zip code – there's a handy finder at Ⓦusps.com. For most destinations outside the US, airmail letters up to an ounce and postcards both cost 98¢. Airmail between the US and Europe may take a week and 12–14 days to Australasia.

The main post office is at 101 Hyde St at Fulton, Civic Center (Mon–Fri 8.30am–5.30pm, Sat 10am–2pm; ☎1 800 275 8777). Two other useful post offices are at Sutter Street Station, 150 Sutter St at Montgomery, Financial District (Mon–Fri 8.30am–5pm), and Rincon Finance Station, 180 Steuart St at Mission, South of Market (Mon–Fri 7am–6pm, Sat 9am–2pm).

Maps

The maps in this book, along with the free city plans you can pick up from the SFCVB in its *Visitors Planning Guide*, will be sufficient to help you find your way around. If you want something more comprehensive, the *Rough Guide Map to San Francisco* ($8.99) is unbeatable – the waterproof paper will last through even the worst of the city's unpredictable weather and the attractions, restaurants and hotels we've listed in the book are all clearly marked.

The city surprisingly has no dedicated travel bookshop but most of the major stores (see p.201) have travel sections. If you'll be travelling around the Bay Area, Rand McNally produces good commercial state maps for around $5 each. The American Automobile Association (☎1 800 222 4357,

W aaa.com) offers free maps to its members, as well as to British members of the AA and RAC.

Money

US currency comes in notes of $1, $5, $10, $20, $50 and $100. All are the same size, so check carefully. The dollar is made up of 100 cents in coins of 1 cent (a penny), 5 cents (a nickel), 10 cents (a dime) and 25 cents (a quarter). Change (quarters are the most useful) is needed for buses, vending machines and public telephones, though automatic machines are increasingly fitted with slots for dollar bills.

As for **exchange rates**, at the time of writing, one pound sterling will buy $1.60–$1.65; one euro fetches $1.45–1.50; one Canadian dollar is worth around $1.04; one Australian dollar is worth around $1.07; and one New Zealand dollar is worth almost 80¢; one South African rand yields about 15¢. You can check the latest exchange rates at W xe.com.

Banks and ATMs

With an ATM card (and PIN number) you'll have access to cash from machines all over San Francisco, though as anywhere, you will be charged a $1.50–4 fee for using a different bank's ATM network. Foreign cash-dispensing cards linked to international networks such as Cirrus and Plus are accepted at just about any ATM and the respective symbol will be on display at the machine.

Most **banks** in San Francisco are open Monday to Friday from 9am to 3pm and a few open on Saturday from 9am to noon. For banking services – particularly currency exchange – outside normal business hours and on weekends, try major hotels: the rate won't be as good but it's the best option in a tight financial corner.

Travellers' cheques

Travellers' cheques should be bought in US dollars only – they are universally accepted as cash in stores or restaurants, as long as you have a photo ID. It's best to bring them in smaller denominations, as some stores will balk at cashing a $100 cheque. The usual fee for travellers' cheque sales is one or two percent, though this fee may be waived if you buy the cheques through a bank where you have an account. You can also buy cheques by phone or online with Thomas Cook and American Express.

Credit and debit cards

For many services in the US, it's simply taken for granted that you'll be paying with plastic. When renting a car or checking into a hotel, you will be asked to show a credit card – even if you intend to settle the bill in cash. Most major credit cards issued by foreign banks are honoured in the US: locally, Visa, MasterCard, American Express and Discover are the most widely used. If you use your credit card at an ATM, remember that all cash advances are treated as loans with interest accruing daily from the date of withdrawal; there will also be a transaction fee on top of this. Not all foreign **debit cards** are valid for transactions in shops in the US.

Visa TravelMoney is a disposable prepaid debit card with a PIN that works in all ATMs that take Visa cards. When your funds are depleted, you simply throw the card away. Since you can buy up to nine cards to access the same funds – useful for couples or families travelling together – it's a good idea to buy at least one extra as a backup in case of loss or theft. You can call a 24-hour toll-free customer service number in the US (T 1 800 847 2911), or visit the Visa TravelMoney website (W usa.visa.com). The card is available in most countries from branches of Thomas Cook and Citicorp.

Phones

Greater San Francisco has a single **area code** – T 415 – and calls within this code are treated as local. You only need to dial the seven digits of the number when calling within T 415. The rest of the Bay Area has no fewer than five codes: East Bay (T 510 and T 925), Wine Country (T 707), Palo Alto (T 650), San Jose (T 408). To phone one area code from another, you'll have to dial a 1 before the number; toll-free calls (prefixed T 800, T 866, T 877, or T 888) also require a 1, no matter where you're calling from. Detailed information about calls, codes and rates in the Bay Area can be found at the front of the telephone directory in the *White Pages*.

In general, telephoning direct from your hotel room is considerably more expensive than using a payphone, costing up to $1 for a local call, though some hotels offer free local calls. Don't even think of calling abroad direct from a hotel phone – you'll be charged a small fortune. Without doubt, the cheapest way of making international calls is to buy a **pre-paid phonecard** with a scratch-off PIN number, available from newsagents and some small supermarkets. These come in denominations of $5 and $10 and can be used from any touchpad phone – hotels rarely charge for accessing the freephone number (but check), although using one from payphones invariably incurs an extra charge of around 50¢. Rates vary but calls to most developed countries only cost a few cents a minute. Another convenient but pricier way of phoning home from abroad is via a telephone **charge card** from your phone company back home. Using a PIN number, you can make calls from most hotel, public and private phones that will be charged to your account: check with your service provider.

Mobile phones

If you are planning to take a mobile phone (universally known as cell phones in America) from outside of the USA, you'll need to check with your service provider whether it will work there. Unless you have a **tri-band or quad-band** phone, it is unlikely that a mobile bought for use outside the US will work. If you do have such a phone, you'll have to contact your service provider's customer care department to ensure it is enabled for international calls. Be aware that you will incur hefty roaming charges for making calls and also be charged extra for incoming calls, as the people calling you will be paying the usual rate. If you want to retrieve messages while you're away, ask your provider for a new access code, as your home one is unlikely to work abroad. As the cost of using mobiles abroad is still fairly prohibitive, you may want to rent a phone if you're travelling to the US; see ⓦ triptel.com for details.

Opening hours and public holidays

The **opening hours** of specific visitor attractions, monuments, memorials, stores and offices are given in the relevant accounts throughout the Guide. Telephone numbers are provided so that you can check current information with the places.

San Francisco might not be a 24-hour city quite like New York and many locals finish work and eat early, yet outside of the Financial District you will find many stores open until 9pm and restaurants in areas such as North Beach, Union Square, Chinatown and the Mission serve food till at least 10–11pm.

Tourist attractions usually have decent hours – most museums will be open 10am–6pm and a few art galleries stay open until 9pm or so once a month. Smaller, private museums close for one day a week, usually Monday or Tuesday.

Public holidays

On the national public holidays listed below, banks and government offices are liable to be closed all day, stores less certainly so. The traditional summer **tourism season**, when many attractions have extended opening hours, runs from Memorial Day to Labor Day.

San Francisco has a huge variety of special **festivals** (see Chapter 15). During some of these events, especially Pride, hotels and hostels will book up quickly, so make sure to arrange accommodation well in advance.

January 1 New Year's Day
January (third Monday) Dr Martin Luther King Jr's Birthday
February (third Monday) President's Day
May (last Monday) Memorial Day
July 4 Independence Day
September (first Monday) Labor Day
October (second Monday) Columbus Day
November 11 Veterans' Day;
November (fourth Thursday) Thanksgiving
December 25 Christmas Day

USEFUL TELEPHONE NUMBERS

Emergencies ⓞ 911 for fire, police or ambulance
Directory enquiries for toll-free numbers ⓞ 1 800 555 1212
Local and long-distance directory assistance information ⓞ 411
Operator ⓞ 0

INTERNATIONAL CALLS TO SAN FRANCISCO

Your country's international access code + 1 for the US + appropriate area code + phone number.

INTERNATIONAL CALLS FROM SAN FRANCISCO

Remember to leave out the initial 0 of the local area code whenever calling home.
Australia ⓞ 011 + 61 + phone number
Canada ⓞ 011 + 1 + phone number
New Zealand ⓞ 011 + 64 + phone number
Republic of Ireland ⓞ 011 + 353 + phone number
South Africa ⓞ 011 + 27 + phone number
UK (including Northern Ireland) ⓞ 011 + 44 + phone number

Senior travellers

Any US citizen or permanent resident aged 62 or over is entitled to free admission for life to all national parks, monuments and historic sites, using a **Senior Pass**, for which a once-only $10 fee is charged; it can be issued at any such site. This free entry also applies to any accompanying car passengers or, for those hiking or cycling, to the passport holder's immediate family. It also gives a fifty-percent reduction on fees for camping, parking and boat launching. Some of these discounts are also extended to seniors of other nationalities. As for **travel**, Amtrak, Greyhound and many US airlines offer percentage discounts to anyone who can produce ID that proves they're over 62: don't expect hefty price breaks, but it's always worth checking. **Museums and art galleries** are better, and most will charge a reduced student/seniors rate, often to those 55 or older.

CONTACTS AND RESOURCES

American Association of Retired Persons 601 E St NW, Washington, DC 20049 ☎ 202 434 2277 or 1 888 687 2247, Ⓦ aarp.org. AARP can provide discounts on accommodation and vehicle rental. Annual fee of US$16.

Saga Holidays 222 Berkeley St, Boston, MA 02116 ☎ 1 800 343 0723 or 617 262 2262, Ⓦ sagaholidays.com. Specializes in worldwide group travel for seniors, with a few domestic trips. Saga's Road Scholar coach tours and their Smithsonian Odyssey Tours to US parks have a more educational slant.

Time

San Francisco, like the rest of California, operates on **Pacific Standard Time**, which is eight hours behind GMT and three hours behind the east coast. Daylight Saving Time (forward one hour) begins at 2am on the second Sunday of March and clocks go back at 2am on the first Sunday of November.

SAN FRANCISCO TOURS

As you'd expect from a city as tourist-friendly as San Francisco, there are plenty of tour operators prepared to show you the sights. Frankly, many of the bus trips are overpriced and worth avoiding – we've listed a few exceptions below. If you want to splash out, there are companies offering aerial tours of the breathtaking Bay; otherwise, try a cruise, but bear in mind that the city's iffy weather can mean some trips amount to little more than an hour adrift in the fog. If you just want to take a loop out under the Golden Gate Bridge and back, several independent boat operators troll for your business along Fisherman's Wharf – you can expect to pay around $10 per person plus tip.

By far the best option is a walking tour: San Francisco is a pedestrian city, and, barring a few hills, the easy pace and knowledgeable guides combine to provide the best value of all. A great way to get to know the quieter, historical side of San Francisco is to take a walking tour. The better ones keep group sizes small and are run by natives who truly love their subject matter. Some, like those sponsored by the library, are free. Reservations are recommended for all walks. The Visitors Information Center (see p.36) can give you a full list of available walks – every neighbourhood has at least one.

AERIAL TOURS

San Francisco Helicopters ☎ 650 635 4500 or 1 800 400 2404, Ⓦ sfhelicoptertours.com. A variety of spectacular flights over the Bay Area; prices start at $160 per person for a twenty-minute flight. Trips depart from SFO airport and land at Sausalito; the company will collect you by bus from the city centre and take you back at journey's end if you wish. The trips may sound pricey but the

soaring views are a five-star introduction to the city.
San Francisco Seaplane Tours ☎ 415 332 4843, Ⓦ seaplane.com. Another high-flying option, this company picks up from Pier 39, Fisherman's Wharf, four times daily for tours of the Bay, Golden Gate Bridge and Downtown. Prices start at $160 per person for a 25-minute flight.

BOAT TOURS

Blue & Gold Fleet ☎ 415 705 5555, Ⓦ blueand goldfleet.com. Offers chilly 75-minute cruises with breathtaking views of the Bay, leaving from Pier 39 and Pier 41 at Fisherman's Wharf – though be warned that everything may

be shrouded in fog, making the price ($25, online $23) less than worth it.
Red & White Fleet From Pier 43 ☎ 415 673 2900, Ⓦ redandwhite.com. Offers a similar service to Blue & Gold Fleet.

Tipping

When working out your daily budget, allow for **tipping**, which is universally expected. You really shouldn't depart a bar or restaurant without leaving a tip of at least fifteen percent (unless the service is utterly disgusting); twenty percent is more like it in upmarket places. About the same amount should be added to taxi fares – and round them up to the nearest 50 cents or dollar. A hotel porter should get $1 a bag, $3–5 for lots of baggage; chambermaids $1–2 a day; valet parking attendants $1.

Tourist information

The main source of city information for tourists is the San Francisco Visitors Information Center (see p.36 for details). Contact it or visit its website before your trip for brochures, maps, guides and event calendars; once in San Francisco, you can visit its walk-in branches. There are also several excellent Bay Area-related websites with current information on tours, museums and the newest restaurants and clubs (see p.36).

Upon arrival, maps and information are available from desks in the airports and at most hotels. Your best first stop, though, is the superb **San Francisco Visitors Information Center**, on the lower level of Hallidie Plaza at the end of the cable-car line on Market Street (Mon–Fri 9am–5pm, Sat & Sun 9am–3pm, closed Sun Nov–April). Its staff are exceptionally knowledgeable and it has free maps of the city and Bay Area, as well as pamphlets on hotels and restaurants. The centre can also help with **accommodation** through its toll-free reservation service (📞1 888 782 9673). Pick up a copy of the **San Francisco Visitors Planning Guide** – terrific for museums and attractions, although less comprehensive on lodging and dining (it lists only SFCVB members).

A great source for **listings** once you're in San Francisco are the weekly freesheets, including *SF*

BUS TOURS

Gray Line Tours 📞 415 434 8687 or 1 800 826 0202, 🌐 graylinesanfrancisco.com. This nationwide tour operator trundles round the city for three and a half fairly tedious hours

WALKING TOURS

Barbary Coast Trail Walking Tour 🌐 sfhistory.org. Self-guided, 3.8-mile tour through San Francisco's oldest and most infamous neighbourhoods, marked by bronze medallions set into the sidewalk. The tour also includes a brief hop onto a cable car.

City Guides 📞 415 557 4266, 🌐 sfcityguides.org. A terrific free series sponsored by the library and covering every San Francisco neighbourhood, as well as themed walks on topics ranging from the Gold Rush to the Beat Generation. Highly recommended.

Cruisin' the Castro 📞 415 255 1821, 🌐 cruisinthecastro .com. This fun tour explains how and why San Francisco became the gay capital of the world. It includes the story of the rise and murder of Harvey Milk, the city's first openly gay politician (see p.294). $35; schedule varies, usually summer only.

Haight-Ashbury Flower Power Walking Tour 📞 1 800 979 3370, 🌐 hippiegourmet.com. Learn about the Human Be-in, Grateful Dead, Summer of Love and the Haight's more distant past as a Victorian resort destination. One of the longest of all the tours. $20 per person; Tues & Sat 9.30am, Fri 11am.

HobNob Tours 📞 650 814 6303, 🌐 hobnobtours.com. Lively and scurrilous tours around the Nob Hill homes and haunts of Silver Kings and Robber Barons. This tour is one of the best in the city and groups are conveniently small. $30; Mon–Fri 10am & 1.30pm.

Mission Mural Walk 📞 415 285 2287, 🌐 precitaeyes.org. Two-hour presentation by mural artists leads around the Mission District's outdoor paintings, taking in over 70 murals. The costlier

for $41, leaving from Transbay Terminal three times daily. It also offers day-trips to Marin, the Wine Country and further afield.

1.30pm tour includes a slide presentation on the history and process of mural art. $12–15 per person; student/senior discounts available; Sat & Sun 11am & 1.30pm.

San Francisco Ghost Tour 📞 415 922 5590, 🌐 sfghosthunt.com. A supernatural tour of haunted hotspots. The first portion of the night is spent telling San Francisco ghost stories inside the *Queen Anne Hotel*. $20 per person; nightly 7pm except Tues.

San Francisco Parks Trust 📞 415 263 0991, 🌐 sfpt.org. Volunteer-led walks round the various attractions in Golden Gate Park, including the windmills and the Japanese Tea Garden, as well as other city green spaces. Free; call for latest schedules.

Vampire Tour of San Francisco 📞 650 279 1840 or 1 866 424 8836, 🌐 sfvampiretour.com. An after-dark stroll through Nob Hill, this two-hour tour is packed with San Francisco history with a fun gothic twist. $20 per person; Fri & Sat 8pm.

Victorian Home Walk 📞 415 252 9485, 🌐 victorianhome walk.com. Leisurely, two-hour tour through Pacific Heights and Cow Hollow where you'll learn to tell the difference between a Queen Anne, Italianate and Stick-Style Vic. $25; transfer bus picks up daily at 11am at the corner of Powell and Post streets.

Wok Wiz Tours 📞 650 355 9657, 🌐 wokwiz.com. A walk through Chinatown run by a knowledgeable team of food experts. Fun and fluffy with plenty of anecdotes, but a little thin on the history. $35, $50 including dim sum lunch; daily 10am.

SAN FRANCISCO ONLINE

craigslist ⓦ craigslist.org. This definitive community website (now operating microsites around the world) began – and is still best – in San Francisco. A terrific resource for everything from jobs to concert tickets.

511.org ⓦ 511.org. A wealth of up-to-the-minute information on Bay Area transport, traffic and cycling. A crucial resource whether you plan to venture beyond or just within San Francisco.

Mister SF ⓦ mistersf.com. An eclectic and well-researched site that's a wonderful repository of San Francisco history.

San Francisco Arts ⓦ sfarts.org. Comprehensive arts listings.

San Francisco Magazine ⓦ sanfranmag.com. Online

version of the local glossy, complete with feature stories. Definitely geared toward the city's "good life".

SFist ⓦ sfist.com. Populist news and culture site. Writers have a ball covering all things San Francisco, from Muni meltdowns and City Hall gossip to entertainment picks and slice-of-life essays. Highly recommended.

SF Station ⓦ sfstation.com. A top online source for local listings – opinionated, up to date, and easy to use. Especially reliable on nightlife.

The Virtual Museum of the City of San Francisco ⓦ sfmuseum.org. An exhaustive source of historical information about the city.

Weekly and *San Francisco Bay Guardian* (see p.27). Details for tourist offices in the wider Bay Area are given in Chapter 16.

STATE AND CITY TOURIST OFFICES

California Travel and Tourism Commission ☎ 1 800 GO CALIF, ⓦ visitcalifornia.com

San Francisco Visitors Information Center 900 Market St at Hallidie Plaza, Union Square ☎ 415 283 0177, ⓦ onlyinsanfrancisco.com

Visit Berkeley 2030 Addison St, Berkeley ☎ 510 549 7040, ⓦ visitberkeley.com

Visit Oakland 463 11th St ☎ 510 839 9000, ⓦ oaklandcvb.com

Travelling with children

San Francisco is primarily a place for adults – more so than, say, LA, where Disneyland and Universal Studios are major attractions. Still, kids can take solace in the fine beaches and neighbourhood parks; other kid-stops in town lean towards the educational – science museums, zoos and the like. If you're looking for **amusement parks**, head across the bay to Vallejo or down the coast to Paramount's

---

THE CITYPASS

The **CityPASS** ($54; ⓦ citypass.net) is a bargain ticket valid for entry to the Exploratorium, the Legion of Honor, Steinhart Aquarium and Academy of Sciences, San Francisco Museum of Modern Art (SFMoMA) and passage on a Blue & Gold Fleet San Francisco Bay cruise – all that, plus a free week's pass on Muni (see p.24). Buy it from the San Francisco Visitors Information Center (see above).

Great America. If you need a **babysitting service**, call the 24-hour hotline ☎ 415 309 5662 for information and rates.

Of San Francisco's few specifically child-oriented **attractions** – all of which are listed in the relevant chapters of this book – the Exploratorium in the Marina District is particularly excellent (the Tactile Dome adventure alone will keep any kid happy for at least half an hour). Otherwise, for natural wonders, head for the Steinhart Aquarium in Golden Gate Park or the newly remodelled San Francisco Zoo with its lush lemur forest and the chance to pet tarantulas. There's also the Aquarium of the Bay at Pier 39 on Fisherman's Wharf, where a moving walkway takes you through the centre of a massive, fish-filled glass tank. The only museum in town expressly designed for kids is the Zeum in Yerba Buena Gardens, although its opening hours are patchy; better to head for the enclosed, old-fashioned carousel next door.

Travellers with disabilities

San Francisco actively caters to the needs of disabled travellers. All public buildings, including hotels and restaurants, are required to have wheelchair-accessible entrances and bathrooms, and the public transit system has kneeling buses to let people aboard – check the comprehensive listings at *Access Northern California* for full details (ⓦ accessnca.com). The one unavoidable disadvantage is steep hills like Nob, Russian and Potrero: Muni buses are a solution for any tough gradients.

Resources

There are several excellent resources for **wheelchair-accessible** accommodation in the city: aside from *Access Northern California*, which rates hotels and sights, the San Francisco Convention and Visitors Bureau produces a free 34-page brochure, *Access San Francisco*, aimed at disabled travellers (☎415 283 0177 or 415 227 2619 TDD, ⓦonlyinsanfrancisco.com/plan_your_trip/access_guide.asp). It offers detailed access information on more than 150 San Francisco hotels, restaurants, museums and attractions, as well as public transport; pick it up from the main Visitors Center on Hallidie Plaza (see opposite), or download from the site directly. The main *Visitors Planning Guide* also includes a special section highlighting hotels that have exceptionally good facilities for disabled visitors. Another terrific resource is the Independent Living Resource Center (☎415 543 6222, ⓦfreed.org), a longstanding disabled advocacy group that can provide similar information.

UNION SQUARE

Downtown San Francisco

Dense with history and humanity, Downtown San Francisco comprises several vibrantly distinct neighbourhoods jammed together between the waterfront and the hills. Most of what the locals call Downtown is clustered within a square mile or two around the northern side of Market Street – San Francisco's main commercial and traffic drag, which cuts a diagonal swath across the city's northeastern corner. The area ends abruptly at the edge of San Francisco Bay, where vistas across the water and beyond came into clear view with the demolition of the Embarcadero Skyway in the early 1990s. Walking is the best means of exploration. It's possible, albeit exhausting, to cover the entire Downtown area in a day, but unless you're on the tightest of schedules, you'll get much more out of it just ambling around.

At the heart of Downtown sits **Union Square**, one of San Francisco's liveliest urban spaces. As the city's main hotel and shopping district, and the junction of its major transportation lines (including cable cars), it makes a logical starting point for wandering Downtown. Immediately west of Union Square, the somewhat quieter **Theater District** is full of old theatres and hotels. Along the waterfront stands the elegant **Embarcadero**, anchored by the Ferry Building and its immensely popular marketplace; the district mostly rests on landfill, partially composed of the remains of ships abandoned by eager forty-niners during the Gold Rush. The Embarcadero rims San Francisco's stalwart Financial District, to the northwest of which is **Jackson Square**, a historical district that's home to several of the city's original structures dating from the mid-nineteenth century. Slightly further from the water, you'll find Portsmouth Square, the site of San Francisco's founding, now all but submerged into frenetic **CHINATOWN**, an enclave boasting authentic pockets of Chinese culture, despite rampant tourism.

Union Square and around

A major hub, **Union Square** is filled with stores, hotels and flocks of tourists. The plaza itself occupies the entire block north of Geary between Stockton and Powell streets, and was radically transformed with the 2002 unveiling of its new, open layout, which replaced the hedge-divided expanse once popular with homeless sleepers. Today, edged by stout palm trees and sprinkled with potted foliage and plenty of seating, it's an ideal place to take a break from the surrounding bustle, although its reliance on granite appears out of step with San Francisco's typically grassy public spaces.

Union Square takes its name from its role as a gathering place for Unionist supporters on the eve of the Civil War, so it's confusing that the 97ft column rising from its centre should celebrate an 1898 victory in the Spanish-American War. The square was built under the direction of Mayor John White Geary, where a massive sand dune known as O'Farrell's Mountain once stood. The first American leader of San Francisco, Geary bequeathed the land to the city for use as a public plaza in 1850. To level off the dune, excess sand was shipped over to the seafront and used to fill Aquatic Park (see p.72), as well as Yerba Buena Cove – in the process helping create what is now the Financial District.

THE LAST EMPEROR

Joshua Norton arrived in San Francisco during the Gold Rush in 1849. Like most other successful entrepreneurs of the time, he didn't mine gold himself, but focused on real estate and commodity speculation through which he amassed an enormous fortune. After failing to corner the rice market in 1854, however, he declared bankruptcy, and vanished.

Five years later, the eccentric and wily Norton reappeared. Gambling on the power of notoriety, he marched into the offices of the *San Francisco Bulletin* dressed in lavish military dress, including a plumed hat and sabre, and proclaimed himself "**Emperor of the United States**", a statement the editor printed on the front page. (A month later, Norton added the title "Protector of Mexico".) His Imperial Palace was a tiny room in a boarding house at 642 Commercial St, and he lived off the currency of his fame – literally, since a local printer started producing 10-, 25-, and 50-cent bills of Emperor Norton money, which most local businesses accepted. He became a mascot for the city and was allocated official funds to replace his uniform each year; local restaurants eagerly claimed that Emperor Norton ate there.

Master of the publicity stunt and brilliantly balanced on the knife edge between nutty and notorious, Norton began issuing headline-grabbing edicts at regular intervals. Among the countless proclamations were a proposal to President Lincoln suggesting he wed Queen Victoria to cement relations between the US and UK, and a call for the building of a bridge to Oakland (prefiguring a route that was realized 75 years later with the completion of the Bay Bridge). He was also said to be the inspiration for the King in Mark Twain's *The Adventures of Huckleberry Finn*. When he died, suddenly, in 1880, his funeral attracted thirty thousand locals who followed the procession of his coffin along San Francisco's streets.

DOWNTOWN SAN FRANCISCO

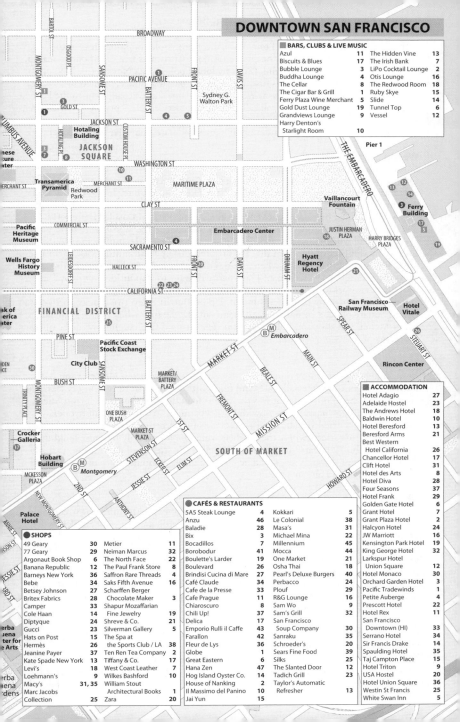

BARS, CLUBS & LIVE MUSIC

Azul	11	The Hidden Vine	13
Biscuits & Blues	17	The Irish Bank	7
Bubble Lounge	3	LiPo Cocktail Lounge	2
Buddha Lounge	4	Otis Lounge	16
The Cellar	8	The Redwood Room	18
The Cigar Bar & Grill	1	Ruby Skye	15
Ferry Plaza Wine Merchant	5	Slide	14
Gold Dust Lounge	19	Tunnel Top	6
Grandviews Lounge	9	Vessel	12
Harry Denton's Starlight Room	10		

CAFÉS & RESTAURANTS

5A5 Steak Lounge	4	Kokkari	5
Anzu	46	Le Colonial	38
Baladie	28	Masa's	31
Bix	3	Michael Mina	22
Bocadillos	7	Millennium	45
Borobodur	41	Mocca	44
Boulette's Larder	19	One Market	21
Boulevard	18	Osha Thai	17
Brindisi Cucina di Mare	27	Pearl's Deluxe Burgers	40
Café Claude	34	Perbacco	24
Cafe de la Presse	33	Plouf	29
Cafe Prague	11	R&G Lounge	16
Chiaroscuro	8	Sam Wo	9
Chili Up!	37	Sam's Grill	32
Delica	17	San Francisco Soup Company	30
Emporio Rulli il Caffe	43	Sanraku	35
Farallon	42	Schroeder's	20
Fleur de Lys	36	Sears Fine Food	39
Globe	1	Silks	25
Great Eastern	6	The Slanted Door	12
Hana Zen	47	Tadich Grill	23
Hog Island Oyster Co.	14	Taylor's Automatic Refresher	13
House of Nanking	2		
Il Massimo del Panino	10		
Jai Yun	15		

SHOPS

49 Geary	30	Metier	11
77 Geary	29	Neiman Marcus	32
Argonaut Book Shop	6	The North Face	22
Banana Republic	12	The Paul Frank Store	8
Barneys New York	36	Saffron Rare Threads	4
Bebe	34	Saks Fifth Avenue	16
Betsey Johnson	27	Scharffen Berger Chocolate Maker	3
Britex Fabrics	28	Shapur Mozaffarian Fine Jewelry	19
Camper	33	Shreve & Co.	21
Cole Haan	14	Silverman Gallery	5
Diptyque	24	The Spa at the Sports Club / LA	38
Gucci	23	Ten Ren Tea Company	2
Hats on Post	15	Tiffany & Co.	17
Hermès	26	West Coast Leather	7
Jeanine Payer	37	Wilkes Bashford	10
Kate Spade New York	13	William Stout Architectural Books	1
Levi's	18	Zara	20
Loehmann's	9		
Macy's	31, 35		
Marc Jacobs Collection	25		

ACCOMMODATION

Hotel Adagio	27
Adelaide Hostel	23
The Andrews Hotel	18
Baldwin Hotel	10
Hotel Beresford	13
Beresford Arms	21
Best Western Hotel California	26
Chancellor Hotel	17
Clift Hotel	31
Hotel des Arts	8
Hotel Diva	28
Four Seasons	37
Hotel Frank	29
Golden Gate Hotel	6
Grant Hotel	7
Grant Plaza Hotel	2
Halcyon Hotel	24
JW Marriott	16
Kensington Park Hotel	19
King George Hotel	32
Larkspur Hotel Union Square	12
Hotel Monaco	30
Orchard Garden Hotel	3
Pacific Tradewinds	1
Petite Auberge	4
Prescott Hotel	22
Hotel Rex	11
San Francisco Downtown (HI)	33
Serrano Hotel	34
Sir Francis Drake	14
Spaulding Hotel	35
Taj Campton Place	15
Hotel Triton	9
USA Hostel	20
Hotel Union Square	36
Westin St Francis	25
White Swan Inn	5

1

The square is now the nexus of one of the most profitable shopping areas in the country, as well as the home of the city's enormous Christmas tree each holiday season, a tradition started back in the mid-1800s by local kook Joshua Norton (see box, p.39). Below the square sits the world's first underground parking garage, opened in 1942; in its earliest days, it doubled as an air-raid shelter. A large stage sits adjacent to the Post Street side of the plaza, while a roll call of San Francisco leaders – pre-cityhood *alcaldes*, as well as mayors – is etched into a granite slab at the plaza's far northeast corner, although reading the vertical rendering of names and dates may give you neck ache.

Westin St Francis Hotel

335 Powell St • ☏ 415 397 7000, ⓦ westinstfrancis.com

On the western face of the square, just across Powell Street, the opulent **Westin St Francis Hotel** is steeped in some of San Francisco's darkest lore. In 1950, Al Jolson died here while playing poker, and just outside, in 1975, President Gerald Ford was nearly assassinated by ex-FBI agent Sara Jane Moore. Parts of **Dashiell Hammett**'s detective stories, including *The Maltese Falcon*, were set in the *Westin St Francis*, where the writer had worked as a private investigator in San Francisco during the 1920s. Indeed, he was part of the team that investigated the rape and murder case against silent film star Fatty Arbuckle when a starlet died after a debauched party in the actor's suite at the hotel in 1921. Fans of Hammett will want to step inside *John's Grill*, at 63 Ellis St at Stockton, the favourite dining spot of Hammett's rugged hero Sam Spade, and also frequented by Hammett himself. Up on Burritt Alley, two blocks north of Union Square plaza, a casually surreal plaque marks the spot where Spade's partner, Miles Archer, was shot and killed by *femme fatale* Brigid O'Shaughnessy in the opening moments of *The Maltese Falcon*.

Maiden Lane

Immediately east of Union Square and usually closed to vehicles, **Maiden Lane** is dotted with gourmet sidewalk cafés and filled with designer stores – a far cry from the latter half of the 1800s, when it was the vice-ridden heart of the city. Morton Street, as it was then known, was choked with bordellos since, in a pirouette of hypocrisy, local lawmakers decided that rather than eradicating prostitution, they would instead relegate it to side streets where the brothels would be found only by those looking for them. After the 1906 earthquake and fire levelled the street and drove away its shady denizens, it went through several name changes until, without a trace of irony, it was christened Maiden Lane in 1922.

140 Maiden Lane

Aside from the small jazz ensembles (or odd accordionist) performing for street-table diners, there's one other sight worth noting on Maiden Lane: the only **Frank Lloyd Wright**-designed building in San Francisco, at no. 140. Its squat exterior of pale brickwork vaguely resembles an ancient temple and lacks Wright's usual obsession with horizontal lines; the interior, however, is extraordinary, with porthole openings in the walls and a gloriously sweeping ramp that's a clear precursor to Wright's famed Guggenheim Museum in New York. Opened in 1948 to house the V.C. Morris Gift Shop, it's now occupied by Xanadu Gallery (Tues–Sat 10am–6pm; ☏ 415 392 9999, ⓦ folkartintl.com), which specializes in premium Asian art pieces.

Lotta's Fountain

Intersection of Market and Kearny streets

Two blocks east of Union Square sits the caramel-coloured – and dry – **Lotta's Fountain**. Reconstructed in 1916 and beautifully restored in 1999, this landmark is named in honour of the actress Lotta Crabtree, who gifted the contraption to her adoptive city in 1875. The fountain was originally intended to provide water to pedestrians and horses (the horse troughs were removed decades ago), but it gained fame for providing a very different form of relief in the wake of the earthquake and fire of 1906, when families used it as an impromptu message centre where they could post news of lost or missing loved ones.

Hallidie Plaza
Three blocks south of Union Square at the junction of Powell and Market streets

The one place in San Francisco through which almost every visitor will pass is Hallidie Plaza. The main San Francisco Visitors Information Center (see p.36) is located on the plaza's lower level, just outside the Powell BART/Muni station; it's

---

SAN FRANCISCO'S CABLE CARS

The brainchild of **Andrew Hallidie**, an enterprising engineer with an eye for the main chance, San Francisco's **cable cars** first appeared in 1873. Scots-born Hallidie is said to have been inspired to find an alternative to horse-drawn carriages when he saw a team of horses badly injured while trying to pull a dray up a steep hill in the rain. In fact, his attention was also drawn to the enormous volume of manure produced and how vocally locals complained about the problem. More than equine welfare was under threat, however – Hallidie's father had patented a strong wire rope that had been extensively used in the mines of eastern California. As the Gold Rush there slowed, Hallidie needed a new application for his family's signature product, and a privately owned transit system like the cable cars offered the ideal solution.

The cable-car pulley system was dubbed "Hallidie's Folly" by doubtful locals. After the first driver to be hired backed out just before the inaugural car ride, Hallidie heroically took the reins himself. Soon the cable-car system had revolutionized the city, launching both a transport and real estate revolution. San Francisco's most elevated areas (such as Nob Hill) suddenly became accessible, and businesses and homes were constructed along cable-car routes, spreading the urban landscape westward. At their peak, just before the 1906 earthquake, more than six hundred cable cars travelled on eight lines and 112 miles of track throughout the city.

Use of the cable-car system began to decline when the increased popularity of cars was compounded by the devastation wrought by the earthquake of 1906, which left large chunks of track wrecked. When it was rumoured that the system would be phased out altogether, local activist Frieda Klussman organized a citizens' committee to save them in the late 1940s. She triumphed nearly two decades later, when the cars were placed on the National Register of Historic Places and the remaining seventeen miles of track (today down to ten) were saved in 1966. Now there are nearly fifty cars in use – each unique – and around 23 miles of moving cable underground.

The **Powell-Mason** and **Powell-Hyde** lines run from Hallidie Plaza off Union Square to Fisherman's Wharf, while the oldest route, the **California Street** line – which underwent a $16 million refit in 2010–11 – climbs Nob Hill along California Street from the Embarcadero and rattles past some of the most upscale hotels in the city. The Powell-Hyde line is the steepest, reaching a hair-raising 21-degree grade between Lombard and Chestnut streets, and if that doesn't sound so frightening, wait until you're hanging off the side of the cable car as you take the white-knuckle plunge seemingly right into the Bay itself.

During their ascents cars fasten on to a moving 2.5-inch cable, which runs continuously beneath the streets and helps the heavy cars maintain a safe, constant speed of about 9.5 mph. The cars' conductors are typically a cheerful lot and receptive to passengers' questions, and each boasts a signature bell-ringing style shown off during the Cable Car Bell Ringing Contest, held every July in Union Square. For more on the cars' history and background, visit the **Cable Car Museum and Powerhouse** (see p.54).

To beat the crowds, arrive early in the day (before 10am). If you do show up during peak hours, head a block or two north along Powell Street to the top of Union Square, since drivers try to leave a bit of extra room on board at the start of the journey. Finally, if the Powell Street lines are just too swarmed, the California Street line (which begins at California and Market streets) crawling up and over Nob Hill is less popular.

1

also the terminus for two cable-car lines that run to the northern waterfront. Hallidie Plaza is a terrific spot from which to admire the grand Flood Building at 870 Market St. This flatiron structure was constructed in 1904 by the silver-mining Flood family and was one of the few structures in Downtown to withstand the 1906 calamities.

The Theater District

The area between Union Square and the grubby Tenderloin is known as the **Theater District**, and despite its proximity to the tourist hub of the city, the neighbourhood is a convenient bolthole from shopping crowds – a secluded place to stay Downtown. The district is anchored by the American Conservatory Theater's eponymous performance venue, and the Curran Theatre immediately next door.

HIDDEN PARKS AND ROOFTOP GARDENS

The result of an urban planning policy that requires newly constructed buildings to provide one square foot of open space for every 50ft of commercial space, several semi-obscure **public open spaces** dot Downtown San Francisco. These humbly sized retreats – far smaller in scale than the likes of Yerba Buena Gardens, Rincon Park and Sidney Walton Park – are open to the public during regular business hours (typically Mon–Fri 9am–5pm), although since each is privately owned, access may be subject to the whims of management. Seating is almost always available, and with the exception of 1 Montgomery Roof Garden (which predates the 1985 mandate's signage guidelines), each location described below has a plaque at street level announcing its use as a public open space. In certain cases where access is through a building's lobby, it doesn't hurt to let the security guard know where you're headed, but you shouldn't be hassled too harshly, if at all.

There are over fifteen such spaces around Downtown; these are the most inviting.

Transamerica Redwood Park Clay St at Sansome. In the immediate shadow of San Francisco's tallest building sits this subtle space flanked by semi-mature redwoods transplanted from the Santa Cruz Mountains south of the city. Two whimsical sculpture pieces – one featuring a small crowd of gravity-defying children jumping through imaginary puddles, the other of frogs leaping about the tiny park's fountain – mingle with workers taking a break in these unlikely woods. It's an utterly unique setting for Northern California's signature tree amid urban commotion.

343 Sansome Sun Terrace Sansome St at California. Fleeting views of Treasure Island and Marin County appear through the forest of high-rises surrounding this promontory. The spacious patio has ample foliage and seating, as well as a colourful obelisk-shaped sculpture by native San Franciscan Joan Brown. Enter through the building's lobby and take the elevator to the fifteenth floor.

1 Montgomery Roof Garden Montgomery St at Post. Space for this elevated hideaway was created when the top of its building was lopped off in the early 1980s. There's a variety of seasonal plants, a lion-headed fountain and even a medieval astrolabe at the southeast corner of the plaza, all overlooking the busy confluence of Market, Montgomery, Post and Second streets. Enter through the lobby of the main building directly below the garden and take the elevator to the top, or via the third floor of Crocker Galleria at 50 Post St (look for the sign on the east side of the centre that reads "Roof Garden").

560 Mission Public Space Mission St at Second. This South of Market nook is wedged between office buildings, but still gets plenty of sun into early afternoon. A number of tables and chairs are available during the day; after hours, you can still have a seat on one of the low stone ledges near the bamboo that rustles in the breeze. Sit and admire the silently mesmerizing sculpture of two round pieces of steel that move with the wind amid the small pool.

1 Sansome Plaza Sansome St at Sutter. Set in the shell of the c.1910 Crocker Bank, this glass-canopied atrium boasts stately palms, lots of marble and plenty of seating. It's an ideal spot if you're looking to relax in the sunlight's warmth, but out of its direct rays.

Empire Park Commercial St at Montgomery. Near the eastern edge of Chinatown, this slender mini-park slices away from Commercial Street under a latticework flanked by hedges and benches. It abuts an older residential building at its north end, so don't be surprised to see someone's laundry drying on a clothesline a few storeys above your head.

American Conservatory Theater

415 Geary St • ⓦ act-sf.org

Taking design cues from a Napoleonic palace, ACT's grand, colonnaded Neoclassical building opened in 1910 and was originally known as the Geary Theater. It sustained significant structural damage in the 1989 Loma Prieta earthquake and did not reopen until seven years later; it was renamed in 2006.

Curran Theatre

445 Geary St • ⓦ shnsf.com/theatres/curran

Next door to the American Conservatory Theater, the Curran dates from 1922 and operated as a vaudeville stage in its earliest days; these days, it hosts crowd-pleasing productions such as *A Chorus Line* and *Hairspray*.

The Financial District

The boundaries of San Francisco's **Financial District** have increasingly blurred in recent years, particularly with the spate of new office high-rises that continue to go up south of Market Street. Its western edge abuts Chinatown at Kearny Street, while to the north it quietly fades into the residential towers, brick offices and inviting parks of the Northeast Waterfront beyond Clay Street. As you'd expect, the often gusty canyons that crisscross its blocks of steel, glass and granite hum most vigorously on weekdays, particularly around lunchtime. Although the Financial District is more relaxed than it used to be – you'll see a higher percentage of dressed-down office workers than you would have in decades past – it's still ground zero for executives whose suits and spirited gaits uphold the district's Wall Street-of-the-West reputation.

Bank of America Center

555 California St at Kearny

Near the northwest edge of the Financial District sits the ominous hulk of the **Bank of America Center**. Though at 779ft not the city's tallest building, this broad-shouldered monolith of dark granite dominates the San Francisco skyline and has divided the city into fans and those who would like to see it razed to the ground; the latter doubtless cheered when it was used for exterior shots of the burning skyscraper in the 1974 film *The Towering Inferno*. Completed in 1969, it challenged the city not only with its size, but also with the startling contrast of its hue, as San Francisco used to be known as "a city of white". Depending on natural lighting and your vantage point, it can look either brown or vaguely reddish.

Wells Fargo History Museum

420 Montgomery St at California • Mon–Fri 9am–5pm • Free • ⓦ wellsfargohistory.com

Around the corner from the behemoth Bank of America Center is the **Wells Fargo History Museum**, where you'll find an unnatural amount of wall space devoted to the history of bank robberies. The display of old letters upstairs will be more intriguing to some – Wells Fargo operated the postal service between San Francisco and the Sierra Nevada foothill mines for a short time during the 1890s – as will be the plush stagecoach you can clamber into, also on the second floor.

Pacific Coast Stock Exchange

301 Pine St at Sansome

An impressive pair of sculptures flanks the steps of the imposing Pacific Coast Stock Exchange building. Sculptor Ralph Stockpole designed these giant artworks, jointly entitled *Progress of Man,* on site to complement one another: on the left stands the feminine half of the piece, "Agriculture", while to the far right, its mate "Industry" is represented by masculine figures. The building itself is striking, its Doric columns

1

THE MONTGOMERY BLOCK

The Transamerica Pyramid stands on the site of one of San Francisco's greatest lost monuments: the **Montgomery Block**, commemorated by a brass plaque in the lobby. Although it initially opened in 1853 as offices for lawyers, doctors and businesspeople, it soon became one of the city's crucial meeting places – a live-in community of bohemian poets, artists and political radicals. Rudyard Kipling, Robert Louis Stevenson, Mark Twain and William Randolph Hearst all rented work space here, while Ambrose Bierce, Bret Harte and Joaquin Miller were frequent visitors to the block's *Bank Exchange* bar and restaurant. A later habitué was Dr Sun Yat-sen, who ran a local newspaper, *Young China*, from his second-floor office; it's been said that Yat-sen wrote the first Chinese constitution here, and even orchestrated the successful overthrow of the Manchu (Qing) Dynasty in 1911. Sadly, the Montgomery Block was demolished in 1959 to eventually make way for today's Transamerica Pyramid.

beautifully intact, but stick your head inside the hall and you'll no longer see frantic neckties: trading operations were moved entirely to an electronic exchange system in 2002. Today the building is a private fitness centre that draws in area workers throughout the day and evening.

City Club
155 Sansome St at Pine

A short walk around the corner from the grand old Pacific Coast Stock Exchange, take the elevator to the tenth floor of what is now the **City Club** (a private gathering place for local business bigwigs) for a look at Diego Rivera's early 1930s mural, *Riches of California*, his first in the US. Depression-era columnists were bemused at the selection of the decidedly anti-capitalist Rivera to decorate the staircase ceiling of what was then the Pacific Stock Exchange Lunch Club; as with Stockpole's sculptures at the Stock Exchange itself, themes of agriculture and industry are major elements in the work. The City Club building, designed by noted San Franciscan Timothy Pflueger (best known locally for his work on San Francisco's Castro Theatre and Oakland's Paramount Theatre), showcases the finest in Art Deco tendencies, from the indulgent ground-floor lobby to the bronze-framed elevator doors. The security officer in the downstairs lobby may ask as to your business upon entry, but visitors are usually permitted to see the artwork upstairs.

Pacific Heritage Museum
608 Commercial St at Montgomery • Tues–Sat 10am–4pm • Free • ☎ 415 399 1124

Where the Financial District meets Chinatown, you'll find the tiny **Pacific Heritage Museum**, hosting rotating shows of Asian art, some better curated than others. The real draw is the structure itself: when the modern, marble-clad office block was built next door, preservationists protected the museum and forced the architect to artfully integrate this squat brick building into the skeleton of the skyscraper.

The Transamerica Pyramid and around
600 Montgomery St at Washington

Anchoring the northwest boundary of the Financial District, the **Transamerica Pyramid** is one of the tallest buildings in the US. Visible on clear days from as far as the Napa Valley hills and Mount Diablo, it's a once-controversial landmark that opened to business tenants in the summer of 1972. Its four triangular sides rise 853ft, and the building is so tall and thin it more resembles a squared-off rocket than a pyramid, particularly with its pair of flanking wings (containing elevator shafts, staircases and a smoke tower) that rise from the 29th floor. Due to security measures, there's no longer public access to the observation deck on the 27th floor, while frustratingly, the ground-level "virtual observation deck" outside the building's lobby – essentially, video monitors that transmit images from the top of the pyramid's spire – is often in need of repair.

I-Hotel
868 Kearny St at Jackson • Tues–Sat 1–6pm • Free • ☎ 415 399 9580, ⓦ manilatown.org

A block west and north of the Transamerica Pyramid, you'll find a chapter of recent history inside the Manilatown Center at the **I-Hotel**. The fourteen-storey 2005 incarnation of the International Hotel stands on the site of its squat predecessor, which played a pivotal role in this formerly Filipino-dominated stretch of Kearny. The original I-Hotel housed low-income Manong (elderly Filipino males) and Chinese for over fifty years until the building's tenants were forcibly evicted one night in August 1977 following a bitter, protracted battle between tenant-activists and city officials. The old building was eventually razed in 1981; however, plans for additional Financial District office space became mired in red tape and were never realized, and an updated version of the original I-Hotel was finally built as a home for low-income seniors. Today, the ground floor houses a public gallery devoted to community art and the history of Kearny Street's former identity as the centre of Filipino culture in San Francisco.

Columbus Tower
916 Kearny St at Columbus

At a sharply angled corner where the Financial District meets North Beach, look for the distinctive green-copper siding of the **Columbus Tower**, owned by director and San Francisco native Francis Ford Coppola. The building is home to *Cafe Zoetrope* (named for Coppola's production company, American Zoetrope) on its ground floor, an inviting, pie-slice-shaped space decorated with Italian paraphernalia and mementos from Coppola's illustrious career.

The Embarcadero

At the northeastern edge of the Financial District, the long stretch of waterfront known as **The Embarcader**o has undergone a remarkable transformation in recent years, largely powered by the renovation of the **Ferry Building** at the end of Market Street. The district has become a coveted location, especially for hotels, restaurants and attractions wishing to take advantage of the spectacular views across San Francisco Bay. It wasn't always this way. Until the 1989 earthquake fatally wounded the double-decker Embarcadero Skyway that blighted the waterfront for over three decades, the area was nothing more than a transport hub; in fact, before the construction of the bridges that connect San Francisco to Oakland and Marin County in the 1930s, the Embarcadero was the main point of arrival for tens of thousands of daily cross-Bay commuters, as well as a teeming port for cargo ships. Once the freeway's demolition was completed, improvements were slowly made to the area: Muni extended its streetcar lines, Harry Bridges Plaza opened between separated lanes of Embarcadero traffic in front of the Ferry Building, and walkers, runners and bikers took to the waterfront paths *en masse*. Several public piers to the north now provide scenic rest stops en route to Fisherman's Wharf (see p.69), while in the other direction lie the South Beach and Mission Bay districts, as well as AT&T Park, home of baseball's San Francisco Giants (see p.223).

San Francisco Railway Museum
77 Steuart St at Mission • Wed–Sun 10am–6pm • Free • ☎ 415 974 1948, ⓦ streetcar.org

A staple of the new Embarcadero is Muni's F-Market line, which exclusively runs restored streetcars plucked from such far-flung cities as Milan, Frankfurt and Louisville. The vintage streetcars cater mainly to city visitors along the Embarcadero section of the line, which rattles between Fisherman's Wharf and the Castro; disembark at the Steuart stop just south of the Ferry Building to visit

1

BONO: SAN FRANCISCO GRAFFITI ARTIST

The Vaillancourt Fountain's most notorious moment came one afternoon in November 1987, near the end of an impromptu set by U2 in Justin Herman Plaza, when vocalist **Bono** – having not yet morphed from rock star to international diplomat – left his artistic mark on it by spray-painting "Rock and roll stops the traffic", as captured in the band's film *Rattle and Hum*. Bono's graffiti stunt drew the ire of then-mayor Dianne Feinstein, who was in the midst of sponsoring an anti-graffiti campaign across the city; the "act of violence" (as it was called by San Francisco police who subsequently confronted Bono) nearly earned the Irishman jail time before cooler heads prevailed. When word reached Vaillancourt in eastern Canada, the feisty Québecois hopped on a plane to the Bay Area, where he backed Bono by appearing on U2's stage three nights later in Oakland, spray-painting "Stop the Madness" on the stage and lauding graffiti as a relevant means of artistic expression.

the **San Francisco Railway Museum**. The small museum, worth a brief visit, offers illuminating artefacts of the city's long rail history, including such ephemera as bygone fare boxes and traffic signals.

Justin Herman Plaza and around

A two-minute walk from the Railway Museum, it's perhaps fitting that **Justin Herman Plaza** – named in honour of San Francisco's father of urban renewal who, in the name of progress, bulldozed acres of historic buildings in the Western Addition after World War II – should be home to San Francisco's least revered modernist work of art. French-Canadian artist Armand Vaillancourt's 1971 *Québec Libre!*, known locally as the **Vaillancourt Fountain**, is a tangled mass of square concrete tubing that looks as if it were inspired by air-conditioning ducts. (One particularly sour local columnist lambasted it as the product of a giant dog with square bowels.) In fact, the visually jumbled statement on provincial sovereignty attempted to echo the Embarcadero Skyway that rimmed its plaza back when the fountain was built; today, with the freeway gone, there's a movement to have the fountain done away with as well.

These days, skateboarders and trick-bike riders share the open concrete square with gulls and lunching office workers. Other events and activities take place here throughout the year, from dance shows and rallies to an outdoor ice-skating oval that appears each winter holiday season.

The Hyatt Regency

5 Embarcadero Center • ☎ 415 788 1234, ⓦ sanfranciscoregency.hyatt.com

An entertaining side trip from Justin Herman Plaza is into the towering, triangular atrium of the adjacent *Hyatt Regency*, where the inverted shape of the terraces above gives the feeling that it could cave in at any moment. Mel Brooks fans will recognize this as the spot where the comic lost his marbles in 1977's *High Anxiety*.

The Ferry Building

1 Ferry Building • ☎ 415 983 8030, ⓦ ferrybuildingmarketplace.com

Now one of San Francisco's true gems, the **Ferry Building**'s makeover is arguably the most impressive of all the recent public space renovations in the city. Once the obstructing Embarcadero Skyway was removed, locals and visitors were able to appreciate the beauty of this Beaux Arts building's extended nave, Corinthian columns and Roman curved windows, as well as its 245ft-tall Moorish clock tower modelled after that of the Giralda in Seville, Spain.

When it was built in 1898, the Ferry Building boasted the largest foundation for a building over water anywhere, and was the first structure to use reinforced concrete; this sort of stout construction enabled it to withstand San Francisco's pair of cataclysmic twentieth-century earthquakes with minimal damage (mainly to the tower in 1906). At its peak in the mid-1930s, the building saw fifty thousand daily ferry commuters pass through its corridors. Once the Bay and Golden Gate bridges opened in 1936–37, however, ferry traffic dried up and the waterfront's longtime linchpin entered an era of sharp decline, its grand, airy nave cordoned off into utilitarian office space in 1955. Two years later, the Ferry Building suffered the ultimate indignation when double-decker slabs of freeway above the Embarcadero severed its physical connection to Market Street and the rest of the city.

After the freeway was demolished in the early 1990s, the stage was set for the Ferry Building's return to splendour, and after a lengthy period of neglect and misguided modification, it emerged immaculately restored in 2003 following a four-year renovation. It now boasts deluxe offices, food shops galore and, once again, a working ferry terminus for an increasingly revitalized commuter service. Now a National Historic Landmark, it has become one of the city's most visited attractions.

Ferry Plaza Farmers' Market
Tues & Thurs 10am–2pm, Sat 8am–2pm • ☎ 415 291 3276, ⓦ ferryplazafarmersmarket.com

The Ferry Building's nave is now a **gourmet marketplace**, and even those who shudder at the concept should visit; the range of merchants here means that almost anyone can find a treat to buy, much of it organic and produced locally. The best time to stop by is during the **Ferry Plaza Farmers' Market**, when local produce is sold from numerous stalls set up in a skirt around the building. Thousands of local food enthusiasts flock here to sample snacks from the city's restaurants, which often set up temporary shacks amid all the fruit and vegetable sellers; there are also regular recipe demonstrations from local name-brand chefs.

Jackson Square and around

The northern flank of what's now the Financial District wasn't known as **Jackson Square** until the 1960s, when interior designers who'd recently opened showrooms here decided on a suitably artsy yet old-fashioned name to replace the notorious Barbary Coast tag. By the late 1800s, the area was full of abandoned ships that had become floating hotels, bars, stores and brothels; as the boats fell into disuse, they were turned into mulched landfill, on which the tiny neighbourhood stands today. The constant stream of sailors provided an endless supply of customers looking for illicit entertainment, and earned the district the nickname "Baghdad by the Bay". It remained raunchy enough into the twentieth century to attract the attention of state lawmakers, who in 1915 passed an anti-vice act designed to stifle further shady activity in the neighbourhood. Certain locals protested unsuccessfully for two years, but the morning after they lost the final legal battle, police barricaded the area and shut down almost every establishment on the spot.

Jackson Square Historical District
Bordered by Washington, Columbus, Sansome and Pacific streets

Visiting the **Jackson Square Historical District** is a good way to imagine what nineteenth-century San Francisco looked like. Here you'll find the sole cluster of Downtown buildings that escaped the great fire of 1906 unharmed, and it's jarring to realize how different the city might have looked without that three-day orgy of destruction. Note the difference between the buildings on either side of Jackson Street: the low-slung, red-brick structures on the northern side date from the 1850s and are relatively simple, while the southern strip, constructed just a decade or so later, shows clear signs of Victorian ornamental excess, its appliqué stonework looking like cubic frosting over the brick base.

1

Hotaling Building

451–455 Jackson St

One of San Francisco's cheekier landmarks, the **Hotaling** (pronounced hote-UH-ling) **Building** is a survivor of the 1906 calamities. During the conflagration that followed the earthquake, when the orders came to dynamite this block as a firebreak, the manager of the wholesale whiskey operation housed here protested vigorously (and rightly) that the five thousand barrels inside were highly flammable. When certain newspapers across the country sermonized that San Francisco's disaster was God's retribution for the city's hedonistic vices, local wag Charles K. Field responded with doggerel that's still repeated with a smirk: "If as they say God spanked the town for being so over frisky, why did he burn the churches down and spare Hotaling's whiskey?"

Pacific Avenue

A block north of Jackson Street, leafy **Pacific Avenue** was the heart of the post-1906 Barbary Coast, nicknamed Terrific Street and filled with dance halls, cabarets and bordellos. It was also the home of San Francisco's first jazz clubs, staffed by refugee musicians who brought their music with them from Storyville, New Orleans' answer to the Barbary Coast. Now the street is home to advertising agencies, interior and graphic design studios, and law offices, with the only hint of its raucous past being the ornate light fixtures outside the old *Hippodrome* nightclub at no. 555.

Chinatown

Bustling, noisy Chinatown is shoehorned into several densely populated blocks between North Beach, the Financial District and Nob Hill. It's home to one of the largest Chinese communities outside Asia, and the oldest such enclave in the US; Chinatown's huge number of residents means that the banks of its river of people are bursting, pouring businesses and residents into surrounding neighbourhoods, especially North Beach. As it grows, its diversity increases, adding Taiwanese, Vietnamese, Korean, Thai and Laotian families; this cultural fusion is most evident in its grocery markets, where alongside traditional Chinese produce, you'll find Italian basil, Mexican kohlrabi bulbs and uniquely Southeast Asian fruits like the super-pungent durian.

Today Chinatown bristles with activity in spite of its increasingly elderly population base and, in sharp contrast to the districts that surround it, a clear lack of wealth. Many of its restaurants and tourist-geared retailers are clustered in its eastern half, while the western and northern sides are much more residential. Due to the crush of commercial and pedestrian traffic, narrow streets and paucity of parking, driving in Chinatown is only for the foolhardy.

A BRIEF HISTORY OF CHINATOWN

Chinatown has its roots in the mostly Cantonese **labourers** who migrated to the area after the completion of the transcontinental railroad, as well as the arrival of Chinese sailors keen to benefit from the Gold Rush. The city didn't extend much of a welcome to Chinese immigrants, however, and they were met by a tide of vicious racial attacks. Shockingly, such attacks were officially ratified under the unapologetically racist **1882 Chinese Exclusion Act** – the only American law ever aimed at a single ethnic group – which prevented Chinese naturalization, barred immigration to most Chinese and forbade thousands of single Chinese men from dating local women or even bringing wives from China. Although a rip-roaring prostitution and gambling quarter controlled by Chinese gangs (*tongs*) developed in the ensuing decades, conditions eventually improved once immigration laws were loosened and finally repealed after World War II, no doubt due to the US and China becoming allies during wartime.

1

Portsmouth Square and around

Between Washington, Clay and Kearny streets stands **Portsmouth Square**, San Francisco's first real city centre, born in the mid-1800s and now, to all intents and purposes, Chinatown's living room. When John Montgomery came ashore in 1846 to claim the land for the United States, he raised his flag here and named the square after his ship; the spot where he first planted the Stars and Stripes is marked by the one often flying in the square today. Two years later, Sam Brannan's cry of "Gold! Gold at the American River!" here sent property prices and development skyrocketing as hungry prospectors poured into the nascent town.

There are a few points of interest in Portsmouth Square, although nothing especially outstanding – the plaza is primarily worth visiting to simply absorb everyday life, with spirited games of cards and Chinese chess played atop cardboard boxes and other makeshift tables, and neighbourhood children letting off steam in the playground. Near Montgomery's flagpole is a replica of the galleon *Hispaniola* from the novel *Treasure Island* – a monument to writer Robert Louis Stevenson, who spent much time observing the locals in Portsmouth Square during his brief sojourn in San Francisco and the Monterey Peninsula in the late 1870s. Across the square, a plaque honours California's first public school, built here in the late 1840s. The most recent addition to the square is the already weathered bronze *Goddess of Democracy* statue near the playground, a replica of a sculpture in Beijing's Tiananmen Square.

Chinese American Telephone Exchange building
743 Washington St

Just outside Portsmouth Square stands a small, red, pagoda-like structure built in 1909 for the Chinese American Telephone Exchange. It's set on the original site of the office of Sam Brannan's *California Star* newspaper, which carried the news of the earliest ore discoveries back to the East Coast in 1848. A team of telephone operators worked here throughout the first half of the 1900s, routing calls solely by memory since no Chinatown phone listings existed; it was restored in 1960 by a bank and remains a financial institution today.

Chinese Culture Center
750 Kearny St • Tues–Sat 10am–4pm • Free • ☎ 415 986 1822, ⓦ c-c-c.org

Best accessed by a direct walkway from Portsmouth Square over Kearny Street is the **Chinese Culture Center**, long sequestered on the third floor inside the *Hilton*'s unappealing poured concrete tower. The exhibition space was granted an overhaul and reopened within the last few years, and continues to feature contemporary art and occasional performances; there's also a gift shop on site.

Grant Avenue and around

The residential overcrowding that has long characterized Chinatown has for decades been compounded by a brisk tourist trade, most of which is centred along **Grant Avenue**, the neighbourhood's main north-south visitor artery. Lined with gold-ornamented portals, brightly painted balconies and some of the tackiest stores and facades around, Grant is one of the oldest thoroughfares in the city. It was originally known as Dupont Street, a wicked ensemble of opium dens, bordellos and gambling huts policed – if not terrorized – by *tong* hatchet men. After the 1906 fire, the city decided to rename it in honour of president and Civil War hero Ulysses S. Grant, and in the process excise the seedy excesses for which it had grown infamous.

Chinatown Gate
A popular way to approach the neighbourhood is through the dramatic Chinatown Gate, which frames Grant Avenue where it meets Bush Street at the northern edge of the Union Square shopping district. Facing south, per feng shui precepts, it's a large,

dragon-clad arch with a four-character inscription that reads, *Xia tian wei gong*, or "The reason to exist is to serve the public good"; it was presented as a gift to the city from the People's Republic of China in 1969. It's hard to see how that idea is carried out in the blocks ahead, however: Grant's sidewalks are lined with plastic Buddhas, cloisonné "health balls", noisemakers and mechanical crickets that chirp above several shop entrances, although a number of gold-ornamented portals and brightly painted balconies provide pleasant counterpoint to the crass commercialism.

Old St Mary's Church

660 California St at Grant • ☎ 415 288 3800, ⓦ oldsaintmarys.org

Two blocks past Chinatown Gate is the red-brick and granite **Old St Mary's Church**, which predates nearly everything around it and abuts Grant Avenue's shopping district. Designed as a replica of a Gothic church in Vich, Spain, it became *Old* St Mary's when the new cathedral of St Mary of the Assumption was dedicated in 1891. In the years that followed, the older church struggled on and was one of the few buildings to weather the 1906 calamities – it survived the earthquake, but the subsequent fire left it as little more than a shell. The church was rebuilt and began ministering to the local Chinese population, as it still does today. Just inside the main doorway behind the banks of pews, there's a fine photo display detailing the 1906 damage to the city and the church.

St Mary's Square

Across California Street from Old St Mary's Church in surprisingly quiet **St Mary's Square** shines a 12ft-high statue of **Dr Sun Yat-sen**, founder of the Chinese Republic in 1911, created by noted sculptor Benjamin Bufano. The small park affords fine views of the Financial District.

Norras and Tien Hou temples

109 and 125 Waverly Place at Clay St • Daily 10am–5pm • Free

One half-block west of Grant Avenue runs parallel Waverly Place, once the heart of Chinatown's extensive network of brothels and now home to two opulent but skilfully subtle **temples: Norras** on the third floor of no. 109, and **Tien Hou** on the fourth f loor of no. 125. The namesake deity of Norras was the first lama from Tibet to teach Buddhism in China, and the temple itself is a calm refuge from the clatter and clang of the streets below. Taoist Tien Hou, a few doors up the street, bills itself as the oldest temple in San Francisco and is dedicated to the Goddess of Heaven; it's more incense-drenched and formally decorated than Norras, but less contemplative when staff members are conducting business at the desk. Still, it's worth the stair climb to see the interior daubed in gold and vermilion and the hundreds of lanterns and tassels suspended from the ceiling. Both Norras and Tien Hou are active temples, but are open to visitors, and although neither charges admission, it's respectful to leave a small donation and refrain from using cameras inside.

Chinese Baptist Church

1 Waverly Place at Sacramento St

South one block of the Norras and Tien Hou temples, look for certain bricks that droop from the Chinese Baptist Church building and are worn smooth – these survivors of the 1906 fire offer tactile evidence of the scorching temperatures that melted everything in their path. You'll find similar "clinker bricks" outside the Donaldina Cameron House at 920 Sacramento, one block up the steep hill.

Chinese Historical Society of America Museum

965 Clay St • Tues–Fri noon–5pm, Sat 11am–4pm • $3 • ☎ 415 391 1188, ⓦ chsa.org

Lodged halfway up the east slope of Nob Hill, the **Chinese Historical Society of America Museum** traces the beginnings of the Chinese community in the US. Housed in a

1

building designed by noted California architect Julia Morgan, its small but worthy collection of photographs, paintings and artefacts are culled from the district's pioneering days of the nineteenth century.

Stockton Street and around
With public housing tenements looming overhead and sidewalks full to bursting with locals on the hunt for that day's meat, fish and produce, **Stockton Street** is the commercial artery for Chinatown locals. Wander into one of the lively markets, where prices range from $1 for a 16-ounce pack of strawberries to shark fin (a much-sought soup delicacy) that can fetch over $350 a pound. Ellison Enterprises, 805 Stockton St at Sacramento, is known as Chinatown's best-stocked herbal pharmacy. Here, you'll find clerks filling orders the ancient Chinese way – with hand-held scales and abacuses – from drug cases filled with dried bark, roots, cicadas, ginseng and other traditional staples.

Chinese Cultural Services Center
832 Stockton St at Sacramento
On the same block as Ellison Enterprises, be sure to take in the striking mural at the **Chinese Cultural Services Center**, commemorating the day in 1869 when a team of 848 Chinese workers laid ten miles of track for the Central Pacific Railway (the usual daily output at the time was about one mile). The heads of certain men in the fresco are wildly disproportional, a design device that makes the piece disarming from any angle.

Golden Gate Fortune Cookie Factory
56 Ross Alley · Daily 7am–8.30pm · Free · ☎ 415 781 3956
Anyone with even a moderate sweet tooth will want to duck down slender Ross Alley and into the fragrant **Golden Gate Fortune Cookie Factory**. True to its name, the cramped plant has been churning out twenty thousand fresh fortune cookies a day since 1962 – by hand. A bag of forty cookies is no more than a few dollars, but it costs 50¢ to snap a photo.

Cable Car Museum and Powerhouse
1201 Mason St at Washington · Daily: April–Sept 10am–6pm; Oct–March 10am–5pm · Free · ☎ 415 474 1887, ⓦ cablecarmuseum.org
Just west of Chinatown, the **Cable Car Museum and Powerhouse** transports visitors back to the smoky world of late-nineteenth-century industry. Informative placards along the raised viewing platforms help even the least mechanically minded person understand how San Francisco's cable-car system operates, while downstairs you can catch a glimpse of the whirring sheaves (giant horizontal gears) working beneath the intersection of Washington and Mason immediately outside. There's also a gift shop, as well as plenty of displays on the cars' history in the city.

VIEW OF COIT TOWER ON TELEGRAPH HILL

North Beach and the hills

Inland North Beach was named when the area sat along San Francisco's original northern waterfront, before the city's landfill expansion above Francisco Street. The neighbourhood is best known as home to the city's Italian community, and you'll certainly hear Italian spoken by some of the older residents and restaurateurs. North Beach was the breeding ground for a number of major-league baseball players (most notably Joe DiMaggio) in the first half of the 1900s; by the 1950s, it had become the home of several Beat poets, thanks to its then-cheap housing and plentiful manual labour. In recent years, North Beach's original blue-collar character has been largely eroded by gentrification; even so, it retains an easy, worn-in feeling, and its sloping residential streets and vibrant main drags are ideal for aimless wandering.

No longer coastal, the sunny neighbourhood would be better known as North Valley, sitting as it does in the cleft between two of San Francisco's most prominent hills, **Telegraph** and **Russian**. These primarily residential neighbourhoods boast many beautiful old homes, as well as hidden gardens tucked away down pathways off steep hillside streets. **Coit Tower** crowns Telegraph Hill, boasting a spectacular panorama of the city, while a few small, lesser-known parks offer promontories from Russian Hill to the west. At the foot of Telegraph Hill's sharp eastern escarpment, reached via the **Greenwich and Filbert steps**, sits the **Northeast Waterfront**, a brick-clad, erstwhile industrial district along the upper Embarcadero reinvented in recent decades as a home to offices, modern condominium towers and a handful of fountain-strewn parks.

South of Russian Hill, you'll find pristine, yet historically snooty **Nob Hill**. Wealthy locals first settled this high mount of cathedrals and opulent hotels after the invention of the cable car, and it clings to its sense of separation as it hovers over the less ritzy neighbourhoods around it, its post-1906 mansions just as grandly imposing as the few original buildings that remain. And of course, even if you've seen it in a thousand pictures, a **cable car ride** up and down Nob and Russian Hills' steep inclines is still an exhilarating, singular experience.

● CAFÉS & RESTAURANTS			
Acquerello	22	La Folie	12
Caffe Sapore	2	Luella	15
Coi	18	The Matterhorn	16
Da Flora	6	Nook	21
Fog City Diner	3	Pat's Cafe	1
Frascati	14	Pesce	17
Grubstake	24	Pier 23 Cafe	4
Harris'	19	Piperade	13
Helman Palace	11	Ristorante Milano	20
Sushi Groove	10		
Sushi on North Beach	5		
Swan Oyster Depot	23		
Swensen's Ice Cream	9		
Trattoria Contadina	8		
Zarzuela	7		

■ BARS, CLUBS & LIVE MUSIC			
Bacchus	3	Red Devil Lounge	8
Bigfoot Lodge	6	Rouge	5
Bimbo's 365 Club	1	Tonga Room &	
The Big Four	10	Hurricane Bar	9
Kimo's	12	Tonic	4
La Trappe	8	Top of the Mark	11

■ GAY BAR	
The Cinch	7

● SHOPS	
Carrots	7
Cris	4
Fields Book Store	8
Graffeo Coffee	
Roasting Co.	1
The Jug Shop	6
Russian Hill Bookstore	2
Smoke Signals	3
Velvet Da Vinci	5

NORTH BEACH AND THE HILLS

■ ACCOMMODATION	
The Fairmont	2
Huntington Hotel	3
InterContinental	
Mark Hopkins	4
San Remo Hotel	1
Stanford Court	
Renaissance	5

North Beach

Sandwiched by Chinatown to the south and Fisherman's Wharf to the north, **North Beach** has always been a gateway for immigrants. Italian immigration to San Francisco was ignited by the Gold Rush, although it gained momentum at the end of the nineteenth century when this area began to develop the characteristics – delicatessens, focaccia bakeries, family restaurants – of a true *Piccola Italia*. Much like Chinatown, San Francisco's Little Italy was populated by expats from one main area of the old country – in this instance, fishermen from Liguria (the region around Genoa), as well as a small contingent from Lucca in nearby Tuscany. The freewheeling European flavour here, coupled with robust nightlife and wide availability of housing thanks to an exodus by wealthier Italians to the nearby Marina district, attracted rebel writers like Lawrence Ferlinghetti, Allen Ginsberg and Jack Kerouac. They made North Beach the nexus of the Beat Generation in the 1950s, which in turn helped make San Francisco a beacon for counterculturalists in the ensuing decades, from flower children in Haight-Ashbury in the late 1960s, to gays in the Castro in the 1970s and warehouse-dwelling ravers in South of Market in the 1990s.

Columbus Avenue

North Beach's lifeline has always been vibrant Columbus Avenue, which cuts diagonally through the neighbourhood's east-west street grid. Originally the route of

THE BEATS IN NORTH BEACH

North Beach has always been something of a literary hangout, serving as temporary home to Mark Twain, Robert Louis Stevenson and Jack London, among other boomtown writers. Despite its later association with Beat literature, however, the San Francisco neighbourhood isn't where the movement emerged – credit for that goes to New York in the 1940s, where bohemian Jack Kerouac joined with Allen Ginsberg and others to bemoan the conservative political climate there. The group soon moved out West, most of them settling in North Beach and securing jobs at the local docks to help longshoremen unload fishing boats. The initial rumblings of interest in the movement were signalled by the 1953 opening of the first bookstore in America dedicated solely to paperbacks: Lawrence Ferlinghetti's **City Lights** (see p.58) drew attention to the area as the latest literary capital of California.

But it wasn't until the publication four years later of Ginsberg's pornographic protest poem *Howl* – originally written simply for his own pleasure – that mainstream America took notice. Police moved in on City Lights to prevent the sale of the book, inadvertently catapulting the Beats to national notoriety – assisted by press hysteria over their hedonistic antics, including heavy drinking and an immense fondness for pot – that matched the fame earned by the literary merits of their work. Ginsberg's case went all the way to the Supreme Court, which eventually ruled that so long as a work has "redeeming social value" it could not be considered pornographic. Within six months, Jack Kerouac's **On the Road**, inspired by his friend Neal Cassady's Benzedrine-fuelled monologues and several cross-country trips, had shot to the top of the bestseller lists, cementing the Beats' fame.

It's said that the term **"Beatnik"** was jokily coined by legendary San Francisco newspaper columnist Herb Caen, who noted that the writers were as far out as the recently launched Soviet satellite, Sputnik. Soon, North Beach was synonymous across America with a wild and subversive lifestyle, an image that drove away the original artsy intelligentsia, many of whom ended up in Haight-Ashbury. In their place, heat-seeking libertines swamped the area, accompanied by tourists on "Beatnik Tours" who were promised sidewalks clogged with black-bereted, goateed trendsetters banging bongos. (The more enterprising fringes of bohemia responded in kind with "The Squaresville Tour" of the neighbouring Financial District, dressed in Bermuda shorts and carrying plaques that read "Hi, Squares".) Soon enough, of course, the Italians who'd once dominated North Beach reclaimed it from the dwindling Beat movement.

The legend of the Beats, though, has yet to die. It's been significantly aided by Ferlinghetti's successful campaign to rename certain smaller North Beach streets after local literary figures – the alley next to City Lights, for example, is now known as Jack Kerouac Alley.

2

CAROL DODA AND TOPLESS WAITRESSING

A mostly unsung pioneer of the Sexual Revolution, **Carol Doda** proudly burned her bra, albeit for very different reasons than the feminists who followed her. Knowing she'd make bigger tips by baring her finest assets, the North Beach cocktail waitress kick-started **topless waitressing** on June 19, 1964, creating a trend that at one point led to almost thirty different topless bars clustered together around the intersection of Columbus and Broadway. It didn't hurt that the Republican Convention was in town at the time – increasing business and fuelling the controversy – or that Doda had a plastic surgeon friend keen for her to showcase his handiwork, which over time boosted her natural bust by ten inches to 44D.

Five years later, on September 3, 1969, Doda broke the final taboo when she started serving stark naked. Her breasts became icons (set in concrete in front of the club), and Doda was awarded Business Person of the Year by a smitten crew from Harvard University. She finally retired from the *Condor* in 1986, turning to TV hosting and rock gigs, singing in a band called Carol Doda and Her Lucky Stiffs. Though the concrete breast impressions are long gone, Carol is commemorated with a bronze plaque on the exterior wall of her one-time workplace – cleverly, the marker is made to resemble an official State of California plaque. These days, Doda owns a lingerie boutique down a quiet courtyard off Cow Hollow's Union Street (see p.204).

the Old Presidio Trail, which connected the commercial settlements downtown with the Spanish fort to the northwest, the road later served as a throughway to the dairy farms of Cow Hollow. Since the early 1900s, however, it's been proudly tagged as San Francisco's Little Italy by the flags painted on each lamppost.

City Lights

261 Columbus Ave at Broadway • Daily 10am–midnight • ☎ 415 362 8193, ⓦ citylights.com

Near Columbus Avenue's southern end stands **City Lights**, the independent bookstore and publishing house opened in 1953 by Lawrence Ferlinghetti; it's still owned by the celebrated Beat poet today. The best reason to drop in is the upstairs poetry room, where you'll find everything from $1 mini-books and poster-size poems from Beat legends to various collections and anthologies, including titles from City Lights' in-house imprint. Across Jack Kerouac Alley from the bookstore is *Vesuvio* (see p.76), an old North Beach watering hole once patronized by the likes of Kerouac and Dylan Thomas that's now simply a popular bar with a colourful past.

Broadway and around

At Columbus's intersection with **Broadway**, you'll find the sites of many bars and comedy clubs from the 1950s – among them the *Hungry I* and the *Purple Onion*, where many of the era's politically conscious comedians, from Mort Sahl and Dick Gregory to Lenny Bruce, once performed. The strip clubs and porn stores that now dominate this stretch of Broadway first arrived with the Beats' exodus, and gained considerable steam with the topless waitress phenomenon kick-started by Carol Doda (see box above) at the **Condor Club** (560 Broadway at Columbus) in 1964. A few pieces of memorabilia from the club's topless heyday remain intact inside the building, including its piano suspended from the ceiling. It commemorates one of the club's choicest legends, the sad tale of a randy bouncer and dancer who climbed on top of that piano together after hours one night in 1983. In the throes of passion, the hydraulic system that raises and lowers the piano was somehow activated, sending the piano up to the ceiling. The man was crushed to death, but he cushioned the woman beneath him, and she survived.

The Saloon

1232 Grant Ave between Vallejo and Broadway • ☎ 415 989 7666, ⓦ sfblues.net/saloon.html

A few steps up Grant Avenue is San Francisco's oldest bar, **The Saloon**. The grungy tavern was first built in the 1860s and survived the 1906 fire; a century on, it persists as a lively, low-brow hardcore blues venue, wonderfully anachronistic among the encroaching boutiques and restaurants along upper Grant's shopping and dining strip.

Caffe Trieste

609 Vallejo St at Kearny • ☎ 415 982 2605, ⓦ caffetrieste.com

North Beach becomes increasingly Italian as you head north from Broadway – expect plenty of cafés, delis and restaurants selling cured meats, strong coffee and plates of *tagliatelle*. One eccentric, minor landmark is **Caffe Trieste**, where the jukebox plays opera classics and, on certain Saturdays, there's live music: jangling mandolin and Italian folk in the morning, and operatic vocalists in the afternoon. Photos of star patrons line *Caffe Trieste*'s walls, and legend has it that Francis Ford Coppola wrote most of the screenplay for *The Godfather* at the table beneath where his portrait now hangs.

National Shrine of St Francis of Assisi

610 Vallejo St at Columbus • ☎ 415 986 4557, ⓦ shrinesf.org

Looping back toward Columbus, you'll find the **National Shrine of St Francis of Assisi**, a neo-Gothic church built on the site of California's first parish. The current building, which dates from 1860, was the Barbary Coast's place of worship, and it's rumoured there was once a bullfighting ring attached. The structure is one of the area's few survivors of the 1906 fire: though its interior was gutted, all the walls held firm, and it was fully restored within twelve years. Behind the rows of pews are a number of compelling archival photographs, and the church itself is brighter, humbler and more contemplative than Saints Peter and Paul Church, a few blocks north (see p.60).

North Beach Museum

1435 Stockton St at Columbus • Mon–Thurs 9am–4pm, Fri 9am–6pm • Free • ☎ 415 391 6210

Plenty of neighbourhood memorabilia awaits at the intimate **North Beach Museum**, located somewhat awkwardly on the mezzanine level of a bank. Its heirlooms and photographs offer a fine look at the district's unique Marco Polo mix of Italian- and Chinese-Americans, although it focuses almost exclusively on the period between 1850 and 1950.

Fugazi Hall

678 Green St at Powell

Just west of Columbus Avenue, **Fugazi Hall** was donated to the community in 1912 by local banker John Fugazi. Once the site of Beat readings, this elaborate, terracotta-ornamented building has hosted San Francisco's

▣ ACCOMMODATION		● SHOPS		▣ BARS, CLUBS & LIVE MUSIC	
Hotel Boheme	2	101 Music	5, 7	15 Romolo	5
Green Tortoise	3	A-B Fits	2	Bamboo Hut	8
SW Hotel	4	Alla Prima		Comstock Saloon	13
Washington		Fine Lingerie	4	Gino and Carlo	3
Square Inn	1	Cavalli Cafe	8	Mr. Bing's	12
		City Lights	10	Rosewood Bar	6
		Coit Liquor	3	The Saloon	4
		Liguria Bakery	1	Savoy Tivoli	1
		Mee Mee Bakery	9	Sip Bar & Lounge	7
		Old Vogue	6	Spec's Twelve Adler Museum Cafe	9
				Tony Nik's	2
				Tosca Cafe	11
				Vesuvio Cafe	10

● CAFÉS & RESTAURANTS			
Cafe Divine	3	Louie's Dim Sum	22
Cafe Jacqueline	7	Mama's	2
Caffe Trieste	16	Mario's Bohemian	
Giordano Bros.	19	Cigar Store Cafe	5
The House	18	Maykadeh	12
Il Pollaio	8	Melt!	1
Italian French Baking	4	Mo's Grill	13
King Cha Cha	15	Molinari	17
L'Osteria del Forno	10	Peña Pachamama	9
Ristorante Ideale	14		
Sodini's	11		
Taqueria Zorro	20		
Tommaso's	21		
Tony's Pizza Napoletana	6		
Yee's	23		

longest-running stage show, *Beach Blanket Babylon* (see p.189), for several years; there's a remarkably lifelike bust of the show's late creator, Steve Silver, just to the right of the main entrance.

Washington Square and around

The soul of North Beach is **Washington Square**, a grassy gathering spot and public back yard that plays host to dozens of older, local Chinese each morning practising tai chi on and around its expansive lawn. Every year in mid-June, the North Beach Festival takes over Washington Square for a weekend with performance stages, food and drink booths and assorted lollygaggery. Local legend Lillie Hitchcock Coit's (see box opposite) none-too-subtle fascination with firefighters can be seen on the Columbus Avenue side of the park in the form of the bronze **statue** she commissioned honouring local volunteer firemen. Near the centre of the green plaza, look for the statue of Benjamin Franklin donated by local dentist/prohibitionist H.D. Cogswell, who ploughed a fortune into this monument by installing taps at the base in the vain hope that people would swill water rather than bootleg liquor.

Saints Peter and Paul Church

666 Filbert St at Powell • ☎ 415 421 0809, ⓦ stspeterpaul.san-francisco.ca.us/church

On the north side of Washington Square, the lacy, cream-coloured spires of **Saints Peter and Paul Church** look like a pair of fairy-tale castles rising from the North Beach flats. Although it's seen as the spiritual home of the local Italian community, the church also offers masses in Cantonese, as well as English and Italian. The interior is a vast nineteenth-century confection, underlit even on sunny days. In 1954, native son Joe DiMaggio and new wife Marilyn Monroe had their wedding pictures taken here, although the actual marriage took place earlier at City Hall since both had been previously divorced.

Joe DiMaggio Playground

Greenwich St at Powell

DiMaggio's legacy lives on a few blocks to the north of Saints Peter and Paul Church at his namesake **playground**, which occupies most of the city block surrounded by Greenwich, Powell, Lombard and Mason. The Yankee Clipper played baseball here as a kid in the 1920s, as did other neighbourhood Italian-Americans such as Frank Crosetti and Tony Lazzeri (as well as DiMaggio's own brothers, Vince and Dominic); each went on to star professionally. Today, the space is mostly paved and given over to basketball and tennis courts, as well as a pair of indoor community swimming pools.

Telegraph Hill and around

#39-Coit Muni bus; there are few parking spots at the top of the hill

Due east of North Beach and named for a semaphore station that once stood atop its 288-foot peak, **Telegraph Hill**'s steep slopes, hidden walkways and lush foliage are capped by one of the city's greatest attractions, Coit Tower. Save for the odd corner market, the hill is entirely residential, but it's well worth exploring for its fantastic views – though you'll need comfortable footwear as it's an unforgiving climb to the top. The most direct path up from North Beach is via Filbert Street; though steep, the short walk up the terraced sidewalk, past clapboard houses and an elementary school, is enjoyable. Once you reach the summit, it's easy to see why the peak was used as a signal tower for ships entering the Golden Gate. Standing where the statue of Christopher Columbus is today, a watchman on the hill would identify the boat's origin and name by the flags flying on the mast, and relay the information via telegraph to the docks along Fisherman's Wharf. The Columbus statue stands in **Pioneer Park**, which was donated to the city by private citizens in 1875 and has a lovely green space on its south side ideal for sitting and picking out the sights below.

Coit Tower

Daily 10am–5pm; mural tours Wed & Sat 11am start at the tower's main entrance • Lobby and tours free, $5 for elevator to top • ☎ 415 362 0808, tours ☎ 415 557 4266, ⊛ sfcityguides.org

Directly above the Columbus statue looms the Moderne-inspired **Coit Tower**, a 210ft-high pillar built in 1933 with a chunk of Lillie Hitchcock Coit's money (see box below) after her death. Provided there isn't too long a wait for the cramped elevator, the trip to the open-air viewing platform is well worth the few dollars – it's a stunning, eight-way panorama with unimpeded vistas in every direction.

Coit Tower's ground-floor lobby is notable for more than its handy restrooms: the **frescoes** wrapped around the interior's base were part of a project overseen by the Public Works of Art Project (a forerunner to the better-known Works Progress Administration), which employed artists to decorate public and government buildings during the Depression. Over two dozen painters were chosen for this project – entitled *Aspects of Life in California* – all of them students of the famous Mexican Communist artist, Diego Rivera. As with much of Rivera's work, the figures here are muscular and sombre, emphasizing the glory of labour, although there's a wide variation in style and quality between panels despite their thematic cohesion. Of particular note is Raymond Bertrand's *Meat Industry*, in which the artist cleverly adapts the building's windows to his scene as sausage smokers; also have a good look at *City Life* by Victor Amantoff, who depicts himself in a fur collar and hat next to a rack full of left-wing newspapers. In 1934, when rumours of "subversive" frescoes like these reached the authorities, the commission in charge of maintaining Coit Tower ordered that a hammer and sickle be removed from one of the pieces, and even tried closing the tower until tempers cooled. It didn't help that, at the same time, there was a contentious dispute between local longshoremen and port management, which escalated dangerously after police killed two demonstrators. A picket of the tower was mounted by local unions, keeping it in the headlines until authorities caved in and allowed the exhibit to open several months later.

The Greenwich and Filbert steps

Coit Tower may be Telegraph Hill's most visible (and visited) attraction, but it's along the **Greenwich and Filbert steps** – a pair of canopied pedestrian paths clinging to the urban peak's eastern flank – that the true identity of this area comes into focus. These lovely, steep walkways pass between oversized bungalows and delightful gardens both wild and manicured.

LOOPY LILLIE, FIREMAN MASCOT

Lillie Hitchcock Coit (1844–1929) first became the patron saint of San Francisco **firefighters** the day she helped the understaffed Knickerbocker Engine Company (No. 5 of the Volunteer Fire Department) tow its truck up Telegraph Hill. The grateful firefighters of the first engine ever to make it up the steep grade made the cheerfully nutty Coit their mascot, nicknaming her Firebelle; in return, she sported a diamond-studded fireman's badge reading "No. 5" all her life and even started signing her name with a five after it. Despite marrying wealthy easterner Howard Coit in 1868, the lifelong tomboy continued attending firemen's balls and playing poker with "her" men of Company No. 5. Coit smoked cigars, gambled avidly and shaved her head so her wigs would fit better, and stories were even told of her dashing away from society balls to chase after clanging fire engines. Oddly, she wasn't ostracized by polite society, but indulged as an amusing eccentric.

Coit's enduring legacy, though, stands on **Telegraph Hill** in the form of the concrete tower that was constructed after her death with the $100,000 she'd left "to be expended in an appropriate manner for the purpose of adding to the beauty of the city which I have always loved". The result, designed by Arthur Brown Jr (architect of City Hall) and Henry Howard, bears an unmistakable (if unintentional) resemblance to a firehose nozzle. Coit's rumoured liaisons with firemen add fuel to the speculation that the tower was actually her parting memorial to another part of a fireman's equipment.

2

The Greenwich steps

The brick **Greenwich steps** drop from the east side of the small Pioneer Park parking lot (look for the street sign) down to a hillside block of Montgomery Street. Lauren Bacall's *Dark Passage* character Irene Jansen lived here in the fine Art Deco apartment building at 1360 Montgomery; around the corner, the real-life former home of **Armistead Maupin** is at 60–62 Alta St, where the writer penned many of the escapades captured in *Tales of the City*.

Near 1440 Montgomery St, the Greenwich steps continue down the sharp slope to Sansome Street; while descending to the east, look for the cleared area to the left of the paved path with a smartly placed bench and, for comic measure, an uprooted parking meter replanted next to it. Also look and listen for the famed flock of **parrots** – hundreds strong – that now calls this side of Telegraph Hill home. The birds' green plumage sometimes makes them difficult to spot in the tall trees, but you can't miss their squawking. For more on this quirky phenomenon, seek out the 2005 documentary film *The Wild Parrots of Telegraph Hill*.

The Filbert steps

A block south of Greenwich, the **Filbert steps** trace an even steeper path up and down Telegraph Hill, with the lengthy stretch of the footpath between Sansome and Montgomery still laid with original wooden planks. There's also boardwalk on the route's most florid offshoot, Napier Lane, which overflows with foliage and is exhilaratingly fragrant with honeysuckle and roses in spring. The cottage at no. 224 Filbert dates from the 1860s and was thoroughly restored in 1978, while many of the other small homes in the immediate area are equally charming. The path continues up to Montgomery before finally cresting adjacent to Pioneer Park.

The Northeast Waterfront

Back on level ground at the foot of both paths, the Embarcadero-adjacent **Northeast Waterfront** is an attractive, if mostly workaday precinct full of restored brick offices made over from industrial warehouses of yesteryear. It's home to **Levi's Plaza**, the west half of which features an ambitious, walk-through fountain and plenty of bench seating; its grassy counterpart across Battery Street has a number of squat, rolling knolls ideal for lounging on sunny afternoons. The main building on the south side of the plaza serves as headquarters for blue-jeans progenitor Levi Strauss & Co, one of San Francisco's original businesses (hence the "SF" on the pocket rivets).

Russian Hill

Bordering North Beach to the west, elegant **Russian Hill** is perhaps San Francisco's quintessential romantic neighbourhood. The area was so named for six unknown Russian sailors who died on an undocumented expedition here in the early 1800s, and were buried near its southeastern tip. Its luxuriant, tree-lined streets, intimate bistros and endless vistas invite wandering and lingering, although like its Telegraph Hill counterpart across the flats below, several of its vertigo-inducing inclines are not for the faint of heart.

> ### THE BIRTH OF TELEVISION
>
> Long before the days of 60-inch flat screens and remote controls, science prodigy Philo Taylor Farnsworth worked in his laboratory in the Northeast Waterfront neighbourhood, where he concocted a video-camera tube – a device that dovetailed directly into his creation of the **world's first television system** here in 1927. Today, there's a plaque on the northwest corner of Green and Sansome streets that commemorates Farnsworth's watershed invention, from which he never became wealthy.

LOMBARD STREET (P.64) >

2

Lombard Street

Russian Hill's most familiar sight, by far, is the one-way block of **Lombard Street** that winds its way between Hyde above and Leavenworth below. It's hardly the white-knuckle drive many make it out to be, however, as the 5mph speed limit prevents any sort of Steve McQueen-like tomfoolery – not that you'll be able to drive much faster even if you tried, given the radius of the street's curves and the hedges that block any potential short-cutting. The best time to enjoy a trip down without having to queue west of Hyde is early morning or, better still, late at night when the city lights twinkle below.

San Francisco Art Institute

800 Chestnut St between Jones and Leavenworth • Daily 9am–8pm • Free • ☎ 415 771 7020, Ⓦ sfai.edu

One block north of Lombard Street, the low-rise, Mission-style building of the **San Francisco Art Institute** clings to the side of vertiginous Chestnut Street. It's easy to miss the place – although certainly not its students, whose freewheeling appearance provides sharp contrast to many of this neighbourhood's conservatively groomed residents. It's the oldest art school in the West; Jerry Garcia and Lawrence Ferlinghetti passed through the school's open studios, and Ansel Adams started its photography department.

Aside from the multi-level annexe in the rear of the school offering terrific rooftop views of northeast San Francisco, the one unmissable sight here is the Diego Rivera Gallery and its outstanding mural, *The Making of a Fresco Showing the Building of a City*. Executed by the painter at the height of his fame in 1931, the piece cleverly includes Rivera himself sitting with his back to the viewer in the centre of the painting – find the chubby figure looking on as others construct a giant human being in front of him.

Macondray Lane and Russell Street

Russian Hill boasts a pair of compelling literary points of interest. Along Taylor Street up the hill from Union, the lush, lower, pedestrian-only section of two-block **Macondray Lane** is widely believed to be the inspiration for Barbary Lane, home to Mrs Madigral and her oddball brood in Armistead Maupin's *Tales of the City* saga. Up and over Russian Hill's crest, branching off from Hyde's busy cable-car line, is

---

SAN FRANCISCO'S STEEPEST (AND TWISTIEST) STREETS

Though no San Francisco street can match Lombard for its fabled curves, there's another, lesser-known twistathon in town, adjacent to the US-101 freeway in the Potrero Hill neighbourhood: **Vermont Street between 20th and 22nd**. Its scenery may not be as picturesque as its Russian Hill counterpart, but it's virtually guaranteed that you won't have to wait in a queue to trundle down its one-way turns.

Another uniquely San Francisco thrill – provided your car's brakes and clutch are up to snuff – is to plummet down (or in certain cases when the streets aren't one-way, slog up) any of the city's **steepest streets**. Much pride among locals hinges on a driver's ability to negotiate San Francisco's most precipitous climbs and drops, particularly with a manual-transmission vehicle.

Below is a rundown of the sharpest drivable grades in town, complete with degree of steepness.
- Filbert Street between Leavenworth and Hyde, Russian Hill (31.5º)
- 22nd Street between Church and Vicksburg, Noe Valley (31.5º)
- Jones Street between Filbert and Union, Russian Hill (29.0º)
- Duboce Avenue between Alpine and Buena Vista Avenue East, Roosevelt Terrace (28.0º)
- Jones Street between Union and Green, Russian Hill (26.0º)
- Webster Street between Vallejo and Broadway, Pacific Heights (26.0º)
- Duboce Avenue between Divisadero and Alpine, Lower Haight (25.0º)
- Jones Street between California and Pine, Nob Hill (25.0º)
- Fillmore Street between Vallejo and Broadway, Pacific Heights (24.0º)
- Third Avenue between Irving and Parnassus, Inner Sunset (23.5º)

Russell Street: Jack Kerouac lived at no. 29 in 1952 where, inspired by the tape-recorded sessions with Neal Cassady for *Visions of Cody*, he produced some of his finest works, including *Doctor Sax* and a revision of *On the Road*.

Russian Hill parks

If you're more interested in green spaces than ghosts, Russian Hill contains some of the loveliest **neighbourhood parks** in the entire city. For picnics, a board game on a wooden tabletop or a few shots on a basketball hoop, **Michelangelo Playground** on Greenwich Street at Jones can't be beat. There's also immaculate **Alice Marble Park** (at Larkin and Greenwich), good for tennis or taking a breather on a bench, as well as the tiny patch of open space where the Vallejo Street pavement ends far above Taylor, for exceptional views of Downtown and the Bay at night. Finally, **Ina Coolbrith Park** is a pleasant outpost of green, named for California's first poet laureate. It's directly below the aforementioned lookout, although views are marred to a degree by the 1950s high-rise apartment tower in its midst.

Nob Hill

The posh hotels, stodgy institutions and multimillion-dollar residences of **Nob Hill**, south of Russian Hill and west of Chinatown, exemplify old San Francisco money in spades. Short on visitor sights but still meriting a quick visit, it's a subdued neighbourhood with oddly deserted streets and a suffocating sense of privacy found in few other parts of the city. Originally called California Street Hill, the 376ft mound was once scrubland occupied by sheep. The invention of the cable car made it accessible to Gold Rush millionaires soon after San Francisco's settlement, and the area garnered its current name which stemmed from any of three sources: "nabob", a Moghul prince; "knob", as in rounded hill; or simply, "snob".

Its status as a stronghold of power and wealth was cemented once Leland Stanford, Collis P. Huntington, Mark Hopkins and Charles Crocker, also known as the "Big Four" (see box, p.66), built the California Street cable line expressly to connect his own and his partners' mansions with Downtown below. Ostentatious showplaces built from Marin redwood were the favoured design among the railroad barons, but none of the young hilltop palaces escaped the 1906 fire. The sole surviving home on Nob Hill belonged to James C. Flood, who bucked his neighbours' trends in 1886 and poured $1 million into his 42-room, fire-resistant brownstone – a nod to his native New York. Today, the silver millionaire's manor, located at 1000 California St at Mason, is known as the **Flood Mansion** and hosts the Pacific-Union Club, an exclusive fraternal organization.

Fairmont Hotel

950 Mason St at Sacramento • ☎ 415 772 5000, ⓦ fairmont.com/sanfrancisco

Along with the Flood Mansion, another significant fire survivor on Nob Hill was the burnt-out shell of the as-yet-uncompleted **Fairmont Hotel**. Its owners tapped noted architect Julia Morgan for the rebuilding, and the design genius raced to complete the task in exactly one year. Note the flags flying above the *Fairmont*'s loggia: they represent nations attending the 1945 meetings held here that led to the formation of the United Nations later that same year. The hotel has a lovely rooftop garden that provides a nice spot to watch the cable cars clank up and down Powell Street far below – to reach it, walk through the plush lobby and down the long, wide corridor to the right of the main desk.

Huntington Park

Around the west side of the Flood Mansion are the primly manicured grounds of **Huntington Park**, designed and laid out after the 1906 fire on the site of

Collis P. Huntington's house. It's a tame plaza popular with contemplative readers and precious toy dogs prancing around its brick and grass surfaces, although its tortoise-covered fountain – a replica of a Renaissance original in Rome – is an enjoyably quirky installation.

Grace Cathedral
1100 California St at Taylor • Mon–Fri 7am–6pm, Sat 8am–6pm, Sun 8am–7pm • ☎ 415 749 6300, ⓦ gracecathedral.org

Overlooking Huntington Park is **Grace Cathedral**, one of the biggest hunks of neo-Gothic architecture in the US. Work began on the poured concrete monolith in 1928, but it wasn't completed until the 1960s as one funding delay after another routinely halted construction. The church's lengthy gestation period explains certain hotchpotch aspects of its Notre Dame-reminiscent design – look no further than the faithful replicas of Ghiberti's doors from the Florence Baptistry adorning the main entrance, which look utterly out of place. Still, the interior feels remarkably European, with a floor labyrinth near the entrance that exactly duplicates the design at Chartres in France (there's another walkable labyrinth to the right of the main entrance) and natural light shining in through the grand, east-facing rose window.

Nob Hill Masonic Center
1111 California St • Call for hours • ☎ 415 776 4702, ⓦ sfmasoniccenter.com

Another sight worth a visit on the hilltop is the modernist **Nob Hill Masonic Center**, across the street from Grace Cathedral. Though the venue is used for concerts and various Mason-approved paid exhibits, it's free to wander into the main hall to admire the astonishing window. Symbolically complex and 1950s naïve, its artwork depicts a group of six men representing the Masonic settlers who arrived in California by land, overlooked by an all-seeing Masonic eye. Though it resembles stained glass, the window is in fact an extremely rare endomosaic, an obscure art that involves sandwiching coloured materials such as twigs and sand between two sheets of clear glass.

THE BIG FOUR AND CALIFORNIA'S EARLY RAILROADS

The "nabobs" who gave Nob Hill both notoriety and name were the so-called Big Four. **Leland Stanford**, **Collis P. Huntington**, **Mark Hopkins** and **Charles Crocker** – the foursome met at a Republican Party political rally – made millions from the Central and Southern Pacific Railroads, a transport monopoly that both fed and strangled the development of California's early economy. Operating an unregulated monopoly that was usually caricatured in the liberal press of the day as a grasping octopus, "The Associates" (as the four men preferred to be known in their day) had by the end of the nineteenth century amassed a fortune worth over $200 million each.

Although they're often lumped together, the four men were vastly different in character. The mastermind was Huntington, a ruthless entrepreneur whose only morals were said to be his scrupulous dishonesty. Vain, self-important Stanford was the makeweight figurehead who had chanced on his wealth when a customer at the grocery store he owned paid off a tab with shares in a mine that soon struck silver. Tiny, penny-pinching Hopkins used to sell vegetables from his cottage garden to neighbours on Nob Hill to make extra money. Crocker was undoubtedly the most appealing of the bunch: a party animal with a popular wife, Mary Ann Deming Crocker, he was known for hands-on supervision of workers, even joining them in ditch-digging. Each man is commemorated with landmarks in the neighbourhood, although poor Crocker's is the posthumous also-ran – while his cohorts had hotels named in their honour, he's instead immortalized with a concrete parking structure.

FISHERMAN'S WHARF

The northern waterfront and Pacific Heights

From east to west, San Francisco's Northern Waterfront begins with crass commercialism, passes through areas of vast wealth and lands cast off by the military, and ends at the city's most famous landmark. Whether you're boarding a ferry to tour the former prison on Alcatraz Island, strolling the inviting paths at Crissy Field or simply browsing the boutiques along Union Street in Cow Hollow – to say nothing of taking in the iconic Golden Gate Bridge or the sandy bluffs and eucalyptus-filled hillsides of the Presidio – this is an area of the city that almost every visitor at least drops into, if not becomes immersed in. Its stunning vistas, opulent (if homogenous) neighbourhoods and even the tourist schlock seem to hold something for everyone.

BOAT TRIPS

Should you want to head out onto the water, **Bay cruises** depart from piers 39, 41 and 43 several times a day (see p.70). In addition, a number of independent boaters along Jefferson Street between Taylor and Jones offer charter tours for small groups; check around, as prices and restrictions may vary. Provided fog isn't too heavy (which can be the case any time of year), any of these excursions will boast excellent views and often pass under the Golden Gate Bridge – an unforgettable experience. Keep in mind that San Francisco Bay can be very cold and choppy, so dress accordingly and expect to get at least a little splashed.

Each year, millions of visitors plough through the overpriced gimmickry of **Fisherman's Wharf** for a glimpse of what remains of a nearly obsolete fishing industry; a few piers down the waterfront is the only point of access to America's most infamous island jail, **Alcatraz**. Immediately west of the Wharf, the area around and including **Aquatic Park** also pays homage to various forms of seafaring (albeit with more dignity), while around and atop the neighbouring bluff sits **Fort Mason**, rescued from the clutches of development and devoted to green space, non-profit organizations and even a hostel.

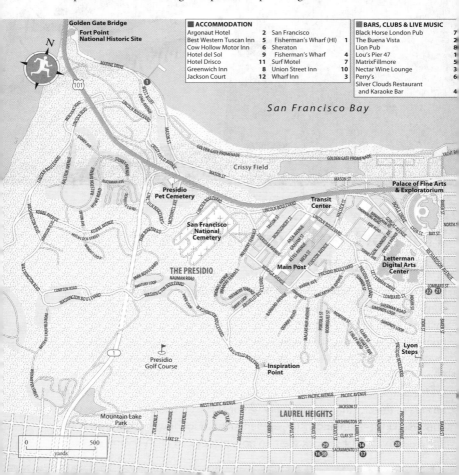

■ ACCOMMODATION			
Argonaut Hotel	2	San Francisco	
Best Western Tuscan Inn	5	Fisherman's Wharf (HI)	1
Cow Hollow Motor Inn	6	Sheraton	
Hotel del Sol	9	Fisherman's Wharf	4
Hotel Drisco	11	Surf Motel	7
Greenwich Inn	8	Union Street Inn	10
Jackson Court	12	Wharf Inn	3

■ BARS, CLUBS & LIVE MUSIC	
Black Horse London Pub	7
The Buena Vista	2
Lion Pub	8
Lou's Pier 47	1
MatrixFillmore	5
Nectar Wine Lounge	3
Perry's	6
Silver Clouds Restaurant and Karaoke Bar	4

Things take a turn for the affluent in the **Marina** and **Cow Hollow** neighbourhoods, where yacht clubs, boutiques and all things upmarket dominate the scene. Perched on the tall hill above these aristocratic districts stands stately, exclusive **Pacific Heights**, home to much of San Francisco's oldest money, and some of its new wealth as well. **The Presidio**'s real estate is equally valuable, but as a former military base that's now part of a national recreational area, it's never been up for private grabs; in fact, its current restoration as a public space (with a few high-profile private lessees) is in full swing. Finally, the **Golden Gate Bridge** lives up to its considerable hype as civic icon *par excellence*.

Fisherman's Wharf

If the districts of San Francisco are a family, then **Fisherman's Wharf** is the boisterous uncle who showed up at the reunion in a ghastly shirt, put a lampshade on his head and was the last to leave. It's the one part of town guaranteed to induce shudders of embarrassment from locals, although many of those same San Franciscans may be quietly thankful for a zone specifically designed to entertain and sequester visitors looking for an amusement park-like setting. San Francisco doesn't go dramatically out of its way to court

THE NORTHERN WATERFRONT AND PACIFIC HEIGHTS

CAFÉS & RESTAURANTS

6	12	Boudin Bakery & Cafe	5	Hime	20	Ristorante Parma	15
a Mandara	6	Dragon Well	9	In-N-Out Burger	4	Scoma's	2
ker Street Bistro	21	Garibaldi's	28	Jackson Fillmore	27	Sociale	30
lboa Cafe	23	Gary Danko	8	Kara's Cupcakes	16	Spruce	29
telnut	26	Ghirardelli		La Canasta	25	Terzo	24
stro Aix	10	Ice Cream and		Liverpool Lil's	22	The Warming Hut	1
ue Barn Gourmet	14	Chocolate Caffe	7	Mamacita	13	Yukol Place	17
boquivari's	19	Greens	3	Mezes	11	Zushi Puzzle	18

●**SHOPS**

American Apparel	8	Kiehl's	12
California Wine Merchant	2	Lululemon Athletica	10
Carol Doda's		My Roommate's Closet	6
Champagne & Lace	7	Patagonia	1
Catherine Jane	14	PlumpJack Wines	3
Chronicle Books	9	Real Food Company	4
D&M Wines & Liquors	15	Repeat Performance	11
Fredericksen's	5	The Ribbonerie	16
Goodbyes	17	Seconds To Go	13

> ### SEA LIONS AT FISHERMAN'S WHARF
>
> Fisherman's Wharf officially includes five **piers** – 39, 41, 43, 43½ and 45 – the numbers of which increase as you head westward. The most endearing sight here are the two dozen or so barking **sea lions** that like to flop upon the floating platforms between piers 39 and 41. Although their number has dropped dramatically since about 2010 – they used to congregate here by the hundreds before a more robust food supply along the Oregon coast lured most of them northward – these wild pinnipeds remain protected by the Marine Mammal Act and are free to come and go as they please; no feeding is allowed.

and fleece tourists, but the scores of tacky souvenir shops and overpriced restaurants that crowd the Wharf expose this area's mission of raking in disposable tourist dollars.

Despite its reputation, Fisherman's Wharf remains a massively popular destination, particularly with visiting families. Naturally, it's at its most crowded in summer and on weekends, but if you're willing to arrive a little earlier in the day than most, it's possible to enjoy its sights and views without having to jostle for position. Be sure to steer clear of unofficial "information centers" along its pavements, which claim to give visitor advice but are really just fronts for shilling overpriced bus tours.

Long before Hooters and the Wax Museum set up shop near the waterfront, Fisherman's Wharf flourished as a serious fishing port – well into the twentieth century, in fact. These days, the few fishermen that can afford the exorbitant mooring charges have usually finished their trawling by early morning and are gone by the time most visitors arrive. You can still find decent seafood here at a few of the better restaurants, but worthwhile sights or remnants of the fishing trade are few and far between.

Aquarium of the Bay

Pier 39 • June–Aug daily 9am–8pm; March–May & Sept–Oct Mon–Thurs 10am–7pm, Fri–Sun 10am–8pm; Nov–Feb Mon–Thurs 10am–6pm, Fri–Sun 10am–7pm • $16.95, children $8 • ☎ 415 623 5300, ⓦ aquariumofthebay.com

There's aquatic life on view at the **Aquarium of the Bay**, conveniently located but, alas, not the finest of its kind. Exhibits here are standard fare for sealife museums, although the petting pool with leopard sharks and bat rays is a nice diversion. The top attraction is "Under the Bay", where you get spectacular close-ups of fish and crustaceans that surround you as you trundle slowly through a 300ft viewing tunnel – assuming you can ignore the cloying muzak overhead.

Boudin Museum & Bakery

160 Jefferson St at Mason • Daily except Tues 11.30am–6pm • $3 • ☎ 415 928 1849, ⓦ boudinbakery.com

Carbohydrate-averse visitors will want to avoid the **Boudin Museum & Bakery** – in fact, it's indeterminate whether even the staunchest supporter of sourdough will find this bubble-headed "museum" truly educational. Bay Area bakery Boudin is famed because its bakers have used the same starter yeast since 1849, when the company was founded. Cheery guides riff on Boudin's extensive history while you watch bakers at work (they churn out two thousand loaves a day), and at tour's end you can gorge on sourdough with ingredients like chocolate and raisin.

Musée Mécanique

Pier 45 • Mon–Fri 10am–7pm, Sat & Sun 10am–8pm • Free • ☎ 415 346 2000, ⓦ museemechanique.org

A sure pick for entertainment at the Wharf is the **Musée Mécanique** on Pier 45, an amusing collection of vintage arcade machines. Set in an enormous shed, this paean to all sorts of gaming – from 1920s analogue to 1980s digital – is home to a number of antique, hand-operated games that are relics from Playland-at-the-Beach, the Ocean Beach amusement park that closed in 1972. If you dare, follow the booming cackling you hear to the giant fibreglass case that houses Laughing Sal, a freakish, gap-toothed veteran of Playland who'll howl forever for a mere quarter.

Fish Alley

Around the corner from the Musée Mécanique and down at the very end of Leavenworth Street, follow your nose to **Fish Alley**, where boats and storage sheds offer a backstage look at a seriously ramshackle world few people care to get more than a quick whiff of: the remaining few working boats of the Wharf's namesake anglers.

Alcatraz

Visible from the waterfront, the islet of **Alcatraz**– colloquially known as "the Rock" – is evocative even from a distance, keenly conjuring up images of bleak isolation. The islet became a military fortress in the late nineteenth century, and by 1912 the US Army had built a jail here. Twenty-two years later, it was turned over to civilian authorities and converted into America's most dreaded **high-security prison**. These days, Alcatraz Island functions as a **museum** (☎415 561 4900, ⊚nps.gov/alcatraz) operated by the National Park Service. Note that you'll be hard-pressed to spend an entire day here – in fact, two hours or so should be plenty, depending on your appetite for convict ephemera.

Brief history

Surrounded by freezing, impassable water, Alcatraz was an ideal place for a jail – this is where many of America's brand-name criminals (such as Al Capone and George "Machine Gun" Kelly) were held, as well as other dangerous oddballs like the fabled "Birdman of Alcatraz", Robert Stroud.

Although conditions softened as time passed – look for the radio jacks installed in each cell in the 1950s – a stay in one of the tiny, lonely rooms must have been psychologically gruelling, especially given the islet's proximity to the glittering lights of San Francisco. The prison's initial policy of silence among inmates also underscored the strict regime, although that law was repealed three years after Alcatraz became a federal prison. Thanks to the violent currents that churn constantly in the chilly Bay waters, escape was virtually unthinkable – in all, nine men managed to get off the island over the years, but none is known to have gained his freedom.

For all its usefulness as a stockade, the island prison turned out to be a fiscal disaster, so US Attorney-General Robert Kennedy closed it in 1963; many of its prisoners were transferred to a new, maximum-security facility in Marion, Illinois. Alcatraz remained abandoned until 1969, when a group of American Indians – citing treaties that designated all federal land not in use as automatically reverting to their ownership – staged an occupation as part of a peaceful attempt to claim the island for their people. US government officials, using all the bureaucratic trickery they could muster, finally ousted the movement in 1971 by claiming the operative lighthouse on the island qualified it as active.

Interestingly, Alcatraz got its name as a result of poor map-reading and questionable diction. An early Spanish explorer christened one island in San

---

TOURING ALCATRAZ

Close to one million visitors take the excellent hour-long **audio tour** of the abandoned prison each year. The tour includes sharp anecdotal commentary, as well as re-enactments of prison life (featuring improvised voices of characters like Capone and Kelly); the real-life stories, such as the man who stayed sane in solitary confinement by endlessly pushing, then searching for, a single button in the darkness, are chilling. Skip the dull twelve-minute introductory film at the dock – you're far better off joining one of the free ranger talks on a variety of themes that run five times daily.

Note that there's no **food** service on the island, but packed lunches are allowed in the designated picnic areas, although the island's scrubby plant life and generally grim mood aren't conducive to a lingering lunch.

Francisco Bay *Isla de Alcatraces* (Island of Pelicans) in honour of the hundreds of birds living on it; however, the island he was referring to is not the one known today as Alcatraz. The pelicans' old home is now called Yerba Buena Island because a clumsy English sea captain became confused when mapping the Bay in 1826. He wrongly assumed that the tiny, rocky islet – set between the mainland and Angel Island, and pelted with guano – must be the birds' home, so he marked it down in mangled Spanglish as "Alcatraz", then assigned the name Yerba Buena to the other island that is today's halfway point of the Bay Bridge.

ARRIVAL AND DEPARTURE

By ferry Alcatraz Cruises operates frequent ferries to Alcatraz (mid-May to late Oct 9am–3.55pm, last ferry returns at 6.25pm; late Oct to mid-May 9am–1.55pm, last ferry returns at 4.25pm; day tour $26, night tour – departs 6.10pm & 6.50pm in summer, 4.20pm in winter – $33; ☎ 415 981 7625, ⓦ alcatrazcruises.com). The port of embarkation is Pier 33, just southeast of Fisherman's Wharf; public transport via Muni's F-Market streetcar is highly recommended. Reservations are essential – by spring, it's virtually impossible to turn up and travel on the same day, and you can expect at least a one-week wait in peak season. The best ferry to catch is the day's first, since the jail will be evocatively empty when you arrive; for unflappable souls, night ferries are available for a few dollars more. A 9.30am trip combining a visit to Alcatraz with a stop at nearby Angel Island is also available for $58.

Aquatic Park and around

West of the Wharf, the pandering tourist trade recedes, although pockets persist next to **Aquatic Park** in the form of caricature portrait artists and dull, occasionally nettlesome street musicians. This area's best asset by far is **San Francisco Maritime National Historic Park**, a low-key complex that includes restored sailing vessels, a superb visitor centre, curving jetties, impressive nautical architecture and a sandy spit.

San Francisco Maritime NHP Visitor Center

499 Jefferson St at Hyde • June–Aug 9.30am–5.30pm; Sept–May 9.30am–5pm • Free • ☎ 415 447 5000, ⓦ nps.gov/safr

The **San Francisco Maritime NHP Visitor Center** shares its huge brick building – formerly a cannery and factory – with the *Argonaut Hotel* (see p.129). Aside from selling tickets for touring the park's docked ships, the space offers an extensive display of local maritime history. Most interesting are the hand-rotated maps that detail changes in the area's shoreline since the nineteenth century, as well as the displays pinpointing shipwreck locations in and around San Francisco Bay.

Aquatic Park

At the end of Jefferson Street

Aquatic Park was established in the 1930s by the Dolphin Club and the South End Club, longstanding private swimming and rowing organizations still based on Jefferson today. Part of this bayside park's sand was originally brought in from Union Square during early 1940s excavations for the underground parking garage there; a few decades prior, this had been the dumping ground for much of the rubble from the 1906 earthquake and fire. You're likely to spot hardy men and women dipping in and out of the bracing water here – this cove is a favoured practice and workout spot for local swimmers. Plenty of benches and grass make this a pleasant spot for a picnic if the weather's agreeable, while the park's southeast corner is the terminus for the Powell-Hyde cable car line, the city's steepest.

Aquatic Park Bathhouse

900 Beach St at Polk • Daily 10am–4pm • Free

The Streamline Moderne-styled **Aquatic Park Bathhouse** commands attention directly behind Aquatic Park. Originally opened in 1939, near the tail end of the Art Deco era, its gently sloping corners and clean lines emulate the sleek ocean liners of the day;

throughout the ensuing decades, it's served as a public bathhouse, World War II troop centre and, these days, a quiet maritime museum. Currently, an ongoing, extensive refurbishment to the upper floors means that the ground-floor lobby is relatively sparse, with just a few displays of model ships and the like – all the better for absorbing its colourful, recently touched-up murals portraying real and mythical sea creatures.

Hyde Street Pier

Daily: June–Aug 9.30am–5.30pm; Sept–May 9.30am–5pm • Free, $5 to board ships

The final notable attraction around San Francisco Maritime NHP is the **Hyde Street Pier** and its painstakingly preserved relics. In its working heyday, the pier itself served numerous ferries that shuttled passengers (and in later years, their cars) between San Francisco and Sausalito, Tiburon and Berkeley, but the 1937 opening of the Golden Gate Bridge quickly rendered these services useless. Today, there's no charge to wander down the wooden slats perched over the Bay and peruse the exhibits, and free ranger tours meet regularly throughout the day at the foot of the pier; however, to board one of the ships, you'll need to pick up a ticket at the Visitor Center (see p.36). Among the half-dozen or so vessels permanently docked here, the Scottish-built *Balclutha* (1886), with its spindly rigging, is the most inviting. Made of solid Douglas fir, this sole survivor of the great sailing ships that journeyed around Cape Horn in the 1800s was put into retirement in 1930, to be dragged out and done up for bit parts in such films as *Mutiny on the Bounty* before settling into its current role as a showboat.

Ghirardelli Square

900 North Point St at Larkin

Across the street but outside the national historic park boundary, looming above the entire scene, is **Ghirardelli Square**, an erstwhile wool mill and chocolate factory sensitively converted in the 1960s into its current incarnation as a superior shopping and dining destination. The complex was among the first in the nation to repurpose disused industrial space as a means for generating new revenue, a trend several US cities have since followed. Its name comes from sweets baron Domenico Ghirardelli, an Italian gold prospector-turned-grocer-turned-chocolatier who arrived in San Francisco via Peru and eventually became patriarch of one of San Francisco's most famous families. When the company moved its manufacturing arm to the East Bay city of San Leandro in 1967, the stage was set for the square's conversion; today, its several restaurants and food- and wine-themed shops, including Ghirardelli Soda Fountain and Chocolate Shops (see p.217), make it a popular gathering spot for city visitors.

Fort Mason

Worth a wander, the rolling lawns, hilltop promontories and renovated piers of **Fort Mason** are sandwiched between Fisherman's Wharf and the Marina. The expansive space is a dog's breakfast of public uses, and the entire complex is part of the sprawling Golden Gate National Recreation Area (see box, p.74).

The headlands and shore here endured a lengthy period of scattershot duty before finally gaining protected status as part of the GGNRA. Known in its early days as both Sand Dune Point and Black Point, Fort Mason was a defence bulkhead during the early Spanish settlement era. Following the Gold Rush, the first occupant of its then-treeless bluff was Selby Smelting, after which the area became littered with the shanty homes of squatters. Fort Mason became a haven of a different sort after the 1906 earthquake and fire, when it served as a refugee centre for the homeless; it was at this point the US military began to actively occupy the site, planting numerous trees and tugging the area under the management auspices of the Presidio about a mile to the west. During World War II, 1.6 million soldiers and 23 million tons of cargo passed through Fort Mason's piers en route to the Pacific Theater, and it served as a logistical support centre during the Korean War in the early 1950s. Following the Army's departure in 1970, it was turned over to public use through the efforts of cantankerous US congressman Phillip Burton, who blocked plans to turn the land over to private development. These days, the space is roughly divided into two sections: **Upper Fort Mason** on the hilltop is parkland, while **Lower Fort Mason** is home to old warehouses and wharves.

Upper Fort Mason

Upper Fort Mason – best accessed via its main entrance at the northern terminus of Franklin Street where it crosses Bay – includes an enormous meadow, hidden picnic areas, housing, a community garden and even a hostel housed in a converted Civil War barracks (see p.134). It's rich with the scent of eucalyptus, and although often windswept, there are some lovely picnic areas to be found around the overgrown hilltop batteries behind the hostel. Closely examine the larger-than-life statue of Burton gesturing animatedly across the meadow, and you'll spot a note protruding from his right jacket pocket. It reads, "*The only way to deal with exploiters is to*", before disappearing into his pocket – a subtle nod to Burton's famously irascible personality, as the late politician always carried a handwritten note reminding him to continually "terrorize" his exploitative opponents.

3

Fort Mason Center

☎ 415 345 7500, ⓦ fortmason.org

At the north end of the meadow, steps lead down to Lower Fort Mason. This waterfront area, better known as **Fort Mason Center**, is almost entirely devoted to cultural and educational organizations, as well as celebrated vegetarian restaurant *Greens* (see p.151). About thirty non-profit groups are headquartered here, including several theatres – for which tickets may be purchased at the main box office on the Middle Pier (Tues & Thurs–Fri 10am–1pm & 2–4pm; ☎ 415 345 7575). Fort Mason Center also houses a handful of galleries and museums, including the **SFMOMA Artists Gallery in Building A** (Tues–Sat 11.30am–5.30pm; free; ☎ 415 441 4777, ⓦ sfmoma.org), presenting about eight shows annually, mostly of locally created contemporary works.

GOLDEN GATE NATIONAL RECREATION AREA

Its funding initiative signed into existence in 1972 by the unlikely hand of President Richard Nixon, the **Golden Gate National Recreation Area (GGNRA)** was the pet project of US congressional Representative Phillip Burton, who spearheaded its birth in an effort to prevent private development from stripping the San Francisco Bay Area of its signature wildlands and historical sites. The ferocious Burton, a staunch Democrat, had surprisingly few partisan enemies in Washington DC, but nonetheless tended to consider land speculators with extreme contempt.

The GGNRA's first acquisitions in the 1970s were **Alcatraz Island** and **Fort Mason** (both purchased from the US Army) and the Marin Headlands (transferred from the Nature Conservancy, which had bought the land from Gulf Oil). Today, the GGNRA's 75,000-plus acres make it one of the largest urban parks anywhere in the world, although its holdings are patchwork and stretch from Tomales Bay in rural west Marin County to the Phleger Estate over thirty miles south of San Francisco. Somewhat confusingly, neither the namesake bridge nor city park is managed by the GGNRA, although much of the land adjacent to each is.

GGNRA holdings offer remarkably wide appeal: from **Muir Woods** and the **Presidio**, to nude bathing at **Golden Gate Beach** and kids' educational exhibits and activities at **Fort Baker**. Visitor centres are located at each of the park's most popular destinations, while the GGNRA's headquarters (☎ 415 561 4700, ⓦ nps.gov/goga) are inside Building 201 in upper Fort Mason. Alcatraz and Muir Woods are the only units of the park to charge admission fees.

The Marina and around

The neighbourhood west of Fort Mason, the **Marina**, enjoys a prime location adjacent to a stretch of waterfront that boasts the Golden Gate Bridge and the Marin Headlands as a backdrop. Today it's one of San Francisco's priciest areas, but its beginnings are far from glamorous, having been created from squelchy land in the Bay in preparation for the Panama–Pacific International Exhibition of 1915. A sea wall was erected parallel to the shoreline north of Cow Hollow, after which the marshland in between was piled high with rubble from the 1906 earthquake and fire, mixed with sand from the ocean floor. Such flimsy foundations ultimately resulted in bitter irony, as the neighbourhood originally built to celebrate the rebirth of the city after the 1906 calamities was the worst casualty of the Loma Prieta earthquake in 1989, when tremors sent many structures collapsing into smouldering heaps. Reconstruction was immediate and complete, however, and today among its townhouses there's barely a speck of evidence of the destruction that ravaged the district.

Short of taking in the **Palace of Fine Arts** and the **Exploratorium**, enjoying a stroll around its dense, beautifully manicured streets, or enjoying its vibrant restaurant scene, the Marina doesn't offer many compelling reasons for visitors to linger; furthermore, its overwhelmingly young, white, professional and straight demographic doesn't make for very interesting people-watching, at least by San Francisco standards. Nearby, its sister district just to the south, quieter **Cow Hollow**, offers a wealth of boutique shopping options.

Palace of Fine Arts

3301 Lyon St

One of San Francisco's most theatrical pieces of architecture lies at the very western edge of the Marina: the **Palace of Fine Arts** is not the museum its name suggests, but rather a huge, classical rotunda by **Bernard Maybeck**, the Berkeley-based architect who was also the mastermind of the Christian Science Church across the Bay (see p.245). To the modern eye, the structure is a mournfully sentimental piece, complete with weeping figures on the colonnade said to represent the melancholy of life without art.

When first erected for the Panama–Pacific International Exhibition in 1915, the palace was brightly coloured with a burnt orange dome, deep red columns and gold capitals, and was widely acknowledged as the most beautiful of all the temporary structures. When the other buildings from the fair, which stretched from here east along the waterfront to Fort Mason, were destroyed to make room for the nascent Marina district, the structure was saved simply because locals thought it too beautiful to lose. A pair of refits over the decades – including a seven-year, $21 million job completed in early 2011 – have recast the structure in reinforced concrete while preserving its original dignity, and it's proudly emerged better than ever. New paths and lovely landscaping around the adjacent lagoon, rich with large white swans, make for a delightful walk.

Exploratorium

3601 Lyon St • Tues–Sun 10am–5pm • $15, children $10–12, free first Wed of the month • ☎ 415 561 0360, Tactile Dome reservations ☎ 415 561 0362, ⓦ exploratorium.edu

Housed in a cramped space behind the Palace of Fine Arts, the **Exploratorium** has been a prime field-trip destination for Bay Area schoolchildren since it opened in 1969. Rather than obscure the fun of science behind simplistic cartoons, curators wisely allow the magic of hundreds of hands-on exhibits to keep young visitors enthralled by demonstrating the principles of electricity, sound waves, lasers and more. The "Exploratorium After Dark" event series (first Thurs of each month; $15) is geared towards adults, while the museum's most popular exhibit for all ages is the Tactile Dome ($20, includes museum admission; reservations essential), a total sensory-deprivation environment explored on hands and knees – definitely not for the claustrophobic.

Wave Organ

About a ten-minute walk from the Exploratorium, at the eastern tip of the jetty that forms the yacht harbour next to the Marina Green, look for San Francisco's most subtle environmental art installation, the **Wave Organ**. The site was constructed in the 1980s from reclaimed marble and granite, and includes more than two dozen scattered "organ pipes" made of PVC tubing and concrete that produce sounds from bay tides. Don't expect theatrical bombast, as the emanated tones generally require sensitive listening. Try visiting at high tide, when the piping produces the most sound.

Cow Hollow

A few blocks inland from the Marina, **Cow Hollow** was originally a small valley of pastures and dairies in the post-Gold Rush years. It takes its name from the days when cows grazed the land between Russian Hill and the Presidio and women brought their loads to one of the only sources of fresh water in town, which came to be known as Washerwoman's Lagoon. Problems with open sewage and complaints from Pacific Heights neighbours about the uninviting odours coming from the cowfields saw the area transformed in the 1950s, when enterprising merchants decided its old clapboard dwellings along **Union Street** had possibilities. Many gorgeous old Victorian homes have since been refitted, and the stretch of Union Street between Van Ness Avenue and Divisadero Street now holds one of the city's densest concentrations of upmarket boutiques. The district is constantly alive with neighbourhood shoppers, and its leafy streets and dearth of tourist sights is what keeps it appealing.

Pacific Heights

Perched on the tall hills that separate Cow Hollow and the Western Addition stands supremely affluent **Pacific Heights**, poised around two lovely parks and home to some of San Francisco's most monumental Victorian residences and stone mansions, as well as much of its social elite. Even when these hills were still bare in the 1860s, their panoramic views earmarked them as potentially fashionable territory once the gradient-conquering cable cars could link them with Downtown.

The district is neatly divided by north-south artery **Fillmore Street**: to its west are the grand chateaux – several of which always seem to be undergoing some sort of construction – that earned the neighbourhood its reputation; to its east, classy Moderne apartment buildings that do little to damage it. Upper Fillmore Street north of Bush is where Pacific Heights locals shop, dine and otherwise spend piles of disposable cash. It's lively and lined with cafés and boutiques, as well as one of the last remaining single-screen movie houses in town, the **Clay Theatre**, which always seems to be on the verge of closing for good.

Haas-Lilienthal House

2007 Franklin St at Jackson • Tours every 20–30min Wed & most Sat noon–3pm, Sun 11am–4pm • $8 • ☎ 415 441 3000, ⓦ sfheritage.org

An 1886 double-size Victorian built by German-born grocer William Haas (the house's hyphenate combines his surname with that of his son-in-law, who later lived here), the **Haas-Lilienthal House** endures as a hushed symbol of old Pacific Heights wealth, although the talky, hour-long tour is more focused on the day-to-day life of Haas and his family than it is on architecture. The house is significant because, unlike many Victorians which were standard designs overseen by builders (see box, p.78), Haas commissioned an architect to custom-design his mansion. Its redwood-faced interior is largely filled with original furniture, including Tiffany art-glass; also note the uniquely stencilled leather wall panelling. Overall, the mansion has stood the test of time remarkably well – look for the crack in the stairwell wall, one of the few signs of damage dating back to the 1906 earthquake.

PALACE OF FINE ARTS (P.75) >

3

VICTORIAN ARCHITECTURE

Constructed from redwood culled from Marin County across the Golden Gate, San Francisco's **Victorian houses** enjoyed their greatest popularity in the late 1800s, thanks to an emerging middle class keen to display its modest wealth as showily as possible on a standard 25' by 125' city lot. By 1906, though, the heyday of the Victorians (and Queen Victoria herself) had already passed, and when many of the all-wood houses went up in flames in April of that year, the axe-stripped hillsides of Marin didn't have enough building material left to replace them.

For a good chunk of the twentieth century, local Victorians became an endangered species. Many were torn down during Justin Herman's hurricane of urban renewal in the Western Addition (see p.112), while others were maimed simply through their owners' economies. By the 1960s, though, grassroots support swelled for the structures, and the **Victorian Alliance** was formed to campaign for their preservation. The effort swiftly succeeded, and Victorian restoration continues to be a lucrative local profession to this day since large numbers of the homes are found in several San Francisco neighbourhoods.

There are three main styles of Victorians to seek out in San Francisco. The earliest is the **Italianate** – look for Corinthian columns, a slanted bay window jutting from the front of the house, and heavy brackets at the roofline, as well as false fronts designed to add height and grandeur. Fine Italianates dating to 1874 are found south of Pacific Heights in the Western Addition, along so-called Cottage Row (2115–2125 Bush St at Webster).

The Italianate was followed in the 1880s by the **San Francisco Stick**. This style is marked by a square bay window, etched or coloured glass, porch columns that resemble furniture legs, and decorative vertical "sticks" appliquéd to the facade; in addition, its millwork is more heavily ornate than its predecessor. There's an excellent cluster of 1889 Sticks along the 1800 block of Laguna Street (between Pine and Bush), a few blocks south of Lafayette Park.

The final – and certainly the most flamboyant – style is the **Queen Anne**, its excesses a rather warped riff on the 1890s vogue. It follows a more diverse architectural template than earlier Victorians, with round turrets, steep roof gables and wooden shingles, as well as whimsical touches such as plaster garlands and fake stucco swallows' nests fixed to the eaves. Well-preserved Queen Annes, painted in muted yellows and greens, can be found at 2000–2010 Gough St at Washington, directly across from Lafayette Park's eastern slope.

Pacific Heights parks

Pacific Heights is home to a pair of sizable, inviting **parks**, with each one anchoring an area just a few blocks off Fillmore. The cypress-dotted peak of **Lafayette Park**, which begins three blocks east of Fillmore at Laguna and Washington Streets, is a terrific spot for a hilltop picnic or frolic; west of the neighbourhood's main street, **Alta Plaza Park** – framed by Jackson, Steiner, Clay and Scott Streets – sees kids romp on the playground structures and dog-walkers exercising pampered local pooches.

The Lyon Steps

At the far west end of Broadway

Six blocks northwest of Alta Plaza Park, the **Lyon Steps** lead down a steep incline along the Presidio and into Cow Hollow. The path passes several grandiose homes (including that of former city mayor and current US Senator, Dianne Feinstein) and offers a magnificent view of the Palace of Fine Arts and other points north over the Bay.

The Presidio

A free shuttle service, PresidiGo, regularly runs buses all around the park from the Transit Center just off the Main Post's square across Lincoln Boulevard (Mon–Fri 6.30am–7.30pm, Sat & Sun 11am–6pm)

Occupying nearly 1500 hilly, forested acres along the northwest tip of San Francisco, the **Presidio** was a military base for over two hundred years before the US Army declared it surplus and handed it over to the National Park Service in the 1990s; like Fort Mason, it's now part of the Golden Gate National Recreation Area (see box, p.74). Along with

Mission Dolores across town, it's the site of the earliest European settlement on San Francisco Bay, where Spanish soldiers established a garrison in 1776 to forestall British and Russian claims in the area. It passed through Mexican hands in the early and mid-1800s before becoming American property along with the rest of California in 1848. The Army began developing the site towards the end of the nineteenth century, and it played a significant deployment role in military embroilments from the Spanish American War on through World War II. Its run as the longest continuously operating military base in the US ended quietly with its 1994 transfer to the NPS, although several relics of its military past remain – most visibly at the sobering **San Francisco National Cemetery**, 1 Lincoln Blvd (daily 7am–5pm; free; ☎650 589 7737, ⓦcem.va.gov), the final resting place of over thirty thousand, and one of San Francisco's only graveyards.

Aside from its stunning setting atop the San Francisco Peninsula, the Presidio is unique as being the only NPS holding with an extensive residential leasing programme. The fact that about 2500 people live here further contributes to its hotchpotch of functions and uses, which range from sprawling green-space playground to home of non-profit organizations and bottom line-geared businesses alike (filmmaker George Lucas's Lucasfilm Ltd operates a sparkling CGI design centre here). As you'd expect in an activist centre like San Francisco, the Presidio's operational diversity hasn't come without conflict: certain park advocates bemoan the park's operating body, the Presidio Trust, as continually kowtowing to business interests, while those in charge of ensuring the Presidio becomes financially self-sufficient by 2012 – a central tenet of its one-of-a-kind Congressional agreement – point to the park's early (2005) achievement of this goal.

3

Main Post and around

Travelling its forested roads and strolling its trails are the best ways to begin to get a sense of the Presidio's vastness. A short distance from the Lombard Gate on the park's east side is the **Main Post**, where a number of handsome, red-brick buildings surrounding the former parade ground (now an enormous parking lot) have been recast as private offices and studios. Just off the Main Post's square across Lincoln Boulevard is the park's **Transit Center**. Due to construction around the Main Post, the Presidio **visitor centre** is temporarily located in Building 105 on the Main Post Parade Ground (Thurs–Sun 10am–4pm; ☎415 561 4323, ⓦnps.gov/prsf).

THE FALL AND RISE OF THE PRESIDIO LANDSCAPE

Though having already been in the firm grasp of Spanish, Mexican and American militaries for over a hundred years, the Presidio was still a hilly, windswept sandbox in the 1880s when US Army Major W.A. Jones initiated his plan to alter its landscape by planting 100,000 cypress, eucalyptus and pine trees. Although the extensive plantings certainly had a beautifying effect and provided sharp contrast with the surrounding city, Jones had other ideas: **forestation** of the Presidio would make it difficult for enemy eyes to scope infantry manoeuvres from afar. The officer's plan also stated that the influx of foliage would make the base appear "immensely larger than it really is", while also "accentuating the power of the Government". Today, however, many of these trees are nearing the end of their lifespan, and there is talk of returning some of the park's falsely forested areas to its original dune habitat.

Throughout its lengthy military era, the Presidio's landscape enjoyed a rare level of **protection** from the urbanization encroaching outside the fort's borders; furthermore, parts of the base were barely (if at all) developed beyond forestation by military brass. By the same token, certain Presidio lands endured untold **abuse** during the US military's nearly 150-year tenure, underscored by the Army contributing tens of millions of dollars towards the removal of toxic waste material and debris once the land changed hands in the 1990s.

Two popular areas of the Presidio that have been returned to their original natural states are **Crissy Field** (see p.80), a former concrete wasteland, and **Coyote Gulch**, an old seaside dump just west of Lincoln Boulevard newly populated by native wildlife.

One of the Presidio's finest lofted vistas is at **Inspiration Point**, just north of the Arguello Gate along Arguello Boulevard, where a platform looks out over the mixed forest northeast across the Bay. Other terrific views are found in the park's western reaches, where sandy bluffs slope down to meet the waters of the Pacific.

Crissy Field

The Presidio's crown jewel – and certainly its most visited – is **Crissy Field**, a bayfront strip of the park that extends west of the Marina. Originally tidal marshland occupied by local Ohlone people, it was landfilled for the 1915 Panama–Pacific International Exhibition. The Army re-appropriated it as an airfield not long after – for evidence of this, look for the old hangars past the west end of the huge expanse of grass. Once it reverted back to the public domain, it became the Presidio's first large-scale reclamation project, with hundreds of volunteers helping restore its lost identity as valuable wetlands in the late 1990s. It's become a wildly popular walking and running destination with striking views all around, and there's even a stretch of sand reserved for dogs (and their guardians).

Presidio Pet Cemetery

Always open • Free

Located near the old stables beneath the Highway 101 flyover, the lovably ramshackle **Presidio Pet Cemetery** is surrounded by a white picket fence amidst a stand of pines. It's a slight side trip inland from Crissy Field to reach the small burial site, which contains the graves of numerous Army pets. Tilted headstones mark the final resting places of Frisky, Smoochy, Skippy and Moocher, among hundreds of others; as you'd expect, dogs and cats were the pets of choice for many Army families, but you're bound to find the odd iguana or hamster grave site if you hunt thoroughly enough.

Fort Point National Historic Site

Fri–Sun 10am–5pm • Free • ☎ 415 556 1693, ⓦ nps.gov/fopo

Located at the end of Marine Drive under the southern terminus of the Golden Gate Bridge, **Fort Point National Historic Site** was built in the 1850s to guard San Francisco Bay. Spectacularly sited, with the great bridge towering above and the Pacific yawning across the west horizon, its well-preserved casemates make a worthy excursion for military buffs, while Alfred Hitchcock fans will recognize the spot just outside the fort where Jimmy Stewart pulled Kim Novak out of the swirling Bay waters in the 1958 thriller *Vertigo*. Fort Point still stands today thanks to Golden Gate Bridge chief engineer Joseph Strauss, who designed the lofted roadway's huge arch to preserve the old brick and granite encampment, which was otherwise slated for demolition. Candlelight tours are held once monthly during winter months – call the information line for details.

Golden Gate Bridge

Muni buses #28-19th Avenue and #29-Sunset stop near the toll plaza on the San Francisco side

The focal point of countless photographs since opening in May 1937, the orange towers of the **Golden Gate Bridge** remain San Francisco's most iconic image. Built in 52 months – and at the cost of eleven workers killed from falls during construction – the span is as much an architectural feat as an engineering marvel. Although the project was overseen by Chicago-born Joseph Strauss, the final design was, in fact, the brainchild of a local-born residential architect, Irving Morrow; at 4200ft, it was the world's first massive suspension bridge, designed to withstand gusts up to 100 miles an hour and swing as much as 27ft (and sag as many as ten) in high winds.

Handsome on a clear day, the Golden Gate takes on an eerie quality when the area's signature thick white fog pours in and obscures it almost completely. Its

CODE 10-31

The Golden Gate is famous for more than just its astonishing span and Art Deco beauty: it's also a leading **suicide** location. On average, someone jumps to their death from one of the bridge's walkways about every two weeks. The first person to leap, World War I veteran Harold Wobber, did so just three months after the bridge opened. Thirty-six years later, in 1973, the number of suicides was set to reach five hundred; there was a circus-like atmosphere fuelled in part by the irresponsible decision of the *Examiner* and *Chronicle* newspapers to chart the countdown publicly. When the number was circling one thousand in the mid-1990s, media reaction was even more callous: one local radio shock jock offered a case of Snapple as a consolation prize to the "winning" victim's family. This time, though, authorities stopped releasing figures so nobody could claim the dubious honour.

It's a four-second, 220ft freefall from the bridge into the swirling sea below; most people hit the water at more than 75mph, and those not killed by the blunt-force trauma of impact are almost invariably swallowed by the treacherous currents – little wonder, then, that only 26 people have ever survived the plunge. Despite the death toll, there's still no safety barrier – it's easy enough to clamber over the 4ft-high retaining wall. Since the 1950s, when the idea of a barrier was first broached, efforts to install one have been repeatedly blocked due to a combination of cost and aesthetics. Instead, the city favours constant patrols by policemen to monitor potential jumpers (known in local police parlance as "**code 10-31**"). The idea of a fixed barrier has been pushed again in recent years, but there's no official word when, or even if, a measure might be passed.

colour was originally intended as a temporary undercoat before the grey topcoat was applied, but locals liked the primer so much that the bridge has remained "international orange" ever since. Surprisingly, the bridge's famed handle – which comes from the namesake strait it spans – predates the Gold Rush by a few years: explorer John C. Fremont saw similarities between San Francisco Bay's entrance and the Golden Horn, the Istanbul strait that connects the Sea of Marmara with the Black Sea. Also, note how the towers aren't the same distance from the centre of the span, as the south anchorage was planted far from shore in treacherously deep waters in order to preserve Fort Point below.

Unlike its more heavily trafficked counterpart, the San Francisco–Oakland Bay Bridge, pedestrians and cyclists are welcome to cross the Golden Gate's Art Deco dedicated walking and cycling pathways; in fact, a walk, run or ride across its 1.7-mile span is the most exhilarating way to experience the bridge's grandeur – and it's free (southbound drivers currently pay $6; northbound is free). Each end of the bridge features a designated vista-point parking lot, both of which become predictably choked with cars at peak times; clear evenings make for particularly grand viewing of city lights from the Marin shore.

CAROUSEL AT YERBA BUENA GARDENS

South of Market, the Tenderloin and Civic Center

The idea of San Francisco as a Victorian-lined utopia holds fast until you wander into the areas to the west and south of Downtown – thoroughly urban places where the flipside of California's prosperity is alive and unwell. After languishing for decades as a warehouse wasteland, South of Market took an upswing in the mid-1990s, when its low rents attracted first art and music communities and then technology employees; in the economic ebb and flow since, the neighbourhood has alternately languished and prospered. Certain areas still boom nightly with the muffled reverberations of underground dance clubs, but nearer to Downtown are some fine museums, as well as the San Francisco Giants' baseball park.

The adjoining **Tenderloin** and **Civic Center** districts reveal harsher realities, with heavy drug traffic and prostitution in evidence, along with a shocking number of homeless people. Their almost constant presence in front of **City Hall** is a stinging reminder of governmental failure to resolve the city's major shortage of affordable housing.

South of Market

The distinctly urban **South of Market** district stretches, fittingly, south of Market Street diagonally from the Mission district on a northeast slant to the waterfront. While the western sections have always been a working-class community (author **Jack London** was born here), the waterfront **Rincon Hill** and the **South Park** areas were home to the first of the city's banking elite. By the 1870s, they were drawn away to Nob Hill by the newly invented cable car, and within thirty years, South of Market had been turned over to industrial development and warehouses. The poorer community that remained was largely driven out by fires following the 1906 earthquake, and Rincon Hill was eventually cleared in 1930 to make way for the new **Bay Bridge**. The decades after World War II saw the area converted almost exclusively into an industrial and shipping district, and oversized grey and brick warehouse complexes still dominate the landscape today.

South of Market's loft spaces and low rents made it a prime location during the dot-com mania of the 1990s – factories and warehouses were relentlessly converted to offices for the fledgling internet industry, drawing young people and creating a more lively neighbourhood. Today, areas of vacant empty office space and after-dark danger persevere – the most notorious being Sixth Street, traditionally a place where drug deals go down day and night.

Still, there are plenty of must-see sights scattered around South of Market. The standout spot is the **Yerba Buena** district, anchored by lovely **Yerba Buena Gardens**; it's surrounded by various museums and cultural spots, including the **Museum of the African Diaspora** and the **Jewish Museum of San Francisco**. Also adjacent is the famed **San Francisco Museum of Modern Art** (SFMOMA), whose building is as much a must-see as its contents. Along the waterfront Embarcadero, the stretch between the Ferry Building and bayside **AT&T Park**, home of baseball's San Francisco Giants, is now a glorious place to stroll.

Rincon Center
Mission St at Spear

A block inland from the waterfront at South of Market's northeastern tip, on the site where Rincon Hill once loomed, stands the **Rincon Center**. Constructed in 1939 as an enormous post office, it was redeveloped as a shopping centre (and food court) in the 1980s. With its smooth but imposing lines, outer simplicity and ornamented interior, the building is a fine example of Depression Moderne architecture. Its lobby is lavishly decorated with murals – commissioned in a contest by the WPA in 1941 – by Anton Refregier, who was selected to paint 27 scenes of California history in the largest project of its kind. His angular style was heavily influenced by leftist Diego Rivera, which, combined with Refregier's Russian origins, ensured that the murals barely made

CUPID'S SPAN

Along San Francisco Bay on the northeast edge of South of Market proper, it's worth taking in one of the city's most eye-popping public art pieces, **Cupid's Span**. This enormous bow-and-arrow was installed in 2003 and is a characteristically playful design by legendary sculptor **Claes Oldenburg**. The bow is partially buried in the ground, while the arrow points downward as a nod to the city's pop-culture lovability. After all, Tony Bennett left his heart here, and it was home to the Summer of Love.

SOUTH OF MARKET, THE TENDERLOIN AND CIVIC CENTER

● CAFÉS & RESTAURANTS

A La Turca	6	Canteen	1	Kyo-Ya	8	Ristorante Umbria	13
Alexander's		Chavo's	30	Le Charm	27	Saha	2
Steakhouse	31	Coco500	33	Manora's Thai	36	Saigon Sandwich	17
Ame	14	Crepes A-Go-Go	37	Maya	21	Shalimar	7
Ananda Fuara	28	Crossroads Cafe	25	Mehfil	19	Taqueria El Castillito	22
Andalé	18	Custom Burger	29	Mochica	32	Thai Stick	11
Asia SF	35	Delancey Street	24	The Old Chelsea	4	Town Hall	5
Brenda's French		Dottie's True Blue Cafe	9	Pagolac	15	Tu Lan	23
Soul Food	16	Farmerbrown	20	Pakwan	12	Yank Sing	3
Caffe Centro	26	Golden Era	10	Primo Patio Cafe	34		

● GAY RESTAURANT

Asia SF	35

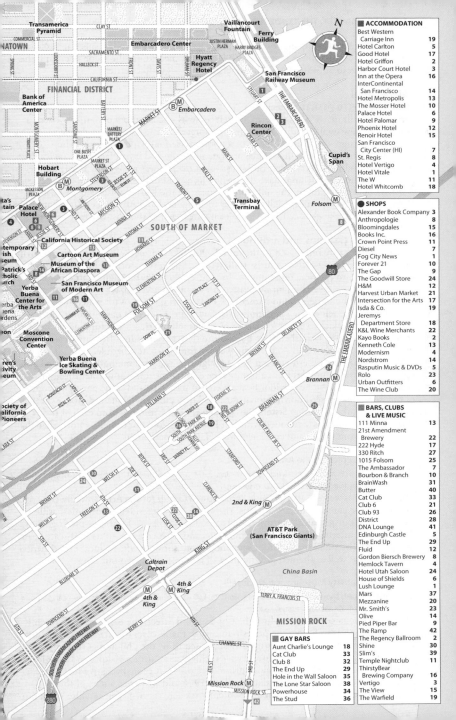

ACCOMMODATION

Best Western Carriage Inn	19
Hotel Carlton	5
Good Hotel	17
Hotel Griffon	2
Harbor Court Hotel	3
Inn at the Opera	16
InterContinental San Francisco	14
Hotel Metropolis	13
The Mosser Hotel	10
Palace Hotel	6
Hotel Palomar	9
Phoenix Hotel	12
Renoir Hotel	15
San Francisco City Center (HI)	7
St. Regis	8
Hotel Vertigo	4
Hotel Vitale	1
The W	11
Hotel Whitcomb	18

SHOPS

Alexander Book Company	3
Anthropologie	8
Bloomingdales	15
Books Inc.	16
Crown Point Press	11
Diesel	7
Fog City News	1
Forever 21	10
The Gap	9
The Goodwill Store	24
H&M	12
Harvest Urban Market	21
Intersection for the Arts	17
Isda & Co.	19
Jeremys Department Store	18
K&L Wine Merchants	22
Kayo Books	2
Kenneth Cole	13
Modernism	14
Nordstrom	14
Rasputin Music & DVDs	5
Rolo	23
Urban Outfitters	6
The Wine Club	20

BARS, CLUBS & LIVE MUSIC

111 Minna	13
21st Amendment Brewery	22
222 Hyde	17
330 Ritch	27
1015 Folsom	25
The Ambassador	7
Bourbon & Branch	10
BrainWash	31
Butter	40
Cat Club	33
Club 6	21
Club 93	26
District	28
DNA Lounge	41
Edinburgh Castle	5
The End Up	29
Fluid	12
Gordon Biersch Brewery	8
Hemlock Tavern	4
Hotel Utah Saloon	24
House of Shields	6
Lush Lounge	1
Mars	37
Mezzanine	20
Mr. Smith's	23
Olive	14
Pied Piper Bar	9
The Ramp	42
The Regency Ballroom	2
Shine	30
Slim's	39
Temple Nightclub	11
ThirstyBear Brewing Company	16
Vertigo	3
The View	15
The Warfield	19

GAY BARS

Aunt Charlie's Lounge	18
Cat Club	33
Club 8	32
The End Up	29
Hole in the Wall Saloon	35
The Lone Star Saloon	38
Powerhouse	34
The Stud	36

it through the McCarthy era. Although some are rather faded today, there are excellent explanations of the subject matter attached to each piece; note the scene depicting the discovery of gold at Sutter's Mill, filled with burly, Fagin-like settlers.

Palace Hotel

2 New Montgomery St • ☎ 415 512 1111, ⓦ sfpalace.com

Originally built in 1875, the enormous **Palace Hotel** was a symbol of San Francisco's swaggering new wealth and its position as the premier American city in the West (even if its design was a direct rip-off of a hotel in Vienna). Upon opening, the extravagant Rococo structure boasted antique furniture and lavish facilities; tragically, however, like almost every other building Downtown, it was ravaged by the 1906 fire, and subsequent remodellings have dampened its excesses. The one exception is the **Garden Court dining room**, the only indoor space on the National Register of Historic Places. Here, you can enjoy high tea under the original 1875 Austrian crystal chandeliers suspended from the glass ceiling, which itself dates back to the post-fire refit of 1909.

Yerba Buena Gardens and around

Until it was socially fumigated in the mid-1990s, Third Street was a crime-ridden strip one block off Market Street's tourist trail; it's since been transformed into the axis of an inviting museum district, **Yerba Buena**. Its centrepiece is **Yerba Buena Gardens** (daily 6am–10pm; free; ⓦ yerbabuenagardens.com), an urban green-space reclamation success story set atop the underground Moscone Convention Center. With waterfalls drowning out much of the street noise, the lawns are a peaceful oasis among all the urban clatter, a place to enjoy a relaxing picnic lunch or stretch out for a nap. The smallish, modernist bandshell here hosts more than two hundred free concerts annually between May and October – check the website for a current schedule.

Along the park's southern face is a 50ft-high granite waterfall **memorial to Martin Luther King, Jr**. The water tumbles from a terrace above, while visitors can wander through a cool, mist-spattered stone corridor behind; etched into glass and stone panels are some of the Reverend's lesser-known quotes translated into different languages. Above on the upper terrace, the charming **Sister Cities garden** is filled with flora from each of the thirteen cities worldwide twinned with San Francisco – look for camellias from Shanghai, marguerites from Osaka and cyclamen from Haifa, among others.

Yerba Buena Center for the Arts

701 Mission St at Third • First Tues of month & Thurs–Sat noon–8pm, Sun noon–6pm • $7, free first Tues of month or with a same-day ticket to an evening performance • ☎ 415 978 2700, ⓦ ybca.org

On the gardens' eastern flank stands **Yerba Buena Center for the Arts**. Initially conceived as a forum for community-art projects, the centre has no resident companies; aside from renting out rehearsal/performance space at a pittance to local non-profit groups, it also brings international touring exhibitions and performances to its 750-seat theatre (see p.189). The small second-floor screening room shows works by local experimental filmmakers, as well as themed programmes of cult and underground films.

Children's Creativity Museum and carousel

221 Fourth St at Howard • **Museum** Wed–Fri 1–5pm, Sat & Sun 11am–5pm • $10, children $8 **Carousel** Daily 11am–6pm • $3 for two rides • ☎ 415 820 3320, ⓦ childrenscreativitymuseum.org

The Yerba Buena complex is split in half by Howard Street; the easiest way to reach its southern chunk is to follow the pedestrian bridge that crosses over Howard. This section's banner attraction was originally supposed to be the **Children's Creativity Museum**, a hands-on science centre, but it's struggled to attract visitors and remains overshadowed locally by the Exploratorium (see p.75). A more evocative hit is the nearby glassed-in **carousel** that dates back to 1906 and was once a part of the long-gone Playland-at-the-Beach amusement park across town. You can also duck into the **Yerba Buena Ice Skating & Bowling Center** (see p.222), the only permanent venue for ice skating in San Francisco.

Society of California Pioneers
300 Fourth St at Folsom • Wed–Fri & first Sat of the month 10am–4pm • Free • ☎ 415 957 1849, ⓦ californiapioneers.org

This low-profile museum is a West Coast answer to the Daughters of the Confederacy, since the **Society of California Pioneers** was founded in 1850 as a club for the city's earliest settlers to reaffirm their Mayflower-style supremacy. Today, exhibitions culled from the organization's extensive holdings of books, manuscripts and paintings are mounted in a smallish hall; though many of its precious documents were lost in 1906, all the pioneer diaries were kept in a fireproof safe, so you can call ahead to see precious items such as John Sutter's day book or early maps of San Francisco.

Old Mint and Mint Plaza
Fifth St and Mission

In disuse for decades, the magnificent **Old Mint** – a Greek Revival behemoth known locally as the "Granite Lady" – remains shuttered, but is slated to become the eventual, long-awaited home of the San Francisco Museum and Historical Society sometime in the next few years, depending on funding. The alley next door, however, has already been renovated into a smartly designed public space called **Mint Plaza**; a venue for festivals and live performances, this stone promenade contains gardens, a steel arbour with climbing vines and plenty of chairs for relaxing.

Contemporary Jewish Museum
736 Mission St near Third • Mon, Tues & Fri–Sun 11am–5pm, Thurs 1–8pm • $10 • ☎ 415 655 7800, ⓦ thecjm.org

Back near Yerba Buena Gardens, you can't miss the striking askew blue cube along Mission Street – an atrium gallery attached to the **Contemporary Jewish Museum of San Francisco**. Inspired by the Hebrew phrase "L'Chaim" ("to life"), architect Daniel Libeskind incorporated two symbolic letters of "chai" (life): "Chet", which shows up in the shape of the cube gallery, and "yud", in the wall relief at the museum's entrance. While the museum has no permanent collection, the space hosts cleverly curated exhibitions spanning Jewish history and culture, as well as installations of visual, aural and multimedia art.

St Patrick's Catholic Church
756 Mission St • Daily 6am–6pm • ⓦ stpatricksf.org

The Contemporary Jewish Museum is set back from Mission Street, and most of the buildings in front of it were cleared out, replaced by the museum's open front plaza and fountain; the one survivor of the recent redevelopment is **St Patrick's Catholic Church**. The parish was conceived in the afterglow of the Gold Rush by Irish immigrant forty-niners, and the current building dates back to 1912 and is now the spiritual centre for the city's Filipino community.

Museum of Craft and Folk Art
51 Yerba Buena Lane • Wed–Sat 11am–6pm • $5 • ☎ 415 227 4888, ⓦ mocfa.org

Around the corner from the Contemporary Jewish Museum, the more modest **Museum of Craft and Folk Art** hosts intriguing exhibitions based on various forms of folk art from around the globe, including fabrics, paper, puppets, ukuleles and tattoos. Every first Thursday of the month sees a "Craft Bar", where visitors can fashion their own memento.

California Historical Society
678 Mission St at Third • Wed–Sat noon–4.30pm • $3 • ☎ 415 357 1848, ⓦ californiahistoricalsociety.org

On the north side of Mission Street heading east from Yerba Buena Gardens, you'll find the squat, blue-and-white home of the **California Historical Society**. This tiny, offbeat gem showcases ephemera from the Golden State's colourful history; its collection is especially strong on the cultural and political fallout from early Spanish settlement.

Museum of the African Diaspora

685 Mission St at Third • Wed–Sat 11am–6pm, Sun noon–5pm • $10 • ☎ 415 358 7200, ⓦ moadsf.org

Across Mission Street from the California Historical Society, the **Museum of the African Diaspora** spotlights everything from traditional African art, through work inspired by the horrors of slavery, to modern pieces in a range of media. The space puts a particular emphasis on hosting educational events and fostering community discussions about history and racism.

Cartoon Art Museum

655 Mission St at New Montgomery • Tues–Sun 11am–5pm • $7 • ☎ 415 227 8666, ⓦ cartoonart.org

A few steps from the Museum of the African Diaspora stands another overlooked attraction, the **Cartoon Art Museum**. Housed in an enormous concrete gallery, the space features rotating exhibits of cells and drawings, usually a sprightly collection of high concept "art-oons" by the likes of French illustrator Moebius; you'll also find staples such as *Peanuts*.

San Francisco Museum of Modern Art

151 Third St • Mon, Tues & Fri–Sun 11am–5.45pm, Thurs 11am–8.45pm • $18, $9 Thurs 6–8.45pm, free first Tues of the month • ☎ 415 357 4000, ⓦ sfmoma.org

Opposite Yerba Buena Gardens to the east across Third Street is the district's – and perhaps the city's – marquee museum. The **San Francisco Museum of Modern Art**, through a host of recently procured gifts and collections (as well as the ongoing presence of top touring shows), now competes with both the Getty and the Museum of Contemporary Art in Los Angeles for the mantle of premier West Coast exhibition space.

Head to the striking structure's upper floors for the standout temporary exhibitions – past shows have included Eva Hesse, Matthew Barney, Alexander Calder, Diane Arbus, Chuck Close and Keith Haring – and make sure to stop by the fine outdoor sculpture garden on the fourth floor. One level down, you'll find photography amid a reasonable selection of permanent works; look for numerous prints by pioneers such as Henri Cartier-Bresson, Ansel Adams and Alfred Stieglitz, not to mention trippy images by Man Ray. The rest of the permanent collection is curated in rotating displays scattered throughout the building, although the second floor is where most exhibitions take place. Fittingly, the **California school** is well represented, with works by Richard Diebenkorn as well as Frida Kahlo and Diego Rivera, who were striking artistic presences in San Francisco during the Depression. There's also a notable collection of **abstract expressionist** works by Mark Rothko, Jackson Pollock and Robert Rauschenberg, as well as a large body of work by Clyfford Still, the cantankerous artist known for once knifing his own painting from its frame in order to reclaim it from an unworthy owner. The museum also possesses part of the world's largest Paul Klee collection – in all, 85 of the 140 works spanning the artist's career.

Furthermore, you'll find paintings and sculptures by Matisse, as well as works by Mondrian, Magritte and Picasso. The **pop art** holdings are also snappy and include the famous gilded porcelain statue of Michael Jackson and his pet chimp by Jeff Koons; another well-known piece of whimsy is **Dadaist** Marcel Duchamp's *Fountain*. Finally, the building itself is always a treat: a huge central skylight floods the space with light, while the upper galleries are connected by a vertigo-inducing metal catwalk made up of tiny slats that challenge the definition of "adventurous" art.

BASEBALL TICKETS

As you'd expect due to the San Francisco Giants' current success, **tickets** can be expensive and quite tricky to come by. If a game is sold out, you can always try buying extra tickets from other fans outside the ballpark the day (or night) of a game; another idea is to queue up for a three-inning standing-room-only spot behind the right field chain-link fence, free of charge.

AT&T Park

90-minute tours: 10.30am & 12.30pm on non-game days; Coca-Cola Fan Lot: June–Aug daily 10am–4pm; Sept–May Sat & Sun only 10am–4pm • Tours $12.50 • ☎ 415 972 2400, ⊕ sfgiants.com • Minimal parking; Muni stops right outside the ballpark along the Embarcadero

For what is inarguably San Francisco's most popular sporting experience, head south down Third Street to the San Francisco Giants' home turf, **AT&T Park**, which debuted to much fanfare in 2000; the venue is a dramatic improvement over the team's former stadium, decrepit and windswept Candlestick Park. AT&T Park, set in one of the sunniest parts of town, boasts modern amenities, terrific food options and an open outfield that reveals stunning Bay views, particularly from the upper seating levels. Most exciting for diehard Giants fans is that, in 2010, the team won its first World Series – Major League Baseball's top prize – since moving west from New York in 1958.

Twice-daily **tours** leave the Giants Dugout Store on Third Street, and even non-sports fans will enjoy these brisk, fact-packed jaunts around the 43,000-seat brick ballpark; you'll even get the chance to stroll out onto the field. Both inside and outside the park, you can't miss the giant Coca-Cola bottle and enormous mitt looming behind left field. The 80ft-long soda bottle, which lights up and shoots bubbles every time the Giants hit a home run, contains slides and is part of the children's play area known as the **Coca-Cola Fan Lot** – it's even open on non-game days. The glove, meanwhile, is a highly detailed 26ft-high replica of a 1927 vintage four-fingered baseball mitt. Back outside the ballpark in the attractive front plaza at the corner of Third Street and King, stop to admire the frozen-in-time sculpture of Giants legend Willie Mays – arguably America's greatest baseball player – ringed by 24 palms, a nod to his jersey number.

China Basin and Mission Rock

South of the Giants' gleaming ballpark, the spirit of blue-collar San Francisco perseveres around the abandoned docks and old shipyards known as **China Basin** and **Mission Rock**. The docks at the switchyards, where the drawbridge crosses China Basin Channel, were the site of deadly clashes between striking longshoremen and the city police in the 1930s, one of the largest labour uprisings in twentieth-century America; to this day, the union maintains a reputation for radicalism. Later, in the 1950s, **Jack Kerouac** worked here as a brakeman while writing material that was later to appear in *Lonesome Traveler*, detailing scenes of South of Market's skid-row hotels and whores.

Folsom Street

Toward the western edge of South of Market, **Folsom Street** is rather drab by day, filled as it is with auto-repair shops and light industry. After dark, however, an eclectic nightlife scene thrives along the thoroughfare between Eighth and 11th streets, where clubs and restaurants cater to seemingly every subculture under the stars. Because it's not the sort of club district where partiers pack the sidewalks (except along 11th) it's best to know which spots you'll be hitting before you arrive. Most of the action happens behind closed doors, and many of the streets – even those where parties are going on – still give the vibe of an isolated warehouse district.

Folsom Street has also been the longtime home to the city's leather community – French postmodernist and renowned S&M fan Michel Foucault claimed to have a near-spiritual relationship with the place – but in reality, the leather scene maintains a relatively low profile most of the year, other than in September for the infamous **Folsom Street Fair** (see p.229).

Defenestration

Sixth St at Howard • ⓦ defenestration.org

Near Folsom Street, the surrounding blocks hide a variety of small art spaces and galleries, though your chances of simply stumbling across them are rather slim. However, if you happen to be here during daytime hours – be aware that the area around Sixth Street and Howard is less than savoury after dark – stop for a look at **Defenestration**, a wonderfully Quixotic piece of public art by local artist Brian Goggin that involves furniture, appliances and even grandfather clocks bolted to the outside of an abandoned building.

The Tenderloin

The **Tenderloin**, an uninviting district on the north side of Market Street between Civic Center and Union Square, has long been one of San Francisco's grittiest sections, overrun with tenement houses and mentally unstable homeless people. Local bureaucratic paralysis has continued to aggravate the problem, and the area is, sadly, rougher than ever. The stretch of Taylor Street around Turk and Eddy is especially unpleasant, day or night, although you should be safe as long as you keep your wits about you and don't mind vagrants asking you for money. There are signs, though, that the neighbourhood is changing: for one, waves of Pakistani and South Asian immigrants have begun transforming the area by establishing numerous cheap restaurants. At its upper edge, gentrification has bled down from ritzy Nob Hill, and realtors have taken to calling the northernmost portion – in a glorious *double entendre* – the Tendernob.

The area's oddball name has never been definitively explained. One tale is that nineteenth-century police were rewarded with choice cuts of steak for serving a particularly perilous tour of duty here. A less flattering version is that, thanks to the constant bribes they collected from the gambling houses and brothels, those same policemen were able to dine in the city's finest restaurants. Still others claim that the name is based on the district's shank shape, or even its notoriety for flesh-flashing brothels. Whatever the answer, it has always been the seediest part of town and the heart of San Francisco's vigorous sex industry (see box, p.92).

Glide Memorial Methodist Church

330 Ellis St at Taylor • Sunday service 9 & 11am • ☎ 415 674 6000, ⓦ glide.org

One of the Tenderloin's brighter places is **Glide Memorial Methodist Church**, which provides a wide range of social services for the neighbourhood's downtrodden, including a shelter and soup kitchen for the homeless. Thanks to the forceful personality of pastor Cecil Williams – a major political figure in the city – the church also conducts a remarkable **Sunday service**, backed by Williams's rollicking choir. It's a high-octane experience full of soul, blues, jazz and R&B music, mind-blowing singing soloists and well-dressed black matrons elbow to elbow with glammed-up drag queens; it's a quintessential San Francisco experience and well worth the effort to attend. If you want to snag a seat in the main auditorium, you'll need to turn up at least an hour beforehand. Otherwise, casual visitors often end up in an adjoining room where they can only watch via live television link. If you're not stopping by on a Sunday, step inside to see the **AIDS Memorial Chapel** – the altarpiece triptych was the last work Keith Haring completed before his death from the disease in 1990.

Lower Polk Gulch

At the western limits of the Tenderloin, along Polk Street between O'Farrell and Bush, lies **Lower Polk Gulch**; this was once a congregating point for the city's transgender community and a hub for the flesh trade, though its sex-soaked past is receding. The area inherited many of the displaced residents and merchants who fled

Haight-Ashbury in the early 1970s. It's now best known for a few historic gay bars that line the street amid slothful gentrification, not to mention its smattering of young hustlers and prostitutes.

Mitchell Brothers O'Farrell Theatre

895 O'Farrell St at Polk • Mon–Sat 11.30am–2am, Sun 5.30pm–1.30am • ☎ 415 776 6686, ⓦ ofarrell.com

The southeast corner of O'Farrell and Polk is home to a neighbourhood landmark of sorts, the strip club known as **Mitchell Brothers O'Farrell Theatre**. The Mitchell boys achieved considerable notoriety in the 1970s when they persuaded young Ivory Soap model Marilyn Chambers to star in their porn film *Behind the Green Door*, which they debuted at the Cannes Film Festival. While the pair slowly slipped back into obscurity over the ensuing decades, they made a tragic return to tabloid fame when Jim Mitchell shot and killed his brother Artie in 1991; the club has managed to soldier on since.

Great American Music Hall

859 O'Farrell St near Polk • ☎ 415 885 0750, ⓦ gamh.com

The most esteemed of Lower Polk Gulch's live music venues is also San Francisco's oldest, the **Great American Music Hall**, right next to Mitchell Brothers O'Farrell Theatre. The 700-person capacity concert hall opened in 1907 as *Blanco's*, a Barbary Coast-era restaurant, bordello and gambling hall with elaborate Victorian balconies, marble columns and ornate frescoes on the ceiling. Fan dancer Sally Rand, who was adored by locals, bought the place in 1936, dubbed it the *Music Box* and hosted popular dance

4

SAN FRANCISCO'S SEX INDUSTRY

San Francisco established itself as a centre of carnal sin long before the Mitchell brothers (see above) set up shop. During the **Gold Rush era**, thousands of unaccompanied men passed through the city before heading off to the Sierra Nevada foothills, and when they returned to town with a bit of gold in their pockets, they often lost it at one of over one hundred houses of ill repute in the city. The twin centres of San Francisco's prostitution industry in those days were the Tenderloin and Barbary Coast, near what's now Jackson Square (see p.49). While the latter is now packed with genteel interior design stores, the sex industry is alive and well in the former.

By the end of the nineteenth century, San Francisco's brothels began to suffocate under the twin engines of women's suffrage and religious fury. The latter was notably embodied in one person, Scottish missionary **Donaldina Cameron**: nicknamed the White Devil, she liberated more than three thousand local women from forcible prostitution. Still, San Francisco's reputation as the **sex capital** of America remained ingrained in popular mythology, and after World War II, the city's massage parlours and strip joints thrived again with the sudden presence of numerous GIs who stayed on after being discharged from service. Once the AIDS pandemic hit in the 1980s, many sex establishments shut down – especially the city's notorious gay bathhouses – only to resurface a decade later in different forms.

For more than thirty years, San Francisco has been at the forefront of sex-positive feminism. In 1977, sex educator Joani Blank opened **Good Vibrations** (see p.215) as a "clean, well-lighted", woman-friendly alternative to the usual spate of lowbrow sex stores. In 1992, the staff of Good Vibrations bought the company from Blank, reorganized as a cooperative and expanded store operations to other neighbourhoods in the city, the East Bay and even Massachusetts. Since the 1990s, San Francisco has also been a leader in the movement to decriminalize prostitution, unionize sex workers and protect them from violence, with local women founding numerous action groups.

Another key element of San Francisco's sex-positive culture is the **Center for Sex & Culture**, a library and seminar space run by eccentric sexologist Dr Carol Queen (1519 Mission St near 11th ☎ 415 255 1155, ⓦ centerforsexandculture.org). Queen regularly hosts discussion groups and sexual self-help shows at her appointment-only centre; she's also well known as ringmistress of the annual Masturbate-a-thon, a one-night event each May that finds dozens of willing participants (and loads of voyeurs) lending a hand to raise funds for the centre.

parties for a decade. Before it reopened as the *Great American Music Hall* in 1972, the spot had other lives as a jazz club and a Moose Lodge. For forty years, the hall has continued to draw big-name performers such as Duke Ellington and the Grateful Dead, as well as successful local acts in every genre from punk and indie rock to jazz, blues and world music.

Civic Center

To the immediate southwest of the grubby Tenderloin stands San Francisco's grandest architectural gesture: the complex of Beaux Arts buildings known as the **Civic Center**. This classical cluster of slate-grey grandiosity was the brainchild of brilliant urban planner Daniel Burnham, a follower of the "City Beautiful" movement – the central tenet of which was that a utopian city built in a vaguely classical style would be so beautiful, it would inspire civic loyalty and upstanding morals in its residents. Before the devastating earthquake of 1906, Burnham had already prepared plans with the help of architect Willis Polk to level San Francisco and rebuild it along Parisian lines. These plans featured boulevard-like traffic arteries fanning out like spokes across the city, extensive subways and a grand civic plaza at the junction of Van Ness Avenue and Market Street. Unfortunately, after the 1906 calamities, the city was choked by bureaucracy, and his plan was heavily diluted until only Civic Center Plaza was passed; even then, it wasn't finished until several years after his death. It's worth pausing here to regard the eighteen flagpoles, each of which displays a flag from California history – including various iterations of Old Glory – with an explanation at its base.

   Despite Burnham's belief that grand architectural answers would silence social questions, Civic Center today is simply a politically reliant version of the Tenderloin with finer building design. Civic Center Plaza is often crammed with homeless people, and although police periodically evict them, most soon return. The contrast here between finely dressed San Franciscans heading in and out of the opera, ballet and symphony – as well as numerous city employees and politicians scurrying about government buildings – and the mentally ill or drug-addicted homeless nearby is painfully glaring.

4

United Nations Plaza

Many visitors arrive at the Civic Center Muni and BART station at the corner of Market and Leavenworth streets and are disgorged immediately into generally uninviting **United Nations Plaza**, constructed in 1975 to commemorate the founding of the UN here thirty years earlier – look for the UN Charter etched on a black stone shard. The plaza is filled with fountains and the homeless, but on Wednesdays and Sundays it's transformed into a buzzing **farmers' market**.

San Francisco Main Library

100 Larkin St at Grove • Mon & Sat 10am–6pm, Tues–Thurs 9am–8pm, Fri noon–6pm, Sun noon–5pm • ☎ 415 557 4400, ⓦ sfpl.org

Adjacent to Civic Center Plaza is the **San Francisco Main Library**, which moved into its current location in 1996. The move was somewhat controversial at the time since the library's sleek design – which includes a large, light-filled central atrium and plenty of space for lounging readers – didn't incorporate enough space for books in the eyes of some; wandering through the extensive stacks today, however, you'll find that such misgivings were unfounded.

   On the top floor, the **San Francisco History Center**, used primarily for research, has a rotating, if ragtag, display of ephemera. Of more unique interest, one level below, is the **James C. Hormel Gay and Lesbian Center** (named in honour of the gay activist and meat magnate), the first of its kind in the nation. Topped by a dome with a mural depicting leading figures in gay rights and literary movements, it's a combined reference library, community centre and exhibition space. The library also has several computer terminals with internet access that anyone can use free of charge for fifteen minutes, available on a first-come, first-served basis; free wi-fi is also provided to visitors with laptops.

Asian Art Museum

200 Larkin St at McAllister • Tues–Sun 10am–5pm, Feb–Sept Thurs till 9pm • $12 • ☎ 415 581 3500, ⓦ asianart.org

Directly across Grove Street from the Main Library stands the **Asian Art Museum**. Originally set in cramped quarters in Golden Gate Park, it reopened here in 2003 in what was the city's original Main Library. The Beaux Arts building, opened in 1917 as part of Daniel Burnham's abortive plans, received a stunning makeover from Gae Aulenti, the same architect who turned a derelict train station in Paris into the Musée d'Orsay. Aulenti opened up the former library's dim interior to allow light to reach every corner, while still preserving details like the multicoloured, ornamental ceiling decorations visible in the upper galleries.

The museum's holdings are vast, and it takes several hours to hit just the highlights; the most famous treasure here is probably the oldest known Chinese Buddha image, dating to 338 AD. Two other items deserve a special look: the White Tara, a gilded, seated female goddess from Nepal with seven eyes – five of which are spread between her palms, feet and forehead; and the wonderful wooden statue of wrathful Japanese god Fudo Myoo, possessing an expression more constipated than thunderous. The best way to tackle the museum is by starting on the third floor and working downward, since the collection is organized by country and loosely arranged so that the upper floor contains religious statuary, while the second holds broader ranges of objects and ephemera. There are free docent talks throughout the day, but be warned that the introductory tours are breathless and hurried – you're better off browsing at leisure with an audio guide.

City Hall

Mon–Fri 8am–8pm; tours Mon–Fri 10am, noon & 2pm • Free • Sign up for tours at the Docent Tour Kiosk on the Van Ness Avenue side of the building, or call ahead on ☎ 415 554 6139, ⓦ sfartscommission.org/tours

Grand **City Hall** stands on Dr Carlton B. Goodlett Place, an honorary designation of one block of Polk Street commemorating a local civil rights leader. This is actually San Francisco's second City Hall – the first, on the site of what's now the Main Library, was constructed of steel and reinforced concrete. Seven years after its 1899 completion, the earthquake and fire gutted the cheaply constructed building, stripping it down to its skeleton and leaving it looking like a charred birdcage. Nothing could be salvaged, other than the statue from the top of the dome, so the building was pulled down and a contest announced for its replacement. (Ironically, the statue shattered after rolling off the flatbed truck in which it was being transported from the site – so ultimately, nothing of the first City Hall survived.) More than seventy local firms submitted designs in hopes of winning the $25,000 prize; the winning plan was submitted by Bakewell and Brown, former students at Paris's Ecole des Beaux Arts, which called for a structure inspired by the gilded dome of that city's Les Invalides.

San Francisco's City Hall cost an astonishing $3.5 million to build, and includes more than ten acres of marble, shipped all the way from New England and Italy. The structure's design is conspicuously sumptuous throughout, notably in the priceless carved Manchurian oak walls in the Board of Supervisors Legislative Chamber. Earthquake retrofitting – which involved sliding giant ball bearings under its foundations – allows the entire structure to wobble more than two feet in either direction during a quake, an almost foolproof defence against destruction.

It was here in 1978 that conservative city supervisor Dan White avoided security by climbing through a window to assassinate, separately, mayor George Moscone and openly gay supervisor Harvey Milk (see box, p.294). The following year, when White was found guilty of manslaughter rather than murder, violent demonstrations took place here as gay protesters set fire to police vehicles and stormed the doors of the building – an event that became known as the "**White Night Riot**". Although you can wander around the first floor

SAN FRANCISCO'S HOMELESS

San Francisco's most intractable social problem is **homelessness**, an issue that's clear even to casual tourists. Downtown, much of Market Street west of Hallidie Plaza is filled with vagrants day or night, drawn here in part by the social service administration buildings that sit on the blocks between Sixth and Eighth streets. In fact, the city has one of the largest homeless populations in the United States, with wanderers attracted by its temperate (if somewhat wet) weather and reputation as a liberal centre. Laws signed by Governor Ronald Reagan in the 1960s and 1970s reformed the state's mental health care system and contributed to the large number of mentally ill living on the streets of San Francisco, and together with those struggling with drug addiction or alcoholism, the sheer volume of people competing for loose change and social services has contributed to a culture of desperation and poverty in the Tenderloin, certain areas of South of Market and even in and around the Financial District.

of City Hall on your own (provided you pass the security checkpoint), the best way to experience the interior of the building is by joining one of the hour-long **tours**, which even include a whistle-stop walk through the mayor's private office.

Museum of Performance & Design

Veterans Building, 401 Van Ness Ave at McAllister • Gallery Wed–Sat noon–5pm, library Wed–Fri noon–5pm • Free • ☎ 415 255 4800, Ⓦ mpdsf.org

Across Van Ness Avenue behind City Hall, the Veterans Building houses two lively museums. Up on the fourth floor, the **Museum of Performance & Design** is an ideal stop for anyone with a love for showbiz. Although it's primarily a research centre boasting the largest collection of performing arts material outside of New York, its museum possesses more than two million painstakingly collected programmes, photographs, posters, books, videos and press clippings. You could spend hours raking through the memorabilia, a highlight of which is the **Isadora Duncan** collection that focuses on the influential dancer, born in San Francisco in 1877.

San Francisco Arts Commission Gallery

Veterans Building, 401 Van Ness Ave at McAllister • Wed–Sat noon–5pm; City Hall space Mon–Fri 8am–8pm • Free • ☎ 415 554 6080, Ⓦ sfacgallery.org

On the ground-level lobby of the Veterans Building, the **San Francisco Arts Commission (SFAC) Gallery** is a terrific place to discover up-and-coming Bay Area artists through provocative exhibitions that often go far beyond the Bay Area sphere. SFAC also hosts a worthwhile satellite space on the lower level of City Hall.

War Memorial Opera House

301 Van Ness Ave at Grove

Directly behind City Hall on Van Ness Avenue is one of San Francisco's cultural mainstays, the c.1932 **War Memorial Opera House**. The ornate building was where the United Nations Charter was signed in 1945; today, the 3100-seat venue is the shared home of both the San Francisco Opera and San Francisco Ballet.

Louise M. Davies Symphony Hall

201 Van Ness Ave at Grove

Contrasting sharply with the understated grandeur of War Memorial Opera House is the giant, Modernist fishbowl that is the **Louise M. Davies Symphony Hall**, one block south on Van Ness. Opened in 1980 with curving lines that may or may not have been inspired by the bridge of the USS *Enterprise*, the hall has its fans in the progressive architecture camp; overall, though, the general consensus is that it's an aberration of the otherwise tastefully harmonious design scheme of Civic Center.

4

DOLORES PARK

The Mission, the Castro and around

Together, the Mission and the Castro make up the beating heart of San Francisco, and here more than anywhere else in the city, a number of cultures exist far outside the boundaries of mainstream America. These compelling neighbourhoods are filled with galleries, murals, one-of-a-kind local shops, vibrant restaurants and thriving nightlife; furthermore, thanks to the hills that shelter them from the chilly coastal fog, these low-lying districts are blessed with some of San Francisco's sunniest weather. Flanking the Mission and the Castro, the manicured streets and inviting sidewalks of mellow Noe Valley offer a glimpse into the everyday lives of well-to-do San Franciscans, while looming up the neighbouring mountain flank to the west, the positively comatose Twin Peaks district offers extraordinary vistas.

While the Mission is the centre of San Francisco's largely working-class **Latino community**, since the 1980s it has experienced a sharp influx of young Anglo artists, writers, musicians and hipsters; furthermore, its lively scene makes it a major weekend destination for young heat-seekers from other parts of town and throughout the Bay Area. Still, the neighbourhood maintains a fierce grip on its Latin American roots, fully evident in the hundreds of murals splashed on buildings and the array of Mexican, Central and South American restaurants, clubs and shops.

West of the Mission at the foot of **Twin Peaks**, the **Castro** is the Bay Area's – some would say America's – epicentre of gay culture. Gentrified by the city's gay community during the 1970s, the area was ground zero for the bacchanalian atmosphere that prevailed on San Francisco's gay scene during that decade. Today, many in the rainbow-flag-bedecked district focus their energies on political organizing instead of the wild life; as a result, the Castro now finds itself increasingly wealthy and politically influential. With this comfort has come a certain conservatism, and while activists argue that residents must still lead the fight on human rights issues such as AIDS funding and legal recognition of gay marriage, many in the area seem increasingly concerned about more immediate quality-of-life issues such as opening new dog parks and keeping chain stores out.

The Mission

Relatively warm and sunny compared to the often fog-shrouded districts further north and west, the **Mission** is a lively, colourful neighbourhood nestled in the flat stretch between the Castro and craggy Potrero Hill. The district takes its name from nearby **Mission Dolores**, built near a lake (since covered) by Spanish missionaries in 1776. In fact, the city of San Francisco – then known as Yerba Buena – was officially founded here that year.

Ever since the United States wrested California territory from Mexico in 1848, the Mission has drawn immigrants – initially Scandinavians, followed during the Gold Rush by a significant Irish influx that also spilled into the Castro. In the 1960s and 1970s, intense political turmoil in Central and South America brought Latin Americans to the Mission in droves; today, the neighbourhood continues to embody a dual identity of Latino *barrio* and Anglo artist stronghold, immediately visible in the way trendy bars and restaurants jostle for space with old taquerias and junk shops, or how flocks of young white hipsters share space with carts selling Mexican ice cream.

For all its eclectic stores, bustling taquerias, bright murals and dynamic energy, the Mission certainly has its dangerous spots, particularly after dark; try not to look overly touristy along 24th and Mission streets, where it's best to avoid wearing bright red or blue, colours that may garner menacing glances from gang members.

Mission Dolores

3321 16th St at Dolores • Daily: May–Oct 9am–4.30pm; Nov–April 9am–4pm • $5 suggested donation • ☎ 415 621 8203, Ⓦ missiondolores.org

Misión San Francisco de Asis, more commonly known as **Mission Dolores**, is one of the city's most authentic historical icons, and is definitely worth a visit. The city's Latin American origins are preserved in the church's adobe walls. Its colloquial name dates back to the nascent city's first European camp: the Spanish arrived on the Friday before Palm Sunday – the Friday of Sorrows – and, finding an ample freshwater supply, decided to pitch their tents here, naming the site *La Laguna de los Dolores* (the Lagoon of Sorrows). The first building they erected didn't last long, but the second, finished in 1791, still stands, having weathered both of the city's major earthquakes – look for the squat, white adobe now dwarfed by the frosted, tiered cake of a basilica next door, added in 1913. When the Mexican government secularized the missions in 1834 Mission Dolores shut down. It was transformed into a tavern and dance hall until finally reconsecrated as a Catholic parish in 1859, and is still active as such today.

5

The **interior** of the small chapel is washed in yellow sunlight, and redwood beams line the ceiling, painted with chevron designs that mimic local Ohlone Indian decorative patterns. A few simple pews face the wooden altar (hand-carved in Mexico around the beginning of the eighteenth century), while plaques on the floor mark the burial sites of prominent locals, including William Leidesdorff, an African-American businessman who funded the construction of the first City Hall.

On the **self-guided tour**, don't miss the diorama of the mission complex as it existed in 1799 – astonishing for its size and isolation – or the wooded cemetery, made famous in Hitchcock's *Vertigo* and filled with rambling roses. The cemetery holds the graves of many local notables, including Francisco de Haro, the first mayor of San Francisco; it also holds the unmarked remains of more than five thousand Native Americans. Note how many of the names on gravestones are now street names across the city.

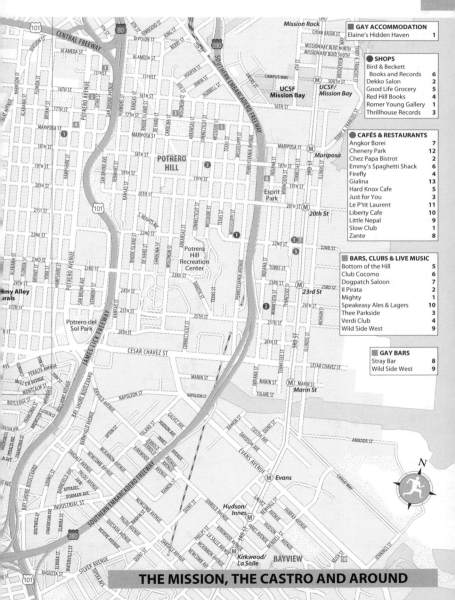

GAY ACCOMMODATION
Elaine's Hidden Haven   1

SHOPS
Bird & Beckett
  Books and Records   6
Dekko Salon   2
Good Life Grocery   5
Red Hill Books   4
Romer Young Gallery   1
Thrillhouse Records   3

CAFÉS & RESTAURANTS
Angkor Borei   7
Chenery Park   12
Chez Papa Bistrot   2
Emmy's Spaghetti Shack   6
Firefly   4
Gialina   13
Hard Knox Cafe   5
Just for You   3
Le P'tit Laurent   11
Liberty Cafe   10
Little Nepal   9
Slow Club   1
Zante   8

BARS, CLUBS & LIVE MUSIC
Bottom of the Hill   5
Club Cocomo   6
Dogpatch Saloon   7
Il Pirata   2
Mighty   1
Speakeasy Ales & Lagers   10
Thee Parkside   3
Verdi Club   4
Wild Side West   9

GAY BARS
Stray Bar   8
Wild Side West   9

THE MISSION, THE CASTRO AND AROUND

THE MISSION AND THE CASTRO: CENTRAL AREA

Dolores Park and around

A few blocks south of Mission Dolores down stately, palm tree-lined Dolores Street, you'll find the rolling hills of **Dolores Park** at 18th Street; once a cemetery for local Jews, it's now a magnet for sun-worshippers. Aside from sprawling Golden Gate Park, this is one of the best green spaces in the city, gracing the area like an unexpected splash of fresh air. It's invariably filled with Castro men, Mission hipsters and local soccer players, as well as hordes of dogs and their owners. The park's southwestern corner provides a spectacular view of the Downtown skyline, while on weekends, this corner becomes known as **Dolores Beach**, where Castro musclemen bronze themselves and show off their bodies to willing onlookers.

Continuing south, the hillsides along Dolores Street between 19th and 24th streets are quilted with a warren of quiet side streets; thanks to the firmer bedrock of the hills, the area holds many Victorians largely untouched by the catastrophic 1906 and 1989 earthquakes. Most are relatively modest, but for ornate standouts, head to **Liberty Street** between 20th and 21st streets. As you slog up and down the hills here, keep your eyes open for ornamental Stars of David, a relic of the area's Jewish past.

The Women's Building

3543 18th St at Guerrero • ☎ 415 431 1180, ⓦ womensbuilding.org

Founded in 1971, **The Women's Building** hosts and sponsors a variety of politicized and progressive community groups, workshops and events, many with a strong feminist or lesbian activism slant – call or check the website for a current calendar. The building is tattooed with an enormous and somewhat awkward mural (known by the horrifically self-conscious name of *Maestrapeace*), designed by seven female designers and executed by a team of one hundred painters. An enormous mother-goddess figure dominates one side, while on the other, there's a gigantic portrait of Rigoberta Menchú, the Guatemalan indigenous activist who won the Nobel Peace Prize in 1992.

Valencia Street

Home to a dynamic mix of high- and low-end culture, **Valencia Street** is the Mission at its most fiercely independent, where boutiques rub shoulders with thrift stores, and chic ethnic restaurants bump up against the Mission's ever-present **taquerias**. Young artists and innovators have brought in small galleries and creative spaces such as **Artists Television Access**, where local directors' projects are screened, and **826 Valencia**, a youth writing workshop launched by author Dave Eggers that's fronted by a pirate supply shop (seriously). Meanwhile, quirky stores specializing in taxidermy, as well as vintage furniture, LPs and books, have popped up alongside Latino apothecaries. Strolling this strip between 15th and 25th streets is one of the city's finest free activities.

Levi's factory building

250 Valencia St near 14th

Just north of the heart of Valencia's humming commercial corridor stands the original **Levi's factory building**, a huge lemon-yellow structure. Though the jeans Levi's makes today bear only a remote resemblance to the original item, invented during the Gold Rush (see box, p.102), their popularity has endured. The building is now home to San Francisco Friends School, a private elementary school.

Mission Street

Running parallel to Valencia Street to the west, **Mission Street** is the **Latino** counterpart to Valencia's Anglo hipster bent. Between 15th and 25th streets, the main drag is lined with five-and-dime shops selling a virtually identical stock of kitschy religious knick-knacks and assorted disposable items. You'll also spot loads of taquerias and a clutch of disused Art Deco movie theatres turned into parking structures and retailers, the faded spire-signs of which are the district's sole high-rise touches. BART's subway

5

SHEER JEAN-IUS

Many men struck gold during the Gold Rush without having to mine for it. Rather than ply the Sierra Nevada foothills with pans and axes, these entrepreneurs concentrated on supplying hopeful forty-niners with everything they needed to pan for their fortunes; grocer/chocolatier Domenico Ghirardelli (see p.73) was one, and drainage specialist Adolph Sutro (see p.117) was another. The most famous, however, was **Levi Strauss**.

Strauss arrived in San Francisco from New York in 1853 as a dry-goods wholesaler, having brought bolts of tan canvas that he planned to sell as tents or wagon covers. Through a combination of savvy and serendipity, Strauss noticed that miners needed stout trousers, and started producing a few pairs for sale. He was so successful that, within seven years, he'd run out of canvas (although it wasn't until 1947 that the company finally gave up on dry-goods wholesaling and focused entirely on jeans). This meant Strauss had to find an alternative, so he turned to *serge de Nîmes*, blue cloth imported from Nîmes, France. The (perhaps fanciful) story goes that the pants he made from this fabric looked like uniforms worn by Italian sailors from Genoa – *Gênes* in French – so his pants were soon colloquially referred to as "jeans". The signature "SF" copper rivets on each pocket were added later at the suggestion of a tailor who'd noticed that gold nuggets shredded the fabric.

Although no production takes place here, Levi's is still headquartered in San Francisco at **Levi's Plaza** (see p.62), home to a disappointing exhibition on the company's history.

rattles directly beneath the strip, the north end of which can be rife with thugs and drug dealers – exercise caution between 16th and 18th streets in particular.

Balmy Alley
Mural tours: Sat & Sun 11.30am &1.30pm • Tours $12–15 • ☏ 415 285 2287, ⓦ precitaeyes.org

East of Mission Street, the pace becomes noticeably slower as blocks get increasingly residential; here, some two hundred murals underscore a strong sense of community pride and Latin American heritage. The greatest concentration of work can be found on **Balmy Alley**, an unassuming passageway between Treat Avenue, 24th, Harrison and 25th streets, where's barely an inch of wall is unadorned. The murals here are painted on wooden fences, rather than stucco walls, and consequently are regularly refreshed and replaced.

Balmy's **mural project** began during a small community-organized event in 1973, but the tiny street has become the spiritual centre of a burgeoning Latino arts movement born out of both the US civil rights struggle and pro-democracy movements in South America. While many of the murals are more heartfelt than either skilled or beautiful, it's nonetheless worth stopping by for a peek. Tours of the artwork are run by **Precita Eyes Mural Arts Center**, which has sponsored most of the paintings since its founding in 1971; the organization also sells maps of the neighbourhood's murals for $5.

Bernal Heights
Buzzing with new arrivals drawn partly by its slightly-out-of-the-way location, and partly by its thriving lesbian scene, **Bernal Heights** is centred on charming Cortland Avenue. The leafy, tree-lined street makes for a pleasant stroll, with its quiet cafés, independent book and clothing stores, and variety of bars and restaurants. Lifting north off Cortland, brave the stiff walk uphill along Folsom Street up to Bernal Heights Park, which offers a lovely, little-seen view of most of the city.

Potrero Hill
East of the Mission, expect a punishing hike to reach **Potrero Hill**, which boasts an incomparably up-close panorama of Downtown and the Bay beyond; it's a strong dichotomy, then, that the neighbourhood possesses an atmosphere more evocative of a country village than a major city. There may be precious little to do here, but Potrero's peaceful, if hilly, streets are terrific for wandering on a sunny morning or afternoon.

A smattering of inviting cafes and restaurants are scattered along a pair of sleepy commercial zones on 18th and 20th streets.

The Castro

A neighbourhood bursting with energy, the **Castro** is a great spot for window-shopping, people-watching, club-hopping or just enjoying a leisurely lunch. Sprawling up and down several hillsides between the Lower Haight, the Mission and Noe Valley, and set in the eastern shadows of Twin Peaks, the district is liveliest along Castro Street between Market and 19th streets. Since its emergence four decades ago as a hub of global **gay culture**, the neighbourhood has consistently lured gay visitors from across the world. It's more upscale than the Mission and presents itself as a blurred fusion of rainbow flags plastered on every retail outlet, shop windows piled high with gay-themed items, and forests of muscular men toting doll-sized dogs. If its jammed sidewalks prove too daunting, head for the scrupulously manicured side streets, lined with neat rows of brightly painted Victorians.

Harvey Milk Plaza
Castro St at Market

Named in honour of the murdered local politician (see box, p.294), **Harvey Milk Plaza** is where the largest **rainbow flag** in the area flutters proudly. This enormous twenty-by-thirty-foot pennant was recently updated by its designer, Gilbert Baker – dubbed "the gay Betsy Ross" – to include the eight colours he'd originally intended. In 1978, tight funds prevented Baker from including turquoise and fuchsia fabrics alongside the shades of red, orange, yellow, green, blue and purple that have become synonymous with gay freedom.

Pink Triangle Park
Market St at 17th • ⓦ pinktrianglepark.org

North across Market Street stands sombre **Pink Triangle Park**, dedicated in 2002 as the first US monument devoted specifically to gay victims of the Holocaust. A pink triangle sits at its heart, filled with rough rose-quartz shingle; around it, amid spiky agave cacti and pink rose bushes, stand fifteen pink triangle-topped granite pylons, each representing one thousand men murdered by the Nazis because of their sexuality. Lesbians aren't included in this number as they were treated differently by Hitler's regime: since they were able to bear children but chose not to, lesbians wore the black triangle of the Antisocials rather than the pink one of the homosexuals (and so weren't sent to the gas chambers in such significant numbers).

Castro Theatre
429 Castro St at Market • ☎ 415 621 6120, ⓦ thecastrotheatre.com

The district's one major sight is the **Castro Theatre**, flagged by the neon sign that towers above the surrounding buildings. Designed by architect Timothy Pflueger, the man behind Oakland's landmark Paramount Theatre (see p.235), the theatre is a stunning example of the Mediterranean Revival style, its exterior marked out by lavish stucco decoration and ornate windows. Inside, the decorative riot continues, thanks to foamy balconies, wall-mounted busts of heroic figures and massive ceiling ornamentation – though you'll have to come for a film to see the interior.

Noe Valley

Dolores Street marks the boundary between the Mission and tidy **Noe Valley**, a pleasant, if inessential diversion. An affluent area filled with thirty- and forty-something, pram-pushing professional couples, the quiet neighbourhood is bedded down between

5

SHE'S GOTTA HABIT

One of the Castro's best sights isn't a bar or a building – rather, it's the **Sisters of Perpetual Indulgence**, an outrageous activist group that dresses up as nuns to promote safe sex and HIV awareness in a gloriously camp pastiche of Catholic pageantry. The Sisters began on Easter Sunday in 1979, when four friends – who'd held onto their habits from a college production of *The Sound of Music* – took to the streets of the Castro in full nun drag, touting water pistols and smoking cigars. The Sisters' ranks soon swelled, and today the group boasts seventy members. A registered charity, the group stages monthly Bada-Bingo fundraisers, doles out free condoms at local gay bars and even guest-teaches courses on human sexuality at San Francisco State University. Sisters of Perpetual Indulgence orders exist across the world and a handful of satellite "convents" are found elsewhere in the United States.

Unsurprisingly, the Sisters have encountered plenty of opposition from Catholic orthodoxy. Proudly placed on the official Papal List of Heretics in the mid-1990s, the group made headlines again after the Catholic Church objected to its application for a party permit to close down Castro Street on Easter Sunday in 1999 for a twentieth-birthday fundraiser. These days, the Sisters' annual alt-Easter bash is held in nearby Dolores Park, and is headlined by the always entertaining Hunky Jesus contest.

steep hills and is centred around the restaurants, cafés and inviting boutiques along its commercial corridor, **24th Street**. Many retail outlets here have benches out front encouraging people to linger and chat along the crowded sidewalks. The ride down from Market Street along Muni's J-Church streetcar line – crucial, unless you want to tackle a killer hill – passes scenic **Dolores Park**. Once you get here, however, odds are you'll be hard-pressed to find anything to do besides sip coffee, have a bite to eat, shop for various furnishings or clothes, or dawdle on one of those benches.

Twin Peaks

To reach Twin Peaks' summit by car, continue uphill on Market Street from the Castro until it turns into Portola Avenue, then turn right on Twin Peaks Boulevard. The #37-Corbett bus goes part of the way, though there's still a significant climb up to the crest

High above Noe Valley, the **Twin Peaks** neighbourhood is safely perched on earthquake-proof granite above the city and boasts one attraction, albeit a major one: **panoramic views** of the city, the Bay and the Pacific Ocean. The North and South hills here are, respectively, the fourth-highest (904ft) and second-highest (910ft) points in the city; they're just pipped by 925ft Mount Davidson to the south. Thanks first to television in the 1970s and, now, cell phone service, the Twin Peaks area now boasts the city's highest landmark, **Sutro Tower**, a massive antenna visible from all over the Bay Area.

Sex-starved Spanish explorers originally named the hills *Los Pechos de la Chola* ("Breasts of an Indian Girl"), but Anglo settlers ultimately agreed on the current, sadly literal name. When architect Daniel Burnham worked on his plans for San Francisco in the early 1900s, he imagined two grand centres for the city. One, at what's now Civic Center, would have contained administrative buildings; the other would have crowned Twin Peaks with an enormous amphitheatre. Unfortunately, only fragments of his Civic Center project were ever completed (including City Hall), and nothing appeared on Twin Peaks.

Tank Hill

A good option for avoiding Twin Peaks' tour-bus rabble lies just downhill, where the small promontory of 600ft **Tank Hill**, along Clarendon Avenue just up the hill from 17th Street, offers equally impressive views – provided the city's infamous fog isn't a suffocating factor. It's named after the enormous 500,000-gallon water tank that used to sit on its peak: note the grove of eucalyptus trees, planted in the early days of World War II to conceal the tank from potential enemy bombing raids.

PIEDMONT BOUTIQUE STOREFRONT

Haight-Ashbury and west of Civic Center

The districts between Civic Center and Golden Gate Park are perhaps the city's most racially and economically diverse; once grubby and crime-ridden, they now make up an eclectic patchwork. Haight-Ashbury began as an upper-class vacation enclave on the city's outskirts long before becoming one of the most famous places in America for a few short summers in the late 1960s, when it was the centre of the hippie movement. These days, businesses along Haight Street have co-opted the neighbourhood's peace-and-love past as a *de facto* marketing campaign, as if offering visitors a chance to encounter the spectre of 1960s rebellion. Nonetheless, it's certainly worth visiting for its fun shops, ethnic restaurants and gorgeous Victorian architecture.

HAIGHT-ASHBURY AND WEST OF CIVIC CENTER

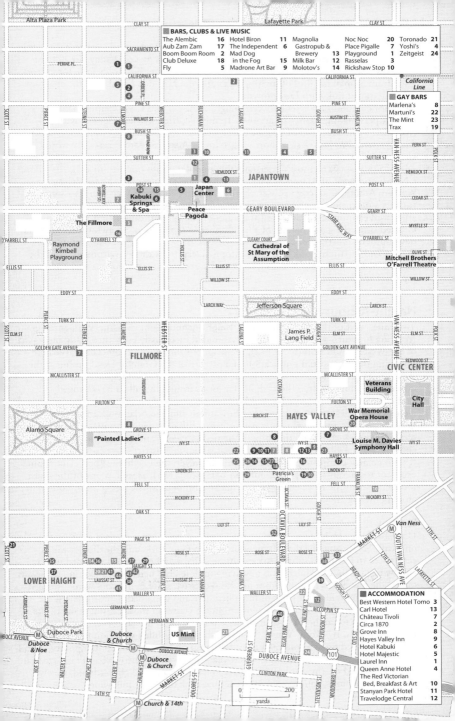

If you're really looking to connect with modern-day counterculture, you're better off in the **Lower Haight**, immediately to the east. Elswhere, Sleepy **Cole Valley**, an affluent nook just south of Haight-Ashbury, is a pleasant diversion, but holds little for visitors aside from a small handful of inviting cafés and the N-Judah Muni line, the area's primary transit link with Downtown.

Other neighbourhoods set between Haight-Ashbury and Civic Center maintain distinct personalities from one another. Trendy, yet friendly **Hayes Valley**, with its tree-lined main street full of upscale boutiques, is a terrific place to while away an empty afternoon. Just west, a short visit to lovely **Alamo Square** is certainly worth a stop, where six restored Victorian houses and a Downtown skyline backdrop provide one of San Francisco's most understandably popular photo opportunities.

North and west of Alamo Square, the landscape gives way to the sprawling **Western Addition**, an edgy subset of which is the **Fillmore**. Once home to some of the city's most notorious housing projects, these heavily African-American areas are still more economically deprived than any of the surrounding neighbourhoods. Grafted onto the eastern edge of the Fillmore is **Japantown**, an awkwardly artificial development mostly comprising a Tokyo-style mall full of sushi bars, tempura houses and Japanese book and paper stores. Despite its drab environs, it's still the heart of the city's Japanese community and a great place to enjoy an authentic Japanese meal.

Haight-Ashbury

Two miles west of the city's downtown, **Haight-Ashbury** lent its name to an entire era, receiving in return a fame on which it has traded mercilessly ever since. Originally part of the Western Addition (see p.112), the neighbourhood was unofficially carved off following the widespread publication of a picture of the Grateful Dead posing at the sign denoting the intersection of Haight and Ashbury streets. Despite the ardent nostalgia of some locals, "The Haight" (as locals invariably call it) has changed dramatically since it emerged in the 1960s as the focus of that decade's countercultural scene; even with its attractive strips of Edwardian and Victorian buildings, today's version feels like a tie-dyed theme park of sorts, full of itinerant homeless people (many of them young), shops offering hippie-themed souvenirs and vintage clothes, and a confrontational vibe hanging in the air that sullies the district's love-is-all sloganeering. It's not an area completely without charms, however: the neighbourhood claims some excellent **restaurants** (see p.163) and fun **bars** (see p.185), as well as one of the finest independent music retailers in the US, massive **Amoeba Music** (see p.202), housed in an old bowling alley.

Brief history

Until 1865, the Haight was no more than a pile of sand dunes marked as "Wasteland" on maps. Soon came the development of Golden Gate Park, and the district was earmarked to form part of the park extension. Victorian houses mushroomed nearby, and by the 1890s, the Haight was a thriving middle-class neighbourhood; in fact, it was one of the few places to profit from the 1906 disaster, since many who were displaced from their homes in other parts of town fled here and remained. Unfortunately, the Depression was a body blow to the lower middle classes in the area, and many of the respectable Victorian homes became low-rent rooming houses as owners defaulted on their mortgages. By World War II, Haight-Ashbury was filled with liquor stores and bars, and limped on as a rundown place for cheap nights out. The contemporary legend of the Haight has its roots in the postwar years, when students from San Francisco State College (located nearby until 1953) began to move into the neighbourhood, slowly creating a rebellious, countercultural scene that took off in the following decade.

JAPANTOWN (P.113) >

6

HIPPIES IN THE HAIGHT

The first **hippies** were an offshoot of the **Beats**, many of whom had moved out of their increasingly expensive North Beach apartments to take advantage of Haight-Ashbury's low rents and large Victorian houses. The post-Beat bohemia that subsequently began to develop here in the early 1960s was initially a small affair, involving drug use and the embrace of Eastern religion and philosophy, together with a marked anti-American political stance and a desire for world peace. Where Beat philosophy had emphasized self-indulgence, the hippies, on the face of it at least, attempted to be more embracing, focusing on self-coined concepts such as "universal truth" and "cosmic awareness". Naturally, it took a few big names to get the ball rolling, and characters such as **Ken Kesey and his Merry Pranksters** were living wildly, challenging authority and dropping out (as they saw it) of the established norms of society. **Drugs**, especially then-legal LSD – which was claimed as an avant-garde art form and the effects of which were just being discovered – were considered an integral part of the movement. LSD was pumped out in private laboratories and distributed by **Timothy Leary** and his network of supporters with a prescription – "Turn on, tune in, drop out" – that galvanized a generation into inactivity.

Before long, life in Haight-Ashbury began to take on a theatrical quality: **Pop Art** found mass appeal, light shows became legion, fashion turned colourfully flamboyant, and **the Grateful Dead**, **Jefferson Airplane** and **Janis Joplin** all made international names for themselves. Backed by the business weight of irascible local promoter **Bill Graham**, San Francisco's **psychedelic music** scene became a genuine force nationwide, and it wasn't long before kids from all over America started turning up in Haight-Ashbury for the free food, free drugs and free love. In no time, "money" became a dirty word, the hip became "heads" and the rest of the world were "straights".

Among other illustrious tenants of the Haight in the 1960s, writer **Kenneth Rexroth** (see p.300) hosted a popular radio show and wrote for the *San Francisco Examiner*. **Hunter S. Thompson**, too, spent time here researching and writing his book *Hell's Angels*, becoming instantly unpopular with neighbours for inviting his biker subjects round to his apartment on Parnassus Avenue for noisy, long and occasionally dangerous drinking and drug-taking sessions.

Things in the neighbourhood inevitably turned sour towards the end of the decade. Some soldiers returning from **Vietnam** brought with them newly acquired **heroin** habits and introduced the drug into local hippie culture. In October 1967, hippies disappointed with the hedonistic, self-centred direction the movement had taken hosted the three-day **Death of the Hippie** event in San Francisco, even though the influx was far from over. Slowly, the outcasts, crazies and villains – who until then had been outnumbered by all the nice middle-class kids who simply wanted to get stoned – started to gain power. The most infamous of these was **Charles Manson**, who recruited much of his "family" in the neighbourhood. The darkening clouds continued to gather in 1969, when the Rolling Stones organized their notorious concert in **Altamont**, California (see p.254). The concert was a tragic failure, and the terrifying image of a fatal stabbing occurring in front of the stage amid the drugged-out crowd is widely considered the end of the hippie heyday.

Upper Haight

The high-profile chunk of Haight-Ashbury wedged between Divisadero Street and Golden Gate Park, commonly known as the **Upper Haight**, is centred on one of San Francisco's top shopping strips, **Haight Street**. Here you'll find a riot of quirky boutiques, thrift stores, souvenir shops, restaurants and cafés; the most striking storefront, **Piedmont Boutique**, at 1452 Haight between Masonic and Ashbury, is marked by a giant pair of fishnet-and-heels-wearing legs hanging from a second-floor window.

Buena Vista Park

Haight St between Baker and Central

A convenient place to begin exploring the chunk of Haight-Ashbury closest to Golden Gate Park is craggy **Buena Vista Park**. This steep, heavily wooded green space marks the unofficial divide between the original chunk of hippie-centric Upper Haight and the grungier Lower Haight. The park is well used by local dog-walkers and is also a prime gay cruising spot, given its dense thicket of trees.

Grateful Dead and Hells Angels houses

Aside from shopping and people-watching, the Upper Haight is a popular place to seek out former homes of 1960s legends. Two of the most notorious are a short distance south of Haight Street, right across the street from one another. At 710 Ashbury St at Waller, the **Grateful Dead**'s 1965–69 home was where the band were photographed around the time of their notorious drug bust. Across Ashbury at no. 715, the **Hells Angels**' former local headquarters in the highly ornate, turreted Queen Anne Victorian demonstrates that, despite opposing ideals, hippies and bikers shared the concept of living outside the law.

6

Diggers house

1775 Haight St at Shrader

When the **Diggers**, a short-lived anarchist art group with anonymous leadership, weren't writing Dadaist manifestos in the late 1960s, they would offer free food and shelter to the increasing numbers of homeless filling the neighbourhood. To this day, the sidewalk in front of their former flophouse remains a popular gathering spot for local wanderers.

Amoeba Music

1855 Haight St at Stanyan

Right before Haight Street comes to a halt at Golden Gate Park, you'll find **Amoeba Music**, a place of pilgrimage for music lovers the world over. Opened in 1997 as a larger counterpart to Amoeba's original Berkeley store, the 24,000-square-foot space holds more than 100,000 items, including new and used CDs, records, DVDs and memorabilia. Free, in-store performances by a variety of acts – from indie rock legends Dinosaur Jr to South African singers Ladysmith Black Mambazo – occur regularly on the store's corner stage.

The Panhandle

Two blocks north of Haight Street, you find the **Panhandle**, a sliver of greenery that leads west to Golden Gate Park. The thin strip was landscaped before the rest of the park in the 1870s, and for a while was the focus of high-society carriage rides. That certainly changed when, following the 1906 earthquake, it became a refuge for some thirty thousand families living here in tents. During the 1960s, it was ground zero for hippie happenings (the Jimi Hendrix Experience performed here in June 1967); today it's rather unkempt, although its bike paths and playgrounds ensure steady use by neighbourhood residents.

Lower Haight and around

East of Buena Vista Park, the intriguing stretch of Haight Street between Divisadero and Laguna is known as the **Lower Haight**. This commercial strip of Haight – and a couple of blocks south of the neighbourhood's main drag along Fillmore – is packed with vibrant restaurants, bars and galleries. A few blocks south of the neighbourhood's heart, at the corner of Steiner Street and Duboce Avenue, you'll find **Duboce Park**, a pleasant patch of green hugely popular with dog lovers since pets can run around leash-free. It's a lovely spot that makes for great, dog-watching fun, but you'll want to take care where you step (let alone sit) on the grass. Close by, at the corner of Duboce Avenue and Webster Street, stands the massive **US Mint** (the Old Mint is in South of Market), one of four currency-producing factories in the country, which rises somewhat menacingly on a granite escarpment.

Cole Valley

A few blocks south of Haight Street is **Cole Valley**, a tiny but welcome residential refuge sandwiched between Haight-Ashbury to the north and the Sunset to the west. Much more buttoned-down than its untucked neighbour, the leafy enclave offers little to see or do, other than eat or drink in one of the few restaurants, cafes or pubs near the junction of Cole and Carl streets.

6 Hayes Valley and around

Just as San Francisco generally received a full-scale facelift after the destruction caused by the great 1906 earthquake, the seeds of Hayes Valley's extraordinary reinvention were sown in the wake of a natural disaster. Prior to the cataclysmic Loma Prieta earthquake of 1989, the neighbourhood was a nowhere-land of sorts – home to crumbling buildings and crime, and awkwardly bisected by an overhead highway. After the highway was demolished due to extensive structural damage, the district below blossomed into a bustling urban village full of clever boutiques, art galleries, cafés and restaurants. Neighbourhood denizens run the gamut from self-made artists, architects and designers, to those struggling to make ends meet in the public housing projects on Hayes Valley's west end. The heart of the district is unquestionably Hayes Street between Franklin and Octavia. Anchored by Patricia's Green – a narrow, unpretentious park – the area is a sublime place to pass through on a sunny day.

Alamo Square and the Painted Ladies

Just to the west of Hayes Valley is manicured **Alamo Square**, a lovely hilltop park surrounded by Hayes, Scott, Fulton and Steiner streets, just uphill from the Lower Haight. A staple of every tour-bus company in town, the park's southeast slope is home to small flocks of amateur photographers eager to snap a picture of the "**Painted Ladies**". These seven Victorian houses, originally built in 1894 and colourfully and attractively restored, have been postcard subjects for years; the largest of the lot, on the corner of Steiner and Grove streets, was placed on the market for $4 million in 2010. Even if you're without a camera, it's still worth a visit for picnicking opportunities and brilliant eastward views that, on a clear day, stretch across the city, the Bay and beyond.

The Western Addition and Fillmore

North of Alamo Square lie two large but loosely organized districts: the **Western Addition** and **Fillmore**, sprawling across the hundred or so blocks between Gough Street, Masonic Avenue, and Bush and Fulton streets. Historically African-American, the districts have also been traditionally troubled by social problems, although new development and a series of beautification projects has leavened the tensions somewhat.

A huge influx of **Japanese immigrants** arrived in the area via Hawaii in the early 1900s, where they had worked on sugar plantations for years. Centred on Geary and Fillmore streets, the community thrived until World War II, when anti-Japanese hysteria swept California following the bombing of Pearl Harbor. Local Japanese-Americans were incarcerated in camps across the western US and forced to sell off their property at below-market prices, only returning to the area in significant numbers following the 1960s construction of **Japantown**.

Many cheap homes in the neighbourhoods were then sold to lower-waged **African-Americans**, and a brief heyday of jazz clubs and black-owned businesses ensued – that is, until the area was levelled by the dual forces of 1960s urban renewal and blunderheaded civic planner **Justin Herman**, who demolished dozens of blocks of precious Victorian housing, replacing them with acres of monolithic concrete apartment blocks.

The Fillmore
1805 Geary Blvd at Fillmore • ☎ 415 346 6000, ⓦ thefillmore.com

There's now little to see in the area other than the famed **Fillmore** concert hall, where promoter Bill Graham put on carnivalesque psychedelic rock shows for hallucinating hippies in the 1960s. It remains an active venue today (see p.182).

The Fillmore Jazz Preservation District
In recent years, San Francisco has dubbed the area around Geary and Fillmore the **Fillmore Jazz Preservation District** as a means to draw attention to the neighbourhood's history. **Yoshi's**, a legendary jazz club in Oakland, opened a sister club here in the mid-2000s, and along with the Fillmore and *Boom Boom Room* (formerly owned by the late John Lee Hooker), the club completes a neighbourhood triumvirate of heavyweights across three genres: jazz, rock and blues.

6

Japantown and around
In 1968, in a conciliatory gesture toward San Francisco's Japanese community, the city built the **Japan Center** as a focal point for the reborn **Japantown**, notched into the northeastern corner of the Fillmore. Stretching three blocks along Post Street between Fillmore and Laguna streets, the complex, officially known as the **Japanese Cultural and Trade Center**, aims to replicate the feeling of modern-day Tokyo – although it's debatable how successful the mall is in that regard. Every aspect of Japanese culture, from old-world kimonos, origami and taiko drums to J-pop cultural mainstays such as anime, robots and colourful fashion, can be explored here.

Despite its artificial origins, the mall is now at the centre of a densely concentrated Japanese community (at around twelve thousand people, one of the largest in the Bay Area); it's also filled with restaurants and shops. To experience the Japan Center at its most vibrant, visit during the annual **Cherry Blossom festival** in April (see p.227).

Peace Pagoda
Japantown's sole sight of note is the 100ft **Peace Pagoda**, which stands in the outdoor central plaza that links the Japan Center's main buildings. Looking like a stack of poured-concrete, space-age mushrooms, many believe its appearance is intended to echo an atomic cloud.

Kabuki Springs & Spa
1750 Geary Blvd at Fillmore • Women-only Sun, Wed, Fri; men-only Mon, Thurs, Sat; unisex Tues 10am–9.45pm • $22–25 •
☎ 415 922 6000, ⓦ kabukisprings.com

Adjacent to the Japan Center, the trendy but appealing **Kabuki Springs & Spa** was once a traditional Japanese bathhouse; thankfully, the huge communal steam room has been preserved. Amenities include a 120°F steam room, a 170°F dry sauna, a small cold plunge pool that's a bracing 55°F and a larger, 104°F hot pool ideal for soaking.

The Cathedral of St Mary of the Assumption
1111 Gough St at Geary • Mon–Sat 6.45am–5pm, Sun 7.30am–5pm • ☎ 415 567 2020, ⓦ stmarycathedralsf.org

Anchoring a corner of the Western Addition fittingly known as Cathedral Hill, the city's most conspicuous Catholic church, the **Cathedral of St Mary of the Assumption**, soars above the city. Opened in 1971 to replace a fire-damaged predecessor, this cathedral has traditionally been the butt of local humour due to a modernist design that many have likened to a washing-machine agitator (hence its nickname, "Our Lady of the Maytag"). Set back from Geary Boulevard by a wide plaza and built one storey above ground, it's a striking building that's even more impressive inside, where the parabolic curves seem to be in constant movement, in part thanks to sunlight playing off the massive metal chandelier. The enormous organ within is a spectacle in and of itself, looking like a pincushion with a Mohawk.

CONSERVATORY OF FLOWERS, GOLDEN GATE PARK

The Richmond, Golden Gate Park and the Sunset

The heart of San Francisco's infamous fog belt, the Richmond and Sunset districts tend to be overshadowed by their beaches and stunning parks. Residents of other local neighbourhoods often sniff about the city's far western settlements, but "the Avenues" comprise a refreshingly real place that provides a welcome contrast from the more tourism-driven areas. North of the Richmond and west of the Presidio, the wild green space of Land's End offers fantastic views of the Golden Gate Bridge and overlooks Baker and China beaches, a pair of fine strands. Nearby Lincoln Park is the site of the grand Legion of Honor art museum, one of San Francisco's undeniable treasures and home to some spectacular Auguste Rodin sculptures.

Wedged between the Richmond and Sunset is the sculpted expanse of **Golden Gate Park**, a true civic jewel. Though the park is home to excellent museums, as well as manicured specialist gardens, nothing compares to the green space itself, an artificial masterpiece laid out in the late 1800s. At the park's western edge, the city's Pacific coastline possesses a hauntingly desolate beauty. Much of the coastal area hereabouts – including the renovated **Cliff House** and forlorn remnants of **Sutro Baths**, both north of Golden Gate Park – once constituted San Francisco's Playland-at-the-Beach. Holding down the city's southwestern corner is blustery **Fort Funston**, a magnet for local hang gliders and dogs; also in the area is **San Francisco Zoo**, a capable, if unspectacular destination where security was called into question a few years ago. Further inland, **Stern Grove** is another lush, green escape from the hustle of the city.

The Richmond and northern beaches

Named by Aussie expatriate (and early San Franciscan) George Turner Marsh after his Adelaide suburb, the **Richmond** stretches more than two miles westward from Arguello Boulevard to the Pacific, filling the gap between Golden Gate Park and the Presidio. It's a melting pot of numerous ethnicities, owing in part to its tremendous size – there are significant Jewish, Irish and Russian communities here, among others. Still, it's the local Chinese residents who lend the area its dominant character, with some locals even referring to the area as "Chinatown West".

Clement Street
The Richmond's vibrant Chinese community is most in evidence along **Clement Street** between Park Presidio and Arguello boulevards. Even on a short stroll, you'll spot dozens of Chinese dim-sum bakeries, grocery stores and restaurants; also, one of the city's top used-book stores, **Green Apple Books** (see p.201), anchors the middle of Clement's commercial zone.

Geary Boulevard
One block south of Clement Street, the Richmond's main traffic thoroughfare, **Geary Boulevard**, showcases the area's European flavour with a myriad of ethnic restaurants. Sadly, it's noisy most of the time and not a pleasant place to dawdle on the sidewalk.

Neptune Society Columbarium
1 Lorraine Court near Anza • Mon–Fri 8am–5pm, Sat & Sun 10am–3pm • Free • ☎ 415 752 7891, ⊛ neptune-society.com
When the **Neptune Society Columbarium** was built in 1898, it stood at the entrance to an exclusive cemetery, and its elaborate decoration – including Tiffany stained-glass windows – is evidence of the money lavished on its construction. The building itself is a natty hybrid of chapel and Roman temple; look for unusual sculptural tributes to the deceased, including a martini shaker and a baseball.

Legion of Honor
100 34th Ave, Lincoln Park • Tues–Sun 9.30am–5.15pm • $10, free first Tues of month • ☎ 415 760 3600, ⊛ thinker.org
One of San Francisco's finest museums, the stately **Legion of Honor** is no less staggering than its dramatic setting high above the bluffs of the Golden Gate. It was built in 1920, and its parade of white columns replicates the Légion d'Honneur in Paris – a firm nod to the heavy French emphasis among the Legion of Honor's holdings. A cast of Rodin's *The Thinker*, set upon a pedestal in the centre of the museum's front courtyard, flags the museum's penchant for the sensual French sculptor.

The Legion's **Rodin holdings** are breathtaking in their depth and range, although there are more bronzes than marble sculptures; with over eighty pieces, it's one of the best collections of its kind in the world, and the Rodin rooms alone make this museum unmissable. Be sure to view the bust of the sculptor by his lover Camille

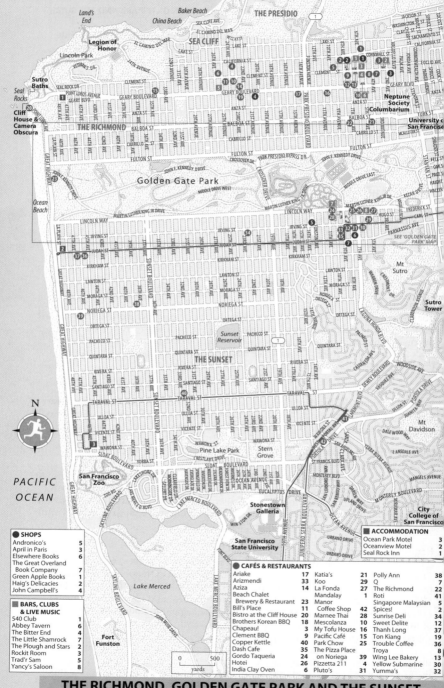

● SHOPS

Andronico's	5
April in Paris	3
Elsewhere Books	6
The Great Overland Book Company	7
Green Apple Books	1
Haig's Delicacies	2
John Campbell's	4

■ BARS, CLUBS & LIVE MUSIC

540 Club	1
Abbey Tavern	6
The Bitter End	4
The Little Shamrock	7
The Plough and Stars	2
Rockit Room	3
Trad'r Sam	5
Yancy's Saloon	8

■ ACCOMMODATION

Ocean Park Motel	3
Oceanview Motel	2
Seal Rock Inn	1

● CAFÉS & RESTAURANTS

Ariake	17	Katia's	21
Arizmendi	33	Koo	29
Aziza	14	La Fonda	27
Beach Chalet Brewery & Restaurant	23	Mandalay	1
Bill's Place	11	Manor Coffee Shop	42
Bistro at the Cliff House	20	Marnee Thai	28
Brothers Korean BBQ	18	Mescolanza	10
Chapeau!	3	My Tofu House	16
Clement BBQ	9	Pacific Café	15
Copper Kettle	40	Park Chow	25
Dash Cafe	35	The Pizza Place on Noriega	39
Gordo Taqueria	24	Pizzetta 211	4
Hotei	26	Pluto's	31
India Clay Oven	6		

Polly Ann	38
Q	7
The Richmond	22
Roti	41
Singapore Malaysian	
Spices!	2
Sunrise Deli	34
Sweet Delite	12
Thanh Long	37
Ton Kiang	19
Trouble Coffee	36
Troya	30
Wing Lee Bakery	13
Yellow Submarine	30
Yumma's	32

THE RICHMOND, GOLDEN GATE PARK AND THE SUNSET

Claudel, whose own outstanding artistic talent was steamrollered by Rodin's monumental personality.

Sadly, the magnificent museum is somewhat let down by its lacklustre collection of **Old Masters**. Many of the artworks, including those by Giambologna, Cellini and Cranach, are "attributed to" or from "the workshop of", rather than bona fide masterpieces. A few bright spots exist, however, including El Greco's chilling *St John the Baptist* and some lively Degas oil sketches among the Impressionist collection. There's also a wide variety of **decorative arts**, including period rooms shipped wholesale from France and a dazzling, gilded ceiling brought to America from the Palacio de Altamira in Toledo. Elsewhere in the museum, you'll find a rotating display of touring shows that vary in quality.

Land's End

From the Legion of Honor, trails curve along the cliffs beneath the museum down to **Land's End**, one of the city's wildest nature corners. Littering the base of the jagged cliffs are the broken hulls of ships that failed to navigate the violent currents; with a little luck, you'll see chunks of the wooden wreckage at low tide. The main trail (a mere 1.25 miles end to end) skirts shady cypress groves and is a popular walking and running path; spectacular views of the Pacific Ocean, Marin Headlands and Golden Gate Bridge abound.

China and Baker beaches

Just north of the Richmond and rimming the western edge of the Presidio, **China** and **Baker beaches** are popular outdoor destinations for locals. Don't expect sun-kissed California boardwalks, though: given the foggy climate, even the sunniest summer days here can be unpredictable. Be advised, too, that since both beaches sit at the mouth of the bay, currents are perilously strong, making swimming very risky (and frigid) any time of year. That said, either beach is an enjoyable place to while away an afternoon, surrounded by an eccentric San Francisco mix of nude sunbathers and families on outings.

A short strip of sand immediately east of Land's End, China Beach got its name in 1870 when it was home to an encampment of Chinese fishermen. Once the government acted on rampant anti-Chinese bigotry and imposed tight restrictions on immigration (see p.289), the beach – supposedly – became a landing place for illegal aliens. These days, it's swankier, more sheltered and has better facilities than Baker Beach further north, including changing rooms and showers.

Sutro Heights Park and around

The western coast of the San Francisco peninsula was a Fisherman's Wharf for the nineteenth century, although these days it's hard to believe, given how little remains from that era. The city's west side began as a working-class seaside resort, and a faded brassiness still lingers here, thanks to scattered pockets of ageing amusements, diners and budget motels. The area was the brainchild of Prussian immigrant (and eventual San Francisco mayor) **Adolph Sutro**, who sold his mining interests at the peak of their value, then invested his subsequent fortune in seaside real estate in San Francisco. In fact, Sutro's former blufftop estate is now picturesque **Sutro Heights Park**, at the western terminus of Geary Boulevard.

Cliff House
1090 Point Lobos Ave • ☎ 415 386 3300, 🌐 cliffhouse.com

The last remnant of Sutro's once-impressive amusement park complex named Playland-at-the-Beach, the **Cliff House** is now a complex of restaurants and minor amusements, with a National Park Service visitor centre thrown in for good measure. Today's incarnation is actually the third to sit on the site – the first two grand buildings were destroyed by fire, and the current, more modest structure (reopened in 2004 after an extensive refit) dates back to 1909. The Cliff House's perennial thrill is undoubtedly its natural setting; seek out the wraparound viewing deck around the rear of the structure for a look at **Seal Rock**, a guano-pelted nesting spot for birds just offshore. Also on this level, below the pair of restaurants, is a Park Service **visitor centre** offering maps and information on Golden Gate National Recreation Area, along with an arresting photographic display of the numerous ships that have run aground on the rocks below.

Camera Obscura

Daily 11am–5pm, weather permitting • $3 • ☏ 415 750 0415, Ⓦ giantcamera.com

On the same landing as the Park Service visitor centre beneath the Cliff House stands the **Camera Obscura**, a longtime oddity listed on the National Register of Historic Places. Using a rotating mirror and a trick of light, the camera affords entrants a panoramic view of the surrounding area, including the birds on nearby Seal Rock.

Sutro Baths

Back toward Land's End and down a path from the Cliff House are the enormous, but decrepit ruins of the **Sutro Baths**, its long-abandoned pools filled with brackish seawater – though photos at the Cliff House's NPS visitor centre reveal what a splendid spa it once was. The baths were a seaside gem where 100,000ft of stained glass covered more than three acres of sculpted pools (some filled with freshwater, others with saltwater) that could accommodate up to twenty thousand people at a time. Sutro packed his "Tropical Winter Gardens" with fountains, gardens, sculptures and historical bric-a-brac from around the world, and the place opened to great fanfare in 1896. But as public baths grew less popular through the decades, the glossy venue frayed, and by 1954, the only remaining open pool was converted to an ice rink. The complex limped along before shutting for good in 1966, when just as it was being readied for demolition, a fire broke out and levelled the entire spread.

After you've imagined the scope of Sutro's grandiose public palace, look for the lengthy tunnel through the rocks just north of the ruins; it fills with the sound of crashing waves during high tide and makes for dramatic exploration.

Golden Gate Park

Daily dawn–dusk • Free • Ⓦ golden-gate-park.com

Developed in the late nineteenth century, many years before most of the neighbourhoods that surround it, **Golden Gate Park** manages to be both a pastoral retreat for San Franciscans and a bastion of local culture, with over one thousand acres of gardens and forest, complemented by some of the city's best museums. Spreading three miles west from Haight-Ashbury to the edge of the continent, the massive green space was designed in 1871 by park commissioner **William Hall**, mimicking the look and feel of Frederick Law Olmsted's Central Park in New York (though Golden Gate Park is larger). Hall used a dyke to protect the park's western side from the sea, while **John McLaren**, the city's Scottish park superintendent for 56 years, planted several thousand trees, in the process sculpting numerous miniature environments from what was then an area of wild sand dunes.

NUDE BEACHES

If you're terrified of tan lines, you'll be relieved to find that the northern end of Baker Beach is mostly given over to **nudists**. Continuing past Baker Beach, you'll soon reach isolated Golden Gate Beach, arguably the area's best spit of sand with a stunning view of the bridge. It, too, is a nudist spot and predominantly gay.

Although the original planners intended to keep the park free of buildings, that proved impossible, and its eastern half is now dotted with several notable sights. Many of the original buildings date from the California Midwinter International Exposition of 1894 (the first world's fair held in California), which was designed as a recession-busting sideshow by local newspaperman Michael H. de Young.

The eastern park

If you're entering Golden Gate Park by car or bike, follow Fell Street west along the Panhandle until it becomes John F. Kennedy Drive, the park's primary roadway along (or near) which most of the major draws are located. Note that this road is closed to autos each Sunday, making it a once-weekly utopia for pedestrians and cyclists.

Conservatory of Flowers

Tues–Sun 10am–4.30pm • $7 • ☎ 415 831 2090, ⓦ conservatoryofflowers.org

The first worthwhile stop along **John F. Kennedy Drive** is the magnificently restored **Conservatory of Flowers**. Manufactured in Ireland for a San Jose millionaire who died before he could take possession of it, the building was eventually donated and shipped piecemeal up to San Francisco. The distinctive structure, with its whitewashed wooden frame, resembles the overblown greenhouse of a well-to-do Victorian country home; highlights include the spindly Andes orchids in the highland tropics section, and the tractor-wheel-sized Victoria waterlilies in the cool, aquatic plant room.

National AIDS Memorial Grove

Daily dawn–dusk • Free • ☎ 415 765 0498, ⓦ aidsmemorial.org

A five-minute walk from the Conservatory of Flowers, the peaceful seven-acre **National AIDS Memorial Grove** was the first garden of its kind in the US, designed to commemorate those who have died of AIDS-related illnesses. Rocks with single names dot the edge of the large oval greenspace, into which you gradually descend from the surrounding paths and roadways.

Music Concourse

Named for the bandshell donated by the sugar magnate Spreckels family set at its western end, Golden Gate Park's **Music Concourse** is filled with symmetrically planted trees and flanked by two sizable museums, the de Young Museum and the California Academy of Sciences (see p.120). Check the park website for performances at the bandshell; otherwise, a few food and drink vendors and an endless supply of benches all invite lingering on a pleasant day.

de Young Museum

50 Hagiwara Tea Garden Drive • Tues–Thurs, Sat & Sun 9.30am–5.15pm, Fri 9.30am–8.45pm • $15, free first Tues of each month • ☎ 415 750 3600, ⓦ thinker.org

Levelled and rebuilt from the ground up between 2001 and 2005, the **de Young Museum** has its origin in the California Midwinter International Exposition of 1894, a venture so successful that the Fine Arts Building from the exhibition was turned over to newspaper publisher Michael H. de Young with the purpose of establishing a permanent museum. By the early 1990s, however, the earthquake-ravaged original structure required several diagonal supports to prop it up. The resulting replacement is a copper-tone building made from interlocking boxes that incorporates both a sculpture garden (look for Louise Nevelson's moody black *Ocean Gate)* and a twisting 144ft tower with impressive views across the park. The entire structure will acquire a greenish patina over the years, intended to blend more harmoniously with the park surroundings.

Among the de Young's American holdings, standouts include canvases by Impressionist Mary Cassatt – a picture of her mother – as well as John Singleton

Copley's *Mrs. Daniel Turner Sargent*. There's also an extensive, hit-and-miss collection of African, Oceanic and South American folk art, mostly holdovers culled from displays at the 1894 fair. Finally, don't miss the four splashy exhibitions commissioned as site-specific installations from contemporary artists, the most noteworthy of which is Gerhard Richter's enormous black-and-white geometric mural sprawling through the main atrium.

California Academy of Sciences

55 Music Concourse Drive • Mon–Sat 9.30am–5pm, Sun 11am–5pm • $29.95 • ☎ 415 379 8000, ⓦ calacademy.org

Across the Music Concourse from the de Young is the even newer home of the **California Academy of Sciences**. Admission is pricey, but definitely worth the investment – there's enough here to occupy a full day, if not more. Most of the original structure was razed in anticipation of an adventurous design by renowned architect Renzo Piano – best known as the designer of Paris's Centre Pompidou – and the justifiably celebrated museum opened to much fanfare in 2008. An airy, glass-encased entrance leads to a full slate of restored and expanded attractions. Top destinations include the **Tusher African Center**, containing a detailed diorama of that continent's zoological landscape, as well as a particularly popular group of South African penguins; the **Swamp**, now boasting a rare white alligator and a lower level from which visitors can watch creatures swim around; and the vastly improved **Morrison Planetarium**, featuring a digital projection system with real-time data from NASA.

The most stunning addition to the new Academy, however, is the glass **Rainforests of the World dome**, a 90ft-diameter space that recreates the warm, humid climate of the tropics. A pathway winds up three storeys around trees and past live animals native to Borneo, Madagascar and Costa Rica; at the top of the canopy, butterflies and birds fly freely. From here, you can take a glass elevator down into the depths of a would-be Amazon River basin before walking into the **Steinhart Aquarium**, an Academy stalwart from its previous incarnation. Finally, the **Living Roof** – over two acres planted with native Bay Area flora – is accessible to visitors and provides the building with natural insulation while preventing two million gallons of water from trickling to waste in storm drains each year.

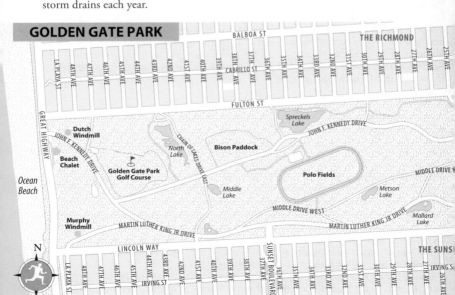

GOLDEN GATE PARK

Japanese Tea Garden

7 Hagiwara Tea Garden Drive • Daily: March–Oct 9am–6pm; Nov–Feb 9am–4.45pm • $7, free before 10am on Mon, Wed & Fri • Ⓦ japaneseteagardensf.com

On the northwestern edge of the Concourse sits an Asian fantasyland of miniature trees and groomed plants. Originally known as the Japanese Village, the **Japanese Tea Garden** proved to be one of the most popular areas of the 1894 World's Fair (for which it was expressly created), after which the Hagiwara family took over to operate the Garden's café until all Japanese-Americans were sent to internment camps in 1942 for the duration of World War II. (The Hagiwaras were also responsible for the invention of the fortune cookie during the Pan-Pacific Exposition of 1915 – despite the prevailing belief that fortune cookies were originally a Chinese concoction.)

The best way to enjoy the Garden is to arrive right when it opens and start with tea and fortune cookies in the teahouse, followed by a stroll among the bridges, statues (including a massive bronze Buddha), footpaths, pools filled with shiny oversized carp, and sublime forests of bonsai and cherry trees before busloads of tourists descend later in the morning; also make sure to climb the humpback bridge and visit the magnificent, if somewhat worn, pagoda.

San Francisco Botanical Garden

Strybing Arboretum, 1199 Ninth Ave • Daily: April–Oct 9am–6pm; Nov–March 10am–5pm; tours meet by the bookstore inside the main gate Mon–Fri 1.30pm, Sat & Sun 10.30am & 1.30pm, or the Ninth Ave entrance Wed, Fri & Sun 2pm • $7; tours free • ☎ 415 661 1316, Ⓦ sfbotanicalgarden.org

A less cramped outdoor alternative to the Japanese Tea Garden, the expansive **San Francisco Botanical Garden** has entrances across from the Tea Garden or near Ninth Avenue and Lincoln Way. This 75-acre hideaway is home to more than seven thousand varieties of plants, with miniature gardens focusing on specimens from regions ranging from desert to tropical; especially appealing is the headily scented garden of fragrance, as well as the towering grove of redwoods towards the garden's west end.

7

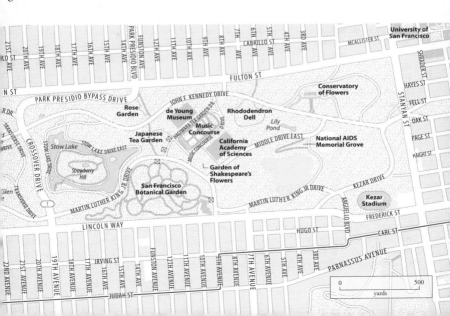

Garden of Shakespeare's Flowers

Martin Luther King Jr Drive and Middle Drive E • Daily dawn–dusk • Free

Adjacent to the Botanical Garden's north entrance, the **Garden of Shakespeare's Flowers** is a tiny, hedged green space, centred on an old-fashioned sundial and dotted with benches. It's a delightful spot that showcases every flower and plant mentioned in Shakespeare's plays and poems, with a metal plaque full of the relevant quotations on a brick wall at the edge of the lawn.

Rose Garden

Behind the de Young Museum on John F. Kennedy Drive • Daily dawn–dusk • Free

Home to more than sixty beds containing all sorts of varieties (including hybrid tea roses and assorted miniatures), Golden Gate Park's **Rose Garden** is another lovely spot to dawdle on the grass. Peak blooms occur in late spring and throughout summer, but a number of roses here show off their colours year-round.

7 The western park

The **western** half of Golden Gate Park is quieter than its sight-filled eastern section; seek out its innumerable flower gardens, lagoons and eucalyptus groves to escape the crowds.

Stow Lake

50 Stow Lake Drive • Daily 10am–4pm • Paddleboats and rowing boats $13–17/hr • ☎ 415 752 0347

If you fancy a float, you can rent a paddleboat or rowing boat on marshy **Stow Lake** in the heart of the park. Sitting at the centre of the algae-strangled water is **Strawberry Hill**, a large fake knoll reached by a pair of footbridges; at the island's eastern end near a crashing cascade is a colourful Chinese pagoda (a gift from the city of Taipei).

Dutch Windmill and Murphy Windmill

At the park's far northwestern edge, the **Dutch Windmill** (c.1902) sits next to a glorious flower patch known as the Queen Wilhelmina Tulip Garden – a terrific spot for a picnic on the lawn or one of the adjacent benches. A second Dutch relic, the **Murphy Windmill**, sits without sails in a state of slothful restoration at the park's southwestern corner.

Beach Chalet

Facing the Great Highway between the two windmills is the **Beach Chalet**, a two-storey, white-pillared building housing a series of 1930s frescoes that depict both the growth of San Francisco and the creation of Golden Gate Park; it also contains a small visitor centre providing information about the park's numerous guided walking tours. Upstairs there's a lively brewery-restaurant, known simply as the *Beach Chalet*, while out back on the lower level is its more relaxed sister pub and grill, the *Park Chalet* (see p.167), with extensive lawn seating.

The Sunset and around

As late as the 1920s, much of what now makes up the **Sunset** remained mile after mile of sand dunes, stretching from today's Upper Haight out to the Pacific. And while residents of the city's more intensely urban districts might say that, in terms of liveliness, not much has changed in the decades since, the truth is that this sprawling neighbourhood is a window into a less-seen side of San Francisco: a comfortable, if at times lethargic, blend of cultures set along the city's western edge.

SAN FRANCISCO'S UNLIKELY BISON

Perhaps the most unusual sight in Golden Gate Park is its **Bison Paddock** (free to view), where a small herd of American bison roams a grassy field north of John F. Kennedy Drive near 38th Avenue, far from their native land over one thousand miles east. The ancestors of these stately, ton-weighing beasts were brought here in 1891 by original park superintendent John McLaren, and have been a popular, if geographically quirky element of the park's landscape ever since. Today, about a half-dozen ageing bison (mostly females cared for by San Francisco Zoo staff) lumber around the twelve-acre paddock, fenced in by hefty metal railings; the closest you can get to the grunting giants is near their feeding area at the far west end.

Irving Street
N-Judah streetcar from Downtown

The Sunset's main commercial corridor, **Irving Street** between Sixth and 11th avenues, is the place for a relaxed night on the town, full of pubs, cafés and all manner of excellent restaurants. Further down Irving just west of 19th Avenue is yet another minor Chinatown, where you can enjoy authentic cuisine and buy bubble tea and silks.

Ocean Beach
At the end of the N-Judah streetcar line

Buffeted – and sometimes blistered – by sea breezes and fog, **Ocean Beach** is home to a small community of hardened surfers and other San Franciscans content to leave the chaos of urbanity to other neighbourhoods around the city. The miles-long strand is particularly popular with runners and dog-walkers, but as with Baker and China beaches, its weather can be more Pacific Northwest than sunny California. Come evening, bonfires are permitted in fire pits set up along the sand.

San Francisco Zoo
Great Highway and Sloat Blvd • Daily: mid-March to early Nov 10am–5pm; mid-Nov to early March 10am–4pm • $15 • ☎ 415 753 7080, ⓦ sfzoo.org

Just inland from the end of Sloat Boulevard is the **San Francisco Zoo**, where the top draws are the Children's Zoo (complete with a beautifully restored carousel), lush Lemur Forest and three-acre African Savannah containing giraffes, zebras, dik-diks and kudus. The zoo's reputation has suffered considerably since a Siberian tiger escaped from its enclosure and fatally mauled a visitor in 2007, although security upgrades have since been put into place.

Stern Grove and West Portal Avenue
19th Ave and Sloat Blvd • Free • Several Muni subway lines from the Castro and Downtown

A leafy ravine of eucalyptus, redwood and fir trees, **Stern Grove** – set a little under two miles inland from Ocean Beach – shelters a natural amphitheatre where a popular free Sunday concert series (see p.228) is held throughout summer. The park is tucked a short walk from **West Portal Avenue**, an invitingly pleasant commercial cluster.

Fort Funston

Down at the extreme southwestern corner of San Francisco, the steep bluff holding scenic **Fort Funston** is popular with dogs and their owners. The dunes that drop off to the beach far below attract scores of hang gliders, and on a gusty day, watching the daredevils swoop and twirl along the cliff face can make for some of the finest free entertainment in town.

LOBBY OF THE WESTIN ST FRANCIS HOTEL

Accommodation

Few things in San Francisco are inexpensive, and accommodation is no exception. Still, there are certainly bargains to be had, particularly out of season. March and November are good months for room availability and potentially agreeable weather, while you're much less likely to find any deals from April to October and around the November and December holidays. Depending on what you've got planned for your visit, certain areas of the city may be a better base than others: Fisherman's Wharf, though unapologetically tacky, is convenient for trips to Alcatraz and Angel Island, while South of Market is good for trendier accommodation. A few hotels near the Embarcadero, meanwhile, offer a mix of luxury and Bay views, and Union Square can't be beat for its variety of options and central location.

If you're on a particularly tight budget, but don't wish to stay in a hostel, your best option is to head to South of Market, the Tenderloin or Civic Center. Be aware, however, that these neighbourhoods can sometimes be dodgy (even during daytime), and the Tenderloin in particular has its share of seedy hotels; we've listed clean and safe budget choices below.

The Bay Area is filled with sumptuous **B&Bs**, most of them housed in historic buildings. You may have to sacrifice a private bathroom for the charms of a home-cooked breakfast, but staying at a B&B is almost the only choice if you're hoping to establish a base in the Castro, Mission or Haight-Ashbury. Most are communal, chatty experiences, so come prepared with conversation and a dressing gown.

Whether privately run or official HI hostels, San Francisco's top-shelf **hostels** are spotless, funky and well equipped, with laid-back rules and welcoming staff. In recent years, there's been a spate of new properties that have opened all over town (including a handy spot in the heart of the Mission district).

Other than a group-only **campground** in the Presidio, there's nowhere legal to camp in San Francisco itself, so if you're determined to sleep underneath the stars, head to any number of parks in the East Bay, down the Peninsula or in Marin County.

For **Bay Area accommodation**, see Chapter 16. For **gay and lesbian accommodation**, see Chapter 12.

ESSENTIALS

ONLINE DEALS
Most hotel websites offer discounts or guaranteed lowest rates, while clearing houses such as ⓦ hotels.com and ⓦ priceline.com sometimes list luxury rooms for a steal.

PARKING
There's little difference between motels and budget hotels in San Francisco. The one advantage at most motels is that parking (often nightmarishly expensive on the street) is included in the overnight rate (a good area to check locally is along Lombard Street in Cow Hollow, the main motel drag in San Francisco).

RATES
The accommodation prices quoted in this chapter are the starting price for the least expensive double room throughout most of the year. Rates are significantly lower in rooms that share baths.

Seasons You can expect generally more affordable rates between January and March, and again in early and mid-November before the holiday season arrives; otherwise, you may be hard-pressed to find bargains, especially around Union Square, Fisherman's Wharf and South of Market. As with most major cities, however, rates can fluctuate wildly, rising steeply during the busiest periods – holidays, summer weekends, popular conventions, etc – or dropping similarly when discounts are offered. Thanks to the glut of accommodation options Downtown, you should

be able to bargain with most of the budget and mid-range hotels in the area during off-peak times, as these places may be scrambling to fill rooms.

Typical rates You should be able to find a room for under (or at least around) $100 throughout the year in the budget hotels around South of Market, the Tenderloin or Civic Center. Downtown, you can expect to pay $110–150 for a standard double room in a budget to midrange hotel, and anywhere from $180 to $320 for similar lodging in one of the many boutique hotels in the area; a night in a luxury hotel can set you back as much as $500. Rates at B&Bs, meanwhile, shouldn't be more than $210. Rates at hostels start around $25 for a bed in a multi-person dorm. Finally, bear in mind that all quoted room rates are subject to a 14 percent local occupancy tax.

RESERVATION SERVICES
Bed and Breakfast San Francisco ☏ 415 899 0060, ⓦ bbsf.com.
Joie de Vivre ☏ 1 800 738 7477, ⓦ jdvhotels.com.
Kimpton Hotels ☏ 1 800 546 7866, ⓦ kimptonhotels .com.
Personality Hotels ☏ 1 800 553 1900, ⓦ personality hotels.com.
San Francisco Reservations ☏ 1 800 677 1500, ⓦ hotelres.com.
San Francisco Visitor Information Center See p.36.

8

HOTELS AND MOTELS

DOWNTOWN
Hotel Adagio 550 Geary St at Jones, Union Square ☏ 415 775 5000, ⓦ jdvhotels.com; map pp.40–41. The

decor here honours the building's ornate Spanish Revival facade with deep reds and ochres, although the interior is surprisingly modern; suite-sized rooms have a calming feng shui vibe and are well appointed with huge televisions, internet and honesty bar. Another advantage is the view across Downtown from the upper floors. $229

The Andrews Hotel 624 Post St at Taylor, Union Square ☎ 415 563 6877 or 1 800 926 3739, ⓦ andrewshotel .com; map pp.40–41. Charming little hotel that, with its small lobby and elegant, shoebox-sized *Fino Bar & Ristorante*, maintains an air of old-fashioned gentility and grace. The room are 1950s retro, with flowered bedspreads, peach walls, green carpeting, avocado-green wooden furniture and tiled bathrooms. Rates include a continental breakfast buffet. Can be a terrific bargain for the location. $109

Baldwin Hotel 321 Grant Ave at Bush, Union Square ☎ 415 781 2220 or 1 800 622 5394, ⓦ baldwinhotel .com; map pp.40–41. Given its bustling location on the edge of Chinatown, this is a surprisingly quiet bolthole offering relief from the noisy streets. The *Baldwin's* rooms are outfitted in oatmeal and taupe colours with simple furnishings and ceiling fans; rates are negotiable during off-peak seasons. $103

Hotel Beresford 635 Sutter St at Mason, Union Square ☎ 415 673 9900 or 1 800 533 6533, ⓦ beresford.com /beresford; map pp.40–41. With its elaborate Victorian interior – cheerful yellow wallpaper and curved banister – this old-fashioned, family-run hotel, home to the *White Horse Tavern and Restaurant*, feels like it belongs in the English countryside. There are 114 guest rooms with satellite TVs and honesty bars, as well as business amenities, free continental breakfast and valet parking. $109

Beresford Arms 701 Post St at Jones, Union Square ☎ 415 673 2600 or 1 800 533 6533, ⓦ beresford.com /arms; map pp.40–41. A vintage hotel where the sumptuous, crushed-velvet lobby belies the rather plain rooms, decorated in dark wood. Each has mirrored wardrobes and window seats – pleasant enough but nothing particularly memorable. Free continental breakfast is included in room rates. $159

Best Western Hotel California 580 Geary St at Jones, Union Square ☎ 415 441 2700 or 1 800 227 4223, ⓦ hotelca.com/sanfrancisco; map pp.40–41. This hotel goes above and beyond standard chain lodging, making it one of the best accommodation values in San Francisco. Its charming rooms, while small, feature gorgeous antique dark wood furniture, hardwood floors and lovely tiled bathroom. There's a free wine and cheese reception from 4–6 pm and a superb vegetarian restaurant, *Millennium*, just off the lobby, while the *pièce de résistance* for some will be the free tequila shot upon check-in. $123

Chancellor Hotel 433 Powell St at Post, Union Square ☎ 415 362 2004 or 1 800 428 4748, ⓦ chancellorhotel .com; map pp.40–41. Built in 1914, this charming boutique hotel offers comfortable beds, a full range of pillows and oversize bathtubs in its small, cosy rooms; *Luques Restaurant and Bar*, just off the lobby, does breakfast, lunch and room service. The *Chancellor's* second floor features a lovely meeting room decked out with murals and a paperback library. $200

Clift Hotel 495 Geary St at Taylor, Union Square ☎ 415 775 4700 or 1 800 697 1791, ⓦ clifthotel.com; map pp.40–41. One of boutique hotel pioneer Ian Schrager's signature efforts, the *Clift* remains the epitome of swish sophistication. Vaguely Asian rooms include quirky touches like Louis XIV-style chairs with mirrors on the seat and back, as well as sleigh beds; pity that the bathrooms are so small. Pricey, ultra-cool and almost disarmingly self-aware – and you ought not expect too many smiles from the staff. Note that the walls are very thin, so bring earplugs. Downstairs is the richly appointed Redwood Room bar (see p.173). $345

★ **Hotel des Arts** 447 Bush St at Grant, Union Square ☎ 415 956 3232 or 1 800 956 4322, ⓦ sfhotelsdesarts .com; map pp.40–41. Buzzy spot that's hybrid art gallery and hotel, where many rooms are custom-decorated by local artists; oversize pieces hang for sale all over the stark white walls that line the hallways. Most rooms are en suite, although the cheaper ones share "European"-style baths down the hallway. It can be noisy, and the space feels – and can sometimes even smell – like a hostel or college dorm, but it's still a fun, bargain place to stay. $89

Hotel Diva 440 Geary St at Taylor, Union Square ☎ 415 885 0200 or 1 800 553 1900, ⓦ hoteldiva.com; map pp.40–41. Boutique hotel that taps into 1980s design with certain touches – black leather sofas and lots of sleek steel – that are part avant-garde new wave and part bachelor pad. Rooms are large and retro minimalist, and the place is particularly well positioned if you're planning to see some theatre, with A.C.T. and the Curran directly across the street. There's also a small fitness centre on site. $195

Four Seasons 757 Market St at Third, Union Square ☎ 415 633 3000, ⓦ fourseasons.com/sanfrancisco; map pp.40–41. The place to stay if you win the lottery (or someone else is paying), this ultra-luxe hotel on Market St affords spectacular views across the city. Its plush rooms are the ultimate indulgence, from the soft blankets to the stand-alone two-person shower stocked with Bulgari beauty products. There's an enormous onsite health club with a pool and vast gym that's free to hotel guests. $545

Hotel Frank 386 Geary St at Mason, Union Square ☎ 415 986 2000 or 1 877 828 4478, ⓦ hotelfranksf.com; map pp.40–41. This 1908 hotel underwent a $10 million

TOP 5 QUIRKY B&BS

Circa 1870 See p.129
Inn San Francisco See p.133
Queen Anne Hotel See p.130
The Red Victorian Bed, Breakfast & Art See p.133
Union Street Inn See p.130

makeover in the late 2000s, and the results bring to mind old-style Hollywood glamour imagining a sleek Jetsons future. Rooms are dominated by a large houndstooth pattern on the floor and emerald green accents; white couches and elegant hanging lamps, as well as large, flat-screen televisions and iPod docking stations, complete the scene. $174

Golden Gate Hotel 775 Bush St at Mason, Union Square ☏ 415 392 3702 or 1 800 835 1118, ⓦ goldengatehotel .com; map pp.40–41. With its adorable yellow facade, beautiful iron elevator and Edwardian interior, this family-operated hotel is a feast for the eyes – and a smart bargain as well. Rooms (some with private bath, for an extra $60) are decorated with antiques and wicker furniture, and many of the bathrooms feature clawfoot tubs. $105

Grant Hotel 753 Bush St at Mason, Union Square ☏ 415 421 7540 or 1 800 522 0979, ⓦ granthotel .net; map pp.40–41. Good value for its location close to Union Square, this hotel has 76 small, but clean rooms that are somewhat overpowered by relentlessly maroon carpeting. Continental breakfast (muffins, coffee, tea) is included in the room rate. Basic but convenient. $95

Grant Plaza Hotel 465 Grant Ave at Pine, Chinatown ☏ 415 434 3883 or 1 800 472 6899, ⓦ grantplaza .com; map pp.40–41. The fair room rates and terrific location – one block inside Chinatown Gate – aren't this hotel's only advantages. Rooms are brighter than at most budget spots, resembling bedrooms from a 1980s sitcom with no shortage of pink and faux pine; what's more, the staff is unstintingly helpful. The main downside is that it can be rather noisy, so be sure to pack earplugs. $109

Halcyon Hotel 649 Jones St at Post, Union Square ☏ 415 929 8033 or 1 800 627 2396, ⓦ halcyonsf.com; map pp.40–41. The rooms and bathroom at this 1912 hotel are extraordinarily small, but serviceable; all are equipped with wireless internet access, along with a clawfoot tub and shower, mini fridge, coffee maker, microwave, toaster and kitchenware. Everything is clean and infused with old-world character, and there's coin-operated laundry available on site. A remarkable bargain, considering the central location. $79

JW Marriott 500 Post St at Mason, Union Square ☏ 415 771 8600 or 1 800 236 2427, ⓦ marriott.com; map pp.40–41. This luxury high-rise hotel one block west of Union Square was the recipient of a thorough redesign once Marriott took the reins. Its rooms are a tech-lover's dream – each is equipped with a 42-inch LCD TV with a plug-in panel, Bose sound system, ergonomic office chair, and wireless internet, plus a 24hr personal butler button. Chocolates on the pillow only sweeten the deal. $269

Kensington Park Hotel 450 Post St at Powell, Union Square ☏ 415 788 6400 or 1 800 553 1900, ⓦ kensingtonparkhotel.com; map pp.40–41. Known for its extraordinarily comfortable beds, this boutique hotel envelops you in *Casablanca* ambience the moment you set foot in the lobby, with its vaulted ceiling and antique

furniture. There's Queen Anne mahogany furniture in the elegant bedrooms, and the hotel offers a complimentary tea and sherry service in the lobby each evening; a 24hr business centre, wireless internet and same-day laundry and dry cleaning services are also available. $215

King George Hotel 334 Mason St at O'Farrell, Union Square ☏ 415 781 5050 or 1 800 288 6005, ⓦ kinggeorge .com; map pp.40–41. Like a less ostentatious version of the *Sir Francis Drake* (see p.128), this Brit-themed hotel boasts heraldic touches in its lobby (think floral carpets and overwrought furniture). Other than a dish filled with candy, the rooms are surprisingly ascetic, if functional – but the central location compensates somewhat. $214

Larkspur Hotel Union Square 524 Sutter St at Powell, Union Square ☏ 415 421 2865 or 1 800 227 3844, ⓦ larkspurhotelunionsquare.com; map pp.40–41. This hotel's airy lobby is like a country house conservatory, with overstuffed (if chintzy) armchairs and a front desk faced with beige marble. The nondescript rooms are much more plain, updated in recent years with modern furniture; en suite bathrooms are utilitarian, but minuscule. $179

Hotel Monaco 501 Geary St at Taylor, Union Square ☏ 415 292 0100 or 1 866 622 5284, ⓦ monaco-sf .com; map pp.40–41. One of Kimpton Hotels' flagship locations, this quirky boutique hotel is housed in a historic Beaux Arts building. Canopied beds enliven each room, and the rest of the decor is equally riotous and colourful; it's a little precious and pricey, but hugely popular. One unusual amenity: the hotel is known for providing complimentary goldfish to keep lonely travellers company in their rooms. $319

Orchard Garden Hotel 466 Bush St at Grant, Union Square ☏ 415 399 9807 or 1 888 717 2881, ⓦ the orchardgardenhotel.com; map pp.40–41. This ground-breaking hotel is a leader in energy-efficient environmental design, thanks to its key card energy control system, in-room recycling, chemical-free cleaning products and low-energy lighting scheme. While the decor is rather unexciting and its "garden" is more of a terrace with a fantastic view, the hotel has much going for it, including a full slate of electronics and organic bath products in each room. A sister boutique, the *Orchard Hotel*, is just up the street at 665 Bush St and offers similar rates. $219

Petite Auberge 863 Bush St at Taylor, Union Square ☏ 415 928 6000 or 1 800 365 3004, ⓦ petiteaubergesf .com; map pp.40–41. An opulent B&B-style hotel at the foot of Nob Hill with 26 rooms decked out in a French country style, full of oak furniture and floral prints; some feature a fireplace. There's complimentary afternoon tea, wine, hors d'oeuvres and a hot breakfast. Luxurious and memorable. $179

Prescott Hotel 545 Post St at Mason, Union Square ☏ 415 563 0303 or 1 866 271 3632, ⓦ prescotthotel .com; map pp.40–41. This small, but sumptuous four-star hotel has rooms decorated in warm woods and rich colours; service is attentive and polite. Still, it's debatable whether

8

the amenities you'll receive by booking one of the 86 club-level rooms and suites – continental breakfast, evening cocktail reception, newspapers, shoe-shine service – make the $50 jump in already-high rates worthwhile. **$289**

Hotel Rex 562 Sutter St at Mason, Union Square ☎ 415 433 4434 or 1 800 433 4434, ⓦ thehotelrex.com; map pp.40–41. Under the guiding hand of Joie de Vivre, the *Rex* has emerged reinvigorated from a major renovation. It's retained its retro, gentlemen's club feel and literary theme – allegedly inspired by the *New Yorker* – with rich wood panelling and various quotations decorating the corridors. *Bar Rex* in the lobby hosts the odd reading and literary event. **$209**

Serrano Hotel 405 Taylor St at O'Farrell, Union Square ☎ 415 885 2500 or 1 866 289 6561, ⓦ serranohotel .com; map pp.40–41. This 17-storey Spanish revival hotel has been painstakingly restored down to its bedazzling lobby. Rooms are decked out in bold reds and golds with Spanish and Moroccan accents; board games are available in the lobby, and there's a nightly wine reception (with free tarot readings). Challenge the desk person to a round of blackjack upon check-in to win appetizers at the hotel restaurant, *Ponzu*. **$149**

Sir Francis Drake 450 Powell St at Sutter, Union Square ☎ 415 392 7755 or 1 800 795 7129, ⓦ sirfrancisdrake .com; map pp.40–41. The *Sir Francis Drake's* lobby is a hallucinogenic evocation of all things heraldic, crammed with faux British memorabilia, chandeliers and overwrought gold plasterwork. Thankfully, the rooms are calmer, with a gentle apple-green colour scheme and full facilities. Aside from its decor and porters dressed in full Beefeater regalia, the hotel is also known for its 21st-floor bar, *Harry Denton's Starlight Room* (see p.173). **$219**

Spaulding Hotel 240 O'Farrell St at Powell, Union Square ☎ 415 397 4924, ⓦ spauldinghotel.com; map pp.40–41. Don't be fooled by the *Spaulding's* boutique-style logo (or put off by its odious elevators and unwelcoming hallways) – this is a reliable, if basic place to stay at Union Square. The budget-priced rooms are clean and nondescript, with dark floral bedspreads and pale wood furniture. All rooms are fitted with mini fridges and private baths. **$95**

Taj Campton Place 340 Stockton St at Sutter, Union Square ☎ 415 781 5555 or 1 866 969 1825, ⓦ campton place.com; map pp.40–41. Upscale and understated hotel that provides utter seclusion despite being located in the heart of Union Square. Each floor is set around a glassed-in central courtyard, while the 110 rooms are decorated in muted russets and greens with Deco-inspired fixtures and deep marble baths; elegant pearwood panels are installed in many rooms' wardrobe areas. **$450**

Hotel Triton 342 Grant Ave at Bush, Union Square ☎ 415 394 0500 or 1 800 800 1299, ⓦ hoteltriton .com; map pp.40–41. An eccentric, smartly located hotel

offering a few choice amenities (such as a 24hr gym), as well as plentiful art on the walls and an arresting lobby mural describing San Francisco's art scene. Rooms themselves are stylish but gaudy, painted in rich clashing colours with plenty of gold. A few guest rooms have been designed by oddball celebrities (Jerry Garcia, Kathy Griffin), while the Häagen-Dazs "Sweet Suite" comes with a freezer cabinet filled with complimentary ice cream. **$233**

★ **Hotel Union Square** 114 Powell St at Ellis, Union Square ☎ 415 397 3000 or 1 800 553 1900, ⓦ hotel unionsquare.com; map pp.40–41. One of the top Art Deco hotels Downtown, this boutique destination features comfortable platform beds, brick walls, mosaics galore and an impeccable overall design; there's even a "Dashiell Hammett Suite". It's set only a couple of blocks south of Union Square proper, with cable cars rattling by directly outside its main entrance. **$255**

Westin St Francis 335 Powell St at Geary, Union Square ☎ 415 397 7000 or 1 800 937 8461, ⓦ westinst francis.com; map pp.40–41. This landmark hotel (see p.42) boasts an extravagant lobby, four restaurants and lounges, a fitness centre and spa. Rooms in the historic main building, which dates to the early 1900s, have high ceilings and chandeliers, while those in the newer tower are contemporary with views across the city. If nothing else, it's worth lingering in the lobby to see the Magneta grandfather clock, gilded ceiling and gaudy painting of Queen Elizabeth amid American celebs. **$303**

White Swan Inn 845 Bush St at Mason, Union Square ☎ 415 775 1755 or 1 800 999 9570, ⓦ whiteswaninnsf .com; map pp.40–41. A delightful B&B-style inn that follows an English manor theme, with a crackling fire in the lobby, oak-panelled walls and a fireplace in each room, and a guest reception featuring wine and hors d'oeuvres each evening. Unsurprisingly, it's particularly popular with Brits looking for a taste of home. **$199**

NORTH BEACH AND THE HILLS

Hotel Boheme 444 Columbus Ave at Green, North Beach ☎ 415 433 9111, ⓦ hotelboheme.com; map p.59. At the heart of North Beach's main commercial corridor, this small, fifteen-room hotel has tiny but dramatic rooms featuring canopied beds and Art Deco-ish bathrooms, all done in rich, dark colours. Columbus Ave can be noisy, so if you're a light sleeper, ask for a room at the back. **$174**

TOP 5 BOUTIQUE HOTELS

Clift Hotel See p.126
Hotel Diva See p.126
Orchard Garden Hotel See p.127
Hotel Union Square See above
Hotel Vertigo See p.131

The Fairmont 950 Mason St at California, Nob Hill ☎415 772 5000 or 1 866 540 4491, ⓦfairmont.com /sanfrancisco; map p.56. The most famous of Nob Hill's landmark hotels, this showy palace has four restaurants and lounges, as well as fantastic views from the rooms – despite being relatively low-rise for the neighbourhood. Don't miss the terrace garden overlooking Powell St, as well as the kitschy splendour of the *Tonga Room* (see p.175) down in the basement. <u>$329</u>

Huntington Hotel 1075 California St at Taylor, Nob Hill ☎415 474 5400, ⓦhuntingtonhotel.com; map p.56. Originally designed as residential apartments, this notably formal hotel was home to Bogart and Bacall for several years. Its common areas are old-money elegant, with chandeliers and vintage prints; the rooms themselves are large, if unexciting, although many have kitchenettes. The hotel's spa lords over the city with spectacular views. <u>$235</u>

InterContinental Mark Hopkins 1 Nob Hill, Nob Hill ☎415 392 3434 or 1 888 424 6835, ⓦichotelsgroup .com; map p.56. Once the chic choice of writers and movie stars, this grand, castle-like hotel – perched at the corner of California and Mason streets – is more corporate these days in both clientele and design, thanks to a beige-heavy renovation. As you might expect, rates rise with each higher floor. The *Top of the Mark* rooftop bar remains popular with tourists (see p.173). <u>$333</u>

San Remo Hotel 2237 Mason St at Chestnut, North Beach ☎415 776 8688 or 1 800 352 7366, ⓦsanremo hotel.com; map p.56. Known for its chatty, helpful staff, this converted three-storey house sits adjacent to Fisherman's Wharf. Rooms are cosy and chintzy – all share spotless bathrooms, and a few have sinks. While there are offbeat additions like massage chairs on each floor, there are no phones or televisions in the bedrooms, and nor is there an elevator. The *Fior d'Italia* restaurant is on site. <u>$75</u>

Stanford Court Renaissance 905 California St at Powell, Nob Hill ☎415 989 3500 or 1 888 236 2427, ⓦmarriott.com; map p.56. The one-time mansion of railroad magnate (and university founder) Leland Stanford, this luxury hotel has undergone a $32 million renovation to give it an even smarter Art Deco upgrade; fortunately, its stunning Tiffany glass dome is still intact. The fairly sizeable rooms are a relative bargain for Nob Hill. <u>$229</u>

SW Hotel 615 Broadway at Grant, North Beach ☎415 362 2999 or 1 888 595 9188, ⓦswhotel.com; map p.59. A well-located bargain on the boundary of Chinatown and North Beach. The decor in the large rooms is modern Asian, with carved armoires and headboards, plus yellow floral bedspreads. Some rooms can be rather dark, but the sparklingly clean bathrooms and willing staff more than compensate. <u>$139</u>

★ **Washington Square Inn** 1660 Stockton St at Filbert, North Beach ☎415 981 4220 or 1 800 388 0220, ⓦwsisf.com; map p.59. This B&B-style hotel overlooking Washington Square has large, airy rooms decorated in modern shades of taupe and cream. The inn's European-flavoured rooms vary widely in price and facilities – some boast bay windows with a sitting area – but all are en suite (albeit mostly shower only). <u>$189</u>

THE NORTHERN WATERFRONT AND PACIFIC HEIGHTS

Argonaut Hotel 495 Jefferson St at Hyde, Fisherman's Wharf ☎415 563 0800 or 1 866 415 0704, ⓦargonaut hotel.com; map pp.68–69. This nautical-themed hotel – an anchor motif runs through much of the decor – set in the Cannery complex has large, lush rooms in brick and timber that feature DVD players, stereos and impressive views. Surprisingly quiet, given its tourist-stampeded location. <u>$263</u>

Best Western Tuscan Inn 425 North Point St at Mason, Fisherman's Wharf ☎415 561 1100 or 1 800 648 4626, ⓦtuscaninn.com; map pp.68–69. Despite its name, this waterfront hotel is more English country manor than Tuscan farmhouse, with cosy rooms decorated in warm colours. Attentive touches such as evening wine receptions, pet-friendly rooms and free limousine service to the Financial District sweeten the deal. <u>$206</u>

Circa 1870 2119 California St at Laguna, Pacific Heights ☎415 928 3224; map pp.106–107. Plush B&B whose period rooms are decorated in fancy Victoriana – rose, oak and vine motifs spring up everywhere, and the fireplaces are quite ornate. Even the bathrooms are old-fashioned, complete with clawfoot tubs. Conveniently for certain European visitors, the innkeepers speak French, German and Finnish. <u>$125</u>

Cow Hollow Motor Inn 2190 Lombard St at Steiner, Cow Hollow ☎415 921 5800, ⓦcowhollowmotorinn .com; map pp.68–69. True to its name, this motor inn features plentiful onsite parking and a convenient (if noisy) location along busy Lombard St. Its common areas are charmingly retro, but the rooms are surprisingly modern, clean and – by San Francisco standards – enormous. <u>$98</u>

Hotel del Sol 3100 Webster St at Greenwich, Cow Hollow ☎415 921 5520 or 1 877 433 5765, ⓦthehotel delsol.com; map pp.68–69. One of the best places for budget cool in the city, this offbeat, updated motor lodge has a tropical theme, all the way down to its small, but inviting outdoor swimming pool (a San Francisco rarity). Amenities include free parking, a pillow-lending library and complimentary handmade aromatherapy soap. <u>$99</u>

Hotel Drisco 2901 Pacific Ave at Broderick, Pacific Heights ☎415 346 2880 or 1 800 634 7277, ⓦhoteldrisco.com; map pp.68–69. Certain rooms and suites at this lavish B&B-style hotel at the peak of Pacific Heights boast spectacular city views, and overall the place feels a bit like a farmhouse dropped into the city. Still, unless you're wedded to staying in this otherwise quiet and residential area, there are better hotels in more centrally located areas. <u>$229</u>

8

8

Greenwich Inn 3201 Steiner St at Greenwich, Cow Hollow ☎415 921 5162, ⓦgreenwichinn.com; map pp.68–69. A sprightly, good-value motel with friendly owners and decent (if slightly dark) rooms. It's one of the more affordable options along the Lombard St motel strip, and its free, off-street parking is a helpful amenity in this area. $89

Jackson Court 2198 Jackson St at Buchanan, Pacific Heights ☎415 929 7670, ⓦjacksoncourt.com; map pp.68–69. With only ten rooms, this B&B-inspired hotel is housed in a converted 1900s brownstone in the heart of Pacific Heights. It's a romantic spot well hidden from the bustle of Downtown – a terrific choice for visitors looking for a quiet bolthole. Breakfast is especially fantastic. $190

Laurel Inn 444 Presidio Ave at California, Laurel Heights ☎415 567 8467 or 1 800 552 8735, ⓦthelaurelinn.com; map pp.106–107. Steps from Sacramento Street's antique shops, and not far from Fillmore St's strip of cafés and stores, the *Laurel Inn* offers small rooms and decor that's a stylish update of 1950s Americana, with muted graphic prints and simple fixtures. Breakfast is included in rates, and the hotel welcomes pets. $199

Hotel Majestic 1500 Sutter at Gough, Pacific Heights ☎415 441 1100 or 1 800 869 8966, ⓦthehotelmajestic.com; map pp.106–107. A gorgeous 1902 building where reams upon reams of drapery are used to decorate the rooms, the more expensive of which feature antique furnishings and fireplaces; many also include clawfoot tubs. There's a huge butterfly collection on display in the lounge, with rare specimens from New Guinea and Africa. $125

★ **Queen Anne Hotel** 1590 Sutter St at Octavia, Pacific Heights ☎415 441 2828 or 1 800 227 3970, ⓦqueenanne.com; map pp.106–107. Gloriously restored Victorian building enjoying its second life as a boutique B&B. Each room is stuffed with gold-accented Rococo furniture and bunches of silk flowers; the parlour (where afternoon tea and sherry are served) is stuffed with museum-quality period furniture. $209

Sheraton Fisherman's Wharf 2500 Mason St at North Point, Fisherman's Wharf ☎415 362 5500 or 1 800 325 3535, ⓦsheratonatthewharf.com; map pp.68–69. This hotel is stylishly done out in cheerful colours and wired with all mod cons, including flat-screen HDTVs and wi-fi. The outdoor "living room" with firepits – as well as the *Spressi* bar and restaurant's community table – both encourage socializing among visitors. $199

Surf Motel 2265 Lombard St at Pierce, Cow Hollow ☎415 922 1950; map pp.68–69. Old-school motel with unbeatable rates and two tiers of bright, simple and clean rooms. Be sure to request a room at the back, since the busy Lombard St thoroughfare roars past the main entrance. $75

Union Street Inn 2229 Union St at Fillmore, Cow Hollow ☎415 346 0424, ⓦunionstreetinn.com; map pp.68–69. Located along Union St's row of trendy boutiques and surrounded by a lush, flower-filled garden, this Edwardian

TOP 5 HOTELS WITH CITY VIEWS

InterContinental San Francisco
  See opposite
Hotel Drisco See p.129
The Fairmont See p.129
Hotel Vitale See p.132
Westin St Francis See p.128

B&B offers six rooms (including a spacious carriage house), gourmet breakfast alfresco (weather permitting), fireplaces, chocolates, fresh flowers, wine and hors d'oeuvres in the evening, and cookies available all day. $249

Wharf Inn 2601 Mason St at Jefferson, Fisherman's Wharf ☎415 673 7411 or 1 877 275 7889, ⓦwharfinn.com; map pp.68–69. This boxy, two-storey motel is a fairly decent option at Fisherman's Wharf, with large, clean and comfortable rooms set along motel-style outdoor walkways and decorated in neutral beige tones. The free off-street parking is a major advantage. $179

SOUTH OF MARKET AND THE TENDERLOIN

Best Western Carriage Inn 140 Seventh St at Mission, South of Market ☎415 552 8600, ⓦcarriageinnsf.com; map pp.84–85. The 48 enormous, elegant rooms here honour unconventional San Francisco legends, including Lillie Coit (see p.61) and the Mitchell Brothers (see p.92); they also offer sofas, flat-screen televisions, iPod docking stations and fireplaces. The main downside is its location on a somewhat sketchy block. $156

Hotel Carlton 1075 Sutter St at Larkin, Polk Gulch ☎415 673 0242 or 1 800 738 7477, ⓦhotelcarltonsf.com; map pp.84–85. One of Joie de Vivre's hotels inspired by literature and magazines; in this case, the globetrotting *Carlton* is a guidebook brought to life. The lobby is filled with objects from the Middle East and Africa, the elevator is plastered with world maps, and the rooms boast rich ochre bedlinen and inlaid wood tables, as well as photographs of Middle Eastern scenes on the walls. $127

★ **Good Hotel** 112 Seventh St at Mission ☎415 621 7001, ⓦthegoodhotel.com; map pp.84–85. One of San Francisco's newest hotels, this fun and eco-aware spot is located within walking distance of several museums. Its 117 rooms (a third of which surround a courtyard) are tastefully decorated and include pet-friendly amenities and iPod docking stations; free bicycles are available to all guests for wheeling around the city. $119

Hotel Griffon 155 Steuart St at Howard, South of Market ☎415 495 2100 or 1 800 321 2201, ⓦhotelgriffon.com; map pp.84–85. This secluded hotel adjacent to the waterfront offers nearly sixty elegant and understated rooms with exposed brick walls, window seats, 32-inch flat-screen televisions and refrigerator, all wrapped in a vaguely Asian theme. Free wireless internet and continental breakfast are included in the room rate. $\underline{\$249}$

Harbor Court Hotel 165 Steuart St at Howard, South of Market ☎ 415 882 1300 or 1 866 792 6283, ⓦharbor courthotel.com; map pp.84–85. Rooms here are grandly decorated in jewel colours such as ruby and deep blue, and many include canopied beds and velveteen cushions; some offer spectacular views across the bay, one block away. There's a free coffee and tea reception each morning, along with discounts to the gym at the neighbouring YMCA. $\underline{\$206}$

Inn at the Opera 333 Fulton St at Franklin, Civic Center ☎ 415 863 8400 or 1 888 298 7198, ⓦshellhospitality .com; map pp.84–85. Centrally located for high-culture aficionados, this 48-room hotel delivers fussy, old-fashioned elegance, with plenty of antiques scattered about. It's located just around the corner from the War Memorial Opera House – hence its lush Symphony and Opera suites. $\underline{\$139}$

InterContinental San Francisco 888 Howard St at Fifth, South of Market ☎ 415 616 6500 or 1 888 811 4273, ⓦintercontinentalsanfrancisco.com; map pp.84–85. Owners of the iconic *Mark Hopkins on Nob Hill* (see p.129), InterContinental opened this sleek, blue 32-storey skyscraper hotel in 2008, and it's certainly caused quite a local stir. Its 500-plus elegant, minimalist rooms feature floor-to-ceiling windows and mahogany furniture; downstairs, *Bar 888* specializes in cocktails made from the Italian spirit grappa, while the bright Tuscany-via-Napa restaurant is aptly named *Luce* (Italian for "light"). $\underline{\$296}$

Hotel Metropolis 25 Mason St at Turk, Tenderloin ☎ 415 775 4600 or 1 800 553 1900, ⓦhotelmetropolis.com; map pp.84–85. Though situated on the far eastern edge of the dodgy Tenderloin district, this hotel – one block from the cable car turnaround at the foot of Powell St – is delightful inside, boasting chic modern decor and a colour scheme that combines neutral tan with eye-popping primaries. Amenities include a cosy reading library, 24hr business centre, wireless internet, a workout room and a "holistic / well-being room" (which you may want to visit after walking the frenetic block leading to the lobby). It's even pet-friendly. $\underline{\$129}$

The Mosser Hotel 54 Fourth St at Mission, South of Market ☎ 415 986 4400 or 1 800 227 3804, ⓦthemosser .com; map pp.84–85. This 166-room hotel is a funky conversion, fusing Victorian touches such as ornamental moulding with mod leather sofas. The chocolate-and-olive rooms (54 with shared bath) may be tiny, but each features double-paned windows – a real advantage in this noisy area – and overall, it's one of the better-value places in South of Market. $\underline{\$99}$

Palace Hotel 2 New Montgomery St at Market, South of Market ☎ 415 512 1111 or 1 888 625 5144, ⓦsfpalace .com; map pp.84–85. Hushed, opulent landmark building known for its *Garden Court* tearoom – favoured by US presidents and heads of state – and its renowned stained glass dome. The hotel's grand lobby and corridors are mismatched with rooms that are awfully small, considering the sky-high prices; most are decorated in lush golds and greens like an English country house. Stay here for snob value, above all. $\underline{\$394}$

Hotel Palomar 12 Fourth St at Market, South of Market ☎ 415 348 1111 or 1 866 373 4941, ⓦhotelpalomar-sf .com; map pp.84–85. The location – above a massive Old Navy store – may be unprepossessing, but the *Palomar* is a chic, neo-Nouveau bolthole in the commercial heart of the city. Decor is dark and smoky, with ebony and leopard print accents; rooms are pleasantly large with full amenities. Note that there's no access from Market St, despite the signage. $\underline{\$280}$

Phoenix Hotel 601 Eddy St at Larkin, Tenderloin ☎ 415 776 1380 or 1 800 248 9466, ⓦjdvhotels.com /phoenix; map pp.84–85. This raucous retro motel conversion features a mixed gay-straight clientele and has been a favourite with touring bands for years. In the central courtyard, there's a small pool (next to which a continental breakfast is served each morning) that gives the place a Sunset Strip feel, while the rooms are eccentrically decorated in tropical colours with changing local artwork on the walls; ask for the "Headliner Suite", which sports a separate living room. At the time of writing, a new bar and lounge was being designed near the hotel pool area. Parking is included in room rates. $\underline{\$129}$

Renoir Hotel 45 McAllister St at Market, Civic Center ☎ 415 626 5200 or 1 800 576 3388, ⓦrenoirhotel.com; map pp.84–85. This wedge-shaped building is a historic landmark with 135 rooms that have been florally, if unexcitingly, refurbished. The superior rooms run $40 more than standard, but if you can snag one of the oddly shaped large rooms at the building's apex, they're definitely worth it. The place is especially popular during Pride weekend each June for its Market St views along the parade route. $\underline{\$129}$

St. Regis 125 Third St at Mission, South of Market ☎ 415 284 4000, ⓦstarwoodhotels.com; map pp.84–85. Located next door to the San Francisco Museum of Modern Art, this luxury hotel naturally has visually stunning modern design aesthetics – it's almost like staying inside a work of art. In addition, rooms are fitted with plasma TVs, 13-inch flat-screen LCD TVs in the bathrooms, Pratesi bed linens, soaking tubs and oversized showerheads in the separate shower. Butlers are also at the beck and call of guests – almost to be expected, since it's often more expensive to stay here than at the Four Seasons. $\underline{\$569}$

★ **Hotel Vertigo** 940 Sutter St at Leavenworth, Polk Gulch ☎ 415 885 6800 or 1 888 444 4605, ⓦhotel vertigosf.com; map pp.84–85. Famous as the place where Alfred Hitchcock filmed the dramatic stairway scenes in *Vertigo* (hence its celebratory name), this swanky spot boasts a mix of classic French style and modern urban

8

sophistication. The *Vertigo* swirl motif is prominent in the shockingly modernist orange, white and black rooms, some of which include flat-screen television, refrigerator and iPod docking station. Bathrooms feature crocodile-patterned tiles, dark walnut vanities and oversize showerheads. Top value for uniquely fun accommodation. **$119**

★ **Hotel Vitale** 8 Mission St at Embarcadero, South of Market ☎ 415 278 3700 or 1 888 890 8688, ⓦ hotelvitale .com; map pp.84–85. Steps from the Ferry Building, this luxury boutique hotel boasts 199 elegant contemporary rooms (many with bay views) and an on-site spa with rooftop soaking tubs. The bar at the ground-level Americano restaurant is a happy-hour favourite of the Downtown crowd, with patio seating along the Embarcadero. **$339**

The W 181 Third St at Howard, South of Market ☎ 415 777 5300, ⓦ starwoodhotels.com; map pp.84–85. South of Market high-rise outpost of the pricey hotel chain that thinks it's a nightclub: loud club muzak, black-clad staffers whispering into headsets and an all-consuming VIP vibe. The minimalist rooms are large and have stunning views across the city, while nifty add-on touches such as Etch-a-Sketches, free tooth-whitening kits and Bliss bath products make them extra welcoming. **$359**

Hotel Whitcomb 1231 Market St at Eighth, South of Market ☎ 415 626 8000, ⓦ hotelwhitcomb.com; map pp.84–85. In the wake of the 1906 earthquake and fire, this c.1911 building temporarily served as San Francisco's City Hall. It's memorably adorned with Tiffany glass, Italian marble pillars and Austrian crystal chandeliers, and possesses one of the city's only parquet dance floors; there's even a piano bar. **$239**

THE MISSION AND THE CASTRO

Beck's Motor Lodge 2222 Market St at Sanchez, Castro ☎ 415 621 8212, ⓦ becksmotorlodge.com; map p.100. Beck's is the rare Castro accommodation option that isn't a gay-oriented B&B, and its clientele is more mixed than you'd expect, given its location; the rooms, too, are plusher than the gaudy yellow exterior suggests. If you're a light sleeper, ask for a room away from the Market St thoroughfare. **$105**

★ **Inn San Francisco** 943 S Van Ness Ave at 20th, Mission ☎ 415 641 0188 or 1 800 359 0913, ⓦ innsf .com; map p.100. Superb, sprawling B&B set in two adjoining historic Victorians. The 15 rooms in the 1872 mansion are dark and stylish, with stunning views across town from the smokers' terrace on the roof; the 1904 extension next door holds six more rooms, chintzier in decor with frilly valances and tapestries. All rooms have phone, fridge, and television, and all but two have private baths (an extra $55). The generous breakfast buffet and redwood hot tub in the garden are also major pluses. **$120**

Travelodge Central 1707 Market St at Valencia, Mission ☎ 415 621 6775 or 1 800 578 7878, ⓦ sanfranciscocentralhotel.com; map pp.106–107.

Very basic, but it couldn't be more conveniently located – everywhere from Downtown to the Castro is an easy walk or bus/trolley ride away. Free off-street parking and low nightly rates compensate somewhat for the slightly worn, floral motel rooms. Free wireless internet, newspapers and coffee. **$89**

HAIGHT-ASHBURY AND WEST OF CIVIC CENTER

Best Western Hotel Tomo 1800 Sutter St at Buchanan, Japantown ☎ 415 921 4000 or 1 800 738 7477, ⓦ jdvhotels.com/tomo; map pp.106–107. A homage to Japanese pop culture, *Hotel Tomo* is a youthful, anime-themed place decked out in neon-bright colours, with action-packed, cartoonish murals on the walls. The "Players Suite" includes a Nintendo Wii or Sony PS3, beanbag chairs and an enormous LCD projection screen. **$144**

Carl Hotel 198 Carl St at Stanyan, Cole Valley ☎ 415 661 5679, ⓦ carlhotel.ypguides.net; map pp.106–107. Plainer than many of the surrounding B&Bs, this hotel is a bargain for its Golden Gate Park-adjacent location. Rooms are small but floral, and are fitted with microwaves and refrigerators; the six with shared bath are especially well-priced; those with private bath cost an extra $45. **$99**

Château Tivoli 1057 Steiner St at Golden Gate, Alamo Square ☎ 415 776 5462 or 1 800 228 1647, ⓦ chateau tivoli.com; map pp.106–107. History figures prominently here, whether in the furniture (one of the beds was owned by Charles de Gaulle), the rooms named for Jack London and Isadora Duncan (among others) or the building itself (built for an early local lumber baron). It's grand and quite serious accommodation, but a luxurious alternative to many of the cosy B&Bs elsewhere in town. **$100**

Grove Inn 890 Grove St at Fillmore, Alamo Square ☎ 415 929 0780 or 1 800 829 0780, ⓦ grovinn.com; map pp.106–107. Friendly B&B housed in a c.1885 Italianate mansion. It's a chic and understated place, with all 15 rooms featuring private bath and television. The knowledgeable innkeepers – very involved in local preservation circles – are always good for a gab. **$120**

Hayes Valley Inn 417 Gough St at Hayes, Hayes Valley ☎ 415 431 9131 or 1 800 930 7999, ⓦ hayesvalleyinn .com; map pp.106–107. Homely, apple-green rooms in a location that feels more secluded than it actually is. Hayes Valley Inn's furnishings are minimal and baths are shared, but the well-stocked kitchen/breakfast room is a terrific place to meet people. **$76**

★ **Hotel Kabuki** 1625 Post St at Laguna, Japantown ☎ 415 922 3220 or 1 800 533 4567, ⓦ jdvhotels.com /kabuki; map pp.106–107. Striking a sophisticated, streamlined look in architecturally drab Japantown, the Kabuki offers a ritual tea service to each guest upon check-in. Each bathroom features a deep, Japanese-style soaking tub, and for a fee, visitors can request any number of bath services.

AIRPORT HOTELS

There's little reason to stay near SFO, unless you're catching an especially early or late flight. If this is the case, the following hotels are good options.

Best Western Grosvenor 380 S Airport Blvd, South San Francisco ☎ 650 873 3200 or 1 800 722 7141, ⓦ grosvenorsfo.com. Large, comfortable hotel with swimming pool and free shuttle service to the airport. $80

Hyatt Regency San Francisco Airport 1333 Bayshore Hwy, Burlingame ☎ 650 347 1234, ⓦ sanfranciscoairport.hyatt.com. Gigantic hotel south

of the airport with several notable amenities (pool, hot tub, bars) and a free shuttle to the airport. $223

La Quinta Inn 20 Airport Blvd, South San Francisco ☎ 650 583 2223, ⓦ laquinta.com. Overnight laundry service, a fitness centre and swimming pool, and complimentary airport shuttle make this a comfortable, affordable stopover. $62

The hotel also offers workshops on Japanese traditions such as taiko drumming and origami, as well as passes to Kabuki Springs & Spa (see p.113) down the street. $144

The Red Victorian Bed, Breakfast & Art 1665 Haight St at Belvedere, Upper Haight ☎ 415 864 1978, ⓦ redvic.com; map pp.106–107. Quirky B&B decorated with the owner's ethnic arts, where the TV-free rooms vary from simple to opulent. Breakfast's a lavish, highly communal affair. Look for the goldfish-filled toilet cistern in one of the shared bathrooms. $129

Stanyan Park Hotel 750 Stanyan St at Waller, Upper Haight ☎ 415 751 1000, ⓦ stanyanpark.com; map pp.106–107. Overlooking the eastern end of Golden Gate Park, this small hotel has 35 sumptuous rooms that are incongruous in its countercultural neighbourhood, busily decorated in country florals with heavy drapes and junior four-poster beds. Continental breakfast and an ample, cookie-filled afternoon tea are included. $155

THE RICHMOND AND THE SUNSET

Ocean Park Motel 2690 46th Ave at Wawona, Parkside ☎ 415 566 7020, ⓦ oceanparkmotel.ypguides.net;

map p.116. All the way across the city from Downtown, San Francisco's oldest Art Deco motel is an outstanding example of Streamline Moderne architecture, and convenient for the zoo, Ocean Beach and Fort Funston. The outdoor hot tub and pleasant garden courtyard are nice touches, and there's even a kids' play area. $118

Oceanview Motel 4340 Judah St at La Playa, Outer Sunset ☎ 415 661 2300, ⓦ oceanviewmotelsf.com; map p.116. Nondescript lodging steps from Ocean Beach. Rooms are on the small side and simply furnished, but there's free off-street parking and quick access to Muni's N-Judah streetcar, which can get you Downtown in about 45 minutes. $104

Seal Rock Inn 545 Point Lobos Ave at 48th, Outer Richmond ☎ 415 752 8000 or 1 800 732 5762, ⓦ sealrockinn.com; map p.116. Well situated for visiting the Cliff House and wandering San Francisco's wild northwest corner, this brown, boxy motel is a good option solely for its views – many rooms look out over the frothy Pacific. Though the standard rooms are fine, the suites (with real log fireplace) are a better option for the extra $20 or so. Just give the on-site restaurant a miss. $135

HOSTELS

Facilities You can expect smart locations across the city, and most hostels offer private rooms along with the usual dorms. Either way, they'll provide a bed and a locker for your valuables.

Membership To stay at an HI hostel, you'll need to purchase an annual membership ($28), available to US citizens and international travellers alike. Even if you're

American, it's worth bringing your passport if you plan on staying at a hostel, as many will insist on seeing it before renting you a bed (a measure designed to preserve accommodation for bona fide travellers). For similar reasons, many hostels also impose a maximum stay of three to five days.

Adelaide Hostel 51 Isadora Duncan Lane off Taylor St at Geary, Union Square ☎ 415 359 1915 or 1 877 359 1915, ⓦ adelaidehostel.com; map pp.40–41. Hidden away on a tiny lane, this former hotel features 100 beds spread across four-, six- and ten-person dorms; some have en suite bathrooms, while others share. Bunks are built into the wall, much like rail sleeper cars, complete with their own curtains. There are also a handful of two- and three-person private rooms. Adelaide's unbeatable facilities include a sizeable, sofa-filled lounge; free wireless internet;

backyard deck; clean kitchen where the hefty continental breakfast is served; and cheap laundry (under $2 per load). Open 24hr. Dorms $23, doubles $60

Elements Hotel 2524 Mission St at 21st, Mission ☎ 415 647 4100 or 1 866 327 8407, ⓦ elementssf.com; map p.100. Mission St hostel that fills a gaping need for any kind of accommodation – budget or otherwise – in the area. En suite dorm rooms mostly sleep four people, and there are men-only, women-only and mixed dorms; couples can opt for one of the few private rooms with twin

8

or double beds. Amenities include 24hr access, wireless internet, movie showings, a hearty continental breakfast in adjacent *Cafe Medjool*, lockers, linens and towels. The extraordinary rooftop terrace view more than compensates for any external noise. Dorms $25, doubles $60

Green Tortoise 494 Broadway at Kearny, North Beach ☎415 834 1000 or 1 800 867 8647, ⓦgreentortoise .com; map p.59. This laid-back hostel has room for 130 people in dorm beds or double rooms (with shared bath), although it's showing its age – especially given the rash of new budget spaces that have opened. Whether you pay for a dorm or a room, you'll get internet access, use of the small onsite sauna, foosball and pool tables, and complimentary breakfast; there's even free dinner three nights a week. There's no curfew, and the front desk is staffed 24hr. Dorms $30, doubles $60

Pacific Tradewinds 680 Sacramento St at Kearny, Chinatown ☎415 433 7970 or 1 888 734 6783, ⓦpactradewinds.com; map pp.40–41. An appealing option well located on the eastern edge of Chinatown, this small hostel offers free internet access, tea and coffee, a clean kitchen, and a large communal dining table that makes for easy chats with fellow travellers. It's certainly an international hub – house rules are posted in almost forty languages, including Afrikaans and Catalan. There are only 38 beds, so book ahead in high season; no lockout or curfew, and check-in is available 8am–11.30pm. Dorms $29.50

San Francisco City Center (HI) 685 Ellis St at Polk, Tenderloin ☎415 474 5721, ⓦsfhostels.com/city-center; map pp.84–85. Converted from a hotel, this large hostel has 200 beds divided into four-person dorms, each with en-suite bath; there are also 15 private rooms, with either double or twin beds. There's no curfew imposed, and overall it's a friendly place to meet other travellers since plenty of activities are laid on (nightly movies, communal pancake breakfasts and walking tours). The main downside is its Tenderloin location – it's not an ideal area for a solo female to walk through after dark. Open 24hr. Dorms $27.50, doubles $89

San Francisco Downtown (HI) 312 Mason St at O'Farrell, Union Square ☎415 788 5604, ⓦsfhostels .com/downtown; map pp.40–41. With nearly 300 beds spread between four- and five-bed dorms, this hostel still fills quickly in peak season, thanks to its central location. The four-person dorms are spotless, sharing bathroom facilities between eight people, while private rooms sleep two. There's a kitchen with microwave and vending machines, a funky little reading room and internet access. Open 24hr. Dorms $28.50, doubles $82

★ **San Francisco Fisherman's Wharf (HI)** Building 240, Fort Mason ☎415 771 7277, ⓦsfhostels.com /fishermans-wharf; map pp.68–69. Housed in a historic former Civil War barracks perched above the bay, and set between the Golden Gate Bridge and Fisherman's Wharf, this is a choice option for outdoorsy travellers. There are 180 beds in both mixed and single-sex dorms, with room capacities ranging from six to twelve people. Note that the disabled-access extension is available to anyone and is the choicest spot – it's effectively a stand-alone apartment with three bedrooms charged at the dorm rate. This hostel may be less centrally located than others, but its terrific amenities include free breakfast, a huge kitchen and, perhaps most notably, breathtaking views over the bay. Dorms $27, doubles $82

★ **USA Hostel** 711 Post St at Jones, Union Square ☎415 440 5600, ⓦusahostels.com/sanfrancisco; map pp.40–41. A safe, friendly and fun hostel in the heart of the city, with colourful walls, affable staff and plenty of opportunities to meet other travellers. Facilities include a huge common area jammed with bright couches and barstools, plus free billiards and foosball tables; other amenities include wireless internet access, free all-you-can-make pancake breakfasts and laundry facilities (complete with free detergent). There are even movie showings in an on-site 45-seat theatre. All dorm rooms have four beds, while private rooms feature one queen bed or two twin bunks. Dorms $29, doubles $82

8

SUSHI RESTAURANT, JAPANTOWN

Cafés and restaurants

With an abundance of nearby farms showering the city's farmers' markets with fresh produce, a culture that increasingly emphasizes sustainable food practices and a local population with a proclivity for eating out, it's little wonder that San Francisco is one of the world's leading restaurant cities. Its dining scene may be remarkably convivial, but this is a city where people take few things more seriously than food. San Francisco has long been known for its five-star fine-dining experiences, and more recently for its wealth of low-end marvels like taquerias, dim sum places and curry houses. However, the city's eating-out habits have gone through a transformation in recent years, with a proliferation of excellent, moderately priced neighbourhood restaurants sending residents flocking to other areas of town.

9

Whereas the restaurant of choice for a big night out used to be one of the high-end **French** or **seafood** places Downtown, it's just as likely now that the same money will be spent on multiple dinners at less formal, but equally stylish restaurants in neighbourhoods away from the city's core (Glen Park, the Marina and Cole Valley, to name a few). The greatest asset of San Francisco's restaurants is the staggering **variety** – not only in types of cuisine, but in price ranges and overall experiences. Our listings reflect the city's dining diversity, from gourmet **vegetarian** restaurants, **steakhouses** and **Italian delicatessens**, to **Spanish tapas** joints, **Mexican taquerias** and a **Portuguese** diner set in an old train car where you can also order meat loaf until 4am – for everyone from big spenders to budget-minded visitors.

Although San Francisco has a well-deserved reputation for exceptional fine dining, many locals believe its strength as a foodie hub is in its informal eating scene. First-rate **sandwich shops** abound, as does an abundance of top-shelf ice-cream places; the city also has no shortage of dim sum and cupcake specialists, as well as numerous **bakeries** that are well worth a visit.

A couple of important notes on San Francisco dining. Firstly, don't plan on enjoying a leisurely cigarette with your aperitif or after-dinner coffee, as California law decrees there's **no smoking** in any public space, including restaurants. Also note that San Francisco has a law providing healthcare for all restaurant employees; to help defray these costs, many local establishments now add a nominal surcharge (usually 2–4 percent) to customers' tabs. A **tip** of at least fifteen percent is expected for good service, although twenty percent is more the norm in San Francisco.

CAFÉS

DOWNTOWN

Chili Up! Crocker Galleria, 50 Post St at Kearny, Financial District ☎415 693 0467; map pp.40–41. Its shopping centre location may be initially off-putting, but this local chainlet is a top Downtown lunch option – its inexpensive gourmet chili (served over basmati rice) is offered in several different varieties, including vegetarian. Mon–Fri 11am–3.45pm, Sat 11am–3pm.

Emporio Rulli il Caffe Stockton St Pavilion in Union Square plaza, Union Square ☎415 433 1122; map pp.40–41. A popular shopping pitstop with mandolin-drenched Italian ballads spilling out of its speakers, this café serves bracingly strong coffee, as well as breakfast and lunch panini starting at around $6. There are scores of tables outside on the square if you feel like lounging. Daily 7.30am–10pm.

Il Massimo del Panino 441 Washington St at Battery, Financial District ☎415 834 0290; map pp.40–41. Stylish café featuring an extensive panini sandwich menu, along with beer, wine and an invitingly cushy couch next to a fireplace. All sandwiches are made on home-made bread and cost $7.45. Branch (with outdoor seating and longer hours): 5 Embarcadero Center at Market, Financial District. Mon–Fri 7am–3pm.

Mocca 175 Maiden Lane at Stockton, Union Square ☎415 956 1188; map pp.40–41. A small, marble-floored café spilling out onto the pedestrianized shopping street, often serenaded by live acoustic jazz. The dapper, mostly Italian staff are decked out in stiff waistcoats and prepare the terrific sandwiches and fresh salads to order (all around

$10–12) with a flourish. Cocktails, beer and wine all available; cash only. Mon–Fri 8am–6pm, Sat 8.30am–4pm.

San Francisco Soup Company 221 Montgomery St at Bush, Financial District ☎415 834 0472; map pp.40–41. Local chain (with a dozen San Francisco outlets) specializing in – you guessed it – gourmet soups. The menu at this large branch includes over a dozen kinds, from vegetarian-friendly staples such as smoky split pea to daily specials such as shrimp bisque. A regular portion is $5.30; add about $1 more for a large portion, and about $1.50 for a fresh-baked bread bowl. Mon–Fri 7am–4pm.

NORTH BEACH AND THE HILLS

Caffe Sapore 790 Lombard St at Taylor, North Beach ☎415 474 1222; map p.56. One block off Columbus, this mellow neighbourhood café serves inexpensive baked goods, fresh sandwiches and all the usual coffee beverages in a sunny room on a corner. Sit and admire the original artwork adorning the walls, or enjoy a glass of wine or beer on one of the outside tables as you watch drivers navigate Lombard's twisting turns just up Russian Hill. Daily 7am–8.30pm.

Giordano Bros. 303 Columbus Ave at Broadway, North Beach ☎415 397 2767; map p.59. Pittsburgh sports-themed shop serves faithful replicas of the "all-in-one" sandwich (about $7) popularized in the blue-collar Pennsylvania city – all the way down to the fries stuffed between each sandwich's Italian bread slices. Given all the impossibly masculine decor of the place, the portions are

9

SAN FRANCISCO COFFEE, INDIE-STYLE

San Francisco has enjoyed a recent proliferation of locally based "microroasters" that offer particularly strong cups of coffee. Listed below are a few espresso bars to seek out if you're looking for a robust kickstart any time of day. You won't find any grande eggnog lattes at these places, but you can expect to get a cup of fresh-drip coffee for a mere couple of dollars. For a wealth of information on San Francisco coffee purveyors, including detailed reviews, visit ⓦ coffeeratings.com.

Blue Bottle Coffee 315 Linden St at Gough, Hayes Valley ☎ 415 252 7535; map pp.106–107. Located down an alley off a main thoroughfare, this quirky spot offers excellent breakfast and desserts, but it's the own-roasted coffee that has taken San Francisco by storm. Cold-brewed coffee makes a surprising appearance on the menu, as do a few milk-based beverages. Mon–Fri 7am–5.30pm, Sat & Sun 8am–5.30pm.

Caffe Trieste 601 Vallejo St at Grant, North Beach ☎ 415 392 6739; map p.59. This local institution is where espresso made its West Coast debut in 1956. Today, it's known almost as much for its Saturday mandolin sessions and opera recitals as for its own-roasted, thick-bodied coffee. It operates a shop next to the café where you can purchase a sack of *Caffe Trieste* beans. Mon–Thurs & Sun 6.30am–11pm, Fri & Sat 6.30am–midnight.

Coffee Bar 1890 Bryant St at Mariposa, Mission ☎ 415 551 8100; map p.100. A huge space on an industrial edge of the Mission that serves a consistently bracing cup. One member of the management team is an avowed oenophile, so the place becomes a wine bar of sorts during

evening hours; salads and sandwiches are served all day long. Mon–Fri 7am–8pm, Sat & Sun 8am–7pm.

Philz Coffee 3101 24th St at Folsom, Mission ☎ 415 875 9370; map p.100. Featuring 20 custom blends (all available by the pound) – to which only owner Phil Jaber and his son know the recipes – Philz has quickly turned into one of San Francisco's most beloved coffee venues. Mon–Fri 6am–8.30pm, Sat & Sun 7am–8.30pm.

Ritual Coffee Roasters 1026 Valencia St at 21st, Mission ☎ 415 641 1024; map p.100. The hipster-chic clientele at this vaunted café can't overshadow the outstanding coffee, roasted on the premises using the company's own beans. The intense espresso boasts flavours of hazelnut and caramel. Mon–Fri 6am–10pm, Sat 7am–10pm, Sun 7am–9pm.

Trouble Coffee 4033 Judah St at 45th, Outer Sunset ☎ 415 690 9119; map p.116. A few blocks in from the coastline sits this pint-sized powerhouse, operated by young eccentrics who are remarkably passionate about their trade. The menu's simple: coffee, coconut, toast. Daily 7am–7pm.

---

surprisingly downsized. Mon & Tues 11.30am–10.30pm, Wed & Thurs 11.30am–midnight, Fri & Sat 11.30am–1.30pm, Sun 11.30am–6pm.

Italian French Baking 1501 Grant Ave at Union, North Beach ☎ 415 421 3796; map p.59. Nestled on a corner along upper Grant's retail drag, this tiny bakery wafts the enticing smell of freshly baked bread up and down the block. Grab a slice of focaccia, a pastry or a flavoured baguette (rosemary, whole wheat), have a seat on one of the stools at the window counter and while away a few minutes watching folks shuffle by on the sidewalk. Mon–Fri & Sun 6am–6pm, Sat 6am–7pm.

★ **Mario's Bohemian Cigar Store Cafe** 566 Columbus Ave at Union, North Beach ☎ 415 362 0536; map p.59. Stogies haven't been sold on these premises for ages, but the chunky, home-made focaccia sandwiches and corner location make this North Beach institution a terrific place to grab a cheap bite and absorb the neighbourhood scene. The pizza and panini aren't bad, either, and the bar's a great, unpretentious spot for a nightcap. Daily 10am–11pm.

Molinari 373 Columbus Ave at Vallejo, North Beach ☎ 415 421 2337; map p.59. Classic Italian deli full of

locals picking up fresh ravioli and tortellini. It doubles as a hearty sandwich shop, so pick the bread of your choice and order a combo to go ($7–8) – try the North Beach Special, with prosciutto, *provolone*, sun-dried tomato and sweet peppers. Mon–Fri 9am–5.30pm, Sat 7.30am–5.30pm.

Nook 1500 Hyde St at Jackson, Russian Hill ☎ 415 447 4100; map p.56. Under the same ownership as *Caffe Sapore* (see opposite), with sleek cream walls, dark wood tables and an inexpensive menu chalked on a blackboard. There are a few seats outside if you want to absorb the Russian Hill street scene, while the short list of sake and soju cocktails sets this warm corner spot apart from the usual café fare. Mon–Fri 7am–10pm, Sat 8am–10pm, Sun 8am–9pm.

Swensen's Ice Cream 1999 Hyde St at Union, Russian Hill ☎ 415 775 6818; map p.56. *Swensen's* global dessert empire got its humble start here at this corner ice-cream shop in 1948, and few things seem to have changed in the decades since – the neon sign, the twinkling lightbulbs and, least of all, the exceptional home-made ice cream. Seating here is non-existent, so arm yourself with napkins and try to enjoy your treats as cleanly as possible. Tues–Thurs & Sun noon–10pm, Fri & Sat noon–11pm.

9

THE NORTHERN WATERFRONT AND PACIFIC HEIGHTS

Blue Barn Gourmet 2105 Chestnut St at Steiner, Marina ☎415 441 3232; map pp.68–69. You can't miss this place when strolling the Chestnut St promenade – just look for the shopfront with the distressed azure slats. The interior's equally ersatz-rustic, but the highly creative made-to-order salads and sandwiches (many under $10) are the real thing, and there's an entire portion of the menu given over to all sorts of grilled cheese panini. Plan to take your items away to enjoy elsewhere, as seating is extremely limited. Mon–Thurs & Sun 11am–8.30pm, Fri & Sat 11am–7pm.

Boudin Bakery & Cafe Pier 39, Fisherman's Wharf ☎415 421 0185; map pp.68–69. Not far from the Boudin Museum (see p.70), this offshoot café serves some of the finest sourdough around. A variety of inexpensive salads, sandwiches and sourdough pizzas are available, in addition to the inevitable chowder in a bread bowl. Mon–Thurs & Sun 11.30am–9pm, Fri & Sat 11.30am–10pm.

Fillmore Bakeshop 1890 Fillmore St at Bush, Pacific Heights ☎415 923 0711; map pp.106–107. Gourmet European-American bakery operated by the Basegio family; house specials include buttery pastries, glistening fruit tarts and a host of seasonal items. There are a few tables near the windows that encourage lingering. Tues–Fri 7am–6pm, Sat 8am–6pm, Sun 8am–4pm.

★ **Ghirardelli Ice Cream and Chocolate Caffe** 900 North Point St at Larkin, Fisherman's Wharf ☎415 771 4903; map pp.68–69. Although the chocolate hasn't been made onsite in decades, this perennially popular, old-fashioned ice-cream parlour is the ideal setting to sample a decadent range of Ghirardelli desserts. The sprawling Earthquake Sundae ($19.06, fittingly) is especially gooey – plan to share it with several friends. Mon–Thurs & Sun 9am–11pm, Fri & Sat 9am–midnight.

Kara's Cupcakes 3249 Scott St at Lombard, Marina ☎415 563 2253; map pp.68–69. These little desserts aren't just for kids' birthday parties anymore. San Francisco adults enjoy heated debates over where to find the best cupcakes, and with its clever selection of own-baked bite-size treats, Kara's is regularly among the elite. Branch: 900 North Point St at Larkin (Ghirardelli Square), Fisherman's Wharf (☎415 351 2253). Mon–Thurs 10am–8pm, Fri & Sat 10am–10pm, Sun 10am–7pm.

The Warming Hut Crissy Field, Presidio ☎415 561 3040; map pp.68–69. Housed in a welcoming white clapboard building near the Torpedo Wharf pier, this café's humble kitchen churns out inexpensive grilled sandwiches, soups and snacks. There are a few seats inside, as well as ample picnic tables on the adjacent lawn in the imposing shadow of the Golden Gate Bridge. Daily 9am–5pm.

SOUTH OF MARKET AND THE TENDERLOIN

Caffe Centro 102 South Park at Jack London, South of Market ☎415 882 1500; map pp.84–85. A neighbourhood favourite serving terrific sandwiches and salads (around $7) in comfort. There are a few tables inside, as well as out on the leafy South Park sidewalk; a take-out window is also available. Mon–Fri 7am–5pm, Sat 8am–4pm.

★ **Crossroads Cafe** 699 Delancey St at Brannan, South of Market ☎415 836 5624; map pp.84–85. Waterfront-adjacent offshoot of the Delancey Street restaurant (see p.154) around the corner. The sprawling, inexpensive menu covers all three meals and ranges from fruit smoothies and egg sandwiches to creative salads and tapas dishes, while the relaxed setting invites lingering – you could easily spend the better part of a morning or afternoon browsing the magazines at the bookshop near the food counter, or enjoying the sunny courtyard along the Embarcadero. Mon–Fri 7am–10pm, Sat 8am–10pm, Sun 8am–5pm.

Saigon Sandwich 560 Larkin St at Eddy, Tenderloin ☎415 474 5698; map pp.84–85. Diminutive shop selling sizeable, made-to-order *bahn mi* (Vietnamese sandwiches) for no more than $3.25: choose between barbecue chicken, barbecue pork and meatballs, then ask the hardworking ladies behind the counter to add lashings of fresh carrot and bundles of coriander (*cilantro*). Expect a line out the door every afternoon. Mon–Sat 6am–6pm, Sun 7am–5pm.

THE MISSION AND THE CASTRO

Bi-Rite Creamery & Bakeshop 3692 18th St at Dolores, Mission ☎415 626 5600; map p.100. This tiny, impossibly popular ice-cream shop hits all the right notes with its artisanal flavours. Usual suspects such as mint chip and chocolate share freezer space with unique concoctions such as toasted coconut and honey lavender; there's also sorbet, as well as cakes, pies and fruity popsicles. Mon–Thurs & Sun 11am–10pm, Fri & Sat 11am–11pm.

Ike's Place 3489 16th St at Sanchez, Castro ☎415 553 6888; map p.100. The staff here take many orders ahead on the phone, so even if there isn't the usual throng milling about, you may have a bit of a wait ahead of you. It's worth it, as the sometimes sloppy, always ambrosial creations ($8–13) are available in a number of ways – meat-stuffed, vegan, gluten-free and slathered (or not) in Ike's secret "Dirty Sauce". And there's a free lollipop with every order. Mon–Sat 10am–7pm.

La Copa Loca 3150 22nd St at Capp, Mission ☎415 401 7424; map p.100. Remarkably authentic gelateria where three delicious scoops will cost you a mere $4. A testament to *La Copa Loca*'s allure: several local Italian restaurants serve its gelato. Mon 1–9pm, Tues–Sat 9am–10pm, Sun 10am–9pm.

La Victoria 2937 24th St at Alabama, Mission ☎415 642 7120; map p.100. This budget bakery sells various *empanadas* (stuffed pastries) and other Mexican delectables, all made onsite and in large batches, so regardless of what time of day you wander in, you're bound to find just about everything on hand. Mon–Fri 6am–9pm, Sat & Sun 7am–9pm.

M & L Market 691 14th St at Market, Castro ☎ 415 431 7044; map p.100. Also known to some as May's Market, this humble deli is run by a small crowd of Korean women who've been known to lose their patience with wishy-washy customers. Be sure to have your order straight before stepping to the counter (specify your desired bread first), and prepare to indulge in a hearty, double-decker doorstop of a meal. Tues–Fri 11.30am–4pm.

Mission Pie 2901 Mission St at 25th, Mission ☎ 415 282 1500; map p.100. Celebrated pie retailer that's gained a fervent local following for its pie variations – ginger pear, strawberry rhubarb – and sustainably minded ethics. Slices and whole pies available. Mon–Thurs 7am–9pm, Fri 7am–10pm, Sat 8am–10pm, Sun 9am–9pm.

★ **Mitchell's Ice Cream** 688 San Jose Ave at 29th, Mission ☎ 415 648 2300; map p.100. Mitchell's produces its extensive selection of flavours onsite, from the mainstream (French vanilla, strawberry) to the leftfield (avocado, sweet bean). Despite its slightly desolate location at the southern end of the neighbourhood, there's often a long wait, particularly on evenings, weekends and warm days. Daily 11am–11pm.

Samovar Tea Lounge 498 Sanchez St at 18th, Castro ☎ 415 626 4700; map p.100. Earthy, cushion-filled café that serves more than a hundred varieties of tea, as well as tasty Asian snacks such as baked tofu with miso chutney; the overstuffed wicker chairs are a great place to curl up with a book for the afternoon. The priciest cup is a $29 brew of gyokuro. Branches: 730 Howard St at Fourth, South of Market (☎ 415 227 9400); 297 Page St at Laguna, Lower Haight (☎ 415 861 0303). Daily 10am–10pm.

★ **Tartine Bakery & Cafe** 600 Guerrero St at 18th, Mission ☎ 415 487 2600; map p.100. Quite possibly San Francisco's most popular bakery, and with good reason: This boulangerie's pies, pastries, hot-pressed sandwiches and bread pudding desserts are some of the finest around. Consequently, lines often twist out the door. Mon 8am–7pm, Tues & Wed 7.30am–7pm, Thurs & Fri 7.30am–8pm, Sat 8am–8pm, Sun 9am–8pm.

HAIGHT-ASHBURY AND WEST OF CIVIC CENTER

Benkyodo 1747 Buchanan St at Sutter, Japantown ☎ 415 922 1244; map pp.106–107. Selling hundreds of snacks daily – from *mochi* (soft rice cakes with filling) to *manju* (floury treats stuffed with red bean paste) – this popular Japanese bakery is one of San Francisco's oldest businesses. It's been in the neighbourhood since 1906, although it was closed through most of the 1940s when its

owners, the Okamura family, were interned during World War II. Items are inexpensive, so it's easy to fill up on dessert for a small sum. Cash only. Mon–Sat 8am–5pm.

Cheese Steak Shop 1716 Divisadero St at Sutter, Western Addition ☎ 415 346 3712; map pp.106–107. Odds are slim you'll bite into a finer cheesesteak sandwich in San Francisco than those you'll get at this immensely popular (if less than creatively named) shop, started by a couple of Philadelphia expats in the early 1980s. The kitchen imports its buns and peppers – and even its Tastykake desserts – from Philly; sandwiches come in three lengths (7-, 10- and 12-in), run the gamut from a bacon cheesesteak to several chicken varieties and cost $5–10. Hoagies (Italian-style sandwiches) are also available. Mon & Sat 10am–9pm, Tues–Fri 9am–9pm, Sun 11am–8pm.

Estela's 250 Fillmore St at Haight, Lower Haight ☎ 415 864 1850; map pp.106–107. This tiny but industrious shop serves more than thirty sandwich options on a variety of breads. Avocado plays a major role, and the vegetarian choices – including sandwiches built around smoked gouda and brie – are especially creative. There's also a choice of smoothies. Mon–Sat 8.30am–5.30pm.

Jubili 1515 Fillmore St at O'Farrell, Western Addition ☎ 415 292 9955; map pp.106–107. An impressive frozen yogurt specialist craftily updating the 1980s frozen-dessert craze with a smattering of flavour choices and a host of nuts, cookie bits and fresh fruit (including blueberries and kiwi) as toppings. Sorbets and parfaits ($5–6) pad the menu. Daily 10am–11pm.

Yasukochi's Sweet Stop 1790 Sutter St at Buchanan, Japantown ☎ 415 931 8165; map pp.106–107. Best known for its heavenly coffee crunch cake ($3.25 for a slice, $26 for a whole cake), this dessert spot inside Japantown's Super Mira Market features other sweet treats in case it sells out of its star attraction (which it sometimes does) – chocolate cake filled with fresh strawberry whipped cream is a smart backup choice. Tues–Fri 9.30am–5.30pm, Sat 9.30am–5pm.

THE RICHMOND AND THE SUNSET

★ **Arizmendi** 1331 Ninth Ave at Irving, Inner Sunset ☎ 415 566 3117; map p.116. The artisanal breads and pastries are reason enough to head to this small, earthy bakery that's an offshoot of Berkeley's famed *Cheeseboard*, but its regular rotation of gourmet pizza is the true surprise treat. Baked goods and pizzas vary daily and everything's inexpensive (pizza slices are $2.50 each), so it's certainly worth visiting more than once. Branch at 1268 Valencia St at 24th, Mission ☎ 415 826 9218. Tues–Fri 7am–7pm, Sat & Sun 7.30am–6pm.

Dash Cafe 420 Judah St at Ninth, Inner Sunset ☎ 415 661 1237; map p.116. The most relaxed café in the area, where the enticing aromas of slow-drip coffee and caramelized waffles ($4–6.50) combine with the sound of bebop jazz to fill

9

the air. Two separate rooms feature comfortable seating, all the better to enjoy a glass of wine, a pint of draught beer or a sweet treat. Mon–Thurs 7.30am–10pm, Fri 7.30am–11pm, Sat 8am–11pm, Sun 8am–10pm.

Polly Ann 3138 Noriega St at 39th, Outer Sunset ☎ 415 664 2472; map p.116. Tidy ice-cream parlour that produces a staggering five hundred flavours, although a rotating selection of a mere 49 is available daily. If you can't decide what to have, ask one of the servers to spin the flavour roulette wheel on the wall behind the counter – you're certain to get something interesting (banana rocky road, sunflower seed, mint marshmallow), and if the spin comes up "lucky", your dessert is on the house. There's only seating for about six. Daily 11am–10pm.

Sunrise Deli 2115 Irving St at 22nd, Outer Sunset ☎ 415 664 8210; map p.116. This drably decorated deli is nevertheless worth a visit for some of the finest Middle Eastern foodstuffs in town, from dolmas and *babaghanouj* to houmous and spinach pies. Branches: 54 Second St at Mission, South of Market (☎ 415 495 9999); 493 Pine St at Kearny, Financial District (☎ 415 362 2800). Mon–Sat 9am–9pm, Sun 10am–8pm.

Sweet Delite 519 Clement St at Sixth, Inner Richmond ☎ 415 386 8222; map p.116. Racks and racks of budget-priced candy from around the world, including Swedish fish with dried fruits and delicately fragranced Asian sweets. The ice-cream counter also serves creamy, scented tea with tapioca balls. Daily noon–9pm.

Wing Lee Bakery 503 Clement St at Sixth, Inner Richmond ☎ 415 668 9481; map p.116. Cheap, no-nonsense Chinese dim sum place, one of several on the Clement St strip. The fillings are more authentic to old-country standards than at other Chinese bakeries around the city, and you can gorge on pearlescent peanut dumplings for only a few bucks. Call for hours.

Yellow Submarine 503 Irving St at Sixth, Inner Sunset ☎ 415 681 5652; map p.116. Premier westside sandwich shop that's light on Beatles memorabilia but heavy on inexpensive, East Coast-style sub sandwiches. Everything's made to order and all meats are freshly grilled, so don't expect to be in and out in a few minutes (although you can phone ahead to speed things up). The grilled pastrami with hot sauce is second to none in town. Mon–Sat 11am–8.30pm, Sun 11am–5.30pm.

RESTAURANTS

DOWNTOWN

While there are certainly still a number of places in and around the Financial District and Union Square to spend upwards of $100 per person on an unforgettable meal, Downtown neighbourhoods have relinquished a bit of their epicurean dominance to outlying areas of town in recent years. That said, Fleur de Lys and *Masa's* are tough to top for formal fine dining, while *Bix* and *Le Colonial* aren't far behind for unapologetic opulence and peerless food. Catering to an enormous daily workforce, this area now features the extraordinary Ferry Building Marketplace (see box, p.144), as well as a handful of other handy lunch spots scattered about. As for Chinatown, the handful of restaurants listed below should steer you clear of the neighbourhood's glut of iffy tourist traps.

AMERICAN

5A5 Steak Lounge 244 Jackson St at Battery, Jackson Square ☎ 415 989 2539; map pp.40–41. *5A5's* contemporary space-age interior is a sharp stylistic departure from the usual men's-club steakhouse design motif, and if Captain Kirk and the Starship Enterprise crew dropped into Downtown San Francisco looking for expertly prepared 8oz cuts of Wagyu New York beef ($72), this is surely where they would reserve a table. DJs and live bands appear in the surprisingly formal lounge at weekends. Dinner Mon–Fri 5.30–10pm, Sat & Sun 5.30–9pm; lounge Mon–Thurs & Sun 5–11pm, Fri 5pm–midnight, Sat 5pm–2am.

Globe 290 Pacific Ave at Battery, Jackson Square ☎ 415 391 4132; map pp.40–41. Look for the wrought-iron globe dangling from the facade of this small,

semi-tucked away spot. It's a late-night favourite for local restaurant industry folks, with a Cal-Ital menu heavy on pizzas (mostly from the wood oven) and fresh fish. Main courses $15–24. Mon–Fri 11.30am–3pm & 6pm–1am, Sat 6pm–1am, Sun 6pm–midnight.

Michael Mina 252 California St at Battery, Financial District ☎ 415 397 9222; map pp.40–41. Postpone the diet and pack your credit card if you want to enjoy the adventurous menu at this five-star restaurant run by the namesake local chef. Mains range from $34 to $48, with specialities stretching from lobster pot pie to braised kurobuta pork; caviar and shellfish menus are also available. Mon–Thurs 11.30am–2.30pm & 5.30–10pm, Fri 11.30am–2.30pm & 5.30–10.30pm, Sat 5.30–10.30pm, Sun 5.30–10pm.

One Market 1 Market St at Steuart, Financial District ☎ 415 777 5577; map pp.40–41. Chef Mark Dommen's daily roast ($20–36) ranges from spice-rubbed pork to leg of lamb, while the roasted sturgeon ($28) and pan-seared scallops ($26.50) are favourites as well. The space itself is gargantuan, yet vivacious, set directly across Harry Bridges Plaza from the Ferry Building. Mon–Fri 11.30am–2pm & 5.30–9pm, Sat 5.30–9pm.

Pearl's Deluxe Burgers 708 Post St at Jones, Union Square ☎ 415 409 6120; map pp.40–41. An overlooked shoebox that cooks up some of San Francisco's finest budget burgers. You can easily sidestep beef by specifying a buffalo meat patty for a couple of dollars extra; chicken, turkey and veggie options are also scattered about the menu. Mon–Thurs 11am–10pm, Fri & Sat 11am–2am, Sun noon–9pm.

9

CALIFORNIA CUISINE

The local slant of cooking, dubbed **California cuisine**, is a development of French *nouvelle cuisine*, preserving the *nouvelle* focus on a wide mix of fresh, locally available foods, but widening the scope of influences considerably. Often, Cal cuisine mates with other ethnic foods, producing such hybrids as Cal-Ital or Cal-Mex, essentially health-conscious reworkings of original recipes. The range of dishes is seemingly endless and could include something as light as a cracker-crusted pizza with shrimp and rocket (arugula), or a heavier selection like herb-crusted rack of lamb with root-vegetable hash and watercress; many local California-style restaurants also often incorporate a pan-Asian edge into recipes.

Sears Fine Food 439 Powell St at Post, Union Square ☎ 415 986 0700; map pp.40–41. This civic legend dates back to pre-World War II San Francisco, and local old-timers say its signature breakfast dish – 18 little Swedish pancakes for $9.50, over 10,000 of which are made daily – hasn't changed at all over the decades. Throngs of people queue up outside to get in; if this is the case, try sneaking by to find a spot at one of the dining counters. Come evening, basics like pasta, steak and fish are a bit pricier ($14–29). Amber chairs and tiled flooring add to the ambience. Daily 6.30am–10pm.

Taylor's Automatic Refresher 1 Ferry Building, Embarcadero ☎ 866 328 3663; map pp.40–41. The immense alfresco dining area at this fancified, yet inexpensive burger stand off the Embarcadero pedestrian path is a major draw on sunny afternoons, along with the touted burgers, sweet-potato fries and super-thick milkshakes. Lines form early for lunch, so consider choosing an off-peak time to visit. Daily 10.30am–9pm.

CALIFORNIA CUISINE

Bix 56 Gold St at Montgomery, Jackson Square ☎ 415 433 6300; map pp.40–41. Hidden on a narrow back-street lined with 160-year-old brick buildings, this dimly lit bar-restaurant has a touch of Deco-inspired glamour in its sophisticated furnishings. The bar – helmed by avuncular men in white jackets and bow ties – is a popular after-work destination, while diners slip into the bi-level, columned supper club to enjoy platters of spice-braised pork shoulder and lobster spaghetti ($30–40) while taking in live jazz. Mon, Tues & Sun 5.30–9.30pm, Wed 5.30–10pm, Thurs & Sat 5.30–10.30pm, Fri 11.30am–2pm & 5.30–10.30pm.

Millennium Hotel California, 580 Geary St at Jones, Union Square ☎ 415 345 3900; map pp.40–41. Catering to San Francisco's sizeable contingent of vegetarians and vegans, this somewhat pricey standby takes kitchen creativity to meat-free heights by using obscure ingredients such as *sambal*, *huitlacoche* and *papazul*. The menu changes frequently – as often as daily – so one night's semolina cake ($23) could be sweet soy and chilli-glazed tempeh ($24) the next. The dark wood-panelled decor is romantic, while the crowd varies from well-dressed opera buffs to young idealists out for a splurge. Mon–Thurs & Sun 5.30–9.30pm, Fri & Sat 5.30–10.30pm.

CHINESE

Great Eastern 649 Jackson St at Kearny, Chinatown ☎ 415 986 2500; map pp.40–41. Behind an impressive pagoda facade and a huge chandelier swinging in the picture window, this elegant, traditional and pricey Chinese restaurant serves geoduck clams and sauteed squab with Chinese broccoli; it's also known for dim sum. Mains hover between $15–22. Daily 10am–1am.

House of Nanking 919 Kearny St at Jackson, Chinatown ☎ 415 421 1429; map pp.40–41. With its red-framed windows and clanking metal cafeteria chairs, this snug spot on the easternmost flank of Chinatown has become a local legend. The line is often long but usually moves quickly; once inside, expect a good and underpriced meal, curt service and the constant clatter of saucepans from the open kitchen. Mon–Fri 11am–10pm, Sat noon–10pm, Sun noon–9pm.

★ **Jai Yun** 680 Clay St at Kearny, Chinatown ☎ 415 981 7438; map pp.40–41. If you're feeling adventurous, book a table at this hotspot, where Chef Nei' Chia Ji tends not to let diners know what they'll be eating until countless northern Chinese dishes appear under their noses. Dinner menus start at $55, and be aware that the chef and staff don't speak much English. Reservations required; cash only. Mon–Wed & Fri–Sun 11am–2pm & 6.30–9.30pm.

Louie's Dim Sum 1236 Stockton St at Pacific, Chinatown ☎ 415 989 8380; map p.59. This tiny shop has glistening, pearly dumplings arranged in vast metal trays before you, and although the variety's limited, they're all very cheap and delicious. There's a small counter for dining in, but most customers take their orders to go. Call for hours.

R&G Lounge 631 Kearny St at Commercial, Chinatown ☎ 415 982 7877; map pp.40–41. Behind frosted windows looms this enormous Hong Kong-style restaurant that draws a diverse crowd. Platters of food (most $14–16) are presented family-style, and there's a heavy bias towards seafood. Call a day ahead to order the house special: a whole chicken hollowed out, stuffed with sticky rice, and deep fried. Daily 11.30am–9.30pm.

Sam Wo 813 Washington St at Grant, Chinatown ☎ 415 982 0596; map pp.40–41. An ever-popular late-night spot where Kerouac, Ginsberg and associates used to hold

9

TOP SAN FRANCISCO RESTAURANTS BY CUISINE

ASIAN
Borobudur Union Square. See p.146
Brothers Korean BBQ Inner Richmond. See p.169
Bushi-tei Japantown. See p.167
Jai Yun Chinatown. See p.141
Le Colonial Union Square. See p.146
Mandalay Inner Richmond. See p.170
Marnee Thai Inner Sunset. See p.170
Sebo Hayes Valley. See p.166
The Slanted Door Embarcadero. See p.146
Spices! Inner Richmond. See p.168

BREAKFAST/BRUNCH
Boogaloos Mission. See p.157
Dottie's True Blue Cafe Tenderloin. See p.154
Just for You Potrero Hill. See p.157
Pat's Cafe North Beach. See p.148
Zazie Cole Valley. See p.165

BAKERIES
Arizmendi Inner Sunset. See p.139
Italian French Baking North Beach. See p.137
La Victoria Mission. See p.138
Tartine Bakery & Cafe Mission. See p.139
Wing Lee Bakery Inner Richmond. See p.140

BURGERS
Burgermeister Cole Valley. See p.164
Custom Burger South of Market. See p.154
Mo's Grill North Beach. See p.146
Pearl's Deluxe Burgers Union Square. See p.140
Taylor's Automatic Refresher Embarcadero.
   See p.141

BURRITOS
El Burrito Express Western Addition. See p.166
Gordo Taqueria Inner Sunset. See p.169
La Espiga de Oro Mission. See p.161
Papalote Mission. See p.162
Taqueria El Castillito Civic Center. See p.155

CALIFORNIA
Frascati Russian Hill. See p.148
Greens Fort Mason Center. See p.151
Jardinière Hayes Valley. See p.164
Nopa Western Addition. See p.165
Pizzetta 211 Outer Richmond. See p.168

COFFEE
See box, p.137

DESSERT
Ghirardelli Ice Cream and Chocolate Caffe
   Fisherman's Wharf. See p.138
La Copa Loca Mission. See p.138
Mission Pie Mission. See p.139
Mitchell's Ice Cream Mission. See p.139
Yasukochi's Sweet Stop Japantown.
   See p.139

FRENCH
Bistro Aix Marina. See p.152
Café Jacqueline North Beach. See p.148
Chapeau! Inner Richmond. See p.168
La Folie Russian Hill. See p.148
Le P'tit Laurent Glen Park. See p.158

---

court. Walk through the kitchen and up the slim stairs to reach the dining room, to which cheap plates of greasy food are hoisted via dumbwaiter. Eat here more for the experience – including famously churlish service – rather than the serviceable (at best) food. Daily 11am–3am.
Yee's 1131 Grant Ave at Pacific, Chinatown ☎415 576 1818; map p.59. Chinatown's answer to a deli, since the food is priced by weight. The menu scrawled on the wall is only in Chinese, but the staff is usually happy to translate. The inexpensive slabs of suckling pig on the lunch counter are particularly succulent, as is the crunchy sweet-and-sour pork. Eat in or take away. Call for hours.

EASTERN EUROPEAN
Cafe Prague 424 Merchant St at Battery, Financial District ☎415 627 7464; map pp.40–41. With goulash,

strudel and several soups ($8–12) on offer, this atmospheric bistro in the shadow of the Transamerica Pyramid exudes warmth the moment you walk in the door. The few outdoor tables just off the alley sidewalk make a nice spot to sip a Czech beer. Mon–Thurs 11am–11pm, Fri & Sat 11am–midnight, Sun 5–10pm.

ECLECTIC
Boulette's Larder 1 Ferry Building, Embarcadero ☎415 399 1155; map pp.40–41. Unique even by Ferry Building standards, this combination shop/restaurant features a lunch menu that draws from a number of culinary cultures; on any given day, you might choose between Sicilian artichoke soup and poached Alaskan black cod ($12–22). Mon–Fri 8–10.30am & 11.30am–2.30pm, Sun brunch 10am–2.30pm.

ITALIAN
Acquerello Russian Hill. See p.148
Café Altano Hayes Valley. See p.166
Delfina Mission. See p.160
Sociale Presidio Heights. See p.152
Trattoria Contadina North Beach. See p.149

LATE-NIGHT
Great Eastern Chinatown. See p.141
Grubstake Polk Gulch. See p.156
Hog & Rocks Mission. See p.158
Liverpool Lil's Cow Hollow. See p.151
Taqueria Can-cún Mission. See p.162

MEDITERRANEAN/MIDDLE EASTERN
Aziza Outer Richmond. See p.169
Goood Frikin Chicken Mission. See p.161
Kokkari Financial District. See p.145
Sunrise Deli Outer Sunset. See p.140
Troya Inner Richmond. See p.169

NEIGHBOURHOOD PLACES
Baker Street Bistro Cow Hollow. See p.152
Bambino's Ristorante Cole Valley. See p.165
Chenery Park Glen Park. See p.157
Liberty Cafe Bernal Heights. See p.157
Ristorante Ideale North Beach. See p.149

PIZZA
Gialina Glen Park. See p.160
Little Star Pizza Western Addition. See p.166
Serrano's Mission. See p.160
Tommaso's North Beach. See p.149
Tony's Pizza Napoletana North Beach. See p.149

SANDWICHES
Cheese Steak Shop Western Addition. See p.139
Ike's Place Castro. See p.138
M & L Market Castro. See p.139
Molinari North Beach. See p.137
Saigon Sandwich Tenderloin. See p.138

SEAFOOD
Anchor Oyster Bar Castro. See p.162
Hog Island Oyster Co. Embarcadero. See p.145
Pacific Café Outer Richmond. See p.170
Swan Oyster Depot Russian Hill. See p.150
Woodhouse Fish Company Castro. See p.163

SOUTH ASIAN
Dosa Mission. See p.163
India Clay Oven Outer Richmond. See p.170
Little Nepal Bernal Heights. See p.163
Shalimar Tenderloin. See p.156
Zante Mission. See p.163

VEGETARIAN
Golden Era Tenderloin. See p.156
Greens Fort Mason Center. See p.151
Herbivore Western Addition. See p.165
Millennium Theater District. See p.141
My Tofu House Inner Richmond. See p.169

WHEN SOMEONE ELSE IS PAYING...
Alexander's Steakhouse South of Market. See p.153
Ame South of Market. See p.155
Gary Danko Fisherman's Wharf. See p.151
Masa's Union Square. See below
Michael Mina Financial District. See p.140

FRENCH
Café Claude 7 Claude Lane at Bush, Union Square ☎415 392 3505; map pp.40–41. Down a tight alley, this impossibly Parisian restaurant features several outdoor tables under umbrellas, heavily accented waiters and live jazz Thurs–Sat evenings. Recommended dishes include the steak tartare ($15) and *porc au miel* (pork filet with honey cream sauce, $20). Mon–Sat 11.30am–10.30pm, Sun 5.30–10.30pm.

Cafe de la Presse 342 Grant Ave at Bush, Union Square ☎415 398 2680; map pp.40–41. An achingly romantic spot set just outside Chinatown Gate, with enormous mirrors and French art enlivening ochre and terracotta walls. Below the gracefully vaulted ceiling, a mix of locals and international visitors enjoy a variety of delightful seafood dishes (including an excellent ahi steak), as well as heavier fare such as leg of lamb with flageolet beans.

There's brunch from 11.30am on weekends. Mains $20–36. Mon–Thurs 7.30–10am, 11.30am–2.30pm & 5.30–9.30pm; Fri 7.30–10am, 11.30am–2.30pm & 5.30–10pm; Sat & Sun 8am–4pm & 5.30–10pm.

Fleur de Lys 777 Sutter St at Jones, Union Square ☎415 673 7779; map pp.40–41. An evening enjoying what is arguably San Francisco's most elegant dining experience will set you back a kingly sum (plan on parting with at least $100 per person), but the superb service, attention to detail and, most importantly, stunning food at this longtime local favourite will help you forget the cost. Four prix-fixe options (including a vegetarian one) are available to enjoy amidst the tented, *Moulin Rouge*-inspired surroundings. Tues–Thurs 6–9.30pm, Fri 5.30–10.30pm, Sat 5–10.30pm.

Masa's 648 Bush St at Stockton, Union Square ☎415 989 7154; map pp.40–41. An intimate, exclusive

9

BEST BITES AT FERRY BUILDING MARKETPLACE

If you want to graze on the go, there's nowhere better for a quick bite Downtown than the **Ferry Building Marketplace** (map pp.40–41). If it's not a market day, there are still plenty of appealing eateries inside selling gourmet treats, including the selected favourites listed below. These establishments are all inexpensive (usually $10 and under); for further details, visit ⓦferrybuildingmarketplace.com.

Ciao Bella Gelato ☎415 834 9330. California outpost of the New York gelato and sorbet company, with a selection of about three dozen varieties among more than two hundred rotating flavours. Try one of the offbeat gelato concoctions (red bean, rum raisin) or, if it's available, the passion fruit sorbet. Take-away pints are available. Mon–Sat 11am–6pm, Sun 11am–5pm.

Cowgirl Creamery's Artisan Cheese Shop ☎415 362 9354. A cheese-lovers' heaven, with piles of an astonishingly wide selection of cheese from producers in the US, Canada and all over Europe. A number of Cowgirl's own creations (made in nearby Point Reyes Station) are also on offer. Mon–Fri 10am–7pm, Sat 8am–6pm, Sun 10am–5pm.

Golden Gate Meat Company ☎415 983 7800. Simple, austere pulled pork and barbecue sandwiches ($6–7) are the stars at this butcher shop and charcuterie; for about the same price, you can also get yourself a pot pie or small rotisserie chicken. Mon–Fri 6.30am–7pm, Sat 7am–5.30pm.

Imperial Tea Court ☎415 544 9830. Drop into this hideaway – complete with black granite counter and dragon sofa – to sit and sip a hot cup of tea. There are over fifty different varieties to choose from, including Jade Fire and Dragon Whiskers, alongside more everyday blends like green, black or herbal. Mon–Fri 10am–6.30pm, Sat 8.30am–6.30pm, Sun 11am–6pm.

Out the Door ☎415 321 3740. Casual, take-out outpost of adjacent Vietnamese legend, *The Slanted Door* (see p.146). It's a much cheaper and quicker option, with a focus on Vietnamese street food such as sandwiches and steamed buns. Minimal counter seating is available, as are take-away dinner boxes. Mon–Fri 10am–6pm, Sat 8.30am–5pm.

Recchiuti Confections ☎415 834 9494. Local artisanal chocolatier, less well known than *Ghirardelli* but of much higher quality. A 16-piece of *fleur de sel* caramels costs $22, while single samples cost about $1.75. Wickedly delicious marshmallows and brownies are also for sale. Mon–Fri 10am–7pm, Sat 8am–6pm, Sun 10am–5pm.

restaurant serving five-star meals in a hushed, white-curtained dining room; prix fixe menus range from $95 to $150. Chef Gregory Short is a veteran of the Napa Valley legend *French Laundry* and has tweaked the menu by pumping up its modern American touches. Reservations recommended; jackets required. Tues–Sat 5.30–9.30pm.

Plouf 40 Belden Place at Bush, Financial District ☎415 986 6491; map pp.40–41. Known for mussels served by the bowlful, this expensive bistro is situated on a busy pedestrian alley and features plenty of alfresco seating. The banana profiteroles served with warm chocolate and caramel sauce are a dessert crowd-pleaser. Mon–Thurs 11.30am–3pm & 5.30–10pm, Fri 11.30am–3pm & 5.30–11pm, Sat 5.30–11pm.

GERMAN

Schroeder's 240 Front St at California, Financial District ☎415 421 4778; map pp.40–41. One of San Francisco's oldest restaurants – it's occupied various locations around town since 1893 – *Schroeder's* continues to draw hearty eaters looking to wolf down sausage platters, ham hocks and, of course, schnitzel; particularly brave souls can order a two-litre boot of German pilsner. Dance off all those calories by timing your visit during one of the restaurant's live polka band performances. Most

dinner mains range from $18–27. Mon–Thurs 11am–9.30pm, Fri 11am–11pm, Sat 4.30–10pm.

ITALIAN

Brindisi Cucina di Mare 88 Belden Place at Pine, Financial District ☎415 593 8000; map pp.40–41. Serving everything from margherita pizza ($11) to more adventurous choices like grilled, pancetta-wrapped quail ($18), this affordable enclave specializes in Pugliese fare. In the unlikely event it's a warm evening, ask for an outdoor table on Belden Place. Mon–Fri 11.30am–2.30pm & 5.30–10pm, Sat 5.30–10pm.

Chiaroscuro 550 Washington St at Montgomery, Financial District ☎415 362 6012; map pp.40–41. This petite eatery sits opposite the Transamerica Pyramid, its industrial-chic interior outfitted with iron arches and pillow-topped concrete seating. The open kitchen produces some of the city's finest gnocchi. Expect to shell out over $20 for a main course. Mon–Thurs 11.30am–2.30pm & 5.30–9.30pm, Fri 11.30am–2.30pm & 5.30–10.30pm, Sat 5.30–10.30pm.

Perbacco 230 California St at Front, Financial District ☎415 955 0663; map pp.40–41. Filling a Downtown void, *Perbacco's* northern Italian cooking has won legions of fans in recent years. The delicate breadsticks are uncommonly delicious, while main courses such as beef short rib *stracotto*

($23) are equally loved by patrons lining the lengthy, narrow room. Mon–Fri 11.30am–10pm, Sat 5.30–10pm.

JAPANESE

Delica 1 Ferry Building, Embarcadero ☎ 415 834 0344; map pp.40–41. This Japanese delicatessen and sushi bar turns the traditional deli concept upside down by offering a variety of small dishes designed to be eaten together. Moderately priced staples such as bento boxes and miso soup are available alongside crab-cream croquettes and sushi rolls. Deli Mon–Fri 10am–6.30pm, Sat 9am–6.30pm, Sun 11am–5pm; sushi bar Mon–Fri 4–9.30pm, Sat 3–9.30pm.

Hana Zen 115 Cyril Magnin St at Ellis, Union Square ☎ 415 421 2101; map pp.40–41. Set in the shadows of the area's high-rise hotels, this popular Japanese grill is best known for its Yakitori skewers – choose from over two dozen, including *sunagimo* (chicken gizzard) and asparagus *maki*; prices range from $5.50 to $12 for a pair. The full bar serves sake and *soju* cocktails. Mon–Thurs & Sun 11.30am–midnight, Fri & Sat 11.30–1am.

Sanraku 704 Sutter St at Taylor, Union Square ☎ 415 771 0803; map pp.40–41. Decorated simply, this sushi purveyor also specializes in favourites such as chicken teriyaki ($14) and tempura prawns ($11). It's one of the more affordable Japanese places in this part of town, and conveniently, one of the best. Branch: 101 Fourth St at Mission (Metreon), South of Market (☎ 415 369 6166). Mon–Sat 11am–10pm, Sun 4–10pm.

MEDITERRANEAN/MIDDLE EASTERN

Baladie 337 Kearny St at Bush, Financial District ☎ 415 989 6629; map pp.40–41. Small, mostly take-out spot on the western edge of the Financial District that's short on plush decor but dishes out good, cheap Med staples like lentil soup and *shawarma*. The spinach pie ($4.50) is a solid choice. Mon–Fri 11am–6pm.

★ **Kokkari** 200 Jackson St at Front, Jackson Square ☎ 415 981 0983; map pp.40–41. Consistently recognized as the top Greek restaurant in town, *Kokkari* relies on Hellenic staples like lamb and aubergine (eggplant), served separately or cooked together in a marvellous moussaka ($21.75). A huge fireplace heats two bedazzling dining rooms decorated with Oriental rugs and goatskin lampshades, leaving the whole place cosy despite its vast dimensions. Mon–Thurs 11.30am–2.30pm & 5.30–10pm, Fri 11.30am–2.30pm & 5.30–11pm, Sat 5–11pm, Sun 5–10pm.

MEXICAN

Andalé 845 Market St at Fifth (San Francisco Centre), Union Square ☎ 415 243 8700; map pp.84–85. Granted, this walk-up counter couldn't be set in a more inauthentic spot – deep in the dimly lit, underground food court of a major shopping centre – but *Andalé*'s fresh Cal-Mex fare is

nobody's punchline. Burritos and plate meals alike are equally special here, even if they cost a few dollars more than most other taquerias in town. Mon–Thurs 10am–9pm, Fri & Sat 10am–10pm, Sun 10am–8pm.

PAN-ASIAN

Anzu Hotel Nikko, 222 Mason St at Ellis, Union Square ☎ 415 394 1100; map pp.40–41. Though it's situated just off a hotel lobby, *Anzu* manages to pull in locals with a number of smoked, tea-spiced meat and fish main courses ($22–38). Thrill-seekers will want to try the Rock ($16) – thinly sliced Wagyu beef sirloin cooked tableside on a sizzling Japanese stone. Sushi is available on the lunch menu, and there's a Sun jazz brunch (10am–2pm). Daily 11am–2.30pm & 5–10pm.

Silks Mandarin Oriental Hotel, 222 Sansome St at Pine, Financial District ☎ 415 986 2020; map pp.40–41. Another Downtown hotel restaurant worth a visit, if you've got the cash and don't mind the subdued – if elegant – atmosphere. The menu's rich with cross-cultural inventions, such as pan-seared onaga snapper with kimchee red beans ($28). Mon breakfast 6.30–10.30am, lunch 11.30am–2pm; Tues–Fri breakfast 6.30–10.30am, lunch 11.30am–2pm, dinner 6–9pm; Sat breakfast 7.30–11am, dinner 6–9pm; Sun breakfast 7.30–11am, brunch 11am–3pm.

SEAFOOD

Farallon 450 Post St at Mason, Union Square ☎ 415 956 6969; map pp.40–41. "Coastal cuisine" (aka seafood) is prepared and served with great fanfare at this local (and quite expensive) notable, although the jellyfish-inspired decor with its dangling luminescent mobiles may not float every visitor's boat. Nonetheless, the food is always excellent and surprising – the champagne-steamed clams are light and tender, while the mackerel tartare and tuna carpaccio are flavour-packed appetizers. Mon–Thurs 5.30–9.30pm, Fri & Sat 5.30–10pm, Sun 5–9.30pm.

Hog Island Oyster Co. 1 Ferry Building, Embarcadero ☎ 415 391 7117; map pp.40–41. This Ferry Building outpost of the Tomales Bay (Marin County) farm hosts mollusc devotees who sit elbow-to-elbow at the wrap-around granite bar, where the lists of oysters, wines and beers are equally impressive. It's about $17 for six oysters, and around $30 for a dozen. The creamy oyster stew ($12) is a perennial hit. Mon–Fri 11.30am–8pm, Sat & Sun 11am–6pm.

Sam's Grill 374 Bush St at Belden, Financial District ☎ 415 421 0594; map pp.40–41. The city's oldest fish house (dating back in various incarnations to 1867), Sam's is known for fresh, moderately priced seafood and cheerfully abrupt service from waiters who look like they helped originally open the place. The onion rings are crunchy and buttery, and there's a mean Hang Town Fry (essentially a bacon/oyster omelette) on the menu for $22. Mon–Fri 11am–9pm.

9

Tadich Grill 240 California St at Front, Financial District ☎ 415 391 1849; map pp.40–41. A Downtown classic originally opened as a coffee stand by three Croatian brothers during the Gold Rush. Its popularity hasn't waned with the decades, and today it's half-diner/half-gentleman's club, with a seasoned group of waiters nearly as stiff as their white jackets. Eat at the endlessly long bar or pull into one of the dark-panelled booths. Most main courses are over $20. Mon–Sat 11am–9.30pm.

SOUTHEAST ASIAN

★ **Borobudur** 700 Post St at Jones, Union Square ☎ 415 775 1512; map pp.40–41. Start with an order of *roti prata* (flaky fried bread) and curry dipping sauce at this Indonesian powerhouse, and you may be hooked for life. The affordable, vegetarian-friendly menu fuses Indian and Thai influences with often extraordinary results – the *kari sayuran* (assorted vegetables in coconut curry sauce) is particularly delicious. Mains $9–18. Mon–Thurs 11.30am–10pm, Fri & Sat 11.30am–11pm, Sun 1–10pm.

★ **Le Colonial** 20 Cosmo Place at Taylor, Union Square ☎ 415 931 3600; map pp.40–41. Upscale Vietnamese dining with a quiet French influence. Le Colonial boasts lush, 1920s-themed dining quarters decked out with tile floors, palm fronds and ceiling fans, while the upstairs lounge is a salon with rattan couches and faded rugs. Exquisitely seasoned appetizers such as tender pork ribs and lettuce-wrapped fried duck rolls are worth a visit alone. Mains over $30. Mon–Wed 5.30–10pm, Thurs & Fri 5.30–11pm, Sat 11.30am–2.30pm & 5.30–11pm, Sun 11.30am–2.30pm & 5.30–10pm.

Osha Thai 4 Embarcadero Center, Financial District ☎ 415 788 6742; map pp.40–41. This hyper-designed eatery is perhaps the *least* stylish among the local chain's seven restaurants scattered around town. Highlights on the extensive menu include Bangkok roti (green curry with beef) and "Osha's Sea" (a seafood melange), and overall the place provides an affordable Southeast Asian option if you're Downtown. Daily 11am–11pm.

The Slanted Door 1 Ferry Building, Embarcadero ☎ 415 861 8032; map pp.40–41. Hosting perennial crowds in his signature bayside space, chef Charles Phan creates a daily menu that's light French-Vietnamese; there's a raw bar and several deliciously fragrant chicken dishes, and the tea list is impressively diverse. Prix fixes are available at both lunch ($42) and dinner ($48). Book a reservation well in advance. Mon–Sat 11am–2.30pm & 5.30–10pm, Sun 11.30am–3pm & 5.30–10pm.

SPANISH

Bocadillos 710 Montgomery St at Jackson, Jackson Square ☎ 415 982 2622; map pp.40–41. At this vibrant restaurant on the edge of North Beach, the *bocadillos*

themselves – tiny, Spanish-style sandwiches ($6) with serrano ham, lamb or Catalan sausage wedged between round buns – are outstanding; the menu gets even more clever with items such as chilled prawns with *huevos diablo* (devilled eggs). Everything is moderately priced. Mon–Wed 7am–10pm, Thurs & Fri 7am–10.30pm, Sat 5–10.30pm.

NORTH BEACH AND THE HILLS

The city's Italian enclave, North Beach, presents the inevitable roster of terrific pasta houses, bakeries, cafés and delis, while in adjacent Russian Hill, you'll find a notable cache of top French and seafood restaurants, as well as a few Italian spots that rival the more celebrated places in North Beach. This area is also home to a pair of fun fondue spots, *Melt!* and *The Matterhorn*.

AMERICAN

Fog City Diner 1300 Battery St at Greenwich, Northeast Waterfront ☎ 415 982 2000; map p.56. It's no longer the prime destination that it was portrayed in 1980s credit card commercials, but this bay-adjacent spot still woos plenty of people into its singular, converted railcar setting. The kitchen's leftfield take on comfort food – beef pot roast with sweet onion jam ($20), garlic *orecchiette* pasta ($17) – offers something for everyone. Brunch on weekends. Mon–Thurs 11.30am–10pm, Fri 11.30am–11pm, Sat 10.30am–11pm, Sun 10.30am–10pm.

Harris' 2100 Van Ness Ave at Pacific, Russian Hill ☎ 415 673 188; map p.56. Proudly old-fashioned, *Harris'* is one of the premier steakhouses in San Francisco. The staff is warm and welcoming (if overly attentive at times), as is the decor: padded chairs, comfy leather booths, thick velvet curtains. There's practically every cut of beef imaginable on the menu – from filet mignon to ribeye (both $45) – and all are buttery and tender. Mon–Fri 5.30–9.30pm, Sat & Sun 5–10pm.

Luella 1896 Hyde St at Green, Russian Hill ☎ 415 674 4343; map p.56. This cosy, family-run restaurant on Russian Hill is decked out in soothing mint green with crisp white tablecloths, while the modern American food is inventive and tasty. The Coca Cola-braised pork shoulder ($21) is a hit whenever it appears on the frequently changing menu. Mon–Sat 5.30–10pm, Sun 5–9pm.

Mama's 1701 Stockton St at Filbert, North Beach ☎ 415 362 6421; map p.59. Order first, then wait to be seated at this inexpensive, immensely popular diner on a corner across from Washington Square. There's always a wait to get in – bring extra patience if you happen to come on a weekend – but the fine "momelettes" and cheery staff (trained to subtly dissuade solo dining, due to limited table space) are usually worth it. Tues–Sun 8am–3pm.

Mo's Grill 1322 Grant Ave at Vallejo, North Beach ☎ 415 788 3779; map p.59. Exclusively cooking Angus beef over

9

a volcanic rock grill, this no-frills shop offers one of San Francisco's best (and chunkiest) hamburgers. The house fries are also noteworthy, while excellent breakfasts are available until mid-afternoon each day. Burgers are about $10; cash only. Mon–Thurs & Sun 9am–10.30pm, Fri & Sat 9am–11.30pm.

Pat's Cafe 2330 Taylor St at Chestnut, North Beach ☎ 415 776 8735; map p.56. This eminently inviting spot is bright and airy, with plenty of wall space devoted to local photography and original artwork. Still, the charming decor doesn't overshadow the delicious, affordable and occasionally rich food – the peppery home fries and banana granola pancakes are especially recommended for morning visitors. Service is often amiably chatty. Mon, Tues & Sun 7.30am–2.30pm; Wed & Thurs 7.30am–2.30pm & 5.30–9pm, Fri & Sat 7.30am–2.30pm & 5.30–10pm.

Pier 23 Cafe Pier 23, Embarcadero ☎ 415 362 5125; map p.56. Sit on this roadhouse's heated deck and enjoy casual seafood and sandwiches along with immediate bay views. There's live music most nights, ranging from jazz to reggae and salsa, and brunch on weekends. Mon–Fri 11.30am–10pm, Sat 10am–10pm, Sun 10am–8pm.

CALIFORNIA CUISINE

Coi 373 Broadway at Montgomery, North Beach ☎ 415 393 9000; map p.56. Pronounced "kwah", this lavish spot stands apart for its adventurous, eleven-course prix-fixe tasting menu ($145) that changes daily. It's one of the most expensive restaurants in the city, and that's no small feat; for cut-rate prices, try the à la carte menu in the adjacent lounge. The 32-seat dining room is padded with calm earth tones and couldn't contrast more with the glut of obstreperous strip clubs down the block. Tues–Fri 6–10pm, Sat 5.30–10pm.

★ **Frascati** 1901 Hyde St at Green, Russian Hill ☎ 415 928 1406; map p.56. Surprisingly intimate considering its prime corner location, this vividly romantic, bi-level bistro has transformed from neighbourhood secret to destination restaurant. It's no wonder, given the menu's uniquely paired mains that still retain a level of comfort – look no further than the maple leaf duck breast with herb *spaetzle* and huckleberry sauce ($26). The wine list is always among the most impressive in town, to boot. Mon–Sat 5.30–9.45pm, Sun 5.30–9pm.

FRENCH

Café Jacqueline 1454 Grant Ave at Union, North Beach ☎ 415 981 5565; map p.59. A romantic, candlelit gourmet experience in an airy dining room that feels like a French country cottage. The menu here is entirely made up of chef-owner Jacqueline Margulis' signature enormous soufflés (well over $20), both savoury and sweet; crab and chocolate are top picks. Since every dish is made to order, plan on making an evening of it. Wed–Sun 5.30–11pm.

★ **La Folie** 2316 Polk St at Green, Russian Hill ☎ 415 776 5577; map p.56. Magnificent Provençal food served without attitude or pretension. There are three different five-course prix-fixe options to choose from, steeply priced ($75–95) but certainly worth it if you fancy a gourmet treat. Regular dishes include frogs' legs as an appetizer, roti of quail and squab as a main course and a wonderful chocolate fondant for dessert. Mon–Sat 5.30–10.30pm.

ITALIAN

Acquerello 1722 Sacramento St at Polk, Russian Hill ☎ 415 567 5432; map p.59. Serving Italian fare unlike anything you'll find over the hill in North Beach, this celebrated, terracotta-toned restaurant welcomes polished crowds into its wood-beamed dining room, which used to serve as a chapel. *Acquerello*'s menu is full of surprises (lobster panzerotti, seared scallops with sugar pie pumpkin), and you can choose between three prix-fixe menus ($64–90). The service, led by co-owner (and Italian wine expert) Giancarlo Paterlini, is peerless. Tues–Sat 5.30–9.30pm.

★ **Café Divine** 1600 Stockton St at Union, North Beach ☎ 415 986 3414; map p.59. Across from Washington Square, this invitingly airy, bistro-inspired café (high ceilings, spindly golden chandeliers, tile flooring) does breakfast, lunch and dinner well – a rarity in this neighbourhood of delis and swanky eateries. The menu's casual and often light, with the six varieties of pizzetta ($11–14) the most popular items here. Outdoor tables flank the corner space along the sidewalks and provide excellent people-watching opportunities. Daily 9am–10pm.

Da Flora 701 Columbus Ave at Filbert, North Beach ☎ 415 981 4664; map p.56. This hopelessly romantic restaurant on North Beach's main artery has been feted as having the neighbourhood's best pasta, and one taste of its trademark sweet potato gnocchi only furthers the claim. Most items on the handwritten menu are distinctly Venetian, and despite all the plaudits, prices remain remarkably reasonable. Tues–Sat 6–9.30pm.

Il Pollaio 555 Columbus Ave at Union, North Beach ☎ 415 362 7727; map p.59. This moderately priced chicken specialist also roasts a few other meats (beef, pork, rabbit, lamb), but it's the perfectly crisped and seasoned poultry that keeps North Beach locals coming back. Mon–Sat 11.30am–9pm.

L'Osteria del Forno 519 Columbus Ave at Green, North Beach ☎ 415 982 1124; map p.59. A postage stamp-sized nook, *L'Osteria del Forno* is a humble refuge from the gaudy tourist traps right across Columbus Ave. The menu's short and driven by whatever's freshest at the market, although the eight or so *focaccine* sandwiches ($6–7) are a standby. Reservations aren't taken, so a wait may be inevitable even at off-peak times. Cash only. Mon, Wed, Thurs & Sun 11.30am–10pm; Fri & Sat 11.30am–10.30pm.

Ristorante Ideale 1309 Grant Ave at Vallejo, North Beach ☎415 391 4129; map p.59. A plate of ravioli is your wisest choice here, although the thin-crust pizzas (which work well as appetizers) are also a sharp move. It's a festive, distinctly Roman dining experience, all the way down to the occasionally lazy service. Mains $16–26. Mon–Thurs 5.30–10.30pm, Fri & Sat 5.30–11pm, Sun 5–10pm.

Ristorante Milano 1448 Pacific Ave at Hyde, Russian Hill ☎415 673 2961; map p.56. It's worth trundling a few blocks off the beaten path for this restaurant's homey service, excellent gnocchi ($17) and delectable tiramisù ($7.50). Italian wines outnumber California varietals by a comfortable margin on the extensive wine list. Mon–Thurs 5.30–10pm, Fri & Sat 5.30–10.30pm, Sun 5–10pm.

Sodini's 510 Green St at Grant, North Beach ☎415 291 0499; map p.59. Light on pretence and heavy on saucy, home-style plates of pasta (around $15), this staple captures the ebullient spirit of North Beach as well as any restaurant in the neighbourhood. Depending on your server, you may or may not get called "hon" or "dear", but it's a near-certainty you'll hear something by Louis Prima or Dean Martin at some point. Reservations not accepted. Mon–Fri 5–10pm, Sat 11.30am–11pm, Sun 11.30–10pm.

Tommaso's 1042 Kearny St at Pacific, North Beach ☎415 398 9696; map p.59. Claiming to be the West Coast birthplace of the wood-fired pizza oven, this North Beach stalwart – marooned on a semi-seedy block near the edge of the district – hasn't lost a step in popularity since opening in 1935 as *Lupo's*. And for good reason: The thin-crust pizzas ($21–27 for a 15-inch large) are sublime, while the seven-layer lasagne ($16) is wonderfully gooey. Expect to wait for a table in the downstairs dining room, as reservations aren't taken. Tues–Sat 5–10.30pm, Sun 4–9.30pm.

★ **Tony's Pizza Napoletana** 1570 Stockton St at Union, North Beach ☎415 835 9888; map p.59. World Pizza Cup champion Tony Gemignani's corner pizzeria bakes up to six hundred pizzas in several styles daily, from his prized, gossamer-thin-crusted Margherita ($19; only 73 made each day) to an extra-saucy New Jersey version. Service is remarkably attentive, and it's best to sit near the brick oven to watch the chefs in action. Wed–Sun noon–11pm.

Trattoria Contadina 1800 Mason St at Union, North Beach ☎415 982 5728; map p.56. Family-owned, with white cloth-swathed tables and photograph-covered walls, warm and charming *Trattoria Contadina* continues to cater to the local Italian-American community. The Powell-Mason cable car will drop you off a few steps from the front door; once seated, try the *fusilli* pasta with sautéed chicken ($18). Daily 5–9.30pm.

JAPANESE

Sushi Groove 1916 Hyde St at Green, Russian Hill ☎415 440 1905; map p.56. Self-consciously stylish restaurant serving inventive and original maki rolls, a sprinkling of Pan-Asian fusion dishes and furiously strong sake martinis. The two downsides are the sometimes sloppy service and the tiny size of the place, which usually translates into long waits for seating. Expect to spend $20–30 for a full meal. Branch: 1516 Folsom St at 11th, South of Market (☎415 503 1950). Mon–Thurs & Sun 5.30–10pm, Fri & Sat 5.30–10.30pm.

Sushi on North Beach 745 Columbus Ave at Filbert, North Beach ☎415 788 8050; map p.56. Cosy, moderately priced place on upper Columbus Ave where you might get a spirited greeting from the whole staff when you step in. Elegantly presented varieties of raw fish, with an impressive list of sakes to match; lunch specials are a particularly good bargain. Mon–Thurs 11.30am–1.30pm & 5–9pm, Fri 11.30am–1.30pm & 5–10pm, Sat 5–10pm, Sun 4.30–9pm.

LATIN AMERICAN

Peña Pachamama 1630 Powell St at Green, North Beach ☎415 646 0018; map p.59. An uncommon find in the city's Italian quarter: organically prepared Bolivian food. Nibble on tapas like *yuca frita* or dive headlong into a full plate of *silpancho* (flattened beef with pico de gallo, fried egg and rice) while taking in a live music performance in the Carnaval-like atmosphere. Nothing on the menu's over $20. Wed–Sun from 5.30pm; closing time varies nightly depending on performance.

MEDITERRANEAN/MIDDLE EASTERN

Helmand Palace 2424 Van Ness Ave at Green, Russian Hill ☎415 345 0072; map p.56. The menu at this popular Afghani restaurant (formerly owned by the brother of Premier Hamid Karzai) is filled with tangy and spicy Afghani staples ($14–23) – try the *kaddo* (caramelized pumpkin on a bed of yogurt) or the *chapandaz* (grilled beef tenderloin). Plenty of vegetarian items are also available. Mon–Thurs & Sun 5.30–10pm, Fri & Sat 5.30–11pm.

Maykadeh 470 Green St at Grant, North Beach ☎415 362 8286; map p.59. A fairly traditional Persian outpost amidst the sea of North Beach trattorias, this is the best place in the area for chicken kebabs ($15.50) and lamb shanks ($16); adventurous types will surely want to opt for the boiled brain ($15). Save room for *bastani* (Persian ice cream). Mon–Thurs 11.45am–10.30pm, Fri & Sat 11.45am–11pm, Sun 11.45am–10pm.

MEXICAN

Taqueria Zorro 308 Columbus Ave at Broadway, North Beach ☎415 392 9677; map p.59. Late-night taqueria with a neon sombrero over its front entrance to match its gaudy strip-joint neighbours. The egg-inclusive breakfast burrito here is reason enough to get to bed early the night before; also, be sure to slather your tortilla chips with some "Salsa Zorro", a roasted vegetable-laden masterpiece.

9

Mon–Wed & Sun 10am–1am, Thurs 10am–2am, Fri & Sat 10am–3am.

PAN-ASIAN

The House 1230 Grant Ave at Columbus, North Beach ☏ 415 986 8612; map p.59. This tiny nook is popular for its self-dubbed "evolutionary Asian food" – expect the likes of Caesar salad with wok-fried scallops or flatiron steak with *wasabi* noodles, all served amidst charmingly austere decor. Mains generally hover around $15–20. Mon–Thurs 11.30am–10pm, Fri & Sat 11.30am–11pm, Sun 5–10pm.

SEAFOOD

Pesce 2227 Polk St at Vallejo, Russian Hill ☏ 415 928 8025; map p.56. Featuring Venetian small plates known as *cicchetti*, the menu at this acclaimed seafood bar tempts the adventurous with options such as *polpo* (braised octopus; $10) and spaghetti with tuna Bolognese sauce ($12). There are more middle-of-the-road choices like penne pasta with garlic and basil ($8) for less chancy eaters; mahogany and teak woodwork add to the room's intimate mood. Mon–Thurs & Sun 5–10pm, Fri & Sat 5–11pm.

★ **Swan Oyster Depot** 1517 Polk St at California, Russian Hill ☏ 415 673 1101; map p.56. Expect no frills at this legendary seafood counter with its huge marble countertop and tiled walls; to find it, follow the smell of fresh fish wafting down the street and duck into the narrow space at the small blue awning. Endure the inevitable wait, grab a stool and hang onto it, and suck down some cheap shellfish, an $8 seafood cocktail or a $5 bowl of chowder. Mon–Sat 8am–5.30pm.

SOUTHEAST ASIAN

King Cha Cha 1268 Grant Ave at Vallejo, North Beach ☏ 415 391 8219; map p.59. A bit more expensive than most Thai places around town, this roomy place is unique in another way: it shares space with an English football pub. The menu includes tried-and-true favourites such as pad thai and beef/basil in curry, with a few diversions sprinkled about – oxtails with peanuts and onion, for instance. Most main courses hover around $15. Daily 11am–3pm & 5pm–2am.

SPANISH

Piperade 1015 Battery St at Green, Northeast Waterfront ☏ 415 391 2555; map p.56. Basque restaurant with rustic, wooden tables and much exposed brick. The robust menu includes cod in smoky broth and the namesake, ratatouille-esque stew, while the warm atmosphere and the affable, attentive service make the place equally inviting. Mains range from $18–30. Mon–Fri 11.30am–3pm & 5.30–10.30pm, Sat 5.30–10.30pm.

Zarzuela 2000 Hyde St at Union, Russian Hill ☏ 415 346 0800; map p.56. This perennially popular (and noisy) small-plates specialist occupies a choice location on one of Russian Hill's liveliest corners. The *tortilla española* – a Spanish tomato and onion omelette ($4.25), served cold – is a terrific appetizer, and the plate of saucy pork medallions ($15.50) anchors the list of main courses. Reservations aren't accepted. Tues–Thurs 5.30–10pm, Fri & Sat 5.30–10.30pm.

SWISS

The Matterhorn 2323 Van Ness Ave at Vallejo, Russian Hill ☏ 415 885 6116; map p.56. Lurking in a nondescript apartment building, this unique restaurant boasts ski-lodge decor that was shipped in pieces from the Swiss motherland, then reassembled onsite. It's known for cheese, beef and chocolate fondues, with the standout being the Fondue Ticinese – a thick and spicy blend of cheeses, *peperoncini* and tomatoes. Beef fondues for two cost $46; cheese fondues for two, $36. Tues–Sun 5–9pm.

Melt! 700 Columbus Ave at Filbert, North Beach ☏ 415 392 9290; map p.59. The calendar here may read like that of a small college-town café – open mic nights, film noir nights, live jazz, free wireless internet – but the reasonably priced fondue is what draws in dippers from all over San Francisco. Extra-sharp cheddar plays a significant role in many varieties; several kinds of sandwiches (including a *croque-monsieur*) are also on offer. Mon–Thurs & Sun noon–10pm, Fri & Sat noon–midnight.

THE NORTHERN WATERFRONT AND PACIFIC HEIGHTS

San Francisco's sharpest-dressed districts enjoy a plethora of celebrated neighbourhood haunts, from hotspots *Boboquivari's* and *Spruce* to veteran favourites *Ella's* and *Bistro Aix*. This area also includes the kitschy tourist confines of Fisherman's Wharf, where a few true gems (*Gary Danko, Ana Mandara*) lurk on the periphery of all the snack kiosks, hot-dog carts and unit-food chain restaurants.

AMERICAN

Balboa Cafe 3199 Fillmore St at Greenwich, Cow Hollow ☏ 415 921 3944; map pp.68–69. This old-fashioned restaurant was first established in 1913; today's throwback touches include waiters in white aprons and black waistcoats. It's known for its meat main courses, so try the oven-roasted pork chop ($23.50) or excellent baguette burger ($12.50). Mon & Tues 11.30am–10pm, Wed–Fri 11.30am–11pm, Sat 9am–3pm & 4–11pm, Sun 9am–3pm & 4–10pm.

★ **Boboquivari's** 1450 Lombard St at Van Ness, Marina ☏ 415 441 8880; map pp.68–69. Laid out over two floors' worth of cosy dining rooms and decorated in rich reds, "Bobo's" serves one of San Francisco's most desired cuts of beef, its bone-in filet mignon ($39), dry-aged from four to six weeks; if you're thinking of investing, call ahead to ensure the cut will be available. Excellent sides such as garlic-studded Swiss chard and fontina-enhanced mac 'n' cheese help round out the meaty menu, which also features crab and iron-skillet roasted mussels. Daily 5–10pm.

The Elite Cafe 2049 Fillmore St at Pine, Pacific Heights ☎415 673 5483; map pp.106–107. This Creole and Cajun restaurant/bar can get frighteningly packed with locals – in fact, it's often easier to sit down for dinners of Louisiana staples (buttery blackened catfish, thick gumbo) in one of the welcoming mahogany booths than it is to cosy up to the bar for a drink. Mains $21–34. Mon–Thurs 5–10pm, Fri 5–10.30pm, Sat 10am–2.30pm & 5–10.30pm, Sun 10am–2.30pm & 5–9pm.

The Grove 2016 Fillmore St at Pine, Pacific Heights ☎415 474 1419; map pp.106–107. Casual diners drop in for serviceable, fairly priced comfort food morning, afternoon and night; it also does double duty as a mellow café in the evenings (wireless internet is available). There's a couch or two near the hearth, and the whole place maintains a cosy mood, even outside at one of the tables along the Fillmore pavement. Branches: 301 Franklin St at Hayes, Hayes Valley (☎415 624 3953); 690 Mission St at Third, South of Market (☎415 957 0558). Mon–Thurs 7am–11pm, Fri 7am–11.30pm, Sat 8am–11.30pm, Sun 8am–11pm.

In-N-Out Burger 333 Jefferson St at Jones, Fisherman's Wharf ☎800 786 1000, ⊛in-n-out.com; map pp.68–69. Yes, it's a fast-food chain, and it couldn't be in a sillier location. Despite all that, this Southern California-based place churns out first-rate burgers for less than the price of 30min parking at the Wharf. Consult the company website for the "secret menu", which includes a few variants on the iconic restaurant's simple formula. Don't pass over the thick shakes. Mon–Thurs & Sun 10.30am–1am, Fri & Sat 10.30am–1.30am.

Spruce 3640 Sacramento St at Locust, Presidio Heights ☎415 931 5100; map pp.68–69. Set in a transformed 1930s auto repair shop, *Spruce's* gorgeous dining room almost trumps its kitchen's glorious (and expensive) New American dishes: charred pork tenderloin ($29), Alaskan cod persillade ($33) and butter poached lobster ($40). The bar menu, while limited, is certainly more affordable. Mon–Thurs 11.30am–2.30pm & 5–10pm, Fri 11.30am–2.30pm & 5–11pm, Sat 5–11pm, Sun 5–10pm.

BRITISH

Liverpool Lil's 2942 Lyon St at Lombard, Cow Hollow ☎415 921 6664; map pp.68–69. Offering a bracingly English menu (liver and onions, lamb shepherd's pie, fish and chips), this Presidio-adjacent pub and restaurant offers a dimly lit alternative to the neighbourhood's otherwise trendy dining scene. Dinner mains range from $12–27. Mon 11am–11pm, Tues–Fri 11am–1am, Sat 10am–1am, Sun 10am–11pm.

CALIFORNIA CUISINE

Ella's 500 Presidio Ave at California, Presidio Heights ☎415 441 5669; map pp.106–107. The wait for weekend brunch at this corner hotspot is among the most notorious in town, so you're better off coming on a weekday when you can generally sit right down. The chicken hash ($10.75) is *Ella's* star item, a delicious loaf of white meat and potato topped with a hearty flurry of green onions and chives. Other top picks include meltingly fluffy pancakes (made with sweet potato to keep them moist) and chunky biscuits. Mon–Fri breakfast 7–11.30am, lunch 11.30am–3pm; Sat & Sun brunch 8.30am–2pm.

Garibaldi's 347 Presidio Ave at Clay, Presidio Heights ☎415 563 8841; map pp.68–69. Amid Presidio Heights' leafy quietude sits this long-popular neighbourhood staple, serving hearty portions of seared California halibut ($28) and *pappardelle* in a pulled pork ragù ($21.50). Dinner often features a three-course prix-fixe "farmer's market" menu for $30. Mon–Wed 11.30am–2.30pm & 5.30–9.30pm, Thurs 11.30am–2.30pm & 5.30–10pm, Fri 11.30am–2.30pm & 5.30–10.30pm, Sat 5.30–10.30pm, Sun 5–9pm.

★ **Gary Danko** 800 North Point St at Hyde, Fisherman's Wharf ☎415 749 2060; map pp.68–69. Don't let the location put you off – this understated oasis regularly vies for the title of best restaurant in food-obsessed San Francisco. Granted, this is performance food served with a flourish, but it's utterly splurgeworthy. The three- to five-course prix-fixe menus ($68–102) allow diners to choose their own items, so if you're a dessert person, you're allowed to order more than one at the expense of an appetizer; whatever you do, though, don't miss the impeccable cheese course. Reserve well in advance. Daily 5.30–10pm.

★ **Greens** Building A, Fort Mason Center ☎415 771 6222; map pp.68–69. San Francisco's original vegetarian restaurant remains popular thanks in no small part to its picturesque pier setting that features massive, gridded windows overlooking the bay; the twisting tree sculpture-cum-bar in the lounge area is equally astonishing. Dinner mains are $19–25, except on Saturday when there's a $49 prix-fixe menu. A takeaway counter, *Greens To Go* (☎415 771 6330) is available during breakfast and lunch hours in the restaurant's lobby. Tues–Sat 11.45am–2.30pm & 5.30–9pm, Sun 10.30am–2pm & 5.30–9pm.

Terzo 3011 Steiner St at Union, Cow Hollow ☎415 441 3200; map pp.68–69. The oft-changing menu at this rustically decorated spot is shaped by a host of cuisines – Spanish, Portuguese, Italian, Moroccan, French and Middle Eastern among them – yet in the end, many of the small and large plates here possess a distinctly California slant. Start with a rocket (arugula) salad with polenta croutons and gorgonzola ($9) before moving on to that evening's selection of fresh meat and fish mains ($20–27). The zinc bar invites

9

lingering with a glass of wine from the Euro-heavy list. Mon–Thurs & Sun 5.30–10pm, Fri & Sat 5.30–11pm.

CHINESE

Dragon Well 2142 Chestnut St at Steiner, Marina ☎ 415 474 6888; map pp.68–69. Although the Marina isn't a hotbed for Chinese cuisine, this inviting spot is the area's best pick for solid, if Americanized versions of such staple dishes as lemongrass chicken and Mongolian beef. Dark wood flooring lends elegance. Dinner mains are very reasonably priced: $9–13. Daily 11.30am–10pm.

FRENCH

Baker Street Bistro 2953 Baker St at Lombard, Cow Hollow ☎ 415 931 1475; map pp.68–69. A cramped, but charming café with a handful of outdoor tables, where a local crowd enjoys simple food served by French staff. Wines are reasonably priced, and the $18.50 prix-fixe dinner (available Tues–Thurs & Sun all evening; Fri & Sat 5.30–6.30pm) is a remarkable bargain. Tues–Fri 11.30am–2.30pm & 5.30–9.30pm, Sat & Sun 9am–2.30pm & 5.30–9.30pm.

Bistro Aix 3340 Steiner St at Lombard, Marina ☎ 415 202 0100; map pp.68–69. The neighbourhood secret about this Gallic bistro is now out all over town – it's been hailed in recent years as one of the top restaurants in San Francisco. Fortunately, success hasn't affected its prices, and the seared ahi tuna with mashed potatoes ($22) is as heavenly as ever; the *bouillabaisse* with halibut ($22) is no slouch, either. Mon–Thurs 5.30–10pm, Fri & Sat 5.30–11pm, Sun 5.30–9.30pm.

ITALIAN

A16 2355 Chestnut St at Divisadero, Marina ☎ 415 771 2216; map pp.68–69. Named after an Italian highway, this hotspot along the Marina's commercial corridor specializes in exceptional, Neapolitan-style pizza, although it's hardly a one-trick pony: house-cured meats, a robust Italian wine list and good old-fashioned buzz combine to pack the narrow space nightly. Individual pizzas and pasta mains go for $11.50–21, while fish and meat mains range from $22–26. Mon & Tues 5.30–10pm, Wed & Thurs 11.30am–2.30pm & 5.30–10pm, Fri 11.30am–2.30pm & 5.30–11pm, Sat 5–11pm, Sun 5–10pm.

Jackson Fillmore 2506 Fillmore St at Jackson, Pacific Heights ☎ 415 346 5288; map pp.68–69. A casual trattoria serving Roman and southern Italian dishes at surprisingly reasonable prices ($16–22), considering the upscale neighbourhood. Go easy on the complimentary bruschetta and save room for one of the sumptuous desserts such as Italian chocolate cake or zabaglione. Wed–Sat 5.30–10pm, Sun 5.30–9.30pm.

Ristorante Parma 3314 Steiner St at Chestnut, Marina ☎ 415 567 0500; map pp.68–69. This slice of *paisano* unpretentiousness has been charming diners with its signature pasta dishes ($14–18) and affordable bottles of Chianti since 1980. Service is suitably welcoming, while the distressed walls provide a bit of Old World ambience. Mon–Sat 5–10.30pm.

★ **Sociale** 3665 Sacramento St at Spruce, Presidio Heights ☎ 415 921 3200; map pp.68–69. Nestled at the end of a verdant pedestrian lane in lovely Presidio Heights, this intimate Italian bistro is worth seeking out for its heated dining courtyard, cosy atmosphere and fontina-stuffed fried olives starter ($8). Chef Tia Harrison also operates Avedano's meat market in Bernal Heights across town, so mains such as the Wagyu bavette steak ($28) and pollo pazzo ($24) are assuredly excellent here; the impressive wine list, meanwhile, is decidedly Italian-leaning. Mon 5.30–10pm, Tues–Sat 11.30am–2.30pm & 5.30–10pm.

SPQR 1911 Fillmore St at Bush, Pacific Heights ☎ 415 771 7779; map pp.106–107. Affiliated with the Marina's A16 (see above) and borrowing its name from a Latin acronym referring to the government of ancient Rome, this highly respected *osteria* sees a rush of patrons nightly. Pasta mains such as *rigatoni* with tomato-braised tripe ($18) are unorthodox but spectacular, while the Italian wine list is one of San Francisco's finest. Mon–Fri 5.30–10.30pm, Sat 11.30am–2.30pm & 5.30–10.30pm, Sun 11.30am–2.30pm & 5.30–10pm.

JAPANESE

Hime 2353 Lombard St at Scott, Marina ☎ 415 931 7900; map pp.68–69. This super-stylish, expensive Japanese spot features strangely glowing bamboo decor and a menu that drifts into Pan-Asian territory on occasion. The excellent, *izakaya*-style sushi rolls, however, anchor the experience. Tues–Thurs 5.30–9.30pm, Fri & Sat 5.30–10.30pm.

Zushi Puzzle 1910 Lombard St at Buchanan, Marina ☎ 415 931 9319; map pp.68–69. Occasionally slipshod service can't sully an evening at this immensely popular, reasonably priced sushi spot. Any of the sashimi options (four pieces for $6.50–8) is a solid order, but if you're a sushi novice, the chef will sometimes offer a tutorial. Daily 5–10.30pm.

LATIN AMERICAN

Fresca 2114 Fillmore St at California, Pacific Heights ☎ 415 447 2668; map pp.106–107. Peruvian ceviche and tapas served in vibrant ambience. Main course-sized portions such as *churrasco* (steak) and salmon are available, but it's in the seafood starters where this restaurant shines most brightly. Most mains are under $20. Two other locations in Noe Valley and West Portal. Mon–Thurs 11am–3pm & 5–10pm, Fri 11am–3pm & 5–11pm, Sat 5–11pm, Sun 5–9pm.

MEDITERRANEAN/MIDDLE EASTERN

Mezes 2373 Chestnut St at Divisadero, Marina ☎ 415 409 7111; map pp.68–69. Moderately priced Greek restaurant with a strong emphasis on small plates of courgette (zucchini) cakes, fried cheese, spinach pie and moussaka; the souvlaki dish (marinated skewers of chicken or pork, with roasted potatoes; $12) is of particular note. The crowd here is typically more diverse than at many other restaurants along Chestnut St. Mon–Thurs & Sun 5.30–9.30pm, Fri & Sat 5–10.30pm.

MEXICAN

La Canasta 3006 Buchanan St at Union, Cow Hollow ☎ 415 474 2627; map pp.68–69. Slightly larger than a walk-in closet, this take-away-only spot has been the area's taqueria of choice since the late 1980s. Quality and value is consistent across the menu, while the spicy salsas will have you wishing you'd ordered a second beverage. Owner/ manager Alberto is one of the friendliest folks you'll meet along Union St. Almost everything's under $10. Daily 11am–9pm.

Mamacita 2317 Chestnut St at Scott, Marina ☎ 415 346 8494; map pp.68–69. Beautifully presented, reasonably priced ($6–18) Mexican cuisine with an emphasis on fresh, local ingredients. The ranchero-decorated dining room can get quite loud, but the kitchen's signature *chilaquiles* – refried tortilla chips with shredded chicken, peppers, *queso fresco* and *chipotle* cream – might be worth losing a bit of hearing for. Mon–Thurs 5.30pm–midnight, Fri–Sun 5pm–midnight.

PAN-ASIAN

Betelnut 2030 Union St at Buchanan, Cow Hollow ☎ 415 929 8855; map pp.68–69. Now a jam-packed institution, *Betelnut* was one of the first restaurants in San Francisco to embrace the small-plates concept, as well as offer well-executed dishes from a number of Asian cultures on a single menu. Choose from Malaysian curries, Indonesian chicken, Penang rice noodles, Sri Lankan fish and more. You should be able to get in and out for less than $30. Mon–Thurs & Sun 11.30am–11pm, Fri & Sat 11.30am–midnight.

SEAFOOD

Scoma's Pier 47, Fisherman's Wharf ☎ 415 771 4383; map pp.68–69. If you can't resist the allure of the tourist-targeting seafood palaces that crowd the Wharf, *Scoma's* is probably your safest choice. Just steel yourself for sky-high prices (the seafood salad alone is $34) and be sure to make a reservation, as it's been one of the most popular restaurants west of the Mississippi for years. Mon–Thurs &Sun 11.30am–10pm, Fri & Sat 11.30am–10.30pm.

SOUTHEAST ASIAN

Ana Mandara 891 Beach St at Polk, Fisherman's Wharf ☎ 415 771 6800; map pp.68–69. Despite overly busy decor and occasionally sloth-like service, this colonial Vietnamese palace occupying a corner of Ghirardelli Square is a fine choice for painstakingly indulgent Franco-Vietnamese. Provided you

can get by the florid names of certain dishes – Enchanting Moments (seared *basa*; $23), Smoke and Seduction (rack of lamb; $32) – you should be in the clear for a terrific, if pricey meal. There's live jazz in the lounge Thurs–Sat. Mon–Thurs 11.30am–2pm & 5.30–9.30pm, Fri 11.30am–2pm & 5.30–10.30pm, Sat 5.30–10.30pm, Sun 5.30–9.30pm.

Yukol Place 2380 Lombard St at Scott, Marina ☎ 415 922 1599; map pp.68–69. An unassuming neighbourhood place with numbered menu items, glass-top tables and uncommonly good Thai curries. The serving staff is friendly and happy to make recommendations. Mains $7–13. Mon–Thurs 11.30am–2.30pm & 5–10pm, Fri 11.30am–2.30pm & 5–10.30pm, Sat 5–10.30pm, Sun 5–10pm.

SOUTH OF MARKET AND THE TENDERLOIN

South of Market's restaurant scene is remarkably varied, from highly sophisticated fine dining (*Boulevard, Kyo-Ya, Ame*) to terrific, informal spots highlighting some of the city's best ethnic cuisine (Crepes A-Go-Go, Manora's Thai). Across Market Street, the gritty Tenderloin and Polk Gulch feature a number of top-grade South and Southeast Asian eateries, as well as a diverse clutch of high-end spots on the Tenderloin's Nob Hill-adjacent blocks.

AMERICAN

Alexander's Steakhouse 448 Brannan St at Fourth, South of Market ☎ 415 495 1111; map pp.84–85. As armies of servers in suits tend assiduously to tables full of well-heeled couples and businesspeople, *Alexander's* sumptuously presented starters and mains – Japanese-influenced small plates, Angus and Wagyu beef and an *omakase* tasting menu – are whimsically followed by candyfloss (cotton candy) at the end of the night. The open kitchen, contemporary design and bi-level layout, meanwhile, lend the large space an inviting feel. Just be sure to bring your credit card: the Wagyu steaks range from $120–200. Mon–Sat 5.30–10pm, Sun 5.30–9pm.

Boulevard 1 Mission St at Steuart, South of Market ☎ 415 563 6084; map pp.40–41. Situated along the Embarcadero and boasting one of the few wood exteriors in the Downtown vicinity to survive the 1906 fire, this impressive space, with its wrought-iron lamps and brick ceiling, is the grand setting for local celebrity chef Nancy Oakes' classic American cuisine. Start with the black cod and lobster bisque ($16.50), and be sure to save room for the terrific desserts. Mains over $30. Mon–Wed 11.30am–2pm & 5.30–10pm, Thurs & Fri 11.30am–2pm & 5.30–10.30pm, Sat 5.30–10.30pm, Sun 5.30–10pm.

★ **Brenda's French Soul Food** 652 Polk St at Eddy, Tenderloin ☎ 415 345 8100; map pp.84–85. Set on one of the more harmless blocks in its grotty neighbourhood, this Creole hideaway dishes out decadent beignets, huge biscuits and fine dinner mains ($11–16), all with New

9

Orleans sass. It's tiny and impossibly popular, so consider dropping in on a less busy weekday. Mon, Tues & Sun 8am–3pm, Wed–Sat 8am–10pm.

Canteen Commodore Hotel, 817 Sutter St at Jones, Tenderloin ☎415 928 8870; map pp.84–85. Canteen's hard-edged decor may lack warmth, and the constantly evolving menu may be short on choices, but this humbly sized nouveau diner has gathered a fervent local following for its clever (if expensive) take on the New American style (such as lamb with fava beans, baby carrots and horseradish; $26.50). The sole constant on the menu is the vanilla soufflé ($9), an unmissable dessert item. Tues 6–10pm, Wed–Fri 11.30am–2pm & 6–10pm, Sat 8am–2pm & 6–10pm, Sun 8am–2pm.

Custom Burger 121 Seventh St at Mission, South of Market ☎415 252 2634; map pp.84–85. Once you step inside this accurately named diner, you select from a choice of buns, patties, toppings and sauces. It's easy to get creative – a particularly adventurous eater could order a salmon burger on a potato bun topped with grilled pineapple and garlic aioli – or simply play it straight. Expect to spend $9–14, and make sure you save room for one of the delectable shakes or desserts. Daily 7am–3pm & 5.30–10pm.

Delancey Street 600 Embarcadero at Brannan, South of Market ☎415 512 5179; map pp.84–85. Largely staffed by individuals recovering from traumatic experiences and attempting to re-enter society on the right foot, this waterfront restaurant's kitchen yields an array of tasty comfort food, from burgers to a variety of noodle dishes. The outdoor patio across the Embarcadero from the bay is a particularly delightful spot on sunny days. Mains $12–13; brunch on Sun. Daily 11am–11pm.

★ **Dottie's True Blue Cafe** 522 Jones St at O'Farrell, Tenderloin ☎415 885 2767; map pp.84–85. An intimate, inexpensive spot that's become immensely popular with locals and visitors – expect to wait regardless of what time you turn up. Still, the oversize home-made pastries and breads (don't leave without trying the chilli cornbread), as well as generous platters of breakfast favourites, make it worth your patience. Check the blackboard for clever specials like chocolate-chip French toast doused in real maple syrup. Mon & Wed–Sun 7.30am–3pm.

Farmerbrown 25 Mason St at Turk, Tenderloin ☎415 409 3276; map pp.84–85. Excellent corner spot that uses organic ingredients from California-based African-American farmers to deliver on its promise of "farm-fresh soul food". A young and diverse crowd packs the copper-and-brick industrial space nightly, as well as for the $16.50 all-you-can-eat weekend brunch featuring live music (Sun only) and stone-ground grits, fried chicken and other Southern staples. Mon–Wed 5–10pm, Thurs & Fri 5–11pm, Sat 10am–2.30pm & 5–11pm, Sun 10am–2.30pm & 5–10pm.

Town Hall 342 Howard St at Fremont ☎415 908 3900; map pp.84–85. An old ship engine-manufacturing building hosts this vibrant restaurant, where New Orleans-inspired dishes such as grilled gulf shrimp are tempered by California cuisine's lighter influence. Mains $16–20. Mon–Thurs 11.30am–2.30pm & 5.30–10pm, Fri 11.30am–2.30pm & 5.30–11pm, Sat 5.30–11pm, Sun 5.30–10pm.

BRITISH

The Old Chelsea 932 Larkin St at Geary, Tenderloin ☎415 474 5015; map pp.84–85. One of the few dedicated chippies in town, the deep fryers at this hole-in-the-wall produce fine chips and capably battered slabs of cod. Staff deliver cheap orders wrapped in the previous day's *Chronicle* to the *Edinburgh Castle* (see p.176) pub around the corner. Mon–Fri 5–11pm.

CALIFORNIA CUISINE

Coco500 500 Brannan St at Fourth St, South of Market ☎415 543 2222; map pp.84–85. Deeply flavourful Cal-Med cuisine in a chic setting warmed by caramel and blue walls adorned with local artwork. Don't miss the beef cheeks – whether as a main course with watercress and horseradish cream ($20), or as a $6 starter whipped into tasty "tacos" with *molé* – and signature house cocktails. Mon–Thurs 11.30am–10pm, Fri 11.30am–11pm, Sat 5.30–11pm.

CARIBBEAN

Primo Patio Cafe 214 Townsend St at Third, Mission Bay ☎415 957 1129; map pp.84–85. A terrific choice for a unique, budget lunch, where sandwiches, burgers and similarly simple dishes are spiced with a subtle Caribbean twist – try the jerk chicken or blackened snapper. The backyard patio offers a pleasant escape from the industrial surroundings. Mon–Sat 9am–4pm.

CHINESE

Yank Sing 49 Stevenson St at First, South of Market ☎415 541 4949; map pp.84–85. One of the better (if pricier) places for dim sum in the city. Though it's routinely packed, the waiters can almost always find a spot for you; come early to select from leftfield varieties such as snow-pea shoot dumplings that populate the circulating carts. Expect to spend at least $25 per person. There's another location in the nearby Rincon Center, 101 Spear St at Mission (☎415 957 9300). Mon–Fri 11am–3pm, Sat & Sun 10am–4pm.

ECLECTIC

Ananda Fuara 1298 Market St at Larkin, Civic Center ☎415 621 1994; map pp.84–85. Situated on a nondescript corner, this affordable and popular vegetarian restaurant casts a wide net – a group of four could easily sample meatless dishes spanning the culinary styles of Mexico, the Middle East, the American South and South

Asia. The "neatloaf" sandwich is a sharp choice, as is any of the creative salads on offer. Most mains under $10. Mon, Tues & Thurs–Sat 11am–8pm, Wed 11am–3pm.

FRENCH

Crepes A-Go-Go 350 11th St at Folsom, South of Market ☎415 503 1294; map pp.84–85. Inexpensive crepe joint with several sweet and savoury and sweet varieties available; in the true Parisian tradition, there's plenty of Nutella on hand. Branch at 1220 Polk St at Sutter, Polk Gulch (☎415 409 4646). Wed–Sun 6pm–3am.

Le Charm 315 Fifth St at Folsom, South of Market ☎415 546 6128; map pp.84–85. Unpretentious and not overly pricey, this light and airy restaurant (with heated rear patio) does southern French bean or fish soups well. Desserts are equally terrific, and the evening three-course prix fixe ($32) is a good deal. Mains $20–30; live jazz every Thurs on the patio. Tues–Fri 5.30–9.30pm, Fri & Sat 5.30–10pm, Sun 5–8.30pm.

ITALIAN

Ristorante Umbria 198 Second St at Howard, South of Market ☎415 546 6985; map pp.84–85. The food at this corner spot is, unsurprisingly, devoted to its namesake Italian region – signature, truffle-inflected starters such as bruschetta misto litter the menu. Several outdoor tables line the sidewalks, where patrons enjoy oven-baked aubergine (eggplant) ($15.75) or spaghetti sauteed with pancetta ($14.75). Mon–Fri 11.30am–2.30pm & 5.30–10.30pm, Sat 5.30–10.30pm.

JAPANESE

Kyo-Ya Palace Hotel, 2 New Montgomery St at Market, South of Market ☎415 546 5090; map pp.84–85. Although it may seem as if *Kyo-Ya* caters exclusively to expense account-wielding Japanese businesspeople, it's also popular with locals glad to venture into one of San Francisco's most storied hotels. Its tranquil setting – rare for a San Francisco restaurant – allows you to hold a conversation without raising your voice. Mains $18–28. Mon–Fri 11.30am–2pm & 6–10pm.

LATIN AMERICAN

Mochica 937 Harrison St at Fifth, South of Market ☎415 278 0480; map pp.84–85. Diminutive Peruvian hideaway specializing in small plates, ceviche and punch-packing sangria. Many dishes, including the warm ceviche with tiger shrimp ($18), benefit from uncommonly flavourful sauces and marinades. Mon & Wed–Sun 11.30am–3.30pm & 5.30–10pm.

MEDITERRANEAN/MIDDLE EASTERN

A La Turca 869 Geary St at Larkin, Tenderloin ☎415 345 1011; map pp.84–85. A highly regarded

Turkish restaurant on one of the Tenderloin's less slummy blocks, *A La Turca* specializes in *pides* – baked flatbread stuffed with vegetables, meat, and/or cheese (all under $10). Overlook the minimal decor and linger for the outstanding *kunefe*, a luscious dessert topped with honey and filled with sweet cheese. Daily 11am–midnight.

Saha Hotel Carlton, 1075 Sutter St at Larkin, Tenderloin ☎415 345 9547; map pp.84–85. Serving food that combines elements of Yemenese Arabic cooking with the fresh ingredients associated with California cuisine, this classy place has become one of the hottest Middle Eastern restaurants in town. There's a three-course prix fixe for $40 (a vegetarian version is only $30), and the wine list is excellent. Tues–Thurs 6–9.30pm, Fri & Sat 6–10.30pm.

MEXICAN

Chavo's 595 Bryant St at Fourth, South of Market ☎415 495 5822; map pp.84–85. Brave the compound-like entrance, cold industrial surroundings and adjacent freeway for some of the finest (and cheapest) Mexican food in the area. This informal place specializes in tender, marinated chicken, and anyone unafraid of lard will want to sample the deliciously tasty refried beans. Mon–Fri 10am–4pm.

Maya 303 Second St at Folsom, South of Market ☎415 543 2928; map pp.84–85. A longtime local favourite out to prove that guacamole *can* be presented in gourmet fashion. Try the shrimp with goat cheese-stuffed chilli, or the pork belly tacos. If you're on a budget, grab a top-rate burrito from the adjacent lunch-only take-away counter. All mains under $20. Mon 11.30am–2.30pm & 5.30–9pm, Tues–Fri 11.30am–2.30pm & 5.30–10pm, Sat 5.30–10pm, Sun 5.30–9pm.

Taqueria El Castillito 370 Golden Gate St at Larkin, Civic Center ☎415 292 7233; map pp.84–85. One of four *El Castillitos* in town, and often overshadowed by higher-profile names in the taqueria-rich Mission, this sparsely decorated bolthole crafts burritos as hearty as any around. Eaters with sizeable appetites will want to plough through a super breakfast burrito, a morning gutbomb that replaces rice with scrambled eggs. Daily 10am–9pm.

PAN-ASIAN

Ame St. Regis Hotel, 689 Mission St at Third, South of Market ☎415 284 4040; map pp.84–85. Sequestered within the luxurious *St. Regis*, this sophisticated spot is recognised locally for its inventive, California-fied take on Far East seafood fare. The custom-built marble bar is a sight in itself, while the large room is lent intimacy by dark wood panelling and gorgeous curtains. Many main courses soar above $35. Mon–Thurs 6–9.30pm, Fri & Sat 5.30–10pm, Sun 5.30–9.45pm.

Asia SF 201 Ninth St at Howard, South of Market ☎415 255 2742; map pp.84–85. Notorious hotspot where gender-illusionist servers perform cheeky dance routines

9

on the bar throughout the evening. The sake martinis are delicious and deadly, while the equally crossbred food (fish burgers, duck quesadillas, truffled *soba* noodles) is surprisingly successful, given the campy surroundings. Prices are moderate, and it's popular with large groups – hen (bachelorette) parties in particular. Wed–Thurs 7–11pm, Fri 7pm–2am, Sat 5pm–2am, Sun 7–10pm.

Golden Era 572 O'Farrell St at Leavenworth, Tenderloin ☎ 415 673 3136; map pp.84–85. Reliably good subterranean restaurant in the heart of the Tenderloin, with all dishes served absent of meat, fish, egg and MSG. The menu swerves through Thai, Chinese and Japanese and features many soy-based items set in quotation marks ("beef", "chicken", etc); alternately, a number of main courses are entirely vegetable-based. Almost all mains are under $10. Mon & Wed–Sun 11am–9pm.

PORTUGUESE

Grubstake 1525 Pine St at Polk, Polk Gulch ☎ 415 673 8268; map p.56. Housed in a decommissioned cable car, this old-fashioned, affordably priced diner serves all the American basics; the brave go for the meat loaf. The real culinary allure of the place, however, are the ten or so Portuguese specialities on offer, including *bacalhau à gomes de sà* (codfish with potato, onion, eggs, parsley and olives). It's a popular late-night destination, so beware of rowdy inebriates once the Polk St bars shut down. Breakfast is served all hours, and there's brunch on weekends. Mon–Fri 5pm–4am, Sat & Sun 10am–4am.

SOUTH ASIAN

Mehfil 600 Folsom St at Second, South of Market ☎ 415 974 5510; map pp.84–85. While the table service at the corner Indian restaurant is fine in its own right, it's the takeaway lunch specials that are the real draw here: choose between a few delectable North Indian specialities, all with basmati rice, for no more than $6 each. Dinners are bit more expensive (about $12–13), but still reasonable. Branch: 2301 Fillmore St at Clay, Pacific Heights (☎ 415 614 1010). Mon–Fri 11am–3pm & 5.30–10pm, Sat & Sun 5.30–10pm.

Pakwan 501 O'Farrell St at Jones, Tenderloin ☎ 415 776 0160; map pp.84–85. Though it's certainly not much to look at on the outside (or the inside, for that matter), the excellent food at this Tenderloin staple has been drawing in plenty of patrons for years. Vegetarian items such as *saag daal* (lentils and spinach) are perennial favourites, as are the various tandoori dishes scattered throughout the menu; mains cost $5.50–8. Combat all the heady spice with a rich mango lassi. Branch: 3180 16th St at Guerrero, Mission (☎ 415 255 2440). Daily 11am–11pm.

★ **Shalimar** 532 Jones St at O'Farrell, Tenderloin ☎ 415 928 0333; map pp.84–85. Another simple South Asian eatery in a neighbourhood rife with such places, *Shalimar* serves delicious dishes made to order. The

chicken tikka masala ($7) is the main attraction – exceptional and generous in its portion. Once you finally emerge, expect to smell as if you yourself have been doused in spices and baked in the tandoor oven. Branch: 1409 Polk St at Pine, Polk Gulch (☎ 415 776 4642). Daily noon–midnight.

SOUTHEAST ASIAN

Manora's Thai 1600 Folsom St at 12th, South of Market ☎ 415 861 6224; map pp.84–85. Light, flavourful Thai food of the highest order, from papaya salad and more ambitious seafood dishes such as *goong-grobb* (in-shell prawns in garlic sauce). It's no surprise that locals pack the place out night after night – the low prices on main courses ($8–15) certainly don't hurt. Mon–Fri 11.30am–2.30pm & 5.30–10.30pm, Sat 5.30–10.30pm, Sun 5–10pm.

★ **Pagolac** 655 Larkin St at Ellis, Tenderloin ☎ 415 776 3234; map pp.84–85. The queue to get into this Little Saigon mainstay can require reserves of patience at peak times, but once you're presented with a plate of *Pagolac's* locally revered imperial rolls, you'll see that it's worth the wait. The tabletop grill meal is a fun DIY option, while the "seven flavors of beef" tasting menu is a fine value at around $15. Tues–Sun 5–10pm.

Thai Stick 925 O'Farrell St at Polk, Tenderloin ☎ 415 776 8858; map pp.84–85. A smart option when other restaurants in the area are too crowded, as the masses seem to continually overlook this quiet winner on an outskirt block of the Tenderloin. *Long song* (sauteed spinach with choice of meat in peanut sauce; $9–10) is a good choice; if it's a foggy evening, go with a soothing bowl of *tom yum* (hot and sour soup with vegetables and lemongrass; $6.50–8). Branches: 2001 Fillmore St at Pine, Pacific Heights (☎ 415 885 6100); 698 Post St at Jones, Union Square (☎ 415 928 7730). Daily 11am–1am.

Tu Lan 8 Sixth St at Market, South of Market ☎ 415 626 0927; map pp.84–85. This cramped, dingy space on one of the seediest blocks in town has been a local legend since superstar chef Julia Child first championed its cheap Vietnamese cooking. Should you sit at the sticky counter, you'll be nearly singed by the flames from the stove; nevertheless, the populist food is consistently fresh and flavourful. Mon–Sat 11am–9.30pm.

THE MISSION AND THE CASTRO

Although the Mission is instantly characterized by many as San Francisco's own Rice and Beans Central, there's much more to the neighbourhood than its famous culinary export, the super burrito. From the inventive New American menus at *Maverick* and *Spork* to San Francisco's most unique and diet-shattering selection of dessert spots, a visitor could spend a week eating well in the Mission and not set foot in a taqueria. In the neighbourhoods around the Mission, you'll find a number of outstanding restaurants slightly off the beaten path, including true-to-form French cuisine at Potrero Hill's *Chez Papa Bistrot*, Himalayan treats at *Little Nepal* in Bernal Heights and top-grade thin-crust pizza at Glen Park's *Gialina*.

AMERICAN

Al's Cafe 3286 Mission St at 29th, Mission ☎ 415 621 8445; map p.100. A time machine that also happens to serve super-calorific comfort food, often brought to your table by veteran hostesses who'll call you "sweetie" while refilling your coffee mug for the third time. Maiden Christina's Special ($8.50) combines nearly every breakfast item under the sun, and it's served at all hours. Mon–Fri 7am–10pm, Sat & Sun 7am–4pm.

Barney's 4138 24th St at Castro, Noe Valley ☎ 415 282 7770; map p.100. Burger standby that's a great place to dive into a patty of beef (or chicken, turkey or portobello). It's tucked away on the western end of 24th St's business strip, with a lovely front patio suitable for lingering. Choose from standard cheeseburgers and leftfield varieties such as the Milano burger, which adds roasted aubergine (eggplant), courgette and pesto sauce. Salads are generously sized and excellent, while the curly fries are justifiably renowned; most items generally hover around $10–12. Branch: 3344 Steiner St at Chestnut, Marina (☎ 415 563 0307). Mon–Thurs 11am–10pm, Fri & Sat 11am–10.30pm, Sun 11am–9.30pm.

Boogaloos 3296 22nd St at Valencia, Mission ☎ 415 824 3211; map p.100. Breakfast is the big draw here: black beans and chorizo feature heavily on the Latinized versions of American diner classics, while the Temple o' Spuds ($6.50) is an orgy of potatoes, melted cheese, sour cream and green onions. Decor is basic, but perked up with bright orange and yellow tables, mosaics and rotating art exhibitions on the walls. The crowd, meanwhile, often borders on the comically self-aware, and can make for hefty waits on weekends. Daily 8am–3pm.

Chenery Park 683 Chenery St at Diamond, Glen Park ☎ 415 337 8537; map pp.98–99. Comfortable neighbourhood haunt that's easily accessed via BART, where friendly servers present modern American dishes with occasional Cajun (spicy seafood gumbo; $18) or Italian flair (wild mushroom gnocchi; $17). The wine list leans heavily towards California varietals. Note that Tues is kids' night. Tues–Thurs 5.30–9.15pm, Fri & Sat 5.30–9.45pm, Sun 5.30–8.45pm.

Firefly 4288 24th St at Douglass, Noe Valley ☎ 415 821 7652; map pp.98–99. Tucked away in the tree-lined folds of sleepy Noe Valley, this unpretentious spot concocts New American dishes from ingredients both local and far-flung. The menu's fun and inventive, with a nice blend of seafood, meat and vegetarian options, and there's a $36 three-course prix-fixe deal Mon–Thurs & Sun. Daily 5.30–10pm.

Hard Knox Cafe 2526 Third St at 22nd, Potrero Hill ☎ 415 648 3770; map pp.98–99. Honest-to-goodness,

moderately priced soul food on the eastern edge of San Francisco – excellent BBQ spare ribs, spicy chicken sandwiches and robust sides such as collard greens and red beans with rice. The interior decor is best described as "Quonset hut moderne", its aluminium walls covered as they are in vintage beverage and traffic signs. Branch: 2448 Clement St at 25th, Outer Richmond (☎ 415 752 3770). Mon–Sat 11am–9pm, Sun 11am–5pm.

★ **Just for You** 732 22nd St at Third, Potrero Hill ☎ 415 647 3033; map pp.98–99. One of San Francisco's true gems, this out-of-the-way spot produces some of the finest, fluffiest (and largest!) beignets outside of New Orleans – take home an extra, all slathered in powdered sugar, for a dollar and change. All breads are home-made (try the raisin cinnamon toast), while the enormous pancakes are the stuff of legend. Service can be as sassy as some of the signs around the place ("We reserve the right to pour coffee on your cell phone; please put it away"). Almost everything's under $10. Mon–Fri 7.30am–3pm, Sat & Sun 8am–3pm.

Liberty Cafe 410 Cortland Ave at Bennington, Bernal Heights ☎ 415 695 8777; map pp.98–99. The front of this three-in-one business is a bakery dishing up delicious pies, both savoury (chicken pot) and sweet (banana cream); the rear is a café serving full meals such as ricotta pizzas and roasted chicken for $14 and up. And on the back patio, a delightful wine bar offers a limited menu. Tues–Fri 11am–3pm & 5.30–10pm, Sat & Sun 9am–3pm & 5.30–10pm.

Maverick 3316 17th St at Mission, Mission ☎ 415 863 3061; map p.100. The menu at this tiny, sparsely decorated spot features old favourites like baked mac 'n' cheese alongside plates of duck breast and day boat scallops. As with many of the Mission's destination restaurants, the crowd is mostly imported from other neighbourhoods, so don't expect much in the way of hipster colour. Mains from $20. Mon–Thurs 5.30–10pm, Fri 5.30–11pm, Sat 10.30am–2.30pm & 5.30–11pm, Sun 10.30am–3pm & 5–9pm.

Range 842 Valencia St at 19th, Mission ☎ 415 282 8283; map pp.98–99. This celebrated restaurant attracts food sophisticates from far and wide for its wonderfully idiosyncratic design (look no further than the polished concrete bar) and top-shelf New American cuisine. The menu is in constant flux, but usually riffs on cosy choices such as asparagus soup and braised Alaskan halibut ($27). Hope that the lemon pudding cake is on the evening's dessert menu. Mon–Thurs & Sun 6–10pm, Fri & Sat 5.30–11pm.

Slow Club 2501 Mariposa St at Hampshire, Mission ☎ 415 241 9390; map pp.98–99. One of the first restaurants in San Francisco to embrace the sustainable slow-food movement – going so far as to work it into its name – *Slow Club*'s decor remains an artful reflection of its industrial-chic environs. The menu relies on clever combinations such as grilled pork loin with Umbrian *farro* ($24), as well as a good old-fashioned

9

burger ($12.50). Mon–Thurs 11.30am–2.30pm & 6.30–10pm, Fri 11.30am–2.30pm & 6.30–11pm, Sat 10am–2.30pm & 6–11pm, Sun 10am–2.30pm.

Spork 1058 Valencia St at 22nd, Mission ☎415 643 5000; map p.100. Named in honour of the two-in-one "wonder utensil" foisted upon the world by this building's previous occupant, Kentucky Fried Chicken, *Spork* packs in culinary scenesters enjoying marvellous, humbly spiced burgers, comically salty (but addictive) smashed potato fries and similar comfort food. Its decor re-imagines items left behind by KFC: a hood that previously cooled deep fryers is now an overhead light. Mains $14–22. Mon–Thurs 6–10pm, Fri 6–11pm, Sat 11am–2pm & 5.30–10.30pm, Sun 11am–2pm & 5.30–9pm.

Woodward's Garden 1700 Mission St at Duboce, Mission ☎415 621 7122; map p.100. Awkwardly sequestered under the Central Freeway, this intimate spot makes patrons forget their exterior surroundings once they make it inside. Gorgeously presented dishes such as lamb shoulder stewed with leeks ($24) rely, in part, on ingredients grown in the restaurant's own garden. Tues–Sat 6–10pm.

CALIFORNIA CUISINE

Foreign Cinema 2534 Mission St at 21st, Mission ☎415 648 7600; map p.100. The "dinner and a movie" concept is redefined at this upscale restaurant, where films are projected onto a large outdoor wall. The menu is as noteworthy as the offbeat concept – the house-cured sardines and vegetables ($9) make for a bracing starter, while the exhaustive oyster-heavy raw bar ($2.50–3.25 per oyster) is showy. Main courses $22–28. Mon–Thurs 6–10pm, Fri 5.30–11pm, Sat 11am–3pm & 5.30–11pm, Sun 11am–3pm & 5.30–10pm.

Universal Cafe 2814 19th St at Bryant, Mission ☎415 821 4608; map p.100. This sunny outpost in a light-industrial enclave of the Mission is still one of the best: wooden tables, chatty waiters, a clientele of twenty- and thirty-somethings and a weekly changing menu of California staples (pasta, meat and fish; $17–25), most of which is sourced from environmentally sustainable farms and ranches. Tues 5.30–9.30pm, Wed & Thurs 11.30am–2.15pm & 5.30–9.30pm, Fri 11.30am–2.15pm & 5.30–10.30pm, Sat 9am–2.15pm & 5.30–10.30pm, Sun 9am–2.15pm & 5.30–9.30pm.

ECLECTIC

Hog & Rocks 3431 19th St at Mission, Mission ☎415 550 8627; map p.100. Surely one of the few ham and oyster bars around, this conceptually unique spot has nevertheless found a niche in this city of adventurous palates. Start with a jar of pickles ($5) before moving on to a shared plate of clams ($12), or just head straight for the Big Piggy Sandwich (pork confit, black forest ham; $10).

The casual mood of the place is buffeted by a list of classy cocktails; the menu changes daily, and there's brunch on weekends. Mon–Fri 5pm–1am, Sat & Sun 11am–1am.

Luna Park 694 Valencia St at 18th, Mission ☎415 553 8584; map p.100. This darkly lit neighbourhood staple is decked out like a lush bordello, with deep red walls and ornamental chandeliers; menus arrive in the shape of little black books. The range of food available is literally all over the map, with most dishes – salads, pastas and meat and seafood mains – priced $14–24; there's a $32 prix-fixe option available as well. Mon–Thurs 11.30am–10.30pm, Fri 11.30am–11.30pm, Sat 10am–11.30pm, Sun 10am–10pm.

Savor 3913 24th St at Sanchez, Noe Valley ☎415 282 0344; map p.100. Stylish, yet affordable spot along Noe Valley's most stroller-choked stretch. The shady rear patio's a terrific place to enjoy a hearty omelette, sandwich or salad (all about $10), while there's a fireplace and plenty of tables inside for when the weather's less cooperative. The diverse menu also features a wide selection of crepes. Mon–Thurs & Sun 8am–10pm, Fri & Sat 8am–11pm.

FRENCH

Chez Papa Bistrot 1401 18th St at Missouri, Potrero Hill ☎415 824 8210; map pp.98–99. This corner bistro off the beaten path has had its veil lifted in recent years. No wonder: the wine list is extensive, the French fare is hearty and the room – brasserie-inspired, with simple decor and a very short bar – always seems to be vibrant and buzzing. Signature dishes include the seafood bouillabaisse ($26) and cassoulet de Toulouse ($22), and outdoor seating is available. Branch: Chez Papa Resto, 4 Mint Plaza (Jessie St at Fifth), South of Market (☎415 546 4134). Mon–Thurs 11.30am–2.30pm & 5.30–10pm, Fri & Sat 11.30am–2.30pm & 5.30–11pm, Sun 5.30–10pm.

Chez Spencer 82 14th St at Folsom, Mission ☎415 864 2191; map p.100. With a vine-swathed cocktail garden outside and a vaulted loft dining space inside, this Francophile destination draws in a mixed crowd from all around town, despite the high prices ($85 for the tasting menu, $125 with wine pairing). You can also choose items à la carte, from truffle-scented Parmesan risotto ($25) to wood-roasted sturgeon ($30). Mon–Thurs 6–10pm, Fri & Sat 5.30–10.30pm, Sun 6–9.30pm.

★ **Le P'tit Laurent** 699 Chenery St at Diamond, Glen Park ☎415 334 3235; map pp.98–99. Carnivores eating at this charming corner spot won't want to miss the meaty cassoulet ($21, complete with full leg of duck). Desserts are memorable, while the service and overall mood of the place are equally warm. Conveniently, it's steps from the Glen Park BART station, making it easily accessible from Downtown or even the East Bay. Mon–Thurs & Sun 5.30–9.30pm, Fri & Sat 5.30–10.30pm.

CLOCKWISE FROM TOP LEFT DINING ALFRESCO ON PIER 39; GOURMET PIZZA; TAYLOR'S AUTOMATIC REFRESHER (P.141) >

9

GERMAN

Walzwerk 381 South Van Ness Ave at 15th, Mission ☎415 551 7181; map p.100. Cramped German eatery serving hearty comfort food – go for the pork schnitzel with seasonal vegetables ($16) or bratwurst with mashed potatoes and sauerkraut ($15). Framed East German pop records and large portraits of twentieth-century Eastern Bloc industry evoke past eras behind the Iron Curtain. Daily 5.30–10pm.

ITALIAN

Bacco 737 Diamond St at Elizabeth, Noe Valley ☎415 282 4969; map p.100. Dark tiled floors and an airy dining space lend elegance to this restaurant that's worth a diversion from the more tourist-alluring parts of town. Try the namesake antipasto ($11), which includes rocket (arugula), radicchio, walnuts, gorgonzola and balsamic dressing; save room for the exceptional tiramisù ($7.50). Main courses $16–29. Mon–Thurs 5.30–9.30pm, Fri & Sat 5.30–10pm, Sun 5–9pm.

★ **Delfina** 3621 18th St at Guerrero, Mission ☎415 552 4055; map p.100. Great fun, this continually buzzing dinner-only restaurant attracts nearly every sort of San Franciscan – it's hard to find someone in town who *hasn't* eaten at *Delfina*. Cal-Ital mains such as roasted duck with sauerkraut and kumquats ($24) rarely miss. Also worth trying is *Pizzeria Delfina* next door (☎415 437 6800, no reservations), featuring nearly a dozen thin-crust varieties ($10–17) at lunch and dinner. Mon–Thurs 5.30–10pm, Fri & Sat 5.30–11pm, Sun 5–10pm.

Emmy's Spaghetti Shack 18 Virginia St at Mission, Mission ☎415 206 2086; map pp.98–99. A dark and funky spot that's always filled with locals who give it a laid-back, unpretentious vibe. The simple, tasty food makes it even more appealing: try a hefty plate of spaghetti and house meatballs for $13. Mon–Thurs & Sun 5.30–10.30pm, Fri & Sat 5.30–11.30pm.

★ **Gialina** 2842 Diamond St at Kern, Glen Park ☎415 239 8500; map pp.98–99. This Neapolitan-style outpost has gained a strong foothold in San Francisco's much-improved pizzeria scene; the menu changes frequently, but there's always a strong emphasis on fresh, seasonal vegetables. Dining quarters are charming but cramped, and since no reservations are taken, expect to take advantage of the wine list to make your wait a bit more enjoyable. Twelve-inch pizzas $13–18. Branch: *Ragazza*, 311 Divisadero St at Page, Lower Haight (☎415 255 1133). Mon–Thurs & Sun 5–10pm, Fri & Sat 5–10.30pm.

Incanto 1550 Church St at Duncan, Noe Valley ☎415 641 4500; map p.100. Stately spot specializing in Northern Italian dishes infused with California sensibilities – spaghetti with cured tuna ($17), asparagus and lemon risotto ($16) and other rustic options abound. The staff is helpful with recommending bottles from the all-Italian wine list. Mon & Sun 5.30–9.30pm, Wed–Sat 5.30–10pm.

Pauline's Pizza 260 Valencia St at 14th, Mission ☎415 552 2050; map p.100. Sit-down pizzeria where the menu ranges from bold (pesto, $20.50 for large) to out-and-out quirky (Louisiana *andouille*, $23 for large), with vegan options available. The house wine is Pauline's own "Pizza Red", while most ingredients are grown in the restaurant's organic garden. Tues–Sat 5–10pm.

Serrano's 3274 21st St at Valencia, Mission ☎415 695 1615; map p.100. You'll be besieged by an overwhelming number of potential toppings at this poorly ventilated, no-nonsense pizza joint between the Mission and Valencia corridors. Slices invariably arrive double-sized and slathered in melted mozzarella. Plastic tables flank the door if you'd like some fresh air with your slices. Mon–Thurs & Sun 11am–midnight, Fri & Sat 11am–1am.

JAPANESE

★ **Nihon** 1779 Folsom St at 14th, Mission ☎415 552 4400; map p.100. Several blocks from the Mission's nexus, you'll find this moderately priced, *izakaya*-style hideaway on a warehouse-laden stretch of Folsom St. Excellent sushi and unusual small plates like *kobe*-wrapped asparagus ($10) are the main magnets, while the upstairs whiskey lounge could encourage you to stick around after the meal. Tues–Sat 5.30pm–1.30am.

Sushi Zone 1815 Market St at Guerrero, Castro ☎415 621 1114; map pp.106–107. Local sushi enthusiasts brave interminable waits to get into this long-popular spot that seats about two dozen. Plan for an early arrival to secure a spot, then choose from an inventive list of rolls incorporating citrus fruits such as mango and papaya. Prices are moderate – under $20. Mon–Sat 5–10pm.

Tokyo Go Go 3174 16th St at Guerrero, Mission ☎415 864 2288; map p.100. There's a celebratory atmosphere at this clubby, brightly lit Japanese spot where signature dishes to share include beef tataki ($14.50) and miso-marinated black cod ($13). The sushi menu focuses on seasonal catches, with the roll call of choices ranging from *hamachi* to *albacore*. Mon–Thurs 5.30–10.30pm, Fri & Sat 5.30–11pm, Sun 5–10pm.

LATIN AMERICAN

El Trébol 3324 24th St at Mission, Mission ☎415 285 6298; map p.100. Excellent Nicaraguan standards – *churrasco* (grilled beef) and *chancho con yucca* (fried pork) – served in a haphazard atmosphere washed with Latin music. The mouth-puckering *tamarindo* beverage is a singular experience. Most dishes cost well under $10. Mon–Fri noon–9pm, Sat noon–8pm.

Limón 524 Valencia St at 16th, Mission ☎415 252 0918; map p.100. The highest-profile of a stylish breed of South American restaurants in San Francisco, Peruvian entry *Limón* wows patrons with small plates of grilled seafood, brazenly seasoned vegetables and flavourful ceviche ($6.75–10); its wallop-packing sangria has also made a local name for itself. Branch: *Limón Rotisserie*, 1001 South Van Ness Ave at 21st, Mission (☎ 415 821 2134). Mon 5.30–10.30pm, Tues–Thurs 11.30am–10.30pm, Fri 11.30am–11pm, Sat noon–11pm, Sun noon–10pm.

Mi Lindo Peru 3226 Mission St at Valencia, Mission ☎ 415 642 4897; map p.100. A colourfully decorated, unpretentious and moderately priced place where the kitchen places an emphasis on the simpler side of Peruvian cooking – expect generous piles of *arroz con pollo*, as well as other dishes built around meat and rice. Make it a destination on a chilly day or night for a huge bowl of seafood soup. Mon–Thurs noon–9pm, Fri & Sat noon–10pm.

Panchita's 3 3115 22nd St at Capp, Mission ☎ 415 821 6660; map p.100. One among a local chainlet of Salvadorean-Mexican fusion restaurants – a bit more upscale than most of the neighbourhood's taquerias, with pygmy palm trees and white tablecloths. Try some of San Francisco's finest Salvadorean *pupusas* (chunky corn tortillas grilled and stuffed with a choice of fillings), all for about the price of a bottle of beer. Daily 4–11pm.

★ **Radio Habana Social Club** 1109 Valencia St at 22nd, Mission ☎ 415 824 7659; map p.100. Quirky Cuban hole-in-the-wall, with a few tables jammed together and walls covered with picture frames and knick-knacks. The food on the short menu is cheap and tasty, especially the chicken tamal; the vivacious crowd's a fun mix of old-timers and hipsters, and almost everyone in the place drinks sangria. Mon 7.30pm–midnight, Wed–Sat 7pm–midnight.

San Miguel 3263 Mission St at 29th, Mission ☎ 415 641 5866; map p.100. The best place in San Francisco for hearty Guatemalan fare: *carne asada* topped with *chirmol* sauce ($10), a rotation of dense seafood soups ($12) and simple sandwiches for around $5. It's family-owned and operated, so you can expect to be treated with warmth. Mon & Tues 11am–9pm, Thurs–Sun 11am–10pm.

MEDITERRANEAN/MIDDLE EASTERN

★ **Goood Frikin Chicken** 10 29th St at Mission, Mission ☎ 415 970 2428; map p.100. Superbly seasoned poultry that warrants the extra 'o' in this airy restaurant's goofy name. Fluffy pitta bread is an ideal accompaniment to the house speciality: a rotisserie half-chicken ($8.95), roasted with an abundance of delectable herbs and spices. The kebab dishes on the menu are just as delicious; the sole downside is the overly bright overhead lighting. Daily 11am–10pm.

La Méditerranée 288 Noe St at Market, Castro ☎ 415 431 7210; map p.100. Neighbourhood staple serving delicious, unexpected dishes such as chicken pomegranate ($13.50) and Lebanese *kibbeh* ($14); the "quiche of the day" option includes three vegetarian slices for $11.75. It's a pleasant place for a relaxed meal, especially when seated at one of the four outdoor tables. Branch at 2210 Fillmore St at Sacramento, Pacific Heights (☎ 415 921 2956). Mon–Thurs & Sun 11am–10pm, Fri & Sat 11am–11pm.

Truly Mediterranean 3109 16th St at Valencia, Mission ☎ 415 252 7482; map p.100. *Truly Med's* inexpensive *shwarmas* are wrapped in thin, crispy *lavash* bread – though there's barely anywhere to sit and eat them inside the tiny windowfront restaurant. The busy staff's spontaneous singing and dancing can be a surprise bonus, though. Mon–Thurs 11am–11pm, Fri & Sat 11am–midnight, Sun 11am–10pm.

MEXICAN

El Metate 2406 Bryant St at 22nd, Mission ☎ 415 285 7117; map p.100. Although *El Metate's* burritos can vary in quality, its tacos and quesadillas ($5–8) have been drawing people to this outer Mission restaurant for several years. The atmosphere's as pleasant as anywhere in the neighbourhood, with the adjoining dining room washed in vibrant yellow and dotted with foliage; there are also several tables outside. Daily 10am–10pm.

El Tonayense Harrison St at 22nd, Mission ☎ 415 550 9192; map p.100. Part of a local fleet of "taco trucks", this kitchen on wheels sets up its mobile shop at this corner daily – look for the small crowd jostling to order miniature tacos on morsel-sized tortillas for less than $2 each (burritos are also available for $6.50). Daily 10am–9pm.

La Espiga de Oro 2916 24th St at Florida, Mission ☎ 415 826 1363; map p.100. As *auténtico* a place as you're bound to find in San Francisco's Latino stronghold, this informal, open-air spot makes its own delectable tortillas; when grilled, they're often the best part of any meal here. Daily 5am–7pm.

La Taqueria 2889 Mission St at 25th, Mission ☎ 415 285 7117; map p.100. Pass on the often sloppy, poorly constructed burritos at this Mission stalwart and head straight for the menu's true strength, the super taco (about $6, including guacamole). The frantic staff is constantly slicing and chopping sizzling pork and beef behind the counter, so if it's crowded (which it usually is), order quickly, then grab a seat at one of the communal benches or the outside counter and enjoy one of the fruitiest *agua fresca* beverages in town. Mon–Sat 11am–9pm, Sun 11am–8pm.

Loló 3230 22nd St at Bartlett, Mission ☎ 415 643 5656; map p.100. Creating a supremely unique menu that borrows liberally from Mexican and Turkish cuisines, as well as other Mediterranean influences, *Loló* is a one-of-a-kind spot – no small feat in San Francisco. Tempting small and large plates abound, from Taco Tropical (panko-dusted shrimp topped with tropical relish and aioli; $9) to Sultan Likes Lolita (beef kofte on a bed of roasted aubergine puree; $14); there's also a dependable *carnitas* plate ($14). The room itself is audaciously vibrant and colourful: one of

9

SAN FRANCISCO'S SUPER BURRITO

Philadelphia has its cheesesteaks, New York its pastrami sandwiches, and Texas its barbecue and 22-oz sides of beef. In San Francisco, the **super burrito** is not only the premier bargain food, but truly a local phenomenon. The city is home to well over 150 **taquerias** – informal Mexican restaurants specializing in tacos, quesadillas, tortas and, of course, burritos – and locals are often heard debating their favourites effusively.

The civic obsession can be traced to September 1961, when El Faro Market's Febronio Ontiveros imaginatively concocted an outsized version of the burrito. Ontiveros' most loyal customers were hungry firemen in his Mission District neighbourhood looking for a bulky, handheld lunch alternative to a sandwich. The take-away-friendly slabs of food were an instant hit, and before the end of the decade, a handful of establishments specializing in this new home-style Mexican-American fast food had popped up around the Mission. By the 1980s, the San Francisco super burrito had reached critical mass, and today taquerias extend from one end of the city to the other.

San Francisco's take on the burrito differs from its Southern California cousin not only in its comparatively gargantuan size, but also in its **ingredient list**. Whereas a San Diego-style burrito can be an austere meal of meat, cheese and salsa scattered about a standard-size tortilla, the best San Francisco version stuffs a jumbo tortilla with any number of grilled or barbecued meats, Spanish rice, beans (choices include whole pinto, black or refried), melted cheese, *pico de gallo* (a splashy mix of diced tomato, onion, jalapeño and cilantro), guacamole or slices of avocado and a splatter of salsa; you may want to pass on sour cream if it's offered, as it often has an adverse effect on the burrito's myriad other elements. And with its emphasis on vegetables, grains and beans, the burrito also easily lends itself to vegetarian and vegan variants.

Most San Francisco taquerias wrap their goods in aluminum foil for easy handling, as the majority of locals eat burritos by hand. Surprisingly to many first-timers, a smartly constructed burrito will create little if any mess, although it's always a good idea to have napkins on hand. Expect to pay anywhere from $5–9 for a super burrito, and to not have much of an appetite for hours afterwards. Additionally, certain taquerias offer free tortilla chips and salsa as an appetizer. Give utensils a miss and order a Mexican beer or non-alcoholic *agua fresca* (fruit drink) with your foiled meal, and you'll fit right in.

A local website, ⓦburritoeater.com, features painstakingly detailed listings of all San Francisco burrito shops and rates each of them, intriguingly enough, in moustaches.

the owners designs furnishings in Mexico. Mon–Thurs 6–10pm, Fri & Sat 6pm–midnight.

★ **Papalote** 2916 24th St at Florida, Mission ☎415 970 8815; map p.100. With a particular emphasis on fresh ingredients and meatless menu options, Papalote serves peerless Cal-Mex cuisine that's remarkably affordable (everything's under $10), given the high quality. There's nary a poor choice to be made, from the marinated tofu burrito to anything that includes the perfectly grilled *carne asada*, while the complimentary offering of warm chips and otherworldly roasted tomato salsa is the real *coup de grace*. Branch: 1777 Fulton St at Masonic, Western Addition (☎415 776 0106). Mon–Sat 11am–10pm, Sun 11am–9pm.

Taqueria Can-cún 2288 Mission St at 19th, Mission ☎415 252 9560; map p.100. Civic standby featuring a rose-strewn shrine to the Virgin of Guadalupe and some of the most celebrated burritos ($5–6) in the Mission. The kitchen staff is uncommonly generous with avocado, while the house-made *horchata* (an unlikely rice-cinnamon drink) is the ideal foil for anything spicy. For a belt-busting eye-opener, drop in for breakfast. Branches: 3211 Mission

St at Valencia, Mission (☎415 550 1414), and 1003 Market St at Sixth, South of Market (☎415 864 6773). Mon–Thurs & Sun 10am–1am, Fri & Sat 10–2am.

Taqueria San Francisco 2794 24th St at York, Mission ☎415 641 1770; map p.100. Perhaps San Francisco's quintessential taqueria. There's a jar of peppery *pico de gallo* on each tabletop and, often, bouncy tuba-pop oozing from the jukebox. Burritos are characterized by generous heft, flaky tortillas and rustic meats such as *al pastor* (rotisserie-grilled pork) and, for the particularly adventurous, *lengua* (tongue) and *sesos* (brain). Daily 11am–9pm.

SEAFOOD

Anchor Oyster Bar 579 Castro St at 19th, Castro ☎415 431 3990; map p.100. Small spot where the salads and shellfish are best enjoyed with a seafood cocktail. Despite having been at this location on a less rambunctious stretch of Castro St for decades, it remains a surprising secret to many locals. It's on the expensive side (you'll spend around $30 per person), but a fun splurge nonetheless. Mon–Fri 11.30am–10pm, Sat noon–10pm, Sun 4–9.30pm.

Weird Fish 2193 Mission St at 18th, Mission ☎ 415 863 4744; map p.100. The fish here isn't particularly weird, but it is delicious, and there aren't many places like this that serve breakfast – you can create your own scramble for only $7 (a bit more if you want oysters). Later meals see a minor hike in prices, but remain adventurous, and there's no shortage of tofu- and veggie- inclusive choices on the menu. Mon, Wed & Sun 6–10pm, Thurs–Sat 6–11pm.

Woodhouse Fish Company 2073 Market St at 14th, Castro ☎ 415 437 2722; map p.100. Everything you'd find on the Maine coast or Cape Cod is available here at this New England-style fish house: lobster rolls ($17), white clam chowder ($5/cup, $7.50/bowl) and the like; if you're looking for a local twist, go for the Dungeness crab (half $11, whole $20) or the cioppino ($20). The corner location's fun for people-watching. Branch: 1914 Fillmore St at Bush, Pacific Heights (☎ 415 437 2722). Mon–Thurs & Sun 11.45am–9.30pm, Fri & Sat 11.45am–10pm.

SOUTH ASIAN

★ **Dosa** 995 Valencia St at 21st, Mission ☎ 415 642 3672; map p.100. *Dosa*'s namesake crepe-like item – and its close cousin, the thicker *uttapam* – are the true stars of the South Indian menu here, although the *sambar*, available as a side dipping soup, is heavenly in its own right. The waitstaff are exceptionally gracious, while the persimmon-coloured dining room and specialized menus (for those allergic to nuts, wheat and dairy) help make this casually stylish restaurant a major winner. Mains cost $10–17.50, with a carefully curated, yet robust wine list. Branch: 1700 Fillmore St at Post, Pacific Heights (☎ 415 441 3672). Mon–Thurs & Sun 5.30–10pm, Fri 5.30–11pm, Sat 11.30am–3.30pm & 5.30–11pm, Sun 11.30am–3.30pm.

Little Nepal 925 Cortland Ave at Folsom, Bernal Heights ☎ 415 643 3881; map pp.98–99. With its pine furniture and crisp white tablecloths, this hospitable neighbourhood eatery is a comfortable place to try Indian-inflected dishes such as *poleko machha* (tandoori-baked salmon, $16) or *tofu tarkari* (tofu and green bean curry, $11). Tues–Sun 5–10pm.

Zante 3489 Mission St at Cortland, Mission ☎ 415 821 3949; map pp.98–99. Getting points for uniqueness, if not for ambience and charm, this scruffy spot at the very south end of the Mission specializes in curry pizzas, a uniquely flavourful invention. The house special ($26 for a large) tops a thick crust with tandoori chicken, lamb, prawns and a host of vegetables and various herbs (spinach, aubergine, ginger). Several meatless options are also available. Daily 11am–3pm & 5–11pm.

SOUTHEAST ASIAN

Angkor Borei 3471 Mission St at Cortland, Mission ☎ 415 550 8417; map pp.98–99. One of the few Cambodian restaurants in San Francisco, *Angkor Borei*'s low prices and alluringly aromatic food make it terrific value. Try the *nhoam lahong* (green papaya salad, $7) or the slices of beef in a peanut curry sauce ($9). Duck in during the afternoon for the lunch specials, when prices are even lower. Mon–Thurs 11.15am–3.30pm & 4–10pm, Fri & Sat 11.15am–3.30pm & 4–10.30pm, Sun 4–10.30pm.

Thai Express 599 Castro St at 19th, Castro ☎ 415 864 5000; map p.100. Street-style Thai food, just like what you'd expect to find in Bangkok. Try the *gui chai* (vegetarian chive cakes, $6) before moving on to a main course of *kao na ped pa-lo* (five-spices duck over rice, $8) or *gang dang* (meat curry over rice, $7.25). Branch: 901 Larkin St at Geary, Tenderloin (☎ 415 441 8038). Daily 11.30am–10.30pm.

Zadin 4039 18th St at Noe, Castro ☎ 415 626 2260; map p.100. As you'd expect in the well-primped Castro, this Vietnamese spot is as chic as can be. The menu incorporates several gluten-free ingredients, but *Zadin*'s pair of chefs (who also happen to be cousins) have ensured authenticity isn't spared: items such as *goi cuon ca* (basa fish rolls; $8) and *thit nuong* (lemongrass pork; $14) hit the mark. Mon 6–9.30pm, Tues–Thurs 6–10pm, Fri & Sat 5.30–10pm, Sun 5.30–9.30pm.

HAIGHT-ASHBURY AND WEST OF CIVIC CENTER

With *Nopa* and *Bushi-tei* having joined the ranks of the city's best-loved dining spots, this area has stepped out of the towering culinary shadows cast by its Downtown and Mission neighbours. It's also notable for its dense concentration of top California restaurants (including longtime favourites *Jardinière* and *Zuni*), as well as one of San Francisco's top pizza destinations, the Western Addition's *Little Star Pizza*.

AFRICAN

Axum Cafe 698 Haight St at Pierce, Lower Haight ☎ 415 252 7912; map pp.106–107. Ethiopian restaurant where you shouldn't expect to keep your hands clean as you stab at deliciously gloopy confections such as *kitfo* (beef simmered in spicy butter, $12) with spongy *injera* bread. Mains can be presented together family-style on a gigantic platter, making the place a good destination for groups. The traditional honey wine (tej), however, is an acquired taste. Mon–Fri 5.30–10pm, Sat & Sun 12.30–10pm.

AMERICAN

Blue Jay Cafe 919 Divisadero St at McAllister, Western Addition ☎ 415 447 6066; map pp.106–107. Neighbourhood diner serving fairly priced comfort food to a clientele that's a signature Western Addition mix of dapper old black men and slouchy white hipsters. Sit at the U-shaped counter or on the pleasant patio, order a vintage soda to start, and follow with some crispy fried chicken, pork chops with apple chutney or saucy ribs – and don't

9

forget the extra-cheesy mac 'n' cheese. Mon–Fri 11.30am–2.30pm & 5.30–10pm, Sat 10am–2.30pm & 5.30–10pm, Sun 10am–2.30pm & 5–9.30pm.

★ **Burgermeister** 86 Carl St at Cole, Cole Valley ☎415 566 1274; map pp.106–107. The original location of this ever-popular local chainlet serves up excellent gourmet burgers (made with Niman Ranch beef); all the usual mainstream choices are available, as well as a handful of unusual options for the adventurous (such as the mango burger). A basic half-pound burger costs $9. Grab a seat of one of the few outdoor tables in front and watch the Muni streetcars rattle by as you eat. Branches: 138 Church St at Duboce, Castro (☎415 437 2874); 759 Columbus Ave at Filbert, North Beach (☎415 296 9907). Daily 11am–10pm.

Kate's Kitchen 471 Haight St at Fillmore, Lower Haight ☎415 626 3984; map pp.106–107. When you first stare down at the monstrous plates of budget breakfast fare served here, it's a little hard to think about saving room for extras. But treat yourself to some hush puppies to take away – deep-fried lumps of corn meal served with honey-touched "pooh butter". Kate's signature item, however, is the "flanched flarney garney" – essentially a hefty, eggy breakfast sandwich that's more than worth the caloric plunge. The place is massively popular on weekends, so just sign your name on the sheet dangling by the door and wait until you're called. Mon–Fri 8am–2.45pm, Sat & Sun 8am–3.45pm.

Memphis Minnie's 576 Haight St at Steiner, Lower Haight ☎415 864 7675; map pp.106–107. Neighbourhood mainstay where all meats are smoked with white oak logs (the irascible owner is vehemently against using gas or electric heat for cooking). In classic southern barbecue fashion, each table is outfitted with a roll of paper towels, to wipe your hands from the saucy slatherings of beef ribs ($17) and 18hr-smoked brisket ($16). The pair of house-ground burgers ($8–11) on the menu are also worth trying, and there's even smoked pecan bacon brittle ($3) for dessert. Mon–Sat 11am–10pm, Sun 11am–9pm.

Momi Tobys Revolution Cafe and Art Bar 528 Laguna St at Hayes, Hayes Valley ☎415 626 1508; map pp.106–107. The name may imply Che-level political fury, but the crowd at this hushed, vaguely Parisian café is more likely to be seen reading the arts section of the *New York Times* than *The Communist Manifesto* over their cups of coffee and plates of chicken tortilla casserole ($9). Tables under awning heaters stretch along the sidewalk for those seeking an alfresco experience. Mon–Thurs 7.30am–10pm, Fri 7.30am–11pm, Sat & Sun 8am–10pm.

Pork Store Cafe 1451 Haight St at Masonic, Upper Haight ☎415 864 6981; map pp.106–107. Grungy hangout on the neighbourhood's main drag that's a good place to spot a mix of locals and weekend visitors. Brave the inevitable lines for hearty portions of brunch standbys like eggs and French toast ($8–10); another artery-clogging option is the house special – two pork chops and suitably greasy hash browns ($9).

Branch: 3122 16th St at Valencia, Mission (☎415 626 5523). Mon–Fri 7am–3.30pm, Sat & Sun 8am–4pm.

Rosamunde Sausage Grille 545 Haight St at Fillmore, Lower Haight ☎415 437 6851; map pp.106–107. Tiny storefront grill with a few stools at the bar, serving inexpensive, top-grade grilled sausages on sesame rolls. Choose from a cherry-laced chicken number to the light flavours of a shrimp, scallop and snapper sausage; the German potato salad's also a knockout. Savvy customers place their order, head next door to *Toronado* (see p.179) and await their sausage's delivery over a beer. Also worth knowing: every Tues at opening time, a limited number of half-pound burgers ($6) go on sale to an early-assembled crowd on the pavement. Branch: 2832 Mission St at 24th, Mission (☎415 970 9015). Daily 11.30am–10pm.

Straw 203 Octavia St at Page, Hayes Valley ☎415 431 3663; map pp.106–107. Featuring self-described "carnival fare", *Straw*'s menu can be playful and quite hearty in one fell swoop – look no further than the fried chicken-and-waffle monte cristo sandwich ($9.75), complete with maple syrup and powdered sugar. A number of other Cajun-inspired items dot the menu as well, including julienne fries and cayenne-dusted corn-on-the-cob. Mon–Fri 5–10pm, Sat 10am–3pm & 5–10pm, Sun 10am–3pm & 5–9pm.

BELGIAN

Frjtz 581 Hayes St at Laguna, Hayes Valley ☎415 864 7654; map pp.106–107. Trendy restaurant serving cones of thick and crunchy Belgian-style fries ($3.25 small, $4.75 large) with dips such as creamy wasabi mayo and spicy yogurt peanut. Sandwiches and crepes are also available under names like "Michelangelo" (roasted red pepper and grilled aubergine sandwich; $9.50) and "Duchamp" (mushroom, chicken and spinach crepe; $9.75). There's also an extensive Belgian beer selection. Branch: 590 Valencia St at 17th, Mission (☎415 863 8272). Mon–Thurs 11.30am–10pm, Fri & Sat 11.30am–11pm, Sun 11am–9pm.

CALIFORNIA CUISINE

Asqew Grill 1607 Haight St at Clayton, Upper Haight ☎415 701 9301; map pp.106–107. This inexpensive local chain offers a refreshing option by specializing in more than a dozen different kinds of grilled skewers – from pork, apple and pear to shrimp, tomato and squash. Save room for a delicious brownie. Branches: 3415 California St at Laurel, Presidio Heights (☎415 386 5608), and 3348 Steiner St at Chestnut, Marina (☎415 931 9200). Daily 11.30am–9.30pm.

Jardinière 300 Grove St at Franklin, Hayes Valley ☎415 861 5555; map pp.106–107. Run by local big-name chef Traci des Jardins, this two-storey brick space caters to a pre-opera/ballet crowd with valet parking and plenty of pomp. It's an indulgent splurge, but worth it. The California-French menu changes regularly (although the aged-cheese platter is a constant), but you can expect innovative dishes like Alaskan halibut with artichokes ($36) or red wine-braised shortribs with horseradish potato purée ($35). A $45 prix-fixe option on Mon includes wine pairings. Mon & Sun 5–10pm, Tues–Sat 5–10.30pm.

★ **Nopa** 560 Divisadero St at Hayes, Western Addition ☎ 415 864 8643; map pp.106–107. One of the most heralded and popular – restaurants in town, *Nopa* (so named for its North of Panhandle home in the Western Addition) is set in a cavernous, yet homey space that formerly housed a laundromat. The Bolognese *pappardelle* pasta ($19) is a proven winner, as is the simple, but near-perfect grass-fed hamburger ($13, with fries). The decibel-sensitive may blanch at the room's noise, but can request a table in the soundproofed area beneath the mezzanine. Mon–Fri 6pm–1am, Sat & Sun 11am–2.30pm & 6pm–1am.

Zuni 1658 Market St at Gough, Hayes Valley ☎ 415 552 2522; map pp.106–107. *Zuni* boasts the most famous Caesar salad ($10) in town – made with home-cured anchovies – and an equally legendary focaccia hamburger ($15, lunch only). The centrally located restaurant's decor is heavy on brick and glass, but the triangular space remains light and airy. If you take a deep breath and go with the custom-roasted chicken for two ($48), be sure to enjoy the company you're with – it takes an hour to prepare. Tues–Thurs 11.30am–11pm, Fri & Sat 11.30am–midnight, Sun 11am–11pm.

CHINESE

Abacus 2078 Hayes St at Cole, Western Addition ☎ 415 387 2828; map pp.106–107. Blonde wood panelling lends an air of elegance to this restaurant's modern Szechuan cuisine. Start with the excellent egg rolls ($5.50 for four) or mushroom medley soup ($5.50) before moving on to fresh takes on favourites such as *kung pao* chicken ($9.50), dressed in bell pepper and peanuts. Mon–Fri 11.30am–2.30pm & 5–9.30pm, Sat 5–9.30pm, Sun 5–9pm.

EASTERN EUROPEAN

★ **Frankie's Bohemian Cafe** 1862 Divisadero St at Pine, Western Addition ☎ 415 567 7899; map pp.106–107. Single-room bar-restaurant on a busy corner that pulls in hearty eaters (and drinkers) to gorge on the house speciality, a hearty Czech mess called *brambory* that piles meat and veggies atop a pan-fried bed of potato and courgettes (zucchini). Like the burgers and salads also on offer, it costs $9–10, while a 20-oz beer goes for about $6. Daily 11am–11pm.

ECLECTIC

Herbivore 531 Divisadero St at Fell, Western Addition ☎ 415 885 7133; map pp.106–107. There's no meat or dairy in sight at this all-vegan restaurant, boasting popular dishes such as lentil loaf with mashed potatoes or giant

bowls of coconut noodle soup; everything's under $11. Large front windows look out onto the endlessly interesting Divisadero St sidewalk. Branch at 983 Valencia St at 21st, Mission (☎ 415 826 5657). Mon–Thurs & Sun 9am–10pm, Fri & Sat 9am–11pm.

FRENCH

Absinthe 398 Hayes St at Gough, Hayes Valley ☎ 415 551 1590; map pp.106–107. Brasserie-cum-bistro with two separate dining areas, both serving robust French food in a trendy atmosphere. Try the onion soup gratinée ($8), California lamb shank ($30), and either the *panna cotta* parfait or single cheese plate (both $9) for dessert. The bar's a cheaper alternative, serving smallish snacks for $3–14 per plate; just avoid the siren call of the pavement tables, as traffic is often punishingly loud. Brunch on weekends. Tues–Fri 11.30am–midnight, Sat 11am–midnight, Sun 11am–10pm.

Sophie's Crepes 1581 Webster St at Post, Japantown ☎ 415 929 7732; map pp.106–107. A solid bet for both savoury and *sucré* crepes, *Sophie's* stuffs its hand-held delicacies ($5–7) with an extensive choice of fillings – the banana-chocolate crepe is devilishly delicious, while the red-bean paste option nods toward this nook's Japantown surroundings. Tues–Thurs & Sun 11am–9pm, Fri & Sat 11am–10pm.

Zazie 941 Cole St at Carl, Cole Valley ☎ 415 564 5332; map pp.106–107. Moderately priced Francophile spot named after Frederic Malle's 1961 comedy of the same name. It's best known for outstanding breakfasts: light, fluffy pancakes ($5–12) and cream cheese coffee cake ($5) are the house specialities. The back patio is the best place to sit on a sunny afternoon, while evening visits are rewarded with a terrific $23.50 prix fixe. Mon–Thurs 8am–2.30pm & 5.30–9.30pm, Fri 8am–2.30pm & 5.30–10pm, Sat 9am–3pm & 5.30–10pm, Sun 9am–3pm & 5.30–9.30pm.

GERMAN

Suppenküche 525 Laguna St at Hayes, Hayes Valley ☎ 415 252 9289; map pp.106–107. Bavarian-inspired fare bang in the centre of San Francisco. This corner spot is constantly bustling, and since you can expect to wait at any hour, you may as well order a German, Austrian or Belgian beer at the bar. Once seated, prepare to indulge in rib-sticking mains such as pickled herring ($10.50), sautéed pork loin in mushroom sauce ($18.50) or, naturally, bratwurst with sauerkraut and mashed potatoes ($14.50). The menu always includes at least two meatless options. Mon–Sat 5–10pm, Sun 10am–2.30pm & 5–10pm.

ITALIAN

Bambino's Ristorante 945 Cole St at Parnassus, Cole Valley ☎ 415 731 1343; map pp.106–107. This inviting spot holds its own on a competitive restaurant block in quiet and reserved Cole Valley. Excellent risotto and pasta dishes

9

($14–19) are presented with subtle flair by the warm staff, while a range of similarly priced seafood pizzas (shrimp and mushroom; a sauceless salmon variety) offers a unique twist. Mon–Thurs 11.30am–10pm, Fri 11.30am–10.30pm, Sat 10am–10.30pm, Sun 10am–10pm.

Café Altano 602 Hayes St at Laguna, Hayes Valley ☎ 415 252 1200; map pp.106–107. Bright and airy corner spot with an enticing handful of pavement tables. Pasta mains are rich and true to form – try the *fettuccine* with pancetta in a thick pesto cream sauce ($14) – while the pork osso bucco ($19.50) is equally robust. Mon–Fri 11.30am–10pm, Sat 11am–11pm.

★ **Little Star Pizza** 846 Divisadero St at McAllister, Western Addition ☎ 415 441 1118; map pp.106–107. One of San Francisco's top pizzerias, this prime destination is packed nightly with locals enjoying its lively bar and jukebox blasting American and British indie rock. The kitchen bakes deep-dish and thin-crust pizzas with equal aplomb; large (12in) pies cost $15.50–23.50. Branch: 400 Valencia St at 15th, Mission (☎ 415 551 7827). Tues–Thurs 5–10pm, Fri 5–11pm, Sat 3–11pm, Sun 3–10pm.

JAPANESE

Grandeho's Kamekyo 943 Cole St at Parnassus, Cole Valley ☎ 415 759 8428; map pp.106–107. Creative, moderately priced sushi dominates the menu at this family-owned spot. The long, wooden sushi bar is popular with Cole Valley and Upper Haight denizens, but if you're in the mood for something other than the house speciality, try the *chasoba* noodles. Branch: 2721 Hyde St at North Point, Fisherman's Wharf (☎ 415 673 6828). Mon–Thurs & Sun 11.30am–10pm, Fri & Sat 11.30am–11pm.

Kiss Sushi 1700 Laguna St at Sutter, Japantown ☎ 415 474 2866; map pp.106–107. With only a dozen or so seats available, you'll need to phone well ahead for a reservation at this signless, blink-and-you'll-miss-it spot. It's also on the expensive side, with a full meal often running upwards of $65 per person. All that said, the expert chef and his wife (the establishment's sole two employees) go out of their way to make customers feel pampered – expect as many as eight courses if you order the *omakase* course (chef's choice) – although stories exist of particularly slow eaters being shown the door. Tues–Sat 5.30–9.30pm.

Maki 1825 Post St at Webster, Japantown ☎ 415 921 5215; map pp.106–107. One of several humbly sized restaurants in the Japan Center serving delicious, moderately priced fare, *Maki* specializes in both *wappan meshi* (a wood steamer filled with vegetables, meat and rice) and *chawan mushi* (savoury custard). It's also notable for its affable owner and extensive sake selection. Tues–Thurs 6–9pm, Fri 5.30–9pm, Sat noon–2pm & 5.30–9pm, Sun noon–2pm & 5.30–8.30pm.

★ **Sebo** 517 Hayes St at Octavia, Hayes Valley ☎ 415 864 2122; map pp.106–107. Despite having two Americans at the helm of the kitchen, this low-key destination serves some of the most authentic sushi in town. Elbow your way to a spot at the six-seat bar and let the chefs lead the way through a multi-course extravaganza; if you prefer, the six-course *omakase* course is $80. No reservations. Sushi Tues–Sat 6–10pm, izakaya (Japanese bar-style dining) Sun 6–11pm.

LATIN AMERICAN

Espetus 1686 Market St at Gough, Hayes Valley ☎ 415 552 8792; map pp.106–107. Brazilian *churrascaria* where the all-you-can-eat menu is a decadently crafted homage to meat on enormous skewers. Servers constantly roam the dining room, offering over a dozen types of meats, in addition to grilled prawns and even pineapple; some, such as the filet mignon and chicken legs, hit the mark more than others, so pick your favourites early and wait for a server to make the rounds. Expect to spend upwards of $50 per person. Mon–Thurs 11.30am–2.30pm & 5–10pm, Fri 11.30am–2.30pm & 5–11pm, Sat noon–3pm & 5–11pm, Sun noon–3pm & 3–9pm.

MEXICAN

Cuco's 488 Haight St at Fillmore, Lower Haight ☎ 415 863 4906; map pp.106–107. Family-operated Mexican-Salvadorean nook known for super-budget prices, fresh-cut *carnitas* (fried pork) and a smirky proprietress who usually double-checks if you'd like your meal extra-spicy. A clever vegetarian option here is the fried plantains burrito, while the home-made chips are oversize and often served warm. Don't come with a large group if you're looking for somewhere to sit – it's a really tiny room. Mon–Sat noon–9pm.

El Burrito Express 1812 Divisadero St at Bush, Western Addition ☎ 415 776 4246; map pp.106–107. One of the most heralded taquerias in town outside the Mission, "EBX" boasts an overwhelming burrito menu that holds something for everyone, with most everything costing about $6–7. The Bronco option passes on the rice, while the Expresso burrito is slathered in cheese and sauce (you'll need a knife and fork). There's a (mostly take-away) branch at 1601 Taraval St at 26th, Outer Sunset (☎ 415 566 8300). Mon & Tues 10am–9pm, Wed–Fri 10am–10pm, Sat 11am–9pm.

★ **Green Chile Kitchen** 1801 McAllister St at Baker, Western Addition ☎ 415 440 9411; map pp.106–107. Deeply flavourful cuisine from the state of New Mexico, further enhanced by robust red and green chillis. A bowl of hearty chicken stew ($7) is the perfect antidote to a chilly San Francisco evening, while a full plate of *tamales* (presented in their husks) with several small side items is $12; request "Christmas" sauce for a dollar extra, and you'll get red and green chilli sauce on (or in) your meal. The inviting corner dining room encourages lingering at the window counter or in one of the booths. Mon–Thurs & Sun 9am–9.30pm, Fri & Sat 9am–10pm.

PAN-ASIAN

★ **Bushi-tei** 1638 Post St at Laguna, Japantown ☎ 415 440 4959; map pp.106–107. Elegant, Japanese-inspired cuisine imbued with accents from other continents: lamb chops with port and *wasabi* ($30); duck with a mascarpone mustard sauce ($28); foie gras over pumpkin pot du crème ($20). The restaurant's gorgeous design includes glass walls that play off wood panelling from nineteenth-century Japan, while certain dishes go so far as to command the use of custom-designed plates and bowls. Mon–Sat 5.30–10pm, Sun 11.30am–2.30pm & 5.30–10pm.

The Citrus Club 1790 Haight St at Cole, Upper Haight ☎ 415 387 6366; map pp.106–107. Vegan-friendly noodle house specializing in sauteed noodles served in a variety of broths; the garlic beef and shiitake mushroom dish is also a solid bet. Budget prices (everything on the menu's well under $10) help seal the deal. Mon–Thurs & Sun 11.30am–10pm, Fri & Sat 11.30am–11pm.

SOUTH ASIAN

Indian Oven 233 Fillmore St at Waller, Lower Haight ☎ 415 626 1628; map pp.106–107. Certainly one of the city's leading Indian restaurants, *Indian Oven* is known for its moderately priced baked tandoori items, but the fluffy naan bread is just as memorable; there's also an impressive selection of Indian beers. Despite its local notoriety, it's large enough that you usually won't have to wait long. Daily 11am–11pm.

SOUTHEAST ASIAN

Thai Place II 312 Divisadero St at Page, Lower Haight ☎ 415 552 6881; map pp.106–107. While this isn't one of San Francisco's major Thai destinations, the upside is that you'll probably be able to sit down immediately for exceptional plates of sizzling beef ($11) or honey-roasted duck on a bed of spinach ($9). Mon–Thurs & Sun 11am–10.30pm, Fri & Sat 11am–11pm.

★ **Thep Phanom** 400 Waller St at Fillmore, Lower Haight ☎ 415 431 2526; map pp.106–107. This corner Thai spot pulls in diners from all over town – and sometimes beyond – for its fragrant and delicious curries ($11–12). The spinach with peanut sauce is sweet and sharp, while the seafood medley in coconut sauce is equally divine. Daily 5.30–10.30pm.

THE RICHMOND, GOLDEN GATE PARK AND THE SUNSET

The west side neighbourhoods may be short on destination restaurants, but they're full of excellent ethnic eateries (*Brothers Korean BBQ, Aziza*) and wonderful niche spots (Pizzetta 211). The area's also home to notables such as

groundbreaking *Thanh Long*, flashy-on-a-budget *Spices!* and unassailable *Gordo Taqueria*, as well as a pair of bustling, if lesser, Chinatowns (and their attendant dining spots) – one along Clement Street in the Inner Richmond, the other along Irving Street in the Outer Sunset.

AMERICAN

Beach Chalet Brewery & Restaurant 1000 Great Highway at John F. Kennedy, Golden Gate Park ☎ 415 386 8439; map p.116. Although the Beach Chalet's singular setting – wedged between Ocean Beach's strand and the far western reaches of Golden Gate Park – will always be its star attraction, this upstairs restaurant's food is eminently enjoyable in its own right. A variety of fish, meat and vegetarian mains ($13–32) pair well with any of the more than half-dozen beers brewed on site. There's a popular brunch on weekends, both here and in the adjacent, more informal Park Chalet in the rear of the historic building's ground level. Mon–Thurs 9am–10pm, Fri 9am–11pm, Sat 8am–11pm, Sun 8am–10pm.

Bill's Place 2315 Clement St at 24th, Outer Richmond ☎ 415 221 5262; map p.116. Classic burger place and soda fountain with a back patio – and a bit of a timewarp feel. Hamburgers are named after local personalities (Carol Doda, Paul Kantner), and most are under $10; the milkshakes and ice-cream sundaes are legendarily thick. Sun–Thurs 11am–10pm, Fri & Sat 11am–11pm.

Bistro at the Cliff House 1900 Point Lobos Ave, Outer Richmond ☎ 415 386 3330; map p.116. The less expensive sibling of downstairs fine-dining restaurant *Sutro's*, this seaside destination can still put a dent in your wallet, as the two restaurants share a similar dinner menu. Reliable choices include the clam chowder ($9.50) and pan-roasted salmon filet ($24.50), while the views of the Pacific are predictably spectacular (coastal fog notwithstanding). Reservations not accepted. Mon–Sat 9am–9.30pm, Sun 8.30am–9.30pm.

Manor Coffee Shop 321 West Portal Ave at 14th, West Portal ☎ 415 661 2468; map p.116. Inexpensive spot that's seemingly as old as the hills, and home to a decidedly local crowd from West Portal and the surrounding neighbourhoods. Breakfast (available well into the afternoon) is the biggest draw here, with staples such as rich omelettes and fluffy pancakes packing customers into cushy booths and a dining counter. Daily 7.30am–8pm.

Pluto's 627 Irving St at Seventh, Inner Sunset ☎ 415 753 8867; map p.116. Walk in through the dining area, pick up a paper menu as you get in line and hand it to the servers behind the counter as you order. Custom salads are the house speciality, as they're among the biggest, best and cheapest ($7.50 or so) in town. The freshly made sandwiches are good but on the small side, while the turkey and stuffing is a soul-warming option any day of the year. Branch: 3258 Scott St at Chestnut, Marina (☎ 415 775 8867). Daily 11am–10pm.

9

Q 225 Clement St at Third, Inner Richmond ☎ 415 752 2298; map p.116. This lively outpost along Clement St's restaurant row is an over-the-top diner, sporting funky features such as a booth where a tree grows through the table. Portions are generous, and the menu mostly consists of comfort food (fried chicken on mashed potatoes; beer-battered catfish), although meatless choices are also available. The most expensive main, a grilled New York steak, is $18. Reservations not accepted. Mon–Fri 11am–11pm, Sat 10am–11pm, Sun 10am–10pm.

The Richmond 615 Balboa St at Seventh, Inner Richmond ☎ 415 379 8988; map p.116. Neighbourhood restaurant serving surprisingly sophisticated meat and seafood mains ($10–25), with a richly varied wine list to match. Wild Pacific salmon is creatively served with aubergine (eggplant) salsa, while vegetarians may opt for the wild mushroom-stuffed puff pastry with chive potatoes. Choose from a variety of wines made by small, family-run California wineries. Mon–Thurs 5.30–9.30pm, Fri & Sat 5.30–10pm.

CALIFORNIA CUISINE

Pizzetta 211 211 23rd Ave at California, Outer Richmond ☎ 415 379 9880; map p.116. Expect inventive and unusual organic thin-crust pizza at this miniscule (only four tables) nook on a residential street. There's a different menu each week, offering whatever's fresh and seasonal – wild rocket (arugula), ricotta and summer squash aren't uncommon toppings. Servers are very amiable and have been known to offer wine and even blankets to those waiting outside on chilly evenings. Pizzas $11–14. Mon & Tues 5–9pm, Wed–Sun noon–9pm.

CHINESE

Clement BBQ 617 Clement St at Seventh, Inner Richmond ☎ 415 666 3328; map p.116. The window of this Hong Kong-style café – managed concurrently with the bare-bones *Clement Restaurant* immediately next door – is filled with glistening ducks and chickens hanging from hooks. There's also other barbecue food sold by the pound for take-away – succulent pork is about $6/lb. Daily 9am–6pm.

★ Spices! 294 Eighth Ave at Clement, Inner Richmond ☎ 415 752 8884; map p.116. This humbly sized Taiwanese-Szechuan upstart is known for brazen dishes such as beef tendon ($4.50) and hot and sour intestine noodle soup ($6.50), although there are plenty of less eyebrow-raising options on the menu. As you'd expect from the name, spice can be added to nearly every dish upon request. Expect crowds of young Asian hipsters, giggly teen servers and MTV Asia burbling on the overhead television. Branch: 291 Sixth Ave at Clement, Outer Richmond (☎ 415 752 8885). Daily noon–midnight.

Ton Kiang 5821 Geary Blvd at 22nd, Outer Richmond ☎ 415 387 8273; map p.116. Gigantic, bi-level restaurant

whose crowd reflects its diverse neighbourhood. A wait is almost inevitable for a table in one of the bustling dining rooms; once inside, try the sliced barbecue pork starter ($9) or spicy aubergine (eggplant) main ($10). Mon–Thurs 10am–9pm, Fri 10am–9.30pm, Sat 9.30am–9.30pm, Sun 9am–9pm.

ECLECTIC

Park Chow 1240 Ninth Ave at Lincoln, Inner Sunset ☎ 415 665 9912; map p.116. This surprisingly huge space features several fun seating options: a terrific upstairs deck, a small enclosed patio and a few fireside tables inside. The menu's all over the globe, from salads, American comfort food (try the burger on a baguette, $11), pizzas and pastas to artisan cheese plates and even a handful of Asian noodle dishes; everything works, though, including the dessert pies and cakes. The original, equally busy *Chow* is at 215 Church St at Market, Castro (☎ 415 665 9912). Mon–Thurs & Sun 8am–10pm, Fri & Sat 8am–11pm.

FRENCH

★ Chapeau! 126 Clement St at Second, Inner Richmond ☎ 415 750 9787; map p.116. Provençal-inspired food on a par with several French restaurants in the city's central neighbourhoods – no surprise, considering the restaurant's name means "Wow!" Mains such as petit poussin and cassoulet de Toulouse are $20–28, with a three-course prix fixe available for $38; there's also a $28 three-course special for early-evening guests (Mon–Thurs & Sun 5–6pm). Mon–Thurs & Sun 5–10pm, Fri & Sat 5–10.30pm.

IRISH

Copper Kettle 2240 Taraval St at 32nd, Outer Sunset ☎ 415 731 8818; map p.116. Excellent doughnuts, pastries and traditional Irish breakfasts (about $10–12) at this homey shop set deep in the Sunset street grid. It's right on the L-Taraval Muni streetcar line – convenient if you're coming from another neighbourhood. Mon–Fri 6am–3pm, Sat 7am–4pm, Sun 8am–3pm.

ITALIAN

Mescolanza 2221 Clement St at 23rd, Outer Richmond ☎ 415 668 2221; map p.116. Affordable neighbourhood trattoria where no main is more than $18. The unassuming exterior gives way to a softly lit interior where Italian classics like chicken *cacciatore* and *pappardelle* with chicken and mushrooms are done right. Mon–Thurs & Sun 5–9.30pm, Fri & Sat 5–10pm.

The Pizza Place on Noriega 3901 Noriega St at 46th, Outer Sunset ☎ 415 759 5752; map p.116. Cleverly named pizzeria set a few blocks off Ocean Beach that's a gathering place for the neighbourhood surfing community. Thin-crust pies ($22–26 for a 20-in large) often include numerous fresh vegetables, while "The

Spicoli" is a nod to the double cheese and sausage pizza that Sean Penn had delivered to his classroom in *Fast Times at Ridgemont High*. Grinders (hearty East Coast sandwiches) are also available during afternoon hours, and there's an inviting back patio. Mon–Thurs & Sun noon–10pm, Fri & Sat noon–10.30pm.

JAPANESE

Ariake 5041 Geary Blvd at 15th, Outer Richmond ☎ 415 221 6210; map p.116. One of the more moderately priced Japanese places you'll find in town. Choose from one of four full sushi dinners ($18–24) available at the bar, with names like Faith, Hope and Love. Other usual suspects such as *gyoza* potstickers ($5.50), tempura plates ($13–14) and steaming bowls of *udon* ($9–10) are also on offer. Mon–Thurs 11.30am–2.30pm & 5–11pm, Fri 11.30am–2.30pm & 5pm–midnight, Sat 11.30am–midnight.

Hotei 1290 Ninth Ave at Irving, Inner Sunset ☎ 415 753 6045; map p.116. This smallish, single-room spot steers away from most local Japanese restaurants' obsession with sushi and focuses its attention on *soba* (buckwheat noodles), *ramen* and titanic bowls of *udon* soup; if you really want sushi, the friendly staff will have it trundled over for you from co-managed *Ebisu* across the street. Most dishes are $12 and under, while two-piece orders of *nigiri* sushi cost $4–5 each. The bubbling indoor fountain is a nice touch. Mon & Wed–Sun 11.30am–10pm.

Koo 408 Irving St at Fifth, Inner Sunset ☎ 415 731 7077; map p.116. The unique Japanese fusion menu at this attractive spot features a combination of cooked plates designed to be shared, as well as plenty of sushi, sashimi and speciality rolls (try the "Flying Kamikaze" – spicy tuna and asparagus wrapped in *albacore*). The grilled aubergine (eggplant) *dengaku* is a top choice. Plan to spend at least $20–30 per person. Tues–Thurs 5.30–10pm, Fri & Sat 5.30–10.30pm, Sun 5–9.30pm.

KOREAN

★ **Brothers Korean BBQ** 4128 Geary Blvd at Sixth, Inner Richmond ☎ 415 387 7991; map p.116. The oldest among a small batch of informal Korean restaurants along Geary Blvd, and one of the few with its name emblazoned in English on the front sign. The decor's certainly nothing to look at, but the moderately priced feasts of marinated meats and myriad, pungent side dishes are worth the visit. Some tables have sunken *hibachis* on which you can cook your own meats, although you may need to towel off the sweat from your brow by meal's end. Daily 11am–midnight.

My Tofu House 4627 Geary Blvd at 11th, Inner Richmond ☎ 415 570 1818; map p.116. Although its name suggests a meatless kitchen, there's in fact a fair amount of dishes here to sate a carnivore. Go with the *bulgogi* (thin-sliced rib-eye with rice and *kimchi*; $8 at lunch,

$18 at dinner); alternatively, vegetarians will want to try one of the many excellent tofu combination items (about $10 each). Mon–Fri & Sun 11am–10pm, Sat 5–10pm.

MEDITERRANEAN/MIDDLE EASTERN

Aziza 5800 Geary Blvd at 22nd Ave, Outer Richmond ☎ 415 752 2222; map p.116. Moroccan fine-dining destination with opulent decor, a superb wine list and fun touches like a rosewater-filled pewter basin presented for pre-meal hand-washing. The menu's packed with California-accented North African specialities: squab with foie gras emulsion ($28) and a couscous plate with goat's milk butter and fava beans ($16) top the list of choices. Arrive early and enjoy a drink at the gorgeously tiled bar. Mon & Wed–Sun 5.30–10pm.

★ **Troya** 349 Clement St at Fifth, Inner Richmond ☎ 415 379 6000; map p.116. Airy corner spot with a lengthy list of Mediterranean meze choices and exceptional main courses. Best bets include the thick courgette (zucchini) cakes with yogurt sauce ($5.95), the hearty beef *turlu* ($12.75) – terrific on a chilly, foggy evening – or any of the numerous kebabs ($12–13) on offer. Mon–Thurs noon–2.30pm & 5–9.30pm, Fri noon–2.30pm & 5–10pm, Sat noon–10pm, Sun noon–9pm.

Yumma's 721 Irving St at Eighth, Inner Sunset ☎ 415 682 0762; map p.116. Excellent Eastern Mediterranean fare for those on a budget. A host of *shawarma* options ($6–8) anchor the menu, while Med staples such as falafel and tabouleh are equally impressive and affordable. Sunny afternoons are ideal for eating on the cosy back patio; there are also a few seats at the window counter. Daily 11am–10pm.

MEXICAN

★ **Gordo Taqueria** 1233 Ninth Ave at Lincoln, Inner Sunset ☎ 415 566 6011; map p.116. This austere shop, just outside Golden Gate Park, lives up to its name (which translates to "fat" in English) by specializing in hefty, stumpy burritos that never miss the mark. The menu's as simple as can be, including only tacos, burritos and quesadillas, and you'll be hard-pressed to spend more than $7 on your meal. If ordering a burrito, be sure to request a grilled (rather than steamed) tortilla. Branches: 2252 Clement St at 24th (☎ 415 387 4484), and 5450 Geary Blvd at 19th (☎ 415 668 8226), both in the Outer Richmond. Daily 10am–10pm.

La Fonda 712 Irving St at Eighth, Inner Sunset ☎ 415 681 9205; map p.116. Inviting taqueria on the neighbourhood's main drag known for its extensive menu and comfortable upstairs dining nook. With a host of meatless options and ten or so meats to choose from (including the rarely seen *cochinita pibil* – marinated pork with *achiote* sauce and banana leaf), you may need a few minutes to decide, but it's hard to go wrong with anything here. Everything's under $10, and there

9

are a pair of two-person tables on the pavement if the weather's agreeable. Daily 9am–10pm.

RUSSIAN

Katia's 600 Fifth Ave at Balboa, Inner Richmond ☎415 668 9292; map p.116. Muscovite restaurant with frilly decor, live acoustic music (accordion, guitar) on occasion, a full slate of Russian teas and almost every Russian dish you'd hope to find in this part of the world. Choose from a bowl of beet borscht ($5) or a golden-baked *piroshki* ($3) as a starter, then move on to a heaping plate of beef stroganoff ($16) or perhaps the poached sturgeon ($19). Wed–Fri 11.30am–2.30pm & 5–10pm, Sat & Sun 5–10pm.

SEAFOOD

Pacific Café 7000 Geary Blvd at 34th, Outer Richmond ☎415 387 7091; map p.116. The decor of this old-fashioned, ever-popular joint has hardly changed since 1974, when it opened. There's frequently a wait for a table, but if the complimentary glass of wine isn't enough of an incentive to invoke reserves of patience, moderately priced dishes such as parmesan-crusted halibut ($27) or lemon-doused crab cakes with red potatoes ($23) should be. Expect a slightly older crowd, and perhaps a family or two. Mon–Thurs & Sun 5–9.30pm, Fri & Sat 5–10.30pm.

SOUTH ASIAN

India Clay Oven 2436 Clement St at 26th, Outer Richmond ☎415 751 2400; map p.116. Delightful curry house catering to adventurous guests unafraid to add "911", the kitchen's highest level of spiciness, to their orders. Medium spice should do the trick for most patrons, however, and there's usually a table available in the lovely, atrium-like dining room. Mains $12–17. Mon–Thurs & Sun 10am–10.30pm, Fri & Sat 10am–11pm.

Roti 53 West Portal Ave at Vicente, West Portal ☎415 665 7684; map p.116. Highly regarded Indian restaurant in a mellow district only two streetcar stops from the bustling Castro. Menu items are smartly prepared, and fish enthusiasts will want to try the tandoori *machchi* ($20), a fresh catch marinated in several spices. Mon–Thurs & Sun 5–9.30pm, Fri & Sat 5–10pm.

SOUTHEAST ASIAN

★ **Mandalay** 4348 California St at Sixth, Inner Richmond ☎415 386 3895; map p.116. A more accessible choice for Burmese food in this area than woefully overcrowded *Burma Superstar* nearby, *Mandalay's* go-to starter is its *balada*, a crispy pancake tailor-made for dipping in its accompanying curry sauce. There's occasional deviation from Burmese on the menu (chow mein, Singapore-style noodles), but overall the cuisine here is a delectable, saucy melange of Thai, Indian and Chinese. Mains rarely exceed $14. Mon–Thurs & Sat 11.30am–3.30pm & 5–9.30pm, Fri & Sat 11.30am–10pm.

Marnee Thai 1243 Ninth Ave at Lincoln, Inner Sunset ☎415 731 9999; map p.116. In a city bursting with neighbourhood Thai restaurants, this humming spot still manages to draw in diners from all over. The kitchen's home-style central Thai cooking rolls with the seasons, so winter visitors may see a markedly different menu from those in summer. Prices for most main courses bob around the $10 mark. Branch: 2225 Irving St at 24th, Outer Sunset (☎415 665 9500). Daily 11.30am–10pm.

Singapore Malaysian 836 Clement St at Ninth, Inner Richmond ☎415 750 9518; map p.116. Treading an uncommon cuisine path found in San Francisco, this gem is often overlooked amid the sea of Chinese and Korean restaurants in its area of the Richmond. It's worth seeking out, however, for fine (and reasonably priced) staples of these Asian regions, including beef *rendang* and coconut curry soup. Daily 11am–10pm.

Thanh Long 4101 Judah St at 46th Ave, Outer Sunset ☎415 665 1146; map p.116. An unlikely destination restaurant, given its location far from the city's core, *Thanh Long* was San Francisco's first Vietnamese restaurant in the early 1970s, and has become increasingly French-inspired and upscale (even offering valet parking on its ramshackle Outer Sunset corner) in the years since. Specialities include an uncommonly delicious soft-shell crab starter ($11.75) and the sizzling claypot main course ($21) – essentially, the day's catch simmered in a medley of vegetables and herbs. The soothing dining room, located bang on the N-Judah streetcar line, is bedecked in blonde wood panelling and earth tones. Tues–Thurs & Sun 5–9.30pm, Fri & Sat 5–10pm.

COCKTAILS IN SOUTH OF MARKET

Bars, clubs and live music venues

Increasingly, in major party cities such as New York or Miami, there's a flexible division between restaurants, bars and clubs – and San Francisco is no different. A top-name DJ might stop by for a quiet session at a neighbourhood bar instead of one of the warehouse clubs, for example, or a savvy promoter might launch a theme night at a local restaurant's bar area instead of a club. Similarly, many popular live music venues in San Francisco are little more than a neighbourhood saloon with a stage in a back corner. Granted, you'll find a smattering of superclubs and larger concert halls (including the landmark Fillmore, prime birthing ground for the psychedelic rock movement of the 1960s), but smaller is often considered better in San Francisco, and even in the biggest venues cover charges usually remain reasonable.

10

ESSENTIALS

ID Most clubs are restricted to those 21 and over. Remember to have your ID on you to prove you're over 21 – since they're serving alcohol, bars and clubs will invariably prevent anyone under that age from entering.

Listings For up-to-date listings, call or check the venue's website; alternatively, pick up one of the local weekly freesheets, *San Francisco Bay Guardian* (wsfbg.com) or *SF Weekly* (wsfweekly.com). Naturally, there are plenty of event websites you can browse, including SF Station (wsfstation .com), Upcoming (wupcoming.yahoo.com) and Flavorpill (wflavorpill.com/sanfrancisco); Nitevibe (wnitevibe.com) is a good resource for DJ happenings in and around town.

Opening hours Depending on neighbourhood and regular clientele, some bars in San Francisco are terrific spots for early-evening happy hours, yet tend to wind down early; others don't begin to fill until after 9pm, if not later (especially on weekends). As for clubs, unlike most other major cities (where the action never gets going until after midnight), most San Francisco clubs close at 2am, so you can usually be sure of finding things well underway around 10pm. Owing to licensing laws, clubs remaining open after 2am must switch to non-alcoholic beverages

after that hour, which makes partying until dawn require a bit of determination and advance planning.

Smoking Smoking is banned in virtually all bars and clubs, although there are a few places around the city with designated smoking sections, noted below. Frankly, you're unlikely to get into trouble for breaking the law, but the glowering glances from other patrons often prove as great a deterrent as the $100 fine.

Tickets Tickets start at around $10 and, unless it's a special gig, top out around $25. The easiest way to buy tickets to live events is online, although with the addition of booking fees, it's by far the most expensive as well. Ticketmaster (t1 800 745 3000, wticketmaster.com) and Tickets.com (wtickets.com) service most major Bay Area venues, while Ticketweb (wticketweb.com) and Ticketfly (wticketfly .com) are prime vendors for smaller clubs. To sidestep steep extra fees, check the venue's website for its box office hours, when fees are often greatly reduced. Some of the Bay Area's largest-scale venues, such as outdoor stadiums and sports arenas, are located in Oakland and San Jose (for which, see Chapter 16), although the San Francisco Giants' AT&T Park hosts a few big shows annually.

BARS

Nowhere are the vastly different identities of San Francisco's neighbourhoods more evident than in its far-reaching bar scene. **Downtown** has dozens of bars packed with office workers in early evening, but lifeless at most other times; many of those same workers – at least those in their 20s and 30s – often adjourn to the countless hotspots in the **Marina** and **Cow Hollow** later in the evening and at weekends. The **Tenderloin** has a few trendy spots and a host of dives amid its grit, while **South of Market** is known more for its clubs than bars. Inevitably, the gay scene (covered in Chapter 12) dominates almost every bar in the **Castro**, while the nearby **Mission** has arguably the city's best selection of watering holes, from grungy corner taverns to hip lounges. Many bars in **North Beach** tend to cater to Bay Areans visiting "the city" for the evening or weekend, although it has a handful of haunts popular with neighbourhood denizens as well. The **Upper Haight**'s bar scene has been revived in recent years, although the neighbouring **Lower Haight** still outshines it. As for the **Richmond** and the **Sunset**, there are a number of pubs and taverns (a disproportionate number of which are Irish) that cater to locals, but few worth a special trip.

DOWNTOWN

Azul 1 Tillman Place at Grant, Union Square t415 362 9750; map pp.40–41. Tucked away down a subtle alley, this bar – and its terrific sangria – makes for a nice getaway from Union Square's retail madness. As the name suggests, its sleek, modern design is awash in soothing blue. Mon & Tues 4pm–midnight, Wed–Sat 4pm–2am.

Bubble Lounge 714 Montgomery St at Columbus, Jackson Square t415 434 4204; map pp.40–41. West Coast outpost of the New York Champagne bar that lures a young, gussied-up crowd to its squishy sofas. There's a vast selection of fizz (divided between light, medium and full-bodied), as well as classic cocktails such as bellinis and chambords. Tues & Wed 5.30pm–1am, Thurs & Fri 5.30pm–2am, Sat 6.30pm–2am.

Buddha Lounge 901 Grant Ave at Washington, Chinatown t415 362 1792; map pp.40–41. With its seemingly die-cut entryway, smattering of ratty stools and

raucous jukebox, this hole-in-the-wall pickup joint feels far removed from urban America, filled as it is with older locals slapping down mah-jong tiles. The namesake Buddha is found in a slapdash mural on the rear wall. Daily 1pm–2am.

The Cigar Bar & Grill 850 Montgomery St at Pacific, Jackson Square t415 398 0850; map pp.40–41. This classy, Spanish-inspired spot feels warm and inviting with its wood-beam ceiling and dark wood bar. The heated brick courtyard is perfect for relaxing, and it's one of San Francisco's few smoking establishments, complete with humidor. Live salsa and Latin jazz performances Thurs–Sat (no cover); pool tables and a late-night menu nightly. Mon–Fri 4pm–2am, Sat 6pm–2am.

Ferry Plaza Wine Merchant Ferry Building Marketplace, Embarcadero t415 391 9400; map pp.40–41. Combination store and wine bar with a vast selection of California varietals that can be sampled either

HOTEL ROOFTOP BARS

Several hotel rooftop bars across San Francisco are designed to make the most of the city's spectacular views – for which, of course, you'll pay a hefty premium.

Grandviews Lounge Grand Hyatt, 345 Stockton St at Sutter, Union Square ☎415 398 1234; map pp.40–41. 36 storeys up in the air and straight out of the 1970s, *Grandviews Lounge* boasts an unforgettable view to the north that allows you to scope out Coit Tower, Alcatraz and beyond. There's a piano player every Fri and Sat, and as long as you nurse a single drink, a visit here won't wallop your wallet. Daily 3pm–1am.

Harry Denton's Starlight Room Sir Francis Drake, 450 Powell St at Sutter, Union Square ☎415 395 8595; map pp.40–41. Look sharp and order a martini at this famed 21st-floor lounge. There's live entertainment most nights ($10–15 cover Wed–Sat) and two drag shows during Sun brunch, for which reservations are recommended. Count on getting turned away at the door if you show up in jeans or sneakers. Tues–Sat 6pm–2am; Sun brunch 11am–5pm.

Medjool Elements Hotel, 2522 Mission St at 21st, Mission ☎415 550 9055; map p.100. This multi-level Mediterranean restaurant-lounge boasts a rooftop perch from which to enjoy wraparound city views. The catch is that there can be lots of posing to contend with; you'll be hard-pressed to find a Mission resident here. Mon–Wed 4–10pm, Thurs 4–11pm, Fri 3pm–2am, Sat 10am–2am, Sun 10am–10pm; Sat & Sun brunch 10am–2pm.

Top of the Mark InterContinental Mark Hopkins, One Nob Hill Circle, Nob Hill ☎415 392 3434; map p.56. San Francisco's most storied rooftop bar opened in 1939, although these days it tends to attract mostly tourists. The martini list includes more than 100 different varieties. Expect to pay a nominal ($5–15) cover Tues–Sat for live entertainment. Bar: Mon–Thurs & Sun 5pm–midnight, Fri & Sat 4pm–1am; brunch: Sun 10am–1pm; tea: Mon–Sat 2.30–5pm.

The View San Francisco Marriott Marquis, 55 Fourth St at Mission, South of Market ☎415 896 1600; map pp.84–85. Set on the 39th floor of the hotel known colloquially as "the Jukebox", this romantic and modern lounge features a spectacular view of South of Market high-rises and the Bay. Mon–Thurs & Sun 4pm–midnight, Fri & Sat 4pm–1am.

10

as tastes ($3–8) or by the glass ($5–12), alongside cheese plates. Mon 11am–8pm, Tues 10am–8pm, Wed–Fri 10am–9pm, Sat 8am–8pm, Sun 10am–7pm.

Gold Dust Lounge 247 Powell St at Geary, Union Square ☎415 397 1695; map pp.40–41. Opened in 1933, this is an enjoyably Disneyesque rendition of the city's Barbary Coast days, decked floor-to-ceiling in gold leaf and filled with red velvet couches and chandeliers. The house band, Johnny Z and the Camaros, regularly performs rock, R&B, blues and country favourites (no cover). Daily 7am–2am.

The Hidden Vine 620 Post St at Taylor, Union Square ☎415 674 3567; map pp.40–41. Intimate and warm, this aptly named wine bar is nestled in the *Fitzgerald Hotel*. Sneak in here for a glass or two of California wine, then sink into one of the comfy armchairs, settle in with a soundtrack of torch songs and gaze out the stained-glass windows. Mon 5–10pm, Tues–Thurs 5pm–midnight, Fri & Sat 5pm–2am.

The Irish Bank 10 Mark Lane at Bush, Union Square ☎415 788 7152; map pp.40–41. An appealing respite from the nearby shopping district, with plenty of alfresco alley seating, pub fare and all the requisite Irish artefacts. It's particularly popular in the early evening with Downtown office workers. Daily 11.30am–2am.

Li Po Cocktail Lounge 916 Grant Ave at Jackson, Chinatown ☎415 982 0072; map pp.40–41. Named after the Chinese poet, charmingly grotty *Li Po* is one of the few places to have a drink in Chinatown. Enter through the false cavern front and grab a drink among the regulars, some of whom may be local literary luminaries. Daily 2pm–2am.

Otis Lounge 25 Maiden Lane at Kearny, Union Square ☎415 298 4826; map pp.40–41. Elegant, if quirky-chic bar popular with Financial District businesspeople and hip, young fashionistas, sipping cocktails in this Art Deco space, decked out in peacock feathers, antlers and snakeskin. Its location makes it a convenient remedy to shopping-induced fatigue. Tues–Fri 5pm–2am, Sat 8pm–2am, Sun 10pm–2am.

The Redwood Room Clift Hotel, 495 Geary St at Taylor, Union Square ☎415 929 2372; map pp.40–41. This clubby landmark has been made over to include lightboxes on the walls that display shifting, fading paintings. It's fun and swanky, if hopelessly pretentious – just don't choke on the comically high drink prices. Mon–Thurs & Sun 5pm–2am, Fri & Sat 4pm–2am.

Slide 430 Mason St at Geary, Union Square ☎415 421 1916; map pp.40–41. Access to this underground homage to the 1920s is via a serpentine slide, which leads to a swish cocktail lounge where DJs spin nightly. Popular with young sophisticates with money to burn on VIP booths and bottle service. Wed–Sun 9pm–2am.

★ **Tunnel Top** 601 Bush St at Stockton, Union Square ☎415 722 6620; map pp.40–41. Vivacious bar atop the Stockton Tunnel with stiff drinks, DJs and a terrific balcony

10

SAN FRANCISCO BEERS

While its nearby countryside may be internationally known for winemaking, the city of San Francisco is renowned for its craft beers. The best-known local product is so-called **steam beer**, a lager-bitter hybrid invented when early local brewers, finding the ice needed for lager production too expensive, instead fermented their yeast at room temperature like an ale. The result was a beer with the lower ABV of lager but the hearty flavour of bitter. (The precise origin of the odd name, unfortunately, has never been established.) To find out more, take one of the engaging, free **tours** at Anchor Steam Brewery, 1705 Mariposa Street at Carolina, Potrero Hill (45min; two daily on weekday afternoons by appointment only; ☎415 863 8350, ⓦanchorbrewing.com), whose namesake product is a local treasure and universally available at bars and stores.

BEST SAN FRANCISCO BREWPUBS

21st Amendment Brewery See opposite
Beach Chalet Brewery & Restaurant See p.167
Gordon Biersch Brewery See p.176

Magnolia Gastropub & Brewery See p.179
Speakeasy Ales & Lagers See p.178
ThirstyBear Brewing Company See p.177

---

that's ideal for taking in the whole scene; gets crushingly crowded at weekends. Daily 5pm–2am.

NORTH BEACH AND THE HILLS

15 Romolo 15 Romolo Place at Broadway, North Beach ☎415 398 1359; map p.59. Tucked away down an alley, this polished, simple and dimly lit bar with no sign is an elegant refuge from the flashing lights and boisterous strip-club crowd on Broadway. The staff is friendly and the jukebox well stocked. Daily 5pm–2am.

Bacchus 1954 Hyde St at Union, Russian Hill ☎415 928 2633; map p.56. Once a spillover bar for nearby *Sushi Groove* (see p.149), this tiny and sleek bar is now a destination in itself; just beware that there are only eight stools, so be prepared to stand. Sake cocktails and upwards of fifty different wines are on offer. Mon, Tues & Sun 5.30–10pm, Wed 5.30–11pm, Thurs 5.30pm–midnight.

Bamboo Hut 479 Broadway at Kearny, North Beach ☎415 989 8555; map p.59. True to its name, this divey bar is nearly covered in bamboo and even sports a 7ft-tall 1948 Tiki icon. With tropical cocktails served in coconut half-shells, it's quite the party destination, so head elsewhere if you're looking for quiet conversation. Tues, Sat & Sun 7pm–2am, Wed–Fri 5pm–2am.

The Big Four Huntington Hotel, 1075 California St at Taylor, Nob Hill ☎415 474 5400; map p.56. Classy hotel bar aimed squarely at an older crowd looking for classic cocktails amid equally old-fashioned environs. Nightly piano entertainment with no cover. Daily 4pm–midnight.

Comstock Saloon 155 Columbus Ave at Pacific, North Beach ☎415 617 0071; map p.59. Bedecked in period decor and darkwood furniture recalling the days of nineteenth-century silver-mining glory, this tavern imagines the convergence of *There Will Be Blood* with the North Beach party-bus crowd. There's a brief food menu of

heavy items (beef shank; broccoli and cheddar casserole), but the savvy drinks menu is the main reason to drop in. Mon–Fri 11.30am–2am, Sat 2pm–2am.

Gino and Carlo 548 Green St at Grant, North Beach ☎415 421 0896; map p.59. Neighbourhood watering hole once popular with overnight pressmen and still beloved by longtime regulars – perhaps because it's open twenty hours a day for them. A welcoming place overall, with pinball and pool available. Daily 6am–2am.

La Trappe 800 Greenwich St at Mason, North Beach ☎415 440 8727; map p.56. The lower level of this two-storey spot is a marvellous dungeon that's a dream come true for Euro-beer enthusiasts. There are about 200 – yes, 200 – beers available in bottles and on tap, so while everything may not exactly be fresh off the truck, you've certainly got your share of options. Pass on the mediocre food. Tues & Wed 6–11pm, Thurs 4pm–midnight, Fri & Sat 3pm–midnight.

Mr. Bing's 201 Columbus Ave at Pacific, North Beach ☎415 362 1545; map p.59. This dirty dive won't win the "Classiest Bar in San Francisco" title anytime soon; nonetheless, it's a North Beach institution with its oddly shaped bar, cantankerous regulars (and sometimes staff) and, perhaps best of all, super-cheap drinks. Daily 10am–2am.

Rosewood Bar 732 Broadway at Stockton, North Beach ☎415 951 4886; map p.59. Best visited on weeknights, this deliberately hidden bolthole doesn't even have a sign outside. The retro interior is complemented by great lounge-core DJs; downsides include the pricey drinks and loads of out-of-towners who pour in at weekends. Mon–Sat 5pm–2am.

Savoy Tivoli 1434 Grant Ave at Green, North Beach ☎415 361 7023; map p.59. Sprawling North Beach landmark dating back to 1907 with a smoker-friendly open-air patio, a couple of pool tables, a beautiful darkwood bar and bizarre decor dotted around the main room. The post-collegiate crowd it draws on weekends belies its Bohemian vibe. Tues & Wed 6pm–2am, Thurs & Fri 5pm–2am, Sat 3pm–2am.

Specs Twelve Adler Museum Cafe 12 Saroyan Place at Columbus, North Beach ☎415 421 4112; map p.51. Known locally as simply "Specs", this friendly dive set just off North Beach's main drag is known for its chatty barstaff and is decked out with oddities from the high seas. Its regulars may be older eccentrics, but it's popular with just about everybody. Mon–Fri 4.30pm–2am, Sat & Sun 5pm–2am.

Tonga Room & Hurricane Bar The Fairmont, 950 Mason St at California, Nob Hill ☎415 772 5278; map p.56. Ultra-campy bar styled like a Polynesian village, complete with pond, simulated rainstorms and grass-skirted band strangling jazz and pop covers to death upon a floating raft. Cocktails are outrageously overpriced, but the happy-hour buffet (under $10) helps compensate. Wed, Thurs & Sun 5–11.30pm; Fri & Sat 5pm–12.30am.

Tonic 2360 Polk St at Green, Russian Hill ☎415 771 5535; map p.56. Set on a Russian Hill corner, this happening little pickup joint is dark and festooned with fresh flowers. Bartenders serve cheap mixed drinks behind the long mahogany bar. Daily 5pm–2am.

★ **Tony Nik's** 1534 Stockton St at Union, North Beach ☎415 693 0990; map p.59. Another legendary watering hole in a neighbourhood full of them, *Tony Nik's* dim, sulky interior and stiff drinks have been summoning North Beach denizens for ages. The bar area is the liveliest spot, while the even darker back area is great for intimate chats. Daily 4pm–2am.

Tosca Cafe 242 Columbus Ave at Pacific, North Beach ☎415 986 9651; map p.59. A bar so classic it feels like a Hollywood set: bartenders in white waistcoats, arias (or perhaps Sinatra) wafting out of the jukebox and a long line of cocktail glasses along the bar filled with the house drink, a brandy-laced cappuccino. Even the average tee-totalling San Franciscan has been here at least once. Tues–Sun 5pm–2am.

Vesuvio Cafe 255 Columbus Ave at Broadway, North Beach ☎415 362 3370; map p.59. Even if it weren't once the regular hangout of Kerouac and company, North Beach's most (in)famous bar would still merit a visit for at least one drink for its inviting atmosphere. Daily 6am–2am.

THE NORTHERN WATERFRONT AND PACIFIC HEIGHTS

★ **Black Horse London Pub** 1514 Union St at Van Ness, Cow Hollow ☎415 928 2414; map pp.68–69. If you can squeeze yourself in, this shoebox-sized, mock-English tavern seems worlds away from the post-collegiate Cow Hollow/Marina scene. It's got old-school San Francisco charm in spades, as well as friendly bar staff

and terrific cheese plates, if a paltry selection of beer and cider. Daily 5pm–midnight.

The Buena Vista 2765 Hyde St at Beach, Fisherman's Wharf ☎415 474 5044; map pp.68–69. The walls at this local landmark are decorated with old newspapers, and the sense of history is reinforced by the bar's claim to have introduced Irish coffee to North America in 1952. Given its location, it easily fills with eager tourists wanting to sample the house special. Mon–Fri 9am–2am, Sat & Sun 8am–2am.

Lion Pub 2062 Divisadero St at Sacramento, Pacific Heights ☎415 567 6565; map pp.68–69. Complete with fireplace and lit candles, this homey neighbourhood spot serves a mixed gay/straight crowd of young professionals. It's known for fresh-pressed juice cocktails and free cheese, crackers and olives set out each evening at happy hour. Note that there's no sign – just look for the olive-green mansion on the corner, and enter via Sacramento St. Daily 4.30pm–2am.

Nectar Wine Lounge 3330 Steiner St at Chestnut, Marina ☎415 345 1377; map pp.68–69. Upscale oenophile haven with a loungey vibe. As with most places in this area, the crowd's youthful and pretty; the wine list, meanwhile, is eclectic and extensive, accompanied by tapas-sized, California cuisine-inspired snacks. Mon–Wed 5–10.30pm, Thurs–Sat 5pm–midnight, Sun 5–10pm.

Perry's 1944 Union St at Laguna, Cow Hollow ☎415 922 9022; map pp.68–69. Made legendary by Armistead Maupin's *Tales of the City series*, this sprawling, multi-roomed institution remains a popular watering hole. If you skip the unspectacular food and take your appetite elsewhere, it's still a friendly place to grab a pint or two, with plenty of sports-tuned TVs and blue-and-white-chequered tablecloths. Mon–Thurs & Sun 9am–11pm, Fri & Sat 11am–midnight.

Silver Clouds Restaurant and Karaoke Bar 1994 Lombard St at Webster, Marina ☎415 922 1977; map pp.68–69. Brash destination notable for its amusingly abrasive staff and raucous karaoke sessions. If you're aching to belt out "Sweet Caroline" or "Like a Virgin", you may want to avoid coming on a weekend night, when you'll be performing almost exclusively for a crush of out-of-towners. Karaoke Tues–Sun 9.30pm–2am.

SOUTH OF MARKET AND THE TENDERLOIN

21st Amendment Brewery 563 Second St at Brannan, South of Market ☎415 369 0900; map pp.84–85. This bright, lively brewpub, right across from South Park and two blocks from the ballpark, turns out a dozen or so fine microbrews, which it serves alongside decent burgers and other pub fare to a down-to-earth crowd. Mon–Thurs 11.30am–midnight, Fri & Sat 11.30am–1am, Sun 10am–midnight.

10

10

222 Hyde 222 Hyde St at Turk, Tenderloin ☎ 415 345 0822; map pp.84–85. Somewhat chic hole-in-the-wall serving cocktails and wine by the glass to a hipster crowd. DJs spin several nights a week, and there's live comedy every Thurs and Sat. Cover around $5. Tues–Fri 6pm–2am, Sat & Sun 9am–2am.

The Ambassador 673 Geary St at Leavenworth, Tenderloin ☎ 415 563 8192; map pp.84–85. Crystal chandeliers, a marble bar and red carpeting give this cocktail lounge an air of old Vegas class, while nightly DJs root the scene firmly in the present. Reserve ahead for one of the high-backed black leather booths, which feature rotary phones to dial up the bar. Tues 6pm–2am, Wed–Fri 7pm–2am, Sat 8pm–2am.

Bigfoot Lodge 1750 Polk St at Washington, Russian Hill ☎ 415 440 2355; map p.56. Watering hole where the decor takes after a 1950s ski lodge – expect plenty of faux wood, hunting trophies and antlers, with the *pièce de résistance* being an enormous papier-mâché statue of Bigfoot himself. Daily 3pm–2am.

Bourbon & Branch 501 Jones St at O'Farrell, Tenderloin ☎ 415 346 1735, ⊛ bourbonandbranch.com; map pp.84–85. A reservations-only bar (book online) that's garnered plenty of buzz for its recreation of a Prohibition-era speakeasy. Give the password at the unmarked door and you'll be whisked into a dimly lit space with wooden booths, burgundy velvet wallpaper and a pressed-tin ceiling. Mon–Sat 6pm–2am.

Butter 354 11th St at Harrison, South of Market ☎ 415 863 5964; map pp.84–85. Fun, stylized "white trash" bar that's nonetheless a hopeless case of forced irony in this warehouse-and-lofts neighbourhood. It's full of imitation trailer-park decor – look no further than the bar covered in shingles – and has a food window that serves only microwaveable junk food (tater tots and the like). Call to confirm opening hours. Wed–Sun 6pm–2am.

Club 93 93 Ninth St at Mission, South of Market ☎ 415 522 0200; map pp.84–85. Terrific dive bar on a gritty block that's great for classic rock and shuffleboard; the marathon weekday happy hour (9am–8pm) doesn't hurt, either. Mon–Thurs & Sun 9am–2am, Fri & Sat 5pm–2am.

District 216 Townsend St at Third, South of Market ☎ 415 896 2120; map pp.84–85. Rekindling the exuberant spirit of San Francisco's dot-com era, this wine bar has high ceilings and exposed brick walls and draws a young, well-heeled crowd. There's an eclectic selection of more than thirty wines by the glass, plus small plates such as pizzettas ($10–14) and salumi ($12). Mon–Fri 4pm–midnight, Sat 5pm–midnight.

Edinburgh Castle 950 Geary St at Polk, Tenderloin ☎ 415 885 4074; map pp.84–85. Evocative Scottish bar filled with Highland memorabilia. The room upstairs regularly hosts live performances of all stripes (music, readings, theatre), while the pub grub (served until 11pm)

comes straight from co-owned chippie *The Old Chelsea* (see p.154) around the corner. Arrive early on Tues for trivia night. Daily 5pm–2am.

Gordon Biersch Brewery 2 Harrison St at Embarcadero, South of Market ☎ 415 243 8246; map pp.84–85. Bayfront outpost of the successful South Bay microbrewery, housed in a converted coffee warehouse with a lovely view of the Bay Bridge. Its patio has heat lamps, so it's habitable even on a chilly evening. Mon–Thurs & Sun 11.30am–midnight, Sat 11.30am–2am.

★ **Hemlock Tavern** 1131 Polk St at Sutter, Polk Gulch ☎ 415 923 0923; map pp.84–85. Fun tavern with a free jukebox heavy on punk, fresh peanut shells on the floor, live music in its back room (see p.183) and a handy, enclosed patio where smokers can puff and sip in peace. Daily 4pm–2am.

House of Shields 39 New Montgomery St at Mission, South of Market ☎ 415 495 5436; map pp.84–85. Certainly one of San Francisco's more changeable spaces, *House of Shields* is an clubby piano bar in early evening, while late nights see DJs and a younger, punk-damaged crowd. Its c.1908 dark wood panelling is inviting any time of day, however. Mon–Fri 2pm–2am, Sat 7pm–2am.

Lush Lounge 1221 Polk St at Sutter, Polk Gulch ☎ 415 771 2022; map pp.84–85. An airy, inviting spot for a sweet cocktail or glass of wine. Long communal tables, hanging ferns and lamps, and a good-looking crowd make it a prime destination along this bar-choked stretch of Polk St. Mon–Fri 3pm–2am, Sat & Sun noon–2am.

Mars 798 Brannan St at Seventh, South of Market ☎ 415 621 6277; map pp.84–85. Quirky, out-of-the-way spot featuring two rooms, a large patio and charmingly retro 1950s colours. The plant-filled patio is perfect for lounging on sunny afternoons, while plenty of heat lamps fend off the night chill. Mon 11.30am–9pm, Tues 11.30am–11pm, Wed & Thurs 11.30am–midnight, Fri 11.30am–2am, Sat 9pm–2am.

Mr. Smith's 34 Seventh St at Market, South of Market ☎ 415 355 9991; map pp.84–85. Step gingerly down this grotty block, then through the small door of this "speakeasy" to take in its main room's chandeliers, exposed brick walls and dark-wood panels. DJs spin funk, soul, house and more Wed–Sat. Tues–Fri 4.30pm–midnight, Sat 8pm–2am.

Olive 743 Larkin St at O'Farrell, Tenderloin ☎ 415 776 9814; map pp.84–85. An elegant, upscale bar (with kitchen) in the heart of the seedy Tenderloin. Olives replace the standard peanuts and art hangs on the walls, while the tapas, thin-crust pizzas and watermelon mojitos are particularly delicious. Mon–Wed 5–11pm, Thurs 5pm–midnight, Fri 5pm–2am, Sat 6pm–2am.

Pied Piper Bar Palace Hotel, 2 New Montgomery St at Market, South of Market ☎ 415 546 5020; map pp.84–85. Named for the Maxwell Parrish mural hovering behind its bar, this mahogany-panelled room is a secluded, elegant place for a martini and a wide range of tasty bar food. Daily 11.30am–midnight.

The Ramp 855 Terry Francois St at Illinois, Mission Bay ☎ 415 621 2378; map pp.84–85. Set way out on the old docks south of the Giants' ballpark, it's worth the trek here from Downtown to sit on the patio and sip beverages while overlooking the evocative disused piers and boatyards. The kitchen serves brunch on weekends. Mon–Fri 11am–10pm, Sat & Sun 9am–10pm.

ThirstyBear Brewing Company 661 Howard St at Second, South of Market ☎ 415 974 0905; map pp.84–85. A combination brewpub and tapas bar, packed in the evenings with local workers; the food's well priced ($7–12 a plate) and tasty – try the fried calamari. Mon–Thurs 11.30am–10pm, Fri 11.30am–midnight, Sat noon–midnight, Sun 5–10pm.

Vertigo 1160 Polk St at Sutter, Polk Gulch ☎ 415 674 1278; map pp.84–85. Electric bar that draws a young crowd revelling in stiff drinks and booty-shaking. As with the *Hemlock Tavern* across the street, it's also popular for its dedicated smoking area. Daily 3pm–2am.

THE MISSION AND THE CASTRO

Argus Lounge 3187 Mission St at Valencia, Mission ☎ 415 824 1447; map p.100. Named after the 100-eyed monster whose eyes were preserved on the peacock, this bar captures the funky-cool Mission aesthetic with fresh-fruit cocktails, cheap beer and amusing decor (look no further than the *Last Supper* paintings). Mon–Sat 4pm–2am, Sun 5pm–2am.

The Attic 3336 24th St at Mission, Mission ☎ 415 643 3376; map p.100. Beloved, small dive that's so dark, it takes your eyes time to adjust to the low lighting. Sure enough, the decor is clearly inspired by a vintage attic, with oddball antiques set in random places. Daily 5pm–2am.

Beauty Bar 2299 Mission St at 19th, Mission ☎ 415 285 0323; map p.100. Unapologetically campy, this San Francisco outpost of New York's original *Beauty Bar* is decorated with memorabilia from a long-gone Long Island hair salon, with plenty of bubblegum pink and rows of retro dryers. DJs bring in youngish crowds most every night of the week. Daily 6pm–2am.

Bender's 806 South Van Ness Ave at 19th, Mission ☎ 415 824 1800; map p.100. This boisterous bar remains as fierce than ever, with pinball machines, pool tables, Sun afternoon barbecues and all kinds of rock on the jukebox. Hope that the bacon-topped mac 'n' cheese sandwich is on

the daily specials menu. Mon– Thurs & Sun 4pm–2am, Fri & Sat 2pm–2am.

Casanova Lounge 527 Valencia St at 16th, Mission ☎ 415 863 9328; map p.100. Cool lamps, easygoing bartenders, a terrific jukebox and some of the city's best DJs (9pm nightly; rarely a cover) attract the young and stylish to this Valencia St linchpin in droves, particularly at weekends. Daily 4pm–2am.

Dalva 3121 16th St at Valencia, Mission ☎ 415 252 7740; map p.100. Alluringly dimly lit, *Dalva* is one of the better finds along 16th St. The wafer-thin space is easy to miss and often crowded; once inside, find space at the bar to order one of the many cheap drinks on offer. In the rear is the *Hideout*, a great spot to hang out if it hasn't been rented to a private party. Daily 4pm–2am.

Doc's Clock 2575 Mission St at 22nd, Mission ☎ 415 824 3627; map p.100. You won't miss this Deco-style bar along Mission St, thanks to the blazing neon sign out front. Shuffleboard's a popular game here, although many regulars are content to nurse drinks at the long bar or in the quieter back area of the lounge. Mon–Sat 6pm–2am, Sun noon–2am.

Elixir 3200 16th St at Guerrero, Mission ☎ 415 552 1633; map p.100. There's been a saloon on this corner for over 150 years – nearly the entire history of San Francisco – and *Elixir* is the latest incarnation. Cocktails are the way to go here – the Bloody Marys in particular are the stuff of local lore. Mon–Fri 3pm–2am, Sat noon–2am, Sun 11am–2am.

The Homestead 2301 Folsom St at 19th, Mission ☎ 415 282 4663; map p.100. With its gold pressed-tin ceiling, rococo wallpaper and pot-bellied stove, this saloon feels like it was transported to modern-day San Francisco from the city's Gold Rush era. It's surprisingly mellow, especially during the week, with a great jukebox and scotch selection to boot. Daily 2pm–2am.

Latin American Club 3286 22nd St at Valencia, Mission ☎ 415 647 2732; map p.100. Cosy place with a neighbourhood feel, great for an early chat over drinks before the crowds arrive later in the evening. The loft space above the entrance is full of piñatas, Mexican streamers and assorted trinkets. Mon–Thurs & Sun 6pm–2am, Fri & Sat 5pm–2am.

Lazslo 2532 Mission St at 21st, Mission ☎ 415 401 0810; map p.100. Industrial-chic bar attached to *Foreign Cinema* (see p.158) whose name, unsurprisingly, is rooted in film – Jean-Paul Belmondo's character's alias in *A Bout de Souffle*, to be exact. DJs spin nightly at 9pm (no cover),

10

GAY BARS AND CLUBS
The bulk of San Francisco's **gay bars** are situated in the Castro, South of Market and Polk Gulch (see pp.196–198); it's worth noting that very few places will shun gay-friendly straight people, provided you don't arrive with an army of "breeders" in tow and try to take over the place for the evening.

10

TOP 5 HISTORIC BARS
The Saloon See p.180
The Little Shamrock See p.179
Gold Dust Lounge See p.173
Aub Zam Zam See p.178
Vesuvio Cafe See p.175

and it's a fine place for a swanky cocktail. Mon–Fri 6pm–2am, Sat & Sun noon–2am.

Little Baobab 3388 19th St at Mission, Mission ☎415 643 3558; map p.100. Homey Senegalese bar where the regulars aren't afraid to dance. Try one of the stiff house cocktails and settle in with a live performance or DJ whose tastes span the African diaspora. Mon–Sat 6pm–2am.

Lime 2247 Market St at Sanchez, Castro ☎415 621 5256; map p.100. Achingly mod destination that transitions from restaurant to mixed gay/straight nightspot later on. The crowd's young, pretty and big on fruity cocktails such as coconut mojitos. Mon–Thurs & Sun 5pm–midnight, Fri & Sat 5pm–1am.

Lone Palm 3394 22nd St at Guerrero, Mission ☎415 648 0109; map p.100. Like some forgotten Vegas revue bar from the 1950s, this candlelit cocktail lounge – less than a block off the well-trod Valencia corridor – is a gem. White cloths cover the raised tables and a TV above the bar plays classic American movies. Daily 4pm–2am.

Lucky 13 2140 Market St at Church, Castro ☎415 487 1313; map p.100. Straight bar on the outskirts of the Castro with an extensive selection of international beers. It's filled with pool players chomping on free popcorn; there's a loud jukebox inside, an inviting balcony and a humble patio out back. Mon–Wed 4pm–2am, Thurs–Sun 11am–2am.

Mission Bar 2695 Mission St at 23rd, Mission ☎415 647 2300; map p.100. Basic, unfussy watering hole in the heart of the Mission with a pool table, pinball machine and a great rock jukebox. Determinedly untrendy, all the way down to the sign above the entrance that simply reads "BAR". Mon–Fri 3pm–2am, Sat & Sun 2pm–2am.

The Phoenix 811 Valencia St at 19th, Mission ☎415 695 1811; map p.100. One of the few decidedly Irish taverns in this area of the city, *The Phoenix* is a large and boisterous place to quaff pints, enjoy pub grub and watch sports. Pull into one of the wooden banquettes and sip your Guinness by the light of the glass chandelier. Mon–Fri 11am–2am, Sat & Sun 10am–2am.

The Phone Booth 1398 South Van Ness Ave at 25th, Mission ☎415 648 4683; map p.100. Significantly more sizeable than its name would suggest, this dark dive bar – known for its cheap drinks and naked-Barbie chandelier – draws all manner of Mission denizens. A pool table is improbably tucked into the place. Daily 1pm–2am.

★ **Revolution Cafe** 3248 22nd St at Bartlett, Mission ☎415 642 0474; map p.100. This hybrid bar and café offers free wireless internet, an upright piano available to anyone, alfresco seating, beer and wine, a light food menu and nightly music ranging from jazz and blues to bluegrass and even classical. It's a quintessential Mission spot, and while the atmosphere may be laid-back, it's often packed, making tables hard to come by. Mon–Wed 9am–12.30am, Thurs & Sun 9am–1am, Fri & Sat 9am–2am.

Speakeasy Ales & Lagers 1195 Evans Ave at Keith, Hunters Point ☎415 642 3371; map pp.98–99. Although it's only open to the public for five hours each week, this spacious warehouse brewery serves terrific beer and offers free tours every Fri at 4pm. It's set in a less than savoury part of town, so keep your wits about you after dark. Fri 4–9pm.

Verdi Club 2424 Mariposa St at Potrero, Mission ☎415 861 9199, ⊚verdiclub.net; map pp.98–99. Founded in 1916 as an Italian-American social club, the *Verdi Club* now hosts musical and spoken word performances – check the website for listings and opening hours. It's also open every Tues for Tuesday Night Jump (swing dancing) and Thurs for Tangozarry (tango), with both nights attracting vintage-obsessives in droves.

★ **Wild Side West** 424 Cortland Ave at Andover, Bernal Heights ☎415 647 3099; map pp.98–99. Unpretentious and friendly tavern at the centre of the Bernal Heights scene, with plenty of kitsch Americana to gaze at. There's a lovely garden out back – one of the best in the city, featuring sculptures, much foliage and a multi-tiered patio – but without heat lamps, you'd be well advised to stay inside on a cold evening. It's known as a lesbian bar, but not so exclusively that straights are unwelcome. Daily 2pm–2am.

Zeitgeist 199 Valencia St at Duboce, Mission ☎415 255 7505; map pp.106–107. This friendly cyclist bar is a Mission institution, with an enormous outdoor beer garden that's wildly popular on sunny afternoons. Come for punk tunes, heavily tattooed bartenders, afternoon cookouts at weekends, hordes of beers on tap and what may be the city's most celebrated Bloody Mary. Daily 9am–2am.

HAIGHT-ASHBURY AND WEST OF CIVIC CENTER

The Alembic 1725 Haight St at Cole, Upper Haight ☎415 666 0822; map pp.106–107. Offering a refreshing break from the dog-eared Haight scene, this small, stylish spot is serious about its liquor, with a wide selection of small-batch bourbons, ryes and gins poured by knowledgeable, friendly bartenders. There's also a short menu of ethnic comfort food (think Moroccan-spiced lamb burgers), along with beers from nearby brewery *Magnolia* (see p.179). Daily noon–2am.

Aub Zam Zam 1663 Haight St at Clayton, Upper Haight ☎415 861 2545; map pp.106–107. Bar regulars purchased this Casbah-style cocktail lounge after the death of its lovably grouchy owner, Bruno, and have just about managed to retain its alternately surly/warm vibe. It's got a great jazz jukebox, and your first drink choice here should be a gin martini. Daily 1pm–2am.

Fly 762 Divisadero St at Fulton, Western Addition ☎415 931 4359; map pp.106–107. This trendy bar-restaurant has no hard liquor licence, so expect creative sake and soju concoctions, as well as a top-notch selection of beer and wine. Walls are decorated with rotating displays of local art, and overall it's one of the more inviting places along this reinvigorated thoroughfare. Daily noon–2am.

★ **Hotel Biron** 45 Rose St at Gough, Hayes Valley ☎415 703 0403; map pp.106–107. Set down a low-profile side street, this wine bar possesses an easy elegance – plenty of cosy nooks, quiet tables, compelling art on the walls and even a leather couch or two. The well-curated wine list is impressive and features a long list of California and international choices; there's also a short menu of cheeses and olives. It's not part of a hotel, despite its name. Daily 5pm–2am.

Mad Dog in the Fog 530 Haight St at Fillmore, Lower Haight ☎415 626 7279; map pp.106–107. Aptly named tavern that's one of the Lower Haight's most loyally patronized bars, with darts, English beer, an outdoor patio, footie on TV (it opens extra-early on weekends for live broadcasts of Premier League matches) and a supremely popular trivia night each Thurs. Mon–Fri 11.30am–2am, Sat & Sun 7am–2am.

Madrone Art Bar 500 Divisadero St at Fell, Western Addition ☎415 241 0202; map pp.106–107. Art lounge and performance space that was once a Victorian-era apothecary. Now with its deep-blue walls, vintage couches and rotating art exhibitions, it's a mellow place to have a drink early in the evening, after which DJs get the nightly party started with Motown, hip-hop, funk and more. Mon & Sun 6am–midnight, Tues–Sat 4pm–1.30am.

Magnolia Gastropub & Brewery 1398 Haight St at Masonic, Upper Haight ☎415 864 7468; map pp.106–107. Perennially popular destination on a highly visible corner where the own-brewed beers and bracing pub fare (try the sausages) bring people in from all over. There's also an extensive wine list, while the best seats in the house are at one of the booths. Mon–Thurs 11am–midnight, Fri 11am–1am, Sat 10am–1am, Sun 10am–midnight.

Molotov's 582 Haight St at Steiner, Lower Haight ☎415 558 8019; map pp.106–107. Longtime neighbourhood stronghold where the jukebox is full of boisterous punk rock, drinks are (relatively) cheap, and pinball and pool are the games of choice. It's co-owned with nearby Lucky 13 (see opposite), another fun rocker bar. Mon–Fri 4pm–2am, Sat & Sun noon–2am.

Noc Noc 557 Haight St at Steiner, Lower Haight ☎415 861 5811; map pp.106–107. Dark, super-groovy

spot with bizarre decor befitting a post-apocalyptic tribal cave, all the way down to the throne-like seats at the bar. It doesn't have a licence to sell spirits, but it does make sake cocktails and boasts a solid range of beers. Daily 5pm–2am.

Place Pigalle 520 Hayes St at Gough, Hayes Valley ☎415 552 2671; map pp.106–107. Decorated in plush, deep reds, this friendly lounge boasts rotating art on the walls and the neighbourhood's most popular pool table. It slowly fills with laid-back regulars nightly who sit at the long bar or find a spot at one of several couches in the place. Mon–Fri 2pm–2am, Sat & Sun noon–2am.

Playground 1705 Buchanan St at Post, Japantown ☎415 929 1471; map pp.106–107. Fun bar and restaurant with a distinctly youthful vibe; it's neon-lit and full of TVs showing Korean pop videos. Ask for karaoke and you'll be led to one of three private rooms upstairs. Mon–Wed & Sun 5pm–midnight, Thurs–Sat 5pm–2am.

Toronado 547 Haight St at Fillmore, Lower Haight ☎415 863 2276; map pp.106–107. Renowned for its vast selection of international beers, this cacophonous tavern should be the first San Francisco stop on any beer aficionado's itinerary. Just don't expect much in the way of warmth from the bartenders. Daily 11.30am–2am.

THE RICHMOND AND THE SUNSET

540 Club 540 Clement St at Seventh, Inner Richmond ☎415 752 7276; map p.116. Artsy punk bar, done up in deep reds and black, that made a name for itself with regular parties such as Catholic School Karaoke and its Sun trivia competition. Selling points include cheap drinks, a good jukebox, dartboards, pool tables and a small outside patio along the Clement St sidewalk. Daily 11am–2am.

Abbey Tavern 4100 Geary Blvd at Fifth, Inner Richmond ☎415 221 7767; map p.116. Quintessentially Irish, this footie-mad bar along the Richmond's main drag is friendly and even a little upscale, often hosting live Irish folk music when there aren't any can't-miss games on TV. Mon–Fri noon–2am, Sat & Sun 10am–2am.

The Bitter End 441 Clement St at Fifth, Inner Richmond ☎415 221 9538; map p.116. One of the more hip (and brightly lit) choices among the scores of Irish bars in this area. *The Bitter End*'s selection of beer, whiskies and single malt scotches is impressively wide, while the cosy fireplace is ideal for huddling around on a frosty San Francisco summer evening. There's pool and darts as well. Mon–Fri 4pm–2am, Sat & Sun 11am–2am.

★ **The Little Shamrock** 807 Lincoln Way at Ninth, Inner Sunset ☎415 661 0060; map p.116. The homey and inviting atmosphere at this Irish pub – San Francisco's second oldest bar – draws regulars with its lived-in couches, fireplace, board games, fresh (and free) popcorn and vast selection of Irish whiskey. Mon–Thurs 3pm–2am, Fri 2pm–2am, Sat & Sun 1pm–2am.

10

Trad'r Sam 6150 Geary Blvd at 26th, Outer Richmond ☎415 221 0773; map p.116. Open since 1939, San Francisco's original tiki bar is a bit of a trek from the central neighbourhoods, but go for the enormous and colourful – and occasionally flaming – cocktails, such as the Scorpion Bowl or the P38, served in a salad bowl with four straws. Daily 10am–2am.

Yancy's Saloon 734 Irving St at Ninth, Inner Sunset ☎415 665 6551; map p.116. One of San Francisco's only bars with a collegiate vibe, this mellow and plant-festooned place boasts dartboards galore, plenty of TVs tuned to sports, cheap drinks and comfortable couches. Mon & Fri 4pm–2am, Tues–Thurs 2pm–2am, Sat & Sun noon–2am.

10 LIVE MUSIC VENUES AND CLUBS

San Francisco's **live music** scene reflects the character of the city as a whole: progressive and ever-evolving, but also a little bit nostalgic. It's never recaptured its crucial 1960s role, though since the 1990s the city has helped launch acid (or beat-heavy) jazz, a classic swing revival and the East Bay punk-pop sound championed by Green Day and Rancid. Options abound here for catching live rock, and young underground bands frequently emerge to make waves beyond the Bay Area. The city is also a prime stop for touring jazz, blues and international acts; as for Latin music, there's little chance of catching authentic performers other than at Roccapulco (see p.184) – surprising given the city's thriving Latino community.

A night out in San Francisco is more of a party than a pose, so while the city's **clubs** will never be confused with more celebrated scenes in Miami or New York, there are a few upsides to its humbler scope: namely that you're unlikely to encounter high cover charges, ridiculously priced drinks or long lines. Very few venues operate any kind of dress code, and only on very busy nights will you have to wait. By far the greatest concentration of places are found among the wide boulevards and warehouses in South of Market (including several with addresses doubling as names), although the Mission also has a handful of spots that get hopping on weekends; North Beach, too, is home to a couple of lounges that veer into club terrain later in the evening.

DOWNTOWN

LIVE MUSIC VENUE

Biscuits & Blues 401 Mason St at Geary, Union Square ☎415 292 2583, ⓦbiscuitsandblues.com; map pp.40–41. It's certainly a tourist trap, but *Biscuits & Blues* is a good place nonetheless to catch a wide range of blues performers. There's also a full menu of serviceable (if overpriced) soul food. $15 and up.

CLUBS

The Cellar 685 Sutter St at Taylor, Union Square ☎415 441 5678, ⓦcellarsf.com; map pp.40–41. Popular with a young, studenty crowd, this brash and kitschy bar-club is decorated with dozens of mirrors. There are slouchy booths where you can lounge and just listen to the DJs once you've danced yourself silly. A no-jeans-and-sneakers dress code is enforced on Fri & Sat, when there's also a $10 cover (free all other nights). Mon–Fri 5pm–2am, Sat & Sun 10pm–2am.

Ruby Skye 420 Mason St at Geary, Union Square ☎415 693 0777, ⓦrubyskye.com; map pp.40–41. The biggest mainstream DJs tend to stop at this gorgeous, spacious Victorian dancehall, where the programming skews towards anything that thumps: trance, house, techno and more. $15 and up. Thurs 7pm–2am, Fri & Sat 7pm–4am.

Vessel 85 Campton Pl at Stockton, Union Square ☎415 433 8585, ⓦvesselsf.com; map pp.40–41. An enormous (4500 square-foot) underground space just around the corner from Union Square proper. Amenities include leather banquettes, an indoor VIP garden and a truly

booming sound system, while the music tends to be mainstream, with renowned DJs such as Graham Funke and Chris Garcia playing sets from time to time. $10 and up. Wed–Sat 9.30pm–2am.

NORTH BEACH AND THE HILLS

LIVE MUSIC VENUE

The Saloon 1232 Grant Ave at Vallejo, North Beach ☎415 989 7666; map p.59. Lively, low-brow and gritty, this hardcore blues venue has survived decades of wear and tear as both a whorehouse and Prohibition-era speakeasy. For the last several decades, it's been a wonderfully anachronistic club where bands play nightly among the boutiques and restaurants along upper Grant's shopping and dining strip. $3 and up. Daily noon–2am.

CLUBS

Rouge 1500 Broadway at Polk, Russian Hill ☎415 286 8621, ⓦrougesf.com; map p.56. *Rouge's* neighbourhood location helps lessen its poser contingent somewhat – at least compared to what you'll encounter in the city's megaclubs – while its red velvet booths lend an elegant touch. Sat is the big night here, when local DJs bump house, club hits and mashups to a casually dressy crowd. $5. Mon, Wed & Thurs 5–11.30pm, Tues 5pm–midnight, Fri 2pm–2am, Sat 11am–2am, Sun 10.30am–10pm.

Sip Bar & Lounge 787 Broadway at Powell, North Beach ☎415 699 6545, ⓦsiploungesf.com; map p.59. Adding a splash of style to the North Beach scene with its

10

MAJOR VENUES

Bimbo's 365 Club 1025 Columbus Ave at Chestnut, North Beach ☎415 474 0365, ⓦbimbos365club .com; map p.56. Named for the grandfather of the current owner, this traditional 1930s supper club – with its plush red decor and tuxedoed bar staff – offers more than just swing bands. Expect underground European acts, kitschy tribute bands and rock acts in equal proportion, as well as sometimes-dour staff. $20 and up.

The Fillmore 1805 Geary Blvd at Fillmore, Western Addition ☎415 346 6000, ⓦthefillmore.com; map pp.106–107. This storied ballroom auditorium was at the heart of 1960s counterculture, masterminded by legendary local promoter Bill Graham. It's still a terrific spot for catching up-and-comers and longtime favourites alike – the sort of place bands love to perform. $20 and up.

★ **Great American Music Hall** 859 O'Farrell St at Polk, Tenderloin ☎415 885 0750, ⓦmusichallsf.com; map pp.84–85. A former bordello converted long ago into a beloved venue for rock, blues and international acts, this gorgeous and intimate venue (capacity is about 700) features an ornately moulded balcony with terrific seats for those who arrive early. $15 and up.

The Regency Ballroom 1290 Sutter St at Van Ness, Tenderloin ⓦtheregencyballroom.com; map pp.84–85. Lovingly restored c.1909 ballroom done up

with fine Beaux Arts design touches and a fine, horseshoe-shaped balcony. Acts run the gamut from '80s metal to current hip-hop stars, but the place remains in the shadow of San Francisco's more storied major venues. $20 and up.

Slim's 333 11th St at Folsom, South of Market ☎415 255 0333, ⓦslims-sf.com; map pp.84–85. Owned by local 1970s hitmaker Boz Scaggs, this cavernous brick space is a top venue to catch an array of indie, alternative and international acts. Sightlines can be dodgy in certain areas, so be sure to stake out a good spot. $15 and up.

The Warfield 982 Market St at Sixth, Tenderloin ☎415 775 7722, ⓦthewarfieldtheatre.com; map pp.84–85. In many ways a counterpart to the iconic, smaller Fillmore across town, this theatre offers a grand setting for enjoying top-tier touring artists. There's reserved balcony seating, as well as general admission tickets that put you close to the stage. $25 and up.

Yoshi's 1330 Fillmore St at Eddy, Western Addition ☎415 655 5600, ⓦyoshis.com; map pp.106–107. Oakland's fabled jazz club and Japanese restaurant opened a chic San Francisco venue in the historic Fillmore Jazz Preservation District in 2007, complete with round stage, balcony and wooden dance floor. Although it continues to draw today's biggest jazz names, its calendar also features hip-hop acts and funk bands. $20 and up.

leather couches and curtained walls, this sophisticated, yet friendly lounge has DJs spinning everything from hip-hop and r'n'b to Top-40 after 10pm several nights a week. Surprisingly, there's neither a dress code nor a cover charge. Fri & Sat 9pm–2am.

THE NORTHERN WATERFRONT AND PACIFIC HEIGHTS

LIVE MUSIC VENUES

Kimo's 1351 Polk St at Pine, Polk Gulch ☎415 885 4535, ⓦkimosbarsf.com; map p.56. The closet-sized performance space up in Kimo's second-storey "penthouse" is decidedly cramped and shabby, and the loyalists who come out for this corner club's nightly loud rock shows wouldn't have it any other way. $5 and up. Daily 11am–2am.

Lou's Pier 47 300 Jefferson St at Jones, Fisherman's Wharf ☎415 771 5687, ⓦlouspier47.com; map pp.68–69. Longtime club set in the heart of San Francisco's tourist zone where you'll find blues on tap seven nights a week, and often two shows daily (4pm and 8pm). $3 and up.

Red Devil Lounge 1695 Polk St at Clay, Polk Gulch ☎415 921 1695, ⓦreddevillounge.com; map p.56. This neo-goth nightspot, kitschly decorated with gargoyles, is a top place to catch a 1980s band – either a

real one on tour (think Dramarama or Colin Hay) or simply a local tribute outfit – in an intimate space. There's also local indie rock, open mic every Tues and the occasional hip-hop act. $2 and up.

CLUB

MatrixFillmore 3138 Fillmore St at Greenwich, Marina ☎415 563 4180, ⓦmatrixfillmore.com; map pp.68–69. Sleek, ever-thronged nightspot supposedly inspired by the original *Matrix* that opened on the same spot in 1965 and hosted many major rock acts of the day (including the Velvet Underground and Jefferson Airplane). The current incarnation is glamorous and more than a little posey, with a young, dressy crowd sipping cocktails in comfortable purple banquettes and preening to mainstream beats. $5. Daily 8pm–2am.

SOUTH OF MARKET AND THE TENDERLOIN

LIVE MUSIC VENUES

BrainWash 1122 Folsom St at Seventh, South of Market ☎415 861 3663, ⓦbrainwash.com; map pp.84–85. Café-cum-laundromat that's also a neighbourhood performance venue, making it one of the more unique multi-tasking destinations citywide. There's live music every Sat and Sun, an open mic night on Tues and comedy every Thurs. Free. Mon–Thurs 7am–10pm, Fri & Sat 7am–11pm, Sun 8am–10pm.

Hemlock Tavern 1131 Polk St at Sutter, Polk Gulch ☎ 415 923 0923, ⊛ hemlocktavern.com; map pp.84–85. All types of hipster-approved music is performed in the shoebox-sized room adjacent to the *Hemlock*'s barroom, including underground pop, noise rock, electro-punk and, of course, ukulele country. Expect nightly bills featuring local and touring bands alike, with the occasional comedy showcase (see p.176). $5 and up. Daily 4pm–2am.

Hotel Utah Saloon 500 Fourth St at Bryant, South of Market ☎ 415 546 6300, ⊛ thehotelutahsaloon.com; map pp.84–85. Singer-songwriters, as well as country and rock bands, take the tiny stage at this cramped, c.1908 locale, where the balcony may induce vertigo in some visitors. Its open mic night every Mon (free) is particularly popular; other shows are $5 and up.

CLUBS

★ **111 Minna** 111 Minna St at Second, South of Market ☎ 415 974 1719, ⊛ 111minnagallery.com; map pp.84–85. Large space that wears multiple hats: bar, locally focused art gallery, DJ club and performance venue. It gets busier, noisier and more raucous as the evening wears on, so go early if you want to chat. Free–$8. Hours vary – check website for booking schedule.

330 Ritch 330 Ritch St at Townsend, South of Market ☎ 415 541 9574, ⊛ 330ritch.com; map pp.84–85. The only constant at this small, out-of-the-way club is its location. Different nights attract wildly varied crowds, from electro DJs to video game nights on the venue's big screen. $5 and up. Tues & Wed 9pm–2am, Thurs 10pm–2am, Fri & Sat 9.30pm–2am.

1015 Folsom 1015 Folsom St at Sixth, South of Market ☎ 415 431 1200, ⊛ 1015.com; map pp.84–85. Multi-level megaclub that's popular across the board for late-night dancing. The music's largely house and trance with big names often spinning on the main floor; Sat is Latin night. $15 and up. Thurs–Sat 10pm–2am.

Cat Club 1190 Folsom St at Eighth, South of Market ☎ 415 703 8965, ⊛ sfcatclub.com; map pp.84–85. This dark, loud space remains one of the city's hotspots, where popular 1980s parties bring in consistent crowds; a wide array of electronic, goth and industrial nights are also often jam-packed. $5 and up. Tues & Sun 9pm–2am, Wed 9.30pm–2.30am, Thurs 9pm–3am, Fri 9.30pm–3am, Sat 10pm–3am.

★ **Club 6** 60 Sixth St at Market, South of Market ☎ 415 863 1221, ⊛ clubsix1.com; map pp.84–85. Long-popular club that focuses on hip-hop and hardcore dance music; the narrow, beer-spattered space downstairs is usually packed with both straights and gays at weekends. It's set on one of the nastier blocks in town, so be careful as you arrive and leave. $5 and up. Mon 7pm–midnight, Tues–Thurs & Sun 9pm–2am, Fri & Sat 9pm–4am.

DNA Lounge 375 11th St at Harrison, South of Market ☎ 415 626 1409, ⊛ dnalounge.com; map pp.84–85. Stalwart club that changes its music style nightly but consistently draws a young, mixed gay/straight crowd. Downstairs is a large dance floor, while the mezzanine is a sofa-packed lounge ideal for chilling. $15 and up. Mon 9.30pm–2.30am, Thurs 9.30pm–3am, Fri & Sat 9pm–3am.

The End Up 401 Sixth St at Harrison, South of Market ☎ 415 646 0999, ⊛ theendup.com; map pp.84–85. This legendary local club has been hosting its "T-Dance" party (6am–8pm every Sun) longer than almost anyone on the scene can remember. The dancefloor is invitingly cramped, and if you need a break from the beat assault, there's an outdoor patio with plenty of seating. $5 and up. Hours vary – check website for booking schedule.

Fluid 662 Mission St at Third, South of Market ☎ 415 615 6888, ⊛ fluidsf.com; map pp.84–85. Dressy "ultra lounge" playing mostly hip-hop and mainstream house. The large first room is the lounge, its mirrored walls illuminated by the neon, flashing floor; the rear room is home to a tiny dancefloor. $5 and up. Thurs–Sat 9pm–2am.

Mezzanine 444 Jessie St at Fifth, South of Market ☎ 415 625 8880, ⊛ mezzaninesf.com; map pp.84–85. Megaclub featuring mainstream, brand-name DJs, as well as gigs by hip-hop, reggae and (very occasionally) indie rock acts, although the massive space's acoustics benefit DJs rather than live bands. There's a VIP lounge with the requisite bottle service if you're feeling flush and flash. $15 and up. Hours vary – check website for booking schedule.

Shine 1337 Mission St at Ninth, South of Market ☎ 415 255 1337, ⊛ shinesf.com; map pp.84–85. It's so dark inside this low-ceilinged lounge that everyone looks good; the floors are hardwood, while the black ceiling is covered in disco balls. Local underground DJs spin house, breaks, techno, house, electro and dubstep for enthusiastic crowds. $5. Wed–Sat 9pm–2am.

Temple Nightclub 540 Howard St at First, South of Market ☎ 415 978 9942, ⊛ templesf.com; map pp.84–85. Walk into this opulent, spacious nightclub, with its tall columns and pristine white couches, and you'll feel as if you've been transported to a high-end, modernist Miami hotel. Descend into the Destiny Lounge and it becomes even more neon-lit and space-agey; by the time you delve even deeper to reach the Catacombs, you'll find yourself in a room resembling a Buddhist-themed cave. Music-wise, Temple is known for its throbbing sound system and separate dance rooms devoted to house, electro, breaks, hip-hop and funk. $10 and up. Thurs–Sat 10pm–4am.

10

10

THE MISSION AND THE CASTRO
LIVE MUSIC VENUES

★ **Amnesia** 853 Valencia St at 20th, Mission ☎ 415 970 0012, ⓦ amnesiathebar.com; map p.100. Duck inside this cosy spot done out speakeasy-style in deep reds and you're bound to find an eclectic crowd of regulars packing the place most nights. Bookings are as all over the stylistic map as the clientele, from bluegrass jams on Mon and open mic on Tues to jazz on Wed and assorted other entertainment through the rest of the week, including cabaret, readings, karaoke and the odd puppet show. There's a wide range of beers on offer, while the house sangria is sure to hit you between the eyes. Free–$15.

Bottom of the Hill 1233 17th St at Missouri, Potrero Hill ☎ 415 621 4455, ⓦ bottomofthehill.com; map pp.98–99. Well off the beaten path, San Francisco's celebrated indie rock stronghold draws crowds nightly for local and nationally touring acts. There's a grungy back patio that's popular with smokers. $8 and up.

Bruno's 2389 Mission St at 20th, Mission ☎ 415 643 5200, ⓦ brunossf.com; map p.100. Like something straight out of a Martin Scorsese film, this retro dance venue is filled with 1960s-style furniture and decor. If it's urban and danceable – hip-hop, r'n'b, soul, funk – you'll hear it here at some point. $10 and up. Fri & Sat 8pm–2am.

★ **Café du Nord** 2170 Market St at Sanchez, Castro ☎ 415 861 5016, ⓦ cafedunord.com; map p.100. This old subterranean speakeasy, built in 1907, retains its Victorian faux panelling and wainscoting – as well as a hand-carved mahogany bar – and is one of San Francisco's top places to catch touring or local rock bands, with the occasional swing and folk act booked for good measure. The amber-walled *Swedish American Hall* upstairs also regularly hosts shows. $10 and up.

Dogpatch Saloon 2496 Third St at 22nd, Dogpatch ☎ 415 643 8592; map pp.98–99. Just east of Potrero Hill, this atmospheric neighbourhood joint – with its sparklingly clean chequered floor and stiff, yet affordable drinks – is an ideal out-of-the-way venue for weekend jazz sessions; call for performance times. $5.

Elbo Room 647 Valencia St at 17th, Mission ☎ 415 552 7788, ⓦ elbo.com; map p.100. A local cradle of acid jazz in the early 1990s, this centrally located venue now hosts a smorgasbord of bands and DJs, from rock to reggae to soul. $6 and up.

El Rio 3158 Mission St at Valencia, Mission ☎ 415 282 3325, ⓦ elriosf.com; map p.100. While it looks like your typical neighbourhood dive up front, *El Rio* has a somewhat hidden side room that plays host to a vastly diverse array of live music, from punk rock, rootsy Americana and metal to samba, salsa and reggae. The event calendar also features burlesque shows and weekly parties aimed at the bar's sizeable lesbian clientele. Free–$10. Mon–Thurs 5pm–2am, Fri 4pm–2am, Sat & Sun 1pm–2am.

The Knockout 3223 Mission St at Valencia ☎ 415 550 6994, ⓦ theknockoutsf.com; map p.100. Oddly shaped bar that brings in garage rockers, honky-tonk bands and retro pop groups, with just as many dance parties (soul, punk, funk and hip-hop) on its calendar. Free–$6. Daily 5pm–2am.

Make-Out Room 3225 22nd St at Mission, Mission ☎ 415 647 2888, ⓦ makeoutroom.com; map p.100. With a larger space lurking beyond the long mahogany bar dominating the entryway, this venerable Mission bar and live music venue books roots and indie rock bands (both local and touring), as well as DJs and literary/storytelling events. Free–$10. Daily 6pm–2am.

The Red Poppy Art House 2698 Folsom St at 23rd, Mission ☎ 415 826 2402, ⓦ redpoppyarthouse.org; map p.100. This humbly sized performance space, brightly lit and draped with white curtains, presents all manner of jazz and international music at weekends, in addition to a wide range of other events (folk, chamber music and film) throughout the week. It's operated as a non-profit where entrance fees are known as "audience grants". $10 and up.

Roccapulco Supper Club 3140 Mission St at Cesar Chavez, Mission ☎ 415 648 6611, ⓦ roccapulco.com; map p.100. Sizeable club (with a decent Mexican restaurant inside) that books salsa and Tejano music, including performers rarely heard in the US. Salsa lessons happen every Fri and Sat night at 8.30pm, and there's a strictly enforced dress code (no jeans or sneakers). $12 and up.

Savanna Jazz 2937 Mission St at 25th, Mission ☎ 415 285 3369, ⓦ savannajazz.com; map p.100. Decked out in vintage records, this intimate nightclub offers live local jazz 5–6 nights a week (closed Mon and some Tues), including Latin and Brazilian nights from time to time. $5 and up.

Thee Parkside 1600 17th St at Wisconsin, Potrero Hill ☎ 415 252 1330, ⓦ theeparkside.com; map pp.98–99. Roomy and relatively clean for a dive, this venue offers everything a greaser or punk could ask for: garage rock, punk, honky-tonk and rockabilly, not to mention delicious burgers. It's also one of the few bars in San Francisco to boast a ping-pong table – head to the large outdoor patio out back. Free–$12.

CLUBS

Bollyhood Cafe 3372 19th St at Mission, Mission ☎ 415 970 0362, ⓦ bollyhoodcafe.com; map p.100. Restaurant and lounge that plays Bollywood movies nonstop and, several nights a week, hosts dance parties that bring out hardcore and novice salsa and tango dancers alike. There's also live jazz every Tues. $3 and up. Hours vary – check website for booking schedule.

Club Cocomo 650 Indiana St at Mariposa, Potrero Hill ☎ 415 824 6910, ⓦ cafecocomo.com; map pp.98–99. The place to be in San Francisco if salsa's your thing. There's an outdoor patio for cooling off, plus salsa dance lessons (included in the cover charge) several nights a week. $5 and up. Opening hours vary, but salsa lessons generally begin at 7pm, with dancing 9pm–2am.

Il Pirata 2007 16th St at Utah, Potrero Hill ☎ 415 626 2626, ⓦ ilpiratasf.com; map pp.98–99. Dive bar-restaurant where the atmosphere morphs into clubbish terrain later in the evening. The decor's on the wacky side – Christmas lights, streamers, etc – but with two rooms and a spacious outdoor patio, there's plenty of room to dance to the DJ sets, whether it's salsa on Fri or electronic and funk other nights of the week. Free. Daily 11am–2am.

Mighty 119 Utah St at 15th, Potrero Hill ☎ 415 762 0151, ⓦ mighty119.com; map pp.98–99. Huddled close to the freeway, this converted warehouse space is a combination art gallery, performance venue, club and lounge; don't miss the frozen vodka bar. As for the music, it's mostly live funk or DJs spinning old-school classic house. $5 and up. Thurs–Sat 9pm–2am.

Skylark 3089 16th St at Valencia, Mission ☎ 415 621 9294, ⓦ skylarkbar.com; map p.100. Club-bar hybrid with low lighting and plenty of booths; it's popular for its intimate vibe, varied DJs and strong and cheap drinks, making it a top choice for an inexpensive night out. During the week, it's more geared toward drinking, while at weekends it becomes a full-scale dance venue. Free. Mon, Tues & Sun 7pm–2am, Wed–Fri 5pm–2am, Sat 9pm–2am.

Som 2925 16th St at Capp, Mission ☎ 415 558 8521, ⓦ som-bar.com; map p.100. Poorly ventilated hotspot in a grotty corner of the Mission that's nonetheless worth checking out. It attracts a diverse crowd that, depending on the night, grooves to house or underground hip-hop, while the friendly bartenders and disarmingly clean restrooms are equally welcome touches. $6 and up. Tues–Fri 5pm–2am, Sat 9pm–3am, Sun 9.30pm–2am.

HAIGHT-ASHBURY AND WEST OF CIVIC CENTER
LIVE MUSIC VENUES

Boom Boom Room 1601 Fillmore St at Geary, Western Addition ☎ 415 673 8000, ⓦ boomboomblues.com; map pp.106–107. Once owned by late blues legend John Lee Hooker, this small, intimate bar with a chequerboard floor plays host to a fine selection of touring blues and funk artists. $7 and up.

> **TOP 5 MUSIC VENUES**
> Café du Nord See p.184
> The Fillmore See p.182
> Great American Music Hall See p.182
> The Independent See p.185
> The Warfield See p.182

★ **Club Deluxe** 1509 Haight St at Ashbury, Upper Haight ☎ 415 552 6949, ⓦ sfclubdeluxe.com; map pp.106–107. Now known just as well for its excellent Neapolitan-style pizza, *Club Deluxe* boasts live entertainment nightly, from comedy on Mon and bossa nova every Sun to jazz on most other evenings. Free.

★ **The Independent** 628 Divisadero St at Hayes, Western Addition ☎ 415 771 1421, ⓦ theindependentsf.com; map pp.106–107. With its disarmingly friendly staff and exceptional sound, this mid-sized club specializes in booking acts both near (Rogue Wave) and far (Vieux Farka Toure), and across all genre boundaries as well, from hip-hop to international folk to electronic. $15 and up.

Rasselas 1534 Fillmore St at O'Farrell, Western Addition ☎ 415 346 8696, ⓦ rasselasjazzclub.com; map pp.106–107. With nightly live acts ranging from jazz and Latin to r'n'b and funk, this club-restaurant has never been considered among the city's first-rank venues, but it still keeps ticking along. It's unique in that you can enjoy fine Ethiopian food during performances. Every Mon sees an open mic and jazz jam. Free–$5.

Rickshaw Stop 155 Fell St at Van Ness, Hayes Valley ☎ 415 861 2011, ⓦ rickshawstop.com; map pp.106–107. Intriguing bar-club whose nondescript exterior reveals an invitingly dark interior swathed in red velvet. It's known for live indie rock shows that mostly showcase touring bands, as well as its monthly bhangra DJ night and queer "Cockblock" dance party on alternating Saturdays. $7 and up.

CLUB

Milk Bar 1840 Haight St at Shrader, Upper Haight ☎ 415 387 6455, ⓦ milksf.com; map pp.106–107. DJ bar and lounge in the unlikely shadow of Golden Gate Park. It boasts white booths, posh drinks and one of the top DJ rosters in the city, spinning hip-hop and soul several nights a week. Free–$10. Mon–Tues & Thurs–Sat 8pm–2am, Sun 2–8pm.

THE RICHMOND AND THE SUNSET
LIVE MUSIC VENUES

Rockit Room 406 Clement St at Fifth, Inner Richmond ☎ 415 387 6343, ⓦ rock-it-room.com; map p.116. Although the Rockit Room's live music programming isn't the most adventurous in the city – it's often dependent on overly earnest rock – it's still one of the better options on San Francisco's west side. There are salsa lessons every Mon, and comedy and karaoke on Tues. $5 and up.

The Plough and Stars 116 Clement St at Second, Inner Richmond ☎ 415 751 1122, ⓦ theploughandstars.com; map p.116. Local Irish expats cram into this terrific pub for pints and live folk, bluegrass and Americana music at 9pm nightly. Nominal cover on Fri & Sat, free other nights.

Performing arts and film

San Francisco rightfully has a reputation for embracing the performing arts
– there are several major symphony orchestras based in the Bay Area, and
the city itself boasts a world-class ballet troupe and a highly respected opera
company. Theatre is also plentiful, though it's unfortunate that many of the
larger venues often fall prey to a schedule of Broadway reruns. The bolder
fringe circuit stages new plays with greater frequency, and while quality can
be uneven, these smaller concerns tend to offer more interesting options
than the crowd-pleasers staged west of Union Square. Thanks largely to an
active club scene, comedy is regaining an audience, with nights built around
stand-up and sketch material. Last but by no means least, film remains nearly
as popular an obsession as eating in San Francisco.

ESSENTIALS

Listings San Francisco's duelling pair of alternative weeklies, *San Francisco Bay Guardian* (ⓦsfbg.com) and *SF Weekly* (ⓦsfweekly.com), each features detailed listings of what's on in the city's arts community each week. San Francisco Chronicle's "Datebook" section is another useful (albeit more mainstream) resource, and is particularly good for film roundups. Finally, check ⓦsfstandup.com for an extensive list of local comedy shows, although there's no guarantee it will have been updated recently.

Tickets Although you'll usually pay dearly (well over $100) for top seats at San Francisco's high-arts events – namely, the symphony, ballet and opera – it's possible to sidestep these steep prices by seeking out standing-room-only and same-day tickets; visit each performing arts company's website for

details. Theatre prices, meanwhile, can range wildly, from $15 for a ticket to watch an original play at the tiny Shelton Theater to upwards of $90 for a prime spot at one of the Curran's major productions. For half-price bargains to shows at major San Francisco theatres, try the Tix Bay Area booth (Tues–Fri 11am–6pm, Sat 10am–6pm, Sun 10am–3pm; ☎415 433 7827, ⓦtheatrebayarea.org), located on the west side of Union Square opposite the *Westin St Francis Hotel*; each day's bargains are listed on the website by 11am. For advance tickets to certain cinemas, try Fandango (ⓦfandango.com) or Moviefone (ⓦmoviefone.com). Film passes generally range from $8–13 around town, while you'll pay anywhere from $5–32 for a comedy show (drinks and bad jokes notwithstanding).

CLASSICAL MUSIC, BALLET AND OPERA

Several first-rate ensembles and troupes keep the city's high-arts scene in top form, including leading lights such as the San Francisco Symphony and Ballet, as well as other widely acclaimed companies like Alonzo King LINES Ballet and the Philharmonia Baroque orchestra. Furthermore, San Francisco Opera's autumn season – and particularly its gala opening night – is one of the region's major annual cultural happenings.

11

MAJOR COMPANIES

Philharmonia Baroque ☎415 252 1288, ⓦphilharmonia.org. This much-lauded company performs early music on traditional European instruments in various San Francisco and Bay Area venues during its autumn and spring seasons. Over the years, the orchestra's repertoire has expanded beyond its strict chronological boundaries, but its sound remains distinctive. Tickets $25–75.

San Francisco Ballet War Memorial Opera House, 301 Van Ness Ave at Grove, Civic Center ☎415 865 2000, ⓦsfballet.org. Founded in 1933, this troupe (the nation's

oldest) was the first to stage full-length productions of *Swan Lake* and *The Nutcracker*. Despite its illustrious origins, however, it faced near-bankruptcy by the 1970s and 1980s; thankfully, the arrival of artistic director Helgi Tomasson (former premier danseur of the New York City Ballet in the 1970s and 80s) ushered in an era of revived prominence. Since it shares the War Memorial with San Francisco Opera, the Ballet's season runs Jan–May, with a run of *Nutcracker* performances anchoring the city's festive holiday season. Tickets begin at around $40, while standing-room tickets are sold two hours before each performance for $10–20.

FREE CONCERTS

A particularly welcome offshoot of San Francisco's thriving performing arts scene is the plenteous free concerts that take place in parks and at venues around town. Naturally, most take place outdoors during the drier months.

Golden Gate Park Band Sun 1pm, early April to early Oct, Spreckels Temple of Music, Golden Gate Park ☎415 831 5500, ⓦgoldengateparkband.org. Since 1882, this populist ensemble has been playing a variety of favourites – Broadway show tunes, marches, folk music – at the bandshell in its namesake park's Music Concourse. Pack a picnic and hum along.

Lindy in the Park Sun 11am–2pm, year-round, John F. Kennedy Drive behind de Young Museum, Golden Gate Park ⓦlindyinthepark.com. Free swing dance gathering that's universally fun – even for confirmed dual left-footers. There's usually a free lesson at noon.

Noontime Concerts Tues 12.30pm, year-round, Old St Mary's Cathedral, 660 California St at Grant,

Chinatown ☎415 777 3211, ⓦnoontimeconcerts.org. Impressive lunch-hour classical concerts showcasing mostly well-known works by the likes of Mozart, Beethoven and Chopin, though there are occasional diversions (such as Baroque chamber works from Italy). A $5 donation is requested.

Stern Grove Festival See p.228.

Yerba Buena Gardens Festival Schedule varies, early May to early Oct, Yerba Buena Gardens, Mission St at Third, South of Market ☎415 543 1718, ⓦybgf.org. More than one hundred daytime concerts – including dance troupes, international music and an occasional appearance by the San Francisco Symphony – take place on the outdoor stage here annually.

San Francisco Opera War Memorial Opera House, 301 Van Ness Ave at Grove, Civic Center ☎415 864 3330, ⓦsfopera.com. A typical season for this internationally regarded company offers a mixture of avant-garde stagings by composers such as John Adams or André Previn, along with acclaimed productions of perennial favourites by Wagner or Puccini. The season runs Sept–Dec, with a short summer season May–July. Tickets start at $40, with same-day tickets available at 11am on the day of performance.

San Francisco Performances ☎415 392 2545, ⓦperformances.org. Known as the most adventurous large company in town, San Francisco Performances schedules a diverse array of classical recitals, jazz and contemporary dance programmes, often with a European emphasis. Spring and autumn programmes shuttle between various local theatres, including the Herbst Theatre, Yerba Buena Center for the Arts and Davies Symphony Hall. Performances vary in both name-recognition and quality. Tickets $15–125.

★ **San Francisco Symphony** Louise M. Davies Symphony Hall, 201 Van Ness Ave at Hayes, Civic Center ☎415 864 6000, ⓦsfsymphony.org. Since the 1995 arrival of conductor Michael Tilson Thomas, this once-musty institution has catapulted to the first rank of American symphony orchestras. Though Thomas's relentless self-promotion can be off-putting, his emphasis on the works of twentieth-century composers has added considerable vibrancy to the company's programming. The season runs Sept–May, with scattered events at the Legion of Honor as well as the Flint Center in Cupertino, near San Jose. Tickets generally range from $40–145, with same-day tickets sometimes available for $15.

SMALLER BALLET COMPANIES

Alonzo King LINES Ballet Yerba Buena Center for the Arts, 701 Mission St at Third, South of Market ☎415 863 3040, ⓦlinesballet.org. A superb contemporary ensemble that started at the San Francisco Dance Center and is now based at the Yerba Buena Center, LINES Ballet also mounts tours around the US and Europe. Expect innovative works – Grateful Dead drummer Mickey Hart was one recent collaborator, while another well-received production brought African pygmy dancers to perform with the troupe. Tickets $25 and up.

Smuin Ballet ☎415 556 5000, ⓦsmuinballet.org. Founded by former San Francisco Ballet director Michael Smuin, this company sasses up traditional dance with bits of jazz and pop – everything from Gershwin to the Beatles to k.d. lang. The roving troupe doesn't have a permanent home, but regularly performs at Yerba Buena Center's Novellus Theater, while also venturing to suburban locales (Walnut Creek and Mountain View) and even Carmel throughout the year. It's perhaps not for ballet purists, but terrific for dance newbies. Tickets $20–62.

THEATRE

With a healthy assortment of theatre companies, venues and, perhaps most crucially, audiences, San Francisco theatre has plenty to offer, from touring Broadway shows to quick-trigger improv – not to mention a veteran mime troupe and the city's famed stage production, Beach Blanket Babylon. Theatre enthusiasts should also consider a trip across the bay, as Berkeley Repertory Theatre is acknowledged as one of the premier stages in California (see p.251). In early September, the San Francisco Fringe Festival (see p.228) takes place at several venues, though the Exit Theatre (see opposite) near Union Square is its primary home.

MAJOR THEATRES

American Conservatory Theater (ACT) 415 Geary St at Mason, Union Square ☎415 749 2228, ⓦact-sf.org. The Bay Area's leading resident theatre group mixes newly commissioned works and innovative renditions of the classics; you can also expect the obligatory holiday season run of *A Christmas Carol*. Particularly noteworthy is the company's inventive set design and staging. Tickets can cost as little as $14 for a preview show, though you'll pay $30–70 most of the time; same-day tickets are generally available from noon on performance days.

The Curran 445 Geary St at Mason, Union Square ☎415 551 2000, ⓦshnsf.com. One of the three San Francisco venues managed by Shorenstein Hays, the Curran is a former vaudeville theatre that now presents both hit Broadway plays and musicals. Pre-Broadway tryouts are common here: Tony magnet *Wicked* was workshopped for several weeks at the Curran before hitting New York. Tickets $30–90.

Golden Gate Theatre 1 Taylor St at Golden Gate Ave, Tenderloin ☎415 551 2000, ⓦshnsf.com. Constructed in the 1920s and restored to its original splendour by owners Shorenstein Hays, this auditorium's elegant Rococo decor frequently outclasses its schedule of touring Broadway productions. Cheap seats cost around $30, while most tickets cost upwards of $45.

Orpheum Theatre 1192 Market St at Eighth, Tenderloin ☎415 551 2000, ⓦshnsf.com. Probably the most spectacular of all the big houses, the third Shorenstein Hays venue is much grander than its lineup of lesser Broadway shows – look for the white gargoyles on the interior moulding. Tickets typically start around $40 for most performances.

Yerba Buena Center for the Arts 701 Mission St at Third, South of Market ☎415 978 2787, ⓦybca.org. This venue struggled to find an identity for several years as it careened between every possible avant-garde performance style in dance, theatre and music. It's finally honing its vision, showcasing local talents in programmes like the Hip-Hop Theater Festival as well as touring shows. Tickets $15–50.

SMALLER SPACES

Actors Theatre 855 Bush St at Mason, Union Square ☎415 345 1287, ⊛actorstheatresf.org. This company presents high-quality, ensemble-based drama in an intimate space – usually big-name plays (*One Flew Over the Cuckoo's Nest*, *A Streetcar Named Desire*) with impressive local casts. Ticket prices usually hover around $30.

African American Art & Culture Complex 762 Fulton St at Webster, Western Addition ☎415 922 2049, ⊛aaacc.org. Thanks to inspiring executive director London Breed, this fledgling cultural space – home to a cluster of black arts associations – has garnered local buzz. Sporadically scheduled stage performances, some presented by AfroSolo Arts Festival (see p.228), take place in the onsite, 210-seat Buriel Clay Memorial Theater. Tickets $10 and up.

★ **BATS Improv** Bayfront Theater, Fort Mason Center ☎415 474 6776, ⊛improv.org. One of the best of its kind anywhere, this celebrated long-form improv company (its titular acronym stands for Bay Area Theatresports) hosts classes, guest groups and an improv competition every Sun night; it also stages its own shows year-round every Fri and Sat. Tickets $5–20.

★ **Beach Blanket Babylon** Club Fugazi, 678 Green St at Powell, North Beach ☎415 421 4222, ⊛beach blanketbabylon.com. Founded by the late Steve Silver, a prominent local personality, *Beach Blanket Babylon* has become a San Francisco institution since debuting in the mid 1970s. The revue-style show, which plays seven times weekly, is *Saturday Night Live* meets *The Daily Show*, injected with a hyperliberal dose of Vegas kitsch – a constantly rewritten pastiche that lampoons celebrities and current events, using the loose framework of a lovelorn Snow White as its base. The massive wigs worn by the mostly veteran cast – including one depicting the entire city skyline – are the true showstoppers. Performances are for those 21 and over, except two Sun matinees. Tickets $25–130.

The Dark Room 2263 Mission St at 19th, Mission ☎415 401 7987, ⊛darkroomsf.com. This multi-use performance space has a varied programming schedule (usually handwritten on a white board on the door): Fri and Sat typically see troupe comedy or live theatre ($10–15), while Sun is Bad Movie Night, for which an unintentionally awful film (*Last Action Hero*, *Waterworld*, etc) is screened for $5. There's also free open improv every Tues.

Exit Theatre 156 Eddy St at Taylor, Tenderloin ☎415 673 3847, ⊛theexit.org. Its Tenderloin address is dodgy, and its houses are tiny – no more than ninety seats in each of its four spaces – but the Exit is one of the best spots in town for cutting-edge theatre. It's known for its DivaFest each spring (an event devoted to women-centric plays and performances), as well as producing and being an anchor venue for September's local Fringe Festival (see p.228). Tickets $20–25.

Footloose Presents at Shotwell Studios 3252-A 19th St at Shotwell, Mission ☎415 920 2223, ⊛ftloose .org. This small company is locally respected for its experimental music and dance shows that often showcase a feminist slant; it also puts on theatre, comedy and multimedia performances. Tickets $15–20.

Intersection for the Arts 925 Mission St at Fifth, South of Market ☎415 626 2787, ⊛theintersection .org. Opened in the 1960s, this is the city's longest-active alternative theatre space, still churning out political, community-oriented productions in its tiny venue. Expect low-budget, high-quality performances, with ticket prices $10–35; "pay what you can" nights occur frequently. There's also a free visual arts gallery (Wed–Sat noon–6pm) with a similarly political bent.

11

Lorraine Hansberry Theatre ☎415 474 8800, ⊛lhtsf.com. Now in its fourth decade, this African-American company showcases mostly new plays, along with the odd classic such as *Porgy and Bess*. Recent seasons have been staged at Fort Mason Center's Southside Theater; however, at the time of writing, its home for the forthcoming season was undetermined – check the website for updated venue information. Tickets $40–50.

Magic Theatre Fort Mason Center ☎415 441 8822, ⊛magictheatre.org. The busiest and largest local company after ACT, the Magic is responsible for some of the top fringe productions in the Bay Area. It specializes in the works of well-known contemporary playwrights, as well as those by emerging new talents. Performances occur at either of two venues at lower Fort Mason: the Northside Theatre or the Sam Shepard Theatre. Tickets $40–45.

The Marsh 1062 Valencia St at 22nd, Mission ☎415 826 5750, ⊛themarsh.org. This longstanding alternative space hosts fine solo shows, many with an offbeat bent. Mon nights are test nights for works in progress. Tickets are often made available on a sliding scale between $15–30.

New Conservatory Theatre Center 25 Van Ness Ave at Fell, Civic Center ☎415 861 8972, ⊛nctcsf.org. Mid-size theatre bang in the centre of the city that's best known for its Pride season of LGBT-themed plays; its programming calendar also includes comedy performances, cabaret productions and even youth programmes. Tickets $18–40.

San Francisco Mime Troupe ☎415 285 1717, ⊛sfmt .org. Founded in 1959, this troupe was an early leader in "people's", or radical, theatre. Its punchy, not-so-subtle political comedies, performed for free at parks throughout the city, have become a summertime tradition from Independence Day through Labor Day – check the website for a performance schedule.

San Francisco Shakespeare Festival ☎ 415 558 0888, ⓦ sfshakes.org. Free productions of the Bard's best usually hit the Presidio's Main Post Parade Ground Lawn in early Sept and are presented all month (see p.228).

Shelton Theater 533 Sutter St at Powell, Union Square ☎ 415 433 1226, ⓦ sheltontheater.com. Improv productions and musicals are staged every Fri and Sat in this tiny showspace just off Union Square proper. It's best known for its long-running local hit, Shopping! The Musical. Tickets $15–29.

Theatre Rhinoceros 2926 16th St at S Van Ness, Mission ☎ 415 861 5079, ⓦ therhino.org. The city's top queer theatre company presents productions that range from heartfelt political drama to raunchy cabaret acts. It's currently in search of a new permanent home, so check the website for performance locations. Tickets $15–25.

Thick House 1695 18th St at Carolina, Potrero Hill ☎ 415 401 8081, ⓦ thickhouse.org. An intimate (under one hundred seats) performing arts and community centre used by several small companies to showcase new, often challenging works by Bay Area playwrights. Tickets $25–28.

COMEDY

Following an era of glory that saw Robin Williams, Margaret Cho and Dana Carvey cut their teeth in local clubs before becoming major stars, San Francisco's **comedy** scene endured a fallow period of venue closures and few national breakthroughs. Things are looking up, however, with the recent proliferation of comedy nights staged at bars, music venues and tiny theatres in the city.

Club Chuckles Hemlock Tavern, 1131 Polk St at Sutter, Polk Gulch ☎ 415 923 0923, ⓦ hemlocktavern.com. Side-splitting, yet frustratingly infrequent shows in the back room of this top Polk Gulch bar. Expect a mixed bag of sketches, musical comedy, stand-up, films and videos. Tickets $5 and up.

Club Deluxe 1511 Haight St at Ashbury, Upper Haight ☎ 415 552 6949, ⓦ liveatdeluxe.com. Mon is comedy night at this terrific Haight St bar and lounge, when regional up-and-comers take the stage. Tickets $5 and up.

Cobb's Comedy Club 915 Columbus Ave at Lombard, North Beach ☎ 415 928 4320, ⓦ cobbscomedy.com. One of two major comedy venues in the city (The Punch Line is the other), this 400-seat room not far from Fisherman's Wharf regularly hosts mid-profile touring comedians. Tickets $19–33, plus two-drink minimum.

The Punch Line 444 Battery St at Clay, Financial District ☎ 415 397 7573, ⓦ punchlinecomedyclub.com. This strangely located cabaret – it's nearly lost amid Maritime Plaza and the poured-concrete environs of the upper Financial District – books nightly shows, many of which feature well-known headliners. Tickets $15 and up, with the obligatory two-drink minimum.

Purple Onion 140 Columbus St at Jackson, North Beach ☎ 415 956 1653, ⓦ liveatdeluxe.com. Once a stage for Lenny Bruce, Woody Allen and Phyllis Diller in the 1950s and 1960s, this eighty-seat cellar venue has been revived and now spotlights local and regional comics; it's co-promoted by the same bookers behind Club Deluxe, and San Francisco Comedy College (see below) also books gigs here from time to time. Tickets $15–20.

San Francisco Comedy College 414 Mason St at Post, Union Square ⓦ clubhousecomedy.com. Organization that not only offers classes and workshops on the art of the laugh, but also puts on weekend shows at various locations around the city and outlying area. Tickets typically run $5–12.

FILM

San Francisco is as much of a film town as ever, judging by the fact that a wide range of cinemas – from old-time, single-screen movie houses to gleaming multiplexes – show all manner of movies, from independent productions to major studio releases. In addition, a strong community of underground filmgoers ensures a slate of truly alternative programming at a few leftfield venues around town.

COMEDY EVENTS

Should you find yourself in San Francisco in either January or September and looking for laughs, a pair of annual comedy happenings bear mention. **SF Sketchfest** (see p.226) is an ever-growing event that books big names (The Kids in the Hall, David Cross) and lesser-knowns alike each January at a host of venues around town; it also promotes other local shows throughout the year. **Comedy Day** (ⓦ comedyday.com) is held annually at Sharon Meadow in Golden Gate Park, usually on one of the last two Sundays in September (when San Francisco weather is often at its most glorious). The free, afternoon-long festival brings together local comedians and nationally known stars such as Paula Poundstone.

MULTIPLEXES

Embarcadero Center Cinema 1 Embarcadero Center, Financial District ☎ 415 267 4893, ⓦ landmarktheatres.com. Immensely popular Downtown complex showing both first-run independents and Oscar contenders. Never mind its location amid the stale Embarcadero Center – its programming definitely makes it worth a visit.

Metreon 16 101 Fourth St at Mission, South of Market ☎ 415 369 6201, ⓦ amctheatres.com/metreon. This multiplex is the one element of the Metreon that locals have welcomed. There are well over a dozen screens (plus an IMAX theatre) and high-definition sound for the bevy of major, first-run films on offer, plus arena-style seating in every auditorium.

San Francisco Centre 9 845 Market St at Fifth, South of Market ☎ 415 538 8422, ⓦ cinemark.com. Expect Hollywood hits galore (and the occasional arthouse surprise), booming sound systems and imitation leather seats at this state-of-the-art complex, set on the fifth floor of the city's Bloomingdales-anchored shopping palace.

★ **Sundance Kabuki** 1881 Post St at Fillmore, Japantown ☎ 415 346 3243, ⓦ sundancecinemas.com /kabuki.html. With advance reserved seating, sustainable-friendly details like "spudware" utensils (compostable/ recyclable cutlery made from potato starch and soy oil), and three eating/drinking destinations inside, this fully facelifted facility is like few other cinemas in the US. Programming varies from mainstream fare to eclectic choices. Validated parking is available at the underground parking garage around the corner on Fillmore St.

Van Ness 14 1000 Van Ness Ave at O'Farrell, Tenderloin ☎ 415 674 4630, ⓦ amctheatres.com/vanness. Dating from the 1920s, when it was an auto showroom topped by warehouses, this enormous multiplex in the heart of the city is ornamented in terracotta and painted metal. Expect mostly mainstream films.

THEATRES

Balboa Theater 3630 Balboa St at 37th, Outer Richmond ☎ 415 221 8184, ⓦ balboamovies.com. On a mellow block in the western reaches of the Richmond, the Balboa has abandoned repertory programming in favour of fresh Hollywood celluloid. It was originally built as a single-screen theatre in 1926 before being split into two viewing spaces in the late 1970s.

Bridge Theatre 3010 Geary St at Blake, Laurel Heights ☎ 415 267 4893, ⓦ landmarktheatres.com. There's one large screen in this old Art Deco cinema, named in 1939 after the then-recently opened Golden Gate Bridge. Programming alternates between Hollywood and independent hits.

★ **Castro Theatre** 429 Castro St at 17th, Castro ☎ 415 621 6120, ⓦ thecastrotheatre.com. San Francisco's signature movie palace (opened in 1922) offers foreign films, classic revivals, seating for over 1400 and the most enthusiastic audience in town; it also serves as hub for a number of local film festivals. Come early for evening screenings to listen to the Wurlitzer organ and gaze at the spectacular chandelier.

Clay Theatre 2261 Fillmore St at Sacramento, Pacific Heights ☎ 415 267 4893, ⓦ landmarktheatres.com. Circa-1910 single-screen cinema showing arthouse and foreign films along the heart of Fillmore St's swanky commercial drag in Pacific Heights. It regularly seems to be on the verge of closing for good, so visit while you can.

Lumiere Theatre 1572 California St at Polk, Polk Gulch ☎ 415 267 4893, ⓦ landmarktheatres.com. This Nob Hill-adjacent theatre, featuring multiple screens and located right on the California cable-car line, offers a mix of short-run rarities and newly released foreign films.

Marina Theatre 2149 Chestnut St at Steiner, Marina ☎ 415 345 1323, ⓦ lntsf.com/marina_theatre. Revitalized in recent years by Lee Neighborhood Theatres (which also operates two other local cinemas), the Marina's two upstairs screens are fine spots to catch mainstream fare like the latest Cameron Diaz vehicle, as well as the occasional independent film.

Opera Plaza Cinema 601 Van Ness Ave at McAllister, Civic Center ☎ 415 267 4893, ⓦ landmarktheatres.com. This is generally the last place in town to catch a movie before it shows up on DVD; the screens in the two smaller of the four theatres can barely be called "big screens". Still, it maintains a certain charm, especially among local hardcore film buffs.

The Red Vic 1727 Haight St at Cole, Upper Haight ☎ 415 668 3994, ⓦ redvicmoviehouse.com. Grab a wooden bowl filled with popcorn and kick your feet up on the natty chairs and couches at this friendly collective, where the calendar is liberally peppered with cult hits, surf movies and directors' cuts of past favourites.

Roxie Theater 3117 16th St at Valencia, Mission ☎ 415 863 1087, ⓦ roxie.com. Although its repertory scheduling has essentially disappeared, this venerable, indie moviehouse is known for adventurous programming – it's always been willing to take a risk on edgy documentaries and little-known foreign directors.

OTHER VENUES

Artists' Television Access 992 Valencia St at 21st, Mission ☎ 415 824 3890, ⓦ atasite.org. A scrappy, non-profit storefront space that shows underground films (often with a political or social theme) about four nights a week for $4 and up.

San Francisco Cinematheque ☎ 415 552 1990, ⓦ sfcinematheque.org. On the local scene for over fifty years, this experimental film and video showcase hosts screenings at a number of local venues, including San Francisco Museum of Modern Art.

11

11

BAY AREA FILM FESTIVALS

February San Francisco IndieFest (see p.226).

March San Francisco International Asian American Film Festival (see p.226).

April San Francisco International Film Festival (see p.227). The San Francisco International Women's Film Festival (ⓦ womensfilminstitute.com) is an event showcasing works by women spanning a number of genres, including documentaries and animation.

May San Francisco Sex Worker Film & Arts Festival (ⓦ sexworkerfest.com): an event for and about the full spectrum of sex workers – dancers, prostitutes, porn performers – that's right at home in a city known for its sexually tolerant mores.

June Frameline (see p.227).

June–September Film Night in the Park (☎ 415 272 2756, ⓦ filmnight.org) offers a variety of crowd-pleasers (*Mary Poppins*, *Vertigo*) and cult faves (*Amelie*, *Caddyshack*)

in Union Square, Washington Square Park and Dolores Park throughout the summer and into early autumn; there are also showings in Marin County. Suggested donation.

July–August San Francisco Jewish Film Festival (☎ 415 621 0556, ⓦ sfjff.org) shows films from throughout the Jewish diaspora – thought-provoking documentaries to racy Israeli soap operas.

September Bicycle Film Festival (ⓦ bicyclefilmfestival .com), a global event showcasing so-called velo-cinema, is a celluloid paean to cycling culture; it annually rolls through the bike-lover's stronghold of San Francisco in early autumn.

October Mill Valley Film Festival (ⓦ mvff.com) brings young lions and big names alike to Mill Valley's Sequoia Theater and San Rafael's Smith Rafael Film Center; independent works and world cinema are heavily emphasized.

Yerba Buena Center for the Arts Screening Room 701 Mission St at Third, South of Market ☎ 415 978 2787, ⓦ ybca.org. Showing experimental films, documentaries and other slipstream works (some from

decades past), this intimate space offers bracing alternatives to what you'll find at the adjacent Metreon and San Francisco Centre multiplexes.

GAY PRIDE PARADE

Gay and lesbian San Francisco

The heart of queer America is, arguably, San Francisco, where it's estimated that up to ten percent of the city's population is gay, lesbian, bisexual or transgender. This concentration has its roots in the permissiveness of the city's Gold Rush era and, more recently, during World War II, when suspected homosexual soldiers, purged by military brass at their point of embarkation, stayed put in town rather than return home to face potential stigma and shame. These beginnings, along with the advent of gay liberation in the early 1970s, nurtured a community with powerful political and social connections. Nowadays, most San Franciscans appreciate the positive cultural and economic impact that gay people have on the city, and a welcoming attitude toward homosexuality predominates pretty much everywhere.

Openly gay politicians or businesspeople in San Francisco are not the issue to straight locals they would be in many other areas of the US; this may also have to do with the fact that most of the gay community has effectively moved from the outrageous to the mainstream, a measure of its political success. Sadly, though (at least to some), the exuberant energy that went into the posturing and parading of the 1970s has taken on a much more sober, down-to-business attitude. Today you'll find more political activists organizing conferences than drag queens throwing parties, but while the city's gay scene has mellowed socially, its parades, parties and street fairs still swing better than most.

Well-kept and relatively safe, the **Castro** remains one of the world's most prominent gay destinations, but is by no means the sole enclave of queer life in San Francisco. Oft-seedy **Polk Gulch** is the city's centre of drag and transgender elements, while leather and fetish scenes continue to flourish in **South of Market**. Although lesbian culture flowered in the city in the 1980s and **Bernal Heights**, **Glen Park**, **Noe Valley** and parts of the **Mission** each contain lesbian communities, many women have migrated across the Bay to Oakland in recent years.

ESSENTIALS

INFORMATION

California HIV/AIDS Service Referrals ☎415 367 2437, ⓦcdcnpin.org/ca. Offers 24hr information and counselling.

Castro Online ⓦcastroonline.com. Robust site featuring travel and calendar listings, original content and discussion boards. A good first stop for gay travellers planning a visit.

Gay & Lesbian Medical Association ☎415 255 4547, ⓦglma.org. Referrals to gay and lesbian physicians.

Gloss ⓦglossmagazine.net. Online lifestyle magazine with interviews, articles, columns and listings.

San Francisco Sex Information ☎415 989 7374, ⓦsfsi.org. Providing free, anonymous and accurate information since 1972. Staffed Mon–Thurs 3–9pm, Fri 3–6pm, Sun 2–5pm.

SFQueer ⓦsfqueer.com. Somewhat ramshackle website devoted to local gay culture; its thorough event listings are the best reason to visit.

The Sisters of Perpetual Indulgence ☎415 820 9697, ⓦthesisters.org. Pope-baiting order of outlandish nuns (see box, p.104) that's been raising hell, safe-sex awareness and piles of money for charitable organizations as diverse as Friends of the Pink Triangle and the Red Cross since 1979. Naturally, it got its start in San Francisco.

RESOURCES

Charles M. Holmes Campus at the Center 1800 Market St at Octavia, Castro ☎415 865 5555, ⓦsfcenter .org. Known to most as simply the Center, this is the local gay community's main large-scale gathering and resource venue. It boasts not only plenty of handy materials at the first-floor information desk, but also regularly hosts workshops and support groups as well as performances by comedy and theatre groups – everything from stand-up and improv to queer-centric film series and kids' programmes. Mon–Thurs noon–10pm, Fri noon–6pm, Sat 9am–6pm.

Dimensions Clinic Castro-Mission Health Center, 3850 17th St at Noe, Castro ☎415 934 7789, ⓦdimensions clinic.org. Affiliated with Lyric (see opposite), this low-cost clinic offers health services to queer youth. Thurs 5–8pm, Sat noon–3pm.

GLBT Historical Society Museum 4127 18th St at Collingwood, Castro ☎415 621 1107, ⓦglbthistory .org. Historical exhibits, programmes and art showings, as well as extensive resource archives and a reading room. Archives and reading room (657 Mission St at New Montgomery, Suite 300, South of Market) available by appointment. $5 museum admission; free first Wed of month. Exhibit galleries open Wed–Sat 11–7pm, Sun noon–5pm.

Lyon-Martin Health Services 1748 Market St at Gough, Suite 201, Lower Haight ☎415 565 7667, ⓦlyon-martin.org. Long-established non-profit clinic focusing on helping low-income and uninsured lesbian/ bisexual and transgender women. Anonymous HIV testing, gynecological care, pregnancy tests, counselling and legal help. At the time of writing, the clinic was facing possible closure due to underfunding. Mon & Wed 11am–7pm, Tues & Fri 9am–5pm, Thurs noon–5pm.

TOP 5 GAY AND LESBIAN PLACES
Castro Theatre See p.198
Harvey's See p.196
Wild Side West See p.198
Charles M. Holmes Campus at the Center See above
Dolores Beach See p.101

TRAVEL CONTACTS

There's barely anywhere in San Francisco that won't welcome handholding gay couples, and hotels or restaurants will comfortably cater to gay travellers. A host of useful resources worldwide are available to help plan your visit.

IN THE US AND CANADA

Damron Box 422458, San Francisco, CA 94142 ☏ 800 462 6654 or 415 255 0404, ⓦ damron.com. Publisher of several guides and apps written specifically for gay travellers, all of which feature in-depth sections on San Francisco.

Gay Travel ⓦ gaytravel.com. Prime information source for international holiday excursions, including trip planning and booking.

Gayellow Pages Box 533, Village Station, New York, NY 10014 ☏ 646 213 0263, ⓦ gayellowpages .com. Useful directory of businesses in the US and Canada. Order a hard copy via post or download the California chapter as a free PDF from the website.

International Gay & Lesbian Travel Association 1201 NE 26th St, Suite 103, Fort Lauderdale, FL 33305 ☏ 954 630 1637, ⓦ iglta.org. Trade group providing information on gay- and lesbian-owned or -friendly travel agents, accommodation and other travel businesses.

IN THE UK

UK Gay Hotel and Travel Guide Box 6991, Leicester LE1 6YS ☏ 08703 455 600, ⓦ gaytravel .co.uk. Top resource for tracking down gay-operated and -friendly accommodation worldwide, with several listings for San Francisco and California.

IN AUSTRALIA

Parkside Travel 70 Glen Osmond Rd, Parkside, SA 5063 ☏ 08 8274 1222. All aspects of gay travel worldwide.

Tearaway Travel 52 Porter St, Prahan, VIC 3181 ☏ 03 9510 6344, ⓦ tearaway.com. Domestic and trans-Pacific travel specialists for gay men and lesbians.

12

Lyric 127 Collingwood St at 18th, Castro ☏ 415 703 6150, ⓦ lyric.org. Discussion groups, trainings, arts, recreation events and assistance with women's issues for LGBT (and questioning) youth aged 24 and under. Call for hours.

Magnet 4122 18th St at Castro, Castro ☏ 415 581 1600, ⓦ magnetsf.com. Health and wellness centre (including rapid HIV testing) combined with a performance space that hosts massage workshops, book readings, social gatherings and performances. Mon, Tues & Sat 11am–6pm, Wed– Fri 11am–9pm.

ACCOMMODATION

Choose any hotel in San Francisco and a single-sex couple won't raise an eyebrow at check-in. Some inns, like the *Queen Anne* (see p.130), attract equal numbers of gay and straight visitors. However, here are a few B&Bs and inns that cater especially to queer travellers. Be sure to check each inn's website for potential online discounts.

24 Henry 24 Henry St at Sanchez, Castro ☏ 415 864 5686 or 800 900 5686, ⓦ 24henry.com; map p.100. This small blue-and-white home, tucked away on a leafy residential street north of Market, is a predominantly gay male guesthouse with five simple rooms, one with private bath. It makes a friendly escape from the cruisey Castro scene nearby. $85–129.

Elaine's Hidden Haven 4005 Folsom St at Tompkins, Bernal Heights ☏ 415 647 2726 or 800 446 9050, ⓦ sfhiddenhaven.com; map pp.98–99. Sequestered on a quiet, sloped street with parking, this private, lesbian-operated suite is attached to the owners' home. There's a hammock and burbling fountain in the back garden, and a kitchen if you'd rather cook your own meals. Children welcome. Rates range from $69 for singles to $139 for four guests.

Inn on Castro 321 Castro St at 16th, Castro ☏ 415 861 0321, ⓦ innoncastro.com; map p.100. Luxurious B&B spread across two nearby houses, with eight rooms and three apartments available – all of which are brightly decorated in individual styles and have private baths and phones. There's also a funky lounge where you can meet other guests. Two-night minimum on weekends, three-night minimum on holidays. Shared bath from $115, private bath from $135.

★ **Parker Guest House** 520 Church St at 17th, Castro ☏ 888 520 7275, ⓦ parkerguesthouse.com; map p.100. This 21-room converted mansion is set in beautiful gardens and features ample common areas, a sunny breakfast room and a sauna; rooms are decorated in flower prints with down comforters. Shared bath from $139, private bath from $159.

Village House 4080 18th St at Castro, Castro ☏ 415 864 5686 or 800 900 5686, ⓦ 24henry.com; map p.100.

Co-managed with *24 Henry*, this delightful Victorian just off the main Castro corridor is a welcoming B&B; complimentary continental breakfast is served each morning. Its rooms are larger and gaudier than those at its counterpart, with primary-coloured walls and plenty of closet space. $105–149.

Willows Inn 710 14th St at Church, Castro ☏ 415 431 4770 or 800 431 0277, ⦿ willowssf.com; map p.100. This Edwardian B&B has a dozen rooms with wicker furniture, armoires and vanity units. Bathrooms are shared, and it's less than a minute's walk from the front door to Market St's bustle. From $99.

CAFÉS AND RESTAURANTS

While you're bound to find people of all sexual orientations at the restaurants and bistros listed below, it's a good bet that gays will outnumber straights at many of these.

Asia SF 201 Ninth St at Howard, South of Market ☏ 415 255 2742; map pp.84–85. The delicious small pan-Asian plates ($10–20) at this sophisticated restaurant/club, are overshadowed by the "gender illusionist" servers, who periodically hop onto the red runway bar to dance. Wed–Thurs 7–11pm, Fri 7pm–2am, Sat 5pm–2am, Sun 7–10pm.

Castro Country Club 4058 18th St at Hartford, Castro ☏ 415 552 6102; map p.100. Low-key social and community space housed on the first floor of an old Victorian. Everyone seems to just hang out on the steps out front, but there's also a TV room, pinball, patio and a coffeehouse that serves cheap snacks and non-alcoholic drinks. Mon–Thurs 7am–11pm, Fri 7am–midnight, Sat 9am–midnight, Sun 9am–10pm.

Catch 2362 Market St between 16th and 17th, Castro ☏ 415 431 5000; map p.100. True to its name, *Catch* specializes in seafood – enjoy seared halibut ($24) on the heated patio while listening to live piano jazz. Oysters on the half shell are available for $2.25 each, and there's a crispy polenta with spinach dish ($15) for landlubbers. Lunch Mon–Fri 11.30am–2.30pm; dinner Mon–Tues & Sun 5.30–9pm, Wed & Thurs 5.30–10pm, Fri & Sat 5.30–11pm; brunch Sat & Sun 11am–3.30pm.

Firewood Café 4248 18th St at Collingwood, Castro ☏ 415 243 8908; map p.100. A casual, quiet place a few blocks off the rambunctious Castro strip, where the thin-crust pizzas ($9–14) and half-chickens ($9) make for one of the most affordable meals in the neighbourhood. Salads (from $7.25) are generously sized. Mon–Thurs & Sun 11am–10pm, Fri–Sat 11am–11pm.

★ **Harvey's** 500 Castro St at 18th, Castro ☏ 415 431 4278; map p.100. A lively, moderately priced restaurant/bar (named in honour of Harvey Milk) that draws a friendly crowd from the neighbourhood and beyond. It's a solid all-around option – there's brunch on weekends, as well as live comedy and piano jazz on certain nights. Be sure to check out the cheeky cocktail list, which riffs wildly on the Bloody Mary concept (the Bloody Mary Tyler Moore has more liquor, of course). Mon–Thurs & Sun 11am–2am, Fri–Sat 9am–2am.

Home 2100 Market St at Church, Castro ☏ 415 503 0333; map p.100. Located on a prime, triangulated Castro corner, this buzzing bar/restaurant serves modern American food that's delicious and reasonably priced; the macaroni and cheese is a popular hit. The crowd is usually a mix of gay men and lesbians, with some straights on hand as well. Weekend brunch features a Build Your Own Bloody Mary bar. Mon–Fri 11am–midnight, Sat & Sun 10am–midnight.

Jumpin' Java 139 Noe St at 14th, Castro ☏ 415 431 5282; map p.100. Modest, low-key café filled with nerdy-cute gay boys and queer grad students, many hovering over their laptops. Mon–Thurs & Sun 6am–7.30pm, Fri–Sat 6.30am–8pm.

Sparky's 242 Church St at 14th, Castro ☏ 415 626 8666; map p.100. Inexpensive diner serving all the usual alcohol-soaking, 3am specialities; there's also a wide array of ice cream and speciality shakes from the soda fountain. The scene can get colourful on weekends, when restaurant-wide singalongs to the jukebox are most likely. Open 24hr.

BARS AND CLUBS

San Francisco's gay bars are many and varied, ranging from cosy cocktail lounges to boisterous leather-and-chain hangouts. Given the flight of large numbers of lesbians to other parts of the Bay Area, the city doesn't have nearly the number of lesbian bars it once did, but a handful of good ones still exist around town, particularly in Bernal Heights, up the hill from the Mission. Many of the bars below may crank up the music later in the evening and transform into mini-clubs; among those listed here, however, only a few are true gay dance clubs. It's a good idea to check websites and the local freesheets before heading out, as new venues seem to come and go all the time. For mixed gay/straight venues, see Chapter 12.

440 Castro 440 Castro St at 17th, Castro ☏ 415 621 8732; map p.100. Address-eponymous bar (known as "the 440") catering to the jeans and leather set – except on Mon, when its underwear party sees bar-goers dressed nearly all the way down. Daily noon–2am.

Aunt Charlie's Lounge 133 Turk St at Taylor, Tenderloin ☏ 415 441 2922, ⦿ auntcharlieslounge.com; map pp.84–85. A refreshingly divey, diverse bar attracting a mixed crowd of ageing drag queens, young hipsters and even a few gym bunnies. Beers are cheap, there are regular drag shows and it's especially popular on Thurs for its 1970s-themed party, "Tubesteak Connection" ($4). Mon–Fri noon–2am, Sat 10am–2am, Sun 10am–midnight.

Badlands 4131 18th St at Collingwood, Castro ☎ 415 626 9320; map p.100. A dance/video bar that attracts a pretty, thirty-something crowd, usually packed at weekends. There's a wide selection of imported beer, and overall it's one of the less sceney places around the Castro. Daily 2pm–2am.

The Café 2369 Market St at 17th, Castro ☎ 415 861 3846, ⓦ cafesf.com; map p.100. With its mainstream DJs, cheap cover, live Sat performance and frequent happy hours (often until 10pm or later), this longtime staple of the Castro club scene remains a crowd-pleaser. Hours vary nightly.

Cat Club 1190 Folsom St at Eighth, South of Market ☎ 415 703 8964, ⓦ sfcatclub.com; map pp.84–85. This dark, loud club gets livelier the later you arrive. Thurs here are known for "The Breakfast Club" party that attracts a mixed crowd for 1980s pop and rock. Hours vary nightly.

The Cinch 1723 Polk St at Washington, Polk Gulch ☎ 415 776 4162; map p.56. Long, narrow bar featuring video games, free pool on Wed and a sizeable patio for smoking. Daily noon–2am.

Club 8 1151 Folsom St at Eighth, South of Market ☎ 415 431 1151, ⓦ eightsf.com; map pp.84–85. With dancefloors on two levels, a trio of full bars and an outdoor patio set aside for smokers, this mid-sized club is a jumping hotspot most weekends. Every Fri sees "Club Dragon", a party that brings out the city's sizeable gay Asian contingent. Fri–Sun 9pm–3am.

★ **El Rio** 3158 Mission St at Valencia, Mission ☎ 415 282 3325, ⓦ elriosf.com; map p.100. Unpretentious bar on lower Mission that considers itself a community centre almost as much as a place to party. Still, the place jumps on Sun afternoons during its weekly salsa dance, live rock shows occur several nights weekly and it's popular with hipsters of all sexual walks. Mon–Thurs 5pm–2am, Fri 4pm–2am, Sat & Sun 1pm–2am.

The End Up 401 Sixth St at Harrison, South of Market ☎ 415 646 0999; map pp.84–85. Best known as the home of Sun's all-day "T-Dance" party (6am–8pm), this stalwart club attracts a mixed bag of hardcore clubbers for after-hours dancing on the always-packed dancefloor. The name's not about end-of-the-night desperation – rather, it was the last gay bar on this drag in the 1970s. Hours vary nightly.

Esta Noche 3079 16th St at Valencia, Mission ☎ 415 861 5757; map p.100. A fun, if dingy Latino drag bar that attracts a youngish, racially mixed clientele. There are raucous drag revues and drink specials nightly, and you can expect to hear Ricky Martin at some point. Daily 5pm–2am.

Hole in the Wall Saloon 1369 Folsom St at Tenth, South of Market ☎ 415 431 4695; map pp.84–85.

Although the *Hole in the Wall* is less outrageous than other places in the neighbourhood, don't be surprised to see an old man in diapers here. The cheap, strong drinks and even cheaper pool table are major draws. Daily noon–2am.

Lexington Club 3464 19th St at Lexington, Mission ☎ 415 863 2052; map p.100. One of the few places in the city where the girls consistently outnumber the boys – often by far. It's a bustling lesbian bar that attracts all sorts with its no-nonsense decor and excellent jukebox. Mon features free pool and $1 cans of Pabst. Mon–Thurs 5pm–2am, Fri–Sun 3pm–2am.

The Lone Star Saloon 1354 Harrison St at Tenth, South of Market ☎ 415 863 9999; map pp.84–85. Large, friendly and welcoming, much like the local bears who make the patio and bar here their second home. Mon–Thurs 4pm–2am, Fri 2pm–2am, Sat–Sun noon–2am.

Marlena's 488 Hayes St at Octavia, Hayes Valley ☎ 415 864 6672; map pp.106–107. An old-school drag bar with high-quality acts, cheap drinks and a deliciously old-fashioned vibe in the heart of boutiquey Hayes Valley. The regulars are mainly thirty- and forty-something guys, plus a few women. Daily noon–2am.

Martuni's 4 Valencia St at Market, Mission ☎ 415 241 0205; map pp.106–107. This two-room piano bar on the edge of the Mission, Castro and Hayes Valley attracts a well-heeled, diverse crowd, with many keen to sing along to classics by Judy, Liza and Edith. The drink menu's full of kitschy choices, including chocolate martinis. Daily 4pm–2am.

The Mint 1942 Market St at Buchanan, Hayes Valley ☎ 415 626 4726; map pp.106–107. Not a gay bar per se, but worth noting for its enduring popularity as San Francisco's go-to karaoke venue. The list of available songs goes far beyond the usual Bette and Barbra ballads – expect to hear everything from "Oops! I Did It Again" to "Emotional Rescue" get completely butchered by soused punters. Mon–Sat 3pm–2am, Sun 3pm–midnight.

Mix 4086 18th St at Castro, Castro ☎ 415 431 8616; map p.100. One of the few gay sports bars in town. Watch games on TV, play pool or enjoy a beer on the back patio. Daily 6pm–2am.

Pilsner Inn 225 Church St at 14th, Castro ☎ 415 621 7058; map p.100. Mature bar filled with a diverse crowd playing pool and darts. There's a large patio out back, and a generally welcoming, open vibe. Mon–Fri noon–2am, Sat & Sun 10–2am.

Powerhouse 1347 Folsom St at Ninth, South of Market ☎ 415 552 8689; map pp.84–85. One of the prime

12

GAY AND LESBIAN FESTIVALS AND EVENTS

Several lesbian- and gay-specific events are held in San Francisco throughout the year – you'll find details in Chapter 15.

JUST MARRIED

San Francisco's position as America's homo heartland was never clearer than in February 2004, when the then-newly elected mayor Gavin Newsom (now California's Lieutenant-Governor) ordered City Hall to start issuing **same-sex marriage licences**. The first couple to wed were a pair of long-term lesbian activists, Del Martin and Phyllis Lyon, who finally sealed their 51-year union with a licence under Newsom's auspices. For 28 days, there were lines outside City Hall as four thousand gay and lesbian couples waited for their own turn; that's when legal challenges from conservative opponents blocked any further same-sex licences.

In late 2004, the California Supreme Court nullified all same-sex marriage licences issued in San Francisco, ruling that Newsom had stepped beyond his authority the previous winter. Around the same time, State Assemblyman Mark Leno, a former supervisor in San Francisco, authored the Marriage Equity Bill, which would have legalized same-sex marriage in California. The bill was approved by both the state's Assembly and Senate, but was vetoed by then-governor Arnold Schwarzenegger. The veto was overturned by the Supreme Court in spring 2008, but the lesbian and gay celebrations were silenced in that autumn's election, when California's official stance on gay marriage was thrust before voters; the resulting initiative, hyper-controversial **Proposition 8**, spearheaded by conservative groups to ban same-sex marriage in the state, gathered 52 percent of votes to pass. Since Proposition 8's watershed ruling, a series of legal actions by same-sex marriage supporters have made minor inroads – the ruling's stay was lifted for four days in August 2010 – but have yet to succeed in repealing the ban; at the time of writing, further appeals await.

12

pick-up joints in the city, this cruisey bar boasts a patio and plenty of convenient dark corners inside. Every Thurs evening here sees a "wet undie" contest. Daily 4pm–2am.
Stray Bar 309 Cortland Ave at Bennington, Bernal Heights ☎415 821 9263; map pp.98–99. A few miles from the hectic Castro and South of Market corridors, this welcoming neighbourhood bar attracts a remarkably mixed crowd, although it's biggest with Bernal Heights lesbians. You may be asked to make room at the stool next to you for a customer's dog. Mon–Wed 4pm–midnight, Thurs 3pm–midnight, Fri 3pm–2am, Sat 1pm–2am, Sun 1pm–midnight.
The Stud 399 Ninth St at Harrison, South of Market ☎415 863 6623, ⓦstudsf.com; map pp.84–85. Legendary club that's been on the scene since the mid 1960s. It's as popular as ever, attracting a diverse, energetic and uninhibited crowd enjoying nightly drink specials. DJs veer from darkwave to industrial to pop, with comedy every Wed and live music every Thurs. Daily 4pm–2am.
Trax 1437 Haight St at Masonic, Upper Haight ☎415 864 4213; map pp.106–107. The Haight's highest-profile gay bar is a dive, though it's been spiffed

up slightly from its grungy yesteryear. You'll find a mix of gays and straights here, so it's much less cruisey than other bars. Daily 2pm–2am.
Truck 1900 Folsom St at 15th, Mission ☎415 252 0306; map p.100. Tavern set off the beaten path that stands out for its everyman quality – relaxed fun without the cruisey vibe of certain places in the Castro and South of Market. There's trivia each Mon. Mon–Thurs & Sun 4pm–2am, Fri & Sat 2pm–2am.
Twin Peaks Tavern 401 Castro St at 17th, Castro ☎415 864 9470; map p.100. Opened in 1972, *Twin Peaks Tavern* is famous as the first gay bar in America to install transparent picture windows, rather than black them out. These days, it's low-key and laid-back, filled with middle-class, older white men. Daily noon–2am.
★ **Wild Side West** 424 Cortland Ave at Andover, Bernal Heights ☎415 647 3099; map pp.98–99. Unpretentious and friendly tavern at the centre of the Bernal Heights lesbian scene, with plenty of kitsch Americana to gaze at. There's a lovely garden out back, but without heat lamps, you'd be well advised to stay inside on a cold evening. Daily 1pm–2am.

PERFORMING ARTS AND FILM

Most venues in San Francisco will host occasional lesbian- or gay-themed plays and movies, but those listed below are especially noted for their queer-centric programming.

Brava! 2781 24th St at York, Mission ☎415 641 7657, ⓦbrava.org. San Francisco's premier women's performance space, with a primary focus on presenting new plays by lesbians and women of colour.

Castro Theatre 429 Castro St at 17th, Castro ☎415 621 6120, ⓦcastrotheatre.com. Gorgeous old movie palace that often hosts revivals of classics, with much audience participation (including hissing at onscreen villains). Come early for evening screenings to listen to the Wurlitzer organ and gaze at the spectacular chandelier.

New Conservatory Theatre Center 25 Van Ness Ave at Market, Civic Center ☎ 415 861 8972, ⓦ nctcsf.org. Highly respected venue that hosts a nearly year-round Pride Season, with theatrical works by local and internationally recognized playwrights.

San Francisco Gay Men's Chorus ☎ 415 865 3650, ⓦ sfgmc.org. Nationally known choral association that performs at several celebrated venues around the city,

including Davies Symphony Hall and its annual "Home for the Holidays" show at the Castro Theatre.

San Francisco Lesbian/Gay Freedom Band ☎ 415 255 1355, ⓦ sflgfb.org. Check this pops-style symphonic ensemble's website for information on performances – including the group's signature *Dance-Along Nutcracker*.

Theatre Rhinoceros ☎ 415 861 5079, ⓦ therhino.org. The city's top queer theatre company presents productions that range from heartfelt political drama to raunchy cabaret acts. It's currently in search of a new permanent home, so check the website for performance locations.

SUNBATHING AND FITNESS

There are two gay **sunbathing** spots in the city: Dolores Beach is a misnomer, as it's actually a rolling green lawn near the southwest corner of Dolores Park (see p.101). Beyond the Richmond is Golden Gate Beach (see p.118), predominantly nude and popular on sunny weekends with its unbeatable view of the Golden Gate Bridge. The pair of gyms listed below have a predominantly gay clientele.

Gold's Gym 2301 Market St at Noe, Castro ☎ 415 626 4488, ⓦ goldsgym.com. Accepts travel cards from other Gold's Gyms. Mon–Thurs 5am–midnight, Fri 5am–11pm, Sat 7am–9pm, Sun 7am–8pm.

The Gym SF 2775 Market St at 17th, Castro

☎ 415 863 4700, ⓦ thegymsf.com. Cruisey gym for men only. It's on the second floor overlooking Market St, so there's a clear view of – and for – passers-by. Print out a free workout pass from the website. Mon–Fri 5am–11pm, Sat 7am–10pm, Sun 8am–8pm.

12

SAN FRANCISCO ANTIQUES STORE

Shopping

Aside from the predictable retail palaces around Union Square – where you'll find everything from Macy's and Neiman Marcus to Saks Fifth Avenue, Tiffany & Co. and practically every major designer label – San Francisco's shopping scene is refreshingly independent, liberally peppered with one-off boutiques selling locally designed clothes, stylish homewares and unique crafts. The city also prides itself on a brilliantly varied (if steadily thinning) selection of independent booksellers and music stores. Another inviting aspect of the shopping scene is its emphasis on outdoor pedestrian access; indeed, the generic, behemoth indoor malls so prevalent elsewhere in the US are few and far between in San Francisco, and many of those that do exist here are certainly more stylish than most.

BOOKS

Unsurprisingly, for a city with such a rich literary history, San Francisco excels in terrific **speciality bookstores** – from the legendary City Lights in North Beach to the new literary hub in the Mission, home to some of the city's more unique and politically charged bookstores. As for **secondhand booksellers**, the city continues to offer a fine selection, but rabid old-book buyers should also head across the Bay to Oakland and Berkeley for equally rich – if not richer – pickings (see p.252).

GENERAL

Alexander Book Company 50 Second St at Market, South of Market ☎ 415 495 2992; map pp.84–85. This centrally located, three-storey independent shop has an especially strong selection of African-American titles. Since Second St is much quieter on weekends, it's only open during regular business hours on weekdays. Mon–Fri 9am–6pm.

Books Inc. 601 Van Ness Ave at Turk, Civic Center ☎ 415 776 1111; map pp.84–85. This highly respected, Bay Area-based independent chain covers all the bases well, from new fiction to other genres such as music and travel. Author events are scheduled from time to time. Three other locations in San Francisco. Mon–Sat 9am–9pm, Sun 10am–8pm.

The Booksmith 1644 Haight St at Cole, Upper Haight ☎ 415 863 8688, ⓦ booksmith.com; map pp.106–107. Good general bookstore stocking mainstream and countercultural titles alike. It's particularly notable for high-profile author events – check the website for a current calendar. Mon–Sat 10am–10pm, Sun 10am–8pm.

City Lights 261 Columbus Ave at Broadway, North Beach ☎ 415 362 8193; map p.59. The world-renowned jewel of North Beach, City Lights remains every bit the excellent bookshop/publisher it's always been since opening its doors in 1953, despite the odd surly staffer. Founded by Beat poet Lawrence Ferlinghetti, the store boasts a redoubtable selection of books, magazines and chapbooks, as well as an excellent upstairs poetry room. Daily 10am–midnight.

★ **Green Apple Books** 506 Clement St at Sixth, Inner Richmond ☎ 415 387 2272; map p.116. A wonderfully browseable store with deft, eccentric touches, such as a section devoted to "Books that will never be Oprah's picks". As long as you don't come looking for bargains, it's a terrific place to rummage. There's a smaller, less impressive music annexe a few doors down the block. Mon–Thurs & Sun 10am–10.30pm, Fri & Sat 10am–11.30pm.

SECONDHAND

Aardvark Books 227 Church St at Market, Castro ☎ 415 552 6733; map p.100. Particularly strong on mysteries, queer fiction and lit-crit, this smartly located neighbourhood favourite carries all sorts of titles. As it continually buys and resells used books, its stock constantly changes. Mon–Sat 10.30am–10.30pm, Sun 9.30am–9pm.

Adobe Bookshop 3166 16th St at Guerrero, Mission ☎ 415 864 3936; map p.100. A jumble of Persian rugs and torn Victorian easy chairs offers readers a respite amid towers of haphazardly stacked books. At the back of the shop, you'll find a reputable, closet-sized art gallery showcasing local artists. Mon–Thurs & Sun 11am–10pm, Fri–Sat 11am–11pm.

Bird & Beckett Books and Records 653 Chenery St at Castro, Glen Park ☎ 415 586 3733; map pp.98–99. Named after icons Charlie "Bird" Parker and Samuel Beckett, this cosy shop is better for its wide range of used books than its smattering of jazz LPs and CDs. The friendly owner, a serious jazz enthusiast who books bands to perform on the shop's stage twice weekly, is generally good for a gab. Mon–Thurs 11am–8pm, Fri & Sat 10am–9pm, Sun 10am–7pm.

Dog Eared Books 900 Valencia St at 20th, Mission ☎ 415 282 1901; map p.100. Bookstore on a vibrant Mission corner with a snappy selection of budget-priced remainders, as well as an eclectic range of secondhand titles, most in terrific condition. Mon–Sat 10am–10pm, Sun 10am–8pm.

Elsewhere Books 260 Judah St at Eighth, Inner Sunset ☎ 415 661 2535; map p.116. This snug, corner shop boasts an extensive collection of pulp fiction, making it a prime destination for lovers of the genre. Wed–Sat 10.30am–6pm, Sun noon–5.30pm.

Forest Books 3080 16th St at Valencia, Mission ☎ 415 863 2755; map p.100. Slightly musty remainder and secondhand bookstore that's strong on history titles and anything Zen – from religious memoirs to self-help volumes. Daily 11am–9pm.

The Great Overland Book Company 345 Judah St at Ninth, Inner Sunset ☎ 415 664 0126; map p.116. Cluttered with piles of books, this is a first-rate, old-fashioned store featuring mint-condition first editions on both its upstairs and downstairs levels; it's also strong on paperback fiction. Daily 11am–7pm.

Phoenix Books 3957 24th St at Noe, Noe Valley ☎ 415 821 3477; map p.100. Neighbourhood store with friendly staff and wide selection of new and used books at knockdown prices – you may well emerge with armloads for $20. Mon–Sat 9am–8pm, Sun 9am–7pm.

Red Hill Books 401 Cortland Ave at Bennington, Bernal Heights ☎ 415 648 5331; map pp.98–99. An amiable pitstop on the main drag in Bernal Heights, with a magazine rack full of mainstream and niche publications, plus plenty of secondhand books – the travel and gender studies sections are the most impressive. You also might stumble upon some long-sought-after CDs and LPs in the small music section. Mon–Sat 9am–8pm, Sun 9am–7pm.

Russian Hill Bookstore 2234 Polk St at Green, Russian Hill ☎ 415 929 0997; map p.56. Combination card store and secondhand bookshop. High-end journals, stationery and greeting cards are widely available, as is a wide range of books spanning art, cooking, history, poetry and even children's titles; it's strongest on fiction. Daily 10am–10pm.

SPECIALITY

Argonaut Book Shop 786 Sutter St at Jones, Union Square ☎415 474 9067; map pp.40–41. San Francisco's best bookstore by far for local history, specializing in volumes on California and the West, from the Gold Rush era to the dot-com days of the 1990s and 2000s. The knowledgeable staff are a major plus. Mon–Fri 9am–5pm, Sat 10.30am–4pm.

Borderlands Books 866 Valencia St at 20th, Mission ☎415 824 8203; map p.100. Large shop crammed full of classic horror, fantasy and science-fiction books, plus graphic novels and a few high-end trinkets. Daily noon–8pm.

Bound Together Anarchist Collective Bookstore 1369 Haight St at Masonic, Upper Haight ☎415 431 8355; map pp.106–107. Store specializing in radical and progressive publications, as well as anarchist posters and everything left of left-wing. Daily 11.30am–7pm.

Cavalli Cafe 1441 Stockton St at Columbus, North Beach ☎415 421 4219; map p.59. Italian-language café and bookstore in the heart of Little Italy, carrying magazines, books and movies from the old country, as well as a few T-shirts. Daily 9am–9pm.

Chronicle Books 1846 Union St at Octavia, Cow Hollow ☎415 345 8435; map pp.68–69. Its shelf space devoted entirely to the local publisher's own titles, this is a fun spot to browse wacky gift books or pop-culture photo specials – expect the likes of an overview of New Wave album covers, Miami Modernist architecture and doga (yoga for dogs), plus a host of cookbooks. There's also a selection of poppy greeting cards and assorted oddities. Mon–Wed & Sun 11am–7pm, Thurs–Sat 11am–8pm.

A Different Light Bookstore 489 Castro St at 18th, Castro ☎415 431 0891, ⊛adlbooks.com; map p.100. Well-stocked gay and lesbian bookshop with an especially strong fiction section (and even a kids' lit corner). Readings and events are held here regularly – check the store's website for upcoming happenings. Mon–Thurs & Sun 10am–10pm, Fri–Sat 10am–11pm.

Fields Book Store 1419 Polk St at Pine, Polk Gulch ☎415 673 2027, ⊛fieldsbooks.com; map p.56. In business since 1932, this old-fashioned bookshop is nonetheless

dedicated to New Age spirituality, from texts on Sufism to yoga workout titles. Check the store's website for events featuring healers and scholars. Tues–Sun 11am–6pm.

Fog City News 455 Market St at First, Financial District ☎415 543 7400; map pp.84–85. Although it's best known locally as having Downtown's widest selection of magazines, this long and narrow shop has also become one of the city's pre-eminent purveyors of premium chocolate bars. Mon–Fri 9am–6pm, Sat 11am–5pm.

Kayo Books 814 Post St at Leavenworth, Tenderloin ☎415 749 0554; map pp.84–85. Glorious vintage paperback store full of bargain classics, including pulpy mysteries, sci-fi and campy 1950s sleaze fiction. Thurs–Sat 11am–6pm; also by appointment.

Kinokuniya 1581 Webster St at Post (Japan Center), Japantown ☎415 567 7625; map pp.106–107. Two-storey shop with a large stock of Japanese and English-language books, as well as assorted Japanese ephemera and an exceptional selection of art titles. Daily 10.30am–8pm.

Marcus Bookstore 1712 Fillmore St at Post, Western Addition ☎415 346 4222; map pp.106–107. Sometimes filled with the smell of incense, this cosy bookstore focuses on African-American literature and magazines. It also regularly hosts Afro-centric readings and author appearances, both here and at its Oakland shop (3900 Martin Luther King Jr Way, ☎510 652 2344). Mon–Sat 10am–7pm.

Modern Times 2919 24th St at Florida, Mission ☎415 282 9246, ⊛mtbs.com; map p.100. Hefty stock of Latin American literature and progressive political publications, as well as a small, but well-chosen, selection of gay and lesbian literature and radical feminist magazines. Mon–Fri 11am–9pm, Sat & Sun 11am–7pm.

Smoke Signals 2223 Polk St at Vallejo, Russian Hill ☎415 292 6025; map p.56. Enormous newsstand stocking just about any magazine (domestic or foreign) you could hope to get your hands on. There's also hefty choice of cigars on hand – hence, the shop's name. Mon–Sat 8am–8pm, Sun 8am–6pm.

William Stout Architectural Books 804 Montgomery St at Jackson, Jackson Square ☎415 391 6757; map pp.40–41. One of San Francisco's most esteemed booksellers, with an excellent range of books on architecture, art and design, as well as urban and building studies. Mon–Fri 10am–6.30pm, Sat 10am–5.30pm.

MUSIC

As has been the case with booksellers in San Francisco (and elsewhere) in recent years, the number of music retailers in the city has also declined – yet a number of worthy **record shops** persevere. Since many are speciality vinyl stores stocking everything from old-school soul and punk rock to bossa nova and 1970s pop, the city still boasts a handful of solid collectors' stores. And in Amoeba Music, San Francisco can lay claim to perhaps the finest independent record store in the US.

GENERAL

★ **Amoeba Music** 1855 Haight St at Stanyan, Upper Haight ☎415 831 1200, ⊛amoeba.com; map

pp.106–107. Housed in an enormous former bowling alley, this renowned emporium is one of the largest independent music retailers in the country. Its encyclopedic collection is a treasure trove for all stripes of music fan, and ploughing through the stacks of new and used vinyl, CDs, DVDs and assorted memorabilia can while away a full afternoon. Check the website for a calendar of terrific (and free) performances on the store's large corner stage. Mon–Sat 10.30am–10pm, Sun 11am–9pm.

Aquarius Records 1055 Valencia St at 21st, Mission ☎ 415 647 2272; map p.100. Inviting shop with a hip, friendly staff who clearly devote hours to the detailed labelling for each artist. There's a proud emphasis on all kinds of underground styles, from noise rock to experimental and electronic, while close to half the stock is vinyl. Mon–Wed & Sun 10am–9pm, Thurs–Sat 10am–10pm.

Rasputin Music & DVDs 69 Powell St at Ellis, Union Square ☎ 1 800 350 8700; map pp.84–85. Light years behind rival Amoeba Music in the local record-store competition, this multi-storey branch of the Berkeley stalwart is conveniently located just south of Union Square. It's best for budget CDs and the odd bargain vinyl LP. Mon–Fri 11am–9pm, Sat 10.30am–9pm, Sun 11am–8pm.

Streetlight Records 2350 Market St at Castro, Castro ☎ 415 282 8000; map p.100. A surprisingly good (and fairly priced) selection of new and used CDs, LPs and DVDs spread over two storeys. Unlike the larger shops around town, it's rarely crowded, even at weekends. Mon–Fri & Sun 11am–7pm, Sat 11am–8pm.

SECONDHAND AND SPECIALITY

101 Music 1414 Grant Ave at Green, North Beach ☎ 415 392 6369; map p.59. Although this street-level shop on Grant Ave is fine enough in its own right for used CDs, guitars and old posters, it's the annexe around the corner at 513 Green St (☎ 415 392 6368) that's an experience in and of itself: a cluttered morass of secondhand speakers and stereo consoles on the main level, and upwards of 100,000 unsorted LPs in the huge basement. Happy hunting. Daily 10am–7pm.

Force of Habit Records 3565 20th St at Lexington, Mission ☎ 415 255 7865; map p.100. The last four digits of this humbly sized corner shop's phone number describe its

TOP SAN FRANCISCO SHOPPING STREETS

San Francisco is stuffed with prime **shopping strips**, and while this isn't an exhaustive list, it should provide a start for shopaholics planning a day of retail therapy.

The Castro Castro Street between 17th and 19th; Market Street between Castro and Church. Gay-oriented boutiques, clubwear and shoes.

Cow Hollow Union Street between Gough and Fillmore. Sweet, if rather conservative, boutiques almost exclusively geared toward women. Also, shoe stores and cute homeware shops.

Hayes Valley Hayes Street between Franklin and Laguna. Trendy but upscale, with edgy boutiques for men and women, as well as jewellery galleries and other high-end goodies.

Inner Richmond Clement Street between Second and 12th. Bustling Chinese grocers, plus home furnishings and one or two good bookstores.

Inner Sunset Irving Street between Seventh and 26th. Book, vintage and designer clothing, shoes and homeware stores.

Jackson Square Jackson Street between Sansome and Montgomery. Home to a cluster of antique-rug, furnishings and clock shops.

Laurel Heights Sacramento Street between Broderick and Spruce. Antique hub of San Francisco that's also good for women's vintage clothes.

The Marina Chestnut Street between Fillmore and Divisadero. Retail thoroughfare catering to the neighbourhood's young, professional set: health-food stores, wine shops and women's clothing boutiques.

The Mission Valencia Street between 14th and 21st. A top choice for urban hipsters, with loads of used furniture and clothing stores, bookshops and handmade gear.

Noe Valley 24th Street between Church and Diamond. Women's clothing, as well as bookstores and homeware shops.

North Beach Grant Avenue between Filbert and Vallejo. Groovy boutiques and homewares – one of the top places in town to find designer apparel.

Pacific Heights Fillmore Street between Jackson and Sutter. Pricey home furnishings, antiques and designer clothes.

Russian Hill and **Polk Gulch** Polk Street between Greenwich and Sutter. Used bookstores and health food shops, with the odd tasteful erotica outlet along the way. The northernmost stretch has the greatest concentration of boutiques.

Upper Haight Haight Street between Stanyan and Central. Clothing, especially vintage and secondhand. Also the home of legendary Amoeba Music (see opposite).

13

selection best – expect to find everything from original Clash vinyl to the latest Green Day smash. Daily noon–7pm.

Groove Merchant Records 687 Haight St at Pierce, Lower Haight ☎ 415 252 5766; map pp.106–107. A smart stop for secondhand soul/funk or jazz; the stock is split clearly between the two categories and is largely vintage vinyl. The shopkeeper is passionate and knowledgeable about his music, so don't be afraid to ask questions. Daily noon–7pm.

Grooves 1797 Market St at Octavia, Mission ☎ 415 436 9933; map pp.106–107. Adorned with coloured LPs on the walls, this vinyl speciality store is crammed with collectable items in all imaginable genres – jazz, classical, blues, comedy, lounge and polka. There are several turntables for giving records test spins before purchasing. Daily noon–7pm.

Jack's Record Cellar 254 Scott St at Page, Lower Haight ☎ 415 431 3047; map pp.106–107. San Francisco's quintessential musty record shop, where you can dig through crates of classic R&B, country and early rock and roll to your heart's content – just call before heading over, as its hours are wildly variable.

★ **Recycled Records** 1377 Haight St at Masonic, Upper Haight ☎ 415 626 4075; map pp.106–107. While mediocre for CDs, this longtime local favourite is best for its extensive vinyl selection, from old film soundtracks to good-condition Stones and Dylan records. Prices are often negotiable. Mon–Fri 10am–8pm, Sat 10am–9pm, Sun 11am–7pm.

Rooky Ricardo's Records 448 Haight St at Webster, Lower Haight ☎ 415 864 7526; map pp.106–107. It's all soul and R&B, all the time at this somewhat dusty, but well-meaning shop in one of San Francisco's oldest African-American neighbourhoods. When you tire of rifling through the vinyl, relax and chat about music at the counter barstool. Daily noon–6pm.

Taiyodo Record Shop 1737 Post St at Buchanan (Japan Center), Japantown ☎ 415 885 2818; map pp.106–107. Tucked away in the uninspiring Japan Center, you'll find this veteran shop carrying a wide range of Asian music beyond simply Japanese pop. It's also a good source for anime DVDs and random items such as Blondie cassettes. Daily 10.30am–6pm.

Thrillhouse Records 3422 Mission St at 30th, Mission ☎ 415 826 0233; map pp.98–99. The stock at this not-for-profit, volunteer-run store reflects punk's DIT spirit – if you're looking for hardcore, this should be your first stop. It also operates a label that puts out releases by local bands, and even hosts live shows on occasion. Daily noon–7pm, but call to confirm.

FASHION

San Francisco may not be quite on a par with US fashion capitals such as New York or Los Angeles, but there's still an impressive range of clothing stores in the city. Aside from the upscale international boutiques that sit elbow to elbow around **Union Square**, there are plenty of local designers who have opened stores in the **Mission**, **Hayes Valley**, **North Beach** and the **Inner Sunset**. It's in its range, variety and quality of **secondhand** and **vintage** stores, however, that San Francisco's fashion scene shines best – at most of these places, you can enjoy rummaging through top-quality cast-offs and picking up armfuls at bargain prices.

ACCESSORIES, SHOES AND JEWELLERY

Alla Prima Fine Lingerie 1420 Grant Ave at Green, North Beach ☎ 415 397 4077; map p.59. Upscale boutique with pale-green walls and an ornate chandelier. There's a wall of pricey, but beautiful frilly bras, fresh flowers everywhere and high-end sex toys (platinum-plated vibrators and the like) by local faves JimmyJane. Branch at 539 Hayes St at Octavia, Hayes Valley. Tues–Sat 11am–7pm, Sun 12.30–5pm.

★ **Alternative Design Studio – ADS Hats** 418 Valencia St at 15th, Mission ☎ 415 503 1316; map p.100. Humbly sized shop at the far northern end of Valencia's retail strip, where the owner frequently hand-stitches hats at the counter. Designs combine practicality – certain hats can be turned and worn inside-out – with distinctive style; many are made from reclaimed cashmere. Wed–Sat noon–7pm, Sun noon–5pm.

April in Paris 55 Clement St at Second, Inner Richmond ☎ 415 750 9910; map p.116. French expat Béatrice Amblard was trained by Hermès, and it shows in the superb quality of the bags she designs and hand-sews at this small Richmond atelier. Staggeringly expensive, but a lifelong treat. Mon–Fri 10am–6pm, Sat 11am–5pm.

Bulo Shoes 418 Hayes St at Gough, Hayes Valley ☎ 415 255 4939; map pp.106–107. Quirky European shoes with an earthy, retro feel. You won't find spike-heeled glamour here, but rather, funky and cool flats that will handle San Francisco's hills with style and ease. There's a branch for men's shoes across the street at 437-A Hayes St. Mon–Sat 11am–7pm, Sun noon–6pm.

Camper 39 Grant Ave at O'Farrell, Union Square ☎ 415 296 1005; map pp.40–41. Local devotees of all things Spanish flock here to get their feet kicking in a wide range of dressy, retro-inspired items from the Iberian peninsula. Tues–Sat 10am–7pm, Sun 11am–6pm.

Carol Doda's Champagne & Lace 1850 Union St at Octavia, Cow Hollow ☎ 415 279 3666; map pp.68–69. Small, boudoir-like store in a flower-filled alleyway off the Union St retail drag, stocking Fredericks of Hollywood-style lacy lingerie personally selected by the Queen of Topless Waitressing herself, Carol Doda (see p.58). Daily 12.30–7pm, but call before setting out, as shop hours are sometimes up to Doda's whims.

13

Cole Haan 324 Stockton St at Post, Union Square ☎ 415 391 1760; map pp.40–41. A smart stop for anyone seeking well-crafted, high-style leather shoes, boots, belts and women's and men's wallets. Daily 10am–7pm.

Five & Diamond 510 Valencia St at 16th, Mission ☎ 415 255 9747; map p.100. Along with browsing this boutique's sexy, distinctively designed punk/Victorian/Wild West gear, you can also get tattoos and piercings in the onsite parlour. Mon–Thurs noon–8pm, Fri & Sat 1–9pm, Sun noon–7pm.

Gimme Shoes 416 Hayes St at Gough, Hayes Valley ☎ 415 864 0691; map pp.106–107. Local shoe chainlet carrying men's and women's shoes from designers such as Paul Smith and Helmut Lang, as well as unusual bags and accessories. You'll find a reliable selection of the season's best, but nothing particularly groundbreaking. Branches at 381 Hayes St at Gough, Hayes Valley (☎ 415 800 8992), and 2358 Fillmore St at Washington, Pacific Heights (☎ 415 441 3040). Mon–Sat 11am–7pm, Sun noon–6pm.

Goorin Brothers 1446 Haight St at Masonic, Upper Haight ☎ 415 436 9450; map pp.106–107. This San Francisco-based haberdasher has been producing its own extensive line of hats for well over a century, but one step inside reveals that its designs have moved with the times. Caps ranging from conservative to brash line the shelves, as do fedoras and a cache of women's hats. Best of all, the staff are often peerlessly helpful, making it fun to try on the numerous styles. Branches at 111 Geary St at Grant, Union Square (☎ 415 362 0036), and 1612 Stockton St at Union, North Beach (☎ 415 402 0454). Mon–Fri & Sun 11am–7pm, Sat 11am–8pm.

Gucci 240 Stockton St at Geary, Union Square ☎ 415 392 2808; map pp.40–41. Sizzling style from this top design – slinky dresses for women, stretchy (often skintight) pants for men. The handmade and high-quality accessories, though, are the real draw; pack your credit cards. Mon–Sat 10am–7pm, Sun noon–6pm.

Hats on Post 201 Post St (sixth floor) at Grant, Union Square ☎ 415 392 3737; map pp.40–41. Intriguing, if odd hats for women. Designs are quite contemporary, but probably only worth shelling out for if you're a serious hat enthusiast. Tues & Thurs–Sat noon–5.30pm, Wed by appointment.

Hermès 125 Grant Ave at Maiden, Union Square ☎ 415 391 7200; map pp.40–41. Top-grade – if somewhat stuffy – French luggage and accessories, augmented by a small selection of apparel. Designs are aimed squarely at proud traditionalists, although a simple Hermès scarf is an undisputed fashion classic. Mon–Sat 10am–6pm.

Jeanine Payer 762 Market St at Grant, Union Square ☎ 415 788 2417; map pp.40–41. Celebrity favourite Payer is known for her poetry-covered jewellery (bracelets, earrings, necklaces). Instead of cutesy greeting card ditties, however, designs here are more like love letters on precious

metal. Mon–Wed, Fri & Sat 11am–6pm, Thurs 11am–7pm, Sun 11am–5pm.

John Fluevog Boots & Shoes 1697 Haight St at Cole, Upper Haight ☎ 415 436 9784; map pp.106–107. Clunky shoes for men and women. Many designs are witty, clog-like shapes – fun, if a little dated. Branch at 253 Grant Ave at Sutter, Union Square (☎ 415 296 7900). Mon–Sat 11am–7pm, Sun noon–6pm.

Kate Spade New York 227 Grant Ave at Post, Union Square ☎ 415 216 0880; map pp.40–41. The patron saint of girly-girls everywhere showcases her stylish, boxy handbags, classic shoes and beauty line. Overpriced and irresistible, all at once. Branch at 865 Market St at Fifth (Westfield San Francisco Centre), Union Square (☎ 415 222 9638). Mon–Sat 10am–6pm, Sun noon–5pm.

Kenneth Cole 865 Market St at Fifth (Westfield San Francisco Centre), Union Square ☎ 415 227 4536; map pp.84–85. Although this mainstream American designer started with shoes, he's branched off into clothes for men and women. Shoes are functional and a little offbeat, but the apparel is cooler and pricier. Mon–Sat 9.30am–9pm, Sun 10am–7pm.

Laku 1069 Valencia St at 22nd, Mission ☎ 415 695 1462; map p.100. Exquisite silk slippers, velvet hair accessories and other superbly designed articles by local designer Yaeko Yamashita. All items in the shop are handmade. Tues–Sat 11.30am–6.30pm, Sun noon–5pm.

★ **Paolo** 524 Hayes St at Octavia, Hayes Valley ☎ 415 552 4580; map pp.106–107. Designer Paolo Lantorno produces extremely limited numbers (about two dozen pairs) of his own men's and women's shoe designs in Italy, then sells them from his two San Francisco stores for around $200 a pair; every style is edgy, yet wearable. Branch at 2000 Fillmore St at Pine, Pacific Heights (☎ 415 771 1944). Mon–Sat 11am–7pm, Sun 11am–6pm.

The Paul Frank Store 262 Sutter St at Grant, Union Square ☎ 415 374 2758; map pp.40–41. Local outpost for the cutesy accessories designer, known for his appliqué designs, 1950s colour palette and extra-wide-mouthed monkey mascot, Julius. Mon–Sat 11am–7pm, Sun 11am–6pm.

Shapur Mozaffarian Fine Jewelry 272 Post St at Grant, Union Square ☎ 415 392 1200; map pp.40–41. Customized fittings for uniquely cut diamonds and various other gems; each piece is created individually. The helpful staff make up for the somewhat slim selection. Mon–Sat 10am–5.30pm.

Shoe Biz 1420 Haight St at Masonic, Upper Haight ☎ 415 861 0313; map pp.106–107. Popular shop along the Haight shopping strip hawking mainstream shoe labels (Diesel, Camper, et al) for both men and women. There's a branch devoted to trainers one block west (1553 Haight at Clayton, ☎ 415 861 3933), and two other locations in Noe Valley and the Mission. Mon–Sat 11am–7pm, Sun 11am–6pm.

13

Shreve & Co. 200 Post St at Grant, Union Square ☎415 421 2600; map pp.40–41. The oldest jeweller in town (dating back to the Gold Rush era), and still one of the best, known for its fine silverware and flawless diamonds. Mon–Sat 10am–6pm, Sun noon–5pm.

Tiffany & Co. 350 Post St at Powell, Union Square ☎415 781 7000; map pp.40–41. Luxurious two-storey site of the legendary retailer, where courteous staff members will let you try items on – even if it's obvious that everything in the place is out of your price range. Mon–Fri 10am–7pm, Sat 10am–6pm, Sun noon–5pm.

CASUALWEAR

American Apparel 2174 Union St at Fillmore, Cow Hollow ☎415 440 3220; map pp.68–69. Guaranteed sweatshop-free T-shirts that are as alluring for their endless colours and soft fabrics as for the company's strong ethics. Branches in Upper Haight and Union Square. Mon–Sat 10am–9pm, Sun 11am–8pm.

Banana Republic 256 Grant Ave at Sutter, Union Square ☎415 788 3087; map pp.40–41. Although there are four other Banana Republic branches around San Francisco, this enormous outpost of Gap's upscale business casual chain is notable as the flagship location. Clothes are well priced, although the womenswear is far more exciting than the bland men's apparel. Mon–Sat 9.30am–8pm, Sun 11am–7pm.

Diesel 800 Market St at Ellis, Union Square ☎415 398 4055; map pp.84–85. Large corner space devoted to the wacky Italian casualwear label that was at the forefront of denim's big comeback. Its jeans wall offers trendy styles in several different washes. Branch at 400 Castro St at 17th, Castro (☎415 621 5557). Mon–Sat 10am–9pm, Sun 11am–8pm.

Forever 21 7 Powell St at Eddy, Union Square ☎415 984 0380; map pp.84–85. Not recommended for the crowd-averse, Forever 21 is a sea of limbs reaching for the nearest trendy, yet inexpensive haltertop or sweater. As the name suggests, its fashions are geared towards the young – and those aspiring to look that way. Branch at Stonestown Galleria, Parkside (☎415 759 8660). Mon–Sat 9.30am–10pm, Sun 10am–9.30pm.

The Gap 890 Market St at Powell, Union Square ☎415 788 5909; map pp.84–85. The behemoth, San Francisco-based casual apparel retailer has carpet-bombed its hometown over the years with outlets that include its myriad sub-brands (babyGap, GapKids, GapBody et al), but this is its local flagship location. Mon–Sat 10am–9pm, Sun 11am–8pm.

H&M 845 Market St at Fifth (Westfield San Francisco Centre), Union Square ☎415 543 1430; map pp.84–85. Love the place or not, even H&M's detractors admit that the chain has introduced a large population of Americans to affordably priced, sartorially considered clothing. It's the ideal destination for anyone who wants to look like a million bucks while having spent very little; if you go, however, just steel yourself for chaotic crowds of shoppers swarming over jackets, jeans and accessories. Two other Union Square branches: 150 Powell St at Ellis (☎415 986 4215) and 150 Post St at Kearny (☎415 986 0156). Mon–Sat 10am–8.30pm, Sun 10am–7pm.

Levi's 300 Post St at Stockton, Union Square ☎415 501 0100; map pp.40–41. Four levels of jeans, tops and jackets, and since this is the iconic label's flagship store, the entire Levi's line is available here. Also on offer is the company's Original Spin service, by which customers can order customized denim. Mon–Sat 10am–8pm, Sun 11am–7pm.

Lululemon Athletica 1981 Union St at Buchanan, Cow Hollow ☎415 776 5858; map pp.68–69. Canadian chain that sells trendy, lycra-heavy togs for yoga-practising men and women – a big hit with the keep-fit crowd in Cow Hollow and the neighbouring Marina. Branch at 327 Grant Ave at Sutter, Union Square (☎415 402 0914). Mon–Wed & Sun 10am–7pm, Thurs–Sat 10am–8pm.

Nomads 556 Hayes St at Laguna, Hayes Valley ☎415 864 5692; map pp.106–107. Britpoppy menswear – skinny, slouchy jeans and zipped cardigans – from the likes of Ben Sherman, Blue Marlin, Jack Spade and Fred Perry. You'll recognize the shop by the sign above its entryway that reads, "You Get Results With". Mon–Sat 11am–7pm, Sun 11am–6pm.

The North Face 180 Post St at Grant, Union Square ☎415 433 3223; map pp.40–41. Rugged fashions and footwear for outdoor enthusiasts (or those who wish to look the part). The Bay Area-based company's lightweight jackets and fleece sweatshirts are particularly popular. Mon–Sat 10am–8pm, Sun 11am–6pm.

Patagonia 770 North Point St at Hyde, Fisherman's Wharf ☎415 771 2050; map pp.68–69. Functional, sweat-wicking performance apparel that boasts more fashion sensibility than many other lines of sportswear. Despite its setting well off San Francisco's retail trail, the shop regularly draws in a sizeable clientele. Mon–Wed & Sun 10am–6pm, Thurs–Sat 10am–7pm.

True 1415 Haight St at Masonic, Upper Haight ☎415 626 2882; map pp.106–107. Urban clothing from Enyce sits alongside a strong selection of classic Nike trainers and watches by Dixon at this boutique owned by Michael Brown, son of former San Francisco mayor Willie. A branch devoted to shoes, True Sole, is just up the block at 1427 Haight St (☎415 626 2600). Daily 11am–7pm.

Upper Playground 220 Fillmore St at Waller, Lower Haight ☎415 861 1960; map pp.106–107. Fiercely San Francisco-based clothing and hip-hop culture boutique whose racks and shelves are full of caps and other streetwear, including no shortage of clever, locally referenced T-shirts. There's artwork for sale in a separate room. Daily noon–7pm.

Urban Outfitters 80 Powell St at Ellis, Union Square ☎ 415 989 1515; map pp.84–85. Slackerwear for the college-aged or -minded. It's great for ironic, irreverent T-shirts and offbeat accessories, and also noted for its affordable and kitschy homewares. Branch at 3322 Fillmore St at Lombard, Marina (☎ 415 409 6497). Mon–Sat 9am–11pm, Sun 11am–8pm.

Villains 1672 Haight St at Cole, Upper Haight ☎ 415 626 5939; map pp.106–107. Youthful, fun clothing from labels such as Ben Sherman, Penguin and Puma. Items aren't cheap, but you may stumble upon a few bargains at Villains Vault at no. 1653 (☎ 415 864 7727) across Haight St, where some sale merchandise is stashed. Daily 11am–7pm.

West Coast Leather 290 Sutter St at Grant, Union Square ☎ 415 362 8300; map pp.40–41. Leather apparel in a staggering range of cuts and styles, from straightforward black leather jackets to revealing outfits for women. Mon–Wed 11am–7pm, Thurs & Fri 10am–7pm, Sat 10am–8pm, Sun noon–6pm.

Zara 250 Post St at Stockton, Union Square ☎ 415 399 6930; map pp.40–41. A continental, runway-inspired antidote to Banana Republic's more conservative fashions. Expect snug fits and reasonable prices for both men's and women's clothing. Mon–Sat 10am–8pm, Sun 11am–6pm.

DESIGNER

A-B Fits 1519 Grant Ave at Union, North Beach ☎ 415 982 5726; map p.59. Imaginative men's and women's jeans boutique, starkly decorated and offering directional clothing at moderate prices. Lines include Band of Outsides and Etro for men; for women, there's fun, girly fashions by Rebecca Taylor and Nanette Lapore, as well as jewellery from local designer Janine Payer. Tues–Sat 11.30am–6.30pm, Sun noon–6pm.

Anthropologie 880 Market St at Powell, Union Square ☎ 415 434 2210; map pp.84–85. Shoppers here can be overheard simultaneously raving about Anthropologie's punchy styles, embroidery and big buttons while complaining about the price tags. The airy store also sells numerous accessories for body and home. Mon–Tues & Thurs–Sat 10am–8pm, Wed 10am–8.30pm, Sun 11am–7pm.

Bebe 21 Grant Ave at O'Farrell, Union Square ☎ 415 781 2323; map pp.40–41. Stretchy, sexy clothes and pertly tailored suits for superskinny women, plus stylish handbags and other accessories. Three other branches in San Francisco: Westfield San Francisco Centre, Marina and Stonestown Galleria. Mon–Sat 10am–7pm, Sun 11am–6pm.

Behind the Post Office 1510 Haight St at Ashbury, Upper Haight ☎ 415 861 2507; map pp.106–107. Low-key women's boutique stocking designer basics by Lily & Jae, Yumi Kim and others. Drop in for the especially wide range of cool T-shirts, as well as handbags and travel accessories. Mon–Thurs & Sun 11am–7pm, Fri & Sat 11am–7.30pm.

Betsey Johnson 160 Geary St at Stockton, Union Square ☎ 415 398 2516; map pp.40–41. Creatively designed apparel in candy colours and floaty fabrics that's surprisingly affordable, compared to other designer boutiques around Union Square. Branch at 2031 Fillmore St at California, Pacific Heights (☎ 415 567 2726). Mon–Sat 10am–7pm, Sun noon–6pm.

Carrots 843 Montgomery St at Jackson, Jackson Square ☎ 415 834 9040; map p.56. Sleek, jazzy boutique featuring understated men's and women's fashions – not to mention housewares, jewellery and accessories – by well-established, independent high-end designers. Tues–Sat 11am–6pm.

Catherine Jane 3490 Sacramento St at Laurel, Presidio Heights ☎ 415 673 5733; map pp.68–69. Distinctly swanky boutique where you'll find luxurious "fog coats" (shawls made from cashmere and angora), as well as fashions in silk dupioni, crêpe de Chine and plenty of other cosy fabrics. Mon–Fri 10.30am–6pm, Sat 11am–6pm, Sun 11am–4pm.

Dema 1038 Valencia St at 21st, Mission ☎ 415 206 0500; map p.100. Feisty, brightly coloured women's clothing done up with plenty of op-artsy prints and retro detailing, mostly designed by shop owner Dema Grim. There's also soft, girly knitwear by the likes of Three Dot and Antoni & Alison. Mon–Fri 11am–7pm, Sat noon–7pm, Sun noon–6pm.

Isda & Co. 21 South Park, South of Market ☎ 415 512 1610; map pp.84–85. Airy outlet selling its own label of Gap-style basics, both classic and casual, in lush natural fabrics such as wool and cotton for both men and women. Tues–Sat 10am–6pm.

★ **MAC – Modern Appealing Clothing** 387 Grove St at Gough, Hayes Valley ☎ 415 863 3011; map pp.106–107. One of the best boutiques in town, this inviting shop stocks unisex apparel from unique designers such as AF Vandervoorst and Martin Margiela, as well as some top local names like Lemon Twist and Dema. It's refreshingly accessible for a high-end boutique, thanks to the homely atmosphere and chatty staff. Branch at 1003 Minnesota St at 22nd, Potrero Hill. Mon–Sat 11am–7pm, Sun noon–6pm.

Marc Jacobs Collection 125 Maiden Lane, Union Square ☎ 415 362 6500; map pp.40–41. The darling of fashionistas worldwide sells his vintage, largely 1940s-inspired separates and accessories at this central boutique; there's also a small selection of his men's line. Expensive but irresistible. There's a Marc by Marc Jacobs branch at 2142 Fillmore St at Sacramento, Pacific Heights (☎ 415 447 9322). Mon–Wed & Fri-Sat 10am–6pm, Thurs 10am–7pm, Sun noon–5pm.

Metier 355 Sutter St at Stockton, Union Square ☎ 415 989 5395; map pp.40–41. A gallery for both up-and-coming and established independent designers where you'll find everything from sweaters and scarves to handbags, jewellery and other accessories. The staff are welcoming and pleasantly unpushy. Mon–Sat 10am–6pm.

13

RAG – Residents Apparel Gallery 541 Octavia St at Hayes, Hayes Valley ☎415 621 7718; map pp.106–107. Innovative co-op specializing in young, local designers, each of whom rents rack space to showcase their ranges. Most are surprisingly affordable, and perhaps the best part is that you'll never see anyone else wearing your same outfit. Mon & Wed–Fri noon–6.30pm, Tues & Sun noon–6pm, Sat 11am–6pm.

Rolo 1301 Howard St at Ninth, South of Market ☎415 578 7139; map pp.84–85. Longtime local retail fixture stocking designer denim and streetwear, although it's downsized considerably in recent years. Branch at 2351 Market St at 17th, Castro. Mon–Sat 11am–7pm, Sun noon–6pm.

Saffron Rare Threads One Embarcadero Center (Sacramento St at Front), Financial District ☎415 433 7233; map pp.40–41. Plenty of classy, attractive apparel to dress the hip professional woman – as well as the hip professional cocktail sipper. Mon–Fri 10am–7pm, Sat by appointment.

Wilkes Bashford 375 Sutter St at Stockton, Union Square ☎415 986 4380; map pp.40–41. Four floors of fabulously classic finery for men, and one floor for women. Wilkes Bashford's savvy store buyers sprinkle compelling new names from Italy among the racks of major-label merchandise. Mon–Sat 10am–6pm.

Zeni 567 Hayes St at Laguna, Hayes Valley ☎415 864 0154; map pp.106–107. Full of designer clothes for men and women, this humbly sized boutique stocks girly fashions from Anna Sui and Nicole Miller, plus a handful of local names. There's also offbeat menswear and a selection of natty sunglasses. Mon & Tues noon–6pm, Wed & Thurs noon–7pm, Fri & Sat 11am–7pm, Sun 11am–6pm.

Zolita 3335 17th St at Mission, Mission ☎415 551 0900; map p.100. Featuring fashion perhaps better suited to the conservative Marina than the hipster neighbourhood it calls home, Zolita has nevertheless carved a niche for itself. It's a great place to find Ted Baker-esque clothes by indie designers – ruffled, super-girly fashions and equally flashy men's clothes. Mon–Fri 11.30am–7pm, Sat & Sun 11.30am–6pm.

VINTAGE AND THRIFT

Buffalo Exchange 1555 Haight St at Clayton, Upper Haight ☎415 431 7733; map pp.106–107. Items here are relatively cheap (if occasionally tatty), but if you've got the patience to rifle through rack after rack of clothing, you may turn up some gems. Branch at 1210 Valencia St at 22nd, Mission (☎415 647 8332). Mon–Sat 11am–8pm, Sun 11am–7pm.

Clothes Contact 473 Valencia St at 16th, Mission ☎415 621 3212; map p.100. Upper Valencia shop with a black awning where local rockers shop for bomber jackets.

You'll pay $10 per pound for clothes, as weighed at checkout on a vintage scale; be prepared to rummage through racks arranged solely by type (shirt, coat, dress, etc.). Daily 11am–7pm.

Community Thrift 625 Valencia St at 17th, Mission ☎415 861 4910; map p.100. Classic thrift store in an enormous warehouse space that's stockpiled with clothes, furniture and others' junk (including old records, magazines, games and books). All proceeds are divided among local charities. Daily 10am–6.30pm.

Cris 2056 Polk St at Broadway, Russian Hill ☎415 474 1191; map p.56. Sumptuous secondhand designer store with a hushed atmosphere, proper fitting rooms and decor reminiscent of a millionaire's tasteful wife – no wonder, since dozens of them must stop by weekly to drop off barely worn samples by every big name. Most items are current season, in excellent condition and shockingly affordable. Mon–Sat 11am–6pm, Sun noon–5pm.

★ **Crossroads Trading Co.** 2123 Market St at Church, Castro ☎415 552 8740; map p.100. This homegrown, now-national chainlet sells vintage clothes and remainders from hip labels at mostly reasonable prices. The selection's equally varied for men's and women's articles, and although prices can be a bit high for the new items scattered around the racks, it's still a great stop for top-condition basics. Three other branches in town: 1901 Fillmore St at Bush, Pacific Heights (☎415 775 8885); 630 Irving St at Eighth, Inner Sunset (☎415 681 0100); 1519 Haight St at Ashbury, Upper Haight (☎415 355 0555). Mon–Thurs & Sun 11am–7pm, Fri & Sat 11am–8pm.

Goodbyes 3483 Sacramento St at Laurel, Presidio Heights ☎415 674 0151; map pp.68–69. Stacked with designer labels, this tucked-away boutique is a first-rate shop where you might find last season's Prada or Chanel at consignment prices. There's a men's shop across Sacramento St at no. 3464 (☎415 346 6388). Mon–Wed, Fri & Sat 10am–6pm; Thurs 10am–8pm; Sun 11am–5pm.

The Goodwill Store 1580 Mission St at Van Ness, South of Market ☎415 575 2240; ⊛sfgoodwill.org; map pp.84–85. Home to an exhaustive selection of junk and gems, there are over a dozen Goodwill outlets scattered across San Francisco. This flagship location stocks everything from shirts and handbags to shoes and suits, in addition to items such as housewares and books. Check the website for a complete list of local shops. Mon–Sat 9am–8pm, Sun 10am–7pm.

Idol Vintage 3162 16th St at Guerrero, Mission ☎415 255 9959; map p.100. Vintage shop boasting helpful staff and an eclectic selection of boots, Western shirts, wigs, hats and other retro accessories and paraphernalia spanning the 1940s to today. Mon–Thurs 12.30–8.15pm, Fri & Sat 11.30am–10.45pm, Sun 12.30–7pm.

Jeremys Department Store 2 South Park at Second, South of Market ☎415 882 4929; map pp.84–85.

13

Oversize, two-storey boutique store specializing in casual and designer clothes for men and women, as well as seconds and fashion show outtakes – no items for sale here are "used" in the traditional sense. It's a San Francisco fashionista favourite where locals often pick up recent-season designer gems at rock-bottom prices; expect plenty of Ralph Lauren and Bergdorf Goodman's own label, as well as a superb selection of women's shoes. Mon–Wed, Fri & Sat 11am–6pm; Thurs 11am–8pm; Sun noon–6pm.

★ **My Roommate's Closet** 3044 Fillmore St at Union, Cow Hollow ☎415 447 7703; map pp.68–69. This inviting, always popular boutique is filled with unworn overstocks from designers such as Ella Moss, Milly and Twelfth Street Cynthia Vincent. Items typically sell for at least fifty percent off regular price, so there's regular turnover on the racks. Mon–Fri 11.30am–6.30pm, Sat 11am–6pm, Sun noon–5pm.

Old Vogue 1412 Grant Ave at Green, North Beach ☎415 392 1522; map p.59. Pricey vintage store along Grant Ave's trendy shopping promenade where the men's selection is especially robust. Look for piles of good-as-new jeans on the upper mezzanine. Mon–Thurs & Sun 11am–7pm, Fri & Sat 11am–10pm.

Painted Bird 1360 Valencia St at 25th, Mission ☎415 401 7027; map p.100. Celebrated by neighbourhood hipsters, this Valencia St boutique is a mine of affordable, smartly selected items: handbags, vests, jackets, owl pendants and jeans. Daily 11am–8pm.

Repeat Performance 2436 Fillmore St at Jackson, Pacific Heights ☎415 563 3123; map pp.68–69. With all its proceeds benefiting the San Francisco Symphony, this volunteer-staffed shop carries both casual and formal wear, as well as a few vintage items – all selling at top dollar, as its Pacific Heights location suggests. There's also jewellery, kitchenware and shoes. Mon–Sat 10am–5.30pm.

Retro Fit 910 Valencia St at 20th, Mission ☎415 550 1530; map p.100. Poppy, sometimes kitschy selection of smart vintage clothes; don't expect bargains, but it's well worth a visit for a chance to fish out that spot-on shirt or just-right jacket. You can also pick a style of blank T-shirt,

then choose custom artwork to be transferred onto it, starting at around $22. Mon, Wed, Thurs & Sun noon–7pm, Fri & Sat noon–9pm.

Schauplatz 791 Valencia St at 19th, Mission ☎415 864 5665; map p.100. With a selection to match the name (German for "happening scene"), Schauplatz's racks are bursting with exceptionally well preserved vintage pieces. The shopkeepers are just as extraordinary – they'll go out of their way to help you find items that flatter your figure. Daily 1–6pm.

Seconds to Go 2252 Fillmore St at Clay, Pacific Heights ☎415 563 7806; map pp.68–69. Boutique selling good-condition clothes and housewares to benefit the nearby Schools of the Sacred Heart. As with other secondhand clothing stores along posh Fillmore St, you'll find the prices higher here than elsewhere. Mon–Sat 10am–5.30pm, Sun noon–5pm.

Thrift Town 2101 Mission St at 17th, Mission ☎415 861 1132; map p.100. Massive corner space with a huge and brightly displayed selection of some of San Francisco's better-quality seconds, all at bargain prices. Come during the week when it's not completely overrun. Mon–Fri 9am–8pm, Sat 10am–7pm, Sun 10am–6pm.

Ver Unica 437 Hayes St (Suite B) at Gough, Hayes Valley ☎415 431 0688; map pp.106–107. Tiny boutique specializing in high-grade secondhand clothing alongside a smattering of new, retro-inspired pieces, mostly by local designers. Mon–Sat 11am–7pm, Sun noon–6pm.

Wasteland 1660 Haight St at Cole, Upper Haight ☎415 863 3150; map pp.106–107. Smart, high-end apparel sorted by style and colour. You'll pay for the ease of browsing, but nonetheless, this is one of the best places to find fashionable, top-condition vintagewear. Mon–Sat 11am–8pm, Sun noon–7pm.

Worn Out West 582 Castro St at 19th, Castro ☎415 431 6020; map p.100. Housed in a classic Victorian along Castro St's retail strip, this shop is devoted to used gay fetish gear. Browse Western wear, leather-studded collars, cuffs and even bow ties. Mon–Fri & Sun noon–7pm, Sat 11am–7pm.

FOOD AND DRINK

Be sure to try such celebrated **local specialities** as Boudin's sourdough bread, Gallo salami and Anchor Steam beer – all of which are affirmed San Francisco treats. If you're looking for everyday essentials, there are **supermarkets** strewn across the city, including several branches of Trader Joe's, an affordable (and immensely popular) grocery store that's a terrific place to find packaged ethnic foods and a large selection of beer, wine and liquor. There are also many Safeway locations in town, although the megachain's goods are less healthy and often poorly presented in cluttered stores. California alcohol laws are liberal: most stores carrying food sell alcohol as well, provided you show **ID** proving you're at least 21 years of age.

DELIS, BAKERIES AND GROCERIES

24th Street Cheese Co. 3893 24th St at Sanchez, Noe Valley ☎415 821 6658; map p.100. Sleepy-looking store hiding behind slatted blinds and heavy awnings; inside, though, the cool space is suffused with

delicate aromas from the dozens of cheeses (both domestic and European) sold by the chunk. There's also a smallish selection of gourmet dried goods – most notably, pasta. Mon–Fri 10am–7pm, Sat 10am–6pm, Sun 10am–5pm.

Andronico's 1200 Irving St at Funston, Inner Sunset ☎415 661 3220; map p.116. Neighbourhood supermarket featuring pricey, but gorgeous produce, plus craft beers, wine, artisan breads, a host of cheeses, an extensive olive bar and a terrific deli. Definitely not for bargain-hunters, although to many locals the quality justifies the store's high prices. Daily 7am–10pm.

Casa Lucas Market 2934 24th St at Florida, Mission ☎415 826 4334; map p.100. If nothing else, visit this market in the Latino heart of San Francisco for its astonishing array of exotic fruits and vegetables, including chilli peppers. Also great for hard-to-find Mexican grocery items. Daily 7am–8pm.

DeLessio Market/Bakery 1695 Market St at Gough, Hayes Valley ☎415 552 5559; map pp.106–107. A beloved local institution featuring gourmet pastries, cakes, heavenly salads and other savoury treats – a worthwhile destination in itself. There's a larger outpost at 302 Broderick St at Oak, Western Addition (☎415 552 8077). Mon–Fri 7am–7.30pm, Sat & Sun 9am–5.30pm.

Good Life Grocery 488 Cortland Ave at Andover, Bernal Heights ☎415 648 3221; map pp.98–99. Neighbourhood gourmet grocer with a vast selection of organic, locally grown produce, along with a great deli and butcher shop. Branch at 1524 20th St at Missouri, Potrero Hill (☎415 282 9204). Daily 8am–9pm.

Haig's Delicacies 642 Clement St at Seventh, Inner Richmond ☎415 752 6283; map p.116. One of the city's oldest international food shops, Haig's shelves are lined with hard-to-find imports from around the globe, from Indian chutneys to Mediterranean mezes. Mon–Fri 9.30am–6.30pm, Sat 9.30am–6pm.

Harvest Urban Market 191 Eighth St at Howard, South of Market ☎415 621 1000; map pp.84–85. Stacked high with largely organic produce from more than two hundred local farmers and bakeries, this healthy and sizeable market is also known for its gourmet salad bar and selection of imported foods. Daily 7.30am–11pm.

John Campbell's 5625 Geary Blvd at 20th, Outer Richmond ☎415 387 1536; map p.116. Staunchly Irish bakehouse where San Francisco rarities like mince pie, soda bread and pasties bring customers back again and again. Cardiologists may not necessarily recommend the Belfast Bap breakfast sandwich ($6) – a giant round filled with cheese, egg, sausage and bacon, so named for proprietor Campbell's former hometown – but you only live once. Mon–Sat 7am–10pm, Sun 7am–8pm.

La Palma Mexicatessen 2884 24th St at Florida, Mission ☎415 647 1500; map p.100. As its unique name implies, this is not only the place to stock up on authentic Mexican spices (such as fresh or dried chillis) and other staples, but there's also a popular take-away food counter toward the back. And in the unlikely event you're in the market for a tortilla press, those are available here as well. Mon–Sat 8am–6pm, Sun 8am–5pm.

★ **Liguria Bakery** 1700 Stockton St at Filbert, North Beach ☎415 421 3786; map p.59. Marvellous old-world bakery with vintage scales and cash registers in its front display windows. Fresh focaccia is the smart order here, and there's no shortage of choices: onion, garlic, rosemary and mushroom, among others. It's best to arrive earlier than later, as it usually closes when the day's goods are sold out. Cash only. Mon–Fri 8am–2pm, Sat 7am–2pm, Sun 7am–noon.

FARMERS' MARKETS

Alemany Farmers' Market 100 Alemany Blvd at Putnam, Bernal Heights ☎415 647 9423. California's very first farmers' market (established in 1943), this weekly event is one of the city's most affordable such affairs – definitely more "of the people, for the people" than many other farmers' markets around the Bay Area. Sat dawn–dusk.

Ferry Plaza Farmers' Market Ferry Building, Embarcadero ☎415 291 3276, ⊕ferryplazafarmers market.com; map pp.40–41. Higher prices accompany the organic produce at this immensely popular bayside market, sold from numerous stalls set up around the landmark building. Thousands of local foodies flock here to sample snacks, and there are also regular recipe demonstrations from local name-brand chefs. Many farmers only sell once a week, so it's worth checking back more than once. Tues & Thurs 10am–2pm, Sat 8am–2pm.

Fillmore Farmers' Market O'Farrell St at Fillmore, Western Addition ☎415 441 6396; map pp.106–107. There are only about a dozen or so stalls set up regularly at this year-round market, and because of its small size, it can feel rather forlorn. The produce, though, is top-quality, and it's not nearly as swarmed by crowds as the city's larger farmers' markets. Sat 9am–1pm.

Heart of the City Farmers' Market Hyde St at Fulton (United Nations Plaza), Civic Center ☎415 558 9455, ⊕hocfarmersmarket.org; map pp.84–85. Huge certified farmers' market (meaning everything is sold by the growers themselves) that's distinguished from other such local ventures by catering to an inner-city, multi-ethnic crowd. Produce prices may be rock-bottom, but quality can be hit-and-miss, so choose carefully. Wed 7am–5.30pm, Sun 7am–5pm.

13

COFFEE BY THE POUND

Several celebrated San Francisco coffee-bean retailers double as cafés (see box, p.137).

Lucca Ravioli 1100 Valencia St at 22nd, Mission ☎ 415 647 5581; map p.100. A fiercely loyal customer base frequents this stalwart market on the edge of San Francisco's Latino stronghold; inside you'll find a fresh pasta factory you can spy on through big picture windows. Mon–Sat 9am–6pm.

Mee Mee Bakery 1328 Stockton St at Broadway, Chinatown ☎ 415 362 3204; map p.59. A little-known gem with an onsite fortune-cookie bakery that fills the space with a hot, sweet aroma. Regular treats are a little over $3 for a half-pound; speciality (biblical, adult) or flavoured (chocolate, strawberry) cookies are $1 more. Daily 8am–6pm.

Miette 449 Octavia St at Hayes, Hayes Valley ☎ 415 626 6221; map pp.106–107. Delightful shop featuring impeccably displayed sweets – including sugar candies, cupcakes, pastries and chocolates – all geared to weaken the sweet tooth of anyone who walks in. Branch at Ferry Building Marketplace, Embarcadero (☎ 415 837 0300). Mon–Fri & Sun noon–7pm, Sat 11am–7pm.

Rainbow Grocery 1745 Folsom St at 13th, Mission ☎ 415 863 0620; map p.100. Ardently progressive politics and organic food rule the scene at this enormous, employee-owned co-op food market; you'll also find a bounty of natural and organic health products, as well as a beauty counter featuring just about every botanical brand and a large selection of products available in bulk. A stone-faced mood can sometimes permeate the place, but the top-grade produce is worth it. Daily 9am–9pm.

Real Food Company 3060 Fillmore St at Filbert, Cow Hollow ☎ 415 567 6900; map pp.68–69. Small local grocer chainlet selling potions and vitamins along with various health foods. There's also an excellent gourmet meat counter and wholewheat pastries – get yourself a sandwich and sit outside on the terrace at one of the wrought-iron picnic tables. Branch at 2140 Polk St at Broadway, Russian Hill (☎ 415 673 7420). Daily 8am–9pm.

Scharffen Berger Chocolate Maker Ferry Building Marketplace, Embarcadero ☎ 415 981 9150; map pp.40–41. A truly mouth-watering array of bars, sauces and other goodies from this famed Berkeley chocolatier. A major draw is the company's limited edition single-origin chocolate bars, available nowhere but here. Mon–Fri 9am–7pm, Sat 8am–7pm, Sun 9am–5.30pm.

COFFEE, TEA AND SPICES

Castro Cheesery 427 Castro St at 17th, Castro ☎ 415 552 6676; map p.100. Despite its name, this shop just up the sidewalk from the Castro Theatre is just as known for its far-ranging selection of reasonably priced coffees, although there's plenty of cheese from around the globe on offer as well. Mon–Sat 8am–10pm, Sun 9am–8pm.

Graffeo Coffee Roasting Co. 733 Columbus Ave at Filbert, North Beach ☎ 415 986 2420; map p.56. Huge sacks of coffee beans are piled around this minimalist, all-granite shop where the Repetto family has been roasting coffee since 1935 – even the caffeine-averse will be enticed by the aroma from a half-block away. Beans of the house blend cost about $15 per pound. Mon–Fri 9am–6pm, Sat 10am–5pm.

San Francisco Herb Co. 250 14th St at South Van Ness, Mission ☎ 415 861 7174; map p.100. Large quantities of fresh herbs and spices – not to mention teas, dehydrated vegetables, nuts, seeds and even essential oils – all at wholesale prices. Mon–Sat 10am–4pm.

Ten Ren Tea Company 949 Grant Ave at Jackson, Chinatown ☎ 415 362 0656; map pp.40–41. Large, inexpensive and well-stocked tea emporium where you can stop in for tea by the pound or a fresh brew to go. The scented iced teas, thick with gloopy tapioca balls, are particularly delicious. Daily 9am–9pm.

WINES AND SPIRITS

California Wine Merchant 2113 Chestnut St at Steiner, Marina ☎ 415 567 0646; map pp.68–69. Before – or perhaps in lieu of – setting off for the Wine Country, pick up a sample selection at this emporium that does double-duty as a highly respected wine bar. Mon–Wed 10am–midnight, Thurs–Sat 10am–1.30am, Sun 11am–11pm.

Castro Village Wine Company 4121 19th St at Castro, Castro ☎ 415 864 4411; map p.100. Laid-back neighbourhood wine retailer featuring weekly tastings. Prices are reasonable and the selection – particularly of California varietals – is enormous. Mon–Thurs 11am–7pm, Fri & Sat 11am–8pm, Sun noon–7pm.

Coit Liquor 585 Columbus Ave at Union, North Beach ☎ 415 362 4444; map p.59. Speciality wine store on a prime North Beach corner, with late-night hours and a strong emphasis on rare Italian vintages. There's a good stock of regular booze as well. Mon–Thurs & Sun 10am–midnight, Fri & Sat 10am–2am.

D&M Wines & Liquors 2200 Fillmore St at Sacramento, Pacific Heights ☎ 415 346 1325; map pp.68–69. Family-owned corner shop that's been in business since the Great Depression. It's known for California wines and champagne, but you'll also find plenty of American whiskey and French brandy on the shelves. Mon–Thurs 10am–8pm, Fri & Sat 10am–10pm, Sun 11am–7pm.

The Jug Shop 1590 Pacific Ave at Polk, Russian Hill ☎ 415 885 2922; map p.56. Large retailer known locally for affordable California wines, although its selection of beer – hundreds strong – is equally diverse and fairly priced. They'll even deliver anywhere within San Francisco if you spend at least $100. Mon–Sat 9am–9pm, Sun 10am–7pm.

K&L Wine Merchants 638 Fourth St at Brannan, South of Market ☎415 896 1734; map pp.84–85. With K&L's deeply knowledgeable staff and seemingly endless stock of wine from around the world, you're bound to track down the right bottle (or case) here. Mon–Fri 10am–7pm, Sat 9am–6pm, Sun 11am–6pm.

PlumpJack Wines 3201 Fillmore St at Greenwich, Cow Hollow ☎415 346 9870; map pp.68–69. If you're looking to surprise the oenophile in your life with an obscure California vintage, this should be one of your first stops – it boasts an exhaustive selection of wines from across the

state. Branch at 4011 24th St at Noe, Noe Valley (☎415 282 3841). Mon–Sat 11am–8pm, Sun 11am–6pm.

★ **True Sake** 560 Hayes St at Laguna, Hayes Valley ☎415 355 9555; map pp.106–107. Selling over a hundred different varieties of Japan's signature booze, this welcoming shop colour-codes each bottle to demonstrate whether it's a light and crisp blend or a heftier, aged sake like port. Mon–Fri noon–7pm, Sat 11am–7pm, Sun noon–6pm.

The Wine Club 953 Harrison St at Sixth, South of Market ☎415 512 9086; map p.84–85. Huge warehouse space – fitting, considering its neighbourhood – where wine is offered in torn cardboard boxes. It's a great place for budget buys, as well as fair-priced vintage specials, and the selection changes daily. Mon–Sat 10am–7pm, Sun 11am–6pm.

HEALTH AND BEAUTY

Benefit 2117 Fillmore St at California, Pacific Heights ☎415 567 0242; map pp.106–107. One of the original boutiques of this popular, San Francisco-based beauty brand that features whimsical, retro touches and excellent personal service. You'll find the complete line of makeup and skin care here, as well as a "brow bar" where you can have your brows waxed or tweezed to perfection. Branch at 2219 Chestnut St at Divisadero, Marina (☎415 567 1173). Mon–Wed 10am–7pm, Thurs & Fri 9.30am–7pm, Sat 9.30am–6.30pm, Sun 10am–6pm.

Common Scents 3920 24th St at Sanchez, Noe Valley ☎415 826 1019; map p.100. This neighbourhood staple offers a wealth of natural skincare accessories, as well as products you can buy in bulk and have refilled. Mon–Fri 10am–7pm, Sat 10am–6pm, Sun 11am–5pm.

Dekko Salon 1325 Indiana St at 25th, Potrero Hill ☎415 285 8848; map pp.98–99. Get a top-notch cut and styling advice at this hip, indie salon that's one of San Francisco's best-kept secrets, tucked away as it is in an industrial area. They also do colour, highlights and keratin treatments. Tues–Wed 11am–5pm, Thurs–Fri 11am–6pm, Sat 10am–5pm.

★ **International Orange** 2044 Fillmore St at California, Pacific Heights ☎415 563 5000; map pp.106–107. This luxurious, eco-friendly spa – named for the paint colour of the Golden Gate Bridge – is both a day spa and yoga studio. Try a customized organic treatment or

pick up something from the array of high-end, green skincare products, candles and accessories. Mon–Fri 9am–9pm, Sat & Sun 9am–8pm.

Kiehl's 2360 Fillmore St at Washington, Pacific Heights ☎415 359 9260; map pp.68–69. Pick up classic, sustainably minded favourites – hand lotions, hair masks, etc – at this flagship store with peerless customer service. Mon–Sat 10am–8.30pm, Sun 11am–6pm.

Nancy Boy 347 Hayes St at Franklin, Hayes Valley ☎415 552 3802; map pp.106–107. Marvellously aromatic shop that's famed for its slogan, "Tested on boyfriends, not on animals". You'll find a full assortment of lotions, moisturizers and bath products, along with one-of-a-kind decor, including furniture and accessories. Mon–Fri 11am–6pm, Sat & Sun 11am–7pm.

Scarlet Sage Herb Company 1173 Valencia St at 23rd, Mission ☎415 821 0997; map p.100. Organic herbal apothecary selling tinctures and treatments made from more than three hundred herbs. You'll also find scented candles and bath oils, and you can even arrange a tarot card reading here. Daily 11am–6.30pm.

The Spa at the Sports Club/LA 747 Market St at Third, Union Square ☎415 633 3900; map pp.40–41. Unwind and relax with a wide variety of facials, massages and beauty treatments (including special offerings each season) at this luxury spa. It's an ideal stop after a workout at the club's expansive, state-of-the-art gym. Mon–Fri 5am–11pm, Sat & Sun 7am–8pm.

ART GALLERIES AND SPECIALITY STORES

It should come as no surprise that San Francisco boasts not only a thriving **art scene**, but no shortage of singular **speciality and gift boutiques**, from a fully fledged pirate supply shop and the West's top ribbon retailer to the most respected sex-toy emporium in the US. A few resources are available to help you avoid the gimmicky tourist trap art galleries strewn about Union Square: the San Francisco Bay Area Gallery Guide (☎415 921 1600, ⊚sfbayareagalleryguide.com) and San Francisco Art Dealers Association (☎415 788 9818, ⊚sfada.com) are good for higher-profile galleries, while ⊚fecalface.com/calendar has extensive listings of younger, edgier openings. If you're around in October, take advantage of the city's annual Open Studios event, for which hundreds of local artists open their creative spaces to the public for free – visit ⊚artspan.org for details.

13

ART GALLERIES

Crown Point Press 20 Hawthorne St at Howard, South of Market ☎ 415 974 6273, ⓦ crownpoint.com; map pp.84–85. Down a South of Market side street, you'll stumble upon this combination gallery/studio, with two showrooms featuring limited editions of prints by internationally recognized artists; there's also a fine bookstore in front. Mon–Sat 10am–6pm.

Galeria de la Raza 2857 24th St at Bryant, Mission ☎ 415 826 8009, ⓦ galeriadelaraza.org; map p.100. Devoted exclusively to Chicano/Latino art, this vibrant space hosts community activities, lectures and socially minded exhibitions featuring artists from as near as the surrounding Mission district, and as far as Los Angeles and even Central and South America. Tues 1–7pm, Wed–Sat noon–6pm.

Intersection for the Arts 925 Mission St at Fifth, South of Market ☎ 415 626 2787, ⓦ theintersection.org; map pp.84–85. Diverse venue that hosts small- and large-scale gallery openings, as well as theatre and dance performances. Shows can vary wildly in quality, but odds are you won't find them humdrum. Wed–Sun noon–6pm.

Mission Cultural Center for Latino Arts 2868 Mission St at 25th, Mission ☎ 415 643 5001; map p.100. Home to one of the Mission's largest galleries, this community mainstay also offers classes, shows documentary films and hosts a wide variety of events. Mon 5–10pm, Tues–Fri 10am–10pm, Sat 10am–5.30pm.

Modernism 685 Market St at Third, Union Square ☎ 415 541 0461, ⓦ modernisminc.com; map pp.84–85. Long-established gallery on the city's main drag hosting exhibitions that encompass futurism, expressionism, Pop Art, minimalism and American modern art; sculpture, photography and even performance art make sporadic appearances here as well. Tues–Sat 10am–5.30pm.

Ratio 3 Gallery 1447 Stevenson St at Duboce, Mission ☎ 415 821 3371, ⓦ ratio3.org; map p.100. Understated upper Mission space hosting solidly curated works by respected names from New York, Los Angeles and Europe, as well as local stars. Wed–Sat 11am–6pm; also by appointment.

Romer Young Gallery 1240 22nd St at Pennsylvania, Potrero Hill ☎ 415 550 7483, ⓦ romeryounggallery .com; map pp.98–99. Committed to contemporary works by emerging artists, this space is located steps from the 22nd St Caltrain station. Expect ambitious exhibitions showcasing photography, sculpture and painting works by the best and brightest up-and-comers. Tues & Thurs 6–9pm, Fri & Sat 11am–5pm.

FIRST THURSDAYS AT 49 AND 77 GEARY

On the first Thursday of every month, the galleries in these two Financial District buildings (map pp.40–41) host openings for often-excellent art shows, making them *the* place to see and be seen in the San Francisco art scene; expect contemporary paintings, sculpture, video art and a host of conceptual installations by artists from around the world. Even if you can't make it for "First Thursday", these conveniently located galleries (less than one block off Market St and a short walk from the Montgomery BART/Muni station) offer exceptional browsing.

49 GEARY

871 Fine Arts ☎ 415 543 5155, ⓦ artbook.com /871store.html. Small-scale sculptures and photographs adjacent to an excellent bookshop. Tues–Sat 10.30am–5.30pm.

Fraenkel Gallery ☎ 415 981 2661, ⓦ fraenkelgallery .com. Late twentieth-century photographers à la Richard Avedon and Diane Arbus. Tues–Fri 9.30am–5.30pm, Sat 10am–5pm.

Gregory Lind Gallery ☎ 415 296 9661, ⓦ gregory lindgallery.com. New York, Los Angeles and local contemporary paintings and sculptures. Tues–Sat 10am–5.30pm.

Robert Koch Gallery ☎ 415 421 0122, ⓦ koch gallery.com. A wide range of photography from the nineteenth century to the present. Tues–Sat 10.30am–5.30pm.

Stephen Wirtz Gallery ☎ 415 433 6879, ⓦ wirtz gallery.com. Works by internationally recognized photographers, both experimental and documentarian. Tues–Sat 10.30am–5.30pm.

77 GEARY

Marx & Zavattero ☎ 415 627 9111, ⓦ marxzav .com. Dedicated West Coast curators exhibiting group and solo shows of paintings, sculptures and installations. Tues–Fri 10.30am–5.30pm, Sat 11am–5pm.

Patricia Sweetow Gallery ☎ 415 788 5126, ⓦ patriciasweetowgallery.com. With a floor to call its own (the "mezzanine"), this raw industrial setting is home to rotating shows of contemporary paintings and drawings. Tues–Fri 10.30am–5.30pm, Sat 10.30am–5pm.

Rena Bransten Gallery ☎ 415 982 3292, ⓦ renabranstengallery.com. Impressive range of established national and international artists in varying media. Tues–Fri 10.30am–5.30pm, Sat 11am–5pm.

Silverman Gallery 804 Sutter St at Jones, Union Square ☎ 415 255 9508, ⓦ silverman-gallery.com; map pp.40–41. Four blocks away from Union Square proper, this gallery presents some of San Francisco's most compelling contemporary photography, installation and film shows by both new and established artists. Tues & Thurs 6–9pm, Fri & Sat 11am–5pm.

Velvet Da Vinci 2015 Polk St at Pacific, Russian Hill ☎ 415 441 0109; map p.56. This sumptuous gallery-cum-jewellery shop stocks art pieces by dozens of international designers. Unique pieces by locals such as Julia Turner are presented alongside work from British furniture maker David Gates. Tues–Sat 11am–6pm, Sun 11am–4pm.

GIFTS AND ODDITIES

★ **826 Valencia** 826 Valencia St at 19th, Mission ☎ 415 642 5905; map p.100. A front for writer/publisher Dave Eggers' non-profit youth writing workshop, this "pirate store" offers everything a swashbuckler could need, from eyepatches and message bottles to spy glasses and Jolly Rogers; naturally, all of Eggers' publications are on sale as well. The store is an adventure unto itself, with treasures scattered about and a fish tank room that's home to Karl the porcupine pufferfish. Daily noon–6pm.

Autumn Express 2071 Mission St at 17th, Mission ☎ 415 824 2222; map p.100. Fair-trade stationery store that's festooned with brightly coloured lanterns and assorted decorations. Much of the high-grade paper is Nepalese, and aside from stationery sold by the sheet, you'll find greeting cards and a smattering of paper-related gifts. Mon–Fri 10am–6.30pm.

Body Manipulations 3234 16th St at Guerrero, Mission ☎ 415 621 0408; map p.100. This shop near a bustling Mission corner is one of San Francisco's most popular destinations for piercing, branding and other body modifications. All services are available on a walk-in basis. Daily noon–7pm.

Britex Fabrics 146 Geary St at Grant, Union Square ☎ 415 392 2910; map pp.40–41. Crammed with bales of every possible fabric, this landmark store has supplied Bay Area designers since the early 1950s. Come for amazing deals on fabric remnants, and considering that it stocks more than 30,000 different styles of buttons, it's also the place to duck into if you lose one during your visit. Mon–Sat 10am–6pm.

★ **Cliff's Variety** 479 Castro St at 18th, Castro ☎ 415 431 5365; map p.100. An emporium like no other, Cliff's Variety has been a neighbourhood fixture since before World War II, and it's little wonder why: only in the Castro would a hardware store carry the expected basics (power drills, toilet paper) alongside hula hoops and feather boas sold by the yard. Mon–Fri 8.30am–8pm, Sat 9.30am–8pm, Sun 11am–6pm.

Cookin' 339 Divisadero St at Page, Lower Haight ☎ 415 861 1854; map pp.106–107. Brave the crabby shopkeeper at this budget gourmet cook's bargain haven, where the shelves are full of good-quality secondhand kitchen items such as cast-iron pans, coffee pots and various oddities. Tues–Sat noon–6.30pm, Sun 1–5pm.

Crystal Way 2335 Market St at Noe, Castro ☎ 415 861 6511; map p.100. Metaphysical boutique in the centre of the city with a small selection of books and a much wider range of crystals, candles, oils and other ephemera; astrology and tarot readings are also available. Mon–Fri noon–7pm, Sat 11am–6pm, Sun 11am–5pm.

Dark Garden 321 Linden St at Gough, Hayes Valley ☎ 415 431 7684; map pp.106–107. Fabulous fetish clothing for men and women, available in ready-to-wear and custom designs. One of the better places in town to find just the right corset. Mon–Wed & Sun 11am–5pm, Thurs–Sat 11am–7pm.

Diptyque 171 Maiden Lane at Stockton, Union Square ☎ 415 402 0600; map pp.40–41. One of only three US locations of this Parisian boutique devoted to own-made deluxe perfume and candles. Its Tuberose (rose) fragrance is a top seller. Mon–Sat 10am–6pm, Sun 10am–5pm.

Flight 001 525 Hayes St at Octavia, Hayes Valley ☎ 415 487 1001; map pp.106–107. Sleek, futuristic travel store selling books, cleverly useful accessories (think chunky, Day-Glo luggage tags and all-in-one shaving kits) and dapper carry-on bags. The place to stock up if you only travel first-class – or at least want to act like it. Mon–Sat 11am–7pm, Sun 11am–6pm.

Fredericksen's 3029 Fillmore St at Union, Cow Hollow ☎ 415 292 2950; map pp.68–69. In business since around the end of the nineteenth century, this hardware and home improvement store is worth a wander for its singular decor – look for the unicorn riding down a rainbow. Mon–Fri 8am–7pm, Sat & Sun 9am–6pm.

★ **Good Vibrations** 603 Valencia St at 17th, Mission ☎ 415 522 5460; map p.100. A glorious emporium designed to destigmatize sex shops and make browsing fun and comfortable for men, women and couples. It's packed with every imaginable sex toy, plus racks of erotica and candy-store-style jars of condoms; all this, plus an antique vibrator museum. Branches at 1620 Polk St at Sacramento, Polk Gulch (☎ 415 345 0400) and 899 Mission St at Fifth, South of Market (☎ 415 513 1635). Mon–Thurs & Sun 10am–9pm, Fri & Sat 10am–11pm.

Just for Fun 3982 24th St at Noe, Noe Valley ☎ 415 285 4068; map p.100. Neighbourhood shop full of kitschy, entertaining gifts and a wide selection of stationery – although what truly sets it apart is its vast range of current and classic board games. Mon–Fri 10am–7pm, Sat 9am–7pm, Sun 10am–6pm.

La Sirena Botanica 1509 Church St at 27th, Noe Valley ☎ 415 285 0612; map p.100. Unique "supply store for matters of the spirit" where curious locals come to peruse Santeria items and have readings done; New Age books,

13

tarot cards, oils and other potent potions are also available. Daily 11am–6.30pm.

Mom's Body Shop 1408 Haight St at Masonic, Upper Haight ☎ 415 864 6667; map pp.106–107. Tattoos and piercings for those who'd like to take home a permanent souvenir from their San Francisco visit, although the place has long been popular with locals as well. Unique for its large selection of Chinese, Celtic and Tibetan scripts; walk-in service available. Daily noon–7pm.

Needles and Pens 3253 16th Street at Guerrero, Mission ☎ 415 255 1534; map p.100. T-shirt, magazine and craft shop that's a perfect introduction to underground Mission style. It's full of locally handcrafted items, while the salon-style wall of constantly changing art is always worth a look. Daily noon–7pm.

Paxton Gate 824 Valencia St at 19th, Mission ☎ 415 824 1872; map p.100. A neo-Victorian ground zero for San Francisco's taxidermy community: mordantly arranged insects, fossils and cute (yet dead) furry fauna. Vintage photos and posters, jewellery, skulls and succulent plants also available. Daily 11am–7pm.

The Ribbonerie 3695 Sacramento St at Spruce, Presidio Heights ☎ 415 626 6184; map pp.68–69. Pitching itself as the West's most complete ribbon retailer, you'll likely agree upon setting foot in this wonderfully specific shop. Every imaginable pattern, width, colour and material is available, along with trims, thimbles and pincushions. Mon–Sat 10am–5.30pm.

Soko Hardware 1698 Post St at Buchanan, Japantown ☎ 415 931 5510; map pp.106–107. An Asian Cliff's Variety (see p.215) of sorts, Soko Hardware carries seemingly every item known to humankind and makes for great browsing fun. Its tools are only a starting point – you'll also find Asian-inspired items for kitchen and home. Mon–Sat 9am–5.30pm.

Super7 1427 Haight St at Masonic, Upper Haight ☎ 415 553 6155; map pp.106–107. With a full range of pop-surreal, grotesque and painfully mawkish wares from Japan lining the shelves, this is the perfect place for addicts of collectable toys to go overboard. Great for hardcore Godzilla fans or anyone with a taste for surprisingly affordable art prints. Daily 11am–7pm.

Under One Roof 518 Castro St at 18th, Castro ☎ 415 503 2300; map p.100. What sets this shop apart isn't its eclectic mix of greeting cards, books and gay-oriented ephemera, but the fact that all its profits go straight to tens of local AIDS services organizations – it's generated over $11 million since 1990. Mon–Wed 10am–8pm, Thurs–Sat 10am–9pm, Sun 11am–7pm.

DEPARTMENT STORES, MALLS AND SHOPPING CENTRES

San Francisco has remained more immune to the establishment of large **shopping malls** than most American cities – and those that have sprouted up are, by and large, reasonably appealing. Downtown plays host to several **department stores** around Union Square, though these are all branches of posh national chains that can be found in most major US cities.

DEPARTMENT STORES

Barneys New York 77 O'Farrell St at Stockton, Union Square ☎ 415 268 3500; map pp.40–41. The famed high-end niche department store finally opened its doors to San Francisco fashionistas in 2007. Sceptics claim that this outpost plays second fiddle to the New York flagship location, but die-hards who are hungry for that Marc Jacobs sweater won't care. Mon–Sat 10am–7pm, Sun 11am–6pm.

Bloomingdales 845 Market St at Fifth, Union Square ☎ 415 856 5300; map pp.84–85. Anchoring the Westfield San Francisco Centre, this shiny haven boasts a Shiseido cosmetics counter, rows of shoes and handbags, and boutiques from the likes of Louis Vuitton and Christian Dior. Mon–Thurs 10am–9pm, Fri & Sat 10am–10pm, Sun 11am–8pm.

Loehmann's 222 Sutter St at Kearny, Union Square ☎ 415 982 3215; map pp.40–41. Root around for terrific designer bargains at this upscale discounter that's often well stocked with same-season DKNY and BCBG. It's known for "The Back Room", where you can pick up budget-priced ballgowns and high-end designer originals at upwards of 65 percent off. Mon–Fri 9am–8pm, Sat 9.30am–8pm, Sun 11am–7pm.

Macy's 170 O'Farrell St at Stockton, Union Square ☎ 415 397 3333; map pp.40–41. In a gigantic glass-fronted building looming over Union Square, Macy's is generally the most affordable of the big-name department stores. The larger shop focuses on mainstream women's and children's wear – reliable for basics, if a bit unexciting; menswear, meanwhile, has been banished to a smaller space on the opposite corner of Stockton St. Mon–Fri 10am–9pm, Sat 9am–9pm, Sun 11am–7pm.

Neiman Marcus 150 Stockton St at Geary, Union Square ☎ 415 362 3900; map pp.40–41. High-end department store housed in a beautiful building with a glass-domed rotunda capping a top-floor restaurant and bar; from there, you can watch shoppers lugging their bags through Union Square far below. Its merchandise is aimed squarely at a well-to-do, middle-aged crowd. Mon–Wed, Fri & Sat 10am–7pm, Thurs 10am–8pm, Sun noon–6pm.

Nordstrom 865 Market St at Powell, Union Square ☎ 415 243 8500; map pp.84–85. Shoppers flock here for the high-quality – and suitably expensive – fashions, while others simply enjoy riding the spiral escalators that climb the four-storey atrium from the Westfield San Francisco Centre below. Mon–Sat 10am–9pm, Sun 10am–7pm.

Saks Fifth Avenue 384 Post St at Powell, Union Square ☎ 415 986 4300; map pp.40–41. A scaled-down version of its parent store in New York, Saks carries a sharper selection of directional fashion than most expect. Great for browsing. Its separate men's store is especially well stocked: 220 Post St at Grant, Union Square (☎ 415 986 4300). Mon–Wed 10am–6pm, Thurs–Sat 10am–7pm, Sun 11am–6pm.

MALLS AND SHOPPING CENTRES

Crocker Galleria 50 Post St at Montgomery, Financial District ☎ 415 393 1505, ⓦ shopatgalleria.com; map pp.40–41. A modern, Italianate atrium, this attractive centre features some very pricey showcase boutiques, including Polo Ralph Lauren. Mon–Fri 10am–6pm, Sat 10am–5pm.

Embarcadero Center Financial District ☎ 415 772 0700, ⓦ embarcaderocenter.com; map p.56. Spread over five blocks between Battery, Sacramento, Drumm and Clay streets, this 1970s mixed-use complex contains well over a hundred stores and a handful of restaurants. You won't find many unusual shops here, and since it's convenient for Downtown workers, it becomes most crowded during weekday lunch hours. Oddly, the centre's four towers are also home to nearly two dozen dental surgeries. Mon–Fri 10am–7pm, Sat 10am–6pm, Sun noon–5pm.

Ghirardelli Square 900 North Point St at Larkin, Fisherman's Wharf ☎ 415 775 5500, ⓦ ghirardellisq .com; map pp.68–69. Anchoring the western end of the brutally crass tourist mile at Fisherman's Wharf, this old brick complex is far more pleasant than you might expect. Its stores may be patchy, but the plaza is a pleasant enough place to linger, and the excellent (if crowded) *Ghirardelli Ice Cream and Chocolate Caffe* is always worth a visit. Call for hours.

Japan Center Japantown ☎ 415 440 1171, ⓦ sfjapan town.org; map pp.106–107. Three-building warren of Japanese restaurants and stores wedged between Geary Boulevard and Fillmore, Sutter and Laguna streets. Despite its dimly lit, soulless design, it's a perennially popular destination and throbs with Japanese-American shoppers, as well as tourists. Daily 7am–midnight, although individual business hours vary.

Metreon 101 Fourth St at Mission, South of Market ☎ 415 369 6000, ⓦ westfield.com/metreon; map pp.84–85. Although it was little more than a futuristic advert for its former owners, Sony, upon its late 1990s debut, this centre has changed over the years to incorporate a few attractions for regular shoppers – a branch of Chronicle Books and a large food court, to name a couple of examples. Its most popular feature, though, has always been its movie multiplex. Mon–Thurs & Sun 10.30am–8.30pm, Fri & Sat 10.30am–9.30pm.

Stonestown Galleria 19th Ave and Winston, Parkside ☎ 415 564 8848, ⓦ stonestowngalleria.com; map p.116. Just north of San Francisco State University, this 130-store complex features a Macy's, Nordstrom and a host of smart clothing and shoe stores, along with the usual mall choices. It's definitely more suburban in nature than any other large shopping centre in the city. Mon–Sat 10am–9pm, Sun noon–6pm.

Westfield San Francisco Centre 865 Market St at Fifth, Union Square ☎ 415 512 5776, ⓦ westfield.com /sanfrancisco; map pp.84–85. Decked out in Italian marble, polished green granite and spiral escalators, and anchored by Nordstrom and Bloomingdales, this glassy shopping centre encompasses the former Emporium department store next door. Its finest attribute may be the basement-level food court, featuring a vast selection of gourmet treats; there's also a large movie multiplex. Upstairs, the Emporium's stunning original glass dome looks better than ever. Mon–Sat 10am–8.30pm, Sun 10am–7pm.

13

SAN FRANCISCO GIANTS AT THE AT&T PARK

Sports and outdoor activities

With its sizeable areas of open water and protected parkland, it comes as no surprise that the Bay Area is full of people who enjoy the region's wealth of outdoor activities. These range from hiking, cycling, swimming or playing tennis to more extreme sports such as hang gliding. The region's three major cities are collectively home to teams in all major American spectator sports and taking in a sporting event is a great way to glimpse a different side of the Bay Area, where its signature sophisticated tastes and intellectualism take a back seat to good old-fashioned cheering (and on occasion, booing). Regardless of how you spend your outdoor time, bear in mind that even when Bay Area skies are grey, the sun's ultraviolet rays still pierce through the clouds and often leave unprepared visitors with a souvenir sunburn.

PARTICIPATORY SPORTS

Upholding coastal California's reputation as a fitness hub, the Bay Area is home to countless acres devoted to outdoor activities of one sort or another. Few urban areas in the US boast as much open space as this region of over seven million residents: numerous parks lend themselves to **hiking and climbing** exploration; miles of country roads offer excellent **cycling routes**; gusty San Francisco Bay itself challenges local riggers and **running paths** line several of the Bay's shores. **Tennis and golf** are popular pursuits in the mild-weather months, while **surfers** attack the mighty Pacific's swells year-round, although waves reach peak power in December and January.

WALKING

For a relaxed walk, simply set out on any of the labyrinthine paths in San Francisco's Golden Gate Park. Crissy Field and Mount Davidson (at 925ft, the city's highest point) are also pleasant spots for off-pavement walks affording expansive vistas. Of course, San Francisco's roadsides make for terrific exploration; best of all with urban hiking, you're never far from comfortably seated refreshment.

BEACHSIDE WALKS

The local chunk of the Pacific coastline doesn't offer an abundance of long seafront spits, but there are a handful of lengthy beaches in and near San Francisco. Anyone looking for a sandy stroll would do well to visit Stinson Beach in Marin County, Half Moon Bay State Beach in San Mateo County or despite its ongoing trash issues, San Francisco's Ocean Beach. Other popular – and paved – paths far inland from the coast's wind and atmospheric fog are Nimitz Way in Berkeley's Tilden Regional Park and the walkways around Oakland's Lake Merritt.

RUNNING

San Francisco remains a big running town, although sometimes not the safest one due to clogged streets and distracted drivers. The above-mentioned pedestrianized areas frequented by walkers are popular with runners as well; add to that list the Embarcadero and the Great Highway, which flank the east and west shores of the city.

EVENTS

Bay To Breakers One of the city's zaniest annual events, this is a 7.5-mile footrace-cum-costume party held each May (see p.227).

Dipsea Race Considerably more serious, Marin's cross-country (w dipsea.org) is held in June, and sees 1500 runners sprint out of Mill Valley before struggling up and

over Windy Gap via 671 discouragingly steep steps. The course then passes through Muir Woods, over Cardiac Hill and down Steep Ravine before mercifully crossing the finish line in Stinson Beach, 7.1 miles from the starting point.

Double Dipsea A few weekends later, the Double Dipsea (w doubledipsea.com) adds to the Dipsea Race's route a run from Stinson Beach to Mill Valley.

CYCLING

Many visitors best experience San Francisco's parks and natural landscapes by cycling through them. Golden Gate Park and the Great Highway Promenade adjacent to Ocean Beach, as well as Crissy Field and the Presidio, all have fine paved trails and some good off-road routes; the bayside Embarcadero is also a popular cycling spot. Along with Mount Tam, serious biking aficionados visiting the Bay Area should consider trips to the Marin Headlands, El Corte de Madera Open Space Preserve in San Mateo County, Mount Diablo State Park in Contra Costa County, and, of course, the Pine Mountain Loop near Fairfax in Marin County. Taking bikes on public transport is not a problem (see p.26); visit w gatetrails.com for details on Bay Area mountain-biking destinations.

BICYCLE RENTALS AND TOURS

Bike and Roll 899 Columbus Ave at Lombard, North Beach ☎ 415 229 2000, w bikeandroll.com. Rates from $8/hr, $32/day with ten-percent online discount. Tours from $60.

Blazing Saddles 1095 Columbus Ave at Francisco in North Beach, and Pier 41 in Fisherman's Wharf ☎ 415 202 8888, w blazingsaddles.com. Rates from $32/day; ten-percent online discount.

Wheel Fun Rentals In the boathouse at Golden Gate Park's Stow Lake ☎ 415 668 6699, w wheelfunrentals .com. Offers all sorts of rolling contraptions for rent, from bikes ($8/hr, $25/day), tandem bikes ($12/hr, $40/day),

BIRTH OF THE MOUNTAIN BIKE

The Bay Area's contribution to cycling was the invention of the **mountain bike** in the early 1970s, when a small group of Tamalpais High School students (known as the Canyon Gang) began cruising down the unpaved roads on Mount Tamalpais on one-speed, coaster-brake Schwinn cruisers. These 45-pound bikes with thick balloon tyres could handle the roads' rough terrain and by 1976, the Repack race was begun on adjacent Pine Mountain; the regular event soon generated major press coverage and led to a national craze but was discontinued in 1984 due to deteriorating trail conditions and other safety issues.

14

and scooters ($5/hr) to a cavalcade of fringed surreys ($20–30/hr, depending on size).

SWIMMING

Swimming is a treacherous activity along much of the Northern California coast, with alarmingly frequent reports of ocean riptides swallowing swimmers. As a result, sea swimming in and around San Francisco can't be recommended, irrespective of your level of expertise. Dipping into the calmer (though hardly calm) waters inside the Golden Gate is a safer move – try Aquatic Park on the city's north shore, where numerous local swimmers train. See the box opposite for a few other options on Bay Area swimming. If you'd prefer not to brave the Bay's cold estuary waters, San Francisco and its outlying communities maintain a number of public pools, some in better condition than others.

PUBLIC POOLS

North Beach Pool Lombard St at Mason ☎ 415 391 0407, ☻ parks.sfgov.org. In the city proper, this newly restored pool offers lap swims for a nominal fee; it's in a covered space with lots of roof windows.

BAY AREA HIKING

The Bay Area's relatively mild year-round weather allows local hikers to set soles to path in any season, although they can get muddy during the wet months of winter and early spring. With a seemingly limitless network of trails accessible in the area – particularly in the Marin Headlands and on Mount Tamalpais in Marin County, along the ridge of the Santa Cruz Mountains in the Peninsula and on Mount Diablo in Contra Costa County – the region boasts wild settings often absent in other metropolitan areas. A particularly helpful resource for finding and planning Bay Area hikes is ☻ bahiker.com; also, Tom Stienstra, the highly respected outdoors writer for the *San Francisco Chronicle*, publishes ideas for outings regularly at ☻ sfgate.com.

San Francisco's northwest corner has a few hikes that don't require much exertion for a payoff of extraordinary views. The **Coastal Trail**, which links Sutro Heights with the Golden Gate Bridge via Baker Beach, follows an old railroad route for part of its length and a spur trail leads steeply downhill to epic vistas at Land's End on the far northwest tip of the San Francisco Peninsula.

Top trailheads on iconic, 2571ft-high **Mount Tamalpais** include Bootjack, Mountain Home and Rock Spring, all of which are on the southern and western flanks of the mountain and easily reached via the Panoramic Highway. Purchase a trail map at the Mount Tamalpais State Park visitor centre (see p.268) and create your own loop hike ranging anywhere from two hours to a full day. Note that trailhead parking lots fill up early, particularly on sunny weekends regardless of season.

A favourite hike among locals, albeit not one for anyone out of shape, is a rigorous seven-mile loop that begins at Stinson Beach and heads up the west side of Mount Tam (as it's known) before descending back around to the seaside village. At the south end of Stinson Beach, look for the **Matt Davis Trailhead**. Climb very steeply (1500ft in a little over two miles) up the Matt Davis Trail, pausing to catch your breath at the ocean vista of Table Rock before continuing to Pantoll through thick forest that eventually opens up into mountainside grassland offering stunning views in three directions. From Pantoll, the approximate halfway point of the hike, drop back down on the aptly named Steep Ravine Trail, a lushly shaded descent featuring ferns, redwoods, a burbling creek and even a 10ft step ladder. Return to Stinson Beach on the vista-laden Dipsea Trail.

San Mateo and **Santa Clara Counties** offer similar grassland/forest landscapes amidst a wealth of uncrowded public parks, many managed by the Mid-Peninsula Open Space District (☎ 650 691 1200, ☻ openspace.org). **Portola Redwoods State Park** (☎ 650 948 9098, ☻ parks .ca.gov), set in a deep and remote canyon on the seaward slope of the Santa Cruz Mountains, requires a slow drive along its curvy entrance road but rewards visitors with excellent hiking and camping in a cool, serene setting.

The **East Bay** counties include a number of trail-rich parks and preserves managed by the East Bay Regional Park District (☎ 888 327 2757, ☻ ebparks.org), while **Mount Diablo State Park** (☎ 925 837 0904, ☻ parks.ca.gov) features its namesake 3849ft peak, from which the total visible land area is second only to Africa's Kilimanjaro due to the expansive valley and delta to Diablo's immediate east. An extensive latticework of hiking trails abounds here as well, but be forewarned that temperatures consistently break into the 90s (and sometimes higher) throughout the summer months. Winter and spring are the best time to visit, particularly for the many waterfalls on the mountain's steep northern flank.

BAY AREA SWIMMING HOLES

These Bay Area swim spots offer the best warm-day alternatives to crashing pool parties in suburban back yards or being sucked undersea by swirling ocean currents.

Bass Lake Point Reyes National Seashore, Marin County ⓣ415 464 5100, ⓦnps.gov/pore. Reached by a moderate three-mile hike from the Palomarin trailhead near Bolinas. Look for rope swings dangling from trees along its south shore. No lifeguard on duty, no fee.

Crown Memorial State Beach Eighth Street at Otis, Alameda ⓣ510 521 7090, ⓦebparks.org. Relatively warm and shallow Bay waters often buffeted by strong breezes. Adjacent bird sanctuary and marine reserve. No lifeguard on duty, picnicking available nearby. $5 parking fee, free to swim.

Lake Anza Tilden Regional Park, Berkeley hills ⓣ510 843 2137, ⓦebparks.org. Sheltered from the wind, and there's even a sandy beach. Changing rooms on-site, lifeguard on duty, picnicking available nearby. $3.50 adults, $2.50 kids and seniors.

Lake Temescal 6502 Broadway Terrace, Oakland hills ⓣ510 652 1155, ⓦebparks.org. In a less wild setting than Lake Anza, but still a nice spot for a dip. Changing rooms onsite, no lifeguards on duty. $3 adults, $2 kids and seniors.

Temescal Pool Oakland Technical High School, 371 45th St ⓣ510 597 5013, ⓦoaklandnet.com. One of Oakland's top spots for an outdoor pool dip on a warm East Bay day.

SURFING

Local coastal waters tend to be chilly, swirling and often rife with sharks, so on a mainstream level, surfing remains more of a Southern California phenomenon. Nonetheless, tightly knit communities of surfers extend from Santa Cruz to Stinson Beach. Certain Bay Area surf spots can sometimes be territorially guarded by locals but overall the scene's fairly welcoming. The San Mateo County coast offers both extremes: Pacifica's Linda Mar Beach is a favourite area for beginners, while down the coast near Princeton-by-the-Sea, the Mavericks break, which hosts a pre-eminent big wave competition most winters, has claimed the lives of some of the world's most accomplished surfers.

SURF SCHOOLS AND EQUIPMENT RENTAL

Aqua Surf Shop 2830 Sloat Blvd at 46th Ave (ⓣ415 242 9283) and 1742 Haight St (ⓣ415 876 2782), ⓦaquasurfshop.com. If you're up for challenging the Pacific's titanic waves, this shop, with branches in Parkside and the Haight, rents and sells a variety of gear and also offers instruction referrals.

Live Water Surf Shop 3448 Hwy 1 in Stinson Beach ⓣ415 868 0333, ⓦlivewatersurfshop.com. Spend any amount of time in West Marin and you're bound to see this shop's iconic "No Sharks" logo stickers on windows, signs and auto bumpers. Offers training and equipment rental.

Sonlight Surfshop 575 Crespi Drive, off Hwy 1 in Pacifica ⓣ650 359 0353, ⓦsonlightsurfshop.com. Located near surf breaks and happy to outfit and train visitors.

OTHER WATERSPORTS

Windsurfing and kitesurfing The best area is around gusty Crissy Field, from where aquatic speed demons race out and around the Golden Gate; other popular windsurfing/kitesurfing spots include the far northern end of Ocean Beach, and the Berkeley Marina. Visit the San Francisco Boardsailing Association's website at ⓦsfba.org for a wealth of information on rental shops and more.

Kayaking and canoeing Possible at several Bay Area locations for anywhere from $15 to $100, depending on vessel size and time allotment. Note that there's no experience needed to rent sit-on-top kayaks, but taking a traditional (closed deck) sea kayak out on the open water will require prior training.

KAYAK TRIPS AND RENTALS

City Kayak Pier 40 at South Beach Harbour and Pier 39 slip A21 ⓣ415 357 1010, ⓦcitykayak.com. In San Francisco, City Kayak operates from two Bayfront locations: the first offers trips and rentals; the second only offers trips.

Sea Trek ⓣ415 488 1000, ⓦseatrek.com. Calmer Bay waters are found near Sausalito, where Sea Trek rents single or double sea kayaks at $20–35 for an hour's worth of paddling.

Stinson Beach Surf & Kayak ⓣ415 868 2739. Fits the bill if you prefer to navigate the waters along the Marin coast.

TENNIS

There are over 150 public tennis courts in San Francisco, and while they can't be reserved by individuals, you shouldn't have too much trouble finding a vacant court somewhere in town. Consult ⓦsftenniscourts.com for a complete list, including photos. Pack your own racket in advance, as rental possibilities are virtually non-existent.

14

GOLF

San Francisco's cash-strapped municipal golf courses are less than the best in terms of maintenance, value and visitor accessibility, so you're probably better off heading out of town if you're looking for a quality round on the links. Disc golf has become a popular activity in the Bay Area in recent years, with nearly a dozen courses scattered around the region. One of the best is set amidst stands of eucalyptus in Golden Gate Park and a second San Francisco course is in the works at McLaren Park. It's recommended you invest $35 or so in "driver" and "putter" discs beforehand, or find a well-equipped partner who's happy to share. Some outlying courses require parking fees, and many have donation boxes. Visit ⦿ sfdiscgolf .org for more information.

GOLF COURSES

Tilden Park Golf Course ☎ 510 848 7373, ⓦ tilden parkgc.americangolf.com. Par-70 course in the Berkeley hills; book online. $20–55.

Metropolitan Golf Links ☎ 510 569 5555, ⓦ play metro.com. A challengingly windy golf course in Oakland; book online. $19–78.

San Geronimo Golf Course ☎ 415 488 4030, ⓦ golf sangeronimo.com. A bucolic, gently rolling course in central Marin County. $39–64.

SKATING

San Francisco's reputation as skateboarding central reached unmanageable proportions in the early 1990s and led to the pursuit being banned from many areas until the opening of the Potrero del Sol skate park, on San Bruno Avenue south of 25th Street at the southeast edge of the Mission (no phone, ⓦ parks.sfgov.org). Outside of town, a fistful of excellent, purpose-built skate parks have sprung up all around the Bay Area; those in Berkeley, Novato (Marin County), and Sunnyvale (Santa Clara County) command the most respect from area shredders. Check ⓦ sk8parklist.com for an exhaustive list. Every Sunday (and in summer, every Sat), lengthy stretches of one of Golden Gate Park's main drags, John F. Kennedy Drive, closes to auto traffic, providing a prime throughway for inline skaters. Marina Green along the Bay and the paved paths that ring Lake Merced in the southwest corner of town also provide good, flat spots to skate. Bay Area ice skaters have access to a few excellent rinks.

SKATE RENTAL

Golden Gate Park Bike & Skate 3038 Fulton St at Sixth in the Inner Richmond ☎ 415 668 1117, ⓦ golden gateparkbikeandskate.com. Rents both skates ($5/hr, $20/day) and inlines ($6/hr, $24/day).

ICE RINKS

Justin Herman Plaza ☎ 415 772 0700, ⓦ embarcadero center.com. In San Francisco, the Embarcadero Center sets up an outdoor oval every holiday season in the Justin Herman Plaza. $9–9.50, skate rental $3.50. Nov–Jan Mon–Thurs & Sun 10am–10pm, Fri & Sat 10am–11.30pm.

Oakland Ice Center 519 18th St at San Pablo ☎ 510 268 9000, ⓦ oaklandice.com. This Olympic-sized rink in Oakland is available for public skating when it's not training big names in figure skating and ice hockey. $8, skate rental $3. Hours vary.

Snoopy's Home Ice Redwood Empire Ice Arena, 1667 West Steele Lane near Hardies ☎ 707 546 7147, ⓦ snoopyshomeice.com. Santa Rosa's rink was built by *Peanuts* creator and local hero Charles M. Schulz in the late 1960s. $9, skate rental $3. Hours vary.

Yerba Buena Ice Skating Center 750 Folsom St at Fourth ☎ 415 820 3532, ⓦ skatebowl.com. This indoor rink operates year-round in a lovely space bathed in natural light atop Moscone Center. $8, skate rental $3. Hours vary.

BOATING AND FISHING

Sailing While Bay sailing is largely a pursuit exclusive to the local financial elite, the Cal Sailing Club (ⓦ cal-sailing .org), located at the south side of the Berkeley Marina, is a beginner-friendly co-op with a fleet of about two dozen vessels. Membership is required ($75 for three months, $225 for a year) but includes instruction and sailboat access for anyone keen to learn the ins and outs of boating.

Fishing Another way to experience the volatile Pacific is by taking a deep-sea fishing cruise. Huck Finn Sportfishing Center (☎ 650 726 7133, ⓦ huckfinnsportfishing.com) runs a variety of such trips out of Half Moon Bay on its fleet of eight boats, and can also service your rod, reel, tackle and fishing licence needs. It also arranges whale-watching expeditions. Expect to shell out $50–120 per person, depending on the boat and trip.

HORSERIDING

Miwok Livery Stables 701 Tennessee Valley Rd in Mill Valley ☎ 415 389 9414, ⓦ miwokstables.com. Offers a one-hour trail ride in the lush Marin County countryside for $75. It's preceded by a thirty-minute lesson and is available at 1.30pm every day except Sun; reservations are required and participants must be 12 years or older.

Sea Horse & Friendly Acres 1828 N Cabrillo Hwy, Half Moon Bay ☎ 650 726 9903, ⓦ horserentals.com /seahorse.html. On the Peninsula coast's Hwy-1, activities include a one-hour trail ride ($55), a ninety-minute beach ride ($65) and a combined beach and trail ride ($75).

HANG GLIDING

The truly daring (and deep-pocketed) will want to consider hang gliding or paragliding flights that swoop down 1500ft to Stinson Beach from the west flank of Mount Tamalpais. The instructors at the San Francisco Hang Gliding Center ($295 weekdays, $325 weekends and holidays; ☎ 510 528 2300, ⓦ sfhanggliding.com) will provide a short instructional session before soaring off the hillside with you on a tandem flight lasting anywhere from ten to thirty minutes, depending on that day's weather. Single lessons from $160 but you'll need to buy your own equipment to fly.

FITNESS CENTRES

A number of San Francisco fitness centres feature daily rates for city visitors – it's best to check each individual gym's website before heading out, as hours can vary wildly from place to place. Some fitness centres cater to a primarily gay crowd (see p.199).

GYMS

Cathedral Hill Plaza Athletic Club 1333 Gough St at Geary, Western Addition ☎ 415 346 3868, ⓦ chpathleticclub.com. Also has swimming and, for an additional fee, tennis. Day pass $15.

Gold's Gym 1001 Brannan St at Ninth, South of Market ☎ 415 552 4653, ⓦ goldsgym.com. Your best choice in or near Downtown. Day pass $20.

Pacific Heights Health Club 2356 Pine St at Steiner in its namesake neighbourhood ☎ 415 563 6694, ⓦ phhcsf.com. Also offers a robust complement of fitness options. Day pass $20.

BOWLING

Presidio Bowling Center 93 Montgomery St at Moraga in the Presidio ☎ 415 561 2695, ⓦ presidiobowl .com. This twelve-lane ex-military alley has remained just as popular since opening to the public. Mon–Thurs & Sun 9am–midnight, Fri & Sat 9am–2am; $4.75–7.25 per game, $4 shoe rental.

Yerba Buena Bowling Center 750 Folsom St at Fourth ☎ 415 820 3532, ⓦ skatebowl.com. Over in South of Market, this colourful alley is easier for most visitors to reach than its Presidio counterpart. Mon–Thurs 10am–10pm, Fri noon–midnight, Sat 10am–midnight, Sun noon–9pm; $5–6 per game, $3 shoe rental.

SPECTATOR SPORTS

For five months a year, the **National Football League** rivals organized religion as America's favourite Sunday activity – the regular season runs from early September through late December, plus a month of playoffs. Each team plays a mere eight competitive home matches, thus elevating each game's urgency to remarkable levels of intensity. The season culminates in the Super Bowl, generally the year's most-watched television event, held on the first Sunday in February. **Major League Baseball**'s regular season begins no later than early April and runs until the end of September, with teams playing a staggering 81 home games. October's eight-team playoffs culminate in the sport's final round, the misleadingly titled **World Series**. On the collegiate level, the University of California, Berkeley (invariably known as "**Cal**" in sports circles) and **Stanford University** in Palo Alto dominate local coverage and attention, with a handful of the area's smaller schools occasionally showing up on the front page of local sports pages.

BASEBALL

San Francisco Giants AT&T Park, 24 Willie Mays Plaza ☎ 415 972 2000, ⓦ sfgiants.com. Since moving at the outset of the millennium to their charming red-brick waterside ballpark, the first major American sports venue in decades to be built with private funds, the Giants' fortunes have finally taken an upturn, and in 2010 they won their first World Series since relocating from New York. Ticket prices range from $8 midweek in the left-field bleachers to $166 for a premier field club box seat; an alternative plan is to stop by the see-through area on the so-called portwalk beyond the right field fence, where you can watch gratis for up to three innings. Muni streetcars stop right in front of the Giants' park, which is an easy walk from Downtown.

Oakland Athletics McAfee Coliseum, 7000 Coliseum Way, Oakland ☎ 510 638 4900, ⓦ oaklandathletics .com. Across the Bay, the once-dominant Oakland Athletics play before smaller, but intensely loyal crowds. Known to most as the A's, the team's glory days of early to mid-1970s, when they won three consecutive World Series, returned in the late 1980s, peaking with their defeat of the Giants in the earthquake-interrupted 1989 World Series. Lacking the financial resources of many other major-league teams, the A's now rely on young talent to keep them in regular contention, though they have not reached a World Series since 1990. Tickets are much more affordable than in San Francisco, however: expect to shell out anywhere from $2–60, depending on the opponent and promotions. Conveniently, BART runs directly to the stadium complex.

FOOTBALL

San Francisco 49ers Candlestick Park, Bayview Heights ☎ 415 656 4900, ⓦ 49ers.com. The toast of the National Football League – and the entire Bay Area – for most of the 1980s and 1990s, the San Francisco 49ers have since fallen on severely hard times. Unlike the waiting list of the glory years, it's now sometimes possible to turn up

14

on game day and pay $70-plus for a seat. It is hoped that the good times will return if the team manages to complete a proposed move to a state-of-the-art stadium in Santa Clara by 2015.

Oakland Raiders McAfee Coliseum ☎ 510 864 5000, Ⓦ raiders.com. The antithesis to the 49ers' outdated image as elegant winners, they revel in their role as the NFL's chief renegades. Although they have been fairly dire since the early 2000s, the team used to be one of the league's most successful, propelled to league titles in 1967, 1976 and 1980 by a motley crew of hilarious misfits and dodgy hoodlums. The Raiders rarely sell out home games these days, although their fans remain among the most boisterous in American sports. Single-game tickets are generally available from around $70.

BASKETBALL

Golden State Warriors Oracle Arena, next door to McAfee Coliseum, Oakland ☎ 888 479 4667, Ⓦ nba .com/warriors. The National Basketball Association's regular season is an 82-game death march from late October to mid-April; the league's equally exhausting, sixteen-team playoff tournament concludes in mid-June. The NBA 1975 season champions and consistently one of the league's most woeful teams since the mid 1990s, the Warriors have improved of late, even enjoying an underdog playoff run in 2007. Tickets $15–140.

ICE HOCKEY

San Jose Sharks HP Pavilion Central San Jose ☎ 408 287 7070, Ⓦ sj-sharks.com. The National Hockey League team plays 41 regular home league games between October and April. Among all Bay Area pro sports franchises, the Sharks have experienced the most consistent success in recent years, though no Stanley Cups (the NHL's league championship trophy that culminates in June) have yet graced the Sharks' tank. The Sharks draw packed crowds for almost every home contest. Tickets cost $40–80.

SOCCER

San Jose Earthquakes Buck Shaw Stadium, Santa Clara University ☎ 408 985 4625, Ⓦ sjearthquakes .mlsnet.com. Although soccer's popularity in the US has yet to catch up to international levels, local professional clubs have enjoyed cult followings over the years. The Earthquakes play in the country's top soccer league, Major League Soccer. Most home games are played in Santa Clara, with a smattering held at Oakland's multi-purpose McAfee Coliseum. Tickets cost $20–60.

COLLEGE SPORTS

California Golden Bears (☎ 800 462 3277, Ⓦ calbears .com) and **Stanford Cardinals** (☎ 800 782 6367 Ⓦ gostanford.com). Football and men's basketball are traditionally the marquee sports in American intercollegiate athletics, although baseball and women's basketball also maintain increasingly devout national followings; bitter rivals Cal and Stanford regularly field excellent teams in several of these sports (in the rugged Pacific-10 athletic conference), with Cal's football squad and Stanford's baseball and women's basketball teams often among the nation's best. Seasons are considerably shorter than at professional levels. Tickets are usually easy to find on the day; check the teams' websites.

AUTO RACING

Infineon Raceway near the junction of Hwys 37 and 121 in southern Sonoma County between Novato and Vallejo ☎ 800 870 7223, Ⓦ infineonraceway.com. Hosts a variety of auto and motorcycle races between May and Oct. The venue's big event is NASCAR's Toyota Save Mart 350 every June, for which thousands of racing fans descend for an entire weekend; other draws throughout the season include the Kawasaki AMA Superbike Showdown in May, Wednesday Night Drags throughout summer and fall, and a regularly scheduled racing drivers' school.

HORSERACING

Golden Gate Fields ☎ 510 559 7300, Ⓦ goldengate fields.com. The Bay Area's lone horseracing track next to the shores of San Francisco Bay in Berkeley soldiers on in the face of declining attendance. Check the racecourse's website for admission details and racing dates, the bulk of which occur between May and July.

Festivals and events

Since San Franciscans need little encouragement to cavort around town, the
city's festivals are uncommonly convivial events. The event calendar's busiest
seasons are summer and autumn, when highlights include San Francisco
Pride and the Stern Grove Festival; in winter, Chinese New Year is justly
well known (if commercialized), although you may have more fun at the
notoriously wild Bay to Breakers shindig come spring. Neighbourhood street
fairs are immensely popular, with those in the Castro and North Beach among
the best. San Francisco's creative spirit means that independent music, film
and literary events are slated on an almost monthly basis. And of course, it
wouldn't be San Francisco without a smattering of absurdities – look no
further than the Valentine's Day Pillow Fight or St Stupid's Day Parade.

15

EVENTS LISTINGS

The San Francisco Convention and Visitors Bureau is a top resource for current festival and event listings (☎415 391 2000, ⓦonlyinsanfrancisco.com).

JANUARY

SF Sketchfest Mid-Jan; ⓦsfsketchfest.com. This weeklong celebration of sketch comedy, held at venues all over the city, gains a higher profile every year, drawing both up-and-coming comedians and major names (Brian Posehn, Eugene Mirman, Patton Oswalt), as well as esteemed troupes such as the Kids in the Hall. $10–40.

Edwardian Ball Late Jan; ⓦedwardianball.com. Inspired by the world of macabre Victorian author/illustrator Edward Gorey, this multi-night event often held at the Regency Ballroom (see p.182) is filled with Tim Burton-esque costumes, so expect lots of corsets, eyeliner and stripey tights. There's also plenty of Edwardian period dress, waltzing, circus performers, burlesque dancers, cabaret music, Grand Guignol-inspired theatre and creepy artwork. $20–32.

Chinese New Year Festival & Parade Late Jan or early/mid-Feb; ☎415 986 1370, ⓦchineseparade .com. The first major ethnic festival in San Francisco's year, this super-hyped event takes over Chinatown for the better part of a week with a colourful flurry of activity. It culminates with the Golden Dragon Parade – one of the biggest of its kind anywhere – featuring floats, lion dancers, martial arts, marching bands and, naturally, a 75ft-long dragon. Free.

Vietnamese New Year's Tet Festival Late Jan or early/mid-Feb; ☎415 351 1038, ⓦvietccsf.org. This far lower-key answer to Chinatown's annual glitzy spectacle takes place along the heart of Little Saigon, Larkin St in the Tenderloin. With food, firecrackers and fun, it can't be beat for authenticity. Free.

FEBRUARY

San Francisco IndieFest Early to mid-Feb; ☎415 820 3907, ⓦsfindie.com. Perhaps the most challenging and intriguing of the city's glut of film festivals, IndieFest allows filmgoers to catch gritty dramas or lo-fi comedies from new filmmakers at a handful of repertory houses around the city. The same organization runs a similar documentary festival, DocFest, in early May, as well as the Hole in the Head festival (focused on horror, sci-fi and fantasy) every June. $9 and up.

San Francisco Bluegrass and Old-Time Festival Mid-Feb; ⓦsfbluegrass.org. Banjo, ukulele, jug and washboard players seize the spotlight at this festival, dedicated to bluegrass and other styles of music popularized in the days before amplification. Shows are held at venues all over San Francisco and Berkeley. Free–$30.

Valentine's Day Pillow Fight Feb 14, 6pm. At the stroke of 6pm every Valentine's Day, hundreds of locals let millions of feathers fly in this mass pillow fight either in front of the Ferry Building or in adjacent Justin Herman Plaza – bring your own pillow to join in. Free.

Noise Pop Late Feb; ⓦnoisepop.com. Now a civic institution, this nationally respected music festival presents legendary independent acts alongside fresh-faced bands. It's thankfully free of the music-industry hype associated with other major festivals such as South by Southwest and CMJ, and in recent years, its schedule has expanded to include film, art, panel discussions and even an exposition of handmade goods. $10 and up.

MARCH

Other Minds Early March; ☎415 934 8134, ⓦother minds.org. Renowned experimental composers such as Laurie Anderson, John Cage and Philip Glass debut their latest works at San Francisco Jewish Community Center's Kanbar Hall. Many performances are preceded by one-hour panel discussions. $20 and up.

San Francisco International Asian American Film Festival Mid-March; ⓦcaamedia.org/festival. Regarded as the nation's premier festival for films both from Asia and by Asian-Americans, this major annual event boasts a varied roster of screenings that range from campy kung-fu flicks to intense political dramas. Most films are shown at the Sundance Kabuki and the Castro Theatre, with a smattering of others appearing in San Jose and Berkeley. $9 and up.

St Patrick's Day Sun before March 17; ⓦsfstpatricks dayparade.com. Given San Francisco's traditionally strong Irish population, it's no surprise that much of the city seems to dress in forty shades of green to celebrate St Patrick's Day. A lengthy parade begins at noon at Market and Second streets and continues to Civic Center; arrive a few hours early for an unencumbered view. The city's innumerable Irish pubs – especially the less-touristed spots in the Richmond and Sunset districts – offer an equally fun experience. Free.

APRIL

St Stupid's Day Parade April 1, noon; ⓦsaintstupid .com. Held on April Fool's Day, this parade starting at Justin Herman Plaza poses as a taunt to all things business- and religion-related, but is really just an absurdist opportunity for locals to act silly. Expect clownish clothes, circus-sideshow antics and other displays of whimsy. Free.

Anarchist Bookfair Early April; ⓦsfbookfair.wordpress .com. True to San Francisco's dissident spirit, this free book fair – presented by Bound Together Anarchist Collective Bookstore (see p.202) – at the San Francisco County Fair Building in Golden Gate Park offers radical literature of all stripes. Speakers, films and panels tackle topics such as the occupation of Palestine and the modern anarchist identity. Free.

WonderCon Early April; ☎619 491 2475, ⓦcomic-con.org/wc. Stormtroopers (among other characters) swarm Downtown San Francisco for this huge, three-day comic convention at the Moscone Center, and it also brings out characters from anime and every sci-fi and fantasy film imaginable. Panels address topics such as misogyny in comics, while comic artists and movie stars make appearances; films are also previewed here. $10 and up.

Northern California Cherry Blossom Festival Early to mid-April; ☎415 563 2313, ⓦnccbf.org. Charming festival that, for two consecutive weekends, transforms Japantown's drab concrete-and-plaster environs into a colourful celebration of all things *Nippon*. Highlights include martial arts demonstrations, food booths, the Queen Program and the vibrant Grand Parade. Free.

Sisters of Perpetual Indulgence Easter Celebration Easter Sun; ☎415 820 9697, ⓦthesisters.org. An irreverent Resurrection celebration in Dolores Park hosted by the original order of the infamous Sisters (see p.104). Bring a picnic lunch – devilled eggs always seem to go down well – to this cross-dressing carnival, where you can enjoy face-painting and egg-hunting (for kids), and live music, burlesque and the fantastic "Hunky Jesus" contest (for adults). Free.

RoboGames Late April; ⓦrobogames.net. The world's largest open robot competition brings in tinkerers from far and wide to the San Mateo County Fairgrounds (twenty miles south of San Francisco) for competitions between combat robots, walking humanoids, soccer bots, sumo bots and kung-fu androids. Tickets $20.

San Francisco International Film Festival Late April to early May; ☎415 561 5000, ⓦsffs.org. This high-profile two-week event screens over two hundred films annually, and while the selection is inevitably eclectic and oddball, it's a great place to discover lesser-known directors from other continents. Primary venues are the Castro Theatre and Sundance Kabuki. $13.

MAY

San Francisco Cinco de Mayo Festival Weekend nearest to May 5; ☎415 206 7754, ⓦsfcincodemayo.com. The Mexican victory at the battle of Puebla is commemorated with a weekend-long fiesta in the Mission. Raucous, booze-filled and fun, activities take place in Dolores Park, while the parade runs along Mission St. Free.

International AIDS Candlelight Memorial Third Sun in May; ⓦcandlelightmemorial.org. An annual tradition since 1983, this hushed procession leads to Civic Center from the intersection of Castro and Market and commemorates the lives of those who have passed away from AIDS.

Bay to Breakers Third Sun in May; ☎415 359 2800, ⓦbaytobreakers.com. Originally founded to raise locals' spirits in the wake of the cataclysmic earthquake and fire of 1906, this campy footrace is still one of the most fun events on the city's calendar. The official race begins at 8am near the Bay (Howard and Spear streets) and ends 12km later at the Pacific Ocean's breakers (specifically, the far west end of Golden Gate Park); really, though, it's just another excuse for San Franciscans to go costume-crazy and drink, and with hordes of side entertainment and food and drink stalls along the route, it's not to be missed. Free to watch.

Maker Faire Late May; ⓦmakerfaire.com. Bay Area science geeks and closet inventors get a chance to shine at this two-day festival held by *Make* magazine. Held at the San Mateo County Event Center, twenty miles south of San Francisco, the enormous event consists of science projects, craft demonstrations, educational workshops and competitions, and features all manner of inventions and oddities, from a pedal-powered bus to a solar-powered chariot pulled by an Arnold Schwarzenegger robot. $25.

Carnaval Memorial Day weekend; ☎415 642 1748, ⓦcarnavalsf.com. San Francisco's answer to Brazil's Carnaval and New Orleans' Mardi Gras, only without the religious context and held in sunny May rather than rainy Feb (all the better for the scantily clad samba dancers). Expect huge feathers, colourful floats and bumping Brazilian music during the parade that runs through the outer blocks of the Mission. $30 for grandstand parade seating; otherwise, free.

JUNE

San Francisco Ethnic Dance Festival Early June to early July; ☎415 474 3914, ⓦworldartswest.org. After auditioning hundreds of Bay Area dance companies, this lengthy festival showcases the finest, performing every kind of dance under the sun: ballet folklorico to belly dance. Tickets $20 and up.

Haight-Ashbury Street Fair Mid-June; ⓦhaightashburystreetfair.org. Signalling the start of San Francisco's street fair season, this single-day schlockfest along Haight St offers yet another chance to pick up a tie-dyed T-shirt or ornamental bong. Still, several local food vendors make it potentially worth checking out. Free.

North Beach Festival Mid-June; ☎415 989 2220, ⓦnorthbeachchamber.com. Centred on Washington Square Park over two days, this is the oldest street fair in the city, and thanks to its pizza-tossing contests, street art and dozens of food stalls, it's retained its decades-old charm. Don't miss the pet-blessing ceremonies in the shrine of St Francis of Assisi. Free.

Frameline Mid-to late June; ☎415 703 8650, ⓦframeline.org. Now well into its fourth decade, this renowned filmfest boasts more than 250 gay- and lesbian-themed works from across the world, from intense documentaries to sloppy romances. Naturally, the Castro Theatre is the main venue. $12 and up.

San Francisco Pride Late June; ☎415 864 0831, ⓦsfpride.org. Crowds of up to half a million pack Market St for what is annually one of the biggest street parties in the

15

US; afterwards, Civic Center Plaza hosts a giant block party, with outdoor discos, live bands and numerous crafts and food stands. Also worth taking part in is Pink Night, an evening when the Castro is virtually pedestrianized by thousands of revellers. Free.

Stern Grove Festival Mid-June to late Aug; ☎415 252 6252, ⓦsterngrove.org. Summer-long programme of Sun afternoon concerts that's a San Francisco institution. Performances span jazz and classical to modern dance and international music, and all take place in a stunning grove of eucalyptus trees where you're free to picnic. For particularly popular acts, arrive early to snag a good spot; also note that it's best to take transit – the #28-19th Ave bus and several Muni streetcars will drop you within close distance. Free.

15

JULY

Fillmore Jazz Festival Early July; ☎1 800 310 6563, ⓦfillmorejazzfestival.com. Billing itself as the largest free-admission jazz festival on the West Coast, this two-day event spans a full dozen blocks along Fillmore St, from affluent Pacific Heights down into the earthier Western Addition. Three stages host continuous performances by more than three hundred artists. Free.

Independence Day July 4; ⓦpier39.com/events. San Francisco's red-white-and-blue fireworks show is viewed by most from a pair of prominent areas along the city's northern waterfront: Crissy Field in the Presidio (arrive early to stake out a spot) and Fisherman's Wharf (mainly for tourists). Free.

Fire Arts Festival Mid-July; ☎415 444 0919, ⓦthecrucible.org. Flames shoot every which way and electric sparks light up the night as the Crucible – an Oakland non-profit centre for industrial arts – hosts this multi-day festival featuring a wide array of interactive fire-sculpture installations. The event was on hiatus at the time of writing, so check the Crucible's website for updates. $40.

Up Your Alley Late July; ☎415 777 3247, ⓦfolsom streetfair.com/alley. The younger – and far more brazen – brother of the Folsom Street Fair (see opposite), Up Your Alley takes over adjacent Dore Alley for one July Sunday with as much raunchy sex and hardcore BDSM as you can handle. Definitely not for the easily shocked. $7.

AfroSolo Arts Festival Late July to mid-Oct; ☎415 771 2376, ⓦafrosolo.org. This music, arts and culture festival – held at various locations around San Francisco over several months – celebrates the works, struggles and achievements of African-Americans and artists from all over the African Diaspora. Ticket prices vary wildly from event to event, so check the festival website.

AUGUST

Nihonmachi Street Fair Mid-Aug; ⓦnihonmachi streetfair.org. Weekend-long Pan-Asian festival in Japantown featuring lion dancers, plenty of kids'

amusements, live music and, in many years, an Asian-American bike show. The biggest draw, though, is the Hawaiian food vendors. Free.

Outside Lands Mid-Aug; ⓦsfoutsidelands.com. Kick-started in the late 2000s, this ambitious three-day music festival at Golden Gate Park's Polo Fields brings in tens of thousands of concertgoers to see major headliners such as Radiohead, Pearl Jam and Arcade Fire. Local underground acts play the smaller stages. $150–200.

Rock Make Festival Late Aug; ⓦrockmake.com. An overwhelmingly popular single-day block party, the Mission's Rock Make brings together close to twenty bands and dozens upon dozens of local food and craft vendors. Free.

Burning Man Late Aug to early Sept; ☎415 863 5263, ⓦburningman.com. Surreal – and surreally expensive – event that takes place hundreds of miles from the Bay Area in northern Nevada's Black Rock Desert, but is listed here since a fair portion of the region seems to attend in increasing numbers each year. Part art installation fest, part extreme camping trip, part headtrip and, above all, a major party, Burning Man offers its thousands of attendees a psychedelic stay in a temporary, money-free civilization. All activities are centred around a 50ft-high sculpture of a man's figure that's ritually burned the night before Labor Day at the end of the festival. $210–320.

SEPTEMBER

San Francisco Shakespeare Festival Early to late Sept; ☎415 558 0888, ⓦsfshakes.org. Staged at the Main Post Parade Ground Lawn in the Presidio, this month-long festival presents Bard classics each Sat and Sun. Plan to arrive at least two hours early to ensure a seat. Check the website for shows and showtimes. Free.

Ghirardelli Square Chocolate Festival Early Sept; ☎415 775 5500, ⓦghirardellisq.com/events. Woefully commercial choco-fest, although at least all proceeds benefit local charity Project Open Hand. If nothing else, it allows you to enter a sundae-eating contest. $20.

San Francisco Fringe Festival Early to mid-Sept; ☎415 931 1094, ⓦsffringe.org. This offshoot of the famed Edinburgh Festival was founded in 1983 when performers were rejected for the Scottish showcase. Don't let the pretensions of certain shows put you off the gems you'll often uncover throughout this twelve-day marathon of more than 250 events. Its performance nexus is the Exit Theatre (see p.189), near Union Square. $8 and up.

Mission Creek Music & Arts Festival Mid-Sept; ⓦmcmf.org. A terrific event for anyone wishing to catch innovative local and underground national rock, psych and folk acts, Mission Creek typically gets going with a few nights' worth of shows in Oakland before moving across the bay to San Francisco for its final five or so days, taking place at smaller venues such as *The Knockout* and *Amnesia* (see p.184). $5 and up.

Folsom Street Fair Last Sun in Sept; ☎ 415 777 3247, ⓦ folsomstreetfair.com. San Francisco's wildest voyeur party takes over Folsom St in South of Market, when upwards of 400,000 come together to celebrate all things fetish. Lashings of leather-related events dominate – don't forget your harness and skin-tight chaps if you plan to attend – but even so, the atmosphere remains remarkably friendly and fun. $10.

OCTOBER

Alternative Press Expo Early Oct; ☎ 619 491 2475, ⓦ comic-con.org/ape. A huge two-day convention for comic book artists held at the Concourse Exhibition Center, where big names and newcomers alike network, participate in workshops and shill their wares. $8–12.

Fleet Week Early to mid-Oct; ☎ 650 599 5057, ⓦ fleetweek.us. For one week every autumn, San Francisco assumes a patriotic, all-American image as it plays host to the US Navy. Citizens get the opportunity to tour military hardware, but the real draw is the aerial acrobatics of the Blue Angels precision-flying squadron as they roar their fighter jets over the bay and city in stunning (if deafening) manoeuvres, best viewed from the Marina Green or Crissy Field along the northern waterfront. Free.

Hardly Strictly Bluegrass Early Oct; ⓦ strictly bluegrass.com. Hugely popular three-day festival that sees icons of country, blues, bluegrass and rock – Emmylou Harris and Elvis Costello are regular headliners – perform under usually sunny skies in Golden Gate Park. A wide range of acts are spread across nearly a half-dozen stages, and thanks to local philanthropist (and bluegrass devotee) Warren Hellman, admission is free.

LovEvolution Early Oct; ☎ 415 820 1423, ⓦ sflovevolution.org. Based on Berlin's enormous Love Parade, this techno music festival and parade is a glorious celebration of dance music. Whether the day event along Market St and in Civic Center Plaza happens or not, its promoters also produce events at various venues through the week, so check the website. Free–$45.

Litquake Early to mid-Oct; ☎ 415 750 1497, ⓦ litquake.org. Local literati such as Lawrence Ferlinghetti, Daniel Handler and Gail Tsukiyama read, give talks or participate in panels in venues all over town at this annual week-long bonding session for writers. There are also workshops for budding novelists, while Lit Crawl (featuring three hundred authors in three hours at various Mission locales) is a popular cap to the week. Free–$10.

SFJazz Early Oct to mid-Nov; ☎ 415 788 7353, ⓦ sfjazz.org. Presenting shows at a range of unique venues throughout the city and Bay Area, SFJazz is one of the top such events in the US. Programming covers all kinds of jazz subgenres while showcasing groundbreaking legends and young lions alike, and its parent organization presents shorter spring and summer seasons as well. $25–75.

Castro Street Fair First Sun in Oct; ☎ 415 841 1824, ⓦ castrostreetfair.org. More arts-and-crafts than ass-and-chaps, this fair – the brainchild of legendary late City Supervisor Harvey Milk in the mid 1970s – features loads of local vendors selling handmade wares, plenty of food stalls and several stages of live entertainment. Definitely in the first-rank among San Francisco's innumerable neighbourhood street fairs. Free.

Treasure Island Music Festival Mid-Oct; ⓦ treasureislandfestival.com. Co-produced by Noise Pop (see p.226), this weekend-long event on Treasure Island in the middle of San Francisco Bay features separate days devoted to electronic/dance acts (Sat) and indie rock bands (Sun). It's an incomparable setting, but the flipside is that there's precious little parking on the island, necessitating a fleet of crowded transit shuttles from AT&T Park on the mainland. $100–120.

Half Moon Bay Art & Pumpkin Festival Mid-Oct; ⓦ miramarevents.com/pumpkinfest. Farmers around the self-proclaimed "World Pumpkin Capital" (see p.259) open their fields to pumpkin hunters, and the town hosts a range of pumpkin-based cooking and eating contests. Expect carvings, parades, costume contests and even weigh-offs between giants of their field. Free.

NOVEMBER

Dia de los Muertos Nov 2; ⓦ dayofthedeadsf.org. A sombre happening in which hordes of skeleton-dressed locals form a candlelit procession through the outer Mission; the contemplative celebration ends at Garfield Park, where participants pay tribute to deceased ancestors and loved ones with flowers and mementoes. A more elaborate event happens around the same time in Oakland's Fruitvale District, where *pan de muerto* (bread of the dead) and papier-mâché skulls and skeletons are widely available from vendors, and multiple stages host traditional Latin music and dance. Free.

Great Dickens Christmas Fair Late Nov to mid-Dec; ⓦ dickensfair.com. Something like a Victorian-era version of the Renaissance Faire – only held at the Cow Palace – this popular annual holiday gathering offers a chance to experience the music and dance of the period while enjoying the finest foods of the British Empire. You're bound to run into characters such as Father Christmas, Ebenezer Scrooge and the three Christmas ghosts as you flit about the unlikely, barn-like venue. $25.

DECEMBER

Bazaar Bizarre Mid-Dec; ⓦ bazaarbizarre.org. Usually held at Fort Mason's Herbst Pavilion, this event presents a handy opportunity to browse and buy one-of-a-kind holiday gifts – from handbags and body products to posters and children's apparel – made by hundreds of artists and crafters; craft workshops are also held. $2.

15

The Bay Area

Of the nearly seven million people who make their home in the San Francisco Bay Area, barely more than one in ten lives in the actual city of San Francisco. Everyone else is spread around one of the many less-renowned cities and suburbs that ring the bay, either down the Peninsula or across one of the two impressively engineered bridges that span the chilly waters of the world's most exquisite natural harbour. There's no doubt about the supporting role these places play in relation to San Francisco – always "the city" – but each has a distinctive character and contributes to the range of people and landscapes that makes the Bay Area one of the most desirable areas in the US.

Across the steel Bay Bridge, eight miles from downtown San Francisco, the **East Bay** is home to the lively, left-leaning cities of **Oakland** and **Berkeley**, which together have some of the best bookshops and restaurants in the greater Bay Area, as well as many live music venues. The weather's generally much sunnier and warmer here, too, and it's easy to reach by way of the BART trains that race under the Bay in a snappy seven minutes. The remainder of the East Bay is contained in Contra Costa County, which includes some leafy valleys and lofty **Mount Diablo**.

South of the city, the **Peninsula** holds some of San Francisco's oldest and most upscale suburbs, spreading down through the densely populated bayside, including **Palo Alto**. The **beaches** and seaside towns such as **Half Moon Bay** to the west, however, are excellent and a couple of youth hostels in old lighthouses perch on the edge of the Pacific.

To the north lie some of California's most beautiful land- and seascapes in **Marin County**, a mountainous peninsula that's half wealthy suburbia and half unspoiled hiking country, with **redwood forests** rising sheer out of the thundering Pacific Ocean. A range of 2500-foot peaks, crowned by **Mount Tamalpais**, divides the county down the middle, separating the yacht clubs and plush bay-view houses of **Sausalito** and **Tiburon** from the nearly untouched Pacific Coast, which culminates in the **Point Reyes National Seashore**.

Further northeast, the **Wine Country** might be your first – indeed your only – taste of Northern California, though it's by no means typical. The two valleys of **Napa** and **Sonoma** unfold along thirty miles of rolling hills and premium real estate, home to California wine barons and San Franciscan weekenders wanting to escape in style.

GETTING AROUND THE EAST BAY

By subway BART subway (☎ 510 465 2278, ⌨ bart.gov) connects Oakland and Berkeley with many other parts of Contra Costa County, as well as San Francisco (see p.25).

By bus AC Transit (☎ 510 817 1717 ext 1111, ⌨ actransit .org) provides a good bus service around the entire East Bay, especially Oakland and Berkeley; the flat fare is $2 but you can pick up a transfer between buses or from BART. Contra Costa County Connection (☎ 925 676 7500, ⌨ cccta .org) also runs buses to most of the inland areas, including the John Muir and Eugene O'Neill historic houses.

By bike One of the best ways to get around the East Bay is by bike. A fine cycle route follows Skyline and Grizzly Peak boulevards along the wooded crest of the hills between Berkeley and Lake Chabot, while within Berkeley itself, the Ohlone Greenway makes for a pleasant cycling or walking route. Bike rental is available in Berkeley (see p.246).

By car A car can be useful for getting to the more distant parts of the East Bay but parking can be a problem in the downtown and business districts of both Oakland and Berkeley, where public transport is the preferred option.

16

Oakland

…what was the use of me having come from Oakland it was not natural for me to have come from there yes write about it if I like or anything if I like but not there, there is no there there.

Gertrude Stein, *Everybody's Autobiography*

As solidly working class as San Francisco is unconventional, **OAKLAND** is one of the busiest ports on the West Coast and the western terminal of the rail network. Though there are few major sights to lure tourists, a quick jaunt over from San Francisco can be justified by the weather alone. Considered one of the best in the US, the East Bay's climate is sunny and mild when San Francisco is cold and dreary, making for great hiking around the redwood- and eucalyptus-covered hills above Downtown.

Oakland has more historical and literary associations than important sights, save for the outstanding **Oakland Museum**. The city is infamous for being the spawning ground of some of America's most unabashedly revolutionary **political movements**, such as the militant **Black Panthers** (see box, p.237) and the Symbionese Liberation Army, who demanded a ransom for kidnapped heiress Patty Hearst in the form of free food distribution to the poor. It's also the birthplace of literary legends **Gertrude Stein** and **Jack London**, who were contemporaries but from entirely different backgrounds – Stein was a stockbroker's daughter, while London, author of *Call of the Wild*, was an orphaned delinquent. The waterfront area where London used to steal oysters and

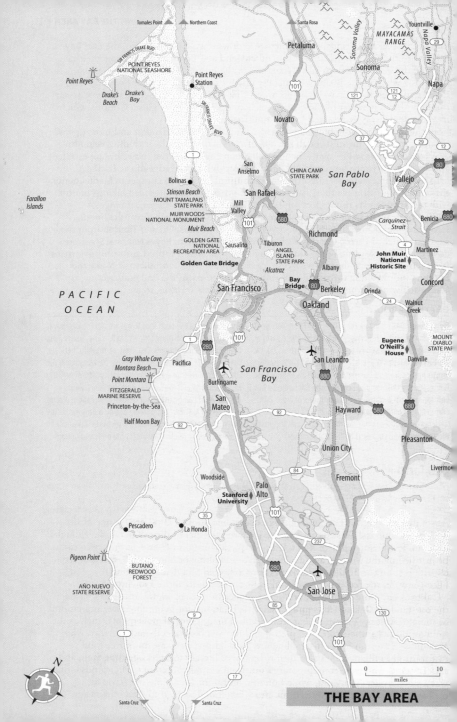

THE BAY AREA

OAKLAND WALKING TOURS

The City of Oakland sponsors free **"discovery tours"** of various neighbourhoods (☎ 510 238 3234); a popular excursion is the Oakland Historical Landmark Tour (Sun 1–3.30pm; free), beginning in front of the Oakland Museum at 10th and Fallon, and covering areas like Chinatown, Lake Merritt, Preservation Park and Jack London Square.

lobsters is now named in his memory, while Stein is all but ignored, unsurprisingly, given her famous proclamation about Oakland cited above.

Nowadays, rents in the increasingly popular **Rockridge** and **Lake Merritt** districts are approaching San Francisco prices. The city has also attracted a significant number of lesbians from San Francisco's Castro and Mission, as well as many artists pushed from their South of Market lofts by sky-high rents into the warehouses of West Oakland.

Downtown Oakland

Easily accessed from the 12th Street–Civic Center BART station, the open-air shopping and office space of **City Center** in the heart of **DOWNTOWN OAKLAND** can seem uncannily deserted outside of rush hours. Downtown's compact district of spruced-up Victorian storefronts overlooked by mostly modern skyscrapers took on its current appearance after entire blocks were cleared of houses following the collapse of the Cypress Freeway in the 1989 earthquake and its replacement by the I-980. At least some efforts were made to maintain the city's architectural heritage, most noticeably in the collection of characterful private properties of **Preservation Park** at 12th Street and Martin Luther King Jr Way.

16

Old Oakland
Along Ninth Street west of Broadway

The late nineteenth-century commercial centre, now tagged **Old Oakland**, underwent a major restoration some years ago. Observing the historic facades, especially between Clay and Washington, provides a glimpse of what Oakland once was. The section between Broadway and Clay is home to a fine **farmers' market** on Fridays (8am–2pm).

Chinatown
Between Seventh and Ninth streets

The bakeries and restaurants of Oakland's **Chinatown** are generally not as lively or picturesque as those of its more famous cousin across the Bay. Except, that is, on the last weekend in August, when the vibrant **Chinatown Street Fest** brings out traditional performing artists, food vendors and cooking and arts demonstrations.

City Hall
14th Street

The city experienced its greatest period of growth in the early twentieth century and many of the grand buildings of this era survive a few blocks north of Chinatown along Broadway, centred on the gigantic grass knoll of **Frank Ogawa Plaza** and the awkwardly imposing 1914 **City Hall**. The first government building designed as a skyscraper, City Hall was restored after the 1989 earthquake and the foundation now rests on 113 giant, but concealed, rubber shock absorbers so that it will sway rather than crumble whenever the next one hits. This area hosts the annual **Art and Soul Festival** over Labor Day weekend, featuring live music and art displays ($5).

The Tribune Tower and the African American Museum & Library

At 13th and Franklin stands Oakland's most unmistakable landmark, the lantern of the **Tribune Tower**, the 1920s-era former home of the *Oakland Tribune* newspaper. A few blocks west, the **African American Museum & Library** (659 14th St; Tues–Sat noon–5.30pm; free; ☎ 510 238 6716, ⊚ oaklandlibrary.org) is housed in an elegant

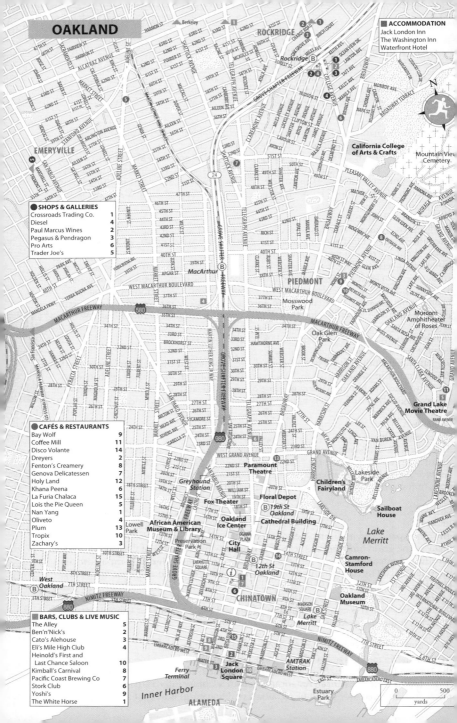

OAKLAND

ROCKRIDGE

EMERYVILLE

Berkeley

PIEDMONT

California College
of Arts & Crafts

Mountain View
Cemetery

Mosswood
Park

Oak Glen
Park

Morcom
Amphitheater
of Roses

Grand Lake
Movie Theatre

Paramount
Theatre

Lakeside
Park

Children's
Fairyland

Greyhound
Station

Fox Theater

Floral Depot

Sailboat
House

Oakland
Ice Center

79th St
Oakland

Cathedral Building

African American
Museum & Library

Lowell
Park

Preservation
Park

City
Hall

12th St
Oakland

Lake
Merritt

Lake
Merritt

Camron-
Stamford
House

West
Oakland

CHINATOWN

Oakland
Museum

Ferry
Terminal

Jack
London
Square

AMTRAK
Station

Estuary
Park

Inner Harbor

ALAMEDA

ACCOMMODATION
Jack London Inn
The Washington Inn
Waterfront Hotel

SHOPS & GALLERIES
Crossroads Trading Co.	1
Diesel	4
Paul Marcus Wines	2
Pegasus & Pendragon	3
Pro Arts	6
Trader Joe's	5

CAFÉS & RESTAURANTS
Bay Wolf	9
Coffee Mill	11
Disco Volante	14
Dreyers	2
Fenton's Creamery	8
Genova Delicatessen	7
Holy Land	12
Khana Peena	6
La Furia Chalaca	15
Lois the Pie Queen	1
Nan Yang	4
Oliveto	4
Plum	13
Tropix	10
Zachary's	3

BARS, CLUBS & LIVE MUSIC
The Alley	5
Ben'n'Nick's	2
Cato's Alehouse	3
Eli's Mile High Club	4
Heinold's First and Last Chance Saloon	10
Kimball's Carnival	8
Pacific Coast Brewing Co	7
Stork Club	6
Yoshi's	9
The White Horse	1

yards   500

OAKLAND ARCHITECTURE

Around the 19th Street BART station are some of the Bay Area's finest early twentieth-century buildings, highlighted by the outstanding Art Deco interior of the 1931 **Paramount Theatre** (2025 Broadway; tours 10am first and third Sat of month; $5; ☎ 510 465 6400, ⓦ paramounttheatre .com). The West Coast's answer to New York City's Radio City Music Hall, the Paramount shows Hollywood classics and hosts various live performances (see p.240). The theatre was designed by **Timothy L. Pflueger**, the San Francisco architect behind the Pacific Coast Stock Exchange, the Castro Theatre and many of the buildings on Treasure Island. The building boasts an eclectic mix of accoutrements, from the illuminated "fountain of light" stained-glass ceiling in the entrance to the mosaics and reliefs which adorn every inch of the interior.

Several buildings near the Paramount Theatre are equally flamboyant, ranging from the wafer-thin Gothic "flatiron" office tower of the **Cathedral Building** at Broadway and Telegraph to the Hindu temple-like facade of the magnificent 3500-seat **Fox Oakland** (see p.240) on Telegraph at 19th – the largest movie house west of Chicago at the time it was built in 1928. Across the street, the 1931 **Floral Depot**, a group of small, modern storefronts faced in black-and-blue terracotta tiles with shiny silver highlights, is also worth a look.

Neoclassical building whose upper floor has a display on the history of African-Americans in California from 1775 to 1900, as well as temporary exhibitions.

Lake Merritt and around

Five blocks east of Broadway, the eastern third of Downtown Oakland comprises **LAKE MERRITT**, a three-mile-circumference tidal lagoon that was bridged and dammed in the 1860s to become the centrepiece of Oakland's most desirable neighbourhood. The lake is also the nation's oldest wildlife refuge, and migrating flocks of ducks, geese and herons break their journeys here. To the north of the water, beyond the MacArthur Freeway, a wide range of cafés and shops line gradually diverging Grand and Lakeshore avenues. Note the huge Art Deco facade of the still-functioning **Grand Lake Movie Theater** (see p.240), a bastion of subversive political film.

Camron-Stanford House

1418 Lakeside Drive • 3rd Wed of month 1–5pm • $5 • ☎ 510 444 1876, ⓦ cshouse.org

Sadly, all that remains of the many fine houses that once circled the lake is this elegant edifice on the southwest shore, a graceful Italianate mansion whose sumptuous interior is open for visits monthly.

Lakeside Park

Sailboat House March–May Mon–Fri 10.30am–6pm, Sat & Sun 10.30am–5pm; summer Mon–Fri 9am–6pm, Sat & Sun 10am–6pm • Boats $10–18/hr, $10–20 deposit • ☎ 510 238 2196, ⓦ sailoakland.com **Gondola Servizio** From $40 for 30min • ☎ 510 663 6603, ⓦ gondolaservizio.com **Children's Fairyland** Times vary • $8 • ☎ 510 452 2259, ⓦ fairyland.org

The north shore of Lake Merritt is lined by **Lakeside Park**, where canoes, rowing boats, kayaks, pedal boats and a range of sailing boats can be rented from the **Sailboat House** or you can splash out to be serenaded on the overpriced but romantic Gondola Servizio. Children will enjoy the puppet shows and pony rides at the **Children's Fairyland**, along Grand Avenue on the northwest edge of the park. The lake is lit up every night by its "Necklace of Lights" and on the first weekend in June the park hosts the **Festival at the Lake**, when thousands enjoy non-stop music and performances.

Oakland Museum

1000 Oak St • Wed–Sun 11am–5pm, Fri till 9pm • $12, free first Sun of month • ☎ 510 238 2200, ⓦ museumca.org • Close to the Lake Merritt BART station

Two blocks south of Lake Merritt, the **Oakland Museum** is undoubtedly Oakland's prime tourist destination, not only by virtue of the exhibits but also for the superb

16

modern building in which it's housed, topped by a terraced rooftop sculpture garden giving great views out over the water and city. The museum covers three topics on as many floors, the first of which treats California's **ecology** in exhibits simulating a walk from the seaside through various natural habitats and climate zones right up to the 14,000-foot summits of the Sierra Nevada mountains. The second floor deals with California's **history**, from Native American habitats through the Spanish colonial and Gold Rush eras, up to the present day; artefacts on display include the guitar that Berkeley-born Country Joe MacDonald played at Woodstock in 1969. The third floor holds a broad survey of California **art and crafts**, including the splendid new Gallery of California Art, showcasing over eight hundred works.

Jack London Square and around

Half a mile south from Downtown Oakland, at the foot of Broadway on the waterfront, **JACK LONDON SQUARE** is Oakland's main concession to the tourist trade. This complex of harbourfront boutiques and restaurants was named after the self-taught writer who grew up pirating shellfish around here – though it's about as distant from the wandering spirit of the man as could be. Apart from the small reconstructed cabin from the Alaska Yukon that London carved his initials into, the site most worth stopping at is **Heinold's First and Last Chance Saloon**, a bar, built in 1883 from the hull of a whaling ship, where Jack London actually drank. The square is also home to a nine-screen multiplex cinema and **Yoshi's World Class Jazz House**, the Bay Area's – if not the West Coast's – premier jazz club (see p.240).

On Sunday, the square bustles with a weekly **farmers' market**. Otherwise, a few short blocks inland lies a warehouse district with a couple of good places to eat and drink lurking among the train tracks; the area is most lively early in the morning, from about 5am, when a daily **produce market** is held along Third and Fourth streets.

Historic vessels

Light Ship Relief Tours: Sat & Sun 11am–4pm · $5 **USS Potomac** Tours: Wed, Fri & Sun 11am–3pm · $10 · ☎ 510 627 1215, ⓦ usspotomac.org

At the western end of Jack London Square, by the foot of Clay Street, are a couple of **historic vessels**; dockside tours are available for both the *Light Ship Relief* and the USS *Potomac*, Franklin D. Roosevelt's famous "floating White House".

West Oakland

WEST OAKLAND may be the nearest East Bay BART stop to San Francisco, but it is light years away from that city's prosperity. The continuing upward mobility of Emeryville, directly to the north, may well point toward a brighter future for the whole area, but for now there's still little to tempt tourists, as it remains an industrial district of warehouses, housing projects from the 1960s, and decaying Victorian houses.

Port View Park

At the end of Seventh Street

A good place to watch the huge container ships that pass by, **Port View Park** stands on the site of the old Transbay ferry terminal. The Black Panthers once held court in West Oakland (see box opposite), and in 1989, their co-founder Huey Newton was gunned down here in a drug-related revenge attack. Now the neighbourhood's dirt-cheap rents and open spaces are finally attracting artists from across the Bay, indicating that the first signs of its surprisingly tardy gentrification are finally afoot.

East Oakland

The bulk of Oakland spreads along foothills and flatlands to the east of Downtown. Gertrude Stein grew up here, though when she returned years later in search of her childhood home it had been torn down and replaced by a dozen Craftsman-style

THE BLACK PANTHERS

Formed amidst the poverty of West Oakland in 1966 by black-rights activists Huey Newton and Bobby Seale, the **Black Panther Party for Self-Defense** captured the media spotlight with its leather-jacketed, beret-sporting members and their militant rhetoric and occasional gun battles with police. The party was started as a civil-rights organization influenced by Malcolm X's call to black Americans to rely on themselves for defence and dignity. Mixing socialism with black pride, the Panthers aimed to eradicate poverty and drug use in America's inner cities and monitor police brutality, arguing that if the government wouldn't do it, they would.

The Panthers' membership grew nationally as the group captured the national spotlight over the trial of Newton for the murder of an Oakland police officer in 1969. Released from prison a year later when his conviction was overturned, Newton sought to revamp the Panthers image by developing "survival programs" in black communities, including the establishment of free medical clinics, breakfasts for children, shelter for the homeless and jobs for the unemployed. But infighting within the party took a heavy toll, and when Newton fled to Cuba in 1974 to avoid prosecution for drug use, a series of resignations ensued. By the end of the 1970s, stripped of its original leadership and under constant attack by the media, the group disbanded.

For more on the Panthers, check out the occasional **Black Panther Tours** ($25; ☎ 505 884 4860, ⓦ blackpanthertours.com), which depart at noon across from the main Downtown library on West 18th Street.

bungalows – the simple 1920s wooden houses that cover most of **EAST OAKLAND**, each fronted by a patch of lawn and divided from its neighbour by a concrete driveway.

16

Joaquin Miller Park
Northeast of Joaquin Miller Rd · AC Transit bus #64 from Downtown

A quick way out from the gridded streets and sidewalks of the city is to head east up into the hills to **Joaquin Miller Park**, the most easily accessible of Oakland's hilltop parks. It stands on the former grounds of "The Hights", the misspelled home of the "Poet of the Sierras", Joaquin Miller, who made his name playing the eccentric frontier American in the literary salons of 1870s London.

Mormon Temple
4770 Lincoln Ave · Museum: daily 9am–9pm; library: daily 7am–8pm · Free · Museum ☎ 510 531 1475; library ☎ 510 531 3200

Perched in the hills at the foot of the park, the pointed towers of the **Mormon Temple** look like missile-launchers designed by the Wizard of Oz – unmissable by day and floodlit at night. In December, speakers hidden in the landscaping make it seem as if the plants are singing Christmas carols. Though only confirmed Mormons can go inside the temple itself, there are great views out over the entire Bay Area from the grounds. There's also a branch of the Mormons' **genealogical research library**, where you can try tracing your family's ancestry, regardless of your faith.

Chabot Space & Science Center
10000 Skyline Blvd · Wed & Thurs, Sun 10am–5pm, Fri & Sat 10am–10pm · $14.95, including one planetarium and one Megadome Theater show · ☎ 510 336 7373, ⓦ chabotspace.org · AC Transit bus #53 from the Fruitvale BART station

Several miles up in the hills behind the Mormon Temple stands the **Chabot Space & Science Center**. This modern museum features interactive displays, a fine **planetarium**, the impressive **Megadome Theater** and a state-of-the-art **observatory**.

North Oakland and Rockridge

The high-priced hills of **North Oakland** suffered the worst damage in the horrific October 1991 Oakland **fire**, which destroyed three thousand homes and killed 26 people. As a result the lush vegetation that made the area so attractive will never be allowed to grow back fully, in order to prevent any more fires.

The Morcom Amphitheater of Roses and around

The **Morcom Amphitheater of Roses**, three blocks east of Broadway on Oakland Avenue (April–Oct daily dawn–dusk; free; ☎ 510 238 3187), has eight acres of pools, trees and roses, which are in full bloom from May to September. Nearby **Piedmont Avenue** is lined by a number of small bookstores and cafés, while a mile north along the avenue is the **Mountain View Cemetery**, laid out in 1863 by Frederick Law Olmsted, designer of New York's Central Park and San Francisco's Golden Gate Park.

Robert Sibley Regional Preserve

Broadway Terrace climbs up to small **Lake Temescal** – where you can swim in summer – and continues to the forested ridge at the **Robert Sibley Regional Preserve**, which includes the 1761-foot volcanic cone of Round Top Peak, offering panoramas of the entire Bay Area. Skyline Boulevard runs through the park and is popular with cyclists, who ride the twelve miles south to Lake Chabot or follow Grizzly Peak Boulevard five miles north to Tilden Park through the Berkeley Hills.

Rockridge

AC Transit #51 bus from Downtown Oakland

Most of the Broadway traffic cuts off onto College Avenue through Oakland's most upscale shopping district, **ROCKRIDGE**. Spreading for half a mile on either side of the Rockridge BART station, the quirky stores and restaurants here, despite their undeniable upwardly mobile overtones, are better than Piedmont's in variety and volume and make for a pleasant afternoon's wander or night out.

16

ARRIVAL AND DEPARTURE
OAKLAND

By plane Oakland Airport ☎ 510 563 2984, automated flight information ☎ 1 800 992 7433, ⓦ oaklandairport .com. The AirBART shuttle van (every 15min; $3; ☎ 510 569 8310) runs to the Coliseum BART station, for connections to Downtown Oakland and beyond. There are numerous door-to-door shuttle buses that run from the airport to East Bay stops, such as A1 American (☎ 1 877 378 3596, ⓦ a1americanshuttle.com); the fare to Downtown Oakland is around $20, only marginally less than a taxi.

By train Amtrak terminates at Second Street near Jack London Square in Downtown Oakland.

By subway Oakland is linked to San Francisco and other points in the East Bay via the BART subway (☎ 510 465 2278 from the East Bay, ⓦ bart.gov).

By bus The Greyhound station is in a dodgy area just north of Downtown Oakland, alongside the I-980 freeway at 2103 San Pablo Ave (☎ 510 832 4730). AC Transit runs buses on a number of routes to Oakland from the Transbay Terminal in San Francisco. These operate all night and are the only way of getting across the Bay by public transport once BART shuts down between midnight and 1am.

By ferry The most enjoyable way to arrive is aboard an Alameda–Oakland ferry ($6.25 each way; ☎ 510 522 3300, ⓦ eastbayferry.com), leaving every hour from San Francisco's Ferry Building and Pier 39 to Oakland's Jack London Square.

By car If you're driving into the East Bay from San Francisco, allow yourself plenty of time: the Bay Bridge and I-80 are jam-packed sixteen hours a day. Having two or more people in the vehicle can save time from 5–9am and 3–7pm on weekdays, when faster car-pool lanes are in effect.

INFORMATION

Tourist information The Visit Oakland office, located next to the enormous *Marriott Hotel* at 463 11th St (Mon–Fri 8.30am–5pm; ☎ 510 839 9000, ⓦ visitoakland.org), is the best source of maps, brochures and information on lodging and activities in the metropolitan area.

Hiking and horseriding For information on hiking or riding horses in the many parks that top the Oakland and Berkeley hills, contact the East Bay Regional Parks District, 2950 Peralta Oaks Court, Oakland (☎ 510 562 7275, ⓦ ebparks.org).

ACCOMMODATION

Oakland offers far fewer hotels and motels than San Francisco but prices are generally lower. There are also fewer B&Bs than in Berkeley but it's still worth checking with the Berkeley & Oakland Bed and Breakfast Network (☎ 510 547 6380, ⓦ bbonline.com/ca/berkeley-oakland).

HOTELS AND MOTELS

Jack London Inn 444 Embarcadero West, Jack London Square ☎510 444 2032 or 1 800 549 8780, ⓦjacklondoninn.com; map p.234. Kitschy motorlodge with a 1950s feel thanks to its wooden lobby fittings; excellent online rates. $40

The Washington Inn 495 10th St, Downtown ☎510 452 1776, ⓦthewashingtoninn.com; map p.234. Best of the Downtown options, this pleasant hotel with a touch of European style offers comfort in a convenient location. $89

Waterfront Hotel 10 Washington St, Jack London Square ☎510 836 3800 or 1 888 842 5333, ⓦjdvhotels .com; map p.234. Plush, modern hotel, with smart, sizeable rooms located on the best stretch of the Oakland waterfront, right among all the amenities. $134

CAMPGROUND

Chabot Family Campground off I-580 in East Oakland ☎510 562 2267 or 1 888 327 2757, ⓦebparks.org. Walk-in, tent-only places, with hot showers and lots of good hiking nearby; reservations recommended in summer; sites for one vehicle and up to ten people from $20

EATING

Oakland is hardly regarded as a gourmet paradise; it does, though, have a tradition of unpretentious all-American diners along with a smattering of good multi-ethnic restaurants. The trendier Rockridge area offers some classier options.

CAFÉS, DELIS AND DINERS

Coffee Mill 3363 Grand Ave, North Oakland ☎510 465 4224; map p.234. A range of great coffee and tasty pastries is served in a spacious room that doubles as an art gallery and often hosts poetry readings. Daily 7am–6pm.

Dreyers 5925 College Ave, Rockridge ☎510 658 0502; map p.234. Oakland's rich ice cream, distributed throughout California, is served at this small, slightly dull Rockridge café. Mon–Thurs & Sun noon–9pm, Fri & Sat noon–10pm.

Fentons Creamery 4226 Piedmont Ave, North Oakland ☎510 658 7000; map p.234. A brightly lit 1950s ice-cream and sandwich shop, with a renowned line in handcrafted versions of both. Mon–Thurs 11am–11pm, Fri & Sat 9am–midnight, Sun 9am–11pm.

Genova Delicatessen 5095 Telegraph Ave, North Oakland ☎510 652 7401; map p.234. This friendly deli serves up superb sandwiches for around $5. Daily 10am–10pm.

Holy Land 677 Rand Ave, Oakland ☎510 272 0535; map p.234. Casual diner-style kosher restaurant just beyond the freeway north of Lake Merritt, serving moderately priced Israeli food, including excellent falafel. Mon–Thurs & Sun 11am–9pm, Fri 11am–sunset.

★ **Lois the Pie Queen** 851 60th St at Adeline, North Oakland ☎510 658 5616; map p.234. Famous around the Bay for its Southern-style sweet potato and fresh fruit pies, this cosy diner also serves massive, down-home breakfasts and Sunday dinners, all for around $10 or less. Mon–Fri 8am–2pm, Sat 7am–3pm, Sun 7am–4pm.

RESTAURANTS

★ **Bay Wolf** 3853 Piedmont Ave, North Oakland ☎510 655 6004, ⓦbaywolf.com; map p.234. Chic restaurant whose menu is influenced by the cuisine of Tuscany, Provence and the Basque country, featuring specials like double mustard-tarragon chicken or grilled Alaska halibut. Most mains over $20. Daily 5.30–10pm.

Disco Volante 347 4th St, Downtown Oakland ☎510 663 0271, ⓦdiscovolanteoakland.com; map p.234. Cool new California-style bistro with frequent live music and specialities like Point Reyes oysters and smoked ribs. Mon–Wed 11.30am–midnight, Thurs & Fri 11.30am–1.30am, Sat 6pm–1.30am, Sun 6pm–midnight.

Khana Peena 5316 College Ave, Rockridge ☎510 658 2300, ⓦthemenupage.com/khanapeenaoakland; map p.234. Fine Indian restaurant in terms of both decor and quality of cuisine. A wide range of curries and tandoori dishes is available, plus a great lunchtime buffet. Daily 11.30am–3pm & 5–9.30pm.

★ **La Furia Chalaca** 310 Broadway, Downtown Oakland ☎510 451 4206, ⓦlafuriachalaca.com; map p.234. Great range of seafood with pasta and various Peruvian sauces, plus some meat dishes such as a fine braised pork stew. Mon–Thurs 11am–3pm & 5–10pm, Fri & Sat 11am–midnight, Sun 11am–9pm.

Nan Yang 6048 College Ave, Rockridge ☎510 655 3298, ⓦnanyangrockridge.com; map p.234. Burmese food served in large, palate-exciting portions. The political refugee owner/chef is willing to discuss all his esoteric delicacies. Mon 5–10pm, Tues–Sat 11am–3pm & 5–10pm, Sun noon–3pm & 5–9.30pm.

Oliveto 5655 College Ave, Rockridge ☎510 547 5356, ⓦoliveto.com; map p.234. Expensive gourmet Italian cuisine is the order of the day in the main dining room; the less pricey basement section has more basic fare on offer. Mon–Thurs 11.30am–2pm & 5.30–9pm, Fri 11.30am–2pm & 5.30–9.30pm, Sat 5.30–10pm, Sun 5–9pm.

Plum 2214 Broadway, Downtown Oakland ☎510 444 7586, ⓦplumoakland.com; map p.234. This highly rated newcomer serves up a range of delights, from oyster stew to beet and goat's cheese salad to hearty pork sandwiches. Mon–Fri 11am–2pm & 5pm–1am, Sat & Sun 5pm–1am.

Tropix 3814 Piedmont Ave, North Oakland ☎510 653 2444, ⓦtropixrestaurant.com; map p.234. Large portions of fruity Caribbean delicacies at reasonable prices,

16

with authentic jerk sauce and mango juice. Tues–Thurs 11.30am–9pm, Fri 11.30am–10pm, Sat 10am–10pm, Sun 10am–9pm.
Zachary's 5801 College Ave, Rockridge ☎ 510 655 6385, ⓦ zacharys.com; map p.234. Zealously defended as the best pizzeria in the Bay Area, *Zachary's* is also one of the only places offering rich, deep-dish, Chicago-style pizza. Mon–Thurs & Sun 11am–10pm, Fri & Sat 11am–10.30pm.

DRINKING, NIGHTLIFE AND ENTERTAINMENT

The widely available *East Bay Express* (issued every Wed; free) has the most comprehensive listings of what's on in the vibrant East Bay music and arts scene.

BARS

The Alley 3325 Grand Ave, North Oakland ☎ 510 444 8505; map p.234. Ramshackle, black-timber piano bar, decorated with business cards and with live old-time blues merchants on the keyboards. Tues–Sat 4pm–2am, Sun 6pm–midnight.

Ben'n'Nick's 5612 College Ave, Rockridge ☎ 510 933 0327; map p.234. Lively and welcoming bar, popular with the student crowd, playing good recorded rock music; tasty food, too. Daily 11.30am–2am.

Cato's Alehouse 3891 Piedmont Ave, North Oakland ☎ 510 655 3349; map p.234. This local alehouse has a good beer selection, as well as pizza and sandwiches, and occasional live music. Mon–Thurs & Sat 11.30am–midnight, Fri 11.30am–1am, Sun 11.30am–10pm.

Heinold's First and Last Chance Saloon 56 Jack London Square, Oakland ☎ 510 839 6761; map p.234. Authentic waterfront bar that's hardly changed since Jack London was a regular. It still has the slanted floor caused by the 1906 earthquake. Mon 3–11pm, Tues–Thurs & Sun noon–11pm, Fri & Sat noon–1am.

★ **Pacific Coast Brewing Co** 906 Washington St, Downtown Oakland ☎ 510 836 2739; map p.234. Oaktown's only real microbrewery, which conjures up a range of decent brews and offers quite an extensive menu too. Attracts Downtown office workers as well as a younger crowd later on. Mon–Thurs 11.30am–midnight, Fri & Sat 11.30am–1am, Sun 11.30am–11pm.

The White Horse 6560 Telegraph Ave at 66th St, North Oakland ☎ 510 652 3820; map p.234. Oakland's oldest gay bar is a smallish, friendly place, with various dance nights and drag events. Wed–Sun 1pm–2am.

LARGE PERFORMANCE VENUES

Center for Contemporary Music Mills College, 5000 MacArthur Blvd, North Oakland ☎ 510 430 2191, ⓦ mills .edu; map p.234. This college performing space is one of the prime centres in the world for experimental music.

Fox Oakland 1807 Telegraph Ave, Oakland ☎ 510 302 2277, ⓦ thefoxoakland.com; map p.234. Recently renovated, this classic old theatre is now a great venue for established and up-and-coming live acts, mostly rock.

Oakland Coliseum Complex at Coliseum BART, near the airport ☎ 510 639 7700, ⓦ www.coliseum.com; map p.234. Mostly stadium shows, inside the 18,000-seat arena or outdoors in the adjacent 55,000-seat Coliseum.

Paramount Theatre 2025 Broadway, Downtown Oakland ☎ 510 465 6400, ⓦ paramounttheatre.com; map p.234. Beautifully restored Art Deco masterpiece, hosting classical concerts, big-name crooners, ballets, operas and a growing roster of rap and rock shows. Ticket office Tues–Sat noon–5pm; tickets $20–85. Some nights they play old Hollywood classics for $8.

LIVE MUSIC VENUES

Eli's Mile High Club 3629 Martin Luther King Jr Way, North Oakland ☎ 510 594 0666, ⓦ elismilehigh.com; map p.234. This gem hidden under the raised freeways has been revamped in minimalist style and now hosts mostly obscure punk, hardcore and psychobilly acts. Cover $8–20.

Kimball's Carnival 215 Washington St, Downtown Oakland ☎ 510 658 2555, ⓦ kimballscarnival.com; map p.234. Black and Latin crossover vibes, either live or with DJs or karaoke. Cover free–$30.

Stork Club 2330 Telegraph Ave, North Oakland ☎ 510 848 0886, ⓦ storkcluboakland.com; map p.234. This place cranks up the volume for its mainly punk, hardcore and metal bands. Cover usually $5.

Yoshi's World Class Jazz House 510 Embarcadero West, Oakland ☎ 510 238 9200, ⓦ yoshis.com; map p.234. The West Coast's premier jazz club, located near Jack London Square, attracts a world-class roster of performers nightly. The place is almost always full. Cover $10–50.

CINEMA

Grand Lake Movie Theater 3200 Grand Ave, Oakland ☎ 510 452 3556; map p.234. The grande dame of East Bay picture palaces, right on Lake Merritt, showing the best of the current major releases, with a special emphasis on politically alternative works.

SHOPS AND GALLERIES

Crossroads Trading Company 5636 College Ave, Oakland ☎ 510 420 1952; map p.234. Men's and women's secondhand clothing of high quality, but more casualwear than vintage apparel. Mon–Thurs 10am–7pm, Fri & Sat 10am–8pm, Sun 11am–7pm.

Diesel 5433 College Ave, Rockridge ☎ 510 653 9965;

map p.234. Dependable bookshop with both fiction and non-fiction, along with the occasional poetry reading. Mon–Thurs 10am–8pm, Fri & Sat 10am–10pm, Sun 10am–6pm.

Paul Marcus Wines 5655 College Ave, Oakland ☎ 510 420 1005; map p.234. Located in trendy Market Hall, where employees are used to matching patrons' gourmet groceries with appropriately sophisticated selections. Mon–Fri 10am–8pm, Sat 10am–7pm, Sun 10am–6pm.

Pegasus & Pendragon Books & Music 5560 College Ave, Rockridge ☎ 510 652 6259; map p.234. College-oriented new and used books, with an emphasis on the fantastic and mysterious. Mon–Thurs 9am–10pm, Fri & Sat 9am–10.45pm, Sun 10am–10pm.

Pro Arts 461 Ninth St, Oakland ☎ 510 763 4361; map p.234. There are changing exhibitions, concentrating on local artists and community issues, six times a year in this bright, modern space. Worth a look, and a good resource for the East Bay art scene. Tues–Fri 11am–6pm, Sat 11am–4pm.

Trader Joe's 5700 Christie Ave in Powell St Plaza, Emeryville ☎ 510 658 8091; map p.234. This popular grocery store has the widest range of affordable wines – many of them imports – in the Bay Area. Daily 8am–10pm.

Berkeley

This Berkeley was like no somnolent Siwash out of her own past at all, but more akin to those Far Eastern or Latin American universities you read about, those autonomous culture media where the most beloved of folklores may be brought into doubt, cataclysmic of dissents voiced, suicidal of commitments chosen – the sort that bring governments down. Thomas Pynchon, The Crying of Lot 49

More than any other American city, **BERKELEY** conjures up an image of 1960s student dissent. When college campuses across the nation were protesting against the Vietnam War, it was Berkeley students who led the charge. In recent decades, despite an influx of more conformist students, a surge in the number of exclusive restaurants and the dismantling of the city's rent-control programme, the progressive legacy has remained in its general political outlook, exemplified in the city's independent **bookstores**.

On top of its ideological rule, the **University of California**, right in the centre of town, physically dominates Berkeley and makes a logical starting point for a visit. Its many grand buildings and thirty thousand students give off a definite energy that spills down the raucous stretch of **Telegraph Avenue** which runs south from the campus and holds most of the student hangouts. Older students and professors congregate in **North Berkeley**. Residents regularly pop down from their woodsy hillside homes here to partake of goodies from **Gourmet Ghetto**, a stretch of Shattuck Avenue crammed with restaurants, delis and bakeries. Of quite distinct character are the flatlands that spread through **West Berkeley** down to the Bay, a poorer but increasingly gentrified district that mixes old Victorian houses with builders' yards and light industrial premises on either side of Fourth Street, with its trendy stores and restaurants. Along the Bay itself is the **Berkeley Marina**, where you can rent sailboards and sailing boats, or just watch the sun set behind the Golden Gate.

The University of California

Tours depart from the University of California's Visitor Services office, 101 Sproul Hall, Sproul Plaza • Tours Mon–Sat 10am, Sun 1pm; 1hr 30min • Free • ☎ 510 642 5215

Caught up in the frantic crush of students who pack the **UNIVERSITY OF CALIFORNIA** campus during the semesters, it's nearly impossible to imagine the bucolic learning environment envisaged by its high-minded founders. When the Reverend Henry Durant and other East Coast academics decided to set up shop here in the 1860s, these rolling foothills were still largely given over to agriculture. They named the institution after an eighteenth-century poem by the Irish bishop and philosopher George Berkeley and the first two hundred students, including 22 women, moved here from Oakland in 1873.

Since then, an increasing number of buildings have been squeezed into the half-mile-square main campus, and the state-funded university has become one of America's most prestigious. UC Berkeley physicists built the first cyclotron and plutonium was

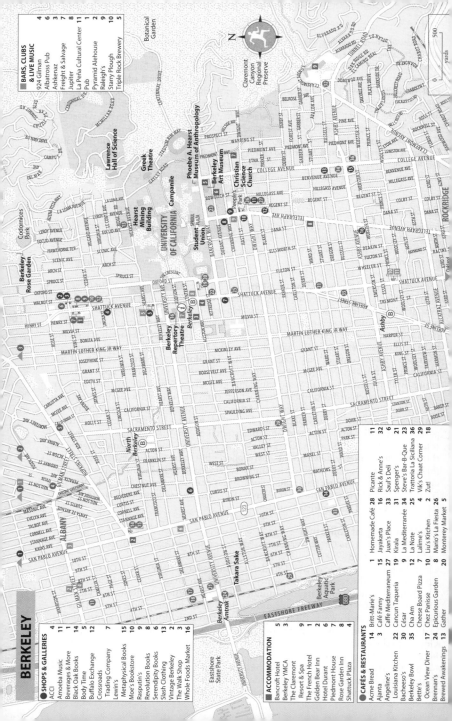

BERKELEY

● SHOPS & GALLERIES

ACCI	4
Amoeba Music	11
Beverages & More	1
Black Oak Books	14
Body Time	5
Buffalo Exchange	12
Crossroads	7
Trading Company	
Lewin's	
Metaphysical Books	15
Moe's Bookstore	10
Rasputin's	9
Revolution Books	8
Serendipity Books	6
Slash Clothing	13
Vintage Berkeley	2
The Walk Shop	3
Whole Foods Market	16

■ BARS, CLUBS & LIVE MUSIC

924 Gilman	4
Albatross Pub	6
Ashkenaz	3
Freight & Salvage	7
Jupiter	8
La Peña Cultural Center	11
Pub	1
Pyramid Alehouse	2
Raleigh's	9
Starry Plough	10
Triple Rock Brewery	5

■ ACCOMMODATION

Bancroft Hotel	5
Berkeley YMCA	3
The Claremont	9
Resort & Spa	
The French Hotel	1
Golden Bear Inn	2
Hotel Durant	6
Piedmont House	7
Rose Garden Inn	8
Shattuck Plaza	4

● CAFÉS & RESTAURANTS

Acme Bread	14	Homemade Café	28
Ajanta	3	Jayakarta	15
Angeline's		Juan's Place	27
Louisiana Kitchen	22	Kirala	19
Bacheso's	30	César	9
Berkeley Bowl	35	Cha Am	12
Bette's		Cheese Board Pizza	1
Ocean View Diner	17	Chez Panisse	7
Brennan's	24	Epicurious Garden	10
Brewed Awakenings	13	Gather	4
Britt-Marie's		La Mediterranée	34
Café Fanny		La Note	25
Caffe Mediterraneum		Lalime's	2
Cancun Taqueria		Liu's Kitchen	10
		Mario's La Fiesta	8
		Monterey Market	20
		Picante	11
		Rick & Anne's	32
		Saul's Deli	6
		Spenger's	21
		Steve's Bar-B-Que	23
		Trattoria La Siciliana	36
		Vik's Chaat Corner	29
		Zut!	18

Botanical Garden

Claremont Canyon Regional Preserve

Lawrence Hall of Science

Greek Theatre

Phoebe A. Hearst Museum of Anthropology

Berkeley Art Museum

Christian Science Church

Hearst Mining Building

Campanile

UNIVERSITY OF CALIFORNIA

Student Union

Sproul Plaza

People's Park

Berkeley Rose Garden

Codornices Park

Berkeley Repertory Theatre

North Berkeley

Takara Sake

Berkeley Amtrak

Berkeley Aquatic Park

Eastshore State Park

EASTSHORE FREEWAY

ROCKRIDGE

ALBANY

N

0   500   yards

discovered here in 1941, along with the elements californium and berkelium later in the decade; as such, it was the setting for sketches for the first atomic bomb. Nuclear weaponry connections and overcrowding aside, the beautifully landscaped campus, stepping down from the eucalyptus-covered Berkeley Hills toward the distant Bay, is eminently strollable, or you can join a free ninety-minute tour.

Sproul Plaza

The best way to get a feel for the place is to follow Strawberry Creek from the top of Center Street across the southeast corner of the campus, emerging from the groves of redwood and eucalyptus trees at **Sproul Plaza**. It's the largest public space on campus, enlivened by street musicians playing for quarters on the steps of the **Student Union** building and conga drummers pounding away in the echoing courtyard below.

The Campanile

Mon–Fri 10am–4pm • $2

Sather Gate, which bridges Strawberry Creek at the north end of Sproul Plaza, marks the entrance to the older part of the campus. Up the hill, past the imposing facade of Wheeler Hall, the 1914 landmark **Campanile** is modelled after the one in the Piazza San Marco in Venice; take an elevator to the top for a great view of the campus and the entire Bay Area. At the foot of the tower stands redbrick **South Hall**, the sole survivor of the original pair of buildings.

Bancroft Library

Mon–Fri 9am–5pm, Sat 1–5pm • Free • ☎ 510 642 3781

Inside the plain white building next door to the Campanile, the **Bancroft Library** displays odds and ends from its exhaustive accumulation of artefacts and documents tracing the history of California, including an imitation brass plaque supposedly left by Sir Francis Drake when he claimed all of the West Coast for Queen Elizabeth I. It also contains a collection of manuscripts and rare books, from Mark Twain to James Joyce – though to see any of these you'll have to show some academic credentials.

16

Morrison Reading Room

Doe Library • Daily noon–5pm

Just inside the arched main entrance to Doe Library, near the Bancroft Library, you'll find the **Morrison Reading Room**, a great place to sit for a while and read foreign magazines and newspapers, listen to a CD, or just ease down into one of the many comfy overstuffed chairs and unwind.

Museum of Paleontology

Valley Life Sciences Building • Mon–Sat 8am–5pm • Free • ⓦ ucmp.berkeley.edu

Worth a quick look is the **Museum of Paleontology**, although only a tyrannosaurus rex skeleton and some other bones and fossils are on general display in the atrium – you need to be on an academic mission to view the wealth of finds within.

The Hearst Mining Building and the Greek Theatre

The Hearst family name appears with disturbing regularity around the Berkeley campus, though in most instances this is due not to the notorious newspaper baron William Randolph but to his altruistic mother, Phoebe Apperson Hearst. She had sponsored the architectural competition that came up with the original campus plan and donated a good number of the campus buildings, some since destroyed. One of the finest survivors, the 1907 **Hearst Mining Building** (daily 8am–5pm; free) on the northeast edge of the campus, conceals a delicate metalwork lobby topped by three glass domes, above ageing exhibits on geology and mining – which is how the Hearst family fortune was originally made, long before scion W.R. took up publishing.

Another Hearst legacy is the nearby **Greek Theatre**, which hosts a summer season of rock concerts (see p.251) and is modelled after the amphitheatre at Epidauros, Greece.

The Botanical Gardens

Daily 9am–5pm, closed first Tues of month • $3, free on Thurs • ☎ 510 643 2755 • UC Berkeley shuttle bus from the campus (free) or Berkeley BART station

Higher up in the hills, above the 80,000-seat Memorial Stadium, the lushly landscaped **Botanical Garden** defeats on-campus claustrophobia with thirty acres of plants and cacti. There are over ten thousand species, representing every continent.

Lawrence Hall of Science

Daily 10am–5pm • $9.50 • ☎ 510 642 3682, ⊕ lawrencehallofscience.org • UC Berkeley shuttle bus from the campus (free) or Berkeley BART station

Near the upper end of campus, with great views out over the Bay, a full-size fibreglass sculpture of a whale stretches out in front of the **Lawrence Hall of Science**, an excellent museum and learning centre featuring earthquake simulations, model dinosaurs and a planetarium, plus hands-on exhibits for kids in the Wizard's Lab.

Berkeley Art Museum

2626 Bancroft Way • Wed–Sun 11am–5pm, Fri until 9pm • $10, free on first Thurs of month • ⊕ bampfa.berkeley.edu

In the southeast corner of the campus, the brutally modern, angular concrete of the **UC Berkeley Art Museum** is in stark contrast to the campus's older buildings. Its skylit, open-plan galleries hold works by Picasso, Cézanne, Rubens and other notables, but the star of the show is the collection of 1950s American painter Hans Hofmann's energetic and colourful abstract paintings on the top floor. The museum is renowned for its cutting-edge exhibitions: the main space hosts a range of major shows, while the Matrix Gallery focuses on lesser-known, (usually) local artists.

Phoebe A. Hearst Museum of Anthropology

Kroeber Hall • Wed–Sat 10am–4.30pm, Sun noon–4pm • $2, free Thurs • ☎ 510 642 3682 ⊕ hearstmuseum.berkeley.edu

Across the road from the Berkeley Art Museum, the **Phoebe A. Hearst Museum of Anthropology** holds a variety of changing exhibits as well as an intriguing display of artefacts made by Ishi, the last surviving Yahi Indian, who was found near Mount Lassen in Northern California in 1911. Anthropologist Alfred Kroeber – father of sci-fi writer Ursula K. Le Guin – brought Ishi to the museum (then located on the UC San Francisco campus), where he lived under the scrutiny of scientists and journalists – in effect, in a state of captivity – until his death from tuberculosis a few years later.

Telegraph Avenue

Downtown Berkeley lies west of the university campus around the Berkeley BART station on Shattuck Avenue – though most activity is centred on **TELEGRAPH AVENUE**, which runs south of the university from Sproul Plaza. This thoroughfare saw some of the worst of the 1960s riots, and today is still a frenetic bustle, especially for the four short blocks closest to the university, which are packed to the gills with everything from cafés and secondhand bookstores to hawkers selling handmade jewellery and subversive bumper stickers, and the requisite down-and-outs.

People's Park

Half a block up from Telegraph Avenue between Haste Street and Dwight Way

People's Park has recovered from a fallow period and is once again a reasonably well-kempt place to hang out, at least during daylight hours – at night it tends to become a haven for the homeless and disenfranchised. In the late 1960s the park was a prime political battleground, when organized and spirited resistance to the university's plans to develop the site into dormitories brought out the military, who shot dead an onlooker by mistake. A mural along Haste Street bears the words of student leader Mario Savio: "There's a time when the operation of the machine becomes so odious... that you can't take part".

Christian Science Church

Across Bowditch Street from People's Park • Open on Sun for worship and for free tours Mon–Sat at 11am

One of the finest buildings in the Bay Area, Bernard Maybeck's **Christian Science Church** was built in 1910. It's an eclectic but thoroughly modern structure, laid out in a simple Greek-cross floor plan and spanned by a massive redwood truss with carved Gothic tracery and Byzantine painted decoration. The interior is open limited hours but the outside is worth lingering over, its cascade of many gently pitched roofs and porticoes carrying the eye from one handcrafted detail to another.

North Berkeley

North Berkeley is a subdued neighbourhood of professors and postgraduate students, its steep, twisting streets climbing up the lushly overgrown hills north of the campus. At the foot of the hills, some of the Bay Area's finest restaurants and delis – most famously *Chez Panisse*, started and run by Alice Waters, the acclaimed "inventor" of California cuisine – have sprung up along Shattuck Avenue to form the so-called **Gourmet Ghetto**, a great place to pick up the makings of a tasty alfresco lunch. **Euclid Avenue**, off Hearst and next to the north gate of the university, is a sort of antidote to Telegraph Avenue, a quiet grove of coffee joints and pizza parlours frequented by grad students, the focal point of the enclave known as **Northside**.

16

Solano Avenue

Where Berkeley meets Albany, **Solano Avenue** is fast catching up as a trendy shopping and dining area, with a variety of stores such as Tibetan craft shops, jewellery emporia and tarot-reading parlours draped along its curved length.

Indian Rock

Far north end of Shattuck Avenue

East of the shops and cafés along Solano, the grey basalt knob of **Indian Rock** stands out from the foot of the hills, challenging rockclimbers who hone their skills on its forty-foot vertical faces; those who just want to appreciate the extraordinary view can take the steps around its back side. Across the street, carved into similarly hard volcanic stone, are the mortar holes used by the Ohlone to grind acorns into flour.

Berkeley Rose Garden

Bayview Place • Daily dawn–dusk • Free • Bus #65 (daily) or #8 (weekdays only) from Shattuck Avenue

Above Euclid Avenue – if you want to avoid the fairly steep walk, take the bus – there are few more pleasant places for a picnic than the **Berkeley Rose Garden**, a terraced amphitheatre filled with three thousand varieties of roses and looking out across the Bay to San Francisco. Built as part of a WPA job-creation scheme during the Depression, a wooden pergola rings the top, stepping down to a small spring.

Tilden Park

Park Daily 8am–10pm; merry-go-round: weekends, daily in summer 8am–10pm • Free **Steam train** Weekends, daily in summer 11am–5pm • $2 • ☎ 510 562 7275 **Lake Anza** Lifeguard on duty: May–Oct daily 11am–6pm • $3.50 **Botanical Garden** Daily 8.30am–5pm • Free **Merry-go-round** $2 • Head southeast from campus on Claremont Avenue (passing the *Claremont Hotel*) or Grizzly Peak Boulevard (signposted from Euclid Ave); AC Transit bus #67 from Downtown (Sat & Sun only; free)

Along the crest of the Berkeley hills, a number of enticing parks give great views over the Bay. The largest and highest of them, **Tilden Park**, encompasses some 2065 acres of near wilderness. Kids can enjoy a ride on the carved wooden horses of the merry-go-round or take the mini-steam train through the grove of redwood trees, at the south end of the park. In the warm months, don't miss a dip in clean and soothing **Lake Anza**. Another attraction is the beautifully landscaped **Botanical Garden**, which features a number of carefully crafted biospheres from temperate rainforest to high desert. Both of the routes from campus – along Claremont Avenue or Grizzly Peak Boulevard – snake 1600ft to the crest of the Berkeley hills, providing stunning views and myriad hiking trails.

West Berkeley

From downtown Berkeley and the UC campus, **University Avenue** runs downhill toward the Bay, lined by increasingly shabby motels and massage parlours. One interesting corner of this **WEST BERKELEY** area is around the the intersection of University and San Pablo avenues, where a community of recent immigrants from India and Pakistan have set up stores and restaurants that serve some delicious curries.

Between San Pablo Avenue and the Bay, you'll find the oldest part of Berkeley, holding remnants of Berkeley's industrial past and where many of the old warehouses and factory premises have been converted into living and working spaces for artists, craftspeople and software companies. The newly polished and gentrified stretch of **Fourth Street** between Gilman and University features upscale furniture outlets and quaint gourmet delis, as well as some outstanding restaurants.

The waterfront

AC Transit bus #51 from University Avenue

At the western edge of Berkeley, I-80 and the still-used rail tracks that run alongside it pretty well manage to cut the town off from its **waterfront**. If you're determined, the best way to get there is to take the bus. The main attraction here is the **Berkeley Marina**, once a major hub for the Transbay ferry services and now one of the prime spots on the Bay for leisure activities, especially windsurfing and kayaking. There's a very long pier where you can chat with the local fishermen and breathe in the fresh salty air while getting a great view of San Francisco and its two bridges. People also stretch their own and their dogs' legs in the green confines of **Cesar Chavez Park**, north of the marina.

ARRIVAL AND DEPARTURE BERKELEY

By subway Berkeley is linked to San Francisco and other points in the East Bay via the BART subway (☎510 465 2278 from the East Bay, ⓦbart.gov).

By bus AC Transit runs buses on a number of routes to Berkeley from the Transbay Terminal in San Francisco. These operate all night and are the only way of getting across the Bay by public transit once BART shuts down.

GETTING AROUND AND INFORMATION

Tourist information The main tourist office is welcoming Visit Berkeley, 2030 Addison St (Mon–Fri 9am–noon & 2–5pm; ☎510 549 7040, ⓦvisitberkeley.com). The University of California's Visitor Services, 101 Sproul Hall, Sproul Plaza (Mon–Fri 8.30am–4.30pm; ☎510 642 5215,

ⓦberkeley.edu), have plenty of info on the Berkeley campus, and organize tours of the university (see p.241).

By bike You can rent bikes at Solano Avenue Cyclery, 1554 Solano Ave (☎510 524 1094, ⓦsolanoavenuecyclery .com; $35/24hr or $140/week).

ACCOMMODATION

Berkeley is without a doubt the most pleasant area to stay in the East Bay. It has a good range of options from cheapish motels to some classy hotels, plus a particularly strong tradition of bed and breakfasts; check with the Berkeley & Oakland Bed and Breakfast Network (☎510 547 6380, ⓦbbonline.com/ca/berkeley-oakland) or get its brochure from the UC's Visitor Services office (see above). There are also two hostels and the possibility of renting student housing in summer.

HOTELS, MOTELS AND B&BS

Bancroft Hotel 2680 Bancroft Way, Berkeley ☎510 549 1000 or 1 800 549 1002, ⓦbancrofthotel .com; map p.242. Small hotel with 22 stylish rooms, a good location right by campus and an attractive

Neoclassical facade. The service is good, and breakfast is included. $129

★ **The Claremont Resort & Spa** 41 Tunnel Rd, Berkeley ☎510 843 3000 or 1 800 551 7266, ⓦclaremontresort.com; map p.242. Built in 1915, the

SAKE TASTING

One place you shouldn't miss in West Berkeley is the **Takara Sake Tasting Room**, just off Fourth Street south of University Avenue at 708 Addison St (daily noon–6pm; $5; ☏ 510 540 8250, ⓦ takarasake.com). Owned and operated by one of Japan's largest producers, this plant is responsible for more than a third of all sake drunk in the US. You can sample any of the dozen or so varieties of California-strain sake (brewed from Californian rice), both warm and chilled. Before tasting, you are ushered into the small museum and then sat down to watch a twelve-minute video presentation of the art of sake brewing.

Claremont is the lap of luxury among Berkeley hotels. Deluxe rooms come with big windows, some overlooking the Bay; the Tower Suite costs over $600. Spa sessions begin around $100/hr for facials or massages. $189

★ **The French Hotel** 1538 Shattuck Ave, North Berkeley ☏ 510 548 9930, ⓦ french-hotel-berkeley.com; map p.242. There's a touch of European class about this small and comfortable hotel with eighteen simple but pleasant rooms in the heart of Berkeley's Gourmet Ghetto. $105

Golden Bear Inn 1620 San Pablo Ave, West Berkeley ☏ 510 525 6770 or 1 800 525 6770, ⓦ goldenbearinn .com; map p.242. The most pleasantly decorated and furnished of the many motels in the "flatlands" of West Berkeley, though somewhat out of the way. $80

Hotel Durant 2600 Durant Ave, Berkeley ☏ 510 845 8981 or 1 800 238 7268, ⓦ jdvhotels.com; map p.242. Upscale hotel at the heart of UC Berkeley, featuring large, airy rooms with refrigerators. $144

Rose Garden Inn 2740 Telegraph Ave, Berkeley ☏ 510 549 2145 or 1 800 992 9005, ⓦ rosegardeninn .com; map p.242. Pleasant, if slightly dull, rooms with fireplaces in a pretty mock-Tudor mansion half a mile south of UC Berkeley. Filling buffet breakfast. $95

Shattuck Plaza 2086 Allston Way, Berkeley ☏ 510 845 7300 or 1 800 237 5359, ⓦ hotelshattuckplaza.com; map p.242. Renovated with an opulent lobby and beautifully furnished rooms, this hotel now competes with the finest in the area, barring the *Claremont*. $219

HOSTELS

Berkeley YMCA 2001 Allston Way ☏ 510 848 9622, ⓦ baymca.org; map p.242. Conveniently close to Downtown Berkeley BART, here you'll find the best single room deals around. No dorms. Rates include use of gym and pool. $65

Piedmont House 2434 Piedmont Ave ☏ 510 849 4800 or 1 888 123 4567, ⓦ berkeleyhostel.com; map p.242. Just three blocks from the campus, this new hostel has very clean facilities. Dorms $32, doubles $55

Summer Visitor Housing 2601 Warring St, Berkeley ☏ 510 642 4444; map p.242. Agency that can arrange summer-only rooms for around $50/night in university residences such as Stern Hall. Weekly rentals are preferred but shorter stays are possible.

16

EATING

With some of the best restaurants in the state, Berkeley is the unofficial home of **California cuisine** and an upmarket diner's paradise. But it's also a college town, so you can eat cheaply and well here, too, especially downtown and around Telegraph Avenue. One of the great joys in Berkeley is languishing in one of its many student **cafés**.

CAFÉS

Bacheeso's 2501 San Pablo Ave, West Berkeley ☏ 510 644 2035; map p.242. Imaginative breakfasts such as egg with artichokes and more filling snacks, as well as a full range of hot beverages, all served with a smile in brightly decorated surroundings. Mon–Sat 7.30am–9pm, Sun 7.30am–4pm.

Brewed Awakenings 1807 Euclid Ave, North Berkeley ☏ 510 540 8865; map p.242. Spacious coffee- and tea-house near the North Gate of campus. Friendly staff, plenty of seating, and lovely artwork on the red-brick walls. Annually confirmed as "Best Café to Study In" by the student press. Mon–Fri 7am–7pm, Sat & Sun 7am–6pm.

Café Fanny 1603 San Pablo Ave, West Berkeley ☏ 510 524 5447; map p.242. Delicious and relatively cheap breakfasts and lunches in a small and unlikely space with sparse industrial decor. Owned by Alice Waters, of *Chez Panisse* fame. Mon–Fri 7am–8pm, Sat 8am–4pm, Sun 8am–3pm.

Caffe Mediterraneum 2475 Telegraph Ave, Berkeley ☏ 510 841 5634; map p.242. Berkeley's oldest café featuring pavement seating. Straight out of the Beat archives: beards and berets optional, battered paperbacks *de rigueur*. Daily 7am–midnight.

DINERS AND DELIS

★ **Bette's Ocean View Diner** 1807 Fourth St, West Berkeley ☏ 510 644 3932, ⓦ bettesdiner.com; map p.242. No views but this popular joint serves up great breakfasts and lunches. Queues at weekends can take up to an hour. Mon–Fri 6.30am–2.30pm, Sat & Sun 6.30am–4pm.

Brennan's 700 University Ave, West Berkeley ☏ 510 841 0960, ⓦ brennansberkeley.com; map p.242. Great downhome self-service meals like roast beef and mash. Also a great place for drinking inexpensive beers and watching sport on TV, including European football. Mon–Wed & Sun 11am–9.30pm, Thurs–Sat 11.30am–10.30pm.

Homemade Café 2454 Sacramento St, Berkeley ☎510 845 1940, ⊛homemade-cafe.com; map p.242. Non-traditional, inexpensive and extremely tasty California-style Mexican and Jewish food served at breakfast and lunch, at shared tables when crowded. Mon–Fri 7am–2pm, Sat & Sun 8am–3pm.

Rick & Ann's 2922 Domingo Ave, South Berkeley ☎510 649 8538, ⊛rickandanns.com; map p.242. Even in Berkeley people sometimes want meatloaf and mashed potatoes instead of rocket and couscous, and as proof, the crowds line up outside this neighbourhood diner every weekend. Mon 8am–2pm, Tues–Sat 8am–2pm & 5.30–9.30pm, Sun 8am–2pm & 5.30–8.30pm.

Saul's Deli 1475 Shattuck Ave, North Berkeley ☎510 848 3354, ⊛saulsdeli.com; map p.242. For pastrami, corned beef, *kreplach* or *knishes*, this is the place. Great sandwiches and picnic food plus a full range of sit-down evening meals. Daily 8am–10pm; closed major Jewish holidays.

AMERICAN AND CALIFORNIA CUISINE

Angeline's Louisiana Kitchen 2261 Shattuck Ave, Berkeley ☎510 548 6900, ⊛angelineskitchen.com; map p.242. Classic New Orleans dishes such as voodoo shrimp and fried catfish are rustled up for around $14 in this lively new place that also has great sounds. Mon 5.30–9pm, Tues–Thurs & Sun 11.30am–9pm, Fri & Sat 11.30am–10pm.

★ **Chez Panisse** 1517 Shattuck Ave, North Berkeley ☎510 548 5525, ⊛chezpanisse.com; map p.242. Chef Alice Waters is widely credited with first inventing California cuisine, with delights like Monterey Bay sardine toast with rocket and fennel, or Sonoma County duck with roasted butternut squash, beets and *tatsoi*. The evening set menu starts at $60 per head on Mon, rising to $95 at weekends, not including drinks. Mon–Thurs 11.30am–3pm & 5–10.30pm, Fri & Sat 11.30am–3.30pm & 5–11.30pm.

Gather 2200 Oxford St, Berkeley ☎510 809 0400, ⊛gatherrestaurant.com; map p.242. Trendy new restaurant whose menus are based on local produce and sustainability, half vegetarian and half high-quality meat and fish. Great lunch deals around $11. Mon–Fri 11.30am–2pm & 5–10pm, Sat & Sun 10am–2.30pm & 5–10pm.

Lalime's 1329 Gilman St, North Berkeley ☎510 527 9838, ⊛lalimes.com; map p.242. A culinary dissertation on irony, as rich leftist Berkeley professors chow down on veal, pâté de foie gras, and other distinctly un-PC fare, in a casual setting. Expect to pay at least $40 per head. Mon–Thurs 5.30–9.30pm, Fri & Sat 5.30–10pm, Sun 5–9pm.

Spenger's 1919 Fourth St, West Berkeley ☎510 845 7771, ⊛spengers.com; map p.242. With a spacious sit-down restaurant and cheap takeaway counter, this is a local institution. As one of the largest chains in the Bay Area, *Spenger's* serves up literally tons of seafood to thousands of customers daily. Mon–Thurs & Sun 11.30am–10pm, Fri & Sat 11.30am–11pm.

ASIAN, AFRICAN AND INDIAN

Ajanta 1888 Solano Ave, North Berkeley ☎510 526 4373, ⊛ajantarestaurant.com; map p.242. The chef rotates dishes from different regions of India every month, such as duck curry Kerala or Kashmiri *dhanwala murg*. Slightly pricey, with most main courses $15–20. Daily 11.30am–2.30pm & 5.30–9.30pm.

Cha Am 1543 Shattuck Ave, North Berkeley ☎510 848 9664; map p.242. Climb the stairs up to this small and popular restaurant for deliciously spicy Thai food at moderate prices. The coconut curries are excellent and cost around $10. Mon–Sat 11.30am–3pm, Mon–Thurs & Sun 5–9.30pm, Fri & Sat 5–10pm.

Jayakarta 2026 University Ave, Berkeley ☎510 841 0884, ⊛jayakartarestaurant.bravehost.com; map p.242. Very simple and inexpensive Indonesian joint that serves up extremely tasty dishes such as *nasi padang*, a mixture of boiled egg, chicken hearts, pork and stinky beans in chili. Daily 11am–10pm.

★ **Kirala** 2100 Ward St, Berkeley ☎510 549 3486, ⊛kiralaberkeley.com; map p.242. Many argue that *Kirala* serves the best sushi in the Bay Area. Others claim that it's the best in the world. Moderate pricing, too – expect to pay little over $20 to get your fill. Mon–Fri 11.30am–2pm & 5.30–9.30pm, Sat 5.30–9.30pm, Sun 5–9pm.

Liu's Kitchen 1593 Solano Ave, North Berkeley ☎510 525 8766; map p.242. Huge helpings of tasty Chinese fare at very reasonable prices – the pot stickers are a meal in themselves. Tues–Sun 11.30am–3pm & 4.30–9.30pm.

Steve's Bar-B-Que Durant Center, 2521 Durant Ave, Berkeley ☎510 848 6166; map p.242. Excellent, low-priced Korean food (the *kimchee* is superb); other cafés in the centre sell Mexican food, sandwiches, deep-fried doughnuts, and pizza – not to mention bargain pitchers of beer. Mon–Thurs & Sun 11am–11pm, Fri & Sat 11am–midnight.

★ **Vik's Chaat Corner** 2390 Fourth St, West Berkeley ☎510 644 4432, ⊛vikschaatcorner.com; map p.242. These brightly coloured new premises still see long queues at weekends. Ever present vegetarian delights such as *masala dosa* or *bhel puri* are supplemented by daily non-veg specials. Tues–Thurs 11am–6pm, Fri–Sun 11am–8pm.

MEDITERRANEAN

Britt-Marie's 1369 Solano Ave, Albany ☎510 527 1314, ⊛brittmariesolano.com; map p.242. Along with a

16

fine selection of mostly California wines by the glass, *Britt-Marie's* serves well-priced, French home cooking – as well as outstanding chocolate cake. Tues–Sat 11.30am–2pm & 5–11pm, Sun 5–10pm.

César 1515 Shattuck Ave, North Berkeley ☎ 510 883 0222, ⓦ barcesar.com; map p.242. Perpetually crowded tapas bar serving small dishes overflowing with taste. Its combination of quality and a relaxed atmosphere has made this a cultish destination for locals. Can get expensive rather quickly, however. Daily noon–midnight.

Cheese Board Pizza 1512 Shattuck Ave, North Berkeley ☎ 510 549 3055, ⓦ cheeseboardcollective.coop; map p.242. Tiny storefront selling top-notch "designer pizza" at very reasonable prices: around $3 a slice, with a different topping every day. Great deli just down the road at no. 1504 too. Tues–Sat 11.30am–3pm & 4.30–8pm.

La Mediterranée 2936 College Ave, Berkeley ☎ 510 540 7773, ⓦ cafelamed.com; map p.242. Good Greek and Middle Eastern dishes, such as Levantine meat tart or various kebabs for $10 or less, served indoors or on the large patio. Mon–Thurs 10am–10pm, Fri & Sat 10am–11pm, Sun 10am–9.30pm.

La Note 2377 Shattuck Ave, Berkeley ☎ 510 843 1535, ⓦ lanoterestaurant.com; map p.242. The appropriately sunny, light cuisine of Provence such as *bouillabaisse Marseillaise* (fish stew) isn't the only flavour you'll find in this petite dining room: musicians from the Jazzschool next door routinely stop in for casual jam sessions. Mon–Wed 8am–2.30pm, Thurs & Fri 8am–2.30pm & 6–10pm, Sat 8am–3pm & 6–10pm, Sun 8am–3pm.

Trattoria La Siciliana 2993 College Ave, Berkeley ☎ 510 704 1474, ⓦ trattorialasiciliana.com; map p.242. Intimate, family-run Italian place with specialities like stuffed beef roll for under $20. Daily 5–10pm.

Zut! 1820 Fourth St, West Berkeley ☎ 510 644 6444, ⓦ zutonfourth.com; map p.242. This smart new place offers a decent range of Mediterranean favourites, from falafel and meze platters to tagliatelli with clams. Mon–Thurs 11.30am–9.30pm, Fri 11.30am–10.30pm, Sat 10.30am–10.30pm, Sun 10.30am–9pm.

MEXICAN

Cancun Taqueria 2134 Allston Way, Berkeley ☎ 510 549 0964, ⓦ sabormexicano.com; map p.242.

Popular, cheap, downtown burrito and taco joint. Self-service but huge portions of tasty food in lively and colourful surroundings. Mon–Fri 10am–10pm, Sat & Sun 10am–10.30pm.

Juan's Place 941 Carleton St, West Berkeley ☎ 510 845 6904, ⓦ mexicanrestaurant.mx; map 242. The original Berkeley Mexican restaurant, with cheap, great food (in huge portions) and an interesting mix of people. Mon–Fri 11am–10pm, Sat & Sun 2–10pm.

Mario's La Fiesta 2506 Haste St, Berkeley ☎ 510 540 9123, ⓦ marioslafiesta.com; map p.242. Always crowded with students and other budget-minded souls who flock here for the heaping portions of inexpensive nachos, quesadillas and so on. Daily 11am–10pm.

Picante 1328 Sixth St, West Berkeley ☎ 510 525 3121, ⓦ picanteberkeley.com; map p.242. Fine and very reasonably priced tacos, plus live jazz on weekends. Nicely decorated with an outdoor patio for fine weather. Mon–Fri 11am–10pm, Sat & Sun 10am–10pm.

FOOD SHOPS AND MARKETS

Acme Bread 1601 San Pablo Ave, West Berkeley ☎ 510 524 1327; map p.242. Small bakery that supplies most of Berkeley's better restaurants; the house speciality is delicious sourdough baguettes. Mon–Sat 8am–6pm, Sun 8.30am–3pm.

Berkeley Bowl 2777 Shattuck Ave, Berkeley ☎ 510 841 6346; map p.242. This converted bowling alley is now an enormous produce, bulk and health-food market. It's the least expensive grocery in town, with the largest selection of fresh food. Mon–Sat 9am–8pm, Sun 10am–6pm.

Epicurious Garden 1511 Shattuck Ave, North Berkeley; map p.242. This indoor mall of top-notch produce and takeaway snacks includes half a dozen independent outlets, such as Alegio Chocolate (☎ 510 548 2466) and Picoso Mexican (☎ 510 540 4811), as well as a Japanese tea garden at the back. Hours vary.

Monterey Market 1550 Hopkins St, North Berkeley ☎ 510 526 6042; map p.242. The main supplier of exotic produce to Berkeley's gourmet restaurants, this boisterous market also has the highest-quality fresh fruit and vegetables available. Mon–Fri 9am–7pm, Sat 8.30am–6pm, Sun 10am–5pm.

DRINKING, NIGHTLIFE AND ENTERTAINMENT

Naturally enough, the area's many bars are frequented mostly by students and teaching staff. The widely available *East Bay Express* (issued every Wed; free) has the most comprehensive listings of what's on in this vibrant area.

BARS

Albatross Pub 1822 San Pablo Ave, West Berkeley ☎ 510 843 2473, ⓦ albatrosspub.com; map p.242. Popular student super-bar, replete with darts, pool, board games and fireplace. Serves a large selection of imported ales. Occasional

jazz and blues music Weds and Sat. Cover free–$5. Mon, Tues & Sun 6pm–2am, Wed–Sat 4.30pm–2am.

Jupiter 2181 Shattuck Ave, Berkeley ☎ 510 843 8277; map p.242. There are many types of lager, ale and cider to select from at this buzzing local favourite, which also offers wood-fired pizza and an outdoor beer garden. Loud disco nights or live jazz at weekends. Mon–Thurs 11.30am–1am, Fri & Sat noon–1.30am, Sun noon–midnight.

★ **Pub (Schmidt's Tobacco & Trading Co)** 1492 Solano Ave, Albany ☎ 510 525 1900; map p.242. Just past the official Berkeley limit, this small, relaxed bar lures a mixture of bookworms and game-players with a good selection of beers. Its other speciality is selling tobacco. Outdoor patio. Daily noon–1am.

Pyramid Alehouse 901 Gilman St, Berkeley ☎ 510 528 9880; map p.242. This huge post-industrial space makes a surprisingly casual spot to sip the suds. Outdoor film screenings on weekend nights during summer. Daily 11.30am–late.

Raleigh's 2438 Telegraph Ave, Berkeley ☎ 510 848 4827; map p.242. Affable pub and grill with a good range of beers on tap, recorded indie music and shuffleboard. Mon–Wed & Sun 11am–midnight, Thurs–Sat 11am–2am.

★ **Triple Rock Brewery** 1920 Shattuck Ave, Berkeley ☎ 510 843 2739; map p.242. Buzzing, all-American microbrewery whose beers (brewed on the premises) are a bit fizzy unless you ask for one of the fine cask-conditioned ales. Great burgers too. Mon–Wed 11.30am–1am, Thurs–Sat 11.30am–2am, Sun 11.30am–midnight.

LARGE PERFORMANCE VENUES

Berkeley Community Theater 1930 Allston Way, Berkeley ☎ 510 845 2308; map p.242. Jimi Hendrix played here, and the 3500-seat theatre still hosts major rock concerts and community events. Tickets through major agents.

Zellerbach Hall/Greek Theatre On the UC Berkeley campus ☎ 510 642 9988, ⓦ calperfs.berkeley.edu; map p.242. Two of the prime spots for catching touring big names in the Bay Area. Zellerbach regularly showcases classical music and dance, while the outdoor Greek theatre welcomes occasional pop and rock acts. Tickets $20–100.

LIVE MUSIC VENUES

924 Gilman 924 Gilman St, West Berkeley ☎ 510 525 9926, ⓦ 924gilman.org; map p.242. On the outer edge of the hardcore punk and metal scene in a bare, squat-like warehouse. Weekends only; cover $5–10.

Ashkenaz 1317 San Pablo Ave, West Berkeley ☎ 510 525 5054, ⓦ ashkenaz.com; map p.242. World music and dance café. Acts range from modern Afro-beat to the best of the Balkans. Kids and under-21s welcome. Cover $10–20.

Freight and Salvage 2020 Addison St, West Berkeley ☎ 510 548 1761, ⓦ www.freightandsalvage.org; map p.242. Since this non-profit organization relocated to this pleasant performance space with a great sound system, it has reestablished its name for showcasing up-and-coming acts, mostly rock bands. Cover $8–35.

La Peña Cultural Center 3105 Shattuck Ave, Berkeley ☎ 510 849 2568, ⓦ lapena.org; map p.242. More folk than rock, along with some Latin, often politically charged. $5–20.

Starry Plough 3101 Shattuck Ave, Berkeley near Ashby BART ☎ 510 841 2082, ⓦ starryploughpub .com; map p.242. Music veers all over the map, from noisy punk to country and traditional Irish folk, and the crowd is just as varied. Open-mic on Wed. Doubles as a friendly saloon and restaurant in the afternoon and early evening. Cover free–$10.

CINEMAS

Act One and Act Two 2128 Center St, Berkeley ☎ 510 548 7200. Foreign films and non-mainstream American options are played in these Downtown movie halls.

Pacific Film Archive 2575 Bancroft at Bowditch, Berkeley ☎ 510 642 5249, ⓦ bampfa.berkeley.edu. The archive's splendid digs plays the West Coast's best selection of cinema. Classic, third world, and experimental films play nightly, plus revivals of otherwise forgotten favourites. Two films a night; tickets $8, $4 additional feature.

UC Theatre 2036 University Ave, Berkeley ☎ 510 843 3456. Popular revival house, with a huge auditorium and a daily double feature featuring funky theme-weeks of *noir*, melodrama and other genres. Tickets $5–7.

THEATRE

Berkeley Repertory Theater 2025 Addison St, Berkeley ☎ 510 845 4700, ⓦ berkeleyrep.org; map p.242. One of the West Coast's most highly respected theatre companies, that presents updated classics as well as contemporary plays. Tickets $30–75; fifty-percent discounts for students and under-30s with advance booking.

Black Repertory Group 3201 Adeline St, Berkeley ☎ 510 652 2120, ⓦ blackrepertorygroup.com. After initial struggles, this politically conscious company has been encouraging new talent with great success. Tickets $15–30.

Julia Morgan Center for the Arts 2640 College Ave, Berkeley ☎ 510 845 8542, ⓦ juliamorgan.org. A variety of touring shows stop off in this cunningly converted old church. Tickets $15–30; some shows "pay what you can".

16

SHOPS AND GALLERIES

ARTS AND CRAFTS

ACCI 1652 Shattuck Ave, Berkeley ☎ 530 843 2527; map p.242. The oldest arts-and-crafts co-operative west of the Mississippi has been exhibiting and selling the work of local artists since 1957. Mon–Sat 11am–6pm, Sun noon–5pm.

BOOKS

Black Oak Books 2618 San Pablo Ave ☎ 510 486 0698; map p.242. Huge selection of secondhand and new books for every interest; also holds regular evening readings by internationally acclaimed authors. Daily 11am–7pm.

Lewin's Metaphysical Books 2644 Ashby Ave ☎ 510 843 4491; map p.242. The best selection on spirituality, religion, astrology and other arcane subjects. Mon–Sat 11am–6pm.

Moe's Bookstore 2476 Telegraph Ave ☎ 510 849 2087; map p.242. An enormous selection of new and used books on four floors, with esoteric surprises in every field of study Fine art section on top floor. Daily 10am–11pm.

Revolution Books 2425c Channing Way ☎ 510 848 1196; map p.242. Wide range of books on political themes, with an emphasis on leftist and anarchist thought. Mon–Fri 10am–6pm, Sat 11am–6pm, Sun 1–6pm.

Serendipity Books 1201 University Ave ☎ 510 841 7455; map p.242. This vast, garage-like bookstore is an absolute must for collectors of first-edition or obscure fiction and poetry, as well as Black American writers. Mon–Sat 9am–5pm.

MUSIC

Amoeba Records 2455 Telegraph Ave, Berkeley ☎ 510 549 1125; map p.242. Berkeley's renowned emporium is one of the largest used-music retailers in America. Stocked to the gills with hard-to-find releases, both new and used, on vinyl and CD. Mon–Sat 10.30am–10pm.

Rasputin's 2350 Telegraph Ave, Berkeley ☎ 510 848 9004; map p.242. Almost as huge as Amoeba, this place is good for jazz, rock and ethnic sounds, especially from Africa. Mon–Thurs & Sun 11am–8pm, Fri & Sat 11am–9pm.

CLOTHES AND ACCESSORIES

Buffalo Exchange 2512 Telegraph Ave, Berkeley ☎ 510 644 9202; map p.242. Part of a secondhand clothing chain, with high-class treasures aplenty, including last year's castoffs from the college crowd,

current fashions and classic Levi's. Mon–Sat 11am–8pm, Sun 11am–7pm.

Crossroads Trading Co 2338 Shattuck Ave, Berkeley ☎ 510 843 7600; map p.242. Large branch of this California chain, with a huge array of men's and women's clothing, shoes and accessories. Mon–Thurs 10am–7pm, Fri–Sat 10am–8pm, Sun 11am–7pm.

Slash Clothing 2840 College Ave, Berkeley ☎ 510 841 7803; map p.242. There's barely room to walk in this tiny, non-trendy basement with secondhand Levi's piled from floor to ceiling. Mon–Sat 11am–7pm, Sun noon–5pm.

The Walk Shop 2120 Vine St, Berkeley ☎ 510 849 3628; map p.242. Down-to-earth but stylish shoes that feel good to walk in. The shop dates back to 1930. Mon–Sat 10am–6pm, Sun 11am–5pm.

HEALTH AND BEAUTY

Body Time 1942 Shattuck Ave ☎ 510 841 5818 & 2911 College Ave, Berkeley ☎ 510 845 2101; map p.242. Natural scents, lotions, soaps, hair products and a collection of other beauty treatments. Mon–Sat 10am–7pm, Sun 11am–6pm.

Whole Foods Market 3000 Telegraph Ave, Berkeley ☎ 510 649 1333; map p.242. For the alternative-remedy addict, an excellent selection of homeopathic herbs and medicinal products. Daily 8am–10pm.

WINES AND SPIRITS

Beverages & More 836 San Pablo Ave, Albany ☎ 510 525 9582, also at Jack London Square, Oakland ☎ 510 208 5126; map p.242. Huge selection of wines, craft brews and spirits; also cigars and party nibbles. Mon–Sat 10am–9pm, Sun 10am–7pm.

Vintage Berkeley 2113 Vine St, North Berkeley ☎ 510 665 8600; map p.242. Excellent outlet for quality domestic and imported wines, mostly under $20, housed in a cute old pump station. The highly knowledgeable staff conduct tastings Mon–Fri 4–7pm, Sat 2–4pm. Mon–Sat 11am–8pm, Sun noon–6pm.

Beyond the urban East Bay

Compared to the urbanized bayfront cities of Oakland and Berkeley, the rest of the East Bay is sparsely populated, and places of interest are few and far between. The area up to the **Carquinez Strait**, which separates the East Bay from the North Bay, is home to some of the Bay Area's heaviest industry – oil refineries and chemical plants dominate the landscape – but there are also a few remarkably unchanged waterfront towns that merit a side-trip. Away from the Bay, the **inland valleys** are a whole other world of dry, rolling hills dominated by the towering peak of **Mount Diablo**. So far the region still feels rural, despite having doubled in population in the past twenty years.

The inland valleys

BART tunnels from Oakland through the Berkeley Hills to the leafy-green stockbroker settlement of **Orinda**, setting for the annual summer-long California Shakespeare Festival (☎510 548 3422, ⓦcalshakes.org), before continuing east through the increasingly hot and dry landscape to **Concord**. In the mid-1990s a peaceful, civilly disobedient blockade here ended with protester Brian Wilson losing his legs under the wheels of a slow-moving munitions train, taking weapons to the controversial nuclear depot. The event raised public awareness and earned Wilson a place in the Lawrence Ferlinghetti poem *A Buddha in the Woodpile*.

John Muir National Historic Site

4202 Alhambra Ave · Wed–Sun 10am–5pm · $3, including museum · ☎ 925 228 8860, ⓦ nps.gov/jomu · Contra Costa County Connection buses leave every thirty minutes from Pleasant Hill BART station

The **John Muir National Historic Site** is just off Hwy-4 two miles south of Martinez. Muir, an articulate, persuasive Scot whose writings and political activism were of vital importance in the preservation of America's wilderness, spent much of his life exploring and writing about the majestic Sierra Nevada mountains, particularly Yosemite. He was also one of the founders of the **Sierra Club** – a wilderness lobby and education organization still active today. His very conventional, upper-class Victorian home, now restored to its appearance when Muir died in 1914, is open five days a week. The bulk of Muir's personal belongings and artefacts are displayed in his study on the upper floor and in the adjacent room an exhibition documents the history of the Sierra Club and Muir's battles to protect America's wilderness.

Behind the bell-towered main house is a large, still productive orchard where Muir cultivated grapes, pears and cherries to earn the money to finance his explorations. Beyond the orchard is the 1849 **Martinez Adobe**, homestead of the original Spanish land-grant settlers and now a small **museum** of Mexican colonial culture.

16

Eugene O'Neill's house

At the foot of Mount Diablo; tours depart from Danville · Wed–Sun 10am & 12.30pm · Free · ☎ 925 838 0249, ⓦ nps.gov/euon

Fifteen miles south of the John Muir National Historic Site, playwright **Eugene O'Neill** used the money he got for winning the Nobel Prize for Literature in 1936 to build a home and sanctuary for himself, which he named **Tao House**. It was here, before he was struck down with Parkinson's disease in 1944, that he wrote many of his best-known plays: *The Iceman Cometh*, *A Moon for the Misbegotten* and *Long Day's Journey into Night*. Readings and performances of his works are sometimes given in the house, which is open to visitors, though you must reserve a place for the **tours**.

Blackhawk Automotive Museum

3700 Blackhawk Plaza Circle, Danville · Wed–Sun 10am–5pm · $10 · ☎ 925 736 2277, ⓦ blackhawkmuseum.org

The tiny town of **Danville**, off I-680 south of Walnut Creek and north of Dublin and San Ramon, is home to the **Blackhawk Automotive Museum**, an impressive collection of classic and antique cars from Britain, Germany, Italy and the US from 1920 to 1960, and artwork inspired by them.

Mount Diablo

Mount Diablo State Park: daily 8am–sunset · Free; parking $6

Majestic **MOUNT DIABLO** rises up from rolling ranchlands to a height of nearly four thousand feet, its summit and flanks preserved within **Mount Diablo State Park**. North Gate Road, the main route through the park, reaches to within three hundred feet of the top, its terminus a popular place to enjoy the marvellous view: on a clear day you can see over two hundred miles in every direction.

Two main entrances lead into the park, both well marked off I-680. The one from the southwest by way of Danville passes by the **ranger station**. The other runs from the

NEMESIS AT ALTAMONT

Uncannily timed in the dying embers of the 1960s and often referred to as "the nemesis of the Woodstock generation", the concert headlined by the **Rolling Stones** at the **Altamont Speedway**, southeast of Mount Diablo, on December 6, 1969 ended in total disaster. The free event had been intended to be a sort of second Woodstock, staged in order to counter allegations that the Stones had ripped off their fans during a long US tour. The band, however, inadvisably hired a chapter of the **Hell's Angels** instead of professional security to maintain order and the result, predictably enough, was chaos. Three people ended up dead, one kicked and stabbed to death by the Hell's Angels themselves.

The whole sorry tale was remarkably captured on film by brothers David and Albert Maysles in their documentary **Gimme Shelter**, released the following year. The footage of the concert clearly shows the deteriorating mood and atmosphere of growing menace in the crowd, exemplified by the scene when **Jefferson Airplane** vocalist Marty Balin jumped down into the crowd to break up a fight, an intervention which earned him a broken jaw. By the time the Stones came on stage matters were blatantly out of hand and after several interruptions and pleas for sanity by Mick Jagger, all hell broke loose during, ironically, *Sympathy for the Devil*. The glint of the knife is plainly seen just before the fatal stabbing, which actually takes place after the following number, *Under My Thumb*. Perhaps even more poignant is the numb look on the faces of Jagger, Richards and company as they watch the evil deed over and over again in the studio during filming.

16

northwest by way of Walnut Creek, and the routes join together five miles from the summit. March and April, when the wildflowers are blooming, are the best months to come and mornings are ideal for getting the clearest view. Keep in mind that in summer it can get desperately hot and dry, so parts of the park are closed because of fire danger.

ARRIVAL AND INFORMATION   MOUNT DIABLO

By car and bike To reach the park, you'll need a car or the ability to cycle a long way uphill.

By organized tour The Sierra Club sometimes organizes day trips; check with the Interpretive Center (see opposite).

Tourist information The Interpretive Center is at the summit (Wed–Sun: March–Oct 11am–5pm, Nov–Feb 11am–4pm; ☎ 925 837 2525, ⓦ mdia.org). The ranger station sells trail maps for $5 listing the best day hikes.

ACCOMMODATION

Three campgrounds with running water and restrooms are open here year-round for RVs and tents (☎ 510 837 2525; ⓦ parks.ca.gov; $30).

The Bay side of the Peninsula

US-101 runs south towards San Jose from San Francisco along the Bay, lined by light-industrial estates and shopping malls, through a series of merging suburban towns from Burlingame to Palo Alto. Parallel to that inland, the surprisingly scenic **I-280** is one of the newer and more expensive freeways in California. Beyond Colma, the scenery improves quickly as I-280 continues past the **Crystal Springs Reservoir**, an artificial lake holding San Francisco's water supply, which is pumped here all the way from Yosemite. An alternative, albeit much slower route south from San Francisco is to take **Hwy-35**, which winds its way majestically along the ridges that divide the Bay from the Ocean. At certain spots, you are rewarded by simultaneous views across both bodies of water.

GETTING AROUND THE PENINSULA

By subway BART only travels down the Peninsula as far as Millbrae.

By bus SamTrans buses (☎ 1 800 660 4287, ⓦ samtrans .com) run south from San Francisco to Palo Alto or along

the coast to Half Moon Bay.

By train CalTrain (☎ 650 817 1717 or 1 800 660 4287, ⓦ caltrain.com) offers an hourly rail service, stopping at most Bayside towns.

Filoli Estate

Just off I-280 on Canada Road, Woodside • Mid-Feb to late Oct Tues–Sat 10am–3.30pm, Sun 11am–3.30pm, last admission 2.30pm • Tours by reservation only $12 • ☎ 650 364 8300 ext 507, ⓦ filoli.org

At the south end of the Crystal Springs Reservoir, in the well-heeled town of **Woodside**, luscious gardens surround the palatial **Filoli Estate**. If the 45-room Georgian-style mansion, designed in 1915 by San Francisco architect Willis Polk, looks familiar, that's because it was used in the TV series *Dynasty*. It's the only one of the many huge houses hereabouts that you can actually visit, although the sixteen-acre grounds featuring formal gardens with reflecting pools are what make it worth coming, especially in the spring.

Palo Alto and Stanford University

Just south of the exclusive communities of Woodside and Menlo Park, leafy and wealthy **PALO ALTO** nestles between I-280 and US-101. Despite its proximity to Stanford University, it has little of the college-town vigour of its northern rival, UC Berkeley. Indeed, Palo Alto has become somewhat of a social centre for Silicon Valley's nouveau riche, as evidenced by the trendy cafés and chic new restaurants that cluster along its main drag, **University Avenue**.

East Palo Alto, on the Bay side of US-101, has a well-deserved reputation for gang- and drug-related violence, with one of the highest per capita murder rates of any US city. Perhaps best known as the childhood home of the Grateful Dead's Jerry Garcia, the area was founded in the 1920s as the utopian Runnymeade Colony, a poultry-raising co-operative; the local preservation society (☎ 650 329 0294) can point out the surviving sites.

Immediately west of Palo Alto, **STANFORD UNIVERSITY** is by contrast one of the tamest places you could hope for. The university is among the most elite and expensive in the United States, though when it opened in 1891, founded by railroad magnate Leland Stanford in memory of his dead son, it offered free tuition. Ridiculed by East Coast academics, who felt that there was little need for a second West Coast university (after UC Berkeley), Stanford was built anyway, a defiant hybrid of Mission and Romanesque buildings on a huge arid campus covering an area larger than the whole of Downtown San Francisco.

16

The Quadrangle

Walking tours depart from the Stanford Visitor Center (see p.256) • Walking tours daily 11am & 3.15pm; golf cart tours daily 1pm • Walking tours free; golf cart tours $5

Approaching from the Palo Alto CalTrain and SamTrans bus station, which acts as a buffer between the town and the university, the campus is entered via a half-mile-long, palm-tree-lined boulevard that deposits you at its heart, the **Quadrangle**, bordered by the phallic **Hoover Tower** (daily 10am–4.30pm; $2), whose observation platform is worth ascending to for the view, and the colourful gold-leaf mosaics of the **Memorial**

CONSERVATIVE OR CUTTING EDGE?

Stanford University, whose reputation as an arch-conservative thinktank was enhanced by Ronald Reagan's offer to donate his video library to the school (the university politely declined), hasn't always been an entirely boring place, though you wouldn't know it to walk among the preppy future-lawyers-of-America that seem to comprise the majority of the student body. **Ken Kesey** came here from Oregon in 1958 on a writing fellowship, working nights as an orderly on the psychiatric ward of one local hospital, and getting paid $75 a day to test experimental drugs (LSD among them) in another. Drawing on both experiences, Kesey wrote *One Flew over the Cuckoo's Nest* in 1960 and quickly became a counter-culture hero, a period admirably chronicled by Tom Wolfe in *The Electric Kool-Aid Acid Test*. To this day, Stanford is at the forefront of pioneering research into the nature of consciousness, including such arcane subjects as lucid dreaming.

Church. Like the rest of the campus, the church was constructed in memory of Leland Stanford Jr, and its elaborate, mosaic entrance has a fittingly elegiac feel.

From here, the campus's covered sidewalks and symmetrical red-roofed brownstone buildings branch out around a central fountain. Free hour-long **walking tours** are conducted by students, or you can take driving tours in a golf cart.

Cantor Arts Center

Intersection of Lomita Drive and Museum Way • Wed–Sun 11am–5pm, Thurs till 8pm • Free • ☎ 650 723 4177, ⊛ museum.stanford.edu

The highlight of any trip to the campus is the **Cantor Arts Center**, one of the finest museums in the Bay Area, comprising 27 galleries spread over 120,000 square feet and containing treasures from six continents, some dating back to 500 BC. Housed in the old Stanford Museum of Art, the refurbished building incorporates the former structure with a new wing, including a bookshop and café. Visiting exhibitions have featured such artists as Duchamp, Oldenburg and Lucian Freud. One of the finest pieces in the permanent collection of photography, painting, sculpture, ceramics and artefacts from around the globe is the stunning *Plum Garden, Kameido* by Japanese wood-block print artist Hiroshige. Another reason to visit is to have a look at its distinguished collection of over two hundred **Rodin sculptures**, including a *Gates of Hell* flanked by a shamed *Adam and Eve*, displayed in an attractive outdoor setting on the museum's south side. There's a version of *The Thinker* here as well, forming a sort of bookend with the rendition that fronts the Palace of the Legion of Honor Museum in San Francisco.

Herbert Hoover Memorial Exhibit Pavilion

Hoover Institution • Tues–Sat 11am–4pm • Free

History buffs will enjoy the **Herbert Hoover Memorial Exhibit Pavilion**, which displays changing exhibits from the vast Hoover collection of posters, photographs, letters and other documents.

ARRIVAL AND INFORMATION   **PALO ALTO**

By train or bus The CalTrain and Sam Trans stations are next to each other just above the University Avenue underpass.

Tourist information The Palo Alto Chamber of Commerce is next to Sam Trans at 400 Mitchell Lane (Mon–Sat 9am–5pm; ☎ 650 324 3121, ⊛ paloaltochamber.com). The Stanford

Visitor Center (Mon–Fri 8.30am–5pm, Sat & Sun 10am–5pm; ☎ 650 723 2560, ⊛ stanford.edu) is at 295 Galvez St.

Listings Look out for the free *Palo Alto Weekly* or see ⊛ paloaltoonline.com, a database of events and services. The free *Stanford Daily* is published on weekdays.

THE ORIGINS OF SILICON VALLEY

Though the name "**Silicon Valley**" is of relatively recent origin, Santa Clara county's history of electronic innovation reaches back to 1909, when **Lee de Forest** completed work on the vacuum tube at Stanford University. Stanford's entrepreneurial spirit was best embodied by **Frederick Terman**, however, a professor of radio engineering who encouraged students to found their own companies rather than bury themselves within massive corporations. After World War II expansions, Terman helped in the foundation of **Hewlett Packard** and the Stanford Industrial Park, earning himself the nickname "Father of Silicon Valley". The unique public–private partnership between the school and its alumni made the Valley central to development of radar, television and microwave products.

It was from these roots that the modern Silicon Valley bloomed in the late 1970s, when the local folks at Intel invented first the **silicon semiconductor** and then the **microprocessor** and initiated the computer revolution. In 1976, the "two Steves", **Wozniak** and **Jobs**, former high-school friends from Los Altos, founded **Apple Computers** in a garage, creating the first hardware for their systems using scavenged parts from calculators and money raised by selling a VW bus; the new computers sold for $666.66 apiece. In 1994, capitalizing on this new market, two young Stanford students named **Steve Yang** and **Jerry Filo** founded Yahoo!, a portal that allowed casual computer users to explore the **internet**, previously a computer network purely for government officials and academics. The rest, as they say, is history.

ACCOMMODATION

The environs of Palo Alto contain a range of accommodation to suit most budgets, mainly used by parents and academics visiting Stanford. Dozens of $50/night motels line El Camino Real (Hwy-82), the old main highway. Hotels by the airport are another option (see box, p.133).

Hotel California 2431 Ash St, Palo Alto ☎ 650 322 7666, ⓦ hotelcalifornia.com. Conveniently placed and with a free shuttle to campus, this friendly hotel has twenty compact but nicely furnished rooms. And yes, the website opens with "Welcome to...". $92

Cardinal Hotel 235 Hamilton Ave, Palo Alto ☎ 650 323 5101, ⓦ cardinalhotel.com. Quaint hotel in the heart of downtown Palo Alto, featuring a winning combination of affordable rates and comfortable rooms, some with shared bathrooms. $85

Cowper Inn 705 Cowper St, Palo Alto ☎ 650 327 4475, ⓦ cowperinn.com. Restored Victorian house with attractive rooms close to University Ave. The cheaper rooms have shared bathrooms. $105

Stanford Park Hotel 100 El Camino Real, Menlo Park ☎ 650 322 1234 or 1 800 368 2468, ⓦ stanfordpark hotel.com. Very pleasant, luxurious hotel in extensive grounds near Stanford University. Sometimes offers good packages and online deals. $369

EATING

For a college town, most places to eat in downtown Stanford around University Avenue are on the chic side, though that's not surprising, given the exclusive nature of the university. Cheaper alternatives tend to cluster around El Camino Real. For a student town, the nightlife in Palo Alto is very low-key.

CAFÉS

★ **Caffé del Doge** 419 University Ave ☎ 650 323 3600. Relaxing, colourful hangout for Palo Alto's intellectual crowd, a branch of the Venetian original. Mon–Wed 7am–11pm, Thurs–Sat 7am–midnight, Sun 8am–11pm.

Da Coffee Spot 235 University Ave ☎ 650 326 9942. Relaxing hangout where punters can puff on a hookah while quaffing a hot beverage or soft drink. Mon–Wed 6pm–1am, Thurs–Sat 6pm–3am.

Printer's Inc Cafe 320 California Ave ☎ 650 323 3347. Fine coffees and a range of meals are served indoors or on the sunny patio. Adjacent to Palo Alto's best bookstore. Mon–Fri 7am–9pm, Sat 8am–9pm, Sun 9am–5pm.

RESTAURANTS

Bistro Elan 448 S California Ave ☎ 650 327 0284, ⓦ bistroelan.com. Elegant Cal cuisine such as duck confit and pan-seared Maine scallops served to the cyber elite. Dinner prices are rather steep at well over $20 for a main course. Tues–Sat 5.30–9.30pm.

Café Brioche 445 S California Ave ☎ 650 336 8640, ⓦ cafebrioche-paloalto.com. Quality fare such as *Cassoulet de Toulouse* are among the delights at this French bistro. Mains mostly under $20. Daily 9am–3pm & 5.30–9.30pm.

Evvia 420 Emerson St ☎ 650 326 0983, ⓦ evvia.net. California/Greek lamb dishes such as *païdakia arnisia* and *arni kapama*, as well as baked fish and other Hellenic faves, served in a cosy yet elegant dining room. Mon–Fri 11.30am–2pm & 5.30pm–10pm, Sat 5–11pm, Sun 5–9pm.

★ **Hyderabad House** 448 University Ave ☎ 650 327 3455, ⓦ hyderabadhouse.com. Inexpensive Indian restaurant combining dishes from both north and south, with touches of ginger and coconut. The lamb *achari ghost*, cooked in a spicy pickle sauce, is a Hyderabadi speciality. Daily noon–3pm & 5–10pm.

Joanie's Cafe 447 California Ave ☎ 650 326 6505, ⓦ joaniescafepaloalto.com. Homestyle breakfasts and lunches are the hallmarks of this comfortable neighbourhood restaurant but dinner sandwiches and burgers are great too. Mon & Sun 7.30am–2.30pm, Tues–Sat 7.30am–2.30pm & 5–9pm.

Krung Siam 423 University Ave ☎ 650 322 5900. Classy but not expensive restaurant serving beautifully presented traditional Thai fare, including red, green and yellow curries for around $10. Mon–Fri 11am–10pm, Sat & Sun noon–10pm.

St Michael's Alley 806 Emerson St ☎ 650 326 2530, ⓦ stmikes.com. One of Palo Alto's hottest bistros features "casual California" cuisine such as seared wild sea scallops and weekend brunch specials for $10–16. A fine wine list too. Tues–Fri 11.30am–2pm & 5.30–9.30pm, Sat 10am–2pm & 5.30–9.30pm, Sun 10am–2pm.

BARS

Gordon Biersch Brewery 640 Emerson St ☎ 650 323 7723. The original branch of one of the oldest Bay Area microbrewery-cum-restaurants; most of its beers are lagers. Mon–Thurs & Sun 11.30am–1am, Fri & Sat 11.30am–2am.

Rose and Crown 547 Emerson St ☎ 650 327 7673. This British-style pub with a mock Tudor facade is festooned inside with European soccer paraphernalia; games are shown on TV too. Daily 11.30am–late.

16

The Peninsula coast

The **coastline** of the Peninsula south from San Francisco is worlds away from the valley of the inland: mostly undeveloped, with a few small towns and countless beaches tracing the 75 miles south to the mellow summer fun of Santa Cruz and Capitola. Along the way, bluffs protect the many nudist beaches from prying eyes and make a popular launching pad for hang-gliding. Hwy-1 is the main route south along the coast and can be a relaxing drive, providing jaw-dropping views of the ocean, although on summer and weekend afternoons it gets clogged with slow-moving traffic. Apart from the possibility of **camping** in the woods by the ocean, those with time to explore the coast can stay in unique **hostels** converted from lighthouses and eat at a number of picturesque restaurants.

Pacifica and around

San Pedro Point, a popular surfing beach fifteen miles south of San Francisco proper, along with the town of **PACIFICA**, marks the southern extent of the city's suburban sprawl. Pacifica is a pleasant stop-off for lunch and wave-gazing around Rockaway Beach.

Ask at the Chamber of Commerce (see p.260) for free maps, including trail guides for **Sweeney Ridge**, from where Spanish explorer Gaspar de Portola discovered the San Francisco Bay in 1769. Also worth a quick look in town is the **Sanchez Adobe** at 1000 Linda Mar (Tues–Thurs 10am–4pm, Sat & Sun 1–5pm; free; ☎650 359 1462), an 1846 hotel and speakeasy, now a museum with various Native American artefacts on display.

The Devil's Slide

A mile south of Pacifica

The continually eroding cliffs make construction along this stretch of coast treacherous at best, as evidenced by the **Devil's Slide**, which has required constant repairs over the decades but will finally close in 2012 when a new tunnel opens. The slide area was also a popular dumping spot for corpses of those who fell foul of rum-runners during Prohibition and is featured under various names in many of Dashiell Hammett's detective stories.

Gray Whale Cove to Venice Beach

The splendid sands of **Gray Whale Cove State Beach** (daily 8am–sunset; free) are clothing-optional. Despite the name, it's not an especially great place to look for migrating grey whales. Two miles south, the red-roofed buildings of the 1875 **Montara Lighthouse**, set among the windswept Monterey pine trees at the top of a steep cliff, have been converted into the *HI-Point Montara Lighthouse* youth hostel (see p.260).

Fitzgerald Marine Reserve

At the end of California Street in the town of Moss Beach • Free • ☎650 728 3584, ⓦ fitzgeraldreserve.org

The **Fitzgerald Marine Reserve** has three miles of diverse oceanic habitat, peaceful trails, and, at low tide, the best tidal pools of the Bay Area. Rangers often give free guided walks through the reserve at low tide, too – call or check the website for low-tide times. At the south end of the reserve, **Pillar Point** juts out into the Pacific.

Mavericks Beach

Mavericks Beach, south of Pillar Point beyond an enormous communications dish, has what are said to be the largest waves in North America, attracting some of the world's best (and craziest) surfers when conditions are right; just watching them can be an exhilarating way to spend an hour or so. The beach hosts the annual **Mavericks Surf Contest**, an event so secretive and dependent on the right wave-creating conditions that invitations are emailed to participants just two days in advance. There's a long breakwater to walk out on but remember never to turn your back on the ocean; rogue waves have crashed in and swept unsuspecting tourists to their deaths.

16

Princeton-By-the-Sea

A little to the east of Mavericks Beach, almost back on Hwy-1, fishing boats and yachts dock at **Pillar Point Harbor**. The surrounding village of **PRINCETON-BY-THE-SEA** has numerous eating options, with a rather anodyne mall-like strip at the harbour, plus some better options a few hundred yards west (see p.261).

Miramar Beach to Venice Beach

There's good surfing at the long strand of **Miramar Beach**. Slightly further south lie **Dunes Beach** and **Venice Beach**, two more beautiful expanses of sand and ocean. You can ride a horse along these beaches from the jointly run **Sea Horse/Friendly Acres Ranches** (☎650 726 9903, ⓦhorserentals.com/seahorse.html), at Hwy-1 one mile north of the intersection with Hwy-92; activities include a one-hour trail ride ($55), a ninety-minute beach ride ($65) and a combined beach and trail ride ($75).

Half Moon Bay

HALF MOON BAY, twenty miles south of the southern reaches of the city, takes its name from the crescent-shaped bay formed by Pillar Point. Lined by miles of sandy beaches, the town is surprisingly rural, considering its proximity to San Francisco and Silicon Valley, and sports a number of ornate Victorians around its centre. The oldest of these, built in 1849, is at the north end of Main Street, just across a little stone bridge over Pillarcitos Creek. **Half Moon Bay State Beach** (daily 8am–sunset; parking $10) is under a mile west of town. Every year in mid-October, Half Moon Bay comes alive for the annual **Pumpkin Festival** (call ☎650 726 9652 for dates), when all manner of competitions are held to find the largest, tastiest and most perfectly shaped pumpkin.

Butano Redwood Forest

If you've got a car and it's not a great beach day, head up into the hills above the coast, where the thousands of acres of the **BUTANO REDWOOD FOREST** feel at their most ancient and primeval in the greyest, gloomiest weather. Any one of a dozen roads heads through endless stands of untouched forest and even the briefest of walks will take you seemingly miles from any sign of civilization. Hwy-84 climbs up from San Gregorio through the Sam McDonald County Park to the hamlet of **LA HONDA**, where Ken Kesey had his ranch during the Sixties and once notoriously invited the Hell's Angels to a party. From here you can continue on to Palo Alto, or, better still, loop back to the coast via Pescadero Road. Another route via Cloverdale Road heads south to **Butano State Park** (daily 8am–sunset; parking $8), where you can hike and camp among the redwoods overlooking the Pacific.

16

AÑO NUEVO STATE RESERVE

From December to March, **Año Nuevo State Reserve**, around ten miles south of Pescadero, offers a chance to see one of nature's most bizarre spectacles – the mating rituals of the **northern elephant seal**. These massive, ungainly creatures, fifteen feet long and weighing up to three tonnes, were once found all along the coast, though they were nearly hunted to extinction by whalers in the nineteenth century. During the mating season the beach is literally a seething mass of blubbery bodies, with the trunk-nosed males fighting it out for the right to sire as many as fifty pups in a season. At any time of the year, though, you're likely to see half a dozen or so dozing in the sands. The reserve is also good for **birdwatching**, and in March you might even catch sight of migrating **grey whales**.

The slowly resurgent Año Nuevo seal population is still carefully protected, and during the breeding season the obligatory **guided tours** – designed to protect spectators as much as to give the seals some privacy – begin booking in October (hourly 8am–4pm; $7 per person, $10 per car; ☎650 879 2025 or 1 800 444 4445, ⓦparks.ca.gov). Otherwise, tickets are usually made available to people staying at the *Pigeon Point Hostel* (see p.260).

Pescadero and around

A mile before Pescadero Road rejoins Hwy-1, you pass through the quaint town of **PESCADERO**, which has one of the best places to eat on the Peninsula – *Duarte's* (see opposite), as well as a petrol station, just about the last place to fill up north of Santa Cruz. Nearby **Pescadero State Beach** is yet another fine spot for a dip, with no time restrictions or parking fee. Five miles south of Pescadero, the grounds of the old **Pigeon Point lighthouse** (daily 8am–sunset; free; ☎650 879 2120) – now a hostel (see below) – are open to visitors. The calmest, most pleasant beach along this stretch is at **Bean Hollow State Beach**, a mile north of the hostel – it's also free but has very limited parking.

ARRIVAL AND DEPARTURE   THE PENINSULA COAST

By bus SamTrans express #DX from San Francisco Transbay Terminal and #16 from Daly City both go to the Linda Mar shopping centre in Pacifica. Here you can connect to #294, which follows Hwy-1 to Half Moon Bay, then Hwy-92 to San Mateo Caltrain station on the Bay. Route #17 runs from Moss Beach via Half Moon Bay to Pescadero.

INFORMATION

Half Moon Bay 235 Main St (Mon–Fri 9am–4pm; ☎650 726 8380, ⓦhalfmoonbaychamber.org); gives out walking-tour maps and information on accommodation.

Pacifica 225 Rockaway Beach Ave (Mon–Fri 9am–5pm, Sat & Sun 10am–4.30pm; ☎650 355 4122, ⓦpacificachamber.com).

ACCOMMODATION

GRAY WHALE COVE TO VENICE BEACH

Farallone Inn 1410 Main St, Montara ☎1 800 818 7316, ⓦfaralloneinn.com. Restored mansion whose rooms vary from extremely cosy to penthouse suites – but all have jacuzzis. Good rates, especially off-season. $85

HI-Point Montara Lighthouse ☎650 728 7177, ⓦnorcalhostels.org. Dorms and rooms in the converted outhouses of an 1875 lighthouse; SamTrans bus #294 from Pacifica. Office hours 7.30am–10pm. Dorms $26 members, $29 non-members; doubles $70

Seal Cove Inn 221 Cypress Ave, Moss Beach ☎1 800 995 9987, ⓦsealcoveinn.com. Splendid inn with the style of an opulent hotel but the friendliness of a B&B. Has a path to the Fitzgerald Marine Reserve. $235

HALF MOON BAY

Cameron's Inn 1410 S Cabrillo Hwy (Hwy-1) ☎650 726 5705, ⓦcameronsinn.com. Three rooms are available at this popular pub (see opposite).

Half Moon Bay State Beach Half Moon Bay ☎650 726 8820; book on ☎1 800 444 7275, ⓦparks.ca.gov. Plenty of tent sites in the woods, right behind the splendid beach. $35, plus hike/bike-in $7

★ **Mill Rose Inn** 615 Mill St ☎650 726 8750 or 1 800 900 7673, ⓦmillroseinn.com. Top of the B&Bs in town is this intricately designed place with luxurious rooms. The beautiful garden contains a huge hot tub. $175

Old Thyme Inn 779 Main St ☎650 726 1616 or 1 800 720 4277, ⓦoldthymeinn.com. A Victorian house with cosy, beautifully furnished rooms, the pricier ones with hot tubs. Easily walkable to the town's restaurants. $139

Landis Shores Oceanfront Inn 211 Mirada Rd, 2 miles north of Half Moon Bay ☎650 726 6644, ⓦlandisshores .com. Overlooking the crashing Pacific waves, this smart modern hotel offers a friendly B&B atmosphere and state-of-the-art amenities. Complimentary afternoon wine from the owner's huge cellar. $285

PACIFICA AND AROUND

Pacifica Motor Inn 200 Rockaway Beach Ave ☎650 359 7700 or 1 800 522 3772, ⓦpacificamotorinn. com. Simple but large pet-friendly motel rooms just a block inland from the beach. Breakfast included. $69

Sea Breeze Motel 100 Rockaway Beach Ave ☎650 359 3903, ⓦnicksrestaurant.net. These small rooms, attached to *Nick's* (see opposite), have the advantage of ocean views. It's also just a few yards to the small but pretty black-sand beach. $80

PESCADERO AND AROUND

Butano State Park Pescadero ☎650 879 2040, book on ☎1 800 444 7275 on ⓦparks.ca.gov. RV and tent spaces located in a beautiful redwood forest. $35

Costanoa Coastal Lodge & Camp 2001 Rossi Rd, just south of Pescadero ☎650 879 1100 or 1 877 262 7848, ⓦcostanoa.com. Offers a pampered night under the stars with accommodation ranging from modest cabins to luxury suites. Cabins $89, suites $325

★ **HI-Pigeon Point Lighthouse Hostel** 5 miles south of Pescadero ☎650 879 0633, ⓦnorcalhostels.org. Stay in the old lighthouse-keeper's quarters and soak your bones in a marvellous hot tub at this hostel. Check-in from 3pm, curfew 11pm; reservations essential in summer. Dorms $24 members, $27–29 non-members; doubles $72

EATING AND DRINKING

PACIFICA

Nick's Seashore Restaurant 101 Rockaway Beach Ave ☎650 359 3903. An all-purpose joint providing cheap breakfasts, moderate pasta options, and pricier steak/seafood dishes. Mon–Thurs 11am–10pm, Fri 9am–10pm, Sat & Sun 8am–10pm, bar till 1am.

Rock'n'Rob's 450 Dundee Way ☎650 359 3663. This simple diner is recommended for its filling burgers and other classic American favourites. Daily 11am–10pm.

GRAY WHALE COVE TO VENICE BEACH

Barbara's Fish Trap 281 Capistrano Rd, Princeton-by-the-Sea ☎650 728 7049. This oceanfront place has an unbeatable view and serves good-value fish and seafood, including a delicious clam chowder. Mon–Thurs & Sun 11am–9pm, Fri & Sat 11am–10pm.

Café Gibraltar 425 Ave Alhambra, El Granada ☎650 560 9039, ⊛cafegibraltar.com. Set back from Hwy-1 but with ocean views, this classy establishment boasts fine decor and finer Mediterranean cuisine made from local organic produce. Delights such as *arni fricasse* (Greek-style lamb) cost around $25. Tues–Thurs & Sun 5–9pm, Fri & Sat 5–9.45pm.

Douglass Beach House Miramar Beach ☎650 726 4143, ⊛bachddsoc.org. On Sunday afternoons this beachfront bar becomes an informal seaside jazz club that attracts surprisingly big names. Sun 4.30–7.15pm; bar hours vary.

★ **Half Moon Bay Brewing Company** 390 Capistrano Ave, Princeton-by-the-Sea ☎650 728 2739, ⊛hmbbrewingco.com. An excellent option where you can wash down a full meal or cheaper bar snack with their own finely crafted ales. Mon–Thurs 11.30am–10pm, Fri 11.30am–11pm, Sat 11am–11pm, Sun 11am–10pm.

Moss Beach Distillery Just off Hwy-1 at Moss Beach ☎650 728 0220, ⊛mossbeachdistillery.com. Top-quality seafood and meat dishes go for around $20–35 at the popular restaurant but there's a cheaper bar menu, or you can enjoy a sunset cocktail from the patio overlooking the ocean. Mon–Thurs noon–8.30pm, Fri & Sat noon–9pm, Sun 11am–8.30pm.

HALF MOON BAY

Cameron's Inn 1410 S Cabrillo Hwy (Hwy-1) ☎650 726 5705, ⊛cameronsinn.com. Decent pub grub, over 20 draught beers from English ales to local microbrews, British football on TV and a unique double-decker bus make this a top spot. Daily 11am–late.

★ **Cetrella** 845 Main St ☎650 726 4090, ⊛cetrella.com. The classiest option in town is this award-winning Mediterranean restaurant, with delights such as braised Australian lamb shank for around $25; live jazz Sat & Sun eves. Tues–Thurs 5.30–9.30pm, Fri & Sat 5.30–10pm, Sun 10.30am–2.30pm & 5.30–9.30pm.

Pasta Moon 315 Main St ☎650 726 5125, ⊛pastamoon.com. Elegant but unpretentious Italian place that serves excellent pizza, pasta and mouthwatering dishes such as seafood *spiedini* (kebabs). Mains $21–28. Mon–Fri 11.30am–2.30pm & 5.30–10.30pm, Sat & Sun noon–3pm & 5.30–10.30pm.

PESCADERO

★ **Duarte's** 202 Stage Rd ☎650 879 0464, ⊛duartestavern.com. One of the best places to eat on the Peninsula, where you can feast on artichoke soup and huge portions of fish in a downhome atmosphere. Great breakfasts too. Daily 7am–9pm.

16

Marin County

North of the Golden Gate Bridge, **MARIN COUNTY** is sandwiched between the top end of San Francisco Bay and the crashing waves of the Pacific. It is one of the USA's wealthiest regions, with chintzy communities such as **Sausalito**, **Tiburon** and **Mill Valley**, and yet also boasts some of the finest natural beauty within easy reach of a major city. This comes principally in the form of redwood-clad **Mount Tamalpais** and the wide-open spaces and shoreline of **Point Reyes National Seashore**.

The Marin Headlands

The largely undeveloped, rugged and dramatically scenic **Marin Headlands** of the **Golden Gate National Recreation Area** (across the Golden Gate Bridge from San Francisco) afford some of the most impressive views of the bridge and the city behind. As the regular fog rolls in, the breathtaking image of the bridge's stanchions tantalizingly drifting in and out of sight and the fleeting glimpses of downtown skyscrapers will abide long in the memory. The first turn as you exit the bridge (Alexander Avenue) takes you up onto steep Conzelman Road, which passes through largely undeveloped land, dotted by the concrete remains of old forts and World War II gun emplacements standing guard over the entrance to the Bay, such as **Battery Wallace**.

Point Bonita Lighthouse

At the end of Marin Headlands • Tours Mon, Sat & Sun 12.30–3.30pm • Free

Standing sentry at the very end of the Headlands is **Point Bonita Lighthouse**. You have to walk the last half a mile from the small parking area down to the beckoning structure, a beautiful stroll that takes you through a tunnel cut into the cliff and across a precarious suspension bridge. The lighthouse casts its beam over 25 miles out to sea.

The inland loop

As Conzelman loops back inland, the left fork, Fort Barry Road, leads to the **Marin Headlands Information Center** (see p.268), offering free maps of popular hiking trails in the area and a **historical walk**, which loops five and a half miles into Gerbode Valley. Just up the hill, the largest of **Fort Barry**'s old buildings has been converted into the spacious but homely *HI-Marin Headlands Hostel* (see p.268), an excellent base for more extended explorations of the Headlands.

Rodeo Beach

#76 MUNI bus from San Francisco (Sun & holidays only)

Northwest from Conzelman, Bunker Road snakes down to wide, sandy **Rodeo Beach**, which separates the chilly ocean from the warm marshy water of **Rodeo Lagoon**, where swimming is prohibited to protect nesting seabirds. North of the lagoon, the **Marine Mammal Center** (daily 10am–5pm; free; ☎415 289 7333, ⊛marinemammalcenter.org) rescues and rehabilitates injured and orphaned sea creatures, especially seals and sea lions. You can visit to learn about the animals and see how caringly they are tended to.

16

Sausalito

SAUSALITO, along the Bay below US-101, is a pretty, snug little town of exclusive restaurants and pricey boutiques along a picturesque waterfront promenade. Expensive, quirkily designed houses climb the overgrown cliffs above **Bridgeway Avenue**, the main road and bus route through town. Sausalito was once a fairly gritty community of fishermen and sea-traders, full of bars and bordellos. Fifty years ago it even served as one of the settings for Orson Welles's murder mystery, *The Lady from Shanghai*. Despite its present pretensions, Sausalito still makes a fun day out from San Francisco by ferry, with boats arriving in the centre of town.

Sausalito waterfront

At the waterfront, the old working wharves and warehouses that made Sausalito a haven for smugglers and Prohibition-era rum-runners are long gone, mostly replaced by tourist restaurants. However, a mile north of the town centre at **Waldo Point**, an ad hoc community of exotic barges and houseboats can be viewed. Some of them have been moored here since the 1950s and many have fanciful appearances – one looks like a South Pacific island, another like the Taj Mahal.

Bay Model Visitor Center

2100 Bridgeway • June–Aug Tues–Fri 9am–4pm, Sat & Sun 10am–5pm; Sept–May Tues–Sat 9am–4pm • Free • ☎415 332 3871, ⊛ spn.usace.army.mil/bmvc

Elevated walkways lead you around a massive working scale model of the Bay, along with its surrounding deltas and aquatic inhabitants, simulating changing tides and powerful currents and offering insight into the vastness and diversity of this confluence of waters.

Bay Area Discovery Museum

557 McReynolds Rd • Tues–Fri 9am–4pm, Sat & Sun 10am–5pm • $10, children $8 • ☎415 339 3900, ⊛ baykidsmuseum.org

One of Sausalito's biggest family draws, situated back towards the Golden Gate Bridge, is the constantly expanding **Bay Area Discovery Museum**. Located in the remodelled barracks of **Fort Baker**, it comprises a series of activities and workshops for youngsters

SAILING AND KAYAKING IN SAUSALITO

If you have sailing experience and enough company, rent a four- to ten-person **sailing boat** at Cass's Marina, 1702 Bridgeway (☎415 332 6789, ⓦcassmarina.com; $119–209 half-day, $181–394 full day). The other main diversion is **sea kayaking**, and Sea Trek (☎415 488 1000, ⓦseatrek.com) rents single or double sea kayaks beginning at $20/35 for an hour's worth of paddling the Bay. It offers sit-on-top kayaks, lessons and safe routes for first-timers, as well as closed kayaks and directions around Angel Island for more experienced paddlers.

from toddlers to those of 10 years old or so, including art and media rooms as well as the outdoor Lookout Cove area, where kids can play in a mini-tidepool, on a shipwreck or on the model of the Golden Gate Bridge as it was during construction – pretty cool as the real one is visible in the distance if it's clear.

The Marin County coast to Bolinas

The **Shoreline Highway**, Hwy-1, cuts off west from US-101 just north of Sausalito, following the old main highway towards Mill Valley (see p.264). The first turn on the left, Tennessee Valley Road, leads up to the less-visited northern expanses of the Golden Gate National Recreation Area. Further along, Hwy-1 twists up the canyon to a crest, where **Panoramic Highway** spears off to the right, following the ridge north to Muir Woods and Mount Tamalpais. Be warned, however, that the hillsides here are more often than not choked with fog until 11am, making the drive both dangerous and visually uninteresting.

Green Gulch Farm and Zen Center

1601 Shoreline Hwy • Public meditation Sun from 8.15am; lecture 10.15am • ☎415 383 3134, ⓦsfzc.org

Two miles down from the crest, a road cuts off to the left, dropping down to the bottom of the broad canyon to the **Green Gulch Farm and Zen Center**, an organic farm and Buddhist retreat, with an authentic Japanese teahouse and a simple but refined prayer hall. On Sunday mornings the centre is open for a public meditation period and an informal lecture on Zen Buddhism.

Muir Beach to Stinson Beach

Golden Gate Transit bus #63 from San Francisco to Stinson Beach (hourly Sat, Sun & holidays only)

The main road down from Mount Tamalpais rejoins Hwy-1 at **Muir Beach**, usually uncrowded and beautifully secluded in a semicircular cove. Three miles north, **Steep Ravine** drops sharply down the cliffs to a small beach, past very rustic cabins and a campground (see p.268). A mile on is the small and lovely **Red Rocks** nudist beach, down a steep trail from a parking area along the highway. **Stinson Beach**, whose wide strand is stunning and justifiably the most popular in the county despite the rather cold water, is a mile further. Unfortunately, it gets packed at weekends in summer.

Bolinas

At the tip of the headland, due west from Stinson Beach, is the village of **BOLINAS**, though you may have a hard time finding it – road signs marking the turn-off from Hwy-1 are removed as soon as they're put up by locals hoping to keep the place to themselves. To get here, take the first left beyond the estuary and follow the road to the end. Bolinas is surrounded by federal property: the Golden Gate National Recreation Area and Point Reyes National Seashore. Even the lagoon was recently declared a National Bird Sanctuary. Known for its leftist hippie culture, the village itself is a small colony of artists, bearded handymen, stray dogs and writers, who have included the late trout-fishing author Richard Brautigan. There's not a lot to see in Bolinas apart from the small **Bolinas Museum** at 48 Wharf Rd (Fri 1–5pm, Sat & Sun noon–5pm; free; ☎415 868 0330, ⓦbolinasmuseum.org), which has a few historical displays and works by local artists in a set of converted cottages around a courtyard.

16

Southern Point Reyes

Beyond Bolinas, the rocky beach at the end of Wharf Road west of the village is great for calm surf waves. **Duxbury Reef Nature Reserve**, half a mile west at the end of Elm Road, is well worth a look for its tidal pools, full of starfish, crabs and sea anemones. Otherwise, Mesa Road heads north from Bolinas past the **Point Reyes Bird Observatory** (informal tours all day; ☎415 868 0655, ⓦprbo.org), the first bird observatory in the US and still an important research and study centre. Beyond here, the unpaved road leads onto the **Palomarin Trailhead**, the southern access into the Point Reyes National Seashore (see p.266). The best of the many beautiful hikes around the area leads past a number of small lakes and meadows for three miles to **Alamere Falls**, which throughout the winter and spring cascade down the cliffs onto **Wildcat Beach**. **Bass Lake**, the first of several lakes along the trail, is a great spot for a swim.

Mount Tamalpais State Park

MOUNT TAMALPAIS dominates the Marin skyline. Hulking over the cool canyons of the rest of the county in a crisp yet voluptuous silhouette, Mount Tam, as it's locally known, divides the county into two distinct parts: the wild western slopes above the Pacific Coast and the increasingly suburban communities along the calmer Bay frontage. Panoramic Highway branches off from Hwy-1 along the crest through the centre of **Mount Tamalpais State Park** (☎415 338 2070, ⓦmttam.net), which has some thirty miles of hiking trails and many campgrounds, though most of the redwood trees which once covered its slopes have long since been chopped down to form the posts and beams of San Francisco's Victorian houses.

Muir Woods National Monument

Daily 8am–sunset · $5 · ☎415 388 2595, ⓦnps.gov/muwo

One 560-acre grove of towering redwoods remains protected as the **MUIR WOODS NATIONAL MONUMENT**, a mile down Muir Woods Road from Panoramic Highway. It's a tranquil and majestic spot, with sunlight filtering through the 300-foot trees down to the laurel and fern-covered canyon below. The canyon's steep sides are what saved it from Mill Valley's lumbermen and today it's one of the few old-growth redwood groves between San Francisco and the fantastic forests of Redwood National Park.

Its proximity to San Francisco makes Muir Woods a popular target, and the **paved trails** nearest the car park are often packed with bus-tour hordes. However, if you visit during the week, or outside midsummer, it's easy enough to leave the crowds behind, especially if you're willing to head off up the steep trails that climb the canyon sides. Winter is a particularly good time to come, as the streams are gurgling and the forest creatures are more likely to be seen going about their business. Keep an eye out for the various species of salamanders and newts that thrive in this damp environment; be warned, though, that some are poisonous and will bite if harassed.

Mill Valley

Golden Gate Transit bus #10 from San Francisco and Sausalito (every 30min)

From the east peak of Mount Tamalpais, a quick two-mile hike downhill follows the **Temelpa Trail** through velvety shrubs of chaparral to **MILL VALLEY**, the oldest and most

---

VISITING THE MUIR WOODS NATIONAL MONUMENT

The only way to get to the Muir Woods National Monument by public transport is to enter the woods from the top by way of a two-mile hike from the **Pan Toll Ranger Station** (Panoramic Highway, on the Golden Gate Transit #63 bus route; ☎415 388 2070). From here, the **Pan Toll Road** turns off to the right along the ridge to within a hundred yards of the 2571-foot summit of Mount Tamalpais, where there are breathtaking views of the distant Sierra Nevadas. Hike the 0.3-mile wood-planked trail up to Gardner Lookout from the car park for an even better view.

CULTURAL MILL VALLEY

Upscale Mill Valley still makes a healthy living out of tourism, especially during the **Mill Valley Film Festival** (☎415 383 5346, ⓦmvff.com) in early October, which draws Bay Area stars like Robin Williams and Sharon Stone. Literature aficionados will not be disappointed by the *Depot Bookstore and Café* (87 Throckmorton Ave; Mon–Sat 7am–10pm, Sun 8am–10pm; ☎415 383 2665), a popular browsing hangout, which also stocks free maps of Mount Tam and hiking trails. Across the street, the Pleasure Principle (74 Throckmorton Ave; ☎415 388 8588) is a reminder of the Northern California eclecticism that lurks beneath Mill Valley's posh facade – this self-declared UFO headquarters also advertises a collection of vintage porn.

enticing of Marin County's inland towns, arranged around an attractive redwood-shaded square. Originally a logging centre, it was from here that the destruction of the surrounding redwoods was organized. The long-defunct **Mill Valley and Mount Tamalpais Scenic Railroad** – according to the blurb of the time, "the crookedest railroad in the world" – became a huge tourist attraction early last century but had folded by 1930. You can, however, follow its old route from the end of Summit Avenue in Mill Valley, a popular trip with daredevils on all-terrain bikes, which were invented here.

Tiburon

TIBURON, five miles southeast of Mill Valley on the other side of US-101, is another ritzy harbourside village to which hundreds of people come each weekend, many of them via direct Blue & Gold Fleet **ferries** from San Francisco (see p.267). It's a relaxed place, a bit less touristy than Sausalito, and sitting out on the sunny deck of one of the many cafés and bars can be idyllic. Or you can browse the galleries and antique shops, the best of which are grouped together in **Ark Row**, at the west end of Main Street. Many of the quirky buildings here are actually old houseboats that were beached here early in the twentieth century. On a hill above the town stands **Old St Hilary's Church** (Apr–Oct Wed–Sun 1–4pm; ☎415 789 0066), a Gothic beauty that is best seen in the spring, when the surrounding fields are covered with multicoloured buckwheat, flax and paintbrush.

Angel Island

The pleasures of Tiburon are soon exhausted, and you'd be well advised to take the Angel Island Ferry (see p.267) a mile offshore to the largest island in San Francisco Bay, ten times the size of Alcatraz. **Angel Island** is now officially a state park but over the years it's served a variety of purposes, everything from a home for Miwok Native Americans to a World War II prisoner-of-war camp. It's full of ghostly ruins of old military installations but it's the nature that lures visitors to the island, with its oak and eucalyptus trees and sagebrush covering the hills above rocky coves and sandy beaches, giving the island a feel quite apart from the mainland. The island offers some pleasant biking opportunities: a five-mile road rings the island, and an unpaved track, plus a number of hiking trails, leads up to the 800ft hump of **Mount Livermore**, with panoramic views of the Bay Area.

For **tours** of Angel Island, contact Angel Island TramTours (☎415 897 0715, ⓦangelisland.com), which organizes one-hour tours ($13.50) and rents mountain bikes ($10/hr, $35/day).

Ayala Cove and Quarry Beach

The ferry arrives at **Ayala Cove**, where a small snack bar provides the only sustenance available on the island – it's best to bring a picnic if you plan to spend the day here. Nearby, the visitor centre (see p.268) is in an old building that was built as a quarantine facility for soldiers returning from the Philippines after the Spanish–American War and has displays on the island's history. Around the point on the northwest corner of the island, **Quarry Beach** is the best on the island, a clean sandy shore that's protected from the winds blowing in through the Golden Gate.

16

Sir Francis Drake Boulevard

Cutting across central Marin County through the dull inland towns of **San Anselmo** and **Fairfax, Sir Francis Drake Boulevard** is the most direct route from the San Rafael Bridge or Larkspur ferry terminal (see opposite) to the Point Reyes National Seashore. The route ends up on the coast thirty miles west at a crescent-shaped bay where, in 1579, Drake supposedly landed and claimed all of "Nova Albion" for England.

San Quentin Prison

Museum: Building 106, Dolores Way • Mon–Fri & Sun 11am–3pm, Sat 11.45am–3pm • $2 • ☎ 415 454 8808

At the very east end of Sir Francis Drake Boulevard, a mile beyond the modern ferry terminal at Larkspur Landing, the monolithic, red-tile-roofed complex you see on the bayfront is the maximum-security **San Quentin State Prison**, which houses the state's most violent and notorious criminals and of which Johnny Cash sang, "I hate every inch of you". The tour of **San Quentin Prison Museum** takes about an hour, during which you'll see a prison cell, a replica of the gas chamber, the original gallows and the solitary confinement pen known as "The Dungeon". At the end of the tour, you can buy prisoner-made artwork and even a collection of the inmates' favourite recipes, collected in the book *Cooking with Conviction*.

Point Reyes Station and around

Ten miles west of Fairfax along Sir Francis Drake Boulevard, **Samuel Taylor State Park** has a range of pleasant trails and alternative camping facilities; five miles more bring you to the coastal Hwy-1 and **Olema**, a hamlet at the entrance to the park with decent food and lodging choices (see p.270). A couple of miles north sits the tourist town of **POINT REYES STATION**, a good place to stop off for a bite to eat or to pick up picnic supplies before heading off to enjoy the wide-open spaces of the Point Reyes National Seashore just beyond.

Point Reyes National Seashore

From Point Reyes Station, Sir Francis Drake Boulevard heads north, for access to the westernmost tip of Marin County at Point Reyes through the **Point Reyes National Seashore**, a near-island of wilderness surrounded on three sides by more than fifty miles of isolated coastline – pine forests and sunny meadows bordered by rocky cliffs and sandy, windswept beaches. This wing-shaped landmass, something of an aberration along the generally straight coastline north of San Francisco, is in fact a rogue piece of the earth's crust that has been drifting slowly and steadily northward along the San Andreas Fault, having started some six million years ago as a suburb of Los Angeles. When the great earthquake of 1906 shattered San Francisco, the epicentre was here and the land shifted over sixteen feet in an instant.

The **Bear Valley Visitors Center** (see p.268) holds engaging displays on geology and natural history, while rangers dish out excellent hiking and cycling itineraries and can give updates on the changeable weather. Nearby, a replica of a native Miwok village has an authentic religious **roundhouse** and a popular hike follows the Bear Valley Trail along Coast Creek four miles to **Arch Rock**, a large tunnel in the seaside cliffs that you can walk through at low tide. North of the visitor centre, Limantour Road heads west six miles to the *HI-Point Reyes Hostel* (see p.268), before continuing another two miles to the coast at **Limantour Beach**, one of the best swimming beaches and a good place to watch the seabirds in the adjacent estuary.

Drake's Beach and around

Eight miles west of Inverness, a turn leads down past **Drake's Bay Oyster Farm** (Tues– Sun 8am–4pm; ☎ 415 669 1149, ⓦ drakesbayfamilyfarms.com), which sells bivalves for less than half the price you'd pay in San Francisco, to **Drake's Beach**, one likely landing spot of Sir Francis in 1579. Appropriately, the coastline here resembles the southern

16

GREY WHALES

The most commonly spotted whale along California's coast, the **grey whale** migrates annually from its summer feeding grounds near Alaska to its winter breeding grounds off Baja California and back again. Some 23,000 whales make the 13,000-mile round-trip, swimming just half a mile from the shoreline in small groups, with pregnant females leading the way on the southbound journey. Protected by an international treaty from hunters since 1938, the grey whale population has been increasing steadily each year and its migration brings out thousands of humans hoping to catch a glimpse of their fellow mammals. Mid-March to April is the best time, as the whales swim closer to the shore on the northbound journey. Point Reyes is a favourite watching spot, as are the beaches along Hwy-1 south to Santa Cruz. For information on whale-watching expeditions or the latest on the migration, contact Oceanic Society Expeditions, Building E, Fort Mason, San Francisco, CA 94123 (☎415 441 1106, ⍵oceanic-society.org).

coast of England – often cold, wet and windy, with chalk-white cliffs rising above the wide sandy beach. The road continues southwest another four miles to the very tip of Point Reyes, where a precariously sited **lighthouse** (Thurs–Sun 10am–4.30pm; tours first and third Sat of each month; free) stands firm against the crashing surf. The bluffs here are an excellent place for watching migrating **grey whales**. Just over a mile back from the lighthouse a narrow road leads to **Chimney Rock**, where you can often see basking **elephant seals** or **sea lions** from the overlook.

Tomales Point and around

The northern tip of the Point Reyes seashore, **Tomales Point**, is accessible via Pierce Point Road, which turns off Sir Francis Drake Boulevard two miles north of Inverness. Jutting out into Tomales Bay, it's the least-visited section of the park and a refuge for hefty **tule elk**; it's also a great place to admire the lupins, poppies and other wildflowers that appear in the spring. The best swimming is at **Heart's Desire Beach**, just before the end of the road. Down the bluffs from where the road comes to a dead end, there are excellent tidal pools at rocky **McClure's Beach**.

16

ARRIVAL AND DEPARTURE

MARIN COUNTY

BY BUS

Golden Gate Transit offers a comprehensive bus service around Marin County and across the Golden Gate Bridge from the Transbay Terminal in San Francisco (☎415 923 2000 in San Francisco, ☎415 455 2000 in Marin, ⍵goldengate.org). It runs every 30min throughout the day, hourly late at night; some areas can only be reached by rush-hour commuter services. Route #40, the only service between Marin County and the East Bay, runs from the San Rafael Transit Center to the Del Norte BART station in El Cerrito. Fares range from $2 to $8.

BY FERRY

To Sausalito, Larkspur and Tiburon Golden Gate Transit ferries (see above for contact information) leave from the Ferry Building to **Sausalito** (Mon–Fri 7.40am–7.55pm, Sat & Sun 10.40am–6.30pm) and Larkspur (Mon–Fri 6.25am–9.40pm, Sat & Sun 12.40–7.15pm); every 30–40min during the rush hour, roughly hourly during the rest of the day and about every 1hr 30min–2hr on weekends and holidays. Tickets cost $8.25 one-way to both destinations. The more expensive Blue & Gold Fleet ferries (☎415 705 8200, ⍵blueandgoldfleet.com; $10 one-way) leave from

Pier 41 at Fisherman's Wharf to Sausalito (Mon–Fri 11.15am–5.10pm, Sat & Sun 11am–7.05pm) and Tiburon (Mon–Fri 10.50am–7.15pm, Sat & Sun 9.40am–7.05pm). Check schedules, as they change frequently.

To Angel Island East Bay Ferries (☎510 747 7963, ⍵eastbayferry.com) run to Angel Island via Pier 39 in San Francisco, departing from Oakland (Sat & Sun mid-May to late Oct 9am, returning at 3.10pm; $14.50 return). Blue & Gold Fleet (see above) provides an additional service direct to Angel Island from Pier 41 (Mon–Fri 2 daily; Sat & Sun 3 daily; $16 return). From Tiburon, there's the Angel Island ferry ($13.50 return, $1 per bicycle; ☎415 435 2131, ⍵angelisland ferry.com; 2–4 daily in summer, weekends only in winter).

BY ORGANIZED TOUR

Gray Line (☎415 558 9400, ⍵grayline.com) offers 4–5hr guided bus tours from the Transbay Terminal in San Francisco, taking in Sausalito and Muir Woods (2 daily 9.15am & 2.15pm; $49, $68 with Bay cruise); the Blue & Gold Fleet ferry (see above) also has a bus trip to Muir Woods (2 daily 9.15am & 2.15pm; 3hr 30min; $56), with an option to return by ferry from Tiburon.

INFORMATION

TOURIST INFORMATION
Angel Island Near Ayala Cove (daily 9am–4pm; ☎ 415 435 1915, ⊛ angelisland.org).
Marin County Signposted off US-101 at 1 Mitchell Blvd, San Rafael (Mon–Fri 9am–5pm; ☎ 415 925 2060 or 1 866 925 2060, ⊛ visitmarin.org).
Mill Valley 85 Throckmorton Ave (Mon–Fri 10am–noon & 1–4pm; ☎ 415 388 9700, ⊛ millvalley.org).
Sausalito 780 Bridgeway Ave (Tues–Sun 11.30am–4pm; ☎ 415 332 0505, ⊛ sausalito.org).

HIKING AND CAMPING INFORMATION
Bear Valley Visitors Center Point Reyes National

Seashore (Mon–Fri 9am–5pm, Sat & Sun 8am–5pm; ☎ 415 464 5100, ⊛ nps.gov/pore).
Marin Headlands 948 Fort Barry (daily 9.30am–4.30pm; ☎ 415 331 1540, ⊛ nps.gov/goga).
Mount Tamalpais State Park 801 Panoramic Hwy, Mill Valley (daily 8am–5.30pm; ☎ 415 388 2070, ⊛ mttam.net).

LISTINGS
Information on cultural events in Marin can be found in the widely available local freesheets, such as the down-to-earth *Coastal Post* (⊛ coastalpost.com) or the New-Agey *Pacific Sun* (⊛ pacificsun.com).

ACCOMMODATION

Sadly, there are relatively few hotels in Marin County and most charge well in excess of $100 a night; motels are also scarce in the best parts of the county, though there are a couple of attractively faded ones along the coast. If you want to stay in a B&B, contact the Bed and Breakfast Exchange (☎ 415 485 1971, ⊛ marinbedandbreakfast.com), which can fix you up with rooms in comfortable private homes all over Marin County from $70/night for two. The best budget accommodation is in two beautifully situated hostels.

MARIN HEADLANDS
★ **HI-Marin Headlands** Building 941, Fort Barry ☎ 415 331 2777, ⊛ norcalhostels.org. Worth the effort for its setting, in cosy old army barracks near the ocean. On Sun and hols only, MUNI bus #76 from San Francisco stops right outside. Closed 10am–3.30pm, except for check-in. Dorms $21, doubles $55
Marin Headlands campsites ☎ 415 561 4304, ⊛ nps .gov/goga. Five campgrounds, the best of which is the very popular *Kirby Cove* (open April–Oct only), at the northern foot of the Golden Gate Bridge (reservations ☎ 1 877 444 6777, ⊛ recreation.gov; $25). Of the remaining sites, one is a group campground ($25), and the other three are free.

MILL VALLEY AND AROUND
Acqua Hotel 555 Redwood Hwy ☎ 415 380 0400 or 1 888 662 9555, ⊛ jdvhotels.com. Sumptuous hotel on Richardson Bay with fifty luxurious rooms and oriental touches in its stylish decor. $159
★ **Mill Valley Inn** 165 Throckmorton Ave ☎ 415 389 6608 or 1 800 595 2100, ⊛ millvalleyinn.com. A gorgeous, European-style inn with elegant rooms, lavishly furnished in period style, and two private cottages. $189
Mount Tamalpais State Par campsites ☎ 415 388 2070, booking ☎ 1 800 444 7275, ⊛ reserveamerica .com. Two separate campgrounds for backpackers, one on the slopes of the mountain and the other towards the coast at Steep Ravine, which also has a few rustic cabins. Camping $20, cabins $65
Mountain Home Inn 810 Panoramic Hwy ☎ 415 381 9000 or 1 877 381 9001, ⊛ mtnhomeinn.com. Located

romantically on the crest of Mount Tamalpais, this B&B offers great views and endless hiking. Some rooms come with hot tubs. Ample cooked breakfasts. $195

MUIR AND STINSON BEACHES
Lindisfarne Guest House Green Gulch Zen Center, Muir Beach ☎ 415 383 3134, ⊛ sfzc.org. Restful rooms in a meditation retreat set in a secluded valley above Muir Beach. Price includes excellent vegetarian meals. $140
★ **Pelican Inn** 10 Pacific Way, Muir Beach ☎ 415 383 6000, ⊛ pelicaninn.com. Comfortable rooms in a romantic pseudo-English country inn, with good bar and restaurant. Two-minute walk from beautiful Muir Beach. $190
Stinson Beach Motel 3416 Shoreline Hwy, Stinson Beach ☎ 415 868 1712, ⊛ stinsonbeachmotel.com. Basic roadside motel right on Hwy-1, with tiny rooms. 5-minute walk to the beach. $90

POINT REYES AND AROUND
★ **Grand Hotel** 15 Brighton Ave, Bolinas ☎ 415 868 1757. Just two budget rooms in a funky, run-down old hotel above a secondhand shop. Shared bath. Unbeatable character, including the quirky owner. $50
HI-Point Reyes Point Reyes National Seashore ☎ 415 663 8811, ⊛ norcalhostels.org. Hard to reach without your own transport: just off Limantour Rd six miles west of the visitor centre and two miles from the beach, it's located in an old ranch house and surrounded by meadows and forests. Closed 10am–4.30pm; office hours 7.30–10am & 4.30–9pm; no check-in after 9.30pm. Dorms $20; double $58

Olema Inn 10000 Sir Francis Drake Blvd, Olema ☎ 415 663 9559 or 1 800 532 9252, ⓦ theolemainn .com. Wonderful little B&B near the entrance to Point Reyes National Seashore, on a site that's been a hotel since 1876. Comfy rooms and absolutely no nightlife or traffic noise to speak of; has its own fine dining. Book by phone only. $150

Point Reyes National Seashore campsites ☎ 415 663 1092. A wide range of hike-in sites for backpackers, near the beach or in the forest. Reserve sites up to two months in advance (weekdays 9am–2pm; ☎ 415 663 8054). $15

Point Reyes Seashore Lodge 10021 Hwy-1, Olema ☎ 415 663 9000 or 1 800 404 5694, ⓦ pointreyessea shore.com. Attractive, largely wooden lodge that's the size of a hotel but with the personal touch of a B&B. All rooms overlook the garden and brook. $135

Ten Inverness Way 10 Inverness Way, Inverness ☎ 415 669 1648, ⓦ teninvernessway.com. Quiet and restful, with a hot tub and complimentary evening wine, in a small village of good restaurants and bakeries on the fringes of Point Reyes. $162

SAUSALITO

Casa Madrona 801 Bridgeway Ave ☎ 415 332 0502 or 1 800 567 9524, ⓦ casamadrona.com. Deluxe, all mod cons hotel with an extension spreading up the hill above the Bay. Spa facilities available. $219

Hotel Sausalito 16 El Portal ☎ 415 332 0700 or 1 888 442 0700, ⓦ hotelsausalito.com. Sixteen rooms, decorated in French Riviera style, with views across the park and harbour. Owned and run by an entertaining Scot. $155

TIBURON AND ANGEL ISLAND

Angel Island State Park Angel Island ☎ 415 435 5390, ⓦ angelisland.org. Camping on Angel Island affords glittering views of San Francisco and the East Bay by night. The nine primitive walk-in (and one kayak-in) sites fill up fast, so reserve well in advance. In summer it's essential to book through Reserve-America (☎ 1 800 444 7275, ⓦ reserveamerica.com). $20

The Lodge At Tiburon 1651 Tiburon Blvd, Tiburon ☎ 415 435 3133, ⓦ thelodgeattiburon.com. Smart, modern hotel with a rustic feel. Comfortable rooms, all with CD/DVD players, and some with Jacuzzis. $169

16 EATING AND DRINKING

Marin County's **restaurants** are as varied in personality as the people who inhabit the county – homely neighbourhood cafés dish out nutritious portions to healthy mountain-bikers, well-appointed waterside restaurants cater to tourists and gourmet establishments serve delicate concoctions to affluent executives. While the Marin County **nightlife** is never as charged as San Francisco's, there are many friendly saloon-like bars. In addition, since many Bay Area musicians have lived here since the 1960s, Marin's few music venues sometimes feature big names in intimate locales.

BOLINAS

Smileys Schooner Saloon 41 Wharf Rd, Bolinas ☎ 415 868 1311, ⓦ smileyssaloon.com. The bartender calls the regulars by name at one of the oldest continually operating bars in the state. Live music Thurs–Sat and open mic Sun. Mon–Fri 8am–2am, Sat & Sun 9am–2am.

LARKSPUR

Marin Brewing Company 1809 Larkspur Landing, Larkspur ☎ 415 461 4677. Lively pub that serves a dozen or so tasty draft ales – try the malty Albion Amber or the Marin Hefe Weiss – all brewed on the premises. Mon–Thurs & Sun 11.30am–midnight, Fri & Sat 11.30am–1am.

★ **Tavern at Lark Creek** 234 Magnolia Ave ☎ 415 924 7766, ⓦ tavernatlarkcreek.com. The contemporary American food here is understandably expensive: delights such as pan-seared sweetbreads and gorgonzola soufflé are exquisite, the service first-rate and the atmosphere charming. Mon–Thurs 5.30–9.30pm, Fri & Sat 5–10pm, Sun 10am–2pm & 5–9.30pm.

MILL VALLEY

142 Throckmorton Theatre 142 Throckmorton Ave, Mill Valley ☎ 415 383 9600, ⓦ 142throckmortontheatre.org.

One of the best live music venues in Marin, showcasing a variety of musical styles, from old acid rockers and newbie indie outfits to chamber choirs. Show times vary.

★ **Avatar's Punjabi Burritos** 15 Madrona St ☎ 415 381 8293. A dastardly simple cross-cultural innovation: inexpensive burritos stuffed with delicious spicy curries. Does a brisk takeaway trade, as there are only two tables inside. Mon–Sat 11am–8pm.

Dipsea Café 200 Shoreline Hwy ☎ 415 381 0298, ⓦ dipseacafe.com. Hearty pancakes, omelettes, sandwiches and salads for breakfast and lunch, as well as a number of Greek classics such as moussaka for dinner. Mon & Tues 7am–3pm, Wed–Sun 7am–9pm.

Dish 507 Miller Ave ☎ 415 388 3474, ⓦ dishmillvalley .com. Typical of Marin, this new diner serves a mixture of down-home and more exotic recipes at affordable prices, while using organic and sustainably-farmed produce. Precede your burger with Thai soup. Mon–Fri & Sun 7.30am–9pm, Sat 7.30am–10pm.

Mill Valley Beerworks 173 Throckmorton Ave, Mill Valley ☎ 415 336 3596. This sleek modern bar would look more at home in the big city. Still, the hand-crafted draught beers and bottled imports are worth investigating. Food served till 10pm. Daily 11am–midnight.

Mountain Home Inn 810 Panoramic Hwy ☎ 415 381 9000, ⓦ mtnhomeinn.com. A place that's as good for the view as for the food, with broiled meat and fish dishes served up in a rustic lodge on the slopes of Mount Tamalpais. Fixed dinner for $38. Mon 11.30am–3pm, Tues 5.30–8pm, Wed, Thurs & Sun 11.30am–3pm & 5.30–8pm, Fri & Sat 11.30am–3pm & 5.30–9pm.

MUIR BEACH

Pelican Inn Hwy-1, Muir Beach ☎ 415 383 6000. Fair selection of traditional English and Californian ales, plus fish'n'chips and rooms to rent in case you overdo it (see p.268). Food served till 9pm. Daily 11.30am–midnight.

POINT REYES AND AROUND

Farmhouse Restaurant 10021 Hwy-1, Olema ☎ 415 663 1264, ⓦ pointreyesseahore.com. The farm-fresh ingredients that go into the downhome cooking make this a good stop for mostly meaty lunches or dinners. Also a friendly bar. Mon–Thurs 9am–5pm, Fri–Sun 9am–6pm.

Station House Café 11180 Hwy-1, Point Reyes Station ☎ 415 663 1515, ⓦ stationhousecafe.com. Serving three meals daily, this local favourite entices diners from miles around to sample their grilled seafood and top-notch steaks. Mon, Tues & Thurs–Sun 8am–9pm.

Vladimir's Czech Restaurant 12785 Sir Francis Drake Blvd, Inverness ☎ 415 669 1021. This relic of rural Bohemia in the far West has been serving up tasty items like Moravian cabbage roll, roast duckling and apple strudel since 1960. Tues–Sun 11am–9pm.

SAUSALITO

Bridgeway Café 633 Bridgeway Ave ☎ 415 332 3426. A good spot to relax over a coffee or grab a gourmet egg breakfast at reasonable prices (by local standards). Daily 7.30am–5pm.

★ **Fish** 350 Harbor Drive ☎ 415 331 3474, ⓦ 331fish .com. This place makes a point of serving sustainable fish and seafood in undoubted style. Follow the Portuguese red chowder with a fish taco plate for only $13. Daily 11.30am–4.30pm & 5.30–8.30pm.

No Name 757 Bridgeway Ave, Sausalito ☎ 415 332 1392. An ex-haunt of the Beats, which hosts live music, mostly jazz, every night beginning at 8pm and on Sundays 3–7pm. Mon–Fri 11am–midnight, Sat & Sun 10am–1am.

Poggio 777 Bridgeway Ave ☎ 415 332 7771, ⓦ poggiotrattoria.com. Excellent Italian cuisine, cooked from many ingredients imported from Italy. Meat and fish main courses range in price from $15 to $65 for a Porterhouse steak. Mon–Thurs 6.30am–10pm, Fri & Sat 11.30am–11pm, Sun 11.30am–10pm.

Sweet Ginger 400 Caledonia St ☎ 415 332 1683, ⓦ sweetgingersausalito.com. Moderately priced small Japanese restaurant that serves sushi, sashimi and main courses like tempura and teriyaki. Tues–Thurs 11am–3pm & 5–9.30pm, Fri & Sat 11am–3pm & 5–10pm, Sun 4.30–9.30pm.

Tommy's Wok 3001 Bridgeway ☎ 415 332 5818, ⓦ tommyswok.com. This Chinese spot specializes in organic vegetables, free-range meats and fresh seafood, prepared to Mandarin, Hunan, and Szechuan recipes. Mon–Thurs 11.30am–3pm & 4–9pm, Fri & Sat 11.30am–3pm & 4–9.30pm, Sun 4–9pm.

TIBURON

New Morning Café 1696 Tiburon Blvd ☎ 415 435 4315. Lots of healthy wholegrain sandwiches with a range of tasty fillings, plus salads and omelettes. Quite a selection of coffee too. Mon–Fri 6.30am–2.30pm, Sat & Sun 6.30am–4pm.

Guaymas 5 Main St ☎ 415 435 6300, ⓦ guaymas restaurant.com. Some of the most unique, inventive but pricey Cal-Mex cuisine in the Bay Area, with spectacular city views. The tamales are especially worth trying. Mon–Thurs & Sun 11.30am–9pm, Fri & Sat 11.30am–10pm.

Sam's Anchor Cafe 27 Main St ☎ 415 435 4527, ⓦ samscafe.com. Popular waterfront spot which serves eggy brekkies, filling lunches and a variety of fish, meat and veg dinners. Bar open nightly till 1.30am. Mon–Fri 11am–10pm, Sat & Sun 9.30–10pm.

16

The Wine Country

Coming from often foggy San Francisco, a trip to the golden, arid Napa and Sonoma valleys, known jointly as the **Wine Country**, can feel like entering another country altogether. With its cool, oak tree-shaded ravines climbing up along creeks and mineral springs to chaparral-covered ridges, it would be a lovely place to visit even without the vineyards. But, as it is, the "Wine Country" tag dominates almost everything here, including many oft-overlooked points of historical and literary interest.

Between the Napa and Sonoma valleys around 30,000 acres of **vineyards**, feeding hundreds of wineries and their upscale patrons, make the area the heart of the American wine industry in reputation, if not in volume. In truth, less than five percent of California's wine comes from the region, but what it does produce is some of America's best. The region is also among America's wealthiest and most provincial, a fact that draws – and repels – a steady stream of tourists. For every grape on the vine there seems to exist a quaint bed-and-breakfast or spa; in fact, tourism is gaining on wine production as the Wine Country's leading industry, so expect clogged highways and full hotels during the lengthy peak season (May–October). Apart from the multiple wine experiences available, quite a few wineries have fun attractions on top of their regular **tastings**. There are also numerous **activities** like ballooning or horse-riding, as well as **historical sights** to be enjoyed.

The Napa Valley

A thirty-mile strip of gently landscaped corridors and lush hillsides, the **NAPA VALLEY** looks more like southern France than the rest of Northern California. In spring the valley floor is covered with brilliant wildflowers which mellow into autumnal shades by grape-harvest time. Local Native Americans named the then fish-rich river flowing through the valley "Napa", meaning "plenty". By the 1850s the town of Napa had become a thriving river port and the first mineral springs resort opened, then in 1870 Jacob Beringer realized that the valley's rocky, well-drained soil resembled that of his homeland, Mainz, a major wine region in Germany, and by 1875 he and his brother had established what has today become America's oldest continually operating winery.

The town of **Napa** itself is rather drab and has little to detain visitors. Continuing northward, however, there are a few places of greater interest, principally **St Helena**, which has retained much of its circa 1900 homestead character, and **Calistoga**, at the top of the valley, famous for its hot springs, massages and spas.

16

Napa

The rather congested town of **NAPA** lacks both excitement and charm, so is best avoided in favour of the wineries and smaller towns north along Hwy-29. It does, though, have a decent number of good restaurants (see p.280). Suburban highway sprawl gives way to the collection of chain stores that anchor the compact Downtown, situated on a curve of the Napa River. The **Napa County Historical Society** at 1219 First St (Tues–Thurs noon–4pm or by appointment; free; ☎707 224 1739, ⓦnapahistory .org) has informative materials and photographic displays on the region's pre-wine era. It's housed in the town's proud old courthouse, which looks like a relic from another era compared to the modern, characterless buildings that comprise the rest of Downtown. Smaller attractions include the **Napa Firefighters Museum** at 201 Main St (Wed–Sat 11am–4pm; free; ☎707 259 0609, ⓦnapafirefightersmuseum.org), or you might want to take in some culture at the newly refurbished **Opera House** at 1030 Main St (tickets $15–60; ☎707 226 7372, ⓦnvoh.org).

Yountville

Nine miles north of Napa on Hwy-29, **YOUNTVILLE** was named in honour of George C. Yount, the valley's first settler of European descent in 1831. There's not much to grab your attention, just some antique shops, restaurants, and the stores at Vintage 1870 (6525 Washington St; daily 10.30am–5.30pm; ☎707 944 2451, ⓦvintage1870 .com), a shopping and wine complex in a former winery.

THE WINE TRAIN

The three-hour **Wine Train** (from $99, including meal; ☎707 253 2111 or 1 800 427 4124, ⓦwinetrain.com) runs two or three times daily from Napa's station at 1275 McKinstry St, east of Downtown. The ten-car train of restored 1950s Pullman cars chugs up the valley to St Helena, with optional stops at the Grgich Hills or Domaine Chandon wineries (tour and tasting cost extra). The scenery en route is pleasant, but the ride is really a wining-and-dining experience for older travellers.

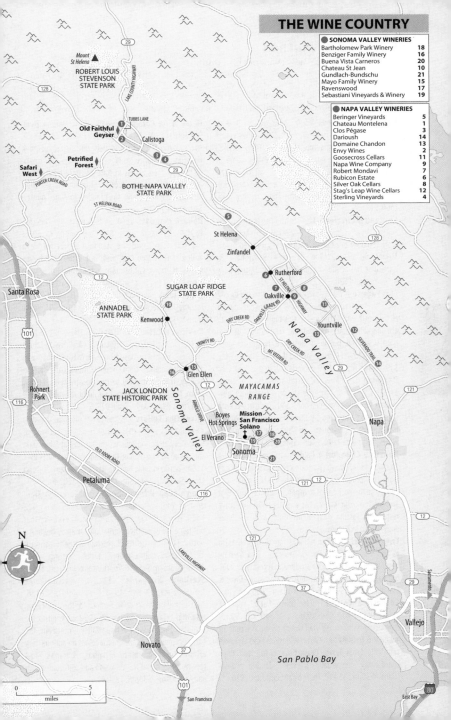

THE WINE COUNTRY

● SONOMA VALLEY WINERIES

Bartholomew Park Winery	18
Benziger Family Winery	16
Buena Vista Carneros	20
Chateau St Jean	10
Gundlach-Bundschu	21
Mayo Family Winery	15
Ravenswood	17
Sebastiani Vineyards & Winery	19

● NAPA VALLEY WINERIES

Beringer Vineyards	5
Chateau Montelena	1
Clos Pégase	3
Darioush	14
Domaine Chandon	13
Envy Wines	2
Goosecross Cellars	11
Napa Wine Company	9
Robert Mondavi	7
Rubicon Estate	6
Silver Oak Cellars	8
Stag's Leap Wine Cellars	12
Sterling Vineyards	4

NAPA VALLEY WINERIES

Almost all of the Napa Valley's **wineries** offer **tastings**, which have become increasingly expensive in recent years; most also offer **tours** of some description. There are more than three hundred wineries in all, of which the following are some long-standing favourites, plus a few lesser-known hopefuls. If you want to buy a bottle, particularly from the larger producers, you can usually get it cheaper in supermarkets than at the wineries themselves, unless you buy in bulk.

Beringer Vineyards 2000 Main St, St Helena ☎ 707 963 7115, ⓦ beringer.com. Napa Valley's most famous piece of architecture, the gothic "Rhine House", is modelled on the ancestral Rhine Valley home of Jacob Beringer. Expansive lawns and a grand tasting room, heavy on dark wood, make for a regal experience. Tasting and tours daily 10am–5pm; tasting $15, tours $15–35.

Chateau Montelena 1429 Tubbs Lane, two miles north of Calistoga ☎ 707 942 9105, ⓦ montelena .com. Smaller but highly rated winery, nestled below Mount St Helena. The Cabernet Sauvignon, in particular, has acquired a fine reputation. Tasting daily 9.30am–4pm; $20.

Clos Pégase 1060 Dunaweal Lane, Calistoga ☎ 707 942 4981, ⓦ clospegase.com. A flamboyant upstart at the north end of the valley, this high-profile winery amalgamates fine wine and fine art, with a sculpture garden around buildings designed by postmodern architect Michael Graves. Tasting daily 10.30am–5pm; $10. Tours daily at 11.30am and 2pm; free.

Darioush 4240 Silverado Trail, northeast of Napa ☎ 707 257 2345, ⓦ darioush.com. Grandiose new winery modelled on Persepolis and constructed with stone blocks imported by the owner from his native Iran. Cabernet Sauvignon and Shiraz are the signature wines. Tasting daily 10.30am–5pm; $12–20.

Domaine Chandon 1 California Drive, Yountville ☎ 707 944 2280, ⓦ chandon.com. Sparkling wines from this progeny of France's Moët & Chandon can challenge the authentic Champagnes from France. Vast and modern, the winery has a gallery and expensive restaurant. Tasting daily 10am–6pm; $18–25. Tours daily 11.30am & 3pm; $12.

Envy Wines 1170 Tubbs Lane, north of Calistoga ☎ 707 942 4677, ⓦ envywines.com. This friendly newcomer first bottled its produce as recently as 2007 but has already received awards. Tasting Mon–Thurs & Sun 10.30am–4.30pm, Fri & Sat 11am–5.30pm; $10.

Goosecross Cellars 1119 State Lane, east of Yountville ☎ 707 944 1986 or 1 800 276 9210, ⓦ goosecross.com. It's well worth taking the time to locate this friendly family-run winery, tucked away off Yountville Cross Road. Crush-time is fun and their Chardonnay especially good. Tasting daily 10am–4.30pm; $5–10. Tours by appointment; $20.

Napa Wine Company 7830–40 St Helena Hwy, Oakville ☎ 707 944 1710 or 1 800 848 9630, ⓦ napawineco.com. Modelled on the cooperative wineries of France, this venture offers 25 small-vineyard owners access to state-of-the-art machinery and also acts as a sales outlet for their vintages. Their tasting room is certainly the broadest in Wine Country. Tasting daily 10am–3.30pm; $10–25.

Robert Mondavi 7801 St Helena Hwy, Oakville ☎ 707 251 4097 or 1 888 766 6328, ⓦ robert mondavi.com. Long the standard-bearer for Napa Valley wines ("Bob Red" and "Bob White" are house wines at many Californian restaurants), they also have one of the most informative and least hard-sell tours. Tours and tasting daily 10am–4.30pm; reservations recommended. Tastings from $15, tours from $25.

Rubicon Estate 1991 St Helena Hwy, Rutherford ☎ 707 968 1100 or 1 800 782 4266, ⓦ niebaum -coppola.com. Purchased by Francis Ford Coppola in 1975, memorabilia from Coppola's movie career are on display in the entryway to the massive wine-tasting room, featuring their signature Rubicon wine. Tasting and tours daily 10am–5pm; $25.

Silver Oak Cellars 915 Oakville Cross Rd, Oakville ☎ 1 800 273 8809, ⓦ www.silveroak.com. Lovers of Cabernet Sauvignon mustn't miss a stop at Silver Oak, the crème de la crème of the heady red that costs over $100 a bottle in some San Francisco restaurants. Tasting Mon–Sat 9am–5pm, Sun 11am–5pm; $20–40.

Stag's Leap Wine Cellars 5766 Silverado Trail, east of Yountville ☎ 707 944 2020 or 1 866 422 7523, ⓦ stagsleapwinecellars.com. The winery that put Napa Valley on the international map by beating a bottle of Château Lafitte-Rothschild at a Paris tasting in 1976. Still quite highly rated. Tasting daily 10am–4.30pm; $15–40. Tours by appointment; $40.

Sterling Vineyards 1111 Dunaweal Lane, Calistoga ☎ 707 942 3344 or 1 800 726 6136, ⓦ sterlingvineyards.com. Famous for the aerial tram ride that brings visitors up the 300-foot knoll to the tasting room; the view of Napa Valley is gorgeous. The extravagant white mansion, modelled on a monastery on the Greek island of Mykonos, is Napa's most recognizable. Aerial tram, tasting and self-guided tour daily 10.30am–4.30pm; $25–40.

16

St Helena

ST HELENA is the largest of all the antique-shop-filled villages you'll encounter heading north; it's also the town that boasts the greatest concentration of wineries and a nice complement of places to stay and eat. Hwy-29 becomes the town's Main Street here, and is lined by some of the Wine Country's finest nineteenth-century brick buildings, most of which stand in prime condition, holding inns, bakeries and shops. It's worth taking a quick detour to see the quaint Craftsman-style homes that line residential **Oak Avenue**, whose past residents include Robert Louis Stevenson and Ambrose Bierce, the nineteenth-century journalist and author.

The **Silverado Museum**, housed in St Helena's former Public Library building at 1490 Library Lane (Tues–Sun noon–4pm; free; ☎707 963 3757, ⍉silveradomuseum.org), has a collection of some eight thousand articles relating to Robert Louis Stevenson, who spent just under a year in the area, honeymooning and recovering from an illness. It's claimed to be the second most extensive collection of Stevenson artefacts in the US, though the only thing of interest to any but the most obsessed fan is a scribbled-on manuscript of *Dr Jekyll and Mr Hyde*. The other half of the building is taken up by the **Napa Valley Wine Library**, a briefly entertaining barrage of photos and clippings relating to the development of local viticulture.

Calistoga

Beyond St Helena, toward the far northern end of the valley, the wineries become prettier and the traffic a little thinner, though it swells again at the very tip of the valley near **CALISTOGA**, a town that takes pride in being the source of the sparkling water that adorns every Californian supermarket shelf. Sam Brannan, the young Mormon entrepreneur who made a mint out of the Gold Rush, established a resort community here in 1860. In his groundbreaking speech, as legend has it, he attempted to assert his desire to create the "Saratoga of California", but got tongue-tied, thus coining the town's name.

Calistoga has one standard tourist attraction, in the shape of the **Sharpsteen Museum and Sam Brannan Cottage** at 1113 Washington St (daily 11am–4pm; suggested donation $3; ☎707 942 5911, ⍉sharpsteen-museum.org). Founded by long-serving Disney producer Ben Sharpsteen, the quaint little museum contains some of his personal effects, including his Oscar for the pearl-diving film *Ama Girls*, as well as a model of the original resort and lots of biographical material on Sam Brannan, plus a full-size recreation of his cottage.

16

SPRINGS AND SPAS

Calistoga's main attraction has always been the opportunity to soak in the calming hot water that bubbles up here from deep in the earth. A multitude of **spas** and volcanic **mud baths**, together with a homely and health-conscious atmosphere, beckon city-dwellers and tourists alike.

Calistoga Spa 1006 Washington St ☎707 942 6269 or 1 866 822 5772, ⍉calistogaspa.com. Mineral bath $45, mud bath $65 and massage treatments from $57.

Dr. Wilkinson's Hot Springs 1507 Lincoln Ave ☎707 942 4102, ⍉drwilkinson.com. Renowned health spa and hotel (treatments from $99) whose heated mineral water and volcanic-ash treatments have been overseen by the same family for almost fifty years.

Golden Haven Hot Springs Spa and Resort 1713 Lake St ☎707 942 6793, ⍉goldenhaven.com.

A number of slightly more down-to-earth establishments are spread along and off the mile-long main drag, Lincoln Avenue, including this place, which offers special one-hour mud baths from $49.

Mount View Spa 1457 Lincoln Ave ☎707 942 5789 or 1 800 772 8838, ⍉mountviewspa.com. This spa can soothe you with a good variety of combined herbal therapies; it also has mud treatments for in excess of $100, as well as shorter but cheaper hydrotherapy sessions.

Old Faithful Geyser

1299 Tubbs Lane · Daily: summer 9am–6pm, winter 9am–5pm · $10 · ☎ 707 942 6463, ⓦ oldfaithfulgeyser.com

More evidence of Calistoga's lively underground activity can be seen on this route at the **Old Faithful Geyser**, two miles north of town on Tubbs Lane, which spurts boiling water sixty feet into the air at nine-to forty-minute intervals, depending on the time of year. The water source was discovered during oil-drilling here in the 1920s, when search equipment struck a force estimated to be up to a thousand pounds per square foot; the equipment was blown away and, despite heroic efforts to control it, the geyser has continued to go off like clockwork ever since. Landowners finally realized that they'd never tame it and turned it into a high-yield tourist attraction, using the same name as the famous spouter at Yellowstone National Park.

The Petrified Forest

Five miles west of Calistoga · Daily: summer 9am–6pm, winter 9am–5pm · $10 · ☎ 707 942 6667, ⓦ petrifiedforest.org

Heading northwest out of Calistoga on Hwy-128 takes you alongside the ridge of the **Mayacamas**, which divide the Napa and Sonoma valleys. On the steep road over the hills to Santa Rosa, the **Petrified Forest** is on the roster of California Historical Landmarks, though Robert Louis Stevenson dubbed it "a pure little isle of touristry among the solitary hills". Indeed, unless you're a geologist or really into hardened wood, you may not fully appreciate the importance of these fossils, some of the largest in the world, up to 150 feet long. The forest here was petrified by the action of the silica-laden volcanic ash, which gradually seeped into the decomposing fibres of trees uprooted during an eruption of Mount St Helena some three million years ago.

The Sonoma Valley

On looks alone the crescent-shaped Sonoma Valley beats Napa Valley hands down. This smaller, altogether more rustic stretch of greenery curves between oak-covered mountain ranges from **SONOMA** a few miles north along Hwy-12 to the hamlet of **Glen Ellen** and **Jack London State Park**, and ends at the booming bedroom community of **Santa Rosa**. The area is known as the "Valley of the Moon", a label that's mined by tour operators for its connection to long-time resident Jack London, whose book of the same name retold a Native American legend about how, as you move through the valley, the moon seems to rise several times from behind the various peaks. Sonoma was claimed, at different moments of its relatively brief recorded history, by Spain, England, Russia and Mexico, before the US took over in 1846 during the Bear Flag Revolt.

Sonoma Valley's **wineries** are generally more intimate and casual than their Napa counterparts, even though Sonoma Valley established the wine industry from which Napa derives its fame. Colonel Agostin Haraszthy first started planting grapes here in the 1850s and his Buena Vista winery in Sonoma still operates today.

Sonoma

Behind a layer of somewhat touristy stores and restaurants, **SONOMA** retains a good deal of its Spanish and Mexican architecture. The town's charm emanates from the grassy plaza at the centre of Downtown, which has lots of shady spots to relax in and a peaceful duck pond. This communal space is at its liveliest on Tuesdays from late March to early November, when there is a weekly **farmers' market** (5–9pm), usually with live music. It is also the site of the 1846 **Bear Flag Revolt**, when thirty settlers proclaimed the Republic of California independent from Mexico, only to see it become an American state three weeks later, when the USA declared war on Mexico and took over the entire West Coast.

A number of historic buildings and relics preserve history in the **Sonoma State Historic Park**, just off Sonoma's plaza (daily 10am–5pm; $3 combined entry). The restored **Mission San Francisco Solano de Sonoma** was the last and northernmost of the California missions, established by Mexican rulers fearful of expansionist Russian fur traders. Half a mile west stands the **General Vallejo Home**, the leader's ornate former residence, dominated by decorated filigree eaves and Gothic-revival arched windows. The storehouse has been turned into a **museum** of artefacts from the general's reign.

Jack London State Park

Daily 9.30am–5pm • $8 per vehicle • ☎ 707 938 5216, ⓦ jacklondonpark.com

Five miles north of Sonoma State Historic Park on Hwy-12, you'll come upon the cosy hamlet of **GLEN ELLEN**, whose main street Arnold Drive loops west and contains a collection of boutique shops and restaurants along the banks of Sonoma Creek. More interestingly, Glen Ellen is the home of **JACK LONDON STATE PARK**, which begins a half-mile up London Ranch Road past the Benziger Family Winery and covers 140 acres of ranchland that the famed author of *The Call of the Wild* owned with his wife. Unfortunately, the park was one of seventy marked for closure by 2012, meaning in effect that it will be accessible but not manned or maintained by the state. There's a possibility that it might be privatized, in which case the three principal buildings within it – the Wolf House, the House of Happy Walls and London's Cottage – will probably stay open.

Santa Rosa

Sixty miles due north of San Francisco on US-101 and about twenty miles from Sonoma on Hwy-12, **SANTA ROSA**, the largest town in Sonoma County, sits at the top end of the Sonoma Valley and is more or less the hub of this part of the Wine Country. It's a very different world from other Wine Country towns, however; much of it is given over to shopping centres and roadside malls. In an attempt to form a central, pedestrian-only focal point, however, **Historic Railroad Square**, a strip of redbrick-facade boutiques, has been developed. Santa Rosa continues to expand both as a bedroom community for San Francisco and site of the Wine Country's cheapest lodging. It also has a decent selection of restaurants and bars, although scant attractions. You can kill an hour or two at the **Luther Burbank Home and Gardens**, 204 Santa Rosa Avenue (gardens: daily 8am–dusk; tours of house Tues–Sun every 30min 10am–3.30pm; gardens: free; tours $5; ☎707 524 5445, ⓦlutherburbank.org), where California's best-known horticulturist is remembered in the house he dwelt in and in the splendid gardens where he created some of his most unusual hybrids. Alternatively, head for **Snoopy's Home Ice** at 1667 West Steele Lane, a skating arena built by *Peanuts* creator Charles Schulz as a gift for the community. It actually comprises two buildings: the ice-skating rink (see p.222) and Snoopy's Gallery (Mon–Fri 11am–5pm, Sat & Sun 10am–5pm, closed Tues in winter; ☎707 546 3385), a museum/gift shop of all things *Peanuts* and a lasting tribute to the much-loved Schulz, who died at the turn of the millennium.

16

THE WINE COUNTRY BY AIR

The most exciting way to see the region is on one of the widely touted **hot-air balloon rides**. These usually lift off at dawn and last sixty to ninety magical minutes, winding up with a Champagne brunch. The most established of the operators is Napa Valley Balloons (☎ 707 253 2224 or 1 800 253 2224, ⓦ napavalleyballoons.com), who fly out of Yountville. Other options in Napa include the slightly cheaper Balloons Above the Valley (☎ 1 800 464 6824, ⓦ balloonrides .com) and Aerostat Adventures (☎ 1 800 579 0183, ⓦ aerostat-adventures.com). The crunch comes when you find out the price – around $200 a head whichever company you use – but it really is worth every cent. Make reservations a week in advance, especially in summer, though with the increasing number of balloon companies, same-day drop-bys are a possibility.

If it's thrills you're looking for, consider taking to the air in a **World War II-era propeller biplane**. The Vintage Aircraft Company, 23982 Arnold Drive, Sonoma (☎707 938 2444, ⓦvintage aircraft.com), operates one- or two-person flights that take in the Sonoma Valley between loops and rolls. The basic choice is between the twenty-minute Scenic Flight ($175) and various forty-minute Explorer Flights ($295): add $50 to either for the extra thrill of some aerobatics.

SONOMA VALLEY WINERIES

Nearly fifty **wineries** are scattered all over the Sonoma Valley, with a good concentration in a well-signposted group a mile east of Sonoma Plaza, down East Napa Street. Tasting charges are generally a little lower than in Napa. If you're tired of driving around, visit the handy **Wine Exchange of Sonoma**, 452 First St E (☎707 938 1794), a commercial tasting room where you can sample the best wines from all over California.

Bartholomew Park Winery 1000 Vineyard Lane ☎707 935 9511, ⓦ bartpark.com. This lavish Spanish-colonial building is surrounded by some great topiary in the gardens. The wines are relatively inexpensive vintages that appeal to the pocket and palate alike. The good little museum of regional history provides an introduction to local viticulture. Self-guided tours of the winery and tastings daily 11am–4.30pm; $10.

Benziger Family Winery 1883 London Ranch Rd, Glen Ellen ☎707 935 3000 or 1 888 490 2739, ⓦ benziger.com. Beautiful vineyard perched on the side of an extinct volcano next to Jack London State Park. There are 5 or 6 daily tram tours through the fields ($15) with an emphasis on viticulture. Tasting daily 10am–5pm; $10–15.

Buena Vista Carneros 18000 Old Winery Rd ☎707 252 7117 or 1 800 926 1266, ⓦ buenavistacarneros .com. Oldest and grandest of the wineries, established in 1857, whose wine has regained a good reputation of late. The tasting room features a small art gallery. Tasting daily 10am–5pm; $5–10 inc glass; free self-guided tours.

Chateau St Jean 8555 Sonoma Hwy, Kenwood ☎707 833 4134 or 1 800 543 7572, ⓦ chateaustjean .com. Attractive estate with an overwhelming aroma of wine throughout the buildings. There's a quirky tower to climb from where you can admire the view. Tasting daily 10am–5pm; $10–25. Tours daily 11am & 2pm; $50.

Gundlach-Bundschu 2000 Denmark St, Sonoma ☎707 938 5277, ⓦ gunbun.com. Gun-Bun, as it's known to locals, has slowly established a fine reputation. The plain, functional building hides some real vintages. Also hosts various theatrical, cinematic and musical events throughout the summer. Tasting daily 11am–4.30pm; $10–20. Tours by appointment; $20–40.

Mayo Family Winery 13101 Arnold Drive, Glen Ellen ☎707 938 9401, ⓦ mayofamilywinery.com. Fairly new winery with a cosy feel and a friendly welcome, matching the small-time production of under five thousand cases annually. Complimentary tasting daily 10.30am–6.30pm; barrel tasting tours Fri–Sun 2 & 4pm.

Ravenswood 18701 Gehricke Rd, Sonoma ☎707 933 2332 or 1 888 669 4679, ⓦ ravenswood-wine.com. Noted for their "gutsy, unapologetic" Zinfandel and advertising a "no wimpy" approach to the wine business, the staff at this unpretentious winery are friendly and easygoing. Sociable summer barbecues. Tastings daily 10am–4.30pm; $10–15. Tour daily 10.30am; $15.

Sebastiani Vineyards & Winery 389 Fourth St E, Sonoma ☎707 938 5532 or 1 800 888 5532, ⓦ sebastiani.com. One of California's oldest family wineries, four blocks from central Sonoma, now boasts a newly renovated hospitality centre, while the rest of the estate is being returned to its original appearance. There is another tasting room on the central square at 103 W Napa St (☎707 933 3291). Tasting daily 10am–5pm; $10–20. Historical tours daily at 11am, 1pm & 3pm; free.

Safari West

Corner of Franz Valley and Porter Creek roads • Jeep tours: daily 9am, 10am, 1pm, 2pm & 4pm in summer, 10am & 2pm in winter • $68 • ☎707 579 2551 or 1 800 616 2695, ⓦ safariwest.com

One enterprise few people would expect to find tucked away in the Wine Country is a full-blown **wildlife refuge** – yet spreading over four hundred acres of the pristine hills between the two valleys, five miles northeast of Santa Rosa, is **Safari West**. Run by wildlife experts Peter and Nancy Lang, the refuge runs breeding programmes for hundreds of rare mammal and bird species. Three-hour African-style **jeep tours** take you through vast open compounds of herd animals, while expert guides supply detailed background on the furry and feathered inhabitants, and you can wander at leisure past large cages of cheetahs and primates or the leafy aviary. Filling buffet meals are served in the mess tent, and you can stay here too (see p.280).

ARRIVAL AND DEPARTURE
THE WINE COUNTRY

By plane From Oakland and San Francisco airports, you can get to Napa with the Evans Airporter Shuttle (8–9 daily; 1hr 30min; $29 one way; ☎707 255 1559, ⓦ evanstransportation.com).

By bus Golden Gate Transit (see p.267) runs commuter buses from San Francisco via Petaluma to Santa Rosa (every

30min–1hr; 2hr 15min); Greyhound (☎ 1 800 231 2222, ⓦ greyhound.com) runs daily to Santa Rosa (1hr 45min).
By tour bus Gray Line run a guided bus tour (1 daily at 9.15am; 9hr; $66; ☎ 415 558 9400, ⓦ grayline.com) from San Francisco Transbay Terminal. The tour covers both

valleys and visits three wineries, including Sebastiani in downtown Sonoma and Sutter Home in St Helena, with a stop for lunch in Calistoga. Blue & Gold also runs a Wine Country bus tour from Pier 43 (1 daily at 9.15am; 9hr; $71; ☎ 415 705 8200, ⓦ blueandgoldfleet.com).

GETTING AROUND

By bus From Santa Rosa, Sonoma County Transit (☎ 707 576 7433, ⓦ sctransit.com) buses serve the entire Sonoma Valley. Napa Valley is served by VINE buses

(☎ 707 251 2800, ⓦ nctpa.net).
By car As the Wine Country's attractions are spread over a fairly broad area, a car is essential for proper touring.

INFORMATION

Calistoga 1458 Lincoln Ave (Mon–Thurs & Sun 9am–5pm, Fri & Sat 9am–6pm; ☎ 707 942 6333, ⓦ calistogachamber .com).
Napa 1310 Napa Town Center, off First Street (daily 9am–5pm; ☎ 707 226 7459, ⓦ napavalley. com).
St Helena 1010 Main St (Mon–Fri 10am–5pm, Sat 10am–4pm, Sun 11am–3pm; ☎ 707 963 4456 or

1 800 799 6456, ⓦ sthelena.com).
Santa Rosa 9 Fourth St (Mon–Sat 9am–5pm, Sun 10am–5pm; ☎ 707 577 8674 or 1 866 918 5685, ⓦ visitsantarosa.com).
Sonoma 453 First St E, on the Plaza (Mon–Sat 9am–5pm, Sun 10am–5pm; ☎ 707 996 1090, ⓦ sonomavalley.com).

ACCOMMODATION

During summer weekends, places fill up well ahead and prices can rise as much as fifty percent, while from November to March rates drop considerably. At peak times, you might need to ask at the tourist office (see above) or make use of an accommodation service such as Bed and Breakfast Inns of Napa Valley (☎ 707 944 4444, ⓦ bbinv.com) or the Bed and Breakfast Association of Sonoma Valley (1 800 969 4667, ⓦ sonomabb.com). There's camping in Sonoma Valley.

16

NAPA VALLEY
CALISTOGA
★ **Calistoga Inn** 1250 Lincoln Ave ☎ 707 942 4101, ⓦ calistogainn.com. Relaxing, excellent-value rooms, most with private bath, in a landmark building with its own restaurant and microbrewery right on the main street, creating a lively atmosphere. $69
Dr Wilkinson's Hot Springs 1507 Lincoln Ave ☎ 707 942 4102, ⓦ drwilkinson.com. Legendary health spa and hotel downtown (see box, p.275). Choose from a variety of spacious, well-lit rooms with sparse furnishings, facing the courtyard or pool patio. $149
Luxe Calistoga 1139 Lincoln Ave ☎ 707 942 9797, ⓦ garnettcreekinn.com. Luxuriously renovated old 1873 house with a wraparound porch, complete with five beautifully decorated, lavishly furnished and welcoming rooms, all with fireplaces. $249

NAPA
Discovery Inn 500 Silverado Trail ☎ 707 253 0892, ⓦ napadiscoveryinn.com. This small motel-style place has adequately furnished modern rooms and is well placed, near Napa and the Silverado Trail wineries. $70
★ **Candlelight Inn** 1045 Easum Drive ☎ 707 257 3717 or 1 800 624 0395, ⓦ candlelightinn.com. Spacious mock-Tudor mansion with a pool in its lovely grounds and a luxurious interior, featuring rooms of

varying sizes, all beautifully decorated. Friendly and informal atmosphere, with free drinks and snacks. $169

ST HELENA
Ambrose Bierce Inn 1515 Main St ☎ 707 963 3003, ⓦ ambrosebiercehouse.com. Luxury accommodation in the 1872 house once inhabited by Bierce himself (see p.275). Breakfast is washed down with complimentary Champagne. $199
El Bonita Motel 195 Main St ☎ 707 963 3216 or 1 800 541 3284, ⓦ elbonita.com. Old roadside motel done up to hotel standard in Art Deco style, with a pool and hot tub. Surrounded by a 2.5-acre garden. $119
Harvest Inn 1 Main St ☎ 707 963 9463 or 1 800 950 8466, ⓦ harvestinn.com. Mock-Tudor cottages at the edge of a vineyard, with huge rooms loaded with perks like a down-feather bed, fireplace and private terrace overlooking the garden or vineyard. Two outdoor heated pools, whirlpool spas and jogging/biking trails too. $329

YOUNTVILLE
Oleander House 7433 St Helena Hwy (Hwy-29) ☎ 707 944 8315, ⓦ oleander.com. Cosy and friendly B&B, with tastefully and simply furnished rooms, in a handy mid-valley location. Quiet enough despite being on the main road, and not too far from restaurants and shops. $175

Vintage Inn 6541 Washington St ☎707 944 1112 or 1 800 351 1133, ⓦvintageinn.com. Huge luxury rooms, all with fireplaces, in a modern hotel complex, plus swimming pool and free bike rental. Handy for Yountville's many fine restaurants but vastly overpriced. $370

SONOMA VALLEY
GLEN ELLEN AND KENWOOD
★ **Gaige House Inn** 13540 Arnold Drive, Glen Ellen ☎707 935 0237 or 1 800 935 0237, ⓦgaige.com. Beautifully restored Queen Anne farmhouse in a quiet country setting. The splendid suites boast individual Japanese gardens and granite tubs. No under-18s. $219
Jack London Lodge 13740 Arnold Drive, Glen Ellen ☎707 938 8510, ⓦjacklondonlodge.com. Modern motel near Jack London State Park, with comfy rooms and a pool. The friendly saloon is a popular local hangout. $95
Kenwood Inn & Spa 10400 Sonoma Hwy, Kenwood ☎707 833 1293 or 1 800 353 6966, ⓦkenwoodinn.com. Deluxe, beautiful and secluded Italian villa-style B&B with a fireplace in all suites, some of which reach over $1000 in season. $575

SANTA ROSA
Astro Motel 323 Santa Rosa Ave ☎707 545 8555, ⓦsterba.com/astro. No-frills motel, but perfectly adequate, conveniently located, and offering some of the cheapest Wine Country rooms around. $55
Hotel La Rose 308 Wilson St ☎707 579 3200 or 1 800 527 6738, ⓦhotellarose.com. Restored lodging in a century-old building on Railroad Square. Rooms are clean and nicely furnished, plus there's a decent bar. $129

Safari West Franz Valley Rd, 5 miles northeast of Santa Rosa ☎707 579 2551 or 1 800 616 2695, ⓦsafariwest.com. Luxury tents, imported from Africa to complete the safari experience(see p.278), hung on stilted wooden decks. Accommodation March–Dec only. $200
Spring Lake Regional Park Newanga Avenue ☎707 565 2267. Sites at this spacious campground by a suburban lake must be reserved at least 10 days in advance. May–Sept daily; Oct–April Sat & Sun. $26

SONOMA
An Inn 2 Remember 171 W Spain St ☎707 938 2909 or 1 800 382 7895, ⓦthistledew.com. This wonderful B&B features elegantly restored rooms, an amazing breakfast and free bike rental. Some rooms offer a fireplace, private hot tub and patio. $175
Bungalows 313 313 First St E ☎707 996 8091, ⓦbungalows313.com. Pleasant collection of six spacious suites arranged round a shady courtyard and period house, each with a private patio and gardens. Gourmet European breakfast included. $219
Cottage Inn & Spa 302 First St E ☎707 996 0719 or 1 800 944 1490, ⓦcottageinnandspa.com. A calm, beautifully decorated downtown B&B, with hot tub and relaxing courtyard. One suite has a full kitchen, another a private patio. $195
Swiss Hotel 18 W Spain St ☎707 938 2884, ⓦswisshotelsonoma.com. A 70-year-old landmark building situated right on the plaza, with a fine restaurant. The five cramped rooms have four-poster queen-size beds and views of either the garden patio or the plaza. $150

EATING AND DRINKING

Fine dining is a Wine Country tradition and the Napa Valley plenty of excellent restaurants, many offering top California cuisine. The Sonoma Valley also has its fair share, particularly around the town of Sonoma and ritzy Glen Ellen.

NAPA VALLEY
CALISTOGA
All Seasons Bistro 1400 Lincoln Ave ☎707 942 9111, ⓦallseasonsnapavalley.net. Exquisite main courses such as roasted monkfish with fava beans and Bohemian pheasant cost $20–30 in this upscale but relaxed bistro. Tues–Sun noon–10pm.
★ **Brannan's Grill** 1374 Lincoln Ave ☎707 942 2233, ⓦbrannansgrill.com. Dishes like pecan-stuffed quail and fresh steamed oysters, plus a wonderful wooden interior, make this rather expensive, high-profile restaurant worth a visit. Daily 11.30am–9pm.
Café Sarafornia 1413 Lincoln Ave ☎707 942 0555, ⓦcafesarafornia.com. Famous for delicious and enormous breakfasts, and filling sandwiches, burgers and pasta for lunch. Expect queues around the block at weekends. Daily 7.30am–2.30pm.

Puerto Vallarta 1473 Lincoln Ave ☎707 942 6563. Heaps of tasty and genuine Mexican grub can be consumed in the shady courtyard of this simple taqueria, tucked in beside the Cal-Mart supermarket. Daily 8am–10pm.
Wappo Bar Bistro 1226 Washington St ☎707 942 4712, ⓦwappobar.com. Creative cuisine, featuring unheard-of combinations like *chile rellenos* with walnut pomegranate sauce or roasted rabbit with gnocchi, makes this restaurant a culinary adventure. Wed–Mon 11.30am–2.30pm & 6–9.30pm.

NAPA
Celadon 1040 Main St ☎707 254 9690, ⓦceladonnapa.com. Quality international nouvelle cuisine with dishes such as truffle and honey-glazed pork chops or Algerian-style lamb, served in an intimate setting. Mon–Thurs 11.30am–9pm, Fri & Sat 11.30am–10pm.

Cole's Chop House 1122 Main St ☎707 224 6328, ⓦcoleschophouse.com. This is the place to come for huge chunks of well-prepared red meat. Very spacious inside, with top service, but the atmosphere is rather stilted. Mon–Thurs & Sun 5–9pm, Fri & Sat 5–10pm.

★ **Downtown Joe's** 902 Main St ☎707 258 2337, ⓦdowntownjoes.com. One of Napa's most popular and lively spots for sandwiches, ribs and pasta, with outdoor dining by the river and beer brewed on the premises. About the only place in town open till at least midnight, with live music some nights. Daily 8.30am–late.

Zuzu 829 Main St ☎707 224 5885, ⓦzuzunapa.com. Not the place to come if ravenous, as portions are modest in size for $4–15, but this popular tapas bar offers tasty fare such as *paella del dia* and a good wine list in its trendy interior. Mon–Thurs 11.30am–10pm, Fri 11.30am–11pm, Sat 4–11pm, Sun 4–10pm.

ST HELENA

Tra Vigne 1050 Charter Oak Ave ☎707 963 4444, ⓦtravignerestaurant.com. Excellent food and fine wines, served up in a lovely vine-covered courtyard or elegant dining room: it feels as if you've been transported to Tuscany. Meat and fish dishes $22–34. Daily 11.30am–9pm.

★ **Wine Spectator Greystone Restaurant** 2555 Main St ☎707 967 1010, ⓦciachef.edu. California/ Mediterranean cuisine served in an elegant ivy-walled mansion, with a tastefully wacky Art Deco interior. Students from the cookery school serve up delicious, large portions of chicken, duck, fish and venison for $20–30. Mon–Thurs & Sun 11.30am–9pm, Fri & Sat 11.30am–10pm.

YOUNTVILLE

Bouchon 6534 Washington St ☎707 944 8037, ⓦbouchonbistro.com. Parisian chic and haute cuisine available at high prices – the *terrine de fois gras* goes for $45, but most mains are around $25–30. Daily 11.30–12.30am.

★ **The French Laundry** 6640 Washington St ☎707 944 2380, ⓦfrenchlaundry.com. The ultimate place for a splurge. World famous chef Thomas Keller creates two 9-course tasting menus daily for a princely $270 each. Dress code. Lunch 11am & 1pm, dinner 5.30–9.15pm.

Mustards Grill 7399 St Helena (Hwy-29) ☎707 944 2424, ⓦmustardsgrill.com. Huge range of starters and main dishes, like the "famous Mongolian pork chop", for around $25. Also does a range of gourmet sandwiches for around $12. Mon–Thurs & Sun 11.30am–9pm, Fri & Sat 11.30am–10pm.

SONOMA VALLEY
GLEN ELLEN AND KENWOOD

Café Citti 9049 Sonoma Hwy, Kenwood ☎707 833 2690, ⓦcafecitti.com. Small, inexpensive trattoria with great Italian food and an intimate, yet casual atmosphere. Lots of salads and "create your own pasta" options. Daily 11am–3.30pm & 5–9pm.

Glen Ellen Inn 13670 Arnold Drive, Glen Ellen ☎707 996 6409, ⓦglenelleninn.com. Husband-and-wife team (not called Glen and Ellen) cook and serve California-style gourmet dishes like West Coast cioppino in a small, romantic dining room. Mon, Tues & Thurs–Sun 11.30am–9pm, Wed 5–9pm.

SANTA ROSA

Gary Chu's 611 Fifth St ☎707 526 5840, ⓦgarychus .com. Large helpings of high-quality Chinese food such as Szechuan lamb at very reasonable prices. Also does Osake Japanese dishes. Tues–Sun 11.30am–9.30pm.

Third Street Aleworks 610 Third St ☎707 523 3060, ⓦthirdstreetaleworks.com. Frequent live music and hearty American grub like burgers and pizza, washed down with microbrewed beer. Mon–Thurs & Sun 11.30am–midnight, Fri & Sat 11.30am–1am.

SONOMA

Coffee Garden Café 421 W First St ☎707 996 6645. Fresh sandwiches are served on the back patio of this 150-year-old adobe, converted into a café with gift shop. Mon–Thurs & Sun 7am–7pm, Fri & Sat 7am–8pm.

★ **The Girl & The Fig** 110 W Spain St ☎707 938 3634, ⓦthegirlandthefig.com. This renowned restaurant offers French dinners and weekend brunch on a weekly fixed three-course menu for $32. Mon–Sat 11.30am–10pm, Sun 10am–10pm.

La Casa 121 E Spain St ☎707 996 3406, ⓦlacasa restaurant.com. Friendly, festive and inexpensive Mexican restaurant just across from the Sonoma Mission. Enjoy an enchilada on the sunny outdoor patio. Mon–Thurs & Sun 11.30am–9.30pm, Fri & Sat 11.30am–10pm.

Rins Thai 139 E Napa St ☎707 938 1462, ⓦrinsthai .com. A good range of spicy curries and other Thai favourites are available at this modest restaurant right on the main square. The *pad ma kuer* is a winner. Tues–Thurs & Sun 11.30am–9pm, Fri & Sat 11.30am–9.30pm.

The Schellville Grill 22900 Broadway ☎707 996 5151, ⓦschellvillegrill.com. No longer *Fords Café* of yore but still an institution with locals, who flock here for the ample burgers and sandwiches, some with surprisingly imaginative touches. Occasional live music (Sat 7–9pm, Sun 10.30am–1.30pm). Mon–Wed 8am–2pm, Thurs–Sun 6am–2.30pm & 5.30–9pm.

16

HIPPIES IN GOLDEN GATE PARK, 1968

Contexts

History

Though its recorded history may not stretch back very far by European standards, in its more than a century and a half of existence San Francisco has done a good job of making up for time. Following its beginnings as an outpost on the Spanish mission trail, the city first really came to life during the legendary California Gold Rush of 1849. The adventurous spirit of that period has been sustained by San Francisco to this day, both in its valuing of individual effort above corporate enterprise and in the often nonconformist policies that have given it perhaps the most progressive image of any US city. Several major cultural movements have had their genesis here too. The following account is intended to give an overall view of the city's development.

Native peoples

For thousands of years before the arrival of Europeans, the **aboriginal peoples** of the Bay Area lived healthily and apparently peacefully on the naturally abundant land. Numbering around 15,000, and grouped in small tribal villages of a few hundred people, they supported themselves mainly by hunting and fishing rather than with agriculture. Most belonged to the coastal **Miwok** tribe, who inhabited much of what is now Marin County, as well as the Sonoma and Napa valleys; the rest were **Ohlone**, who lived in smaller villages sprinkled around the Bay and down the south coast of the Peninsula.

Very few artefacts from the period survive and most of what anthropologists have deduced is based on the observations of the early explorers, who were by and large impressed by the Indian way of life – if not their "heathen" religion: one of the first colonists characterized them as "constant in their good friendship and gentle in their manners." Indian boats, fashioned from lengths of tule reed, were remarkably agile and seaworthy. Of the buildings, few of which were ever intended to last beyond the change of seasons, the most distinctive was the *temescal*, or sweat lodge. Kule Loklo, a replica Miwok village in the Point Reyes National Seashore, provides a good sense of what their settlements might have looked like.

Since there was no political or social organization beyond the immediate tribal level, it did not take long for the colonizing Spaniards effectively to wipe them out, if more through epidemics than through outright genocide. Nowadays no Bay Area Native Americans survive on their aboriginal homelands.

Exploration and conquest

Looking at the Golden Gate from almost any vantage point, it's hard to imagine that anyone might fail to notice such a remarkable opening to the Pacific. Nevertheless, dozens of **European explorers**, including some of the most legendary names of the

Circa 4000BC	1579	1603
The first native people inhabit the Bay Area, in the region of today's Emeryville.	Sir Francis Drake arrives at Point Reyes, north of San Francisco, in the Golden Hinde.	Sebastian Vizcaino charts the California coast but misses the San Francisco Bay.

New World conquest – Juan Cabrillo, Sir Francis Drake and Sebastián Vizcaíno – managed to sail past for centuries, oblivious to the great harbour it protected. Admittedly, the passage is often obscured by fog and even on a clear day the Bay's islands and the East Bay hills that rise up behind do disguise the entrance to the point of invisibility.

Sir Francis Drake came close to finding the Bay when he arrived in the *Golden Hinde* in **1579**, taking a break from plundering Spanish vessels in order to make repairs. The "white bancks and cliffes" of his supposed landing spot – now called Drake's Bay, off Point Reyes north of San Francisco – reminded him of Dover. Upon going ashore, he was met by a band of Miwok, who greeted him with food and drink and placed a feathered crown upon his head; in return, he claimed all of their lands, which he called Nova Albion (New England), for Queen Elizabeth. He was supposed to have left behind a brass plaque (since proved a fake) – even so, a copy remains on display in the Bancroft Library at the University of California in Berkeley.

Fifteen years later the Spanish galleon **San Augustín** – loaded to the gunwales with treasure from the Philippines – moored in the same spot but met with tragically different results. After the crew renamed Drake's Bay to honour their patron saint, San Francisco de Asis (Francis of Assisi), the ship was dashed against the rocks of Point Reyes and wrecked. The crew was able to salvage some of the cargo and enough of the ship to build a small lifeboat, on which they travelled south all the way to Acapulco, hugging the Pacific Coast for the entire voyage and still sailing right past the Golden Gate. Indeed, it was not until the end of 1769 that European eyes set sight on the great body of water now called San Francisco Bay.

Colonization: the mission era

The **Spanish occupation** of the West Coast, which they called "Alta California", began in earnest in the late 1760s, following the Seven Years' War. Although this was partly owing to military expediency to prevent another power from gaining a foothold, the conquest was fuelled more by religious fervour: both Catholic missionary zeal to convert the heathen Indians, and Franciscan eagerness to replace the Jesuits who'd been expelled from all Spanish dominions by King Don Carlos III in 1767. Early in 1769, a company of three hundred soldiers and clergy, led by Father **Junípero Serra**, set off from Mexico in Baja California to establish an outpost at Monterey; half travelled by ship, the other half overland. A number stopped to set up the first Californian mission at San Diego, while an advance party – made up of some sixty soldiers, mule skinners, priests and Indians, under the leadership of **Gaspàr de Portola** – continued up the coast, blazing an overland route. It was hard going, especially with their inadequate maps, and not surprisingly they overshot their mark, ending up somewhere around Half Moon Bay. Ironically, after two centuries of sea voyages designed to map the coastline, it would be this landlocked expedition that would first sight the magnificent San Francisco Bay.

Trying to regain their bearings, Portola sent out two scouting parties, one north along the coast and one east into the mountains. Both groups returned with extraordinary descriptions of the Golden Gate and the great Bay, which they thought must be the same "Bahia de San Francisco" where the *San Augustín* had come to grief almost two centuries earlier. On November 4, 1769, the entire party gathered together on the ridgetop, overwhelmed by the incredible sight: Father Crespi, their priest, wrote that the Bay "could hold not only all the armadas of our Catholic Monarch, but also all

1769	1776	1777
Spanish expedition under **Gaspàr de Portola** are the first Europeans to see the San Francisco Bay.	The Spaniards establish the Presidio of San Francisco, overlooking the Golden Gate.	First Bay Area pueblo established near Mission Santa Clara at the southern end of the Peninsula.

those of Europe." Portola's band barely stayed long enough to gather up supplies before turning around and heading back to Monterey; that mission was to become the capital and commercial centre of Spanish California.

It took the Spanish another six years to send an expedition 85 miles north to the bay Portola had discovered. In May 1775, when he piloted the *San Carlos* through the Golden Gate, Juan Manuel de Ayala became the first European to sail into San Francisco Bay. The next year **Captain Juan Bautista de Anza** returned with some two hundred soldiers and settlers to establish the **Presidio of San Francisco** overlooking the Golden Gate. His party also set up a mission three miles to the southeast beside a lake, which they named *Laguna de los Dolores* – "The Lake of Our Lady of Sorrows" – because it was settled on the so-called Friday of Sorrows before Palm Sunday. From this came the mission's popular – and still current – name, **Mission Dolores**; the first Mass at the mission also marks the official founding of the city later known as San Francisco.

Over the coming years four other Bay Area **missions** were established along the El Camino Real, or the "Royal Road": it was built between 1769 and 1823 to link the 21 missions in the chain, running along the Californian coast from San Diego up to the final outpost in Sonoma. **Santa Clara de Asis**, forty miles south of Mission Dolores, was founded in 1777; **San José de Guadalupe**, set up in 1797 near today's Fremont, grew into the most successful of the lot. In 1817, the *asistencia*, or auxiliary mission, **San Rafael Arcangel**, was built in sunny Marin County as a convalescent hospital for priests and Indians who had been taken ill at Mission Dolores. The last, **San Francisco Solano**, built at Sonoma in 1823, was the only mission established under Mexican rule.

Each of the mission complexes was broadly similar, with a church and cloistered residence structure surrounded by irrigated fields, vineyards and more distant ranchlands, the whole protected by a small contingent of soldiers. Indian catechumens were put to work making soap and candles, but were treated as retarded children, often beaten and never educated. Objective facts about the missionaries' treatment of the Indians are hard to come by, though mission registries record twice as many deaths as they do births, and their cemeteries are packed with Indian dead in their thousands, most of them in unmarked graves. Many of the missions suffered from Indian raids, as evidenced by the red-tiled, fire-resistant roofs that replaced earlier thatch designs.

To grow food for the missions and the forts or presidios, **towns** – called *pueblos* – were established, part of the ongoing effort to attract settlers to this distant and as yet undesirable territory. The first was laid out in 1777 at San Jose in a broad fertile valley south of the Mission Santa Clara. Though it was quite successful at growing crops, it had no more than a hundred inhabitants until well into the 1800s. Meanwhile, a small village – not sanctioned by the Spanish authorities – was beginning to emerge between Mission Dolores and the Presidio, around the one deepwater landing spot, southeast of today's Telegraph Hill. Called **Yerba Buena**, "good grass," after the sweet-smelling minty herb that grew wild over the windswept hills, it was little more than a collection of shacks and ramshackle jetties. This tiny outpost formed the basis of today's city, though it wasn't officially tagged as San Francisco until 1847, when opportunistic settlers on the East Bay, looking to capitalize on their closeness to bustling Sacramento, planned a town called Francisca, after the San Francisco Bay. In response, Yerba Buena bigwigs – anxious to flag their pre-eminent position on the coast – quickly renamed their town San Francisco to eclipse the upstarts.

1822	1823	1835
Englishman William Richardson was the first European entrepreneur to set up business in embryonic San Francisco.	The El Camino Real road, linking the area's missions, is completed after 54 years.	Having been solely a male pioneer's preserve, San Francisco's first child to European parents is born.

The Mexican revolutions and the coming of the Americans

The emergence of an independent **Mexican state** in 1821 spelled the end of the mission era. In 1834, the new republic had secularized the missions, the excuse being that they were originally intended only as temporary places to "train" Indians in good Christian ways before letting them run their affairs. The Mexican government didn't pass the land onto native peoples – instead, in a politically savvy manoeuvre, it bequeathed the territory to the few powerful families of the "Californios" – mostly ex-soldiers who had settled here after completing their military service. Mexico exerted hardly any control over distant Yerba Buena, and was generally much more willing than the Spanish had been to allow foreigners to remain as they were, so long as they behaved themselves.

A few trappers and adventurers had passed by in the early 1800s, and, beginning in the early 1820s, a number of British and Americans started arriving in the Bay Area, most of them sailors who jumped ship, but also including a few men of property. The most notable of these immigrants was **William Richardson**, an Englishman who arrived on a whaling ship in 1822 and stayed for the rest of his life, marrying the daughter of the Presidio commander and eventually coming to own most of southern Marin County. Here, he started a profitable shipping company and ran the sole ferry service across the tricky Bay waters. In Richardson's wake, dozens followed – almost without exception males who, like him, tended to fit in with the existing Mexican culture, often marrying into established families and converting to the Catholic faith.

As late as the mid-1840s, Monterey was still the only town of any size on the entire West Coast, and tiny Yerba Buena, with a population around two hundred, made its livelihood from supplying passing ships, mainly Boston-based whaling vessels and the fur-traders of the British-owned **Hudson's Bay Company**. Though the locals lived well, the Bay Area was not obviously rich in resources, and so was not by any means a major issue in international relations. However, from the 1830s onwards, the US government decided that it wanted to buy all of Mexico's lands north of the Rio Grande, California included, fulfilling the "Manifest Destiny" of the United States to cover the continent from coast to coast. Any negotiations were rendered unnecessary when, in June 1846, the **Mexican–American War** broke out in Texas and US naval forces quickly took over the entire West Coast, capturing San Francisco's Presidio on **July 9, 1846**.

Just before this, however, a historically insignificant revolt in the Bay Area left an unusual, lasting legacy for California. An ambitious US Army captain, John C. Fremont, had been working to encourage unhappy settlers to declare independence from Mexico and to set himself up as their leader. By assembling an unofficial force of some sixty sharpshooting ex-soldiers, and by spreading rumours that war with Mexico was imminent and unstoppable, he managed to persuade settlers to take action, leading to the **Bear Flag Revolt**. On June 14, some thirty farmers and trappers descended upon the abandoned Presidio in Sonoma and took the retired commandant captive, raising a makeshift flag over the town's plaza and declaring California independent. The flag – which featured a roughly drawn grizzly bear above the words "California Republic" – was eventually adopted as the California state flag, but this "Republic" was short-lived. Three weeks after the disgruntled settlers hoisted their flag in Sonoma, it was replaced by the Stars and Stripes, and California was thereafter **US territory**.

Ironically, just nine days before the Americans took formal control, **gold** was discovered on January 24, 1848, in the Sierra Nevada foothills a hundred miles east

1846	1847	1848
During the Mexican-American War the US navy captures the San Francisco Presidio and whole West Coast.	Tycoon Sam Brannan publishes The California Star, the West Coast's first local newspaper.	Gold is discovered in the nearby Sierra Nevada foothills, leading to the following year's Gold Rush.

of the city – something that was to change the face of San Francisco forever. Gold would eventually be discovered in 54 out of California's 58 counties; ironically San Francisco – the city whose identity and future were forged in the heat of the Gold Rush – stands in one of the four barren counties.

The Gold Rush

At the time gold was discovered, the Bay Area had a total (non-native) population of around two thousand, about a quarter of whom lived in tiny **San Francisco**. By the summer of 1848, rumours of the find attracted a trickle of gold seekers and when news of their subsequent success filtered back to the coast, soldiers deserted and sailors jumped ship.

The first prospectors on the scene made fantastic fortunes – those working the richest "diggings" could extract more than an ounce every hour – but the real money was being made by merchants charging equally outrageous prices for essentials. (This is how jeans genius Levi Strauss made his fortune, and how Domenico Ghirardelli turned chocolate into gold.) Even the most basic supplies were hard to come by, and what little was available cost exorbitant amounts: a dozen eggs for $50, a shovel or pickaxe twice that. Exuberant miners willingly traded glasses of gold dust for an equal amount of whiskey – something like $1000 a shot. Though it took some time for news of the riches to travel, soon men were flooding into California from all over the globe to share the wealth. Within a year, some 100,000 men – known collectively as the **forty-niners** – had arrived in California: it was the greatest peacetime migration in modern history, and for a time, the men arrived in such numbers that San Francisco's population doubled every ten days. About half of the hopefuls came overland, after a three-month slog across the continent – they headed straight for the mines. The rest arrived by ship and landed at San Francisco, expecting to find a city where they could recuperate before continuing on the arduous journey. They must have been disappointed with what they found: hulks of abandoned ships formed the only solidly constructed buildings; rats overran the filthy streets; and drinking water was scarce and often contaminated.

Few of the new arrivals stayed very long in ruthless San Francisco, but, if anything, life in the mining camps proved even less hospitable. As thousands of moderately successful but worn-out miners returned to San Francisco, especially during the torrential rains of the **winter of 1849–50**, the shanty-town settlement began to grow into a proper city. It suffered six infernos in the six months following Christmas 1849, the last of which spurred the formation of the first Committee of Vigilance. Ex-miners set up foundries and sawmills to provide those starting out with the tools of their trade, and traders arrived to profit from the miners' success, selling them clothing, food, drink and entertainment. The city where the successful miners came to blow their hard-earned cash was a place of luxury hotels and burlesque theatres, which featured the likes of Lola Montez, whose semi-clad "spider dance" enthralled legions of fans. Throughout the early 1850s immigrants continued to pour through the Golden Gate, and although the great majority hurried on to the mines, enough stayed around to bring the city's population up to around 35,000 by the end of 1853. Of these, more than half were from foreign parts – a wide-ranging mix of Mexicans, Germans, Chinese, Italians and others.

Within five years of the discovery of gold, the easy pickings were all but gone. As the freewheeling mining camps evolved into increasingly large-scale, corporate operations,

1849	1856	1865
San Francisco's population balloons to over 30,000 from just several hundred the previous year.	The Committee of Vigilance takes effective control of San Francisco to quell its increasing anarchy.	The Confederate ship Shenandoah was poised to attack San Francisco when the Civil War ended in August.

THE RISE AND FALL OF SAM BRANNAN

Sam Brannan was one of the smartest and most ruthless of the Gold Rush's business tycoons; Levi Strauss and Domenico Ghirardelli may be more famous now, but Brannan was both more notorious and wealthier in their time. He arrived in San Francisco via New York in 1846 as the leader of a 230-strong Mormon missionary group, who fled here by boat hoping to found a new settlement free from what they considered the United States' religious intolerance (while the group was at sea, sadly, California was annexed and its plans scuppered). It's unlikely to have troubled Brannan deeply as he was an iffy Mormon at best – eventually excommunicated from the church for dipping into its cash reserves for his own treats. However, on arriving, Brannan's followers were industrious enough to put up more than two hundred buildings; while he himself used the printing press he'd hauled from the East Coast to publish the first local newspaper, *The California Star*, in 1847.

As the Gold Rush era's answer to Citizen Kane, he was in an ideal position to fan – and profit from – the hysteria that emerged on the discovery of the first deposits. Never one to let scruples get in the way of sheckels, Brannan effectively orchestrated the entire thing. Aside from his printing press, Brannan owned a dry-goods and supply store, and realized he could make a fortune from hordes of get-rich-quick types needing hammers, pails and tents for prospecting. He waited until his warehouses were full of products and then published a special issue of the *Star* in 1848 that focused on local gold mining. His strategy was flawless, and it earned him $36,000 in just nine weeks; he sold prospecting equipment at such a premium, Brannan later became California's first-ever millionaire.

He used the money for two things: first, to buy chunks of local land for a town he was planning, later named Calistoga. The official reason for the name was a combination of New York's Saratoga and California; the more likely basis is that Brannan named it during a speech he gave while drunk on whisky. After all, liquor was the second thing he spent his fortune on – so much so, in fact, that he frittered away his business, was married and divorced three times and ended up living in Mexico, selling pencils on the streets to earn a few pennies. When he died, his body lay in a vault for a year until the money to bury him could be found.

San Francisco swelled from frontier outpost into a substantial city, with a growing industrial base, a few newspapers, and even its own branch of the US Mint. When revenues from the gold fields ceased to expand in the late 1850s, the speculative base that had made so many fortunes quickly vanished. Lots that had been selling at a premium couldn't be given away, banks went bust, and San Francisco had to declare itself **bankrupt** as a result of years of corrupt dealings. The already volatile city descended into near-anarchy, with vigilante mobs roaming the streets. By the summer of 1856, the Committee of Vigilance, led by William Coleman and Sam Brannan and composed of the city's most successful businessmen, was the **de facto government** of the city, having taken over the state militia. It installed itself inside its "Fort Gunnybags" headquarters on Portsmouth Square, outside which it regularly hanged petty criminals (admittedly after giving them a trial), to the amusement of gathered throngs.

Events reached a boiling point when the future California Supreme Court Justice **David Terry** shot a committee member (Terry would go on to shoot the state's first senator a few years later), bringing the vigilantes into direct confrontation with the official government. A few of the most radically minded proposed secession from the US, but calmer heads prevailed, and the city was soon restored to more legitimate

1869	1873	1887
The transcontinental railroad is completed, largely by the labour of Chinese immigrants.	Scottish immigrant Andrew Halliday invents the first cable car to tackle the city's infamous hills.	William Randolph Hearst becomes the owner of the *San Francisco Examiner* newspaper.

governance. Ironically, the task of defending the rabidly pro-slavery Terry fell to a failed banker and young local military commander named **William Sherman**, who would later go into the history books for razing much of the state of Georgia during the Civil War.

The boom years (1860–1900)

In the 1860s, San Francisco enjoyed a bigger boom than that of the Gold Rush, following the discovery of an even more lucrative band of precious **silver ore** in the Great Basin Mountains of western Nevada. Discovered just east of Reno in late 1859 and soon known as the **Comstock Lode**, it was one of the most fantastic deposits ever encountered. A single, solid vein of silver, mixed with gold, it ranged from ten to over a hundred feet wide and stretched a little over two miles long, most of it buried hundreds of feet underground. Mining here was in complete contrast to the freelance prospecting of the California gold fields, and required a scale of operations unimagined in the Californian mines. Many of San Francisco's great engineers, including George Hearst, Andrew Hallidie and Adolph Sutro, put their minds to the task.

As the mines had to go increasingly deeper to get at the valuable ore, the mining companies needed larger and larger amounts of capital, which they attracted by issuing shares dealt on the burgeoning **San Francisco Stock Exchange**. Speculation was rampant, and the value of shares could rise or fall by a factor of ten, depending on the day's rumours and forecasts; Mark Twain got his literary start publicizing, for a fee, various new "discoveries" in his employers' mines. Hundreds of thousands of dollars were made and lost in a day's trading, and the cagier players, like James Flood and James Fair, made millions.

While the Comstock silver enabled many San Franciscans to enjoy an unsurpassed prosperity throughout the 1860s, few people gave much thought to the decade's other major development, the building of the **transcontinental railroad**, completed in 1869 using imported Chinese labourers. Originally set up in Sacramento to build the western link, the **Central Pacific** and later **Southern Pacific** railroad soon expanded to cover most of the West, ensnaring San Francisco in its web. Wholly owned by the so-called **Big Four** – Charles Crocker, Collis P. Huntington, Mark Hopkins and Leland Stanford – the Southern Pacific "octopus," as it was caricatured in the popular press, exercised an essential monopoly over transportation in the Bay Area. Besides controlling the long-distance railroads, they also owned San Francisco's streetcar system, the network of ferries that crisscrossed the Bay and even the cable-car line that lifted them up California Street to their Nob Hill palaces (see box, p.66).

Not everyone, however, reaped the good fortune of the Nob Hill elite. The coming of the railroad usurped San Francisco's primacy as the West Coast's supply point, and products from the East began flooding in at prices well under anything local industry could manage. At the same time the Comstock mines ceased to produce such enormous fortunes and a depression began to set in. The lowering of economic confidence was compounded by a series of droughts that wiped out agricultural harvests and by the arrival in San Francisco of thousands of now unwanted **Chinese workers**. As unemployment rose throughout the late 1870s, frustrated workers took out their aggression in racist assaults on the city's substantial Chinese population. Railroad baron **Leland Stanford** campaigned for governor on an anti-immigrant platform (though his company's employment of masses of Chinese labourers on

1889	1892	1906
Pioneering Gold Rush entrepreneur Sam Brannan dies in penury.	The Sierra Club is founded, with naturalist John Muir as its first President.	The USA's most powerful earthquake ever and the ensuing fires demolish two thirds of the city.

construction gangs seriously undercut his candidacy), and at mass demonstrations all over the city, thousands rallied behind the slogan "The Chinese Must Go!"

Though San Francisco was popularly seen as powered by ignoble motives and full of self-serving money-grabbers, there were a few exceptions, even among its wealthiest elite. **Adolph Sutro**, for example, was a German-born engineer who made one fortune in the Comstock mines and another buying up land in the city – in 1890 he was said to own ten percent of San Francisco, even more than the Big Four. But Sutro was an unlikely millionaire, as compassionate and public-spirited as the Big Four were ruthlessly single-minded; in fact, when the Southern Pacific tripled fares to a quarter on the trolley line out to Golden Gate Park, Sutro built a parallel line that charged a nickel. He also built the Sutro Baths and the Cliff House and in 1894 was elected mayor of San Francisco on the Populist Party ticket. Campaigning on an anti-Southern Pacific manifesto, he promised to rid San Francisco of "this horrible monster which is devouring our substance and debauching our people, and by its devilish instincts and criminal methods is every day more firmly grasping us in its tentacles." Sutro died in 1898, with the city still firmly in the grasp of the "octopus."

The early twentieth century

San Francisco experienced another period of economic expansion in the **early years of the 1900s**, owing in equal part to the Spanish–American War and the Klondike Gold Rush in Alaska. Both of these events increased ship traffic through the port, where dockworkers were beginning to organize themselves into **unions** on an unprecedented scale; the mighty longshoremen's association they formed was to become a political force to be reckoned with for years to come. The fight to win recognition and better wages was long and hard; unrest was virtually constant, and police were brought in to scare off strikers and prevent picket lines from shutting down the waterfront. But this economic instability was nothing compared to the one truly earth-shattering event of the time: the **Great Earthquake of 1906.**

During the ensuing ten years, San Francisco was rebuilt with a vengeance, although the grand plan drawn up by designer Daniel Burnham just a year before the disaster was ignored in favour of the old city layout. The city council had given its approval to this plan, which would have replaced the rigid grid of streets with an eminently more sensible system of axial main boulevards filled in with curving avenues skirting the hills and smaller, residential streets climbing their heights. However, such was the power and influence of the city's vested interests that the status quo was quickly reinstated, despite the clear opportunity afforded by the earthquake. At least cartographers cleaned up the mishmash of street names here – in 1910, by city ordinance, duplicates (often pioneer names like Sutter) were eliminated and dozens of streets renamed for clarity.

To celebrate its recovery and the opening of the Panama Canal – a project that had definite implications for San Francisco's trade-based economy – the city fathers set out to create the magnificent **1915 Panama–Pacific International Exhibition**. Land was reclaimed from the Bay for the exhibition, and an elaborate complex of exotic buildings was constructed on it, including Bernard Maybeck's exquisite Palace of Fine Arts and centring on the 100-yard-high, gem-encrusted Tower of Jewels (a few of its dazzling gems can be seen in the Wells Fargo History Museum). Hundreds of thousands visited the fair, which lasted throughout the year, but when it ended all the buildings, save the

1910	1915	1920
Angel Island is opened as the West Coast's Ellis Island, to process immigrants.	The Panama-Pacific International Exhibition drew hundreds of thousands, marking recovery from the earthquake.	ACLU founded to protect civil liberties, bolstering San Francisco's reputation as a liberal bastion.

THE GREAT EARTHQUAKE AND ITS AFTERMATH

The **quake** that hit San Francisco on the morning of April 18, 1906, was, at 8.1 on the Richter Scale, the most powerful ever to hit anywhere in the US, before or since (over ten times the force of the 1989 earthquake). It destroyed hundreds of buildings, but by far the worst destruction was wrought by the **post-earthquake conflagration**, as ruptured gas mains exploded and chimneys toppled, starting fires that spread rapidly across the city. Temperatures often reached 2000°F, which meant that spontaneous ignition could occur at distances of up to 125ft. The fire all but levelled the entire area from the waterfront, north and south of Market Street, and west to Van Ness Avenue, whose grand mansions were dynamited in a politically daring move to form a firebreak. The statistics are staggering: 490 city blocks and 28,000 buildings were destroyed, causing $300–500m worth of damage – at the time, two-thirds of the property value of the city and one-third of the taxable property in all California. Half of San Francisco's population – some 100,000 people – were left homeless and fled the city. Many of those who stayed set up camp in the barren reaches of what's now Golden Gate Park, where soldiers from the Presidio undertook the mammoth task of establishing and maintaining a tent city for about 20,000 displaced San Franciscans. The official death toll has long been touted at only 500 people, but historians have challenged such figures and upped estimates to at least 3000 dead and likely thousands more.

Palace of Fine Arts, were torn down, and the land was sold off for housing, forming the area now known as the Marina.

The great success of the exhibition proved to the world that San Francisco had recovered from the earthquake. But the newly recovered civic pride was tested the next year when, on the eve of America's involvement in **World War I**, a pro-war parade organized by San Francisco's business community was devastated by a **bomb attack** on Steuart Street near the Ferry Building, that killed ten marchers and severely wounded another forty. In their haste to find the culprit, the San Francisco police arrested half a dozen radical union agitators. With no evidence other than perjured testimony, activist **Tom Mooney** was convicted and sentenced to death, along with his alleged co-conspirator **Warren Billings**. Neither, fortunately, was executed, but both spent most of the rest of their lives in prison; Billings wasn't pardoned until 1961, 45 years after his fraudulent conviction.

The Roaring Twenties

The war years had little effect on San Francisco, but the period thereafter, the **Roaring Twenties**, was in many ways the city's finest era. Despite Prohibition, the jazz clubs and speakeasies of the Barbary Coast district were in full swing: San Francisco was still the premier artistic and cultural centre of the West Coast, although it would relinquish that role to Los Angeles by the next decade. Furthermore, its status as an international financial hub (the two major international credit-card companies – Visa and Access – started here) equalled that of New York City. The strength of San Francisco as a banking power was highlighted by the rise of Bank of America – founded as the Bank of Italy in 1904 by A.P. Giannini in North Beach – into the largest bank in the world.

The buoyant 1920s gave way to the Depression of the 1930s, but, despite the sharp increases in unemployment, there was only one major battle on the industrial-relations front. On "**Bloody Thursday**" – July 5, 1934 – police protecting strike-breakers from

1933	1934	1937
Alcatraz, the craggy rock off the tip of San Francisco, is turned into a prison.	The shooting of union pickets by police on "Bloody Thursday" led to a four-day general strike.	The Golden Gate Bridge, one of the world's most iconic structures, goes into operation.

angry picketers fired into the crowd, wounding thirty and killing two longshoremen. The Army was sent in to restore order, and in retaliation the unions called a **General Strike** that saw some 125,000 workers down tools, bringing the Bay Area economy to a halt for four days. It was one of the largest strikes in the nation's history. Otherwise there was remarkably little unrest, and some of the city's finest monuments – Coit Tower, for example, and, most importantly, the two great bridges – were built during this time under **WPA sponsorship**. Before the **Bay and Golden Gate bridges** went up, in 1936 and 1937 respectively, links between the city and the surrounding towns of the Bay Area were provided by an impressive network of **ferry boats**, some of which were among the world's largest. In 1935, the ferries' peak year, some 100,000 commuters per day crossed the Bay by boat; just five years later the last of the boats was withdrawn from service, unable to compete with the increasingly popular automobile.

World War II

The Japanese attack on Pearl Harbor and US involvement in **World War II** transformed the Bay Area into a massive war machine, its industry mobilizing quickly to provide weaponry and ships for the war effort. **Shipyards** opened all around the Bay – the largest, the Kaiser Shipyards in Richmond, was employing more than 100,000 workers on round-the-clock shifts just six months after its inception – and men and women flooded into the region from all over the country to work in the lucrative concerns. In fact, in 1943, for perhaps the first and only time in its history, the city was so crowded that civic groups discouraged conventions and tourists. Entire cities were constructed to house the workers, many of which survive – not least Hunter's Point, on the southern edge of the San Francisco waterfront, which was never intended to last beyond the end of hostilities but still houses some 15,000 of the city's poorest people. A more successful example is Marin City, a workers' housing community just north of Sausalito, which – surprisingly, considering its present-day air of leisured affluence – was one of the most successful wartime shipyards, able to crank out a ship a day.

Certainly, there was a strong male-only culture in San Francisco that dated back to the time of the forty-niners, but it was the war that inadvertently established the city as a **gay centre**. Young men, barred from embarkation under suspicion of homosexuality were discharged before they saw combat others, whose sexuality had come under question while overseas, were summarily discharged when they docked in San Francisco. Both groups received distinctive blue-coloured discharge papers – vital to show a new employer – marked with a large red H to denote "homosexual"; little wonder so many dismissed in that way chose to settle in the city and try to make new lives here rather than return home. In the process, those disgraced military men helped found the roots of the current community.

The 1950s... and the Beats go on

After the war, thousands of GIs returning from the South Pacific came home through San Francisco and many decided to stay. The city spilled out into new districts and, especially in suburbs like the Sunset, massive tracts of identical dwellings, subsidized by federal loans and grants, were thrown up to house the returning heroes – many of whom still live here. The accompanying economic prosperity continued unabated well into the 1950s, and in order to accommodate increasing numbers of cars on the roads,

1945	1950	1952
The United Nations Charter is signed here on June 26.	After entering the NFL for the first time, the 49ers win only three games.	One of America's first public broadcasting companies, forerunner of KQED, is launched.

TRIPPY HIPPIES

The main difference between the Beats and the early hippies, besides the five years that elapsed, was that the hippies had discovered – and regularly experimented with – a new hallucinogenic drug called LSD, better known as **acid**. Since its synthesis, LSD had been legally and readily available, mainly through psychologists who were interested in studying its possible therapeutic benefits. Other, less scientific, research was also being done by a variety of people, many of whom, from around 1965 onwards, began to settle in the **Haight-Ashbury district** west of the city centre, living communally in huge low-rent Victorian houses in which they could take acid and "trip" in safe, controlled circumstances. Music was an integral part of the acid experience, and a number of bands – the **Charlatans**, **Jefferson Airplane**, and the **Grateful Dead** – came together in San Francisco during the summer of 1966, playing open-ended dance music at such places as the Fillmore Auditorium and the Avalon Ballroom.

Things remained on a fairly small scale until the spring of **1967**, when a free concert in Golden Gate Park, the "Human Be-In," drew a massive crowd and, for the first time, media attention. Articles describing the hippies, most of which focused on their prolific appetites for sex and drugs, attracted a stream of newcomers to the Haight from all over the country, and within a few months the **Summer of Love** was well under way, with some 100,000 young people descending upon the district (see box, p.110).

huge **freeways** were constructed, cutting through the city. The Embarcadero Freeway in particular formed an imposing barrier, perhaps appropriately dividing the increasingly office-oriented Financial District from the declining docks and warehouses of the waterfront, which for so long had been the heart of San Francisco's economy.

As the increasingly mobile and prosperous middle classes moved out from the inner city, new bands of literate but disenchanted middle-class youth began to move into the areas left behind, starting, in the middle part of the decade, in the bars and cafés of North Beach, which swiftly changed from a staunch Italian neighbourhood into the Greenwich Village of the West Coast. The **Beat Generation**, as they became known, reacted against what they saw as the empty materialism of Fifties America by losing themselves in a bohemian orgy of jazz, drugs and Buddhism, expressing their disillusionment with the status quo through a new, highly personal and expressive brand of fiction and poetry. The writer **Jack Kerouac**, whose *On the Road* became widely accepted as the handbook of the Beats, both for the style of writing (fast, passionate, unpunctuated) and the lifestyle it described, was in some ways the movement's main spokesman, and is credited with coining the term "Beat" to describe the group. Later, columnist Herb Caen somewhat derisively turned "Beat" into "Beatnik," after Sputnik, since the rebellious youngsters' behaviour was as "far out" as the Russian satellite. San Francisco, and particularly the **City Lights Bookstore**, at the centre of North Beach, which was opened by poet Lawrence Ferlinghetti in 1953, became the main meeting point and focus of this diffuse group, though whatever impetus the movement had was gone by the early 1960s (see box, p.57).

The socially and politically radical 1960s

If the 1950s belonged to the Beats, then the 1960s were ruled by the inexperienced but enthusiastic young people who followed in their hedonistic footsteps – derisively

1953	1957	1964
Early Beat poet Lawrence Ferlinghetti opens the legendary City Lights bookstore in North Beach.	Jack Kerouac's pivotal Beat Generation novel *On The Road* is published.	The city's cable cars are declared the USA's only moving National Historic Landmark.

THE ASSASSINATION OF HARVEY MILK

In 1977, eight years after New York's Stonewall riots cast a spotlight on gay political activism, Castro camera-shop owner **Harvey Milk** was elected as the city's first openly gay supervisor (or councillor) and quickly became one of the most prominent gay officials in the country. A celebrated figure for the city's gay community, the New York native was nicknamed the "Mayor of Castro Street"; however, his political career was horrifyingly cut short in 1978 when former supervisor Dan White entered City Hall and shot both supervisor Milk and **mayor George Moscone** dead.

The conservative White saw himself as a spokesman for San Francisco's many blue-collar Irish families and, as an ex-policeman, also saw himself at the vanguard of the traditional family values he believed gay rights risked damaging. Throughout the ensuing trial, the prosecution never once mentioned the word "assassination" or recognized a political motive for the killings, and White was ultimately sentenced to only five years' imprisonment for manslaughter. The gay community exploded when White's light sentence was handed down, and the "White Night" **riots** that followed – which saw protesters torch police cars and storm City Hall – were among the most violent San Francisco has ever witnessed. White was released from prison in 1985 and, unwelcome in San Francisco and unable to find a job, committed suicide shortly afterwards.

The anniversary of the murder of Milk and Moscone is marked by a **candlelight procession** from the Castro to City Hall every November 27.

christened junior hipsters, or **hippies**. The first hippies appeared in the early Sixties, in cafés and folk-music clubs around the fringes of Bay Area university campuses. Like the Beats they eschewed the materialism and the nine-to-five consumer world. But while the Beats were nitty-gritty, their successors were hippy-dippy, preferring an escapist fantasy of music and marijuana that morphed into a half-baked political indictment of society and where it was going wrong.

In contrast to the hippie indulgence of the Haight-Ashbury scene, across the Bay in Berkeley and Oakland **revolutionary politics**, rather than drugs, were at the top of the agenda. While many of the hippies opted out of politics, the student radicals threw themselves into political activism, beginning with the Free Speech Movement at the University of California in 1964. The FSM, originally a reaction against the university's banning of on-campus political activity, laid the groundwork for the more passionate **anti-Vietnam War** protests that rocked the entire country for the rest of the decade. The first of what turned out to be dozens of **riots** occurred in June 1968, when students marching down Telegraph Avenue in Berkeley in support of the Paris student uprising were met by a wall of police, leading to rioting that continued for days. Probably the most famous event in Berkeley's radical history took place in **People's Park**, a plot of university-owned land that was taken over by local people. Four days later an army of police, under the command of Edwin Meese – later head of the US Department of Justice during the Reagan years – tear-gassed and stormed the park, accidentally killing a bystander and seriously injuring more than one hundred others.

Probably the most extreme element of late-1960s San Francisco emerged out of the impoverished flatlands of Oakland – the **Black Panthers**, established by Bobby Seale, Huey Newton and Eldridge Cleaver in 1966 (see box, p.237). The Panthers were a heavily armed but numerically small band of militant black activists with an

1964	1966	1967
The Free Speech Movement is founded by radical students at Berkeley's University of California.	The militant Black Panther movement is formed in Oakland to fight for civil rights.	The first "Human Be-in" is held in Golden Gate Park, heralding the hippy Summer of Love.

announced goal of securing self-determination for America's blacks. From their Oakland base they set up a nationwide organization but the threat they posed and the chances they were willing to take in pursuit of their cause, were too great. Thirty of their members died in gun battles with the police and the surviving Panthers lost track of their aims: Eldridge Cleaver later became a right-wing Republican, while Huey Newton was killed over a drug deal in West Oakland in 1989.

The gay decade

The unrest of the 1960s continued into the **early 1970s**, if not at such a fever pitch. One last headline-grabber was the kidnapping in 1974 of heiress Patty Hearst from her Berkeley apartment by the Symbionese Liberation Army, or **SLA**, a hardcore bunch of revolutionaries who used their wealthy hostage to demand free food for Oakland's poor. Hearst later helped the gang to rob a San Francisco bank, wielding a submachine gun (she was sent to jail for her crime, although later pardoned). Otherwise, the 1970s were quiet times (certainly compared to the previous decade). They saw the opening of the long-delayed **BART** high-speed transportation system, as well as the establishment of the **Golden Gate National Recreation Area** to protect and preserve 75,000 acres of open space on both sides of the Golden Gate Bridge.

Throughout the 1970s, it wasn't so much that San Francisco's rebellious thread had been broken but rather that the battle lines were being drawn elsewhere. The most distinctive political voices were those of the city's large **gay and lesbian communities**. Inspired by the Stonewall Riots in New York City in 1969, San Francisco's homosexuals began to organize themselves politically, demanding equal status with heterosexuals. Most importantly, gays and lesbians stepped out into the open and refused to hide their sexuality behind closed doors, giving rise to the gay liberation movement that has prospered worldwide. One of the leaders of the gay community in San Francisco, **Harvey Milk**, won a seat on the Board of Supervisors, becoming the first openly gay man to take public office. When Milk was **assassinated** in City Hall, along with Mayor George Moscone, by former supervisor Dan White in 1978 (see box opposite) the whole city was shaken. The fact that White was found guilty of manslaughter, not murder, caused the gay community to erupt in riotous frustration, burning police cars and laying siege to City Hall.

The onslaught of AIDS and the 1989 earthquake

The **1980s** saw the city's gay community in retreat to some extent, with the advent of **AIDS** in the early part of the decade devastating the confidence of activists and decimating its population. City Hall, led by Mayor **Dianne Feinstein** (nicknamed Di-Fi), who took over after the death of Moscone, responded to the crisis more quickly and efficiently than other cities hard hit by the virus, supporting the community's Herculean efforts with well-funded urban relief and education programmes. Together, they managed to stabilize new infection rates by the 1990s. Treatment and caretaking efforts for those infected by HIV, meanwhile, remained largely driven by volunteers' fundraising efforts, nearly exhausting the energies of the community, which became almost exclusively focused on the crisis.

At the same time, Feinstein oversaw the construction of millions of square feet of office towers in Downtown's Financial District, despite angry protests against the

1972	1978	1981
Construction on the Transamerica Pyramid, the city's tallest and most iconic skyscraper, is completed.	Gay public official Harvey Milk and Mayor George Moscone are assassinated in City Hall.	The first symptoms of what was to become known as AIDS appear, mainly in the gay community.

Manhattanization of the city. Although Feinstein's attempts to spend the city out of its financial slump dumped a tangled mess of financial worries into the lap of her successors, she went on to become senator in 1992 and remains one of the most prominent female politicians in America today.

But before the already tough 1980s came to an end, the city was shaken by a major **earthquake** in October 1989, 7.1 on the Richter Scale. The event, which collapsed a freeway in Oakland, was watched by a hundred million people on nationwide TV, since it hit during a World Series game between the San Francisco Giants and the Oakland Athletics.

It's a wired, wired world – the 1990s

Following this rather grim decade, the **1990s** seemed sunnier, at least for some of the city's residents. A national boom in high-tech industries, initiated by companies such as Apple, Oracle, Netscape and Yahoo, based south of the city in **Silicon Valley**, proved particularly lucrative for the Bay Area. The rush for new-technology jobs – at one peak moment, the valley was supposedly cranking out 63 new millionaires per day – created a region-wide population boom. In San Francisco, the influx of wealthy young computer professionals into an incredibly tight housing market led to the rapid **gentrification** of certain city neighbourhoods (Hayes Valley and parts of the Mission, to name two), where rents skyrocketed by as much as a hundred percent per year; meanwhile, an entirely new upscale community sprung up along the South Beach waterfront, adjacent to a sparkling new (and privately financed) baseball stadium.

Merrily riding the wave of prosperity in 1996 was **Willie Brown**, self-dubbed "da Mayor," who began his remarkable climb to power from being a child of African-American sharecroppers in Texas by driving a cab to fund his law degree, eventually becoming the most influential man in California's state senate and one of the most powerful black politicians in the nation. Brown noisily focused on ambitious programmes to fix the city's overburdened mass-transit system and ageing public housing. His detractors, however, pointed out the lack of substance behind his style and the failure of the city's newfound wealth to solve such longstanding problems as homelessness argued in their favour. Evidence that gentrification hadn't completely killed the city's liberal spirit came during Brown's campaign for re-election in 1999, when write-in candidate Tom Ammiano, a popular gay stand-up comedian and President of the city's Board of Supervisors, nearly staged an upset with his progressive agenda. The victory may have been Brown's, but it was a pyrrhic one, as in his second term he struggled to balance the extravagant campaign promises he made to help the disenfranchised while protecting corporate interests.

Across the Bay, the successes of Oakland mayor **Jerry Brown**, elected in 1998, showed up "da Mayor's" failings all too acutely. Jerry's deft populist approach contrasted with Willie's ham-fisted tub-thumping and easily earned him a second term in office during the 2002 election. A former governor of California, Jerry's political platform centered on turning central Oakland, drained by suburban exodus and dogged by second-fiddle status to San Francisco, into a lively town crammed with amenities and residential space – a concept he called "elegant density." He made some progress before handing Oakland mayoral duties off to current city chief **Ron Dellums** in 2006, but the city's continued economic shortcomings indicate there's still plenty left to do.

1989	**1996**	**1998**
Another major earthquake hits the Bay Area, causing a freeway to collapse in Oakland.	Willie Brown completes his rise from impoverished roots to become "Da Mayor" of San Francisco.	Ex-Governor Jerry Brown is elected mayor in Oakland and sets about a programme of urban regeneration.

San Francisco in the new millennium

The torrid **internet industry** imploded in 2000–01, and the end of the dot-com boom left savage marks on San Francisco's cityscape, from empty warehouse offices in South of Market to the closure of new restaurants now devoid of patrons. The city stumbled on for a few years, with housing rates deflating, a marked drop in population and a general listlessness uncharacteristic of San Francisco. By the middle of the decade, however, much of the city's energy had returned, thanks to a rebounded economy fuelled in no small part by a flurry of Web 2.0 companies intent on learning from their predecessors' – or in some cases, their own – prior overindulgences.

The city's rediscovered youthful exuberance was symbolized by the inauguration of native son **Gavin Newsom**, a suave restaurateur turned young-lion politico, as mayor at the age of 36 in early 2004. Newsom focused on social issues like homelessness, not to mention his surprisingly staunch stance on gay marriage (see box, p.198), which found him bucking state laws to wed hundreds of same-sex couples at City Hall. Despite a flurry of controversy over personal issues in the early months of 2007, Newsom's popularity at the polls soared and he ran virtually unopposed, winning a second term easily with over 72 percent of all votes cast. Unsurprisingly then, many of the San Franciscans who had backed him felt somewhat betrayed when he resigned from the mayorship a year early to become Lieutenant Governor of California, the second highest position in the state.

His successor, **Edwin Lee**, had the distinction of being the first Asian-American to hold the position of mayor, even though he was not elected but appointed by the Board of Supervisors, whose president was **David Chiu**, another member of the politically rising Chinese community. Having initially declared he would not run in the November 2011 mayoral elections, public approval of his handling of the role had led to Lee reconsidering his position at the time of writing. Chiu was also in the running, as was state senator **Leland Yee**, completing a strong trio of Asian-American candidates. At the same time there has been a fair degree of optimism that the Bay Area economy is showing signs of recovering from the recent global gloom, though there are no real hard statistics to back that up.

2000	**2001**	**2011**
The San Francisco Giants move to their new bayside ballpark, now renamed AT&T Park.	The dot-com bust leads to a recession across the Bay Area and housing prices downturn sharply.	Edwin Lee is appointed as the first Asian-American mayor, following the resignation of Gavin Newsom.

Books

Travel and impressions

★ **Jack Kerouac** *On the Road*. The book that launched a generation with its "spontaneous bop prosody," it chronicles Beat life in a series of road adventures, featuring some of San Francisco and a lot of the rest of the US. His other books, many set in the Bay Area, include *Lonesome Traveler*, *The Dharma Bums*, and *Desolation Angels*.

Jack London *Martin Eden*. Jack Kerouac's favourite book, a semi-autobiographical account tracking the early years of this San Francisco-born, Oakland-bred adventure writer. The lengthy opus tells of his rise from waterfront hoodlum to high-brow intellectual and of his subsequent disenchantment with the trappings of success.

John Miller (ed) *San Francisco Stories: Great Writers on the City*. Patchy collection of writings on the city with contributions from Lewis Lapham, Tom Wolfe, Dylan Thomas and Hunter S. Thompson, to name but a few.

Czeslaw Milosz *Visions from San Francisco Bay*. Written in Berkeley during the unrest of 1968, these dense and somewhat ponderous essays show a European mind trying to come to grips with California's nascent Aquarian Age.

Mick Sinclair *Cities of the Imagination: San Francisco*. Fact-crammed and immensely readable, but its thematic, rather than linear, history can make the narrative frustratingly circular and repetitive.

★ **Mark Twain** *Roughing It*. Vivid, semi-fantastical tales of frontier California, particularly evocative of life in the silver mines of the 1860s Comstock Lode, where Twain got his start as a journalist and storyteller. His descriptions of San Francisco include a moment-by-moment description of an earthquake.

★ **Tom Wolfe** *The Electric Kool-Aid Acid Test*. Wolfe at his most expansive, floridly riding with the Grateful Dead and Hell's Angels on the magic bus of Ken Kesey and the Merry Pranksters as they travel through the early 1960s, turning California onto LSD. Wolfe's *Radical Chic & Mau Mauing the Flak Catchers* digs at radical politics and white guilt in City Hall.

History, politics and society

Nan Alamilla Boyd *Wide Open Town: A History of Queer San Francisco to 1965*. This gay history is sadly rather heavy going and academic in its analysis; where it shines is in the first person oral histories, scattered throughout the book, which are interviews with everyday gays and lesbians who lived here in the early and mid-twentieth century.

Walton Bean *California: An Interpretive History*. Blow-by-blow account of the history of California, including all the shady deals and backroom politicking, presented in accessible, anecdotal form.

Mark Bittner *The Parrots of Telegraph Hill*. Homeless drifter-cum-hippie befriends the flock of parrots living on the power lines in this neighbourhood, gains local notoriety and then has his story recorded by a documentary filmmaker. A charming, low-key gem.

Gray Brechin *Imperial San Francisco*. Crisply written, tough-minded account of the questionable dealings that helped drive the city's rapid growth around the end of the nineteenth century.

Herb Caen *Baghdad by the Bay*; *The Best of Herb Caen*. Two collections by the city's most indefatigable promoter. Though rather light, Caen's bemused writing always portrays the city as a charming, cosmopolitan stomping ground.

Barnaby Conrad *Name Dropping: Tales from My Barbary Coast Saloon*. Author, bullfighter, and once-proud owner of the happening 1950s Bay Area bar *El Matador* spills the beans on his celebrity clientele, which included the likes of Kerouac, Sinatra and Marilyn Monroe. Conrad has also edited a book about one of his long-time pals, *The World of Herb Caen*.

Peter Coyote *Sleeping Where I Fall*. The author, a minor actor, chronicles his hippie days giving out food as a member of the Diggers and directing radical theatre with the SF Mime Troupe.

★ **Joan Didion** *Slouching Toward Bethlehem*. Selected essays from one of California's most renowned journalists, taking a critical look at the West Coast of the 1960s, including San Francisco's acid culture. In a similar style, *The White Album* traces the West Coast characters and events that shaped the 1960s and 1970s, including The Doors, Charles Manson and the Black Panthers.

Dave Eggers *A Heartbreaking Work of Staggering Genius*. Most of Eggers' manic memoir takes place in the Bay Area of the early 1990s, providing a highly personalized, entertaining and at times harrowing window into the dawn of the internet age and Generation X.

Philip L. Fradkin *The Great Earthquake and Firestorms of 1906: How San Francisco Nearly Destroyed Itself*. Stunning overview that brings fresh insight to a well-known topic; local journalist Fradkin follows not just the mistakes which led to the city's devastation (essentially, ignoring every earthquake warning) but also the political power struggles that erupted in the wake of the disaster.

★ **Joshua Gamson** *The Fabulous Sylvester: The Legend, the Music, the 70s in San Francisco*. Gamson uses an early disco diva, the flamingly gay Sylvester, as an entry point into the "Anything Goes" San Francisco of the 1970s. Sylvester's story is compelling even for casual readers: a kid from the hood in LA becomes a falsetto-voiced, fabulous drag star in San Francisco before succumbing to AIDS in the late 1980s.

Milton Gould *A Cast of Hawks*. Juicy but overcooked account of San Francisco's early days, when the distinction between crook and statesman was at its vaguest; the book's details on the city's vigilante government are interesting.

Joyce Jansen *San Francisco's Cable Cars*. An informal history of the city's most prominent moving landmarks, with some good historic photos of them.

David A. Kaplan *The Silicon Boys*. A witty, entertaining and thorough account of the history and culture of the Silicon Valley.

★ **Dan Kurtzman** *Disaster!*. Hour-by-hour account of the Great Fire of 1906, crisply told as a gripping narrative focusing on the fate of a handful of local residents.

Pat Montandon *The Intruders*. Breathless true-life account of the supposed curse society hostess Montandon endured in the late 1960s, taking in the mysterious deaths and rattling around her Pacific Heights home. Hokey but great trashy fun.

Charles Perry *The Haight-Ashbury*. Curiously distant but detailed account of the Haight during the Flower Power years, written by an editor of *Rolling Stone*.

Rand Richards *Historic San Francisco*. Part history and part guidebook, this is a superb introduction to the city's odd narrative. The sight descriptions are rather redundant but the intriguing, oddball historical digressions illuminate.

★ **Randy Shilts** *The Mayor of Castro Street: The Life and Times of Harvey Milk*. Exhaustively researched epic biography of Milk that explores the assassinated supervisor's place in the struggle for gay rights. Shilts also wrote the most thorough account of the early days of the AIDS epidemic, *And the Band Played On*.

Jay Stevens *Storming Heaven: LSD and the American Dream*. An engaging account of psychedelic drugs and their effect on American society through the 1960s, with an epilogue covering "designer drugs" – Venus, Ecstasy, Vitamin K, and others – and the inner space they help some modern Californians to find.

Susan Stryker and Jim Van Buskirk *Gay by the Bay*. Pithy illustrated history of the city's gay and lesbian community. Though they touch on the city's history, the authors focus their attention on the post-World War II boom in the gay scene and the subsequent movement for artistic expression and political liberation.

Pam Tent *Midnight at The Palace: My life as a Fabulous Cockette*. Tent was one of the pan-sexual, LSD-fuelled performance artists known as *The Cockettes* who scandalized and symbolized early 1970s San Francisco; she was unusual mostly for being a woman. Tent's anecdotal, affectionate recap of the troupe and era is surprisingly sweet.

★ **Hunter S. Thompson** *Hell's Angels*. The book that put the late Thompson's "gonzo" journalism on the map, as he chronicles violent parties with the notorious biker gang. *The Great Shark Hunt* is a collection of often barbed and cynical essays on 1960s American life and politics that's thought-provoking and hilarious. *Generation of Swine* is a more recent collection of caustic musings on the state of America and those who control it, assembled from his columns in the *San Francisco Examiner*.

William T. Vollman *The Rainbow Stories*. Brutal, gut-level portraits of street life: Tenderloin whores, Haight Street skinheads, beggars, junkies and homeless Vietnam vets. Engaging stuff for those who can handle it.

Specific guides

★ **Daniel Bacon** *Walking San Francisco on the Barbary Coast Trail*. A fantastic, enthusiastic resource on the early days of San Francisco that's amusing, highly detailed and informative. Highly recommended.

Adab Bakalinsky *Stairway Walks in San Francisco*. This guide details pretty back streets and stairways through San Francisco's hills. It's excellent for turning up lesser-known spots on a walking tour.

Bicycle Rider Directory Low-cost guide to do-it-yourself bicycle touring around the Bay Area and Napa and Sonoma valleys, with good fold-out route maps.

Jack Boulware *San Francisco Bizarro*. As its name suggests, this is a poppy, snappy survey of the offbeat and strange; some of Boulware's information is a little out of date, but his gossip approach is appealing.

★ **Don Herron** *The Literary World of San Francisco*. A walk through the San Francisco neighbourhoods associated with authors who have lived in and written about the city. Detailed and well presented, it's an essential handbook for anyone interested in San Francisco's literary heritage. If you're a hard-bitten crime hound, try *The Dashiell Hammett Tour* by the same author.

Grant Peterson *Roads to Ride*. As its subtitle says, this is a bicyclist's topographic guide to the whole Bay Area and is particularly good on the back roads of Marin County.

Sidra Sitch *Art Sites San Francisco*. An exhaustive overview of the city's architecture, whether classic Victorians or modern skyscrapers Downtown. A little po-faced and dry but packed with information.

★ **Walking the West Series**: *Walking the California Coast and Walking California's State Parks* and others. Well-written and -produced paperbacks, each covering over a hundred excellent day walks from two to twenty miles. They're strong on practical details (maps, route descriptions and so on), and boast inspiring prose and historical background.

Peggy Wayburn *Adventuring in the San Francisco Bay Area*. If you're planning to spend any time hiking in the Bay

Area's many fine wilderness regions, pick up this fact-filled guide, which also details a number of historical walks through the city's urban areas.

Fiction and poetry

James d'Alessandro *1906: A Novel*. Rollicking page-turner using the disaster of 1906 as a backdrop. The vivid story is narrated by a feisty Italian-American reporter Annalisa Passarelli and fuses factual chunks with inventive subplots (including one starring world-famous tenor Enrico Caruso, who was indeed performing here during the disaster).

Philip K. Dick *The Man in the High Castle*. Long-time Berkeley- and Marin County-based science-fiction author imagines an alternative San Francisco, following a Japanese victory in World War II. Of his dozens of other brilliant novels and short stories, *Bladerunner* and *The Trans-migration of Timothy Archer* make good use of Bay Area locales.

John Dos Passos *USA*. Massive, groundbreaking trilogy, combining fiction, poetry and reportage to tap the various strands of the American Experience. Much of the first part, *The 42nd Parallel*, takes place around the Sutro Baths and Golden Gate Park.

William Gibson *Virtual Light* and *All Tomorrow's Parties*. Two books showcasing the cyberpunk sci-fi author's futuristic vision of the city, complete with squatters on the Golden Gate Bridge and heroic bike messengers.

Allen Ginsberg *Howl and Other Poems*. The attempted banning of the title poem assured its fame; *Howl* itself is an angry rant that often descends into wince-inducing Beatnik jive, but a Whitmanesque voice often shines through.

Oakley Hall *Ambrose Bierce and the Queen of Spades*. Rich mystery of old-time San Francisco, in which colourful characters of the city's late-nineteenth-century cultural scene collide against a backdrop of murder, corruption, big business and investigative journalism.

★ **Dashiell Hammett** *The Four Great Novels* (Random House/Picador). Seminal detective stories including *The Maltese Falcon* and starring Sam Spade, the private investigator working out of San Francisco. See also Diane Johnson's absorbing *The Life of Dashiell Hammett*.

★ **Maxine Hong Kingston** *Chinamen*. Hugely popular and affecting magical-realist depiction of one family's immigration from China to the gold coast. Kingston manages to combine both telling period details and the larger mythic quality of the passage of generations.

David Lodge *Changing Places*. Thinly disguised autobiographical tale of an English academic who spends a year teaching at UC Berkeley (renamed in the book) and finds himself bang in the middle of the late-1960s student upheaval.

Armistead Maupin *Tales of the City; Further Tales of the City; More Tales of the City; Babycakes; Significant Others; Sure of You*. Six twisty, plot-crammed novels that wittily

detail the sexual (and emotional) antics of four housemates – Michael (the gay one, Maupin's alter ego), Brian (the stud), MaryAnn (the virgin) and Mona (the flower child). The story, based on Maupin's newspaper columns, takes the characters from free-living and -loving late-1970s San Francisco to the hard realities of the late 1980s.

Ken McGoogan *Kerouac's Ghost*. Beat homage in which the author raises Kerouac from the dead and sticks him in the 1970s to write about Haight-Ashbury and play mentor to a struggling French-Canadian writer.

Seth Morgan *Homeboy*. Novel charting the sleazy San Francisco experiences of the former junkie boyfriend of Janis Joplin.

John Mulligan *Shopping Cart Soldiers*. Fictionalized memoir of a homeless vet who hangs out in Washington Square, where he meets the ghost of Robert Louis Stevenson. Offbeat and well written.

Fae Myenne *Ng Bone*. Well-crafted first novel that gives a good taste of living rough in San Francisco's Chinatown.

Frank Norris *McTeague: A Story of San Francisco*. Dramatic, extremely violent but engrossing saga of love and revenge in San Francisco at the end of the nineteenth century; later filmed by Erich von Stroheim as Greed. Norris's *Octopus* tells the bitter tale of the Southern Pacific Railroad's stranglehold over the Californian economy.

Thomas Pynchon *The Crying of Lot 49*. Obtuse but sharp and quite hilarious novel that follows the labyrinthine adventures of conspiracy freaks and potheads in 1960s California.

Kenneth Rexroth *An Autobiographical Novel*. Rather stiffly written account of the influential poet and translator's freewheeling life and times. A leading figure in San Francisco's postwar artistic community, Rexroth's experimental nature was an inspiration to a younger generation of Beat writers.

Douglas Rushkoff *The Ecstasy Club*. Cyberculture pundit concocts a frothy, well-paced novel ribboned with conspiracy theories and occult esoterica. Ravers, Deadheads and other Bay Area riffraff wander in and out of the plot.

Vikram Seth *The Golden Gate*. Slick novel in verse, tracing the complex social lives of a group of San Francisco yuppies.

Gary Snyder *Left Out in the Rain*. One of the original Beat writers and the only one whose work ever matured, Snyder's poetry is direct and spare, yet manages to conjure up a deep animistic spirituality underlying everyday life.

★ **Amy Tan** *The Joy Luck Club*. Set in San Francisco, four Chinese-American women and their daughters gather together to look back over their lives. The mothers' lyrical tales of life in China dance with Tan's vivid and imaginative touch; the daughters' stories are soapier and less transporting.

San Francisco on film

Ten classic San Francisco films

Barbary Coast (Howard Hawks 1935). Set in misty, fog-bound, c.1900 San Francisco, where Edward G. Robinson finds he has competition when he tries to seduce the exotic dancer played by Miriam Hopkins. A brawling adventure film that captures the spirit of a lawless San Francisco.

Bullitt (Peter Yates 1968). Steve McQueen is the star but San Francisco steals the show in the definitive high-speed car chase the film revolves around. It was filmed mostly on the steep streets of Pacific Heights and Potrero Hill.

The Conversation (Francis Ford Coppola 1974). Local boy Coppola directs this brilliant Watergate-era thriller, starring Gene Hackman as a surveillance expert slowly descending into paranoia. A foggy Union Square provides the perfect backdrop.

Days of Wine and Roses (Martin Manulis 1962). Jack Lemmon plays a likeable drunk who drags his wife into alcoholism too, only to leave her there once he's on the road to recovery. Smart satirical comedy that occasionally slips into melodrama.

Dirty Harry (Don Siegel 1971). Sleek and exciting sequel-spawning thriller casting Clint Eastwood in his definitive role as a quasi-fascist San Francisco cop. Morally debatable, but technically dynamic.

Greed (Erich von Stroheim 1924). Legendary, lengthy silent masterpiece based on Frank Norris's *McTeague* (see opposite) detailing the squalid, ultimately tragic marriage between a blunt ex-miner with a dental practice on Polk Street and a simple girl from nearby Oakland.

The Lady From Shanghai (Orson Welles 1948). Orson Welles' brief marriage to Rita Hayworth resulted in this twisted mystery about a double-crossing couple. The finale, shot in a hall of mirrors, is one of the most famous scenes in film history.

The Maltese Falcon (John Huston 1941). Possibly the greatest detective movie of all time, starring a hard-bitten Humphrey Bogart as private dick Sam Spade and Peter Lorre (stroking a remarkably suggestive cane).

Out of the Past (Jacques Torneur 1947). Real-life, lantern-jawed tough guy Robert Mitchum stars in this iconic film *noir* about one man's date with destiny.

Vertigo (Alfred Hitchcock 1958). Known during production as the "San Francisco movie," Hitchcock's remarkable film looks at fear, obsession and voyeurism. Jimmy Stewart gives an uncharacteristically dark performance as an ex-cop slowly becoming unhinged because of a romantic obsession. Excellent use of locations, including Nob Hill, Fort Point, Muir Woods and Mission Dolores.

Documentaries

Berkeley in the Sixties (Mark Kitchell 1990). Well-made documentary about the heyday of political protest in Berkeley. Combination of modern-day interviews with startling clips showcasing nearly every movement that occurred back in the day.

Crumb (Terry Zwigoff 1994). Disturbing portrait of Robert Crumb, the wildly eccentric comic artist, whose Mr Natural became a 1960s icon, and his even more bizarre relatives.

Gimme Shelter (David & Albert Maysles/Charlotte Zwerin 1970). Legendary film about the Rolling Stones' Altamont concert (see box, p.254). Lots of shots of Mick Jagger looking bemused during and after the notorious murder.

Jimi Plays Berkeley (Peter Pilafian 1971). The historic Memorial Day Jimi Hendrix concert in Berkeley, interspersed with lots of shots of rampaging students waving their peace signs. Hendrix ignores the peripheral action and just plays.

Last Call at Maude's (Paris Poirier 1993). Sweet ode to a bygone lesbian bar – a window into over twenty years of Bay Area lesbian history.

Neighborhoods: the Hidden Cities of San Francisco (Peter L. Stein 1997). A popular four-part mini-series on the history of San Francisco, focusing on Chinatown, the Castro, the Fillmore and the Mission.

The Times of Harvey Milk (Robert Epstein 1984). Academy Award-winning documentary chronicling Milk's career in San Francisco politics and the aftermath of his 1978 assassination.

The Wild Parrots of Telegraph Hill (Judy Irving 2005). While living in a Telegraph Hill cottage, former homeless musician Mark Bittner made friends with the flock of cherry-headed conures, also called red-masked parakeets, who populate the neighbourhood. The film won Sundance and Emmy awards.

Thrillers

48 Hours (Walter Hill 1982). Eddie Murphy puts in a slick comic performance as the criminal sidekick to Nick Nolte's tough-talking cop, who has 48 hours to wrap up a homicide case. Fantastic shots of San Francisco and quick-witted dialogue make this fast-paced comedy-thriller immensely entertaining.

Basic Instinct (Paul Verhoeven 1992). Sharon Stone is vampish as a pickaxe-wielding, bisexual writer pursued by bug-eyed Michael Douglas around the dramatic city landscape in this conventional murder mystery. The movie drew howls of protest from San Francisco's gay and lesbian community over alleged homophobia.

Dark Passage (Delmer Davies 1947). Classic couple Humphrey Bogart and Lauren Bacall steam up foggy San Francisco as they try to clear the wrongfully accused Bogey's good name. Good locations and camerawork.

D.O.A. (Rudolph Mate 1949). A thriller with a terrific gimmick that makes excellent use of its San Francisco and LA locales: a poisoned man with only a few hours to live searches to uncover his murderer.

Escape from Alcatraz (Don Siegel 1979). Clint Eastwood reteams with Dirty Harry director Don Seigel for this well-made retelling of a true-life escape attempt.

Experiment in Terror (Blake Edwards 1962). The inspiration for David Lynch's *Twin Peaks*, this entertaining Cold War period piece has dozens of FBI agents trying to track down an obscene phone caller in Twin Peaks.

Fog over Frisco (William Dieterle 1934). Bette Davis plays a wayward heiress who is kidnapped in this thriller.

High Crimes (Carl Franklin 2002). Ashley Judd plays yet another feisty woman in peril in this Marin County-set thriller – picturesque and fun but formulaic.

Interview with the Vampire (Neil Jordan 1994). Jordan's stylish adaptation of Anne Rice's hugely popular novel is well filmed, even if the leading actors, Tom Cruise and Brad Pitt, are miscast. Pivotal scenes were shot on the Golden Gate Bridge and along Market Street.

It Came From Beneath the Sea (Charles Schneer 1955). A giant octopus attacks the city and tries to destroy Golden Gate Bridge in this B-grade monster flick.

The Lineup (Frank Cooper 1958). Film adaptation of the TV series *San Francisco Beat*, about the SFPD capturing a junkie gunman. An unconvincing plot, but polished acting and fantastic shots of San Francisco.

The Organization (James Webb 1971). Sidney Poitier returns again as uptight cop Virgil Tibbs, from *In the Heat of the Night*, and ends up breaking the law to help a radical group trying to stop the flow of heroin into the inner city.

The Rock (Michael Bay 1996). Embarrassingly enjoyable action adventure starring Nicholas Cage as an FBI scientist trying to save the city from biological warheads hidden on Alcatraz. Sean Connery, as the only man ever to escape from the island prison, looks on with droll amusement during the absurd proceedings. Look out for the geographically impossible car chase.

They Call Me Mister Tibbs! (Gordon Douglas 1970). Another benign follow-up to *In the Heat of the Night*, with Sidney Poitier as Virgil Tibbs, the black San Francisco cop who sleuths his way to unravelling a murder mystery.

Time After Time (Nicholas Meyer 1979). Courtesy of the Time Machine, Malcolm McDowell chases Jack the Ripper into twentieth-century San Francisco accompanied by a lot of cheap jokes and violence.

The Towering Inferno (John Guillermin/Irwin Allen 1974). An all-star cast – including Steve McQueen, Faye Dunaway, Fred Astaire and Paul Newman – gets alternately burned, blown-up, smashed or dropped from great heights in this borderline-camp disaster epic about a fire in the world's tallest building.

Zodiac (David Fincher 2007). This thriller starring Jake Gyllenhaal and Robert Downey Jr meticulously re-creates the details of the *San Francisco Chronicle*'s relationship to and investigation into the Zodiac Killer crimes.

Drama

Birdman of Alcatraz (John Frankenheimer 1962). Earnest but overlong study of real-life convicted killer Robert Stroud (Burt Lancaster) who becomes an authority on birds while kept in America's highest-security prison.

The Frisco Kid (Samuel Bischoff 1935). James Cagney stars in this rough-and-tumble tale of a shanghaied sailor who rises to power on the rough 1860s Barbary Coast.

Gentleman Jim (Raoul Walsh 1942). Rich evocation of 1880s San Francisco with Errol Flynn playing the charming, social-climbing boxer, Gentleman Jim Corbett.

Hammett (Wim Wenders 1982). German director Wenders, never known for keeping things short and sweet, financially ruined Coppola's Zoetrope production company with this tribute to Dashiell Hammett's quest for material in the back alleys of Chinatown.

Joy Luck Club (Wayne Wang 1993). Epic weepy based on the bestselling novel about first-generation Chinese women's struggle to make it in America.

La Mission (Peter Bratt 2009). Poignant social drama, shot around the Mission district. The story of macho Mexican immigrant Che Rivera, played by the director's brother Benjamin, rearing his only son Jes after his wife's death and struggling to come to terms with Jes's homosexuality.

Murder in the First (Marc Rocco 1995). Draining courtroom drama based on the true story of an incarcerated petty thief driven to a jailhouse murder by years of solitary confinement and torture. There are ample period trappings, including antique streetcars.

My Name Is Khan (Karan Johar 2010). This voyage of personal discovery, whose central character is played by Bollywood superstar Shahruck Khan, follows an Indian immigrant to San Francisco on his quest to personally deliver a message to the US President after he and his family are subject to post 9-11 anti-Muslim prejudice.

The Pursuit of Happyness (Gabriele Muccino 2006). This drama tells the real-life story of Chris Gardner (Will Smith), a down-on-his-luck salesman who ends up homeless with a young son. Gardner keeps his child fed by hitting the soup kitchen at Glide Memorial Church every night while he works an internship at a brokerage firm.

Star Trek IV – The Voyage Home (Leonard Nimoy 1986). In a surprising twist, this warm-hearted comic instalment of the sci-fi series sends Kirk and company back in time to contemporary San Francisco in order to save some whales.

Comedy and romance

40 Days, 40 Nights (Michael Lehmann 2002). Heart-throb vehicle for Josh Hartnett, who gives up sex in the city of the Summer of Love – days before meeting his dream girl. Passably funny, but most notable for its loving shots of San Francisco.

Dim Sum (Wayne Wang 1985). Appealing film about a more-or-less Westernized Chinese family in San Francisco. Fittingly, given the title, it's a small, delicious treat.

Guess Who's Coming to Dinner (Stanley Kramer 1967). Well-meaning but slightly flat interracial comedy in which Spencer Tracy and Katharine Hepburn play the supposedly liberal but bewildered parents of a woman who brings home the black man (Sidney Poitier) she intends to marry.

Harold and Maude (Hal Ashby 1971). Black comedy about a romance between a death-obsessed teenager and the 80-year-old woman he befriends at various funerals. Intolerable for some, a cult classic for others.

High Anxiety (Mel Brooks 1977). Mel Brooks's spoof on *Vertigo*, and psychiatry in general, is one of the director's best – if you have a high tolerance for rampant silliness.

I Love You, Alice B. Toklas (Hy Averback 1968). Long before Austin Powers hit the screen, Peter Sellers' performance in this groovy film, set the standard for Swinging Sixties farces. By today's standards, though, the film's portrayal of women seems almost as dated as the wardrobe.

Just Like Heaven (Mark Waters 2005). Reese Witherspoon plays a busy San Francisco doctor who lives in a swank wood-panelled Victorian condo in Russian Hill. After her car is hit by a truck, her apartment is rented to an architect (Mark Ruffalo) who falls in love with her ghost, which happens to be haunting the space. Dolores Park and *Caffe Trieste* are featured.

Nina Takes a Lover (Alan Jacobs 1996). Small, independently produced romantic comedy about love and loneliness, well shot against the backdrop of San Francisco.

Petulia (Richard Lester 1968). San Francisco surgeon George C. Scott takes up with unhappily married kook Julie Christie in richly detailed, deliberately fragmentary comedy-drama set in druggy, decadent society.

Play It Again, Sam (Herbert Ross 1972). Woody Allen leaves his beloved New York and enters film history as a nerdy young cinephile obsessed with Humphrey Bogart in this sweet, mildly amusing comedy.

The Princess Diaries (Garry Marshall 2001). This innocent teen romantic comedy stars Anne Hathaway as a San Francisco Catholic school student who discovers she's the unlikely heir to the throne of the fictional European country of Genovia. San Francisco, from its hills and beaches to Cliff House and cable cars, shines.

Sucker Free City (Spike Lee 2005). Shot in Chinatown, the Mission and Hunters Point, this two-hour film, originally intended as a pilot for a Showtime series, shows the urban underside to San Francisco, rarely seen on film. A gritty, realistic look at the street gangs made up of white, Asian and African-American members.

Psych-Out (Richard Rush 1968). Pumped out quickly to capitalize on the Summer of Love, this movie offers good performances from Jack Nicholson and Bruce Dern; but they can't save what is basically a compendium of every hippie cliché in the book.

San Francisco (W.S. Van Dyke 1936). Elaborate, entertaining hokum about a Barbary Coast love triangle circa 1906. The script is upstaged by the climactic earthquake sequence.

Serial (Bill Persky 1980). Sharply observed comedy about social neurosis among wealthy ex-hippies in Marin.

Skidoo (Otto Preminger 1968). Carol Channing, Jackie Gleason and friends drop acid on Alcatraz, under the observant eye of a stoned God, played by Groucho Marx, plus a soundtrack by Harry Nilsson.

Sweet November (Pat O'Connor 2001). Charlize Theron plays a libertine who attempts to teach advertising executive Keanu Reeves what's important in life. Her bohemian Victorian flat in Potrero Hill is contrasted to his sleek Pacific Heights penthouse.

Tales of the City (Alastair Reid 1993). Widely loved mini-series based on Maupin's popular books. When it was first shown on public television, there were hurricanes of controversy over its gay content which no doubt helped it go on to become the most popular programme ever aired on PBS.

The Wedding Planner (Adam Shankman 2001). Charmingly old-fashioned romantic comedy, implausibly featuring the steely Jennifer Lopez as an ambitious wedding planner who's love-challenged in her personal life. There's terrific footage of San Francisco's hills.

What's Up, Doc? (Peter Bogdanovich 1972). Wildly likeable screwball comedy pastiche starring Barbra Streisand and Ryan O'Neal as a cook and a naive professor, with a famous moment shot in Alta Plaza park.

The Woman In Red (Gene Wilder 1984). Initially sophomoric comedy about one man's lust for a beautiful stranger. Takes a pleasant twist when Wilder's character realizes there's more to love than physical attraction and more to parking on San Francisco's hills than shifting to P.

Small print and index

A ROUGH GUIDE TO ROUGH GUIDES

Published in 1982, the first Rough Guide – to Greece – was a student scheme that became a publishing phenomenon. Mark Ellingham, a recent graduate in English from Bristol University, had been travelling in Greece the previous summer and couldn't find the right guidebook. With a small group of friends he wrote his own guide, combining a highly contemporary, journalistic style with a thoroughly practical approach to travellers' needs.

The immediate success of the book spawned a series that rapidly covered dozens of destinations. And, in addition to impecunious backpackers, Rough Guides soon acquired a much broader readership that relished the guides' wit and inquisitiveness as much as their enthusiastic, critical approach and value-for-money ethos.

These days, Rough Guides include recommendations from budget to luxury and cover more than 200 destinations around the globe, as well as producing an ever-growing range of eBooks and apps.

Visit **roughguides.com** to see our latest publications.

Rough Guide credits

Editors: Natasha Foges, Ann-Marie Shaw
Layout: Jessica Subramanian
Cartography: Ed Wright
Picture editor: Sarah Ross
Proofreader: Stewart Wild
Managing editor: Mani Ramaswamy
Assistant editor: Prema Dutta
Production: Rebecca Short
Cover design: Nicole Newman, Harriet Mills
Photographers: Greg Roden, Angus Oborn, Paul Whitfield
Editorial assistant: Lorna North

Senior pre-press designer: Dan May
Design director: Scott Stickland
Travel publisher: Joanna Kirby
Digital travel publisher: Peter Buckley
Reference director: Andrew Lockett
Operations coordinator: Becky Doyle
Operations assistant: Johanna Wurm
Publishing director (Travel): Clare Currie
Commercial manager: Gino Magnotta
Managing director: John Duhigg

Publishing information

This ninth edition published February 2012 by
Rough Guides Ltd,
80 Strand, London WC2R 0RL
11, Community Centre, Panchsheel Park,
New Delhi 110017, India
Distributed by the Penguin Group
Penguin Books Ltd,
80 Strand, London WC2R 0RL
Penguin Group (USA)
375 Hudson Street, NY 10014, USA
Penguin Group (Australia)
250 Camberwell Road, Camberwell,
Victoria 3124, Australia
Penguin Group (NZ)
67 Apollo Drive, Mairangi Bay, Auckland 1310,
New Zealand
Rough Guides is represented in Canada by Tourmaline
Editions Inc. 662 King Street West, Suite 304, Toronto,
Ontario M5V 1M7
Printed in Singapore
© Charles Hodgkins, Nick Edwards 2012

Maps © Rough Guides
No part of this book may be reproduced in any form
without permission from the publisher except for the
quotation of brief passages in reviews.
328pp includes index
A catalogue record for this book is available from the
British Library
ISBN: 978-1-40538-607-4
The publishers and authors have done their best to
ensure the accuracy and currency of all the information
in **The Rough Guide to San Francisco & the Bay Area**,
however, they can accept no responsibility for any loss,
injury, or inconvenience sustained by any traveller as a
result of information or advice contained in the guide.
1 3 5 7 9 8 6 4 2

MIX
Paper from
responsible sources
FSC™ C018179

Help us update

We've gone to a lot of effort to ensure that the ninth edition
of **The Rough Guide to San Francisco & the Bay Area** is
accurate and up-to-date. However, things change – places
get "discovered", opening hours are notoriously fickle,
restaurants and rooms raise prices or lower standards. If
you feel we've got it wrong or left something out, we'd like
to know, and if you can remember the address, the price,
the hours, the phone number, so much the better.

Please send your comments with the subject line
"**Rough Guide San Francisco & the Bay Area Update**" to
mail@uk.roughguides.com. We'll credit all contributions
and send a copy of the next edition (or any other Rough
Guide if you prefer) for the very best emails.

Find more travel information, connect with fellow
travellers and book your trip on roughguides.com

ABOUT THE AUTHORS

Nick Edwards Since graduating in Classics & Modern Greek from Oxford, Nick spent many years living in Athens and travelling widely, especially in India. He later settled in Pittsburgh with spouse Maria, until they returned to his native south London in 2008. He's a lifelong Spurs fan, psych music aficionado and believer in universal Oneness.

Charles Hodgkins Charles regularly adventures to other places, but every itinerary leads back to his lifelong home, the Bay Area. He has co-authored or contributed to several other Rough Guides, including *California*, *the USA* and *Yellowstone & Grand Teton*. He lives in San Francisco, where the punishing hills and doorstop burritos offer the finest caloric offset imaginable.

Acknowledgements

Charles Thanks to my frequent co-author Nick Edwards, always an infinite pleasure to work with; Natasha Foges and Annie Shaw for improving the text at every turn and navigating the churning redesign waters with grace and aplomb; Mani Ramaswamy for keeping me as busy as humanly possible the last couple years; Ed Wright, cartographer extraordinaire; Tom Walton and Kelly Chamberlin for making my research a little more convivial and fun; Andrew Rosenberg, Gregory Dicum and Jeff Cranmer for helping get me into this mess in the first place; Linda Kelly and Tim Scanlin for all the understanding and cooperation; and Todd, Emily, Tyler and Aaron for being pals among pals.

Nick Thanks to Barbara and Adele of Visit Berkeley; Kelly Chamberlin for setting things up in Half Moon Bay; Peter, Nancy and Aphrodite at Safari West; and Kristina Hjelsand of Joie de Vivre Hotels. Mucho gratzias to my co-author Charles for expert burrito guidance in the city and growing friendship. Thanks once again to Clint, Erin, Laramie and Wendi for great hospitality at Bonita Hollow and to the rest of the Berkeley circle for fine evenings at *Pub*. Good to see my old friend Alexandra on my break down south in Santa Barbara. As ever a heartfelt scratch on the back to Maria for keeping the hearth warm back in London.

Readers' letters

Thanks to all the readers who have taken the time to write in with comments and suggestions (and apologies if we've inadvertently omitted or misspelt anyone's name):

Howard Chabner, Brad Chelin, Kay Clayton, Jeremy Keighley, Rob Marsh, Catherine McHugh, Shivu Rao, Sascha Schneider and Hugh Sutherland.

Photo credits

All photos © Rough Guides except the following:
(Key: t-top; b-bottom; c-centre; l-left; r-right)

p.2 Jean-Pierre Lescourret/Corbis
p.4 Sharon Hitman/Fotolia
p.7 Eros Hoagland/ZUMA Press/Axiom (t); Mitchell Funk/Getty (b)
p.8 Harris Shiffman/Fotolia
p.11 Donald Smith/Alamy (c); Paul Chinn/San Francisco Chronicle/Corbis (b)
p.12 Holler, Hendrik/the food passionates/Corbis (b)
p.13 Danita Delimont/Alamy (t); Steve Stock/Alamy (b)
p.14 Stars and Stripes/Alamy (c); Macduff Everton/Corbis (b)
p.15 Gabriel Buoys/AFP/Getty Images (tl); Alison Wright/Corbis (br)
p.16 Can Balcioglu/Fotolia (tl)
p.55 Robert Harding World Imagery/Alamy
p.105 Fabian Gonzales/Alamy
p.109 Ei Katsumata/Alamy (t)

p.114 Danita Delimont/Alamy
p.147 Carlos Avila Gonzalez/Corbis (tl)
p.159 Richard T. Nowitz/Corbis (tl); Dhanraj Emanuel/Alamy (tr); Rich Iwasaki/Alamy (b)
p.171 Aurora Photos/Alamy
p.186 Alex Washburn/San Francisco Chronicle/Corbis
p.193 Robert Galbraith/Reuters/Corbis
p.209 Kim Kulish/Corbis (tl)
p.218 Michael Macor/San Francisco Chronicle/Corbis
p.225 Judy Bellah/Alamy
p.230 Lee Foster/Alamy
p.249 Walter Bibikow/Getty (t); David H Collier/Getty (bl); Aerial Archives/Alamy (br)
p.269 Kim Kulish/Corbis (t); Chris A Crumley/Alamy (bl); Judy Bellah/Alamy (br)
p.282 Bettmann/Corbis

Index

Maps are marked in **grey**

Maps

Index

Listings key

■ Accommodation

● Café/restaurant

■ Bar/club/live music

● Shop/gallery

City plan

The **city plan** on the pages that follow is divided as shown:

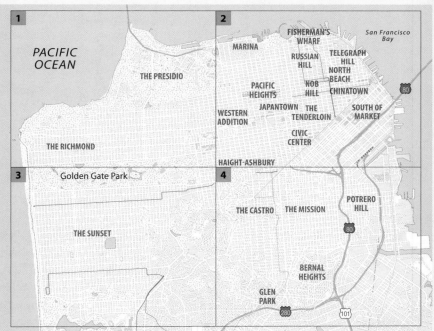

Map symbols

ⓘ Information office	∙∙∙→ California Line cable car	✈ Airport
🅿 Parking	∙∙∙→ Powell–Hyde Line cable car	🗼 Lighthouse
▦ Building	∙∙∙→ Powell–Mason Line cable car	⛰ Mountain range
⛪ Church	— MUNI line F-Market & Wharves	▲ Mountain peak
♦ Place of interest	— MUNI line J-Church	+ Cemetery
⊠ Entrance gate	— MUNI line K-Ingleside	Park/forest/open land
≈ Bridge/tunnel	— MUNI line L-Taraval	Marsh
⛳ Golf course	— MUNI line M-Ocean View	
Ⓜ MUNI metro station	— MUNI line N-Judah	
Ⓑ BART station	— MUNI line T-Third St	

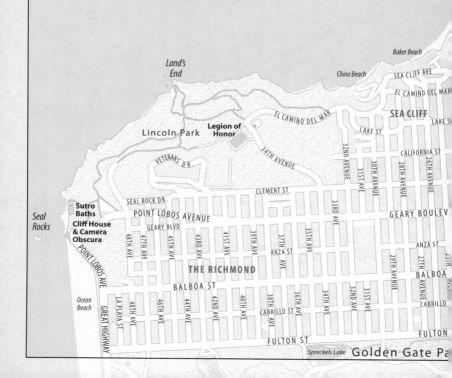

1

PACIFIC OCEAN

South Bay

Baker Beach

China Beach

SEA CLIFF AVE

EL CAMINO DEL MAR

SEA CLIFF

LAKE S

Land's End

EL CAMINO DEL MAR

Legion of Honor

Lincoln Park

34TH AVENUE

32ND AVENUE

31ST AVENUE

30TH AVENUE

28TH AVENUE

26TH AVENUE

LAKE ST

CALIFORNIA ST

VETERANS DR.

CLEMENT ST.

33RD AVE

35TH AVE

GEARY BOULEV

SEAL ROCK DR.

POINT LOBOS AVENUE

GEARY BLVD.

37TH AVE

39TH AVE

41ST AVE

43RD AVE

45TH AVE

47TH AVE

48TH AVE

ANZA ST

ANZA ST

29TH AVENUE

27TH

Sutro Baths

Cliff House & Camera Obscura

Seal Rocks

POINT LOBOS AVE

THE RICHMOND

BALBOA ST.

32ND AVE

34TH AVE

36TH AVE

38TH AVE

40TH AVE

42ND AVE

44TH AVE

46TH AVE

LA PLAYA ST

31ST AVE

BALBOA

Ocean Beach

GREAT HIGHWAY

CABRILLO ST.

CABRILLO

FULTON ST.

FULTON

Spreckels Lake Golden Gate Pa

2

FISHERMAN'S WHA

Pier 45 Musée Mecaniqu

Hyde Street Pier

Fish Alley
JEFFERSON ST

Bo
Museu
Ba

Fort Mason Center

Aquatic Park

BEACH ST

YACHT ROAD

Marina Green

FORT MASON

Ghirardelli Square

MARINA BOULEVARD
CASA WAY
RICO W.AY

BEACH ST

Russian Hill Park

San Francisco Art Institute

JEFFERSON ST
PRADO ST
CERVANTES BLVD

NORTH POINT ST

BRODERICK ST

FILLMORE ST

WEBSTER ST

BEACH ST

MARINA

BAY ST

NORTH POINT ST
DIVISADERO ST
SCOTT ST
CAPRA WAY
MALLORCA WAY
MILEY

FRANCISCO ST

Alice Marble Park

Lombard St

BAY ST
BAY ST

ALHAMBRA ST
TOLEDO WAY

LOMBARD ST

GREENWICH ST

RUSSIAN H

FRANCISCO ST

CHESTNUT ST

MAGNOLIA ST

VAN NESS AVENUE

FILBERT ST

LARKIN ST

LEAVENWORTH ST

MACONDRA

RICHARDSON AVE

LOMBARD ST
MOULTON ST

UNION ST

GREEN ST

Powell-Hyde Line

JON

BROADW
BE

LOMBARD ST

GREENWICH ST
PIXLEY ST

FILBERT ST

SCOTT ST

PIERCE ST

STEINER ST

FILLMORE ST

UNION ST

WEBSTER ST

BUCHANAN ST

LAGUNA ST

OCTAVIA ST

GOUGH ST

FRANKLIN ST

POLK ST

VALLEJO ST

BROADWAY

MORRELL ST

LYNCH ST

LYON ST

BAKER ST

BRODERICK ST

COW HOLLOW

GREEN ST

VALLEJO ST

BROADWAY

PACIFIC AVENUE

JACKSON ST

WASHINGTON ST

NOB

Lyon Steps

PACIFIC AVENUE

JACKSON ST

Haas-Lilienthal House

CLAY ST

SACRAMENTO ST

Cath

PRESIDIO AVENUE

DIVISADERO ST

Alta Plaza Park

WASHINGTON ST

CLAY ST

PACIFIC HEIGHTS

Lafayette Park

CALIFORNIA ST

FRANKLIN ST

AUSTIN ST

PINE ST

SACRAMENTO ST

BRODERICK ST

LYON ST

BAKER ST

SCOTT ST

PIERCE ST

STEINER ST

FILLMORE ST

CALIFORNIA ST

PINE ST

BUSH ST

BUCHANAN ST

LAGUNA ST

OCTAVIA ST

GOUGH ST

FERN ST

BUSH ST

SUTTER ST

HEMLOCK ST

CEDAR ST

POLK ST

LARKIN ST

HYDE ST

POST ST

GEARY ST

WESTERN ADDITION

PINE ST

BUSH ST

SUTTER ST

POST ST

JAPANTOWN

Japan Center

MASONIC AVENUE

GEARY BOULEVARD

GEARY BLVD

O'FARRELL ST

ELLIS ST

Cathedral of St Mary of the Assumption

MYRTLE ST

OLIVE ST

WILLOW ST

LARCH ST

O'FARRELL ST

ELLIS ST

EDDY ST

TH
TENDE

TERRA VISTA AVENUE
ENCANTO AVE
FORTUNA AVE
BAKER ST
BARCELONA AVE
ANZA VISTA AVE

TURK ST

GOLDEN GATE AVENUE

MCALLISTER ST

Jefferson Square

TURK ST

GOLDEN GATE

O'FARRELL ST

TURK ST

GOLDEN GATE AVENUE

MCALLISTER ST

CIVIC CENTER

MCALLI

CENTRAL
AVE

MCALLISTER ST

FULTON ST

PIERCE ST

STEINER ST

FILLMORE

FILLMORE

WEBSTER ST

FULTON ST

GROVE ST

HAYES VALLEY

FRANKLIN ST

VAN NESS AVENUE

City Hall

CIVIC CENTER PLAZA

GROVE ST

NORTH OF THE PANHANDLE

GROVE ST

LYON ST

BAKER ST

BRODERICK ST

DIVISADERO ST

Alamo Square

IVY ST

HAYES ST

LINDEN ST

OCTAVIA ST

GOUGH ST

MARKET ST

MASONIC AVENUE

HAYES ST

FELL ST

FELL ST

HICKORY ST

OAK ST

HICKORY ST

OAK ST

BUCHANAN ST

LILY ST

PAGE ST

Van Ness

SOUTH VAN NESS AVENUE

MISSION ST

MINNA ST

NATOMA

BRADY ST

OTIS ST

GOUGH ST

LAFAYETTE ST

12TH ST

ROSE

The Panhandle

OAK ST

PAGE ST

PIERCE ST

ROSE ST

PAGE ST

ROSE ST

HAIGHT-ASHBURY

PAGE ST

LOWER HAIGHT

HAIGHT ST

WALLER ST

LAUSSAT ST

MCCOPPIN ST

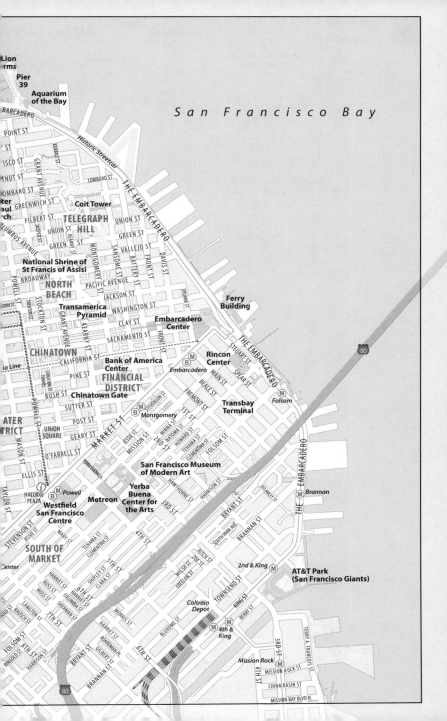

Lion
arms

Pier
39

Aquarium
of the Bay

San Francisco Bay

BARCADERO

POINT ST

ISCO ST

KEARNY ST

GRANT ST

NUT ST

LOMBARD ST

OMBARD ST

GREENWICH ST

er
aul
ch

Coit Tower

FILBERT ST

TELEGRAPH
HILL

UNION ST

KEARNY ST

COLUMBUS AVENUE

GREEN ST

HYDE ST

GREEN ST

GRANT AVENUE

MONTGOMERY ST

SANSOME ST

VALLEJO ST

BATTERY ST

FRONT ST

DAVIS ST

National Shrine of
St Francis of Assisi

BROADWAY

NORTH
BEACH

PACIFIC AVENUE

Ferry
Building

POWELL ST

JOHN ST

Transamerica
Pyramid

JACKSON ST

WASHINGTON ST

STOCKTON ST

GRANT AVENUE

CLAY ST

Embarcadero
Center

THE EMBARCADERO

CHINATOWN

KEARNY ST

SACRAMENTO ST

FRONT ST

ia Line

CALIFORNIA ST

Bank of America
Center

Rincon
Center

STEUART ST

STOCKTON TUNNEL

PINE ST

FINANCIAL
DISTRICT

ⓑ
Embarcadero

MAIN ST

SPEAR ST

ⓜ
Folsom

POWELL ST

BUSH ST

Chinatown Gate

BEALE ST

ATER
RICT

SUTTER ST

FREMONT ST

POST ST

ⓑ
Montgomery

1ST ST

Transbay
Terminal

MASON ST

UNION
SQUARE

GEARY ST

MARKET ST

JESSIE ST

MISSION ST

2ND ST

MINNA ST

NATOMA ST

HOWARD ST

TEHAMA ST

CLEMENTINA ST

FOLSOM ST

THE EMBARCADERO

O'FARRELL ST

STEVENSON ST

ELLIS ST

YERBA BUENA LA

San Francisco Museum
of Modern Art

HAWTHORNE ST

HARRISON ST

TAYLOR ST

HALLIDIE
PLAZA

ⓘ ⓜ Powell
ⓑ

Metreon

Yerba
Buena
Center for
the Arts

3RD ST

ⓜ Brannan

STEVENSON ST

JESSIE ST

Westfield
San Francisco
Centre

MARY ST

BRYANT ST

DE HARO ST

Center

SOUTH OF
MARKET

TEHAMA ST

CLEMENTINA ST

4TH ST

5TH ST

SOUTH PARK AVE

BRANNAN ST

2nd & King ⓜ

AT&T Park
(San Francisco Giants)

HARRIET ST

RUSS ST

MOSS ST

6TH ST

HARRIET ST
COLUMBIA ST

SHIPLEY ST

CLARA ST

RITCH ST

ZOE ST

WELSH ST

TOWNSEND ST

KING ST

BERRY ST

ARD ST

LANGTON ST

7TH ST

SHERMAN ST

MORRIS ST

BLUXOME ST

Caltrain
Depot

3RD ST

TERRY A FRANCOIS ST

RINGOLD ST 8TH ST

HARRISON ST

HARRIET ST

BOARDMAN PL

GILBERT ST

6TH ST

ⓜ 4th &
King

FREELON ST

ⓜ Brannan

Mission Rock

MISSION ROCK ST

80

BRYANT ST

BRANNAN ST

4TH ST

CHINA BASIN ST

MISSION BAY BLVD N

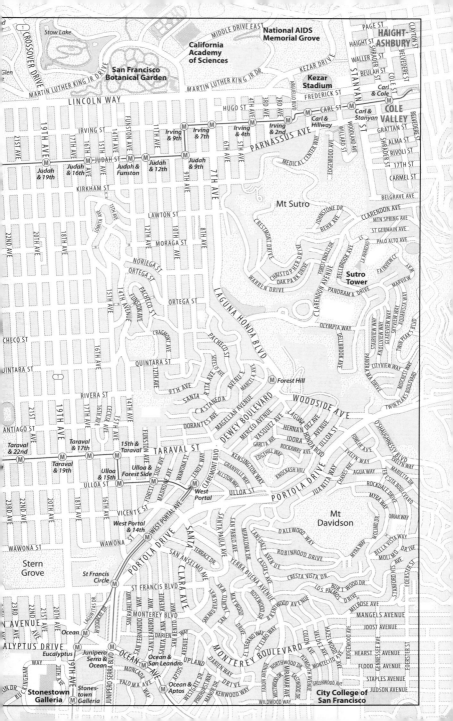

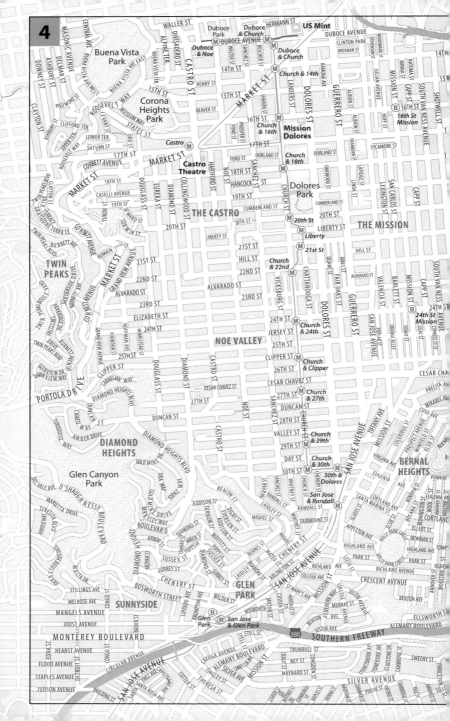

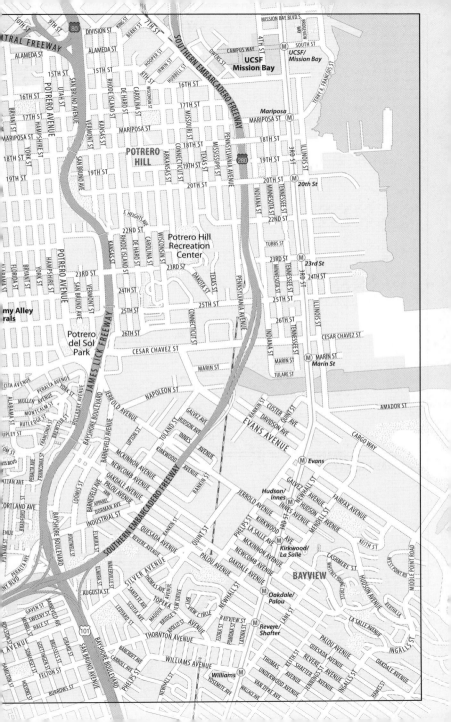

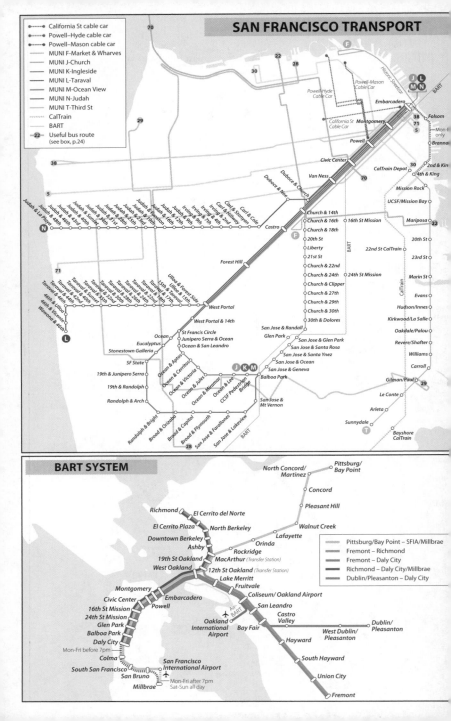

ROUGH GUIDES

SO NOW WE'VE TOLD YOU
HOW TO MAKE THE MOST
OF YOUR TIME, WE WANT
YOU TO STAY SAFE AND
COVERED WITH OUR
FAVOURITE TRAVEL INSURER

WorldNomads.com

keep travelling safely

GET AN ONLINE QUOTE
roughguides.com/insurance

RECOMMENDED BY

ROUGH GUIDES

MAKE THE MOST OF YOUR TIME ON EARTH™

MAKE THE MOST OF YOUR CITY BREAK

    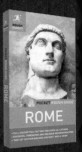

BARCELONA LONDON NEW YORK CITY PARIS ROME

FREE PULL OUT MAP WITH EVERY SIGHT AND LISTING FROM THE GUIDE

ESSENTIAL ITINERARIES AND RELIABLE RECOMMENDATIONS

ROUGH
GUIDES

MAKE THE MOST
OF YOUR GADGETS

roughguides.com/downloads

THE ROUGH GUIDE to
Barcelona

THE ROUGH GUIDE
Thailand
Beaches & Is

Rome
ROUGH GUIDES

ROUGH
GUIDES

Android

Cloud
Computing

iPhone

iPods
& iTunes

FROM
ANDROID
TO **iPADS** TO
WINDOWS 7

BOOKS | EBOOKS | APPS

MAKE THE MOST OF YOUR TIME ON EARTH™

ROUGH GUIDES

GET LOST

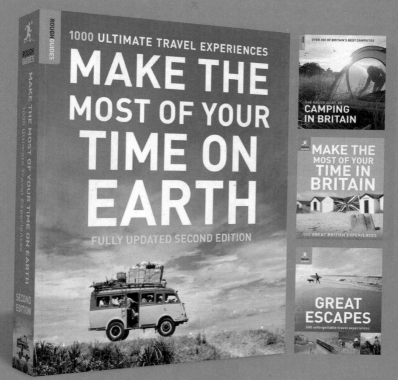

ESCAPE THE EVERYDAY
WITH OVER 700 **BOOKS**, **EBOOKS** AND **APPS**
YOU'RE SURE TO BE INSPIRED

Start your journey at **roughguides.com**
MAKE THE MOST OF YOUR TIME ON EARTH™